The Handbook of Aging and Cognition

Third Edition

The Handbook
of Aging and Cognition

Third Edition

Edited by

Fergus I. M. Craik
University of Toronto

Timothy A. Salthouse
University of Virginia

Psychology Press
Taylor & Francis Group
NEW YORK AND HOVE

Published in 2008
by Psychology Press
270 Madison Avenue
New York, NY 10016
www.psypress.com

Published in Great Britain
by Psychology Press
27 Church Road
Hove, East Sussex BN3 2FA

Psychology Press is an imprint of the Taylor & Francis Group, an informa business

Typeset by RefineCatch Limited, Bungay, Suffolk, UK
Printed and bound by Edwards Brothers, Inc. in the USA on acid-free paper

10 9 8 7 6 5 4 3 2 1

Library of Congress Cataloging-in-Publication Data
The handbook of aging and cognition / edited by Fergus I.M. Craik & Timothy A. Salthouse. – 3rd ed.
    p. cm.
  Includes bibliographical references and indexes.
  ISBN-13: 978-0-8058-5990-4 (hardcover : alk. paper)
  ISBN-10: 0-8058-5990-X (hardcover : alk. paper)   1. Cognition in old age.
2. Cognition—Age factors.   I. Craik, Fergus I. M.   II. Salthouse, Timothy A.
  BF724.85.C64H36 2007
  155.67′13–dc22

                                                                    2007021218

ISBN: 978-0-8058-5990-4 (hbk)

Contents

Preface

This is the third edition of what has proven to be a popular and respected handbook. From the beginning, the goal was to select chapter authors on the basis of their expertise in a specific research area, and then ask them to prepare a scholarly review of contemporary research on that topic. Unlike many edited volumes, the authors were encouraged to adopt a broad perspective, and not merely summarize their own research. In our opinion this approach has been successful given that previous editions of *The Handbook of Aging and Cognition* have been recognized as authoritative sources in the field of cognitive aging. The present authors are almost entirely different from the group who wrote chapters for the previous two editions, so this is not an update or revision, but constitutes an entirely new volume.

Some topics, such as attention, memory, and language, have persisted throughout every edition of the Handbook, although with different authors adopting somewhat different perspectives. However, in keeping with shifts in the field, there have also been changes in the chapter topics. For example, there was very little discussion of neuroscience in the 1992 book, but two chapters focused on this topic in the 2000 book, and the current edition not only contains several chapters with an explicit neuroscience focus, but some mention of neuroscience is included in most of the chapters. New topics have also been introduced in successive editions to reflect changing emphases in the field, such as the chapters on behavioral genetics by McGue and Johnson (chapter 2), on knowledge by Ackerman (chapter 9), and on within-person variability by Hultsch and colleagues (chapter 10).

The first chapter, by Dennis and Cabeza, reviews structural and functional neuroimaging research in aging. A particularly useful feature of this chapter is an attempt to link neuroimaging results to major theories of cognitive aging. The next chapter, by McGue and Johnson, focuses on genetic influences in cognitive functioning at different periods in adulthood. They describe major methodological approaches to investigating genetic determinants on cognition, and review major findings in this area. In chapter 3, Albert provides a clinical perspective on cognition and dementia, with a valuable discussion of how cognitive assessments are used in the diagnosis, and in the monitoring of change, in neuropathology.

There has been considerable interest in recent years in the concept of brain reserve, which is an idea proposed to account for the observation that an individual's level of cognitive functioning is often higher than what would be expected based on the amount of pathology in the brain. In chapter 4, Christensen, Anstey, Leach, and Mackinnon provide a comprehensive review of this topic, including an informative discussion of how the concept has been formulated and tested, and a meta-analysis of results relevant to different versions of the brain reserve hypothesis. Chapter 5, by Kramer and Madden, reviews recent research on age differences in attention, not only from the perspective of behavioral studies but also from a neurobiological perspective. The topic of memory is the focus of chapter 6 by McDaniel, Jacoby, and Einstein. Their chapter contains a detailed coverage of age differences in prospective memory, and an extensive discussion of factors that might be associated with variation in memory performance among older adults, including cognitive training, physical exercise, and dietary nutrients. Two of the most popular topics in contemporary research in aging and cognition, working memory and executive control, are the focus of chapter 7 by Braver and West. These authors review major behavioral and neuroimaging findings in this area, and also describe how different research approaches to these topics might be integrated.

In chapter 8, Burke and Shafto provide a thorough and up-to-date review of the literature on adult age differences in the comprehension and production of language. Although it is sometimes claimed that language abilities are unaffected by aging, this chapter provides a more nuanced perspective on the relations of age to aspects of language. Another domain often assumed to be spared with aging is knowledge, although the amount of research specifically focusing on age differences in knowledge has been quite limited. In chapter 9, Ackerman provides a historical perspective on the topic of knowledge, and also reviews contemporary research relating age to different domains of knowledge. A new focus in research on cognitive aging emphasizes the variation around an individual's average level of functioning in addition to his or her average level of functioning. In chapter 10, Hultsch, Strauss, Hunter, and MacDonald provide a very scholarly discussion of the theoretical and methodological issues in this area, as well as a review of empirical research relating aging to within-person variability in cognitive functioning. In the final chapter, Craik and Bialystok provide an overview of some of the similarities and differences in cognitive development across different periods in the lifespan. This perspective is valuable because researchers in cognitive aging and cognitive development are both concerned with change in cognition, and they often emphasize similar constructs, but there has been very little integration across the two areas.

Acknowledgments

We are grateful to a number of people for their help and encouragement. In Toronto, we thank Johanna Lake and Lynn Luo for their work on organizational materials and manuscripts. We also thank Lori Handelman, Tony Messina and Steve Rutter from the editorial department of Lawrence Erlbaum Associates, Inc. for their help, and extend an especially warm thank you to Larry Erlbaum himself for his continuing support of the project over the years. We wish him well in his retirement. Paul Dukes from Psychology Press saw the volume through the production process, and we are grateful for his help and guidance. We thank the Natural Sciences and Engineering Research Council of Canada and the National Institute of Aging in the United States for grant support during the course of preparing the book for publication. As always, we are most grateful to our outstanding authors who have given us such excellent reviews of their research areas.

We are very pleased with the scope and quality of the chapters in this third edition of *The Handbook of Aging and Cognition*. As with previous editions, we believe that the current volume will be valuable to researchers in the field and to students in graduate seminars because this collection of chapters represents a comprehensive summary of the contemporary field of cognitive aging.

Timothy A. Salthouse
Fergus I. M. Craik

1

Neuroimaging of Healthy Cognitive Aging

Nancy A. Dennis
Roberto Cabeza
Duke University

Cognitive aging research and theory has, until recently, been based upon behavioral measures of cognitive performance such as response time and accuracy. Results from behavioral methodologies have indicated a general age-related decline in cognitive functions such as speed of processing, attention, perception, working memory, and cued and free recall—and age invariance when assessing cognitive processes associated with vocabulary and semantic memory. Recently, advances in the area of neuroimaging have allowed for the examination of the relationship between cognitive and neural differences in the aging brain. Given that cognitive processes depend on brain anatomy and physiology, it is natural to expect that previously observed behavioral differences in aging are intimately linked to age-related changes in the integrity of cerebral architecture and function.

By using in vivo neuroimaging techniques such as positron emission tomography (PET) and magnetic resonance imaging (MRI), researchers can tap into the neural substrates of cognitive aging linking behavior and function. As this technology has improved over the last two decades, significant advances have been made in the field of functional neuroimaging of cognitive aging. Research has shown us that, despite a common notion that everything declines in aging, neural activity associated with cognitive aging is characterized by both age-related *increases* as well as age-related *decreases* in brain activity. Failure on the part of older adults to activate brain regions typically recruited by younger adults during cognitive tasks is usually characterized as neurocognitive decline. However,

1

additional neural recruitment by older adults during task performance, beyond that seen in younger adults, is typically characterized as functional compensation. Examination of both types of neural activity is necessary for developing a better understanding of the plasticity of both the aging brain and cognitive aging in general.

There are two basic neuroimaging approaches to link the effects of aging on the brain and on behavior. The first is to correlate a *resting neuroimaging* measure, such as an MRI measure of brain volume or a PET measure of resting blood flow, to a behavioral measure obtained outside the scanner, such as performance in a memory test. The second is to use a *task-related neuroimaging* technique, such as functional MRI (fMRI), to measure activity in the scanner while participants are performing a cognitive task. Both approaches have strengths and weaknesses and complement each other. In the first major section of this chapter, we provide a brief overview of resting neuroimaging studies of aging, and in the second major section, which is the core of the chapter, we review functional neuroimaging studies of aging in various cognitive domains. The chapter ends with a section linking consistent neuroimaging findings to major theories of cognitive aging.

RESTING NEUROIMAGING STUDIES OF AGING

Resting neuroimaging measures include measures of brain volume, white matter integrity, resting blood flow and metabolism, and neurotransmitter function. These different measures are considered in separate sections below.

Measures of Brain Volume

Understanding age-related atrophy is essential to the understanding of functional differences between age groups. However, as it is not the main focus of this chapter, only a very brief overview of volumetric MRI studies of healthy aging is presented here (for a more complete review of age-related structural decline see Raz, 2005). While earlier studies of structural differences in aging have used a cross-sectional approach, more recent studies have used a longitudinal design. Despite this inherent bias towards healthier and more stable samples, longitudinal estimates of decline usually exceed those of cross-sectional studies. One explanation is that in cross-sectional analyses, intrapersonal change is masked to some degree by the noise associated with age-independent individual differences, whereas longitudinal studies are able to exclude both individual differences and cohort effects (Raz et al., 2005). The current section will focus on these more recent assessments of gray matter change across time.

Changes in whole brain volume as a function of aging have been examined in over 14 studies to date (Raz, 2005). In general, these changes are not linear, but become steeper in old age. For example, the cerebral cortex as a whole declines at a rate of 0.12% per year in younger adults but at a rate of 0.35% per year in adults over 52 years of age. Similarly, ventricles expand at a rate of 0.43% in younger adults but at a rate of 4.25% after the age of 70.

From a cognitive neuroscience perspective, the most interesting finding is that age-related atrophy differs across regions. With an average decline rate of between 0.9% and 1.5% per year, the frontal lobes show the steepest rate of atrophy (Pfefferbaum, Sullivan, Rosenbloom, Mathalon, & Lim, 1998; Raz et al., 2005; Resnick, Pham, Kraut, Zonderman, & Davatzikos, 2003). Moreover, frontal atrophy has been shown to correspond with cognitive deficits mediated by frontal regions. For example, Gunning-Dixon and Raz (2003) found that in a large group of older adults perseveration errors on the Wisconsin Card Sorting Task, a measure of executive functioning, negatively correlated with prefrontal volume.

The parietal lobes show the second steepest decline in function (Pfefferbaum et al., 1998; Raz, 2005; Resnick et al., 2003), with an annual rate between 0.34 and 0.90%. Compared to frontal and parietal lobes, the occipital lobe shows small or nonsignificant age-related atrophy. Additionally, atrophy rates also differ among subregions of each lobe. For example, there is evidence that within frontal and parietal cortex, more inferior subregions show the steepest rates of decline (Resnick et al., 2003).

Due to their role in memory function, the medial temporal lobes (MTL) have elicited more focal examinations over the years. Like other brain regions, longitudinal estimates of temporal lobe shrinkage exceed those of cross-sectional data (Scahill, Frost, Jenkins, Whitwell, Rossor, & Fox, 2003). Additionally, subregions of the temporal lobes (e.g., entorhinal cortex, hippocampus, parahippocampal gyrus) exhibit differential rates of decline. For example, a recent longitudinal study found that in healthy older adults, the hippocampus showed substantial atrophy whereas the entorhinal cortex did not (Raz et al., 2005). Furthermore, studies have shown that the rate of hippocampal atrophy increases with age (Raz, Rodrigue, Head, Kennedy, & Acker, 2004; Scahill et al., 2003). In one study, for example, this rate was an average of 0.86% per year in the whole sample (26–82 years) but 1.18% when considering only individuals over 50 years of age (Raz et al., 2004). A review of 12 studies estimated that after the age of 70 this rate may be as high as 1.85% per year (see Raz, 2005). These findings are very interesting because the entorhinal cortex is one of the regions first affected by Alzheimer's disease (AD; Braak, Braak, & Bohl, 1993). As discussed later, together with recent fMRI evidence of dissociations between hippocampal and rhinal functions in aging (Daselaar, Fleck, Dobbins, Madden, & Cabeza, 2006), these findings have implications for the early diagnosis of AD. (See Figure 1.1.)

Correlating structure with function, Rodrigue and Raz (2004) acquired both volumetric measures of the prefrontal cortex (PFC), hippocampus, and entorhinal cortex and measures of episodic memory across a 5-year interval in a large group spanning 26–83 years of age. While the volume of hippocampus and PFC correlated with age at baseline and follow-up, once the effects of age were controlled for, neither predicted memory performance. However, increased shrinkage of entorhinal cortex was associated with poorer memory performance at follow-up. Results support previous work showing a correlation between entorhinal cortex shrinkage and memory performance in the very old (Du et al., 2003). Additionally, Persson and colleagues (2006) found reduced hippocampal

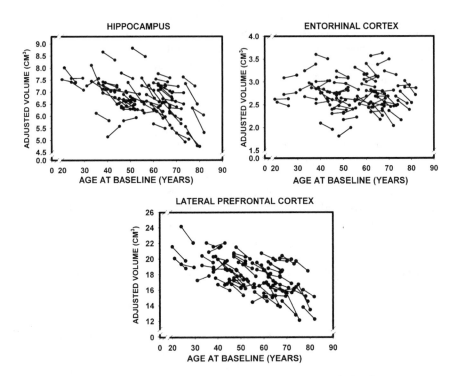

FIG. 1.1. Longitudinal changes in adjusted volumes of the hippocampus, entorhinal cortex, and lateral prefrontal cortex as a function of
baseline age. Reproduced by permission of Oxford University Press from
Raz et al. (2005). Regional brain changes in aging healthy adults: General
trends, individual differences and modifiers. *Cerebral Cortex*, 15(11), 1676–
1689.

volume in a group of older adults whose episodic memory performance declined across a decade compared to that of a group whose memory performance remained stable.

Subcortical atrophy in healthy aging is also prevalent, with longitudinal studies showing age-related striatal decline beginning in early adulthood. Four studies assessing decline in younger adults (average age = 29 yrs) showed caudate shrinkage that exceeds 1% per year (Chakos et al., 1994; Lang et al., 2001; Lieberman et al., 2001; Tauscher-Wisniewski, Tauscher, Logan, Christensen, Mikulis, & Zipursky, 2002) (but see DeLisi, Sakuma, Tew, Kushner, Hoff, & Grimson, 1997). Only one study to date has assessed striatal shrinkage in a group that included older adults. Following 53 adults (ranging in age from 26 to 82 at time 2) over five years, researchers see a more modest 0.83% decline in caudate volume per year (Raz et al., 2003). However, caudate decline is not representative of decline in other striatal nuclei. When assessed separately, the caudate exhibits a steeper rate of decline compared to the putamen, which shows less decline than the globus pallidus (Lang et al., 2001; Raz, Rodrigue, Kennedy, Head, Gunning-Dixon, & Acker, 2003). When correlating motor speed and striatal atrophy in a large sample of older adults (129 older adults ranging in age from 64 to 74 years), Soderlund, Nyberg, and Nilsson (2004) concluded that atrophy in the caudate nucleus predicted poorer performance in women, but not men.

Several metencephalic structures (e.g., cerebellum, vermis, pons) also show decline with age (Raz, 2005). While most longitudinal studies in this area have been conducted within a small age range (e.g., either younger or older adults), they generally show significant age-related shrinkage across all metencephalic structures. On average the cerebellum shows the greatest shrinkage, followed by the vermis, with the pons showing the smallest decline.

Finally, age-related decline has also been seen within the corpus callosum. Though cross-sectional studies show only modest shrinkage in the corpus callosum (Driesen & Raz, 1995), longitudinal studies show more significant age-related reductions (e.g., Sullivan, Pfefferbaum, Adalsteinsson, Swan, & Carmelli, 2002; Teipel et al., 2002), around 0.90% per annum. Furthermore, thinning of the corpus callosum over a 4-year period has been shown to correlate with performance on the Stroop task (Sullivan, Pfefferbaum et al., 2002) in older adults. A later study by Sullivan, Adalsteinsson, and Pfefferbaum (2006) found that fronto-callosal fibers showed a steeper rate of age-related decline than posterior fibers. Results support the view that age-related callosal degradation contributes to functional decline and that anterior regions are more vulnerable than other regions.

Interestingly, gender differences in volumetric decline across time appear nonexistent (Raz et al., 2005; Resnick et al., 2003), except perhaps in the caudate (Raz et al., 2005) which may show greater decline in women compared to men. There is also some evidence that volume loss is attenuated (though not absent) in the healthiest of individuals (Resnick et al., 2003). Overall, results support differential aging of individual cortical and subcortical regions.

Measures of White Matter Integrity

Postmortem studies suggest that age-related white matter loss occurs throughout the brain, and in particular in the frontal lobes, with white matter loss more extensive than gray matter loss (Double et al., 1996; Esiri, 1994; Kemper, 1994). In contrast, in vivo studies find no significant loss in healthy aging (Raz, 1996; Raz et al., 1997; Sullivan, Marsh, Mathalon, Lim, & Pfefferbaum, 1995), albeit some evidence suggests loss restricted to frontal regions (Raz et al., 1997; Salat, Kaye, & Janowsky, 1999). Several studies examining white matter differences across the entire lifespan (Courchesne et al., 2000; Pfefferbaum, Mathalon, Sullivan, Rawles, Zipursky, & Lim, 1994; Sullivan, Rosenbloom, Serventi, & Pfefferbaum, 2004) show decline beginning only in the seventh decade (but see Liu & Cooper, 2003).

Beyond overall volume measurements, it is also possible to measure white matter integrity. One method is to assess the number of white matter hyperintensities (WMHs) in the aging brain. While the exact cause of WMHs is unknown, they are posited to arise both from neural and vascular pathologies (for a review see Pantoni & Garcia, 1997). A review of 49 studies of healthy aging found the mean correlation between age and severity of WMHs to be .37 (Gunning-Dixon & Raz, 2000). Other risk factors for WMHs include hypertension (Gunning-Dixon & Raz, 2000), elevated systolic blood pressure (DeCarli et al., 1995), and apolipoprotein E-4 (e.g., Kuller et al., 1998; but see Schmidt et al., 1996).

In addition to correlating prefrontal volume with executive functioning, Gunning-Dixon and Raz (2003) also found that WMHs in the prefrontal cortex are independently associated with perseveration errors on the Wisconsin Card Sorting Task. Additionally, in an extensive study including 1254 participants ranging in age from 64 to 76 years, Soderlund, Nyberg, Adolfsson, Nilsson, and Launer (2003) found that periventricular WMHs and subcortical atrophy predicted lower performance on both motor speed and the Stroop task. Results remained stable after controlling for demographic factors (e.g., age, gender, education).

An advent of recent years, diffusion tensor imaging (DTI) has been employed to identify the structural integrity of white matter tracts in the brain. DTI measures assess changes in the MR signal due to the movement of water molecules. In healthy myelinated fiber tracts, water molecules travel along the internal membrane, not across the fiber walls. With degradation of myelin sheath in normal aging, the probability and speed of diffusion along the fiber walls diminish. Two measures, fractional anisotropy (FA) and apparent diffusion coefficient (ADC), quantify these changes and, in turn, white matter integrity. Reduced FA and increased ADC are indicative of degraded micro-structural tissue integrity.

Several studies have investigated age-related differences in FA and ADC in numerous brain regions (Abe et al., 2002; Madden, Whiting, Huettel, White, MacFall, & Provenzale, 2004; Madden et al., 2007; Pfefferbaum, Sullivan, Hedehus, Lim, Adalsteinsson, & Moseley, 2000; Salat et al., 2005; Sullivan et al., 2001). Significant age-related decline in white matter integrity was found in the centrum semiovale (white matter in the medial 55% of the left and right hemispheres), frontal white matter tracts, the posterior limb of the internal capsule, and the genu of the corpus callosum. Furthermore, evidence suggests that age-related decline in anisotropy and diffusivity is more pronounced in anterior, as opposed to posterior, regions. Correspondingly, two studies focusing specifically on alterations of prefrontal white matter (Pfefferbaum, Adalsteinsson, & Sullivan, 2005; Salat et al., 2005) showed that prefrontal FA was reduced in older adults compared to younger adults. Furthermore, Salat et al. (2005) found that prefrontal FA values were significantly correlated with prefrontal volume measures in individuals over the age of 40. Within prefrontal regions, ventromedial and deep prefrontal regions showed a greater reduction compared to other regions. Similar to this finding, Pfefferbaum et al. (2005) also found significant age-related FA decline in restricted frontal regions, whereas posterior and inferior white matter was largely preserved. The authors suggest that this pattern of frontal dysfunction may account for age-related behavioral deficits in frontally based processes. Additionally, Head et al. (2004) found age differences in FA and ADC in anterior and posterior corpus callosum and all four cortical lobes. Age-related differences were greater in anterior compared to posterior callosal white matter as well as frontal vs. temporal, parietal, and occipital white matter. Results suggest an anterior–posterior gradient for decline in the structural integrity of white matter. (See Figure 1.2 in color plate section.)

Like cortical atrophy, declines in white matter volume and integrity also exhibit correlations with cognitive performance in older adults. Following the aforementioned anterior–posterior gradient, these correlations are often more prevalent in anterior regions. Accordingly, declines in frontal white matter (e.g., FA values) have been associated with measures of processing speed (Symbol Digit Modalities Test) and reasoning

(Raven's Progressive Matrices Test; Stebbins et al., 2001) and memory performance (Persson et al., 2006). Taken together, results indicate that degradation of both white and gray matter within the frontal lobes contributes to decline in cognitive processes mediated by this region.

However, studies have found relationships between white matter integrity and performance in other brain regions as well. For example, Madden et al. (2004) found that FA in the splenium (most posterior portion of the corpus callosum) was a significant predictor of reaction time (RT) for younger adults, whereas FA in the anterior limb of the internal capsule predicted RT in older adults. Results not only suggest that slower responding is correlated with decline in FA values, but that performance in older adults is more dependent on the integrity of the fronto-striatal circuitry than on the frontal circuitry alone. Persson et al. (2006) found that word reading correlated with ADC and FA values in premotor/ precentral callosal bundles, with FA and fiber length in postcentral bundles, and with number of fibers in posterior parietal and superior temporal bundles. The authors suggest that age-related degradation in the corpus callosum may impede bilateral recruitment—recruitment necessary for enhanced performance in older adults (Cabeza, 2002).

Measures of Resting Blood Flow and Metabolism

In addition to age-related differences in both gray and white matter, research has examined differences in cerebral blood flow (CBF) and metabolic activity in aging. As suggested by the aforementioned volume data, age-related differences are observed in resting functional imaging as well. Early research using nontomographic methods (Kety, 1956) first indicated CBF and metabolic activity decline with age. Furthermore, this decrease paralleled decreases in cortical density. Kety suggested that age-related decreases in metabolic activity were indicative of neuronal loss.

More recent evidence from imaging methodologies suggests mixed results in regards to CBF and metabolic activity in healthy aging (for a review see Madden & Hoffman, 1997). However, when present, age differences indicated decline in both measures as a function of age. For example, assessing regional cerebral metabolic rate for glucose (rCMR-glc), several studies indicated no change across age (e.g., de Leon et al., 1983; Duara et al., 1983; Haxby et al., 1986), whereas others noted an age-related decline in rCMRglc in frontal (e.g., Azari et al., 1992; Horwitz, Duara, & Rapoport, 1986; e.g., Kuhl, Metter, Riege, & Phelps, 1982; Riege, Metter, Kuhl, & Phelps, 1985) and parietal regions (e.g., Azari et al., 1992; Horwitz et al., 1986; e.g., Kuhl et al., 1982). When compared directly, greater decline was observed in frontal regions (de Leon et al., 1987; Kuhl et al., 1982). More recently, studies have shown that glucose regulation may have a significant impact on cognition in older adults (e.g., Kaplan, Greenwood, Winocur, & Wolever, 2000; Messier & Gagnon, 2000). For example, Kaplan et al. (2000) found that glucose regulation was associated with both verbal declarative memory and visuomotor performance in healthy older adults.

Regional cerebral metabolic rate for oxygen ($rCMRO_2$) also shows mixed results, with some studies finding no difference across age (e.g., Herscovitch, Auchus, Gado, Chi, & Raichle, 1986; Itoh et al., 1990) and others showing age-related decreases in multiple regions (e.g., Leenders et al., 1990; Pantano, Baron, Lebrun-Grandie, Duquesnoy, Bousser, & Comar, 1984; e.g., Yamaguchi et al., 1986). Like rCMRglc, $rCMRO_2$ decline was often observed in frontal and parietal regions (e.g., Pantano et al., 1984). Furthermore, most decreases in $rCMRO_2$ showed linear declines with age.

Finally, regional CBF (rCBF) also showed both stability (e.g., Herscovitch et al., 1986; Itoh et al., 1990; Yamaguchi et al., 1986) and decline (e.g., Frackowiak, Lenzi, Jones, & Heather, 1980; Leenders et al., 1990; Marchal et al., 1992) across early aging studies. This controversy has remained in more recent assessments. For example, Larsson et al. (2001) found an age-related decrease in rCBF across 28 gray and white matter regions when assessing middle-aged (40 yrs), young-old (75 yrs), and old-old (88 yrs), with the annual reduction in rCBF increasing from .10% from middle-aged to young-old to .13% from young-old to the old-old adults. However, a study by Meltzer and colleagues (2000) suggests that apparent age-related reductions in rCBF can be removed by correcting for partial-volume effects (see also Inoue et al., 2005). Thus, the authors suggest that age-related cerebral atrophy may confound interpretation of metabolic measurements in previous studies, and thus must be first corrected for when interpreting difference in rCBF among groups.

More recent PET and fMRI studies have also found age-related differences in the blood oxygen level dependent (BOLD) signal and hemodynamic response (HDR) amplitude. Assessing HDR in visual cortex during photic stimulation, Ross and colleagues (1997) observed a decrease in HDR amplitude, but not in the volume of cortical activation. Other studies have found mixed results in regards to age-related differences in HDR. For example, Brodtmann, Puce, Syngeniotis, Darby, and Donnan (2003) did not observe age-related differences in the HDR until the ninth decade, suggesting that these age-related differences in HDR may be restricted to only the oldest-old. Buckner, Snyder, Sanders, Raichle, and Morris (2000) found age-related reductions in the amplitude of the HDR in visual cortex, but not in other brain regions (e.g., motor cortex). The authors concluded that the summation of the HDR overall was highly similar between age groups. Two other studies (D'Esposito, Zarahn, Aguirre, &

Rypma, 1999; Huettel, Singerman, & McCarthy, 2001) also observed age equivalent HDR, but reductions in the number of activated voxels. The authors suggest reductions in activated voxels in older adults may be due to increased physiological noise in older adults. Despite the absolute differences in some resting measures mentioned above, recent work suggests that relative activation changes should be preserved with age and that functional neuroimaging designs that employ group comparisons between task conditions or parametric manipulations are valid and can be an effective means of assessing age-related differences in functional and anatomical measures (Buckner et al., 2000; Huettel et al., 2001).

Measures of Neurotransmitter Function: The Case of Dopamine

Much of the research assessing neurotransmitter differences in aging has focused on the role of dopamine (DA). There are two main families of DA receptors, D_1 and D_2. In the presynaptic terminal, the DA transporter protein regulates the synaptic DA concentration. Dopamine systems are critical for higher order cognitive functions. For example, patients with DA deficits (Huntington's and Parkinson's disease) often show cognitive deficits—which can be modulated by dopamine agonists and antagonists. The role of DA in cognition is also supported by computational models, and by ontogenetic and phylogenetic evidence.

Like the aforementioned structural decline, in vivo measurements of DA decline exceed those of in vitro studies. In vivo studies (Antonini & Leenders, 1993; Ichise et al., 1998; Suhara et al., 1991; Wang et al., 1998) using PET and single photon emission computerized tomography (SPECT) have found loss of striatal D_1 and D_2 receptor binding across adulthood, with age-related decreases ranging between 7–10% per decade. Additionally, age-related decreases in striatal DA transporter protein binding have been measured in vivo at a rate of 4.4 to 8% per decade (Rinne, Sahlberg, Ruottinen, Nagren, & Lehikoinen, 1998; van Dyck et al., 1995).

The relationship between age-related changes in DA and age-related cognitive differences has been examined in only a small number of studies. Despite the paucity of data, findings are remarkably consistent. Age deficits in striatal DA have been associated with reduction in episodic memory (Bäckman et al., 2000; Erixon-Lindroth, Farde, Wahlin, Sovago, Halldin, & Bäckman, 2005), executive function (Erixon-Lindroth et al., 2005; Mozley, Gur, Mozley, & Gur, 2001; Volkow et al., 1998), and motor performance (Mozley et al., 2001; Wang et al., 1998). Furthermore, several studies have also found that striatal DA markers served as a significant predictor of cognitive performance, after controlling for the effects of age (Bäckman et al., 2000; Volkow et al., 1998), and also, that age-related cognitive deficits were completely mediated by reductions in striatal DA functioning (Erixon-Lindroth et al., 2005).

DA loss in aging has also been observed in frontal, temporal, and occipital cortices as well as in hippocampus and thalamus (Inoue et al., 2001; Kaasinen et al., 2000). The magnitude of extrastriatal DA decline mirrors that observed within the striatum itself. Given the cognitive role of fronto-striatal loops, age-related striatal DA deficits could also account for age-related cognitive deficits associated with PFC dysfunction. Moreover, age-related deficits in DA binding have been observed in PFC, as well as in posterior cortical and hippocampal regions.

Evidence is mixed as to whether these declines are linear (see Reeves, Bench, & Howard, 2002) or exponential (Antonini & Leenders, 1993; Bannon & Whitty, 1997; Rinne et al., 1998) across adulthood. The correlation between declines in DA receptor binding and DA transporter protein binding may reflect a common causal mechanism for age-related DA loss (e.g., DiGirolamo et al., 2001).

Summary

Taken together, resting neuroimaging measures suggest significant age-related differences. Both white and gray matter decline show similar patterns in aging, with structural decline appearing most prominent in advanced aging and anterior regions showing greater decline compared to posterior regions. Age-related decline in both pre- and post-synaptic DA markers also tends to follow this anterior–posterior gradient of decline. Both patterns coincide with behavioral data findings that show greater age-related performance decrements in cognitive functions mediated by frontal functioning (see West, 1996) and greater cognitive decline in advanced aging (for a review see Park, 2002). Furthermore, resting blood flow and metabolism measures (i.e., in rCMRglc, rCMRO$_2$ and CBF) also show age-related decline in healthy adults. However, caution should be used when interpreting these findings, for they also may reflect changes caused by age differences in cerebral atrophy.

In addition to resting neuroimaging measures, several studies have also examined cognitive performance—finding significant correlations between structure and function. Thus, results underscore the need to not only consider age-related differences within a given measure, but also to assess its relationship with behavioral measures of cognition. One of the strongest approaches to understanding the neural mechanisms for age-related cognitive decline will be to consider the interaction of several methodologies in assessing age-related cognitive deficits.

TASK-RELATED ACTIVATIONS IN NEUROIMAGING
STUDIES OF AGING

Before reviewing the findings of studies in each cognitive domain, it is useful to describe first two patterns of age-related differences in brain activity that are consistently found in several domains. First, several studies, particularly in the visual perception domain, have found an age-related decrease in occipital activity coupled with an age-related increase in PFC activity. This pattern, which we call *posterior–anterior shift in aging* (PASA), can be easily identified in Table 1.1 (minus signs in occipital lobe, plus signs in frontal lobe). Grady et al. (1994) were the first to noticed this pattern, and they suggested that older adults compensated for visual processing deficits (occipital decrease) by recruiting higher order cognitive processes (PFC increase). In this study older and younger adults were matched in accuracy but differed in RTs, so the authors further suggested that additional recruitment of PFC functions allows older adults to maintain a good accuracy level at the expense of slower reaction times. Most subsequent studies that found PASA endorsed Grady et al.'s compensatory account of age-related PFC increases.

Second, in many studies across several different cognitive domains (perception, attention, working memory, episodic memory encoding, epi-

TABLE 1.1
PASA (Posterior–Anterior Shift in Aging)

			Occipital	*Frontal*
BP	Perception	Grady 94	−	+
BP	Perception	Grady 94	+/−	+
BP	Perception	Grady 00	−	+/−
BP	Perception	Levine 00	+/−	+
BF	Perception	Gunning-Dixon 03	−	+
EF	Perception	Iidaka 02	−	+/−
BP	Attention	Madden 97	−	+
EF	Attention	Cabeza 04	−	+
EF	Working Memory	Cabeza 04	−	+
BP	Problem Solving	Nagahama 97	−	+/−
EF	Encoding	Meulenbroek 04	−	+/−
EF	Encoding	Gutchess 05	−	+
EF	Retrieval	Cabeza 04	+/−	+
BP	Retrieval	Grady 02	−	+
BP	Retrieval	Anders 00	+/−	+/−
BP	Retrieval	Cabeza 00	−	+/−

Significant activation in older compared with younger adults. Plus signs represent age-related activity increases and minus signs, decreases. BP = blocked PET; BF = blocked fMRI; EF = event-related fMRI.

TABLE 1.2
HAROLD

			Younger		Older	
			L	R	L	R
BF	Encoding	Stebbins 02	++	+	+	+
BF	Encoding-inc	Logan 02	++	+	++	++
BF	Encoding-inc	Rosen 02	++	+	+	+
EF	Encoding-inc/Dm	Morcom 03	+	–	++	++
BF	Encoding-int	Logan 02	+	+	+	+
BP	Encoding-int	Cabeza 97	++	–	+	+
EF	Inhibitory Control	Nielson 02	–	+	+	+
EF	Language	Perrson 04	+	–	+	+
BP	Perception	Grady 94 exp 2	–	+	++	++
BP	Perception	Grady 00a	+	+++	++	++
BP	Retrieval	Cabeza 97	–	++	+	+
BP	Retrieval	Bäckman 97	–	+	+	+
BP	Retrieval	Madden 99	–	+	++	++
BP	Retrieval	Grady 00b	–	++	+	+
BP	Retrieval	Cabeza 02	–	+	+	+
EF	Retrieval	Maguire 03*	–	+	+	+
BP	Working Memory (letter)	Reuter-Lorenz 00	+	–	+	+
BP	Working Memory (location)	Reuter-Lorenz 00	–	+	+	+
BP	Working Memory	Dixit 00	+	+++	++	++
EF	Working Memory	Cabeza 04b	+	+	+	+
BP	Working Memory	Grady 98	+	++	+	+

Plus signs represent significant activity in the left and right PFC, and minus signs represent non-significant activity. The number of plus signs is an approximate index of the relative amount of activity in left and right PFC in each study, and it cannot be compared across studies. inc = incidental; int = intentional; Dm = subsequent memory paradigm; BF = blocked fMRI; BP = blocked PET; EF = event-related fMRI; *activation differences within MTL.

sodic memory retrieval, inhibitory control, etc.) older adults showed a more bilateral (less asymmetric) pattern of PFC activity than younger adults. This pattern was conceptualized as a *Hemispheric Asymmetry Reduction in OLDer Adults* (HAROLD) model (Cabeza, 2002; see Table 1.2). The HAROLD pattern was originally described by Cabeza et al. (1997) and attributed to a compensatory mechanism. This *compensation account* is consistent with evidence that bilateral activity in older adults is positively correlated with successful cognitive performance (Reuter-Lorenz et al., 2000), and is found in high-performing rather than in low-performing older adults (Cabeza, 2002; Rosen et al., 2002). However, an alternative account is that a more widespread activation pattern reflects an age-related difficulty in engaging specialized neural mechanisms (e.g., Li & Lindenberger, 1999; Logan, Sanders, Snyder, Morris, & Buckner, 2002). This *dedifferentiation account* is consistent with an age-related increase in correlations across tasks (Lindenberger & Baltes, 1994). In general, the available evidence tends to be more consistent with the compensation than with the dedifferentiation account (Daselaar, Veltman, Rombouts, Raaijmakers, & Jonker, 2005) but further research is certainly required.

Visual Perception

Visual perception studies often find age-related reductions in activations in visual cortex regions, as well as in more anterior regions of the ventral pathway, such as the parahippocampal gyrus (Iidaka et al., 2002; Levine et al., 2000) and also the amygdala (Fischer et al., 2005; Gunning-Dixon et al., 2003; Iidaka et al., 2002). MTL decreases may reflect an extension of occipital decreases or specific deficits in memory or emotion-related processes. Additionally, other studies show age-related increases in more anterior brain regions such as PFC (Grady et al., 1994; Grady, McIntosh, Horwitz, & Rapoport, 2000), anterior cingulate (Gunning-Dixon et al., 2003), and insula (Fischer, Sandblom, Gavazzeni, Fransson, Wright, & Bäckman, 2005) (see Table 1.3). Researchers suggest that the frontal increases compensate for the occipital decreases. As noted earlier, a compensation hypothesis is common in explaining age-related shifts in neural activation. However, like other compensation theories, the specific cognitive operations recruited by older adults have yet to be identified.

Attention

In general, attention studies also show age-related compensation in the form of the PASA pattern (Cabeza, Daselaar, Dolcos, Prince, Budde, & Nyberg, 2004; Madden & Hoffman, 1997) as well as other forms of compensation such as activation of deep gray matter regions (Madden et al., 2004; see Table 1.3). For example, when cueing selective attention, both spatial (Madden & Hoffman, 1997) and color (Madden et al., 2002) visual cues elicited weaker occipital activity in older adults, but stronger PFC activation. Similar results have been found for sustained attention (Cabeza et al., 2004). In this study, the PASA pattern was simultaneously found for visual attention, verbal working memory, and verbal episodic retrieval (see below), supporting the generality of this phenomenon.

However, not all attention studies show anterior increases. As noted, age-related increases in deep gray matter regions (striatum, thalamus, insula) were seen for an odd-ball task where activation in frontal regions showed no age-related differences (Madden, Whiting, Provenzale, & Huettel, 2004). In the single study to date focusing on the effects of aging on auditory attention using a dichotic listening task (Thomsen, Specht,

TABLE 1.3
PET/fMRI Studies of Visual Perception/Attention

| | | Left Hemisphere | | | | | | | Right Hemisphere | | | | | | |
| | | Occipital | | | Left PFC | | | | Right PFC | | | | Occipital | | |
		17	18	19	P	VL	DL	A	A	DL	VL	P	19	18	17
Visual Perception															
BP	Grady 94 — face: matching – bl		●		○	○						○		●	
BP	Grady 94 — location: match – bl			○							○			●	
BP	Grady 00 — face-ndgr: match – bl		●	●	○	○	○			○	●	○		●	
BP	Levine 00 — form perception – bl		○		○	○	○	○	●					○	
BF	Gunning-Dixon 03 — face expression: discrim. – bl	●							●						●
EF	Iidaka 02 — face expression: perception – bl		●	●								●	●	●	
EF	Fischer 05 — face expression: angry vs. neutral							○	○		○	●	●	●	
Attention															
BP	Madden 97 — visual srch: divided – central		●					●	●			○	●	●	
BP	Madden 02 — visual srch: covariate w/ perform		●	●									●		●
EF	Cabeza 04 — visual sustained attention – bl		●		○	○		○	○		○	○		●	
EF	Thomsen 04 — dichot. listening: attend-left			○	●	●		●	●		●				

● only young/young > old; ○ only old/old>young; BP = blocked PET; BF = blocked fMRI; EF = event-related fMRI; bl = baseline; srch = search; dichot = dichotic; P = posterior; VL = ventrolateral; DL = dorsolateral; A = anterior.

Hammar, Nyttinges, Ersland, & Hugdahl, 2004), older adults showed a reduction in left dorsal PFC (BA 8/9) activation. Cortical thickness in this region was also reduced in older adults, suggesting both functional and structural changes underlie age-related attentional deficits.

Language/Semantic Processing

To date, the majority of studies in this domain have investigated simple linguistic and semantic processes using words as stimuli. Two studies by Madden and collaborators investigating lexical decisions (word/ nonword) found age-related reductions in ventral pathway activity (Madden et al., 1996, 2002). Unlike studies of perception and attention, these studies did not show compensatory increases in frontal regions. Johnson and Jusczyk (2001) also showed that simple auditory semantic and phonological decisions may not require compensatory PFC activity. Additionally, the work of Persson, Sylvester, Nelson, Welsh, Jonides, and Reuter-Lorenz (2004) and Grossman and colleagues (2002a, 2002b) suggests that age-related differences are minimal when the demands for mediating age-sensitive cognitive functions are low. For example, during a study of sentence comprehension across different working memory loads, both younger and older adults recruited a similar set of regions, independent of working memory demands, including the left temporal and ventrolateral PFC regions, and bilateral occipital cortex—and common activation in left ventrolateral PFC was associated with increased working memory load. However, overall, older adults showed weaker task-related activity in parietal cortex but greater activity in left dorsal PFC, right temporal, and bilateral anteromedial PFC regions. According to the authors, the latter age-related increases reflect up-regulation of portions of rehearsal (Broca's area) and material-specific (right temporoparietal cortex) aspects of a large-scale working memory network supporting complex sentence comprehension. The preservation of cortical regions mediating core language functions appears robust enough to posit that healthy aging is not associated with cortical reorganization or compensation related to language abilities. Rather, it is the increased demands of working memory and visual perceptual skills in aging that account for observed age-related differences.

Working Memory

Working memory (WM) involves a composite of cognitive operations, including maintenance of information over a brief delay, manipulation and monitoring of information, and executive processes involved in problem solving and reasoning tasks. We will review each of these components separately.

Maintenance and Manipulation

Overall, maintenance and manipulation of information in WM results in age-related reductions in activity in PFC regions engaged by younger adults but greater activity in other PFC regions, such as contralateral PFC regions (i.e., the PFC hemisphere less engaged by younger adults). Typically referred to as HAROLD, these age-related increases in frontal bilaterality have been seen in both verbal (e.g., Cabeza et al., 2004; Reuter-Lorenz et al., 2000) and visuospatial WM tasks (Park et al., 2003; Reuter-Lorenz et al., 2000). See Table 1.4 for an overview of WM studies. For example, Reuter-Lorenz et al. (2000) examined simple maintenance operations in aging using both verbal and spatial stimuli. Whereas the verbal task resulted in reduced left and increased right PFC activity, the spatial task showed reduced right and increased left PFC activity in older adults. Thus, in both instances, older adults showed a more bilateral pattern of PFC activity consistent with the HAROLD model. Often, such contralateral recruitment in older adults is interpreted as compensatory, frequently cited as reflecting a response to increased task demands (Grady, McIntosh, Bookstein, Horwitz, Rapoport, & Haxby, 1998) or retrieval effort (Park et al., 2003), as well as decreased activation in other brain regions such as PFC and MTL (e.g., Cabeza et al., 2004; Haut, Kuwabara, Leach, & Callahan, 2000; Park et al., 2003; Rypma, Prabhakaran, Desmond, & Gabrieli, 2001).

Age-related reductions in MTL regions have been observed in three nonverbal WM studies (Grady et al., 1998; Mitchell, Johnson, Raye, & D'Esposito, 2000; Park et al., 2003) but never in verbal WM studies. For example, in a study by Mitchell et al. (2000) older adults showed equivalent performance to young in a single item WM task, but a marked decrease in performance for the combination (location plus object) condition. This performance deficit was accompanied by decreased activity in the left anterior hippocampus and anteromedial PFC (right BA 10) compared to younger adults. Suggesting that a disruption in hippocampal-PFC circuitry may underlie age-related deficits in the combination condition, the authors concluded that aging not only affects the overall magnitude of brain activity, but also can disrupt activations amongst regions (see also Della-Maggiore, Sekuler, Grady, Bennett, Sekuler, & McIntosh, 2000; McIntosh et al., 1999). Interpreting the lack of MTL decreases in verbal WM studies, it is possible that nonverbal tasks were more dependent on hippocampal-mediated relational memory processing, and hence more sensitive to age-related deficits in these regions.

TABLE 1.4
PET/fMRI Studies of Working Memory (WM) and Executive Functioning

			Left Hemisphere				Right Hemisphere			
			Left PFC				*Right PFC*			
			P	VL	DL	A	A	DL	VL	P
Verbal WM										
BP	Reuter-L. 00	letter: WM – bl (VOIs)					○			○
BF	Rypma 01	letter: WM: 6–1 letter load	●	○	●		●	●	●	●
BF	Rypma 00	letter: WM Enc, main, retr	●							●
EF	Cabeza 04	word: WM – bl	○		○		○		○	○
BP	Haut 00	number: self-ordering > ctrl								●
BP	Haut 00	number: ext.-ordered > ctrl	○							
EF	Johnson 04	word: refresh > repeat/read	●							
EF	Sun 05	fwd & bkwd digit span						○		
Visuospatial WM										
BP	Reuter-L. 00	locat: WM – bl (VOIs)	○		○					
BP	Grady 98	face: WM – bl	○	●					●	
BP	Grady 98	incr w/long delays							●	●
EF	Mitchel 00	objects.: combo > obj / loc					●			
EF	Park 03	scenes: maint or probe		○	○		○	○		
BF	Lamar 04	DMTS – ctrl			●		●			●
BF	Lamar 04	DNMTS – ctrl	●		●		●		≈	
Executive Functioning										
EF	Nielsen 02	no-go > base	○	○			○	≈		
BF	Milham 02	Stroop: incong > others	●	○			●		○	
BF	Langenecker 04	Stroop: incong > neutral	○		○		○		○	
BP	Nagahama 97	WCST – bl	●		●		●	○	○	
BP	Esposito 99	WCST (corr w/ age)	●							○
BP	Esposito 99	RPM (corr w/ age)	○	○					○	

● only young/young > old; ○ only old/old > young; ≈ young~old; BP = blocked PET; BF = blocked fMRI; EF = event-related fMRI; bl = baseline; Enc = Encoding; retr = retrieval; fwd = forward; bkwd = backward; obj = object; loc = location; ctrl = control; dscr = discrimination; incr = increasing; incong = incongruent; corr = correlation; WCST = Wisconsin Card Sorting Task; P = posterior; VL = ventrolateral; DL = dorsolateral; A = anterior.

Executive Functions

The effects of aging on brain activity associated with executive functions have been measured with tasks that tap such processes as inhibitory control, task switching, dual-task performance, and reasoning. The most consistent finding across all studies to date has been age-related increases in PFC activation (Jonides, Marshuetz, Smith, Reuter-Lorenz, Koeppe, & Hartley, 2000a; Langenecker, Nielson, & Rao, 2004; Milham et al., 2002;

Nielson, Langenecker, & Garavan, 2002; Smith, Geva, Jonides, Miller, Reuter-Lorenz, & Koeppe, 2001). PFC increases in these executive tasks were more prevalent than those seen in simpler WM tasks, possibly reflecting greater cognitive demands for executive function tasks. This notion conforms to the compensation account suggested in several studies. Fittingly, in several of the studies, age-related PFC increases led to bilateral PFC activations in older adults (HAROLD). Also consistent with this account, PFC regions were differentially engaged by younger adults with limited cognitive resources (Smith et al., 2001). However, in some cases, age-related increases in PFC activity may indicate a failure to inhibit irrelevant information presented earlier (Milham et al., 2002). In regards to parietal activity, the results are mixed, with some studies finding age-related increases in parietal activity (Nielson et al., 2002) and others showing decreases (Esposito, Kirby, Van Horn, Ellmore, & Faith Berman, 1999; Milham et al., 2002; Nagahama et al., 1997).

Implicit Memory

Several neuroimaging studies have investigated effects of aging on implicit memory using such tasks as word stem completion priming (Bäckman, Robins-Wahlin, Lundin, Ginovart, & Farde, 1997; Daselaar et al., 2005), repetition priming (Lustig & Buckner, 2004), sequence learning (Aizenstein et al., 2006; Daselaar, Rombouts, Veltman, Raaijmakers, & Jonker, 2003), and probabilistic categorical learning (Fera et al., 2005). Overall, results indicate that memory functions in this domain are relatively preserved in older adults. Three studies found age equivalent activations (Bäckman et al., 1997; Daselaar et al., 2003; Lustig & Buckner, 2004) and two others found similar regions activated in young and older adults, but reduced activity within these regions in older adults (Daselaar et al., 2005; Fera et al., 2005). When present, age differences in activation during implicit memory using such tasks involve age-related decreases in frontal and striatal regions (Aizenstein et al., 2006; Fera et al., 2005). Whereas priming is known to be mediated by frontal and occipital regions (Buckner et al., 1995), sequence and categorical learning are attributed to activation in fronto-striatal circuitry (Daselaar et al., 2003; Grafton, Hazeltine, & Ivry, 1995). Thus, the aforementioned dissociation in preserved vs. impaired neural functioning may be a result of age differences in the neural circuitry supporting different types of implicit tasks.

Episodic Memory Encoding

Episodic memory is one of the cognitive functions most affected by aging, and accordingly it is the focus of a large number of functional neuroimaging studies. An important advantage of functional neuroimaging is that, unlike behavioral methods, it provides separate measures of encoding and retrieval processes. This section considers studies that measured brain activity during encoding, and the next section those that measured activity during retrieval.

Encoding studies typically fall into one of three groups: intentional encoding studies, incidental encoding studies (both using blocked designs), and subsequent memory studies. During intentional encoding studies, participants are scanned while attempting to memorize words, faces, objects, or spatial routes, whereas, during incidental encoding, participants are usually asked to make a judgment (i.e., semantic, size) concerning stimuli during encoding, with no overt attempts at memorizing. Finally, in subsequent memory studies, activity associated with successful encoding operations is identified by comparing activity for items that are subsequently remembered to items that are subsequently forgotten (for a review see Paller & Wagner, 2002). The most common results, spanning all three methods, are discussed below. See Table 1.5 for an overview of all encoding studies.

The most consistent finding within blocked designs is an age-related reduction in left PFC activity (Anderson, Iidaka, Cabeza, Kapur, McIntosh, & Craik, 2000; Cabeza et al., 1997; Daselaar et al., 2003b; Grady, Bernstein, Beig, & Siegenthaler, 2002; Grady et al., 1995; Logan et al., 2002; Morcom, Good, Frackowiak, & Rugg, 2003; Nyberg et al., 2003; Rosen et al., 2002; Stebbins et al., 2002). This finding is more prevalent in intentional compared to incidental encoding studies (see Table 1.5), suggesting that the environmental support provided by a deep encoding task may attenuate the age-related decrease in left PFC activity. This difference highlights a strategic component in age-related memory decline. However, recent subsequent memory studies using event-related fMRI show increased age-related activity in dorsolateral and orbito-prefrontal cortex (Dennis, Daselaar, & Cabeza, 2006; Gutchess et al., 2005; Morcom et al., 2003). One explanation for this difference in PFC activity may be accounted for by differences in blocked vs. event-related designs, which measure sustained and transient encoding-related activity, respectively. In support of this theory, Dennis et al. (2006) showed that while younger and older adults recruited a similar set of regions for transient successful encoding, they recruited qualitatively different regions supporting sustained successful encoding.

A second common finding within encoding studies is that of age-related increased activity in right PFC regions, resulting in a more bilateral pattern of PFC activity (i.e., HAROLD) (Anderson, Iidaka, Cabeza, Kapur, McIntosh, & Craik, 2000; Cabeza et al., 1997; Daselaar et al., 2003b; Grady, et al., 2002; Logan et al., 2002; Rosen et al., 2002; Stebbins

TABLE 1.5

PET/fMRI Studies of Episodic Memory Encoding

		Left Hemisphere						Right Hemisphere					
		MTL		Left PFC				Right PFC				MTL	
		PHG	HC	P	VL	DL	A	A	DL	VL	P	HC	PHG
Intentional encoding													
BP Grady 95	face: Enc – 2 bl											●	
BP Cabeza 97	word pair: Enc – Rn/Rc			●	●						○		
BP Anderson 00	word pairs: FA Enc – FA Rc			●	●		●	●	○		○		
BF Logan 02 exp 1	words: intent Enc – bl				●		●	○					
BP Madden 99	words: Enc – bl							○					
BP Schiavetto 02	obj ident Enc > obj loc Enc		●										
BF Iidaka 01	object pairs: abstract Enc – bl												
BP Nyberg 03	loci mnemonic: training – pretest					●							
Incidental encoding													
BP Grady 02	face: Enc – Rn				●								
BF Stebbins 02	word: deep – shallow			●	●		●	○					
BF Logan 02 exp 2	word: deep – shallow						●	○					
BF Daselaar 03b	word: deep – shallow		●										
BF Rosen 02	Old-high, word: deep – shallow		●							●	○		
EF Daselaar 03c	Old-low, word: rem – bl	●	●										
Subsequent memory													
EF Morcom 03	word Dm: Y long delay – O short delay					○		○	○				
EF Gutchess 05	picture Dm	●	●					○	○				●
EF Dennis 06	word Dm: Transient activity	●	●			○		○	○				
EF Dennis 06	word Dm: Sustained activity						●		●		●		

● only young/young > old; ○ only old/old > young; BP = blocked PET; BF = blocked fMRI; EF = event-related fMRI; bl = baseline; Enc = Encoding; obj = object; P = posterior; RC = recall; Rn = recognition; VL = ventrolateral; DL = dorsolateral; A = anterior.

et al., 2002). While the aforementioned decreases were often interpreted as reflecting a disturbed encoding network (i.e., the typical set of regions associated with encoding in young adults) in older adults, increased contralateral recruitment was often interpreted as compensatory. Two studies that divided older adults into high- and low-performers found the HAROLD pattern only in the high-performing group (Daselaar et al., 2003b; Rosen et al., 2002), supporting a finding previously reported for retrieval (Cabeza, Anderson, Locantore, & McIntosh, 2002). These results provide direct support for the compensation account of HAROLD.

A third common finding is decreased MTL activity in older compared to younger adults (Daselaar, Veltman, Rombouts, Raaijmakers, & Jonker, 2003a, Daselaar et al., 2003b; Dennis, Daselaar, & Cabeza, 2006; Grady et al., 1995, 2002; Gutchess et al., 2005; Iidaka et al., 2002). Taken together, decreases in left PFC and MTL are often interpreted as reflecting a disturbed encoding network in older adults. For example, Grady and colleagues (1995) found that younger but not older adults showed a highly significant correlation between MTL and left PFC activity. Based on these results, the authors concluded that aging is accompanied by reduced neural activity and diminished connectivity between PFC and MTL areas. Supporting the aforementioned theory of age-related disruptions in the encoding network, Gutchess et al. (2005) found that older adults exhibited a significant negative correlation between inferior frontal and parahippocampal activity, whereas younger adults did not. These results suggest that older adults who engage less hippocampal activity conversely engage more frontal areas, suggesting that a selective recruitment of left PFC may compensate for MTL dysfunction. Furthermore, Daselaar and colleagues (2003b) were able to directly link reductions in MTL activity to reduced memory performance. Taken together, these findings indicate that reduced MTL function accompanies frontal differences and also contributes to age-related memory decline.

Finally, it should be noted that older adults also exhibit decreases in posterior parietal (Iidaka et al., 2001; Schiavetto, Kohler, Grady, Winocur, & Moscovitch, 2002) and visual regions (Iidaka et al., 2001; Meulenbroek, Petersson, Voermans, Weber, & Fernandez, 2004; Schiavetto et al., 2002) compared to younger adults. Studies by Schiavetto et al., Iidaka et al., and Meulenbroek et al. suggest age-related deficits in visuospatial processing associated with reduced activity in parietal regions. These studies suggest that age-related reductions in parietal activity were associated with deficits in encoding of visuospatial information, thus suggesting that attentional deficits may play a role in decline of visuospatial memory. Furthermore, decreased activation in posterior brain regions and increased PFC activity suggest a reduction in functional specialization with age.

Episodic Memory Retrieval

As with encoding, the literature regarding aging and imaging in retrieval can also be broken down into three main categories of study: recognition, recall, and context memory. In recognition studies participants are shown items presented at encoding along with new items and asked to judge whether they recognize the item as old or new, whereas recall studies require participants to freely generate that which was presented during encoding. Finally, context memory involves remembering not just the individual item presented at encoding, but also in what context (i.e., temporal order, color, location) it was presented. Again, the most consistent findings from all three types of retrieval studies are discussed below (see Table 1.6).

Several studies report finding similarly activated regions for recognition across age groups (Daselaar et al., 2003b; Grady et al., 1995; Tisserand, McIntosh, van der Veen, Backes, & Jolles, 2005). Such results have led researchers to suggest that age effects are more pronounced for encoding than retrieval. However, despite this relative stability, age differences do arise. For example, in a recent study by Cabeza et al. (2004), older adults showed decreases in occipital and parietal regions coupled with increases in PFC regions (i.e., the PASA pattern). Several studies find age-related decreases in right PFC activity (Anderson et al., 2000; Bäckman et al., 1997; Cabeza, Anderson, Houle, Mangels, & Nyberg, 2000; Cabeza, Dolcos, Graham, & Nyberg, 2002; Cabeza et al., 1997; Schacter, Savage, Alpert, Rauch, & Albert, 1996; Schiavetto et al., 2002). Overall, older adults show larger age deficits as task difficulty increases (i.e., context> recall>recognition tasks).

Reduced right PFC activity in older adults often resulted in a more bilateral pattern of PFC in older adults than in younger adults (i.e., HAROLD). This age-related bilaterality has also been observed in MTL regions during recall of words (Bäckman et al., 1997) and autobiographical memories (Maguire & Frith, 2003), suggesting that HAROLD may generalize to other brain regions outside of PFC. Like left PFC decreases, retrieval resulting in the HAROLD pattern has been found more frequently in studies using demanding recall and context memory tasks than during simpler item recognition. Overall, results suggest a three-way interaction between age, task difficulty, and frontal laterality. Importantly, distinguishing between old-high performing and old-low performing adults, a study by Cabeza et al. (2002) showed that only the old-high performers showed this frontal bilaterality, providing direct evidence for the compensation account of HAROLD.

Regarding MTL activity during retrieval, several studies reported increases in MTL activity with age (Bäckman et al., 1997; Cabeza et al.,

TABLE 1.6
PET/fMRI Studies of Episodic Memory Retrieval

			Left Hemisphere						Right Hemisphere					
			MTL		Left PFC				Right PFC				MTL	
			PHG	HC	P	VL	DL	A	A	DL	VL	P	HC	PHG
Recognition														
BP	Cabeza 97	word pair: Rn – Enc						○	○	○	●			
BP	Madden 99	word: Rn – bl				○		○	○	○	○	○		
EF	Daselaar 03c	Old-high, word: Rn – bl				○								
EF	Cabeza 04	Rn – bl	○	●	○			○	○		○	○	●	
Recall														
BP	Schacter 96	stem Rc: low – high					●	○		●				
BP	Cabeza 97	pair Rc: Rc – Enc		○	○		○							
BP	Backman 97	stem Rc: Rc – bl			○	○								
EF	Maguire O3	autobio events – publ event											○	○
BP	Anderson 00	pair Rc: FA – FA Enc			○	○	●			●		●		
Context memory														
BP	Cabeza 00	word: Context – Rn					●			●		○		
BP	Cabeza 02	Old-high, word: Context – Recall					●			●	○	○		
BP	Schiavetto 02	object: loc Rn > obj Rn		○		●						○		

● only young/young > old; ○ only old/old > young; BP = blocked PET; BF = blocked fMRI; EF = event-related fMRI; bl = baseline; Enc = Encoding; Rc = recall; Rn = recognition; obj = object; loc = location; FA = full attention; P = posterior; VL = ventrolateral; DL = dorsolateral; A = anterior.

2004; Maguire & Frith, 2003; Meulenbroek et al., 2004; Schiavetto et al., 2002). Consistent with behavioral findings, results reported by Cabeza and colleagues suggest that these increases may reflect a greater reliance on familiarity-based retrieval in aging (Cabeza et al., 2004; Daselaar et al., 2006). For example, Cabeza et al. (2004) found a dissociation between the hippocampus, which showed weaker activity in older adults, and the parahippocampal gyrus, which showed greater activity in older adults. Given the evidence linking the hippocampus to recollection and cortical MTL regions to familiarity (see Yonelinas, 2001), these results fit with the hypothesis that older adults are more impaired in recollection than in familiarity (e.g., Jennings & Jacoby, 1993; Parkin & Walter, 1992) and suggest that they may compensate for recollection deficits by relying more on familiarity. Consistent with this speculation, older adults had a larger number of *Know* responses than did younger adults, and these responses were positively correlated with parahippocampal activation in older adults. The effects of aging on recollection vs. familiarity were further investigated in a study by Daselaar et al. (2006), which is described at the end of the chapter.

Summary

In summary, our review of functional neuroimaging studies of cognitive aging has identified considerable age-related differences in activity during all cognitive tasks reviewed. Despite the abundance of age-related differences presented, several patterns emerge from these findings. First, several studies in visual perception (e.g., Grady et al., 1994), attention (e.g., Madden et al., 2002), and recognition memory (e.g., Cabeza et al., 2004) show age-related occipital decreases accompanied by frontal increases (PASA). Additionally, studies spanning the domains of WM (e.g., Reuter-Lorenz et al., 2000), attention (e.g., Cabeza et al., 2004), language (e.g., Persson et al., 2004), encoding (e.g., Cabeza, McIntosh, Tulving, Nyberg, & Grady, 1997), and retrieval (e.g., Cabeza et al., 1997) show age-related decreases in hemispheric asymmetry (HAROLD). Still others (e.g., Gutchess et al., 2005) show age-related reductions in MTL activity accompanied by increases in frontal activity.

Despite differences in the pattern of age-related differences in neural activity, one common thread prevails—the occurrence of both age-related decreases as well as *increases* in neural activity. For the most part these increases are viewed as beneficial to performance in older adults. This view postulates that older adults compensate for decreases in neuronal activity in one brain region by recruiting additional resources to perform a cognitive task (see Cabeza, 2002). However, as seen by the aforementioned patterns this compensation can occur in several forms. As in the case of studies showing HAROLD, older adults compensate for declines in neural activity by recruiting cortical regions responsible for similar functioning as areas showing decline (e.g., the contralateral hemisphere). Older adults may also recruit cortical regions responsible for related cognitive operations (e.g. familiarity vs. recollection). Finally, in the case of subsequent memory studies and studies showing PASA, older adults can compensate for relatively automatic sensory and encoding processes with more strategic and elaborative processing associated with frontal functioning. One might wonder if recruitment of additional brain regions is compensatory, then why don't younger adults show such patterns of activation as well? One answer is that compensation or the recruitment of additional brain regions may come with a cost (Bäckman & Dixon, 1992; Cabeza, 2002). For example, recruitment of contralateral hemispheres may reduce the brain's ability to perform simultaneous tasks. Evidence supporting this view comes from studies showing age-related reductions in performance under dual task or divided attention conditions (e.g., Anderson, Craik, & Naveh-Benjamin, 1998). Given the nature of neural compensation in aging, it is not only important to evaluate activation associated with age-related cognitive decline in order to understand what brain areas/processes are most vulnerable to the effects of aging, but also to evaluate age-related increases in activity to assess how and when older adults are able to cope with these declines—and at what possible cost.

LINKING BRAIN DATA AND COGNITIVE AGING THEORIES

Although the number of functional neuroimaging studies of cognitive aging has dramatically increased during the last decade, very few of these studies have made direct contact with cognitive aging theories. One reason is that cognitive aging theories were originally developed to account for age-related differences in behavior, and hence they do not usually make predictions regarding the effects of aging on brain activity. A second reason is that these theories typically try to explain deficits in cognition and they rarely include hypotheses regarding compensatory mechanisms. In contrast, the notion of compensation is a central concept in the domain of functional neuroimaging of aging.

Thus, in order to link functional neuroimaging findings to cognitive aging theories one must "expand" these theories with additional assumptions regarding (a) the brain correlates of relevant cognitive processes, and (b) compensatory mechanisms. In this section, we illustrate this "theory expansion" using as examples five popular cognitive aging theories. The first four are general cognitive aging theories that apply to all cognitive functions: the sensory deficit theory (Lindenberger & Baltes, 1994); the resources deficit theory (Craik, 1986); the speed deficit theory (Salthouse, 1996); and the inhibition deficit theory (Hasher & Zacks, 1988). The fifth theory is specific to the memory domain: the recollection deficit theory (Johnson, Hashtroudi, & Lindsay, 1993; Naveh-Benjamin, 2000; Parkin & Walter, 1992). For each theory, we describe how the theory may be expanded by incorporating assumptions regarding brain mechanisms and regarding functional compensation, and how the resulting "expanded theory" may account for the available functional neuroimaging evidence.

Sensory Deficit Theory

According to the sensory deficit theory, age-related deficits in sensory processing play a major role in age-related cognitive decline (Lindenberger & Baltes, 1994). Consistent with this view, older adults show considerable deficits in basic sensory functioning, including simple vision and auditory processing (for a review, see Schneider & Pichora-Fuller, 2000). The main evidence for the sensory deficit theory comprises findings of strong correlations between age-related differences in sensory and cognitive measures (e.g., Baltes & Lindenberger, 1997; e.g., Lindenberger & Baltes, 1994).

Adding Assumptions regarding Brain Mechanisms and Compensation

To link the sensory deficit theory to functional neuroimaging data, one must expand this theory with assumptions regarding neural mechanisms. In general, discussions regarding the sensory deficit theory have contrasted a *cascade view* (Figure 1.3A), in which sensory organ degeneration leads to sensory deficits and eventually to cognitive decline, to a *common cause view* (Figure 1.3B), in which sensory and cognitive deficits are both mediated by widespread neural degeneration (for a review, see Schneider & Pichora-Fuller, 2000). A third possibility is that age-related sensory decline reflects a decline in the function of sensory cortices (Cabeza, Dolcos, Prince, Budde, & Nyberg, 2004; Grady et al., 1994). This assumption leads to the prediction of age-related reductions in sensory cortex function (e.g., visual cortex activity). As for compensation, given that perception reflects the interaction of bottom-up sensory processing and top-down cognitive processing, one may hypothesize that deficits in the former may be compensated by greater reliance on the latter. Assuming that top-down cognitive operations are partly mediated by PFC, this idea predicts an age-related increase in PFC activity (Cabeza et al., 2004; Grady et al., 1994).

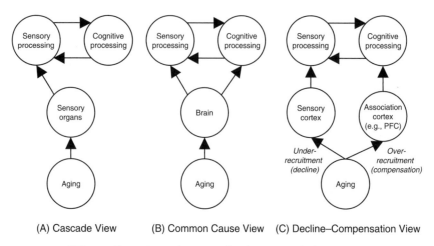

(A) Cascade View   (B) Common Cause View   (C) Decline–Compensation View

FIG. 1.3.   Three views of perceptual and cognitive decline in aging.

Thus, if one enlarges the sensory deficit theory with assumptions regarding brain mechanisms and functional compensation, this theory predicts that under-recruitment of sensory processing in sensory cortex may be compensated by over-recruitment of top-down processes mediated by PFC (see Figure 1.3C). Thus, the expanded theory predicts that, *compared to younger adults, older adults will tend to show reduced visual cortex activity but increased PFC activity.* As described in the next section, this prediction has been confirmed by many functional neuroimaging studies.

Neuroimaging Evidence for the Expanded Sensory Deficit Theory

Consistent with the expanded sensory deficit theory, several functional neuroimaging studies have found the pattern previously described as PASA: an age-related decrease in posterior activity coupled with an age-related increase in PFC activity (see Table 1.1). This finding was first reported by Grady et al. (1994) during face matching and location matching tasks. According to the authors, older adults compensated for visual processing deficits (occipital decrease) by recruiting higher order cognitive processes (frontal increase). Given that in this study older adults were as accurate as younger adults but significantly slower than younger adults, Grady et al. further suggested that additional PFC recruitment allowed older adults to maintain a good level of performance *at the expense* of slower RTs. As indicated by Table 1.1, the PASA pattern has been found during perception, attention, working memory, problem solving, and episodic memory tasks.

The fact that PASA has been found across a variety of cognitive func-

tions is consistent with the assumption of the sensory deficit theory that age-related sensory deficits have a global impact on cognitive functions. However, there is considerable variability in the localization of occipital decreases and frontal increases. In order to demonstrate that the PASA pattern is truly general, it is necessary to compare the effects of aging on brain activity during different cognitive tasks, directly and within participants. This was the main goal of an fMRI study in which we directly compared age-related differences in activity during working memory, visual attention, and episodic retrieval (Cabeza et al., 2004). To identify task-independent age effects, we used a conjunction procedure that isolated age-related differences in activity that occurred in each and every cognitive task.

As illustrated by Figure 1.4 (see color plate section), conjunction analyses yielded the PASA pattern: whereas the visual cortex showed an age-related reduction in activity in all three tasks, the prefrontal cortex showed an age-related increase in activity in all three tasks. These findings demonstrate that exactly the same occipital and PFC regions can display identical age-related differences in activity across different cognitive tasks. Task-independent, age-related decreases in visual cortex activity provide strong support for the sensory deficit theory, while task-independent, age-related increases in PFC activity are consistent with Grady et al.'s (1994) hypothesis that age-related increases in PFC activity could compensate for age-related decreases in visual cortex activity.

To investigate the idea of compensation more directly, we calculated the correlations between age-related differences in occipital and PFC activity. In the working memory task, we found a significant negative correlation between these two effects ($r = -0.5$, $P < 0.02$). In other words, those older adults who showed the weakest occipital activations tended to also show the strongest PFC activations. This finding is relevant to the distinction between common cause (Figure 1.3-B) and cognitive neuroscience (Figure 1.3-C) views of the sensory deficit theory. Whereas the common cause view predicts that the neural correlates of age-related sensory and cognitive deficits should be *positively* correlated, the cognitive neuroscience view, which assumes that top-down cognitive processes may compensate for sensory deficits, predicts negative correlations between sensory and PFC activity in older adults. Thus, our findings were more consistent with the cognitive neuroscience view.

The expanded sensory deficit theory predicts that, compared to younger adults, older adults will tend to show reduced occipital activity (sensory deficit) but increased prefrontal activity (compensatory top-down cognitive processes). This idea is supported by many functional neuroimaging studies showing age-related decreases in occipital activity coupled with age-related increases in frontal activity (PASA pattern). In

one study, the PASA pattern was found in the same participants across three different tasks, and a negative correlation consistent with the compensation idea was found between age-related differences in occipital and frontal regions (Cabeza et al., 2004). Finally, if one assumes that sensory deficits may appear not only as a general reduction in sensory processing but also as difficulty in recruiting specialized sensory operations, the sensory deficit theory would be consistent with recent evidence of age-related dedifferentiation in stimulus-specific processing in ventral temporal regions (Park et al., 2004).

Resources Deficit Theory

Craik and collaborators (Craik, 1983, 1986; Craik & Byrd, 1982) suggested that aging is associated with a reduction in the amount of attentional resources, which results in deficits in demanding cognitive tasks. A corollary of the resources deficit theory, the *environmental support hypothesis* (Craik, 1983, 1986), predicts that age-related differences should be smaller when the task provides a supportive environment which reduces attentional demands. Among other findings, the resources deficit theory is supported by evidence that when attentional resources are reduced in younger adults, they tend to show cognitive deficits that resemble those of older adults (Anderson et al., 1998; Jennings & Jacoby, 1993).

Adding Assumptions regarding Brain Mechanisms and Compensation

Regarding neural correlates, Craik (1983) originally suggested that older adults' deficits in processing were related to a reduction in the efficiency of frontal lobe functioning. On the basis of this assumption, the resources deficit theory can predict weaker PFC activity in older adults than in younger adults. However, if one further assumes the effects of aging can be detected only in the PFC regions recruited by a particular task, then the foregoing prediction could be specified as follows: older adults will tend to show reduced activity in PFC regions recruited by younger adults. Moreover, given that the most dramatic differences in PFC activity across tasks are differences in lateralization, the prediction could be stated as follows: *older adults will tend to show reduced activity in the PFC hemisphere differentially engaged by younger adults.*

Regarding compensatory mechanisms, one way in which older adults could counteract deficits in the particular pool of cognitive resources required by a cognitive task is to tap into other pools of cognitive resources. Returning to the notion of lateralized cognitive functions, if one task is particularly dependent on cognitive processes mediated by one hemisphere, the other hemisphere represents an alternative pool of

cognitive resources. Thus, in the case of PFC-mediated cognitive resources, if older adults have deficits in PFC activity in one hemisphere, they may compensate for these deficits by recruiting contralateral PFC regions. Combining the first prediction of age-related decreases in the PFC hemisphere differentially engaged by younger adults with the assumption of a compensatory mechanisms involving contralateral PFC recruitment, the expanded resources deficit theory makes the following second prediction: *older adults will tend to show a more bilateral (less asymmetric) pattern of PFC activity (i.e., HAROLD)*. Both the first prediction and the second prediction have received considerable support from functional neuroimaging studies.

Neuroimaging Evidence for the Expanded Resources Deficit Theory

The first prediction that older adults will show reduced activity in the PFC hemisphere differentially engaged by younger adults is supported by many functional neuroimaging studies. For example, during tasks in which younger adults recruit mainly right PFC, such as visuospatial working memory (e.g., Grady et al., 1998; Lamar, Yousem, & Resnick, 2004; Mitchell et al., 2000), older adults often show weaker activations in right PFC. Conversely, during tasks in which younger adults recruit primarily left PFC, such as episodic encoding tasks (e.g., Cabeza et al., 1997; Grady et al., 1995, 2002; Logan et al., 2002; Schiavetto et al., 2002), older adults frequently display weaker activity in left PFC. Consistent with the resources deficit hypothesis there is evidence that under conditions of divided attention younger adults show reductions in PFC activity that resemble those associated with aging. In the aforementioned PET study by Anderson and collaborators (2000), younger and older adults were scanned during encoding and retrieval of word pairs both under full attention and under divided attention. As shown by Figure 1.5, during encoding, activity in a region known to be critical for successful encoding operations, the left ventrolateral PFC, was similarly reduced by aging and by divided attention. This finding suggests that older adults' difficulty with encoding is partly due to a reduction in resources, such as that displayed by younger adults under divided attention.

There is also functional neuroimaging evidence supporting the corollary of the resources deficit theory: the environmental support hypothesis. With additional brain assumptions, this corollary predicts that age-related differences in activity will tend to be larger in conditions that require more self-initiated processing resources and smaller in conditions that provide more environmental support. Consistent with this prediction, age-related reductions in left PFC activity during episodic retrieval tend to occur more frequently for recall than for recognition tasks. Moreover, a study

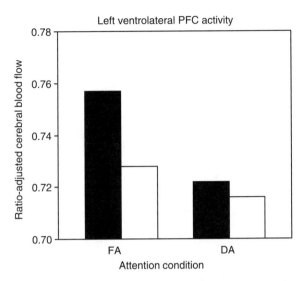

FIG. 1.5. Ratio-adjusted blood flow values during encoding in left ventro-lateral prefrontal cortex (PFC) as a function of age group and attentional condition (FA = full attention, DA = divided attention). Adapted from Anderson et al. (2000).

that directly compared the effects of aging on recall activity vs. recognition activity found larger deficits in the more demanding recall task (Cabeza et al., 1997). Differences related to environmental support can also be found during encoding. As is clear in Table 1.3 and previously discussed in the encoding section, age-related reductions in left PFC activity tend to be more frequent for intentional learning (Anderson et al., 2000; Cabeza et al., 1997; Grady et al., 1995, 2002; Logan et al., 2002; Schiavetto et al., 2002) than for incidental learning conditions (see however, Stebbins et al., 2002). Consistent with this idea, an fMRI study that directly compared intentional vs. incidental encoding conditions found age-related decreases in left PFC activity in the former but not the latter (Logan et al., 2002). This finding provides strong support for the environmental support hypothesis.

Finally, there is also functional neuroimaging evidence supporting the second prediction made by the expanded resources deficit theory, that is, that older adults may compensate for resource deficits in one hemisphere by recruiting the contralateral hemisphere. As reviewed before, this finding (HAROLD) has been consistently observed in many cognitive domains, including perception, attention, language, semantic memory, episodic encoding and retrieval, working memory, and inhibitory control processes (Cabeza, 2002). Consistent with the expanded resources theory, the HAROLD pattern has been linked to compensatory mechanisms.

First, it has been found to be positively correlated with cognitive performance (Reuter-Lorenz et al., 2000). Second, it has been found to be more pronounced in high-performing than in low-performing older adults (Cabeza et al., 2002; Daselaar et al., 2003b; Rosen et al., 2002). Finally, a recent study using transcranial magnetic stimulation (TMS) found that in younger adults episodic retrieval performance was impaired by TMS of right PFC but not of left PFC, whereas in older adults it was impaired by either right or left PFC stimulation (Rossi, Miniussi, Pasqualetti, Babiloni, Rossini, & Cappa, 2004). This result indicates that the left PFC was less critical for younger adults, and was used more by older adults, consistent with the compensation hypothesis.

The expanded resources deficit theory predicts that, compared to younger adults, older adults will show reduced activity in the PFC hemisphere differentially engaged by younger adults, particularly under conditions providing less environmental support, but that older adults will compensate for this deficit by recruiting contralateral PFC regions. Consistent with the first prediction, older adults often show reduced activity in right PFC during visuospatial working memory and episodic retrieval, and reduced left PFC activity during episodic encoding. Also, the latter reduction was observed in younger adults under divided attention conditions (Anderson et al., 2000). Moreover, consistent with the notion of environmental support, age-related PFC reductions tend to be smaller for recognition than for recall (Cabeza et al., 1997) and for semantic encoding than for intentional encoding conditions (Logan et al., 2002). Finally, consistent with the second prediction, there is converging evidence from many different cognitive domains that older adults compensate for reductions in PFC activity in one hemisphere by recruiting the contralateral PFC hemisphere (HAROLD).

Speed Deficit Theory

One of the most popular cognitive aging theories is that older adults' cognitive deficits reflect a general reduction in the speed of cognitive processes (for a review, see Salthouse, 1996). According to Salthouse (1996), low processing speed is assumed to impair cognitive performance because of two mechanisms: the time required by early operations reduces the time available for later operations (*limited time mechanism*), and the products of early operations are lost or irrelevant by the time later operations are completed (*simultaneity mechanism*). This view is supported by evidence that processing speed declines steadily with age, that this slowing shares considerable variance with age-related deficits in cognitive measures, and that processing speed is a strong mediator of cognitive decline in structural equation models (for a review, see Salthouse, 1996).

Adding Assumptions Regarding Brain Mechanisms and Compensation

One possible neural mechanism for age-related slowing is white matter deterioration. The whitish appearance of white matter tracts is due to the fat-containing glial cells forming the myelin sheath around axons connecting gray matter regions. The myelin sheath dramatically increases the speed of neural transmission along axons, and hence its deterioration can lead to a slowing in neural communication. Thus, the speed deficit theory predicts that older adults' increased RTs in cognitive tasks should be correlated with measures of white matter deterioration. In addition to white matter decline, there is another way in which brain changes may lead to age-related slowing: an increase in the size of the neural network supporting cognitive performance. In general, it is reasonable to assume that a larger network involving more brain regions or more distant brain regions will tend to be slower than a smaller, circumscribed network. Thus, the aforementioned evidence that older adults tend to recruit frontal regions even for relatively simple sensory/perceptual tasks (PASA) can also be interpreted as consistent with the speed deficit theory. As Cheryl Grady speculated, older adults' recruitment of frontal regions may allow them to maintain accuracy at the expense of slower RTs (Grady et al., 1994). Given that this evidence was reviewed within the context of the sensory theory, we will focus here on the prediction regarding white matter changes. As for compensatory mechanisms, if one assumes that older adults may recruit additional brain regions to support performance, then one could predict that activation in these brain regions may lead to faster RTs in older adults but not in younger adults. In sum, with the addition of assumptions regarding neural mechanisms and compensation, the expanded speed deficit theory predicts that *in older adults reduced speed is correlated with white matter deficits and that they may show activations predicting faster RTs that are not displayed by younger adults.*

Neuroimaging Evidence for the Expanded Speed Deficit Theory

Consistent with the expanded speed deficit theory, several studies have found significant correlations between age-related slowing and measures of white matter integrity, such as WMHs and DTI. As reviewed earlier in this chapter, Soderlund and colleagues (Soderlund et al., 2003) found that periventricular WMHs were associated with reduction in motor speed. Also, the DTI measures of fractional anisotropy (FA) and diffusivity (ADC) were found to predict slower RTs in older adults. For example, Madden and colleagues (2004) found a significant relationship between age-related FA decline and RT during visual detection—with older adults showing a greater dependence on fronto-striatal circuitry than younger

adults. Additionally, performance on tasks assessing executive functioning and processing speed show significant correlations with DTI
measures in older adults (O'Sullivan, Jones, Summers, Morris, Williams,
& Markus, 2001; Persson et al., 2006; Stebbins et al., 2001). Again, declines
in speeded performance show a strong correlation with declining white
matter integrity in frontal regions (see Figure 1.6). Results suggest that
degradation in white matter underlies age-related decline in processing
speed and cognitive tasks dependent upon frontal functioning.

Whereas the results of structural MRI studies suggest that white matter
deficits may lead to age-related slowing, the results of functional MRI
studies suggest that older adults may boost speed by recruiting PFC
regions. For example, Reuter-Lorenz et al. (2000) found that in conditions
in which PFC activity was unilateral in younger adults, those older adults

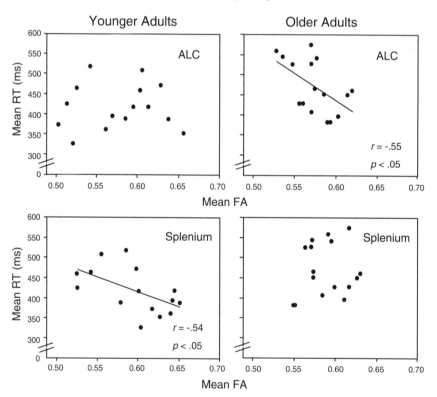

FIG. 1.6. Correlations between mean response time (RT) and mean fractional anisotropy (FA) for the anterior limb of the internal capsule (ALC)
and the splenium. Reprinted from Madden et al. (2004). Diffusion tensor
imaging of adult age differences in cerebral white matter: relation to
response time. *Neuroimage, 21*(3), 1174–1181, © 2004, with permission from
Elsevier.

who showed bilateral PFC activations were faster during a working memory task. Thus, under certain conditions, increased PFC activity in older adults may help them increase the speed of their cognitive processes. This finding may seem inconsistent with the aforementioned suggestion that a larger network that includes anterior brain regions may be slower than a more circumscribed posterior set of regions (Grady et al., 1994). One way in which these two ideas can be harmonized is to assume that involving anterior brain regions may slow down responses in younger adults but speed them up in older adults. This pattern was reported by Rypma and D'Esposito (2000) during a working memory task.

The expanded speed deficit theory predicts that in older adults reduced speed is correlated with white matter deficits and that they may show activations predicting faster RTs that are not displayed by younger adults. Consistent with the first prediction, several structural MRI studies have found significant correlations between RT slowing in older adults and measures of white matter integrity, such as WMHs and DTI measures. Consistent with the second prediction, a few PET and functional MRI studies have associated increased PFC activity in older adults with faster RTs. It has been suggested that the relationship between PFC activity and speed may change with aging so that greater PFC activity may be associated with slower RTs in younger adults but with faster RTs in older adults. Thus, PFC recruitment may compensate for age-related slowing due to white matter decline.

Inhibition Deficit Theory

A fourth popular theory of cognitive aging is the inhibition deficit theory, which attributes age-related cognitive deficits to a decline in the inhibitory control of working-memory contents (Hasher & Zacks, 1988; Zacks, Hasher, & Li, 2000). When inhibitory control fails, goal-irrelevant information gains access to working memory, and the resulting "mental clutter" impairs working-memory operations, including the encoding and retrieval of episodic information (Zacks et al., 2000). Evidence supporting the inhibition view includes results showing that, compared to young adults, older adults make more indirect semantic associations and better remember disconfirmed solutions and to-be-forgotten information (for a review, see Zacks et al., 2000).

Adding Assumptions Regarding Brain Mechanisms and Compensation

The brain basis of inhibition may be described at very different levels of analysis, from inhibitory synapses, to inhibitory neurohormonal systems, to inhibitory functional connections among regions in a distributed

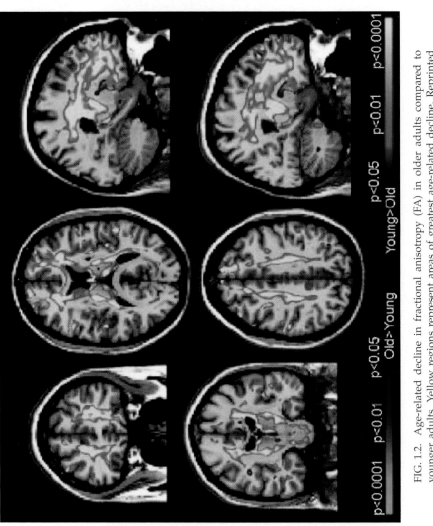

FIG. 1.2. Age-related decline in fractional anisotropy (FA) in older adults compared to younger adults. Yellow regions represent areas of greatest age-related decline. Reprinted from Salat et al. (2005). Age-related alterations in white matter microstructure measured by diffusion tensor imaging. *Neurobiology of Aging, 26*(8), 1215–1227, © 2005, with permission from Elsevier Inc.

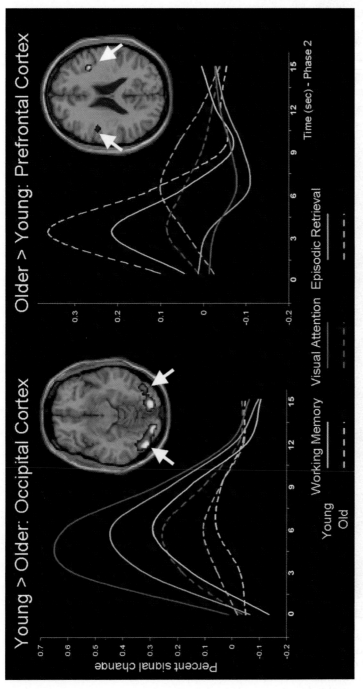

FIG. 1.4. Task-independent age effects. Compared to younger adults, older adults showed weaker activity in occipital cortex, but greater activity in frontal regions. The time-course plots are from left BA19 (x, y, z = −23, −84, −8) and right BA45 (x, y, z = 41, 12, 21). Reproduced by permission of Oxford University Press from Cabeza et al. (2004b). Task-independent and task-specific age effects on brain activity during working memory, visual attention and episodic retrieval. *Cerebral Cortex, 14*(4), 364–375.

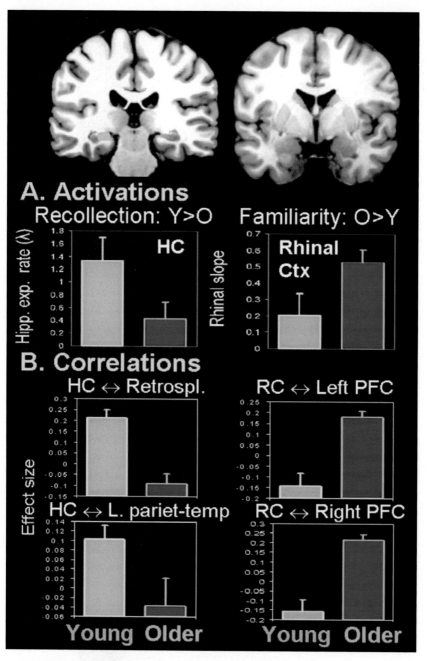

FIG. 1.8. Double dissociation between recollection-related activity in the hippocampus, attenuated by aging, and familiarity-related activity in the rhinal cortex, enhanced by aging. Reproduced by permission of Oxford University Press from Daselaar et al. (2006). Effects of healthy aging on hippocampal and rhinal memory functions: An event-related fMRI study. *Cerebral Cortex, 16,* 1771–1782.

network. Given that neuroimaging can only investigate the latter, here we focus only on inhibitory effects within large-scale networks. At this level, it is generally assumed that an important function of PFC is to inhibit activity in posterior associative cortices and in sensory and motor cortices. Therefore, when expanding the inhibitory deficit theory with assumptions regarding brain activity, it is critical to distinguish between the *regions that exert the inhibition* (inhibitory control regions), whose activity should increase when inhibition occurs, and the *regions affected by the inhibition* (inhibited regions), whose activity should decrease when inhibition occurs. Accordingly, the expanded inhibitory deficit theory predicts that *older adults should show weaker activity than younger adults in inhibitory control regions but greater activity than younger adults in inhibited regions* (i.e., a disinhibition phenomenon). Conversely, if one assumes that older adults may compensate for these deficits, one may also expect an *age-related increase in alternative inhibitory control regions.*

Neuroimaging Evidence for the Expanded Inhibition Deficit Theory

Consistent with the expanded inhibition deficit theory, there is evidence that older adults show reduced activity in inhibitory control regions and greater activity in inhibited regions than younger adults. As an example of the former, Jonides and colleagues have shown an age-related decrease in the activity of a region associated with controlling interference during verbal working memory, the left ventrolateral PFC (Jonides, Marshuetz, Smith, Reuter-Lorenz, Koeppe, & Hartley, 2000b). In each trial of the task, subjects maintained four target letters for 3 sec and then decided whether a probe matched any of the four target letters. In a high-recency condition, half of the probes did not match any target letter in the current trial but matched a target letter in the immediately preceding trial. In the low-recency condition, in contrast, the probe did not match any target letter in the two preceding trials. Thus, inhibitory control was critical in the high-recency but not in the low-recency condition. The high-recency minus the low-recency condition yielded an activation in the left PFC. An ROI analysis indicated that in older adults this activation was significantly weaker than in young adults and was not reliable. A combined measure of accuracy and reaction times yielded an interference effect for negative trials in which the probe matched a target letter in the preceding trial. Since this interference effect was larger for older than for young adults, the authors concluded that aging diminishes the efficacy of the left PFC in inhibiting the interfering effects of prepotent processes.

There is also evidence supporting the prediction that older adults will show greater activity than younger adults in regions that must be inhibited. For example, in an early PET study we found that an insular

region that is often deactivated during memory tasks showed greater activity in older adults than in younger adults during an episodic encoding task (Cabeza et al., 1997). Unlike the case in which increased activity in older adults is associated with better performance, this activation showed a *negative* correlation with subsequent recall performance, suggesting that engaging insular regions during encoding is detrimental for encoding and could reflect a lack of inhibition in older adults. More recently, Gazzaley, Cooney, Rissman, and D'Esposito (2005) investigated the effects of aging on the inhibition of stimuli-specific regions during a working memory task. Participants were presented with alternating faces and scenes under three instruction conditions: remember the faces and ignore the scenes, remember the scenes and ignore the faces, and passively view faces and scenes. As illustrated by Figure 1.7, in younger adults, activity in brain regions sensitive to scene processing was enhanced by the instruction to remember scenes and suppressed by the instruction to ignore the scenes, compared to the passive view condition, whereas in older adults only the former instruction produced an effect. In other words, older adults' selective attention was able to up-regulate task-relevant activity but failed to down-regulate task-irrelevant activity.

Finally, there is evidence that older adults may compensate for reduced activity in inhibitory control regions recruited by younger adults by recruiting other additional brain regions, such as areas in the contralateral PFC hemisphere. For example, such evidence was found for the *Go/No-go* task. In this task, participants must respond to targets (*Go* trials) while inhibiting prepotent responses to distractors (*No-go* trials). In younger adults, inhibitory control in the Go/No-go task is usually associated with activity in right PFC (e.g., Garavan, Ross, & Stein, 1999). In an fMRI study, Nielson et al. (2002) found that in older adults, inhibitory control elicited significant activity not only in right PFC but also in left PFC. This finding is consistent with the HAROLD model, and provides support for the idea that older adults may compensate for inhibitory control deficits by recruiting additional brain regions.

The expanded inhibition deficit theory predicts that, compared to younger adults, older adults will show weaker activity in inhibitory control regions but greater activity in inhibited regions (i.e., a disinhibition). Regarding compensation, this view predicts that older adults will compensate for deficits in recruiting the inhibitory deficits activated by younger adults by activating alternative inhibitory control regions. Consistent with the first prediction, activity in regions associated with inhibitory control in younger adults, such as left ventrolateral PFC during verbal working memory (Jonides et al., 2000b), was found to be reduced in older adults. In contrast, older adults showed increased activity in regions that show the effect of inhibition, such as the insula during

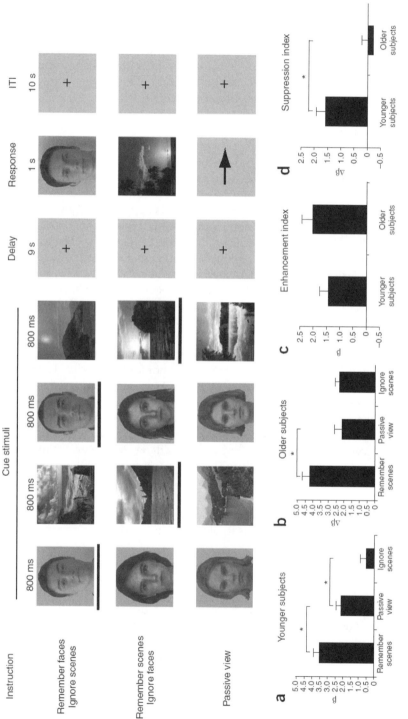

FIG. 1.7. Experimental framework indicating the three task conditions/instructions and response requirements. In the response period of the two memory tasks participants were required to report with a button press whether the stimulus matched one of the previously presented stimuli. Below are fMRI data showing a selective deficit of top-down suppression in older adults. Reprinted by permission from Macmillan Publishers Ltd: *Nature Neuroscience* (Gazzaley et al. (2005)), © 2005.

encoding (Cabeza et al., 1997) and stimuli-specific ventral temporal regions during working memory (Gazzaley et al., 2005). Possibly compensating for these inhibitory deficits, older adults have been found to show bilateral PFC activations during inhibition tasks that show lateralized activations in younger adults (Nielson et al., 2002).

Recollection Deficit Theory

Whereas the sensory, resources, speed, and inhibition deficit theories are general cognitive aging theories that apply to all cognitive domains, the recollection deficit theory is specific to the episodic memory domain. *Recollection* refers to the retrieval of a past event that is accompanied by the recovery of specific associations or contextual details, whereas *familiarity* refers to the feeling that an event occurred in the past even in the absence of specific associations or contextual details. Among other methods, recollection and familiarity can be distinguished using the *remember–know procedure* (for a review, see Gardiner, 2001; Tulving, 1985), in which subjects use introspection to distinguish between test cues that elicited recollection (*Remember response*) and those that elicited familiarity (*Know response*). According to the recollection deficit theory, episodic memory deficits in older adults are larger for recollection than for familiarity, and in some cases they are significant only for recollection and not for familiarity. This view is also supported by evidence that older adults are more impaired in recollection than in familiarity (Yonelinas, 2002), which has been demonstrated using the Remember/Know paradigm (Bastin & Van der Linden, 2003; Davidson & Glisky, 2002; Java, 1996; Mäntylä, 1993; Parkin & Walter, 1992), ROC curves (Howard, Bessette-Symons, Zhang, & Hoyer, 2006), and the process-dissociation procedure (Jennings & Jacoby, 1993). Given that recollection involves the retrieval of associations between core and contextual elements of an episode, this evidence is also consistent with theories that postulate associative (Naveh-Benjamin, 2000) and source memory (Johnson et al., 1993) deficits in older adults.

Adding Assumptions Regarding Brain Mechanisms and Compensation

Adding brain assumptions to the recollection deficit theory is straightforward because several researchers have proposed differences between the neural correlates of recollection and familiarity. Within MTL, one popular idea supported by lesion, electrophysiology, and functional neuroimaging studies with laboratory animals and human participants is that recollection (or relational memory) is more dependent on the hippocampus, whereas familiarity (or item memory) is more dependent on cortical MTL regions (Eichenbaum, Otto, & Cohen, 1994), such as the

perirhinal cortex (Aggleton & Brown, 1999; Brown & Aggleton, 2001). Thus, on the basis of this idea, one could link older adults' deficits in recollection to hippocampal dysfunction. As for compensation assumptions, if one assumes that familiarity and rhinal regions are less affected by aging, then recollection deficits in older adults could be attenuated by greater reliance on familiarity and rhinal functions. As illustrated by Figure 1.1, a recent longitudinal volumetric MRI study found that age-related atrophy was significant in the hippocampus but not in rhinal cortex. In sum, if one expands the recollection deficit theory of aging with assumptions regarding the neural mechanisms and functional compensation, this view predicts that, *compared to younger adults, older adults will tend to show reduced recollection-related activity in the hippocampus but increased familiarity-related activity in rhinal cortex.*

Neuroimaging Evidence for the Expanded Recollection Deficit Theory

We recently found fMRI evidence supporting the recollection deficit theory in a study in which participants were scanned while recognizing words studied before scanning. Brain activity associated with recollection and familiarity were distinguished using confidence ratings under the assumption that most recollection-based responses are mainly "definitely old" responses whereas the frequency of familiarity-based responses increases gradually from "definitely new" to "definitely old." Therefore, recollection-related activity was identified with a quasi-exponential function and familiarity-related activity with a linear function. The main finding of the study was a double dissociation between recollection-related activity in hippocampus, which was reduced by aging, and familiarity-related activity in rhinal cortex, which was increased by aging (see Figure 1.8 in color plate section). In addition, regression analyses based on individual trial data showed that changes in hippocampal activity predicted recognition performance in both younger and older adults, whereas changes in rhinal activity predicted recognition only in older adults. Finally, network analyses that linked hippocampal and rhinal activity to activity in the rest of the brain yielded a dissociation in functional connectivity: whereas connectivity within a hippocampal-retrosplenial/parietotemporal network was reduced by aging, connectivity within a rhinal-frontal network was increased by aging. These findings indicate that older adults compensate for hippocampal deficits by relying more on rhinal cortex, possibly through a top-down frontal modulation. This finding has important clinical implications, since early AD impairs both hippocampus and rhinal cortex and in its earliest stages it often affects rhinal cortex to a greater extent than the hippocampus.

The expanded recollection deficit theory predicts that, compared to

younger adults, older adults will show reduced recollection-related activity in the hippocampus but increased familiarity-related activity in rhinal cortex. Consistent with this prediction, during a recognition memory test, we found that hippocampal activity that showed an exponential pattern associated with recollection was attenuated in older adults, whereas a rhinal region that showed a linear pattern associated with familiarity was enhanced in older adults. Consistent with the idea of compensation, the rhinal activation predicted recognition performance only in older adults, and it was more directly linked to frontal activity in older adults than in younger adults.

Summary

In sum, with the addition of assumptions regarding neural mechanisms and functional compensation, existing cognitive aging theories can be easily linked to available functional neuroimaging data. The expanded versions of these theories yield specific predictions that can be investigated in structural and functional neuroimaging studies, and in general these predictions are consistent with the extant evidence.

CONCLUSIONS

In the first section of the chapter we reviewed resting neuroimaging studies of aging. Results indicate that while the brain undergoes significant structural change with age, age-related atrophy differs across and within regions. Regarding volumetric measures of gray matter, studies have shown that the frontal lobes exhibit the steepest rate of decline, followed by the parietal, then temporal lobes, with the occipital lobes showing little if any volume loss. Measures of white matter volume and integrity (i.e., FA) also showed differential aging effects throughout the brain. Similar to gray matter decline, age-related white matter degradation and DA dysfunction are greater in anterior compared to posterior regions. Correlations between these measures and cognitive function emphasize the importance these changes have on cognitive functions.

In the second section of the chapter we reviewed PET and fMRI studies of aging in the domains of visual perception, attention, language, working memory, implicit memory, and episodic memory encoding and retrieval. In addition to many task-specific differences, these studies revealed two consistent patterns of age-related differences in brain activity: a posterior–anterior shift in activity in older adults (PASA), and a general reduction in the asymmetry of brain activity (HAROLD). Furthermore, studies exhibiting both activation patterns make the same general

conclusion—increased activation in prefrontal regions acts as a compensatory mechanism for age-related deficits in other brain regions (in PASA studies, occipital regions, and in HAROLD studies, contralateral PFC regions). This increased recruitment of higher order cognitive processes may be indicative of: (a) alternate strategies employed by older adults when presented with cognitively demanding tasks; and (b) the subtle rearrangement of neural networks. As discussed, direct support for the compensation accounts of PASA and HAROLD has come from functional neuroimaging studies that correlated individual activation patterns with performance, or that directly compared high- and low-performing older adults.

In the final section of the chapter we integrated both the structural and functional neuroimaging measures with traditional theories of cognitive aging. As noted, the majority of cognitive aging theories were constructed to account for behavioral differences among age groups and did not consider neural activations. However, in order for a theory to continue to be informative in regards to neuroimaging methodologies, it must be expanded to both explain and be predictive of neuroimaging studies. The theories mentioned above have just that capability. As is the case with the behavioral literature, different aspects of the neuroimaging literature support each of the "extended" major theories of cognitive aging. This provides a rich foundation on which we can continue to build our understanding of cognitive aging. Advancements in neuroimaging and development of other methodologies must continually be integrated with theory development in order to not only understand *what* changes occur in aging, but *why* these changes take place.

ACKNOWLEDGMENTS

This work was supported by grants from the National Institute of Aging (R01AG19731 & R01AG023770; R. Cabeza, primary investigator and T32 AG000029 awarded to N. Dennis). The authors wish to thank Amber Baptiste Tarter for help in preparation of this manuscript.

REFERENCES

Abe, O., Aoki, S., Hayashi, N., Yamada, H., Kunimatsu, A., Mori, H., et al. (2002). Normal aging in the central nervous system: Quantitative MR diffusion-tensor analysis. *Neurobiology of Aging*, 23(3), 433–441.

Aggleton, J. P., & Brown, M. W. (1999). Episodic memory, amnesia, and the hippocampal-anterior thalamic axis. *Behavioral & Brain Sciences*, 22(3), 425–444; discussion 444–489.

Aizenstein, H. J., Butters, M. A., Clark, K. A., Figurski, J. L., Stenger, V. A., Nebes, R. D., et al.

(2006). Prefrontal and striatal activation in elderly subjects during concurrent implicit and explicit sequence learning. *Neurobiology of Aging, 27,* 741–751.

Anderson, N. D., Craik, F. I. M., & Naveh-Benjamin, M. (1998). The attentional demands of encoding and retrieval in younger and older adults: I. Evidence from divided attention costs. *Psychology and Aging, 13,* 405–423.

Anderson, N. D., Iidaka, T., Cabeza, R., Kapur, S., McIntosh, A. R., & Craik, F. I. (2000). The effects of divided attention on encoding- and retrieval-related brain activity: A PET study of younger and older adults. *Journal of Cognitive Neuroscience, 12*(5), 775–792.

Antonini, A., & Leenders, K. L. (1993). Dopamine D2 receptors in normal human brain: Effect of age measured by positron emission tomography (PET) and [11C]-raclopride. *Annals of the New York Academy of Sciences, 695,* 81–85.

Azari, N. P., Rapoport, S. I., Salerno, J. A., Grady, C. L., Gonzalez-Aviles, A., Schapiro, M. B., et al. (1992). Interregional correlations of resting cerebral glucose metabolism in old and young women. *Brain Research, 589*(2), 279–290.

Bäckman, L., Almkvist, O., Andersson, J., Nordberg, A., Winblad, B., Rineck, R., et al. (1997). Brain activation in young and older adults during implicit and explicit retrieval. *Journal of Cognitive Neuroscience, 9*(3), 378–391.

Bäckman, L., & Dixon, R. A. (1992). Psychological compensation: a theoretical framework. *Psychological Bulletin, 112*(2), 259–283.

Bäckman, L., Ginovart, N., Dixon, R. A., Wahlin, T. B., Wahlin, A., Halldin, C., et al. (2000). Age-related cognitive deficits mediated by changes in the striatal dopamine system. *American Journal of Psychiatry, 157*(4), 635–637.

Bäckman, L., Robins-Wahlin, T. B., Lundin, A., Ginovart, N., & Farde, L. (1997). Cognitive deficits in Huntington's disease are predicted by dopaminergic PET markers and brain volumes. *Brain, 120*(Pt 12), 2207–2217.

Baltes, P. B., & Lindenberger, U. (1997). Emergence of a powerful connection between sensory and cognitive functions across the adult life span: A new window to the study of cognitive aging? *Psychology and Aging, 12*(1), 12–21.

Bannon, M. J., & Whitty, C. J. (1997). Age-related and regional differences in dopamine transporter mRNA expression in human midbrain. *Neurology, 48*(4), 969–977.

Bastin, C., & Van der Linden, M. (2003). The contribution of recollection and familiarity to recognition memory: A study of the effects of test format and aging. *Neuropsychology, 17*(1), 14–24.

Braak, H., Braak, E., & Bohl, J. (1993). Staging of Alzheimer-related cortical destruction. *European Neurology, 33*(6), 403–408.

Brodtmann, A., Puce, A., Syngeniotis, A., Darby, D., & Donnan, G. (2003). The functional magnetic resonance imaging hemodynamic response to faces remains stable until the ninth decade. *Neuroimage, 20*(1), 520–528.

Brown, M. W., & Aggleton, J. P. (2001). Recognition memory: What are the roles of the perirhinal cortex and hippocampus? *Nature Reviews Neuroscience, 2*(1), 51–61.

Buckner, R. L., Petersen, S. E., Ojemann, J. G., Miezin, F. M., Squire, L. R., & Raichle, M. E. (1995). Functional anatomical studies of explicit and implicit memory retrieval tasks. *Journal of Neuroscience, 15*(1 Pt 1), 12–29.

Buckner, R. L., Snyder, A. Z., Sanders, A. L., Raichle, M. E., & Morris, J. C. (2000). Functional brain imaging of young, nondemented, and demented older adults. *Journal of Cognitive Neuroscience, 12,* Supplement 2, 24–34.

Cabeza, R. (2002). Hemispheric asymmetry reduction in older adults: The HAROLD model. *Psychology and Aging, 17*(1), 85–100.

Cabeza, R., Anderson, N. D., Houle, S., Mangels, J. A., & Nyberg, L. (2000). Age-related differences in neural activity during item and temporal-order memory retrieval: A positron emission tomography study. *Journal of Cognitive Neuroscience, 12,* 1–10.

Cabeza, R., Anderson, N. D., Locantore, J. K., & McIntosh, A. R. (2002). Aging gracefully: Compensatory brain activity in high-performing older adults. *Neuroimage, 17*(3), 1394–1402.

Cabeza, R., Daselaar, S. M., Dolcos, F., Prince, S. E., Budde, M., & Nyberg, L. (2004). Task-independent and task-specific age effects on brain activity during working memory, visual attention and episodic retrieval. *Cerebral Cortex, 14*(4), 364–375.

Cabeza, R., Dolcos, F., Graham, R., & Nyberg, L. (2002). Similarities and differences in the neural correlates of episodic memory retrieval and working memory. *Neuroimage, 16*(2), 317–330.

Cabeza, R., Grady, C. L., Nyberg, L., McIntosh, A. R., Tulving, E., Kapur, S., et al. (1997). Age-related differences in neural activity during memory encoding and retrieval: A positron emission tomography study. *Journal of Neuroscience, 17*(1), 391–400.

Cabeza, R., McIntosh, A. R., Tulving, E., Nyberg, L., & Grady, C. L. (1997). Age-related differences in effective neural connectivity during encoding and recall. *Neuroreport, 8*(16), 3479–3483.

Chakos, M. H., Lieberman, J. A., Bilder, R. M., Borenstein, M., Lerner, G., Bogerts, B., et al. (1994). Increase in caudate nuclei volumes of first-episode schizophrenic patients taking antipsychotic drugs. *American Journal of Psychiatry, 151*(10), 1430–1436.

Courchesne, E., Chisum, H. J., Townsend, J., Cowles, A., Covington, J., Egaas, B., et al. (2000). Normal brain development and aging: Quantitative analysis at in vivo MR imaging in healthy volunteers. *Radiology, 216*(3), 672–682.

Craik, F. I. M. (1983). On the transfer of information from temporary to permanent memory. *Philosophical Transactions of the Royal Society, London, Series B, 302,* 341–359.

Craik, F. I. M. (1986). A functional account of age differences in memory. In F. Lix & H. Hagendorf (Eds.), *Human memory and cognitive capabilities, mechanisms, and performances* (pp. 499–422). Amsterdam: Elsevier.

Craik, F. I. M., & Byrd, M. (1982). Aging and cognitive deficits: The role of attentional resources. In F. I. M. Craik & S. Trehub (Eds.), *Aging and cognitive processes* (pp. 191–211). New York: Plenum.

Daselaar, S. M., Fleck, M. S., Dobbins, I. G., Madden, D. J., & Cabeza, R. (2006). Effects of healthy aging on hippocampal and rhinal memory functions: An event-related fMRI study. *Cerebral Cortex, 12,* 1771–1782.

Daselaar, S. M., Rombouts, S. A., Veltman, D. J., Raaijmakers, J. G., & Jonker, C. (2003). Similar network activated by young and old adults during the acquisition of a motor sequence. *Neurobiology of Aging, 24*(7), 1013–1019.

Daselaar, S. M., Veltman, D. J., Rombouts, S. A., Raaijmakers, J. G., & Jonker, C. (2003a). Deep processing activates the medial temporal lobe in young but not in old adults. *Neurobiology of Aging, 24*(7), 1005–1011.

Daselaar, S. M., Veltman, D. J., Rombouts, S. A., Raaijmakers, J. G., & Jonker, C. (2003b). Neuroanatomical correlates of episodic encoding and retrieval in young and elderly subjects. *Brain, 126*(Pt 1), 43–56.

Daselaar, S. M., Veltman, D. J., Rombouts, S. A., Raaijmakers, J. G., & Jonker, C. (2005). Aging affects both perceptual and lexical/semantic components of word stem priming: An event-related fMRI study. *Neurobiology of Learning and Memory, 83*(3), 251–262.

Davidson, P. S., & Glisky, E. L. (2002). Neuropsychological correlates of recollection and familiarity in normal aging. *Cognitive, Affective & Behavioral Neuroscience, 2*(2), 174–186.

DeCarli, C., Murphy, D. G., Tranh, M., Grady, C. L., Haxby, J. V., Gillette, J. A., et al. (1995). The effect of white matter hyperintensity volume on brain structure, cognitive performance, and cerebral metabolism of glucose in 51 healthy adults. *Neurology, 45*(11), 2077–2084.

de Leon, M. J., Ferris, S. H., George, A. E., Christman, D. R., Fowler, J. S., Gentes, C., et al.

(1983). Positron emission tomographic studies of aging and Alzheimer disease. *American Journal of Neuroradiology, 4*(3), 568–571.

de Leon, M. J., George, A. E., Tomanelli, J., Christman, D., Kluger, A., Miller, J., et al. (1987). Positron emission tomography studies of normal aging: A replication of PET III and 18-FDG using PET VI and 11-CDG. *Neurobiology of Aging, 8*(4), 319–323.

DeLisi, L. E., Sakuma, M., Tew, W., Kushner, M., Hoff, A. L., & Grimson, R. (1997). Schizophrenia as a chronic active brain process: A study of progressive brain structural change subsequent to the onset of schizophrenia. *Psychiatry Research: Neuroimaging, 74*(3), 129–140.

Della-Maggiore, V., Sekuler, A. B., Grady, C. L., Bennett, P. J., Sekuler, R., & McIntosh, A. R. (2000). Corticolimbic interactions associated with performance on a short-term memory task are modified by age. *Journal of Neuroscience, 20*(22), 8410–8416.

Dennis, N. A., Daselaar, S., & Cabeza, R. (2006). Effects of aging on transient and sustained successful memory encoding activity. *Neurobiology of Aging.*

D'Esposito, M., Zarahn, E., Aguirre, G. K., & Rypma, B. (1999). The effect of normal aging on the coupling of neural activity to the bold hemodynamic response. *Neuroimage, 10*(1), 6–14.

DiGirolamo, G. J., Kramer, A. F., Barad, V., Cepeda, N. J., Weissman, D. H., Milham, M. P., et al. (2001). General and task-specific frontal lobe recruitment in older adults during executive processes: A fMRI investigation of task-switching. *Neuroreport, 12*(9), 2065–2071.

Double, K. L., Halliday, G. M., Kril, J. J., Harasty, J. A., Cullen, K., Brooks, W. S., et al. (1996). Topography of brain atrophy during normal aging and Alzheimer's disease. *Neurobiology of Aging, 17*, 513–521.

Driesen, N. R., & Raz, N. (1995). Sex-, age-, and handedness-related differences in human corpus callosum observed *in vivo. Psychobiology, 23*, 240–247.

Du, A. T., Schuff, N., Zhu, X. P., Jagust, W. J., Miller, B. L., Reed, B. R., et al. (2003). Atrophy rates of entorhinal cortex in AD and normal aging. *Neurology, 60*(3), 481–486.

Duara, R., Margolin, R. A., Robertson-Tchabo, E. A., London, E. D., Schwartz, M., Renfrew, J. W., et al. (1983). Cerebral glucose utilization, as measured with positron emission tomography in 21 resting healthy men between the ages of 21 and 83 years. *Brain, 106* (Pt 3), 761–775.

Eichenbaum, H., Otto, T., & Cohen, N. J. (1994). Two component functions of the hippocampal memory system. *Behavioral and Brain Sciences, 17*, 449–517.

Erixon-Lindroth, N., Farde, L., Wahlin, T. B., Sovago, J., Halldin, C., & Bäckman, L. (2005). The role of the striatal dopamine transporter in cognitive aging. *Psychiatry Research: Neuroimaging, 138*(1), 1–12.

Esiri, M. (1994). Dementia and normal aging: Neuropathology. In F. A. Huppert, C. Brayne, & D. W. O'Connor (Eds.), *Dementia and normal aging* (pp. 385–436). Cambridge: Cambridge University Press.

Esposito, G., Kirby, G. S., Van Horn, J. D., Ellmore, T. M., & Faith Berman, K. (1999). Context-dependent, neural system-specific neurophysiological concomitants of ageing: Mapping PET correlates during cognitive activation. *Brain, 122*, 963–979.

Fera, F., Weickert, T. W., Goldberg, T. E., Tessitore, A., Hariri, A., Das, S., et al. (2005). Neural mechanisms underlying probabilistic category learning in normal aging. *Journal of Neuroscience, 25*(49), 11340–11348.

Fischer, H., Sandblom, J., Gavazzeni, J., Fransson, P., Wright, C. I., & Bäckman, L. (2005). Age-differential patterns of brain activation during perception of angry faces. *Neuroscience Letters 386*(2), 99–104.

Frackowiak, R. S., Lenzi, G. L., Jones, T., & Heather, J. D. (1980). Quantitative measurement of regional cerebral blood flow and oxygen metabolism in man using 15O and positron emission tomography: Theory, procedure, and normal values. *Journal of Computer Assisted Tomography, 4*(6), 727–736.

Garavan, H., Ross, T. J., & Stein, E. A. (1999). Right hemispheric dominance of inhibitory control: An event-related functional MRI study. *Proceedings of the National Academy of Sciences of the United States of America, 96*(14), 8301–8306.

Gardiner, J. M. (2001). Episodic memory and autonoetic consciousness: A first-person approach. *Philosophical Transactions of the Royal Society of London—Series B: Biological Sciences, 356*(1413), 1351–1361.

Gazzaley, A., Cooney, J. W., Rissman, J., & D'Esposito, M. (2005). Top-down suppression deficit underlies working memory impairment in normal aging. *Nature Neuroscience, 8*(10), 1298–1300.

Grady, C. L., Bernstein, L. J., Beig, S., & Siegenthaler, A. L. (2002). The effects of encoding task on age-related differences in the functional neuroanatomy of face memory. *Psychology and Aging, 17*(1), 7–23.

Grady, C. L., Maisog, J. M., Horwitz, B., Ungerleider, L. G., Mentis, M. J., Salerno, J. A., et al. (1994). Age-related changes in cortical blood flow during visual processing of faces and location. *Journal of Neuroscience, 14*(3, Pt 2), 1450–1462.

Grady, C. L., McIntosh, A. R., Bookstein, F., Horwitz, B., Rapoport, S. I., & Haxby, J. V. (1998). Age-related changes in regional cerebral blood flow during working memory for faces. *Neuroimage, 8*(4), 409–425.

Grady, C. L., McIntosh, A. R., Horwitz, B., Maisog, J. M., Ungerleider, L. G., Mentis, M. J., et al. (1995). Age-related reductions in human recognition memory due to impaired encoding. *Science, 269*(5221), 218–221.

Grady, C. L., McIntosh, A. R., Horwitz, B., & Rapoport, S. I. (2000). Age-related changes in the neural correlates of degraded and nondegraded face processing. *Cognitive Neuropsychology, 217*, 165–186.

Grafton, S. T., Hazeltine, E., & Ivry, I. (1995). Functional mapping of sequence learning in normal humans. *Journal of Cognitive Neuroscience., 7*, 497–510.

Grossman, M., Cooke, A., DeVita, C., Alsop, D., Detre, J., Chen, W., et al. (2002a). Age-related changes in working memory during sentence comprehension: An fMRI study. *Neuroimage, 15*(2), 302–317.

Grossman, M., Cooke, A., DeVita, C., Chen, W., Moore, P., Detre, J., et al. (2002b). Sentence processing strategies in healthy seniors with poor comprehension: An fMRI study. *Brain & Language, 80*(3), 296–313.

Gunning-Dixon, F. M., Gur, R. C., Perkins, A. C., Schroeder, L., Turner, T., Turetsky, B. I., et al. (2003). Age-related differences in brain activation during emotional face processing. *Neurobiology of Aging, 24*(2), 285–295.

Gunning-Dixon, F. M., & Raz, N. (2000). The cognitive correlates of white matter abnormalities in normal aging: A quantitative review. *Neuropsychology, 14*(2), 224–232.

Gunning-Dixon, F. M., & Raz, N. (2003). Neuroanatomical correlates of selected executive functions in middle-aged and older adults: A prospective MRI study. *Neuropsychologia, 41*(14), 1929–1941.

Gutchess, A. H., Welsh, R. C., Hedden, T., Bangert, A., Minear, M., Liu, L. L., et al. (2005). Aging and the neural correlates of successful picture encoding: Frontal activations compensate for decreased medial-temporal activity. *Journal of Cognitive Neuroscience, 17*(1), 84–96.

Hasher, L., & Zacks, R. T. (1988). Working memory, comprehension, and aging: A review and a new view. In G. H. Bower (Ed.), *The psychology of learning and motivation* (Vol. 22, pp. 193–225). New York: Academic Press.

Haut, M. W., Kuwabara, H., Leach, S., & Callahan, T. (2000). Age-related changes in neural activation during working memory performance. *Aging, Neuropsychology, and Cognition, 7*(2), 119–129.

Haxby, J. V., Grady, C. L., Duara, R., Robertson-Tchabo, E. A., Koziarz, B., Cutler, N. R., et al.

(1986). Relations among age, visual memory, and resting cerebral metabolism in 40 healthy men. *Brain Cognition, 5*(4), 412–427.

Head, D., Buckner, R. L., Shimony, J. S., Williams, L. E., Akbudak, E., Conturo, T. E., et al. (2004). Differential vulnerability of anterior white matter in nondemented aging with minimal acceleration in dementia of the Alzheimer type: Evidence from diffusion tensor imaging. *Cerebral Cortex, 14*(4), 410–423.

Herscovitch, P., Auchus, A. P., Gado, M., Chi, D., & Raichle, M. E. (1986). Correction of positron emission tomography data for cerebral atrophy. *Journal of Cerebral Blood Flow and Metabolism, 6*(1), 120–124.

Horwitz, B., Duara, R., & Rapoport, S. I. (1986). Age differences in intercorrelations between regional cerebral metabolic rates for glucose. *Annals of Neurology, 19*(1), 60–67.

Howard, M. W., Bessette-Symons, B., Zhang, Y., & Hoyer, W. J. (2006). Aging selectively impairs recollection in recognition memory for pictures: Evidence from modeling and receiver operating characteristic curves. *Psychology and Aging, 21*(1), 96–106.

Huettel, S. A., Singerman, J. D., & McCarthy, G. (2001). The effects of aging upon the hemodynamic response measured by functional MRI. *Neuroimage, 13*(1), 161–175.

Ichise, M., Ballinger, J. R., Tanaka, F., Moscovitch, M., St George-Hyslop, P. H., Raphael, D., et al. (1998). Age-related changes in D2 receptor binding with iodine–123-iodobenzofuran SPECT. *Journal of Nuclear Medicine 39*(9), 1511–1518.

Iidaka, T., Okada, T., Murata, T., Omori, M., Kosaka, H., Sadato, N., et al. (2002). Age-related differences in the medial temporal lobe responses to emotional faces as revealed by fMRI. *Hippocampus, 12*(3), 352–362.

Iidaka, T., Sadato, N., Yamada, H., Murata, T., Omori, M., & Yonekura, Y. (2001). An fMRI study of the functional neuroanatomy of picture encoding in younger and older adults. *Brain Research: Cognitive Brain Research, 11*(1), 1–11.

Inoue, K., Ito, H., Goto, R., Nakagawa, M., Kinomura, S., Sato, T., et al. (2005). Apparent CBF decrease with normal aging due to partial volume effects: MR-based partial volume correction on CBF SPECT. *Annals of Nuclear Medicine, 19*(4), 283–290.

Inoue, M., Suhara, T., Sudo, Y., Okubo, Y., Yasuno, F., Kishimoto, T., et al. (2001). Age-related reduction of extrastriatal dopamine D2 receptor measured by PET. *Life Sciences, 69*(9), 1079–1084.

Itoh, M., Hatazawa, J., Miyazawa, H., Matsui, H., Meguro, K., Yanai, K., et al. (1990). Stability of cerebral blood flow and oxygen metabolism during normal aging. *Gerontology, 36*(1), 43–48.

Java, R. I. (1996). Effects of age on state of awareness following implicit and explicit word-association tasks. *Psychology and Aging, 11*(1), 108–111.

Jennings, J. M., & Jacoby, L. L. (1993). Automatic versus intentional uses of memory: Aging, attention, and control. *Psychology and Aging, 8*(2), 283–293.

Johnson, E. K., & Jusczyk, P. W. (2001). Word segmentation by 8-month-olds: When speech cues count more than statistics. *Journal of Memory and Language, 44*(4), 548–567.

Johnson, M. K., Hashtroudi, S., & Lindsay, D. S. (1993). Source monitoring. *Psychological Bulletin, 114*(1), 3–28.

Jonides, J., Marshuetz, C., Smith, E. E., Reuter-Lorenz, P. A., Koeppe, R. A., & Hartley, A. (2000a). Age differences in behavior and PET activation reveal differences in interference resolution in verbal working memory. *Journal of Cognitive Neuroscience, 12*(1), 188–196.

Jonides, J., Marshuetz, C., Smith, E. E., Reuter-Lorenz, P. A., Koeppe, R. A., & Hartley, A. (2000b). Brain activation reveals changes with age in resolving interference in verbal working memory. *Journal of Cognitive Neuroscience, 12*, 188–196.

Kaasinen, V., Vilkman, H., Hietala, J., Nagren, K., Helenius, H., Olsson, H., et al. (2000). Age-related dopamine D2/D3 receptor loss in extrastriatal regions of the human brain. *Neurobiology of Aging, 21*(5), 683–688.

Kaplan, R. J., Greenwood, C. E., Winocur, G., & Wolever, T. M. (2000). Cognitive performance is associated with glucose regulation in healthy elderly persons and can be enhanced with glucose and dietary carbohydrates. *American Journal of Clinical Nutrition, 72*(3), 825–836.

Kemper, T. L. (1994). Neuroanatomical and neuropathological changes during aging and in dementia. In M. L. Albert & E. J. E. Knoepfel (Eds.), *Clinical neurology of aging* (2nd ed., pp. 3–67). New York: Oxford University Press.

Kety, S. S. (1956). Human cerebral blood flow and oxygen consumption as related to aging. *Journal of Chronic Diseases, 3*(5), 478–486.

Kuhl, D. E., Metter, E. J., Riege, W. H., & Phelps, M. E. (1982). Effects of human aging on patterns of local cerebral glucose utilization determined by the [18F]fluorodeoxyglucose method. *Journal of Cerebral Blood Flow and Metabolism 2*(2), 163–171.

Kuller, L. H., Shemanski, L., Manolio, T., Haan, M., Fried, L., Bryan, N., et al. (1998). Relationship between ApoE, MRI findings, and cognitive function in the Cardiovascular Health Study. *Stroke, 29*(2), 388–398.

Lamar, M., Yousem, D. M., & Resnick, S. M. (2004). Age differences in orbitofrontal activation: An fMRI investigation of delayed match and nonmatch to sample. *Neuroimage, 21*(4), 1368–1376.

Lang, D. J., Kopala, L. C., Vandorpe, R. A., Rui, Q., Smith, G. N., Goghari, V. M., et al. (2001). An MRI study of basal ganglia volumes in first-episode schizophrenia patients treated with risperidone. *American Journal of Psychiatry, 158*(4), 625–631.

Langenecker, S. A., Nielson, K. A., & Rao, S. M. (2004). fMRI of healthy older adults during Stroop interference. *Neuroimage, 21*(1), 192–200.

Leenders, K. L., Perani, D., Lammertsma, A. A., Heather, J. D., Buckingham, P., Healy, M. J., et al. (1990). Cerebral blood flow, blood volume and oxygen utilization. Normal values and effect of age. *Brain, 113*(Pt 1), 27–47.

Levine, B. K., Beason-Held, L. L., Purpura, K. P., Aronchick, D. M., Optican, L. M., Alexander, G. E., et al. (2000). Age-related differences in visual perception: A PET study. *Neurobiology of Aging, 21*(4), 577–584.

Li, S.-C., & Lindenberger, U. (1999). Cross-level unification: A computational exploration of the link between deterioration of neurotransmitter systems dedifferentiation of cognitive abilities in old age. In L.-G. Nilsson & H. J. Markowitsch (Eds.), *Cognitive neuroscience of memory* (pp. 103–146). Seattle, WA: Hogrefe & Huber.

Lieberman, J., Chakos, M., Wu, H., Alvir, J., Hoffman, E., Robinson, D., et al. (2001). Longitudinal study of brain morphology in first episode schizophrenia. *Biological Psychiatry, 49*(6), 487–499.

Lindenberger, U., & Baltes, P. B. (1994). Sensory functioning and intelligence in old age: A strong connection. *Psychology and Aging, 9*(3), 339–355.

Liu, T., & Cooper, L. A. (2003). Explicit and implicit memory for rotating objects. *Journal of Experimental Psychology: Learning, Memory, and Cognition, 29*(4), 554–562.

Logan, J. M., Sanders, A. L., Snyder, A. Z., Morris, J. C., & Buckner, R. L. (2002). Underrecruitment and nonselective recruitment: Dissociable neural mechanisms associated with aging. *Neuron, 33*(5), 827–840.

Lustig, C., & Buckner, R. L. (2004). Preserved neural correlates of priming in old age and dementia. *Neuron, 42*(5), 865–875.

Madden, D. J., & Hoffman, J. M. (1997). Application of positron emission tomography to age-related cognitive changes. In K. R. R. Krishnan & P. M. Doraiswamy (Eds.), *Brain imaging in clinical psychiatry* (pp. 575–613). New York: Marcel Dekker.

Madden, D. J., Langley, L. K., Denny, L. L., Turkington, T. G., Provenzale, J. M., Hawk, T. C., et al. (2002). Adult age differences in visual word identification: Functional neuroanatomy by positron emission tomography. *Brain and Cognition, 49*(3), 297–321.

Madden, D. J., Spaniol, J., Whiting, W. L., Bucur, B., Provenzale, J. M., Cabeza, R., et al. (2007). Adult age differences in the functional neuroanatomy of visual attention: A combined fMRI and DTI study. *Neurobiology of Aging*, *7*, 907–915.

Madden, D. J., Turkington, T. G., Coleman, R. E., Provenzale, J. M., DeGrado, T. R., & Hoffman, J. M. (1996). Adult age differences in regional cerebral blood flow during visual word identification: Evidence from H2150 PET. *Neuroimage*, *3*(2), 127–142.

Madden, D. J., Turkington, T. G., Provenzale, J. M., Denny, L. L., Langley, L. K., Hawk, T. C., et al. (2002). Aging and attentional guidance during visual search: Functional neuro-anatomy by positron emission tomography. *Psychology and Aging*, *17*(1), 24–43.

Madden, D. J., Whiting, W. L., Cabeza, R., & Huettel, S. A. (2004). Age-related preservation of top-down attentional guidance during visual search. *Psychology and Aging*, *19*(2), 304–309.

Madden, D. J., Whiting, W. L., Huettel, S. A., White, L. E., MacFall, J. R., & Provenzale, J. M. (2004). Diffusion tensor imaging of adult age differences in cerebral white matter: Relation to response time. *Neuroimage*, *21*(3), 1174–1181.

Madden, D. J., Whiting, W. L., Provenzale, J. M., & Huettel, S. A. (2004). Age-related changes in neural activity during visual target detection measured by fMRI. *Cerebral Cortex*, *14*(2), 143–155.

Maguire, E. A., & Frith, C. D. (2003). Aging affects the engagement of the hippocampus during autobiographical memory retrieval. *Brain*, *126*(7), 1511–1523.

Mäntylä, T. (1993). Knowing but not remembering: Adult age differences in recollective experience. *Memory & Cognition*, *21*(3), 379–388.

Marchal, G., Rioux, P., Petit-Taboue, M. C., Sette, G., Travere, J. M., Le Poec, C., et al. (1992). Regional cerebral oxygen consumption, blood flow, and blood volume in healthy human aging. *Archives of Neurology*, *49*(10), 1013–1020.

McIntosh, A. R., Sekuler, A. B., Penpeci, C., Rajah, M. N., Grady, C. L., Sekuler, R., et al. (1999). Recruitment of unique neural systems to support visual memory in normal aging. *Current Biology*, *9*(21), 1275–1278.

Meltzer, C. C., Cantwell, M. N., Greer, P. J., Ben-Eliezer, D., Smith, G., Frank, G., et al. (2000). Does cerebral blood flow decline in healthy aging? A PET study with partial-volume correction. *Journal of Nuclear Medicine*, *41*(11), 1842–1848.

Messier, C., & Gagnon, M. (2000). Glucose regulation and brain aging. *Journal of Nutrition, Health, and Aging*, *4*(4), 208–213.

Meulenbroek, O., Petersson, K. M., Voermans, N., Weber, B., & Fernandez, G. (2004). Age differences in neural correlates of route encoding and route recognition. *NeuroImage*, *22*(4), 1503–1514.

Milham, M. P., Erickson, K. I., Banich, M. T., Kramer, A. F., Webb, A., Wszalek, T., et al. (2002). Attentional control in the aging brain: Insights from an fMRI study of the Stroop task. *Brain and Cognition*, *49*(3), 277–296.

Mitchell, K. J., Johnson, M. K., Raye, C. L., & D'Esposito, M. (2000). fMRI evidence of age-related hippocampal dysfunction in feature binding in working memory. *Brain Research: Cognitive Brain Research*, *10*(1–2), 197–206.

Morcom, A. M., Good, C. D., Frackowiak, R. S. J., & Rugg, M. D. (2003). Age effects on the neural correlates of successful memory encoding. *Brain*, *126*(1), 213–229.

Mozley, L. H., Gur, R. C., Mozley, P. D., & Gur, R. E. (2001). Striatal dopamine transporters and cognitive functioning in healthy men and women. *American Journal of Psychiatry*, *158*(9), 1492–1499.

Nagahama, Y., Fukuyama, H., Yamaguchi, H., Katsumi, Y., Magata, Y., Shibasaki, H., et al. (1997). Age-related changes in cerebral blood flow activation during a card sorting test. *Experimental Brain Research*, *114*, 571–577.

Naveh-Benjamin, M. (2000). Adult age differences in memory performance: Tests of an

associative deficit hypothesis. *Journal of Experimental Psychology: Learning, Memory and Cognition, 26*(5), 1170–1187.

Nielson, K. A., Langenecker, S. A., & Garavan, H. (2002). Differences in the functional neuroanatomy of inhibitory control across the adult life span. *Psychology and Aging, 17*(1), 56–71.

Nyberg, L., Sandblom, J., Jones, S., Neely, A. S., Petersson, K. M., Ingvar, M., et al. (2003). Neural correlates of training-related memory improvement in adulthood and aging. *Proceedings of the National Academy of Sciences of the United States of America, 100*(23), 13728–13733.

O'Sullivan, M., Jones, D. K., Summers, P. E., Morris, R. G., Williams, S. C., & Markus, H. S. (2001). Evidence for cortical "disconnection" as a mechanism of age-related cognitive decline. *Neurology, 57*(4), 632–638.

Paller, K. A., & Wagner, A. D. (2002). Observing the transformation of experience into memory. *Trends in Cognitive Sciences, 6*(2), 93–102.

Pantano, P., Baron, J. C., Lebrun-Grandie, P., Duquesnoy, N., Bousser, M. G., & Comar, D. (1984). Regional cerebral blood flow and oxygen consumption in human aging. *Stroke, 15*(4), 635–641.

Pantoni, L., & Garcia, J. H. (1997). Cognitive impairment and cellular/vascular changes in the cerebral white matter. *Annals of the New York Academy of Sciences, 826*, 92–102.

Park, D. C. (2002). Aging, cognition, and culture: a neuroscientific perspective. *Neuroscience & Biobehavioral Reviews, 26*(7), 859–867.

Park, D. C., Polk, T. A., Park, R., Minear, M., Savage, A., & Smith, M. R. (2004). Aging reduces neural specialization in ventral visual cortex. *Proceedings of the National Academy of Sciences of the United States of America, 101*(35), 13091–13095.

Park, D. C., Welsh, R. C., Marshuetz, C., Gutchess, A. H., Mikels, J., Polk, T. A., et al. (2003). Working memory for complex scenes: Age differences in frontal and hippocampal activations. *Journal of Cognitive Neuroscience, 15*(8), 1122–1134.

Parkin, A. J., & Walter, B. M. (1992). Recollective experience, normal aging, and frontal dysfunction. *Psychology and Aging, 7*, 290–298.

Persson, J., Nyberg, L., Lind, J., Larsson, A., Nilsson, L. G., Ingvar, M., et al. (2006). Structure-function correlates of cognitive decline in aging. *Cerebral Cortex, 7*, 907–915.

Persson, J., Sylvester, C. Y., Nelson, J. K., Welsh, K. M., Jonides, J., & Reuter-Lorenz, P. A. (2004). Selection requirements during verb generation: Differential recruitment in older and younger adults. *Neuroimage, 23*(4), 1382–1390.

Pfefferbaum, A., Adalsteinsson, E., & Sullivan, E. V. (2005). Frontal circuitry degradation marks healthy adult aging: Evidence from diffusion tensor imaging. *Neuroimage, 26*(3), 891–899.

Pfefferbaum, A., Mathalon, D. H., Sullivan, E. V., Rawles, J. M., Zipursky, R. B., & Lim, K. O. (1994). A quantitative magnetic resonance imaging study of changes in brain morphology from infancy to late adulthood. *Archives of Neurology, 51*(9), 874–887.

Pfefferbaum, A., Sullivan, E. V., Hedehus, M., Lim, K. O., Adalsteinsson, E., & Moseley, M. (2000). Age-related decline in brain white matter anisotropy measured with spatially corrected echo-planar diffusion tensor imaging. *Magnetic Resonance in Medicine, 44*(2), 259–268.

Pfefferbaum, A., Sullivan, E. V., Rosenbloom, M. J., Mathalon, D. H., & Lim, K. O. (1998). A controlled study of cortical gray matter and ventricular changes in alcoholic men over a 5-year interval. *Archives of General Psychiatry, 55*(10), 905–912.

Raz, N. (1996). Neuroanatomy of aging brain: Evidence from structural MRI. In E. D. Bigler (Ed.), *Neuroimaging II: Clinical applications* (pp. 153–182). New York: Academic Press.

Raz, N. (2005). The aging brain observed in vivo: Differential changes and their modifiers. In

R. Cabeza, Nyberg, L., & Park, D. (Ed.), *Cognitive neuroscience of aging* (pp. 19–57). New York: Oxford University Press.

Raz, N., Gunning, F. M., Head, D., Dupuis, J. H., McQuain, J., Briggs, S. D., et al. (1997). Selective aging of the human cerebral cortex observed in vivo: Differential vulnerability of the prefrontal gray matter. *Cerebral Cortex, 7*(3), 268–282.

Raz, N., Lindenberger, U., Rodrigue, K. M., Kennedy, K. M., Head, D., Williamson, A., et al. (2005). Regional brain changes in aging healthy adults: General trends, individual differences and modifiers. *Cerebral Cortex, 15*(11), 1676–1689.

Raz, N., Rodrigue, K. M., Head, D., Kennedy, K. M., & Acker, J. D. (2004). Differential aging of the medial temporal lobe: A study of a five-year change. *Neurology, 62*(3), 433–438.

Raz, N., Rodrigue, K. M., Kennedy, K. M., Head, D., Gunning-Dixon, F., & Acker, J. D. (2003). Differential aging of the human striatum: Longitudinal evidence. *American Journal of Neuroradiology, 24*(9), 1849–1856.

Reeves, S., Bench, C., & Howard, R. (2002). Ageing and the nigrostriatal dopaminergic system. *International Journal of Geriatric Psychiatry, 17*(4), 359–370.

Resnick, S. M., Pham, D. L., Kraut, M. A., Zonderman, A. B., & Davatzikos, C. (2003). Longitudinal magnetic resonance imaging studies of older adults: A shrinking brain. *Journal of Neuroscience, 23*(8), 3295–3301.

Reuter-Lorenz, P. A., Jonides, J., Smith, E. E., Hartley, A., Miller, A., Marshuetz, C., et al. (2000). Age differences in the frontal lateralization of verbal and spatial working memory revealed by PET. *Journal of Cognitive Neuroscience, 12*(1), 174–187.

Riege, W. H., Metter, E. J., Kuhl, D. E., & Phelps, M. E. (1985). Brain glucose metabolism and memory functions: Age decrease in factor scores. *Journal of Gerontology, 40*(4), 459–467.

Rinne, J. O., Sahlberg, N., Ruottinen, H., Nagren, K., & Lehikoinen, P. (1998). Striatal uptake of the dopamine reuptake ligand [11C]beta-CFT is reduced in Alzheimer's disease assessed by positron emission tomography. *Neurology, 50*(1), 152–156.

Rodrigue, K. M., & Raz, N. (2004). Shrinkage of the entorhinal cortex over five years predicts memory performance in healthy adults. *Journal of Neuroscience, 24*(4), 956–963.

Rosen, A. C., Prull, M. W., O'Hara, R., Race, E. A., Desmond, J. E., Glover, G. H., et al. (2002). Variable effects of aging on frontal lobe contributions to memory. *Neuroreport, 13*(18), 2425–2428.

Ross, M. H., Yurgelun-Todd, D. A., Renshaw, P. F., Maas, L. C., Mendelson, J. H., Mello, N. K., et al. (1997). Age-related reduction in functional MRI response to photic stimulation. *Neurology, 48*(1), 173–176.

Rossi, S., Miniussi, C., Pasqualetti, P., Babiloni, C., Rossini, P. M., & Cappa, S. F. (2004). Age-related functional changes of prefrontal cortex in long-term memory: A repetitive transcranial magnetic stimulation study. *Journal of Neuroscience, 24*(36), 7939–7944.

Rypma, B., & D'Esposito, M. (2000). Isolating the neural mechanisms of age-related changes in human working memory. *Nature Neuroscience, 3*(5), 509–515.

Rypma, B., Prabhakaran, V., Desmond, J. E., & Gabrieli, J. D. (2001). Age differences in prefrontal cortical activity in working memory. *Psychology and Aging, 16*(3), 371–384.

Salat, D. H., Kaye, J. A., & Janowsky, J. S. (1999). Prefrontal gray and white matter volumes in healthy aging and Alzheimer disease. *Archives of Neurology, 56*(3), 338–344.

Salat, D. H., Tuch, D. S., Greve, D. N., van der Kouwe, A. J., Hevelone, N. D., Zaleta, A. K., et al. (2005). Age-related alterations in white matter microstructure measured by diffusion tensor imaging. *Neurobiology of Aging, 26*(8), 1215–1227.

Salat, D. H., Tuch, D. S., Hevelone, N. D., Fischl, B., Corkin, S., Rosas, H. D., et al. (2005). Age-related changes in prefrontal white matter measured by diffusion tensor imaging. *Annals of the New York Academy of Sciences, 1064*, 37–49.

Salthouse, T. A. (1996). The processing-speed theory of adult age differences in cognition. *Psychological Review, 103*(3), 403–428.

Scahill, R. I., Frost, C., Jenkins, R., Whitwell, J. L., Rossor, M. N., & Fox, N. C. (2003). A longitudinal study of brain volume changes in normal aging using serial registered magnetic resonance imaging. *Archives of Neurology, 60*(7), 989–994.

Schacter, D. L., Savage, C. R., Alpert, N. M., Rauch, S. L., & Albert, M. S. (1996). The role of hippocampus and frontal cortex in age-related memory changes: A PET study. *Neuroreport, 7*(1165–1169).

Schiavetto, A., Kohler, S., Grady, C. L., Winocur, G., & Moscovitch, M. (2002). Neural correlates of memory for object identity and object location: Effects of aging. *Neuropsychologia, 40*(8), 1428–1442.

Schmidt, H., Schmidt, R., Fazekas, F., Semmler, J., Kapeller, P., Reinhart, B., et al. (1996). Apolipoprotein E e4 allele in the normal elderly: Neuropsychologic and brain MRI correlates. *Clinical Genetics 50*(5), 293–299.

Schneider, B. A., & Pichora-Fuller, M. K. (2000). Implications of perceptual deterioration for cognitive aging research. In F. I. M. Craik & T. A. Salthouse (Eds.), *Handbook of cognitive aging II* (pp. 155–219). Mahwah, NJ: Lawrence Erlbaum Associates, Inc.

Smith, E. E., Geva, A., Jonides, J., Miller, A., Reuter-Lorenz, P., & Koeppe, R. A. (2001). The neural basis of task-switching in working memory: Effects of performance and aging. *Proceedings of the National Academy of Sciences of the United States of America, 98*(4), 2095–2100.

Soderlund, H., Nyberg, L., Adolfsson, R., Nilsson, L. G., & Launer, L. J. (2003). High prevalence of white matter hyperintensities in normal aging: Relation to blood pressure and cognition. *Cortex, 39*(4–5), 1093–1105.

Soderlund, H., Nyberg, L., & Nilsson, L. G. (2004). Cerebral atrophy as predictor of cognitive function in old, community-dwelling individuals. *Acta Neurologica Scandinavica, 109*(6), 398–406.

Stebbins, G. T., Carrillo, M. C., Dorfman, J., Dirksen, C., Desmond, J. E., Turner, D. A., et al. (2002). Aging effects on memory encoding in the frontal lobes. *Psychology and Aging, 17*(1), 44–55.

Stebbins, G. T., Poldrack, R. A., Klingberg, T., Carrillo, M. C., Desmond, J. E., Moseley, M. E., et al. (2001). Aging effects on white matter integrity and processing speed: A diffusion tensor imaging study. *Neurology, 56*(3), A374.

Suhara, T., Fukuda, H., Inoue, O., Itoh, T., Suzuki, K., Yamasaki, T., et al. (1991). Age-related changes in human D1 dopamine receptors measured by positron emission tomography. *Psychopharmacology (Berlin), 103*(1), 41–45.

Sullivan, E. V., Adalsteinsson, E., Hedehus, M., Ju, C., Moseley, M., Lim, K. O., et al. (2001). Equivalent disruption of regional white matter microstructure in ageing healthy men and women. *Neuroreport, 12*(1), 99–104.

Sullivan, E. V., Adalsteinsson, E., & Pfefferbaum, A. (2006). Selective age-related degradation of anterior callosal fiber bundles quantified in vivo with fiber tracking. *Cerebral Cortex, 7*, 1030–1039.

Sullivan, E. V., Marsh, L., Mathalon, D. H., Lim, K. O., & Pfefferbaum, A. (1995). Age-related decline in MRI volumes of temporal lobe gray matter but not hippocampus. *Neurobiology of Aging, 16*(4), 591–606.

Sullivan, E. V., Pfefferbaum, A., Adalsteinsson, E., Swan, G. E., & Carmelli, D. (2002). Differential rates of regional brain change in callosal and ventricular size: A 4-year longitudinal MRI study of elderly men. *Cerebral Cortex, 12*(4), 438–445.

Sullivan, E. V., Rosenbloom, M., Serventi, K. L., & Pfefferbaum, A. (2004). Effects of age and sex on volumes of the thalamus, pons, and cortex. *Neurobiology of Aging, 25*(2), 185–192.

Tauscher-Wisniewski, S., Tauscher, J., Logan, J., Christensen, B. K., Mikulis, D. J., & Zipursky, R. B. (2002). Caudate volume changes in first episode psychosis parallel the effects of normal aging: A 5-year follow-up study. *Schizophrenia Research, 58*(2–3), 185–188.

Teipel, S. J., Bayer, W., Alexander, G. E., Zebuhr, Y., Teichberg, D., Kulic, L., et al. (2002). Progression of corpus callosum atrophy in Alzheimer disease. *Archives of Neurology, 59*(2), 243–248.

Thomsen, T., Specht, K., Hammar, A., Nyttingnes, J., Ersland, L., & Hugdahl, K. (2004). Brain localization of attentional control in different age groups by combining functional and structural MRI. *Neuroimage, 22*(2), 912–919.

Tisserand, D. J., McIntosh, A. R., van der Veen, F. M., Backes, W. H., & Jolles, J. (2005). Age-related reorganization of encoding networks directly influences subsequent recognition memory. *Brain Research: Cognitive Brain Research, 25*(1), 8–18.

Tulving, E. (1985). Memory and consciousness. *Canadian Psychology, 25,* 1–12.

van Dyck, C. H., Seibyl, J. P., Malison, R. T., Laruelle, M., Wallace, E., Zoghbi, S. S., et al. (1995). Age-related decline in striatal dopamine transporter binding with iodine-123-beta-CITSPECT. *Journal of Nuclear Medicine, 36*(7), 1175–1181.

Volkow, N. D., Wang, G. J., Fowler, J. S., Ding, Y. S., Gur, R. C., Gatley, J., et al. (1998). Parallel loss of presynaptic and postsynaptic dopamine markers in normal aging. *Annals of Neurology, 44*(1), 143–147.

Wang, Y., Chan, G. L., Holden, J. E., Dobko, T., Mak, E., Schulzer, M., et al. (1998). Age-dependent decline of dopamine D1 receptors in human brain: A PET study. *Synapse, 30*(1), 56–61.

West, R. L. (1996). An application of prefrontal cortex function theory to cognitive aging. *Psychological Bulletin, 120*(2), 272–292.

Yamaguchi, T., Kanno, I., Uemura, K., Shishido, F., Inugami, A., Ogawa, T., et al. (1986). Reduction in regional cerebral metabolic rate of oxygen during human aging. *Stroke, 17*(6), 1220–1228.

Yonelinas, A. P. (2001). Components of episodic memory: The contribution of recollection and familiarity. *Philosophical Transactions of the Royal Society of London. Series B, Biological Sciences, 356*(1413), 1363–1374.

Yonelinas, A. P. (2002). The nature of recollection and familiarity: A review of 30 years of research. *Memory and Language, 46,* 441–517.

Zacks, R. T., Hasher, L., & Li, K. Z. H. (2000). Human memory. In F. I. M. Craik & T. A. Salthouse (Eds.), *The handbook of aging and cognition* (2nd ed.). Mahwah, NJ: Lawrence Erlbaum Associates, Inc.

2

Genetics of Cognitive Aging

Matt McGue
University of Minnesota and Southern Denmark University

Wendy Johnson
University of Edinburgh and University of Minnesota

OVERVIEW

Numerous large-scale, cross-sectional and longitudinal investigations have helped to characterize the basic nature of age differences and age changes in cognitive functioning across much of the adult lifespan. We know, for example, that average cognitive test performance declines in adulthood, although the specific age when decline first emerges varies across abilities and in some cases may occur earlier than previously appreciated (Salthouse, 2004). We also know that the timing and rate of decline vary markedly across individuals (Salthouse & Ferrer-Caja, 2003). Although the target of considerable research, the origins of individual differences in the aging of cognitive abilities remain largely unknown (Anstey & Christensen, 2000). In the search for the sources of individual differences in cognitive aging, some researchers emphasize the importance of neurobiological processes (Hedden & Gabrieli, 2005), while others emphasize the importance of psychosocial factors (Pushkar, Etezadi, Andres, Arbuckle, Schwartzman, & Chaikelson, 1999). Although these two approaches are distinct, they need not be incompatible as late-life cognitive functioning is likely the result of a complex interplay between neurobiological changes and psychosocial adaptations (Baltes & Baltes, 1990).

In this chapter we review findings from behavioral genetic research on cognitive aging, with a particular focus on normal-range cognitive functioning as opposed to dementia or late-life cognitive impairment.

Although there is emerging evidence that cognitive changes can begin as early as age 30 (Salthouse, 2004), our review will focus primarily on late-life functioning (e.g., after age 65), which has been the focus of most behavioral genetic research in this area. The centrality of heritability estimation in much behavioral genetic research has likely contributed to the view held by some that the field is narrowly conceived. We seek to show, however, that behavioral genetic methods are especially well suited to exploring a range of questions concerning the origins of individual differences in cognitive aging (Table 2.1). We organize our review around three broad types of research: (1) biometrical approaches, which seek to identify, quantify, and characterize the major factors contributing to individual differences in cognitive functioning; (2) gene identification approaches, which seek to identify the specific genes underlying the heritable effects identified using biometrical approaches; and (3) in-

TABLE 2.1
Behavior Genetic Research on Cognitive Aging

Research Question	Typical Research Design
Biometrical Approaches	
What are the magnitudes of genetic and environmental contributions to individual differences?	Cross-sectional Twin Studies
Do the magnitudes of genetic and environmental contributions vary with age?	Cross-sectional and Longitudinal Twin Studies
What are the overall contributions of genetic and environmental factors to trait stability and change?	Longitudinal Twin Studies
What are the neurobiological systems and processes that underlie heritable effects on cognitive functioning?	Multivariate Twin Studies
Gene Identification	
What are the specific genes that influence individual differences in cognitive functioning?	Candidate-gene studies of unrelated individuals
What are the specific genes that account for change in cognitive functioning?	Longitudinal candidate-gene studies of unrelated individuals
Gene–Environment Interplay	
What are the specific environmental factors that influence individual differences in cognitive functioning?	Discordant Twin Studies
How do environmental factors interact with genetic factors to influence individual differences in cognitive aging?	Candidate Gene and Twin Studies

vestigations of gene–environment interplay, which seek to explore the combined effects of genetic and environmental factors on cognitive aging.

At the outset it is useful to consider the alternative mechanisms by which genetic factors might influence individual differences in late-life cognitive functioning. First, there is overwhelming evidence of the existence of genetic influences on intellectual performance in childhood and early adulthood (McGue, Bouchard, Iacono, & Lykken, 1993). Genetic influences on late-life intellectual functioning may be due in part to the stability of cognitive ability throughout the lifespan. Second, beyond their influence on the enduring aspects of cognitive functioning, genetic factors may also influence the timing and rate of late-life changes. This second form of influence is most directly linked to what is meant by genetic influences on cognitive aging. The development of growth model methods, and especially their biometric extensions, has contributed greatly to behavioral genetic investigations of the influence of genetic factors on both initial level as well as change in cognitive functioning. Finally, the influence of genetic factors on late-life cognitive functioning may be indirect, the result of genetic influences on late-onset disorders like dementia that impair cognitive functioning.

Although our review focuses on the genetics of normal-range, late-life cognitive functioning, we cannot completely rule out the possibility that the research findings we review have been affected in part by the inclusion of individuals in the early stages of dementia. The prevalence of Alzheimer's disease (AD) is 1% among individuals age 60–64 but increases exponentially after age 65, with approximately 25–30% of those age 85 or older being affected (Blennow, de Leon, & Zetterberg, 2006). Subtle cognitive deficits attributable to the very early stages of AD may precede the actual onset of the disorder by more than a decade (La Rue & Jarvik, 1987), making it difficult to distinguish cognitive declines that are due to AD from those due to "normal" age-related processes. Consequently, a representative sample of older adults is likely to include some individuals with mild cognitive impairment attributable to incipient dementia, even if the sample has been screened for dementia (Bondi, Monsch, Galasko, Butters, Salmon, & Delis, 1994). Given the well-established existence of genetic influences on risk for dementia (Pedersen, Gatz, Berg, & Johansson, 2004), the inclusion of preclinical cases of dementia in a genetic study of "normal aging" could add to estimates of the heritability of late-life cognitive functioning. Nonetheless, the impact of preclinical cases of dementia on heritability and other parameter estimates is likely to be minimal because the proportionate representation of such cases in the sample is likely to be small (McGue & Christensen, 2001).

A second assessment issue concerns the well-established finding of an

accelerated decline in a broad range of human abilities, including cognitive functioning, shortly before death, a phenomenon termed terminal decline (Bosworth & Siegler, 2002). The inclusion of individuals in a longitudinal sample who are suffering terminal decline could lead to an overestimate of normative cognitive declines and attenuate twin similarity for cognitive functioning if twins are not concordant for the onset of terminal decline. Both terminal decline and the potential contamination of results on normal aging by the inclusion of preclinical cases of dementia serve to illustrate the ambiguity surrounding heritability estimation in cognitive aging research. While establishing a heritable basis for cognitive aging would direct our attention towards some etiological mechanisms and away from others, heritability estimation alone does not constitute a theoretical explanation. Rather, behavioral genetic research must build on the observation of heritable effects to develop research investigations and models of how genetic and environmental influences combine to influence late-life cognitive functioning.

We begin this chapter with an overview of alternative theoretical perspectives on the role of genetic factors in normative aging. Most behavioral genetic research in cognitive aging has used a twin-study design, so we next describe the logic, validity, and feasibility of this method. Our review of the substantive literature is organized around the three broad themes identified above, and leads us to conclude that while much has been accomplished, much remains to be done if we are to fully understand the contribution of genetic factors to cognitive aging.

THEORETICAL PERSPECTIVES

Evolutionary Models of Biological Aging

The eminent evolutionary biologist, Theodosius Dobzhansky, titled his most celebrated essay "Nothing in biology makes sense except in light of evolution" (Dobzhansky, 1973). Dobzhansky's adage is nowhere more applicable than in the study of the genetics of aging. Identifying the mechanisms that underlie the evolution of aging has long been a focus of biogerontological research, and findings from this research have direct relevance to models of genetic influences on the aging of psychological, and especially cognitive, function.

Although at one time popular, there is no longer widespread support for the proposition that, like early human development, human aging evolved as a tightly regulated program of senescence (Austad, 2001). Rather, several alternative mechanisms are thought to underlie the evolution of human biological aging. First, throughout most of human

evolutionary history, predation and infectious disease ensured that the cumulative probability of survival declined with age even in the absence of senescence. Consequently the force of natural selection is much stronger in early life, when there are many organisms alive, than in late life, when there are few, and selection is relatively inefficient in eliminating from the human genome deleterious mutations that only express in late life. The *Mutation Accumulation* model of biological aging hypothesizes that post-reproductive biological deterioration occurs because over time there have been many deleterious and unselected late-acting genetic mutations that have accumulated in the population (Hamilton, 1966). Alternatively, Williams (1957) noted that genetic mutations that confer a reproductive advantage early in life will be selectively favored even if they have deleterious effects in late life. This latter evolutionary model of biological aging, called *Antagonistic Pleiotropy*, characterizes biological deterioration in late life as the price organisms pay for fitness in early life. Consistent with the proposition that no single evolutionary mechanism is likely to account for all aspects of biological aging, there is empirical support for both evolutionary models.

These evolutionary models have implications for behavioral genetic models of psychological aging. Specifically, both the Mutation Accumulation and the Antagonistic Pleiotropy models posit the existence of age-specific genetic influences that underlie dimensions of biological aging. If the aging of cognitive abilities is in part a manifestation of the aging of basic biological processes, then we would expect there to be genetic influences specific to changes in cognitive functioning in late life. Indeed, since both evolutionary models posit the existence of genetic influences unique to late life, they raise the possibility that the overall contribution of heritable factors to cognitive functioning may be greater in late life than at earlier life stages.

While both models lead to the expectation of increasing genetic influence with age, they differ significantly in how those influences are characterized. Under the Mutation Accumulation model, mutations with specific late-life deleterious effects accumulate because they cannot be eliminated through natural selection. Mutations that are not selectively advantageous are generally not expected to be common in the general population, although they might be common in isolated or newly formed populations due to mechanisms like genetic drift and founder effects (Wright, Charlesworth, Rudan, Carothers, & Campbell, 2003). Thus, under the Mutation Accumulation model, biological aging is hypothesized to be due to a large number of mutations, many of which will be at low frequency in the population (called private mutations, Partridge & Gems, 2002). Alternatively, the mutations hypothesized to underlie biological aging in the Antagonistic Pleiotropy model have been selected for

their advantageous effects at earlier ages. Consequently, these genetic mutations are expected to be relatively few in number and common in the population (i.e., public mutations, Partridge & Gems, 2002). As we discuss later, methods currently used for gene identification in humans are most likely to be successful for the detection of common gene variants. Antagonistic Pleiotropy consequently provides a more hopeful model for identifying specific genetic effects on late-life cognitive decline than Mutation Accumulation. As we will see, whether such optimism is justified remains to be determined.

Quantitative Genetic Theory

The major aim of a quantitative genetic analysis is to identify and quantify the major contributors to individual differences in a complex phenotype. Individual differences are typically indexed by the phenotypic variance, V_P, a quantitative model for which was first proposed by Fisher (1918):

$$V_P = V_G + V_E + 2cov(G,E) + V_{G \times E}$$

where V_G is the variance attributable to genetic effects, V_E is the variance attributable to environmental effects, $cov(G,E)$ corresponds to the covariance of the genetic and environmental effects, and $V_{G \times E}$ is the variance attributable to the interaction of genetic and environmental effects. Typically, the variance attributable to genetic effects is further decomposed into portions associated with additive genetic factors (i.e., the independent effects of genes at specific loci added up over loci) and nonadditive genetics factors (i.e., either the interaction of gene effects at a specific locus— dominance—or the interaction of gene effects at different loci—epistasis), while the environmental variance is decomposed into a shared (i.e., environmental influences that contribute to phenotypic similarities among reared-together relatives) and a nonshared (i.e., environmental influences that contribute to phenotypic differences among reared-together relatives) component (Plomin, DeFries, McClearn, & McGuffin, 2001).

Elaborate statistical procedures, called biometrical methods or models, have been developed to estimate the parameters of the variance decomposition model from observations on twins and other pairs of relatives (Neale & Cardon, 1992). At the initial stages of inquiry, simplifying assumptions (e.g., no gene environment interaction or correlation) are often made to make the system mathematically tractable and enable estimation of the proportion of phenotypic variance associated with genetic (i.e., the heritability) and environmental factors. At subsequent stages of inquiry, the basic biometric model can be elaborated to investigate, for example, whether heritability varies with age, or the extent to which gen-

etic and environmental effects are shared across multiple behavioral phenotypes. The existence of untested assumptions implies, however, that the parameters of the basic biometric model, including the heritability coefficient, can only be estimated approximately. Nonetheless, these estimates have proven to be useful in characterizing the major factors contributing to phenotypic variance and have typically been found for many traits to be replicable across alternative behavioral genetic designs that rely on different assumptions. This suggests some degree of robustness against failure to meet assumptions (e.g., Loehlin, 1992). As such, the biometric estimates provide a useful initial step in trying to understand the major factors influencing individual differences in behavior.

Models of Gene–Environment Interplay

A set of recent influential findings has helped developmental researchers move beyond the simplistic dichotomy that was the basis of the Nature–Nurture debate to consider models for the joint influence of genetic and environmental factors on behavioral development (Rutter & Silberg, 2002). Several developments are especially relevant to behavioral genetic models of cognitive aging. First, there is growing theoretical interest in the importance of genotype–environment interactions (G×E) in psychological development in general and aging in particular (Grigorenko, 2005). Of greatest relevance to behavioral genetic models of cognitive aging is the finding that heritable influences on cognitive ability appear to be diminished in especially impoverished environments (Turkheimer, Haley, Waldron, D'Onofrio, & Gottesman, 2003). While this finding is based on a sample of twin children, it suggests that heritable influences on cognitive aging might be minimized when individuals do not have access to the economic and social resources needed to allow them to express their genetic potentials fully. The systematic investigation of G×E effects is only at the initial stages of inquiry, especially in the behavioral domain, although there are potentially many interactions of interest to gerontology researchers (Kelada, Eaton, Wang, Rothman, & Khoury, 2003).

A second aspect of gene–environment interplay is based on the recognition that environments are not experienced randomly. Rather, the environment an individual experiences is in part a function of her or his interests, abilities, and motivations. To the extent that the behavioral factors that guide experiential choices are genetically influenced, this induces a correlation between genetic and environmental effects, a phenomenon behavioral geneticists term genotype–environment (G–E) correlation. Deater-Deckard and Mayr (2005) have discussed how traditional theories of psychological aging can be incorporated into a G–E correlational framework. For example, the well-known Selective

Optimization with Compensation model of Baltes and Baltes (1990) can be framed as describing how individuals structure their environments to accommodate for the onset of genetically influenced diseases and disabilities.

The regulation of gene expression provides another vehicle for modeling gene–environment interplay. Although the same DNA resides in the nucleus of every somatic cell, all genes are not expressed in all cells at all times. Rather gene expression varies by cell type and stage of development, and is influenced not only by the cell's biological environment but also by the individual's psychological environment. A recent elegant demonstration of epigenetic influences on behavior comes from the work of Weaver et al. (2004), who reported that differential maternal treatment of rat pups in infancy resulted in differential expression of glucocorticoid receptor genes. This differential expression in turn resulted in differential response to stress that persisted into adulthood. The expression of particular genes is also likely to be influenced by other genes, as, in the aggregate, the regulation of genetic expression appears to be substantially under genetic influence (York, Kendler, Jackson-Cook, Bowman, & Eaves, 2005). These processes which geneticists call epigenesist are potentially powerful contributors to normative aging processes (Fraga, 2005).

THE TWIN STUDY METHOD

There is a variety of research designs for drawing inferences about the existence of genetic and environmental contributions to individual differences in behavior (Plomin et al., 2001). Nonetheless, aging researchers have relied almost exclusively on the twin design because of the difficulties presented by the very long time periods necessary to assess aging phenotypes in multigeneration family structures. The study of monozygotic (MZ) and dizygotic (DZ) twins has been very fruitful in generating both information and testable hypotheses about the sources of individual differences in cognitive function in general and changes in cognitive function during aging in particular. A twin study is based on the well-documented and accepted understanding that MZ twins share the same genotype while DZ twins share on average half the genes segregating in their families.

Univariate Biometric Twin Model

The relative similarity between the two types of twins has been used to estimate the amounts of variance in an observed trait that can be attributed to genetic and environmental influences. The basic idea is that

genetic influence is indicated when MZ twins are more similar than DZ twins and environmental influence is indicated when the MZ twins are not exactly alike. Under the model that is usually implemented (Figure 2.1), variance attributed to genetic influences can be divided into additive (A) and nonadditive components. In traits to which many genes contribute, termed polygenic traits, genetic variance is additive when the genes influencing the trait do so independently of each other. Genetic variance is nonadditive when genetic influences reflect dominance (D; the interaction between allele effects at individual loci), or epistasis (the interaction among allele effects at multiple loci).

Variance attributed to environmental influence can also be divided into two components. One component is termed shared environmental variance (C). This reflects experiential factors common to two members of a twin pair and operating to make them similar. It could include experiences such as lifetime effects of parental socioeconomic status and

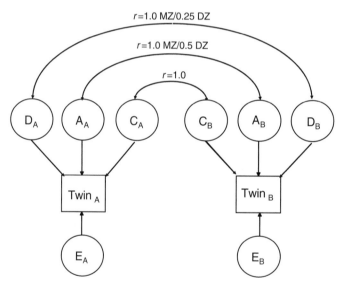

FIG. 2.1. Univariate Biometric Twin Model. The model shows how the biometric components of variance contribute to the phenotypic variance and covariance for two members of a twin pair (subscripts A and B). Variance in the observed phenotype is decomposed into additive genetic effects (A), dominance genetic effects (D), shared environmental effects (C), and nonshared environmental effects (E). Covariance in the additive and dominance components of variance for monozygotic (MZ) and dizygotic (DZ) twins is specified by quantitative genetic theory. C components are assumed to be perfectly correlated for reared-together twins regardless of zygosity, while E effects are uncorrelated. With data on reared-together twins only, both C and D cannot be estimated.

common religious adherence. The other component is termed nonshared environmental variance (E). This reflects experiential factors unique to each member of a twin pair and operating to make them different. Such experiences may include injuries and illnesses, having different jobs, and participating in different leisure activities. The distinction between the two kinds of environmental variance is sometimes subtle. For example, co-twins may experience the same event (e.g., long-term care and then death of an elderly parent) but that event is only a shared environmental influence to the extent that it makes the co-twins similar (Turkheimer & Waldron, 2000). Variance attributable to measurement error cannot be distinguished from nonshared environmental variance.

In the absence of environmental effects, additive genetic variance makes MZ twins twice as similar as DZ twins, while nonadditive genetic variance makes MZ twins more than twice as similar as DZ twins. Conversely, in the absence of genetic influence, MZ and DZ twins will be similar to the same degree when only shared environmental variance is present, and not similar at all when only nonshared environmental variance is present. Usually, of course, there is evidence for both genetic and environmental influences. With only MZ and DZ twins reared together, however, it is not possible to distinguish between nonadditive genetic and shared environmental variance because both reflect departures from the expectation that the ratio of the covariance between MZ twins to the covariance between DZ twins will be 2:1, like the ratio of their shared genes (100%:50%). Thus, biometric models of reared-together twin data estimate either shared environmental or, less frequently, nonadditive genetic variance, but not both. When shared environmental variance is estimated, the expected phenotypic variance and covariances between two members of MZ and DZ twin pairs can be specified as:

$$VAR = A + C + E$$

$$COV_{(MZ)} = A + C$$

$$COV_{(DZ)} = .5*A + C$$

the parameters of which can be estimated from observations on reared-together MZ and DZ twins using standard structural equation software (Neale, Boker, Xie, & Maes, 1999).

Assumptions Underlying the Twin Model

This kind of evaluation of co-twin similarity rests on several assumptions. First, we assume that genetic and environmental influences are additive and independent. This implies that there are no interactions or correl-

ations between genetic and environmental influences that would act to create differing degrees of genetic and environmental variance within different subgroups of the sample. The overall approach is not, however, invalidated by the presence of such interactions or correlations. Rather, the existence of G×E and G–E correlations renders the estimates of the variance components from the standard biometric model to be approximate. The biases in the estimates depend on the nature of the interaction or correlation. Specifically, an interaction between genetic and shared environmental influences acts to increase estimates of genetic influence, while an interaction between genetic and nonshared environmental influences acts to increase estimates of nonshared environmental influence. Conversely, a correlation between genetic and shared environmental influences acts to increase the estimates of shared environmental influence, but a correlation between genetic and nonshared environmental influences acts to increase estimates of genetic influence (Purcell, 2002).

A related assumption is that the environments of MZ and DZ twins are equally similar. Known as the Equal Environments Assumption (EEA), this means that we assume that people do not treat MZ twins more similarly than they do DZ twins simply because of their zygosity status, at least in any way that has an impact on the trait in question, here cognitive function in later life. In evaluating the appropriateness of the EEA, it is important to distinguish between treatment evoked by the twins through their behavior or appearance and treatment systematically provided by parents, friends, job supervisors, etc. MZ twins may elicit more similar experiences and treatment than DZs from their environments due to their greater genetic similarity. This is, however, generally considered to be another expression of their greater genetic similarity. Many studies of the EEA have been carried out, and they support its validity (Kendler & Gardner, 1998; Plomin et al., 2001). Moreover, the absence of any relationship between measured intelligence and physical attractiveness, either in individuals (Feingold, 1992) or MZ twins (Rowe, Clapp, & Wallis, 1987), implies that greater physical similarity could not be the basis for any greater intellectual similarity of MZ as compared to DZ twins.

The standard biometric model also relies on the assumption that parents are not more similar to each other for cognitive functioning than are randomly paired individuals. There is considerable evidence that this assumption is generally violated for cognitive function (Vandenberg, 1972). Assortative mating increases the phenotypic similarity of DZ twins because it reduces the genetic variation within families relative to the genetic variation between families but is not expected to similarly affect resemblance between genetically identical MZ twins. We can adjust the model shown above to account for this, but such adjustments are not often

made. Failure to adjust has the effect of understating estimates of genetic variance and overstating estimates of shared environmental variance. For cognitive function in later life, however, estimates of shared environmental variance have generally been negligible (McGue et al., 1993), suggesting little need for adjustment.

Finally, the importance of the twin study in an epidemiological context relies on the understanding that, except for the fact that they were born "together," twins are ordinary folks. Although there are ways in which this is not true—for example, twins are more likely to have low birthweight (Hall & Lopez-Rangel, 1996), and developmental difficulties in language and attention in early childhood (Levy, McLaughlin, Wood, Hay, & Waldman, 1996)—twins do not appear to age differently than nontwins (Christensen, Vaupel, Holm, & Yashin, 1995). Moreover, and of more direct relevance to cognitive aging, any cognitive deficits associated with being a twin appear to be modest in older birth cohorts (Ronalds, De Stavola, & Leon, 2005) and nonexistent in more recent birth cohorts (Christensen, Petersen, Skytthe, Herskind, McGue, & Bingley, 2006; Posthuma, De Geus, Bleichrodt, & Boomsma, 2000).

Ascertaining Twins for Studies on Aging

Assuming that twins are ordinary folks who happen to have been born together, one of the primary goals of most twin studies is to generate a sample that is representative of the population from which it is drawn. There are two components to this: the twins must span the same demographic range as singletons so that the sample can be considered representative of the overall population, and the twin sample must appropriately represent the incidence of twin births. Twin births are, of course, relatively rare: in western nations they have historically occurred in about 1 out of 80 live births (Segal, 2000), and after childhood it is uncommon for them to share residence. This makes adult twins relatively difficult to locate. Most of the prominent twin samples in use today have been ascertained using state-maintained and publicly available birth records, which has generally been considered a reasonable way to generate a sample that representatively spans the demographic range of singletons. It is for this reason that many twin studies have been carried out in the Scandinavian countries, which have long histories of consistent birth and residency records and relatively geographically stable populations. The extent to which twin study findings from Scandinavia, where access to health care is universal and rates of poverty low, generalize to countries like the US, where access to health care is uneven and poverty more common, is uncertain.

Multivariate Biometric Twin Model

The standard biometric twin model for one trait can be extended to assess associations among genetic and environmental influences on two or more traits, or on the same traits at different time points (i.e., biometric growth models). Figure 2.2 provides a schematic representation of a bivariate biometric model. For convenience, only one member of a twin pair is represented in the model. The central aim of a bivariate biometric analysis is to identify the genetic and environmental contributions to the covariance between two phenotypes, which are parameterized in terms of r_a, the correlation in additive genetic factors; r_c, the correlation in shared environmental factors; and r_e, the correlation in nonshared environmental factors. Bivariate biometric methods have been instrumental for investigating the neuropsychological and neurological factors mediating heritable influences on cognitive functioning.

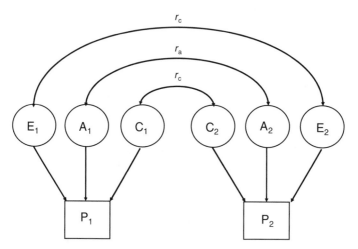

FIG. 2.2. Bivariate Biometric Model. The diagram gives a schematic for the biometric model accounting for the correlation in two observed phenotypes (subscripts 1 and 2). For convenience only one member of the twin pair is depicted. The correlation between the two phenotypes is modeled in terms of correlated additive genetic effects (A), correlated shared environmental effects (C), and correlated nonshared environmental effects (E).

USING THE TWIN METHOD TO CHARACTERIZE THE MAJOR SOURCES OF INDIVIDUAL DIFFERENCES IN LATE-LIFE COGNITIVE FUNCTIONING

Cross-sectional Twin Studies

Cross-sectional twin studies of late-life cognitive functioning have tended to focus on estimation and comparison of genetic and environmental influences on general and specific cognitive function, with the intents of establishing baseline estimates and determining whether the genetic and environmental associations among general and specific cognitive abilities in late life are similar to those in young and middle adulthood. These studies have consistently found that genetic influences on general cognitive functioning in old age are substantial. In a sample of 312 pairs of Swedish twins with an average age of 65.6 years, for example, Pedersen, Plomin, Nesselroade, and McClearn (1992) reported an estimate of 81% for the heritability for the first principal component of a battery of 13 tests of fluid and crystallized intelligence. This estimate is consistent with the hypothesis that the heritability of general cognitive ability increases from childhood through at least early adulthood (McGue et al., 1993). Studies of very-old twins, however, suggest that the heritability of cognitive ability may decline in very late life. McClearn et al. (1997) reported a heritability estimate of 62% (95% confidence interval of 29–73%) for the first principal component of a diverse set of verbal and nonverbal cognitive ability tests assessed in a sample of 240 pairs of like-sex Swedish twins aged 80 years and older. This finding of lower heritability at older ages was replicated by McGue and Christensen (2001), who reported a heritability estimate of 54% (95% confidence interval of 27–63%) for a composite of five brief cognitive tests of memory and fluency in a sample of 365 like-sex Danish twins aged 75 years and older. In the only cross-sectional study to formally assess age moderation, Finkel, Pedersen, McGue, and McClearn (1995) reported heritability estimates for the first principal component of four subscales (Information, Block Design, Digit Symbol, and Digit Span) from the Wechsler Adult Intelligence Scale—Revised (WAIS-R, Wechsler, 1981) in two adult samples, one from Sweden and the other from the US. The heritability for the principal component was stable at 81% across the two samples from age 27 to 65 but decreased significantly after age 65 to 54% in the Swedish sample. No evidence for an age-related decline in heritability was observed in the US sample, however. In all these studies, nonshared environmental factors were identified as the predominant source of nongenetic influence. Thus, the observation of decreasing heritability implicates the increasing importance of nonshared environmental factors in late life.

When measured separately without consideration of the role of general cognitive ability, tests of memory have tended to show somewhat less genetic influence than tests of overall cognitive ability in older twin samples (McGue & Christensen, 2001; Swan et al., 1999). This is also true, however, at younger adult ages (Johnson et al., 2006). Moreover, multivariate studies have generally found that genetic influences on general cognitive ability account for much of the correlation between general and specific cognitive abilities, including memory. Using data from the Swedish Adoption/Twin Study of Aging (SATSA) project, Finkel and colleagues failed to find evidence for genetic influences on perceptual speed (Finkel & Pedersen, 2000; Finkel, Pedersen, & Harris, 2000) and memory (Finkel et al., 1998) distinct from genetic influences on general cognitive function. Similarly, in a study of twins age 80 years and older Petrill et al. (1998) concluded that once the genetic influence on overall cognitive ability had been taken into account there were no residual genetic influences on verbal, spatial, memory, and speed ability measures. These results stand in contrast to findings from twin studies on younger adults, where ability-specific genetic influences have been observed, and provide some evidence for the widely held assumption that cognitive abilities become less differentiated with age.

Longitudinal Studies of Late-life Cognitive Functioning

The Growth Curve Approach

As noted above, the univariate biometric model can be extended to assess associations among genetic and environmental influences on the same traits at different time points. This kind of longitudinal analysis has been used to carry out some of the most interesting work on genetic and environmental influences on cognitive functioning. The model used most commonly makes use of latent growth curves to describe changes in cognitive function over time. The curves employed provide estimates of overall population effects derived from the average pattern from the sample as a whole (fixed effects) as well as estimates of the extent to which individuals in the sample vary around these overall estimates (random effects). In general, individual scores at any one point in time are considered to be functions of an initial level, or intercept, and linear patterns of deviation from that initial level over time (or slope). Sometimes terms reflecting curvilinear (e.g., quadratic) patterns of change or changes in slope at particular ages are estimated as well. These models can be specified to reflect each participant's age at assessment individually so that variations in age within the sample at time of assessment can be taken into consideration. In addition, the models allow for missing data by giving

greater weight to participants with more data points. Participants with only single data points contribute to the estimates of initial level, but not to the estimates of change. Once the growth curve model is established, the variances of the initial level, slope, any other change parameters, and the covariances among them can be decomposed into components reflecting genetic and environmental influences (Neale & McArdle, 2000). These variance components provide information that can be used to test hypotheses generated by different theories of the effects of aging on cognitive function.

Longitudinal Studies of Genetic and Environmental Influences on Cognitive Aging

Longitudinal research is inherently difficult to undertake, and this difficulty is compounded by the need to sample large numbers of older twin pairs for behavioral genetic research on aging. It is consequently not surprising that longitudinal twin research on cognitive aging is restricted primarily to three samples. The Swedish Adoption/Twin Study of Aging (SATSA, Pedersen et al., 1991) constitutes a subset of twins from the population-based Swedish Twin Registry. It is made up of all pairs of twins who indicated that they had been separated before the age of 11 and reared apart, matched on gender, date, and county of birth to a group of reared-together twins. From this group, pairs of twins aged 50 and older were invited to participate in 4-hour, in-person testing sessions of health and cognitive abilities. Cognitive abilities were measured using a battery of WAIS-R subtests and a standard Swedish ability battery. Second and third waves of testing were conducted 3 and 6 years after the first, and a fourth wave occurred 7 years after the third. Twin pairs who reached the age of 50 after the first wave were invited to participate in later waves as eligible. The first wave included 595 participants, and numbers of participants declined slowly over the waves so that there were 517 during the fourth wave.

The Longitudinal Study of Aging Danish Twins (LSADT) was started in 1995 with the assessment of members of same-sex twin pairs born in Denmark prior to 1920 (Christensen, Holm, McGue, Corder, & Vaupel, 1999). These twins were thus at least age 75 at time of initial assessment. They were recruited without regard to the mortality status of their co-twins, so many pairs in the sample are incomplete. The assessment included five brief individual cognitive measures of fluency, forward and backward digit span, and immediate and delayed word recall. Follow-up assessments on this group were carried out in 1997, 1999, 2001, 2003, and 2005. In addition, twins at least age 73 in 1997 and at least age 70 in 1999 and 2001 were added to the study in those years. In all, 4731 individual

twins and 1152 twin pairs have completed an LSADT intake assessment, either through in-person interview, usually in the home, or by proxy.

The third study consists of participants from the National Heart, Lung, and Blood Institute Twin Study. The sample was drawn from a population-based registry of twin pairs of Caucasian men born between 1917 and 1927 who were World War II veterans, and originally included 514 pairs. These twins have been followed periodically over a 32-year span. A small numbers of twin pairs (23 MZ and 23 DZ) completed a 5-year longitudinal assessment of cognitive assessment in the 1980s (Swan, LaRue, Carmelli, Reed, & Fabsitz, 1992), and another small sample from this cohort (34 MZ and 37 DZ twin pairs) received structural brain MRIs in both 1995–1997 and 1999–2001 (Pfefferbaum et al., 2004).

The first longitudinal study of genetic and environmental influences on cognitive function in later life was carried out by Plomin, Pedersen, Lichtenstein, and McClearn (1994) using SATSA. At that time, there had been only two assessments. Given that the average age of the participants was relatively young for a study of aging (64.1 at first assessment) and the period between assessments was only 3 years, the focus of this study was on sources of stability in cognitive function rather than change. Results showed large genetic influences on cognitive abilities, particularly general cognitive ability as measured by the first principal component from a battery of 11 cognitive tests, which yielded a heritability estimate of 80%. In addition, 90% of the correlation of .92 between general cognitive abilities at the two time points appeared to be under genetic influence.

Since this initial investigation, the SATSA sample has been assessed two more times, bringing the maximal retest interval to 13 years, and the LSADT sample has been compiled and assessed several times. These two samples have generated several studies investigating different aspects of genetic and environmental influences on stability and change for the various cognitive measures used in these two studies (Finkel & Pedersen, 2004; Finkel, Pedersen, Reynolds, Berg, de Faire, & Svartengren, 2003a; Finkel, Reynolds, McArdle, Gatz, & Pedersen, 2003b; Finkel et al., 2005; McGue & Christensen, 2002; Reynolds et al., 2002, 2005) that provide the basis for several general conclusions. These studies have consistently shown greater individual differences in level of cognitive functioning than in rate of change in cognitive functioning, or slope. The same pattern has been observed with respect to genetic influences on cognitive functioning: they are substantial for initial level of cognitive functioning but modest or insignificant for slope. For the five-test composite measure of general cognitive ability in LSADT, heritability was estimated to be 76% for the intercept parameter as compared to 6% for the slope (McGue & Christensen, 2002). Similarly, for the first principal component measure of

general cognitive ability from SATSA, heritability was estimated to be 91% for the intercept as compared to 1% for the slope (Reynolds et al., 2005). The SATSA sample shows evidence for moderate genetic influences on quadratic change in cognitive function (Finkel, Reynolds, McArdle, Gatz, & Pedersen, 2003b; Finkel et al., 2005; Reynolds et al., 2005), suggesting that genetic factors might influence the acceleration, even if they do not affect the overall rate, of cognitive decline. Nonetheless, it is important that the SATSA findings on quadratic change be replicated in other samples.

The failure to find significant genetic influences on rate of cognitive change could be interpreted as providing evidence that cognitive aging is largely a stochastic environmental rather than systematic genetic process. This interpretation gains further support from the consistent findings from longitudinal research, which replicate findings from cross-sectional research, that genetic influences on cognitive functioning generally decline while nonshared environmental influences increase with age (Finkel et al., 1998; McGue & Christensen, 2002; Reynolds et al., 2002). Nonetheless, several factors caution against concluding at this time that late-life change in cognitive functioning is due entirely to environmental factors. First, retest intervals for the vast majority of participants in the existing large-scale longitudinal twin studies generally fall in the 4–8 year range, which may be too limited a time period to allow for reliable assessment of individual change. Indeed, a study of a small sample of twins that spanned a 16-year interval found greater evidence for heritable influences on cognitive change than has been reported in the larger twin studies (McArdle, Prescott, Hamagami, & Horn, 1998).

Second, as discussed earlier, cognitive assessments in late life can be confounded by the effects of impending death (i.e., terminal drop, Bosworth & Siegler, 2002). The existence of terminal drop presents particular difficulties for twin studies because differences in the timing with which it occurs for co-twins will attenuate their similarity at individual points in time, reducing estimates of genetic influence while increasing estimates of environmental influence. Consistent with this proposition, Johansson et al. (2004) reported that nearness to death moderated twin correlations of cognitive ability in a sample of Swedish twins aged 80 years and older. Third, several researchers have noted practice effects on measures of cognitive ability, even in older samples over extended periods of time (Rabbitt, Diggle, Holland, & McInnes, 2004; Reeve & Lam, 2005; Singer, Lindenberger, & Baltes, 2003). None of the behavioral genetic studies we have reviewed has taken practice effects into account, and it is possible that individual differences in these effects may mask genetic influences on change in cognitive ability. Finally, failure to find genetic influences on individual differences in rate of cognitive change does not rule out the

existence of species-typical genetic influences on the shared population trajectory.

Multivariate Analyses: Identifying the Basis of Heritable and Nonheritable Effects

Health and Psychological Function

Several SATSA studies have explored how genetic and environmental contributions to physical aspects of aging compare to those on cognitive aging. For example, in a growth curve analysis using SATSA data Finkel et al. (2003a) reported substantial genetic contributions (heritability estimates all exceeded .50) to rate of linear change in mean arterial pressure, forced expiratory volume (FEV), and a motor functioning composite. Consequently, the failure to observe similar heritable contributions to change in measures of cognitive functioning in SATSA does not appear to be some artifact of the SATSA design. Reynolds et al. (2002) provide additional evidence from SATSA of the need to distinguish aspects of cognitive aging from aspects of physical aging. These researchers investigated the relationship between FEV (a measure of lung capacity) and three measures of cognitive functioning (block design, picture memory, and digit symbol substitution). The relationship between FEV and initial level of cognitive functioning (i.e., the intercept) was primarily genetically mediated, while the relationship between FEV and change in cognitive functioning (i.e., the slope) was primarily environmentally mediated. These data make clear that there is no unitary genetically controlled program of aging across all body systems, and suggest that exogenous stochastic processes may be a major source of the timing and rate of change in late-life cognitive functioning.

Finkel and colleagues (Finkel & Pedersen, 2000, 2004; Finkel et al., 2005) have used SATSA data to explore how the genetic and environmental pathways involved in the association between processing speed and general cognitive ability vary with age. These studies indicate that processing speed plays an increasingly important role in general cognitive ability with increasing age. They also suggest that the genetic influences on general cognitive ability increasingly reflect genetic influences on processing speed, particularly for fluid abilities. Specifically, as much as 70% of the genetic variance in cognitive functioning in later life can be accounted for by genetic effects on perceptual speed (Finkel & Pedersen, 2000). This provides some evidence in support of the proposition that cognitive abilities become less differentiated with age and increasingly reflect basic neurological processes as manifested in cognitive speed (Salthouse, 1996).

Brain Imaging Studies

The relationship of processing speed to cognitive functioning suggests that neurobiological structures and processes may mediate heritable effects on late-life cognitive functioning. A recent significant development on the genetics of cognitive aging is the linking of genetic research designs with brain imaging approaches in order to investigate this possibility. Several independent twin studies of young adults have revealed that brain morphology measures are highly heritable (e.g., 80–90%; Toga & Thompson, 2005). Moreover, brain volumetric measures are moderately correlated with cognitive test performance (McDaniel, 2005), and common genetic factors appear to be the primary basis for this correlation (Posthuma, De Geus, Baare, Pol, Kahn, & Boomsma, 2002; Thompson et al., 2001). Thus, an emerging hypothesis is that one mechanism by which genetic factors influence individual differences in cognitive ability is through their effects on brain structure (Gray & Thompson, 2004).

Investigation of the interrelationships among brain aging, genetics, and cognitive functioning is only at the initial stages of inquiry. In a sample of male twins aged 68–78, Pfefferbaum Sullivan, and Carmelli (2000) reported heritability estimates of approximately 80% for both total intracranial volume and lateral ventricle size. Age-related brain volume loss has been observed consistently in cross-sectional (Raz, 2000) and longitudinal research (Raz et al., 2005) among intact as well as cognitively impaired elderly (Resnick, Pham, Kraut, Zonderman, & Davatzikos, 2003). Some might hypothesize that the failure to find genetic influences on change in cognitive function might be a consequence of environmentally mediated reductions in brain volume. Nonetheless, a 4-year follow-up of the Pfefferbaum et al. (2000) sample revealed that genetic factors contributed to both stability and change in individual differences in brain morphology (Pfefferbaum et al., 2004). Moreover, counter to what would be expected if environmental factors exerted an increasing influence on brain morphological measures, heritability estimates were not lower at follow-up than at intake. Carmelli, Swan, DeCarli, and Reed (2002b) also reported strong heritable effects on brain morphological measures in a sample of 139 male twins aged 69–80 years old. They further reported that less than 50% of the genetic variance in an executive function factor that loaded on measures of digit-symbol substitution and trail making could be accounted for by heritable effects on brain morphology. These findings thus indicate that purely structural measures can account for a portion but not all of the heritable variance in late-life cognitive functioning.

Carmelli and colleagues have also investigated the relationship between white matter hyperintensities (WMHs) and cognitive functioning

in their sample of elderly male twins. WMHs increase with age, are correlated with risk for dementia, and are thought to be reflections of ischemic damage (Breteler, Claus, Grobbee, & Hofman, 1994). WMHs also appear to be strongly heritable, with heritability estimates of 73–92% (Carmelli et al., 1998). Carmelli, Reed, and DeCarli (2002a) showed that WMHs are modestly but significantly correlated ($r = -.20$) with an executive function composite they derived from four neuropsychological tests: Trail Making A and B, Digit-Symbol Substitution, Verbal Fluency, and Color-Word Interference in normal aging twins. Common genetic factors were found to be the primary basis for this correlation. Nonetheless, again most of the heritable variance in cognitive functioning could not be accounted for by the brain imaging measures.

The behavioral genetic literature on late-life cognitive functioning and brain morphology, although limited, appears to be consistent with findings based on younger adults. That is, genetic influences on brain morphological measures appear to be substantial and account statistically for some but by no means all of the heritable influences on cognitive functioning. The inclusion of functional as well as structural measures in future research may help to better characterize the neurogenetic basis of late-life cognitive functioning. Of interest are the findings that the magnitude of genetic influence does not appear to change with age and that genetic factors appear to contribute to both stability and change in late-life brain morphology. This latter observation may appear to be somewhat inconsistent with findings from studies of cognitive functioning, where there was limited evidence for genetic influences on cognitive change. It is well to note, however, the limitations of longitudinal twin research on both brain morphology (a single study of male twins) and cognitive functioning (narrow retest intervals).

IDENTIFYING SPECIFIC GENETIC CONTRIBUTIONS TO LATE-LIFE COGNITIVE FUNCTIONING: CANDIDATE-GENE STUDIES

The Human Genome and Behavioral Genomics

In February 2001, the two leading scientific publications in the world simultaneously published the draft sequence of the human genome, providing the tools needed to identify genes influencing complex phenotypes, including behavior (Plomin & Crabbe, 2000). The human genome spans approximately three billion bases of DNA and approximately 20,000 functioning genes (Collins, Lander, Rogers, & Waterston, 2004). Although the vast majority of the human genome is invariant across individuals, approximately ten to twelve million of the DNA bases are

polymorphic (i.e., they vary across individuals in the population, Crawford, Akey, & Nickerson, 2005). These variations at the DNA level, called single nucleotide polymorphisms (SNPs), represent one likely source of genetic influences on individual differences in behavior. Of course sorting through the millions of SNPs to find the small number of relevance to individual differences in any one trait of interest has been accurately likened to finding the proverbial needle in a haystack.

Genetic epidemiologists have primarily made use of two research strategies to identify genes affecting complex phenotypes. The first involves determining whether a specific region of a human chromosome, identified through known genetic markers, is associated with the transmission of a phenotype within families. This strategy, which is called linkage analysis, identifies regions of the human genome that are likely to harbor genes affecting the phenotype in question. Although linkage analysis has been a major strategy for mapping genes for behavioral disorders like schizophrenia (Lewis et al., 2003), bipolar disorder (Segurado et al., 2003), and Alzheimer's disease (AD; Kehoe et al., 1999), its use to map genes for normal range variation in behavioral traits has been more limited. Indeed, there is only one published systematic linkage study of cognitive ability, and this study, which identified two chromosomal regions as possibly containing genes affecting individual differences in cognitive ability, is based on adolescent and young adult samples (Posthuma et al., 2005).

The second strategy for gene identification, a candidate-gene or genetic association study, has been widely applied throughout the behavioral sciences, including gerontology. A candidate-gene study seeks to associate individual differences in a phenotype with genetic polymorphisms in candidate genes targeted because the biological effects of that gene are hypothesized to be directly relevant for the phenotype being investigated. The logic of the candidate-gene approach is relatively straightforward: if there are genetic variants influencing individual differences in a behavioral phenotype, then these variants should be predictably associated with phenotypic outcomes. In this section we review candidate-gene studies of normal-range, late-life cognitive functioning beginning with apolipoprotein E (APOE), the most widely investigated candidate gene in the gerontological literature. Table 2.2 provides a qualitative summary of existing candidate-gene research on cognitive aging.

Apolipoprotein E (APOE)

One of the most robust genetic associations in the gerontological field is that between APOE and risk of late-onset AD (Corder et al., 1993). APOE codes for a protein involved in cholesterol transport and maps to human chromosome 19q. There are three allelic forms of the APOE gene: ε2, ε3, and ε4, with the ε4 allele being associated with increased risk for develop-

TABLE 2.2
Candidate Genes that have been Investigated in Late-life Cognitive Functioning

Gene	Rationale	Strength of Evidence
Apolipoprotein E (APOE)	Risk factor for cardiovascular disease and AD. Involved in neuronal repair and lipid transport	+
Angiotensin I Converting Enzyme (ACE)	Risk factor for hypertension and AD	+/−
Catechol-O-methyltransferase (COMT)	Involved in the degradation of released catecholamines. Associated with working memory function in younger adults	+/−
Methylenetetrahydrofolate Reductase (MTHFR)	Involved in the metabolism of homocysteine, which has been associated with cognitive impairment and cardiovascular health	−
Methionine Synthase (MTR)	Involved in the metabolism of homocysteine	+/−
Klotho	Implicated in accelerated aging	IE
Cathepsin D	Involved in cell apoptosis	IE
Lactotransferrin	Antioxidant defense	IE
Nicastrin	Transmembrane glycoprotein	IE
Prion gene (PRNP)	Antioxidant defense	IE
Serotonin Transporter	Thought to affect memory function	IE
DISC	Risk factor for schizophrenia; thought to affect hippocampus function	IE

AD = Alzheimer's Disease; + = combined evidence supports existence of an association; +/− = evidence for association is inconsistent; − = combined evidence does not support existence of an association; IE = insufficient evidence, only one published study.

ing AD, principally by advancing its age of onset, and the ε2 allele appearing to be protective. As compared to risk among noncarriers, the odds of developing AD are approximately 3-fold higher among carriers of a single ε4 allele and nearly 15-fold higher among ε4/ε4 homozygotes (Farrer et al., 1997). The ε4 allele has a large attributable risk because it is relatively common, with a frequency that is approximately 15% among individuals of European ancestry and even higher among Nigerians, Finns, Sudanese, and African Americans (Hallman et al., 1991). APOE appears to exert its influence on AD risk by its involvement in the repair of neuronal damage. Specifically, the ε2 and ε3 alleles may be relatively effective in facilitating repair of neuronal damage while the ε4 allele is not (Mahley & Rall, 2000). There is some evidence to suggest that the primary effect of the APOE ε4 allele is to advance the age of onset but not otherwise increase the overall risk of AD (Meyer et al., 1998). For example, Khachaturian, Corcoran,

Mayer, Zandi, and Breitner (2004) reported that APOE genotype was not associated with lifetime risk for AD, which was estimated to be 72% through to age 100, but possession of one and especially two copies of the ε4 allele accelerated the age of AD onset. Interestingly, APOE may provide an example of the Antagonistic Pleiotropy model of aging. The ε4 allele that is a risk factor for dementia may be common in part because it appears to protect young children from the physical and cognitive impairments that are a consequence of severe diarrhea (Oriá, Patrick, Blackman, Lima, & Guerrant, 2007).

The association of APOE with normal-range cognitive functioning has also been extensively investigated. There are several reasons why APOE might be associated with general cognitive functioning in addition to its association with AD. The neuronal repair mechanism thought to be the basis for APOE's association with AD could also be the basis for a more general association with late-life cognitive functioning. Alternatively, a representative sample of older individuals will include some individuals who are at risk for developing AD and thus may show preclinical signs of cognitive impairment at the time of assessment (Bäckman, Jones, Berger, Laukka, & Small, 2005), inducing an association, albeit one that is likely to be weak, between cognitive functioning and APOE.

Typical of genetic association research with other phenotypes and polymorphisms, research on the association of APOE with normal-range cognitive functioning has yielded a bewildering pattern of positive (e.g., Deary et al., 2003; Wilson, Bienias, Berry-Kravis, Evans, & Bennett, 2002a) and negative (e.g., Kim et al., 2002; Yip, Brayne, Easton, & Rubinsztein, 2002a) results. To resolve inconsistencies in genetic association studies like those found with APOE and late-life cognitive functioning, geneticists have increasingly made use of meta-analytic methods. Small, Rosnick, Fratiglioni, and Bäckman (2004) recently undertook a comprehensive meta-analysis of 38 cross-sectional studies relating APOE to normal-range cognitive functioning in older adults. Carriers of at least one copy of the ε4 allele were found to perform significantly more poorly than noncarriers on measures of general cognitive ability, although the magnitude of the associated effect size was quite modest (standardized effect size, $d = -.09$). In terms of specific cognitive abilities, only episodic memory ($d = -.03$) and executive functioning ($d = -.09$) showed significant meta-analytic associations, although again the magnitude of the effects was quite small even if statistically significant.

The meta-analysis also identified age as a significant moderator of the APOE's association with both general cognitive and episodic memory ability. In both cases, the effect of APOE decreased with increasing age over the range of mean ages spanned by the studies included in the meta-analysis (approximately 45 to 89 years). A recent large study of nonagenarians provides further confirmation that APOE is not associated with

normal-range cognitive functioning at very advanced ages (Bathum, Christiansen, Jeune, Vaupel, McGue, & Christensen, 2006). In addition, APOE does not appear to be related to normal-range cognitive functioning at the other end of the lifespan, as studies of APOE and cognitive functioning in children have consistently failed to find any association (Deary et al., 2003; Turic, Fisher, Plomin, & Owen, 2001). Taken together, these studies along with the meta-analysis suggest that an association of APOE with normal-range cognitive functioning may only exist among the so-called young-old (i.e., 50–70), and even here the effect size is at best modest. This underscores the possibility that the association of APOE with normal-range cognitive functioning might actually be due to the inclusion of preclinical cases of AD that investigators have been unable to screen out of samples of the young-old but which become increasingly likely to be screened out in older samples.

Because of the limited number of published longitudinal studies, the Small et al. (2004) meta-analysis was limited to cross-sectional research and consequently did not consider whether APOE is associated with cognitive change. Several longitudinal studies of APOE and cognitive functioning have been published subsequent to the Small et al. (2004) review and, when combined with earlier longitudinal research, suggest a small effect of APOE on cognitive change. Anstey and Christensen (2000) reviewed ten early longitudinal studies on the relationship between APOE status and cognitive change. Most of the studies focused on neurological screens like the Mini Mental State Examination (MMSE) rather than comprehensive cognitive assessments, and an effect of APOE was not observed in every study. Nonetheless, Anstey and Christensen's qualitative review of longitudinal research led them to a conclusion quite similar to that which emerged from the quantitative review of cross-sectional research: carriers of the ε4 allele experience greater cognitive decline in late life than non-ε4 carriers, especially on measures of memory and processing speed. Recent longitudinal research further shows the consistency of findings from longitudinal and cross-sectional research on APOE. That is, the association of APOE with cognitive decline appears in general to be modest, primarily to involve memory (Christensen et al., 2004; Hofer et al., 2002; Wilson *et al.*, 2002b) and perceptual speed (Wilson et al., 2002b) abilities, and not to be evident among either the very old (Bathum, Christiansen et al., 2006) or younger adults (Zhao et al., 2005).

Other Genetic Polymorphisms

The associations between polymorphisms in several other candidate genes and late-life cognitive functioning have also been investigated. These genes have been targeted because they have been associated with

risk of AD or other diseases that might affect cognitive functioning (e.g., cardiovascular disease), or because they have been associated with cognitive functioning in samples of young adults.

Angiotensin I Converting Enzyme (ACE)

ACE is a key component of the renin–angiotensin system, and consequently the regulation of blood pressure (Wright & Harding, 1994). An insertion (I)/deletion (D) polymorphism has been identified in the ACE gene such that the D allele is associated with higher circulating levels of ACE and increased risk of cardiovascular disease (Hessner, Dinauer, Kwiatkowski, Neri, & Raife, 2001). ACE inhibitors are used in the treatment of hypertension and there is some evidence they may improve cognitive functioning (Zuccala et al., 2005). The association of ACE with risk for AD has been extensively investigated, and a recent large meta-analysis of 40 relevant studies concluded that the I allele is associated with a significant but modest elevation in risk (Lehmann et al., 2005).

Richard, Berr, Amant, Helbecque, Amouyel, and Alperovitch (2000) were the first to investigate whether ACE was associated with cognitive functioning in nondemented older (age 59–71) adults. They reported that individuals homozygous for the D allele scored significantly lower on the MMSE at intake and were more likely to experience cognitive decline at 4-year follow-up. Nonetheless, although poorer cognitive performance among carriers of the D allele has been reported in at least one other study (Bartres-Faz et al., 2000), most studies have failed to find an association of ACE with either normal-range cognitive functioning (Visscher et al., 2003) or cognitive change (Frederiksen et al., 2003; Stewart, Powell, Prince, & Mann, 2004; Yip, Brayne, Easton, & Rubinsztein, 2002b). The relevance of ACE for normal cognitive aging consequently remains at this time unclear. Adding to the ambiguity is the finding that the I variant is associated with increased risk for AD but the D variant has been associated, albeit inconsistently, with poorer cognitive performance in nondemented adults. Although these paradoxical associations may appear to be inconsistent, they need not be. Rather than being directly causal, the I/D polymorphism may only be a marker for the causal influence of another functional mutation in the ACE gene or another nearby gene (a phenomenon geneticists call linkage disequilibrium). Resolving this possibility will require systematic assessment of genetic variation in the ACE region beyond the I/D polymorphism in future investigations.

Catechol-O-methyltransferase (COMT)

COMT codes for an enzyme involved in the degradation of released catecholamines and has been a major target in neuropsychiatric and neuro-

genetic research. A SNP in the COMT gene results in a valine (Val) →
methionine (Met) exchange in the resulting protein. The Met version of
COMT results in a protein with approximately one-fourth of the enzymatic activity of the Val version. In multiple studies with young adults (i.e.,
college-aged), the Met allele has been generally, albeit not consistently,
associated with better working memory (Goldberg et al., 2003) and executive functioning (Malhotra, Kestler, Mazzanti, Bates, Goldberg, & Goldman, 2002). In a longitudinal study of men initially aged 35–85 (mean of
58), de Frias and colleagues reported that carriers of the Met allele performed better on measures of episodic memory (de Frias, Annerbrink,
Westberg, Eriksson, Adolfsson, & Nilsson, 2004) and executive functioning and that their cognitive performance was more stable over a 5-year
interval than men who were homozygous for the Val allele (de Frias,
Annerbrink, Westberg, Eriksson, Adolfsson, & Nilsson, 2005). In a sample
of 460 individuals born in 1921 and assessed at an average age of 79,
Harris, Wright, Hayward, Starr, Whalley, and Deary (2005) also reported a
significant association of COMT genotype with verbal memory. In this
case, however, Val/Met heterozygotes performed significantly better than
both homozygote groups, a paradoxical finding. The relevance of COMT
for late-life cognitive functioning remains unclear.

Methylenetetrahydrofolate Reductase (MTHFR) and Methionine Synthase (MTR)

High levels of homocysteine, a sulphur containing amino acid, have
been associated with cardiovascular disease (Tucker, Qiao, Scott, Rosenberg, & Spiro, 2005). Elevated levels of homocysteine have also been consistently associated with late-life cognitive impairment (Troen & Rosenberg, 2005). Although homocysteine levels are clearly influenced by diet,
the enzymes MTHFR and MTR are both involved in the metabolism of
homocysteine. Common polymorphisms in genes for both MTHFR (the T
allele in the 677C>T polymorphism) and MTR (the A allele in the
2756A>G polymorphism) are associated with elevated plasma concentrations of homocysteine, and thus constitute reasonable targets for candidate-gene analysis. Studies of the common polymorphism in MTHFR
have consistently failed to find an association with late-life cognitive
functioning or change (Almeida, Flicker, Lautenschlager, Leedman,
Vasikaran, & van Bockxmeer, 2005; Bathum, Hjelmborg, Christiansen,
McGue, Jeune, & Christensen, 2007; Gussekloo, Heijmans, Slagboom,
Lagaay, Knook, & Westendorp, 1999; Visscher et al., 2003), while the
common polymorphism in MTR has yielded inconsistent findings
(Bathum et al., 2007; Beyer, Lao, Latorre, Riutort, Matute, & Fernandez-
Figueras, 2003).

Other Gene Systems

Associations between late-life cognitive functioning and polymorph-isms in several additional genes have also been investigated. These include: Klotho, a gene implicated in accelerated aging (Deary *et al.*, 2005b); Cathepsin D, a gene implicated in apoptosis (Peyton et al., 2003); Lactotransferrin, a gene involved in iron absorption and antioxidant defense (Kachiwala et al., 2005); DISC, a gene that has been associated with risk of schizophrenia and is thought to affect hippocampus function (Thomson et al., 2005); PRNP, the prion gene thought to be involved in antioxidant activity (Kachiwala et al., 2005); the serotonin transporter gene, thought to be a modulator of memory function (Payton et al., 2005); and Nicastrin, a gene for a transmembrane glycoprotein (Deary *et al.*, 2005a). In each case, the evidence for or against an association with cogni-tive functioning is based on a single study. Since candidate-gene associations are not considered credible until replicated (Newton-Cheh & Hirschhorn, 2005), we do not discuss these studies further here but have included them for readers interested in a comprehensive survey of candidate-gene studies that have been undertaken in late-life cognitive functioning.

The Challenges of Gene Identification with Complex Aging Phenotypes

The mapping of the human genome brought with it a surge of optimism over the likelihood of identifying the specific genes that underlie heritable effects on behavior (Gottesman, 1997; Plomin & Crabbe, 2000). Nonethe-less, over the past 5 years progress in identifying genes affecting human behavior has been generally modest (Kendler, 2005). It is important to recognize that behavioral phenotypes are not unique in this regard. The reliable identification of genes for many complex medical and physical phenotypes has been more difficult than initially anticipated (Ioannidis, Ntzani, Trikalinos, & Contopoulos-Ioannidis, 2001). This is certainly the case for late-life cognitive aging, where currently there is limited evidence for genes other than APOE with specific genetic effects. Even in this case we cannot altogether rule out the possibility that the gene association arises because of preclinical cases of AD rather than a true effect on normal-range cognitive functioning.

While the current yield of replicable genetic associations in the cognitive aging field may be somewhat disappointing, future research in this area is likely to benefit greatly from what we have learned about the limitations of candidate-gene studies from existing research. First, it is now widely recognized that the genetic basis of complex phenotypes likely constitutes the effect of many, rather than just one or two, genes.

Consequently the phenotypic effect of any single gene is likely to be small (perhaps as little as 1–2% of phenotypic variance at most). Detecting gene effects of this magnitude will require larger samples than have been used thus far in the cognitive aging field (Gauderman, 2002). Second, although behavioral phenotypes are the result of a complex developmental interplay between genetic and environmental factors, environmental factors have typically not been considered in efforts to identify gene effects on cognitive aging. The successful incorporation of environmental measures into genetic research on other behavioral phenotypes may serve as a model for future research in the cognitive aging field (Moffitt, Caspi, & Rutter, 2005). Third, progress in understanding the nature of genetic variation at the DNA level did not end with the sequencing of the human genome. There is a growing recognition that the power of candidate gene studies is enhanced by comprehensively assessing all the genetic variance in the targeted gene by typing multiple rather than just one genetic polymorphism (Cardon & Abecasis, 2003). Findings from the International HapMap project (International HapMap Consortium, 2005) and the International SNP consortium (Syvänen, 2005) will be important resources in the design of the next generation of candidate-gene studies on cognitive aging.

Even if future candidate gene studies on cognitive aging involve large samples, simultaneously model genetic and environmental effects, and take advantage of recent developments in genetic epidemiology, it is still possible that few replicable genetic associations will be found. Standard methods of gene identification are effective in detecting the influence of common (i.e., variants carried by at least 5% of the population) but not rare gene variants (Pritchard & Cox, 2002). The Mutation Accumulation model predicts that genetic influences on aging will be attributable primarily to the effects of multiple genetic variants, each of which is likely to be rare because it has not been selected for or against. Consequently, although molecular approaches to normal cognitive aging represent an exciting recent development, we must be cautious not to overstate the likelihood that research in this area will yield multiple replicable genetic associations over the next 5 years.

INVESTIGATING MODELS OF GENE–ENVIRONMENT INTERPLAY

Discordant Twin Studies

Instead of focusing on co-twin similarity, the second kind of natural twin experiment makes use of differences between co-twins. A major issue in investigations of the effects of environmental influences or lifestyle choices on function in later life is the problem of common causation. This

is likely to be of great importance given findings from twin similarity studies indicating that environmental influences are the predominant source of change in late-life cognitive functioning. For example, pursuit of leisure-time activities involving intellectual engagement such as crossword puzzles may be associated with higher cognitive function or slower deterioration in cognitive function in later life, but it is never clear that the pursuit of the leisure-time activities is causing the higher cognitive function or slower deterioration. The direction of causation may of course flow in the opposite direction, and the association may also be due to some cause common to both factors such as higher education or greater intelligence. This latter possibility is often handled by "controlling for" or adjusting for the covariance shared with potential third-variable common causes. The possibility always remains, however, that there is some unmeasured third variable that is responsible for the residual association.

There is a related and potentially more significant problem. Termed the "selection problem," it is the possibility that the association between environment/lifestyle and later-life function reflects the kinds of choices typically made by people who differ genetically or in some aspect of childhood environment such as socioeconomic status. For example, if pursuit of leisure-time activities involving intellectual engagement is associated with higher cognitive function in later life, this may be because genetic or childhood environmental differences make it easier and thus more pleasurable for some people to engage in leisure-time activities involving intellectual engagement than it is for others throughout the lifespan. Alternatively, it may be that people at genetic or childhood environmental risk for late-life cognitive impairment reduce their pursuit of such leisure-time activities as their cognitive function begins to deteriorate. In a critical review of research linking lifestyle factors with cognitive aging, Salthouse (2006) concludes that limitations with existing research preclude strong inferences about the nature and strength of causal influence.

The discordant twin study relies on the fact that MZ twins share all of their genes and, when raised together, their childhood environments to address these possible confounding factors by using one twin as control for the other. To the extent that their shared genetic and childhood background is of importance, they should be equally likely to select relevant environments or lifestyles, so any differences between them must result from nonshared environmental influences independent of all genetic and shared environmental influences. DZ twins can also be included in studies of this type, with the recognition that DZ co-twins will differ more from each other than MZ co-twins because DZ twins share only half their segregating genes.

Despite the potential power of the design, there have been only a few discordant twin studies involving cognitive aging. Three of these studies involved members of the Swedish Twin Registry discordant for AD in particular and dementia in general. Although these studies did not consider normal-range cognitive functioning, the primary focus of our review, we include discussion of them here to illustrate the utility of this approach. Gatz, Svedberg, Pedersen, Mortimer, Berg, and Johansson (2001) showed that low education was a risk factor for AD, but not for dementia in general, in both unrelated controls and within twin pairs discordant for AD. The discordant twin pairs showed longstanding differences in intellectual involvement, with less involvement by the twin who developed AD. Complexity of main life occupation showed similar results (Andel et al., 2005), with AD twins having less intellectually demanding occupations than their unaffected co-twins. Participation in leisure activities appears also to be protective against both AD and dementia in general (Crowe, Andel, Pedersen, Johansson, & Gatz, 2003), and participation in intellectual-cultural activities was associated with lower risk of AD in women, but not in men.

These studies are particularly valuable as the reports of participation and occupation date back 20 years prior to the observation of dementia status, so retrospective bias should not have influenced results. They implicate environmental influences on AD risk in particular, but it is less clear that the forms of participation in question were the particular environmental influences involved, as the longstanding differences in participation as well as the difference in late-life cognitive function may have resulted from the existence of differences in other characteristics that contributed to willingness or ability to participate in the relevant activities.

Only a single study has used the discordant-twin study to investigate normal-range cognitive functioning. Osler, McGue, and Christensen (2006) categorized 1266 like-sex Danish twin pairs aged 46 years and older as either concordant or discordant for adult socioeconomic status (working class versus upper class). Within DZ twin pairs discordant for socioeconomic status, the upper class twin performed significantly better on a measure of general cognitive ability. Within MZ twin pairs discordant for socioeconomic status, however, there was no difference in the general cognitive performance of the upper and working class twins. The absence of an effect in the discordant MZ group suggests that adult social class does not exert an environmental influence on cognitive functioning. Alternatively, the existence of an effect in the discordant DZ group implies that genetic factors mediate the association of adult socioeconomic status and cognitive functioning. The Danish study on normal-range cognitive functioning appears to be at odds with the Swedish study on AD and dementia. The methodological differences between the two

studies, however, could account for the differences. Additional research is clearly needed.

Genotype–Environment Interaction

Despite the growing interest in the investigation and characterization of G×E interactions within the behavioral sciences (Moffitt et al., 2005), there has been very little G×E research in the cognitive aging field. We consequently illustrate this approach by describing G×E research on the relationship between APOE and risk of cognitive impairment. As discussed above, APOE is a well-established risk factor for cognitive impairment and dementia. It appears also to be a powerful modulator of other environmentally mediated risk factors. Several studies have shown that carriers of the high-risk ε4 are more susceptible to the cognitive impairing effects of chronic head trauma (Jordan, Relkin, Ravdin, Jacobs, Bennett, & Gandy, 1997) and stroke (Heyer et al., 2005). The ε4 allele also appears to diminish the impact of protective factors, as carriers of the high-risk allele are less likely to experience the beneficial effects of physical exercise (Podewils et al., 2005) or educational attainment (Seeman, Huang, Bretsky, Crimmins, Launer, & Guralnik, 2005). Although this research on cognitive impairment again lies somewhat outside our primary focus on normal-range cognitive functioning, it serves to illustrate how G × E approaches can help explicate the origins of individual differences in late-life outcomes.

The investigation of epigenetic phenomena in neurological and cognitive aging is at the very initial stages of inquiry so that there is relatively little research for us to review. We know that gene expression patterns in human brain vary by age and region (Fraser, Khaitovich, Plotkin, Pääbo, & Eisen, 2005). These expression differences may be causes of neurological aging; they may also be consequences. Gene expression differences in AD have been studied extensively, and several dozen genes appear to be reliably down-regulated and a smaller number up-regulated in AD versus non-AD controls (Blalock et al., 2005). The finding that the expression of APOE appears to be associated with risk for AD (Lahiri, Sambamurti, & Bennett, 2004) indicates that it will be important to explore not only what is inherited but also how what is inherited is expressed to understand brain aging.

CONCLUSION

Genetic research on cognitive aging has made substantial progress in addressing several of the questions outlined in Table 2.1. Other questions,

however, have only begun to be addressed. We know that genetic factors contribute substantially to individual differences in late-life cognitive functioning. Nonetheless, the magnitude of that influence appears to diminish after age 75–80, as the impact of nonshared environmental factors influences increases. These findings suggest that environmental factors might counteract an increase in genetic variance with age that is hypothesized by basic evolutionary models of aging. Somewhat unexpectedly, twin studies have consistently failed to find strong genetic influences on cognitive change. Whether this is because the environment is the major determinant of change or because the longitudinal twin studies have not been of sufficient duration to allow reliable assessment of change remains to be determined. Notably, in the samples that have been assessed beginning at older ages, we have no way of knowing to what degree cognitive decline had begun even before initial assessment. We thus know virtually nothing about genetic influences on the long-term changes that are the hallmark of cognitive functioning.

We know that heritable influences on late-life cognitive functioning overlap extensively with, and by extension are likely to be mediated by, heritable influences in cognitive speed and brain morphology. We know little about the specific genes that underlie heritable effects on late-life cognitive function beyond the notably overall modest effect of APOE. Nonetheless, the Human Genome Project has helped to position this area of research well for advances in the next 5 years, but only if the relevant genetic polymorphisms are relatively common in the general population. A consideration of basic evolutionary models of aging suggests that this latter possibility is far from certain.

The least progress has been made in the exploration of gene environment models of cognitive aging. This is especially unfortunate, since it is in this area that the potential for significant contribution is arguably the greatest. Genetic designs like the discordant twin design provide powerful tools for characterizing the nature of environmental risk, while the exploration of GxE and epigenesis should help us ultimately understand the unique and individual nature of late-life development. The major impediment to progress in this area is the general failure both to consider environmental factors in studies focused on genetics and to consider genetic factors in studies focused on the environment. There are hopeful signs that this limitation to existing research is disappearing and that 5 years from now we will be in a much better position to describe how genes and the environment jointly affect individual differences in late-life cognitive function.

REFERENCES

Almeida, O. P., Flicker, L., Lautenschlager, N. T., Leedman, P., Vasikaran, S., & van Bock-xmeer, F. M. (2005). Contribution of the MTHFR gene to the causal pathway for depression, anxiety and cognitive impairment in later life. *Neurobiology of Aging, 26*(2), 251–257.

Andel, R., Crowe, M., Pedersen, N. L., Mortimer, J., Crimmins, E., Johansson, B., et al. (2005). Complexity of work and risk of Alzheimer's disease: A population-based study of Swedish twins. *Journals of Gerontology Series B—Psychological Sciences and Social Sciences, 60*(5), P251–P258.

Anstey, K., & Christensen, H. (2000). Education, activity, health, blood pressure, and apolipoprotein E as predictors of cognitive change in old age: A review. *Gerontology, 46,* 163–177.

Austad, S. N. (2001). Concepts and theories of aging. In E. J. Masoro & S. N. Austad (Eds.), *Handbook of the biology of aging* (5th ed., pp. 3–22). San Diego: Academic Press.

Bäckman, L., Jones, S., Berger, A. K., Laukka, E. J., & Small, B. J. (2005). Cognitive impairment in preclinical Alzheimer's Disease: A meta-analysis. *Neuropsychology, 19*(4), 520–531.

Baltes, P. B., & Baltes, M. M. (1990). On the imcomplete architecture of human ontogeny: Selection, optimization, and compensation as a foundation of developmental theory. In P. B. Baltes & M. M. Baltes (Eds.), *Successful aging: Perspectives from the behavioral sciences* (pp. 1–34). New York: Cambridge University Press.

Bartres-Faz, D., Junque, C., Clemente, I. C., Lopez-Alomar, A., Valveny, N., Lopez-Guillen, A., et al. (2000). Angiotensin I converting enzyme polymorphism in humans with age-associated memory impairment: Relationship with cognitive performance. *Neuroscience Letters, 290*(3), 177–180.

Bathum, L., Christiansen, L., Jeune, B., Vaupel, J., McGue, M., & Christensen, K. (2006). Apolipoprotein E genotypes: Relationship to cognitive functioning, cognitive decline, and survival in nonagenarians. *Journal of the American Geriatrics Society, 54*(4), 654–658.

Bathum, L., Hjelmborg, J. V. B., Christiansen, L., McGue, M., Jeune, B., & Christensen, K. (2007). Methylenetetrahydrofolate reductase 677C>T and Methionine syntase 2756A>G mutations: No impact on survival, cognitive functioning or cognitive decline in nonagenarians. *Journal of Gerontology: Medical Sciences, 62,* 196–201.

Beyer, K., Lao, J. I., Latorre, P., Riutort, N., Matute, B., & Fernandez-Figueras, M. T. (2003). Methionine synthase polymorphism is a risk factor for Alzheimer disease. *Neuroreport, 14*(10), 1391–1394.

Blalock, E. M., Chen, K. C., Stromberg, A. J., Norris, C. M., Kadish, I., Kraner, S. D., et al. (2005). Harnessing the power of gene microarrays for the study of brain aging and Alzheimer's disease: Statistical reliability and functional correlation. *Ageing Research Reviews, 4*(4), 481–512.

Blennow, K., de Leon, M. J., & Zetterberg, H. (2006). Alzheimer's disease. *Lancet, 368*(9533), 387–403.

Bondi, M. W., Monsch, A. U., Galasko, D., Butters, N., Salmon, D. P., & Delis, D. C. (1994). Preclinical cognitive markers of dementia of the Alzheimer type. *Neuropsychology, 8,* 374–384.

Bosworth, H. B., & Siegler, I. C. (2002). Terminal change in cognitive function: An updated review of longitudinal studies. *Experimental Aging Research, 28,* 299–315.

Breteler, M. M. B., Claus, J. J., Grobbee, D. E., & Hofman, A. (1994). Cardiovascular disease and distribution of cognitive function in elderly people: The Rotterdam Study. *British Medical Journal, 308,* 1604–1608.

Cardon, L. R., & Abecasis, G. R. (2003). Using haplotype blocks to map human complex trait loci. *Trends in Genetics, 19*(3), 135–140.

Carmelli, D., DeCarli, C., Swan, G. E., Jack, L. M., Reed, T., Wolf, P. A., et al. (1998). Evidence

for genetic variance in white matter hypersensitivity volume in normal elderly male twins. *Stroke, 29*(6), 1177–1181.

Carmelli, D., Reed, T., & DeCarli, C. (2002a). A bivariate genetic analysis of cerebral white matter hyperintensities and cognitive performance in elderly male twins. *Neurobiology of Aging, 23*, 413–420.

Carmelli, D., Swan, G. E., DeCarli, C., & Reed, T. (2002b). Quantitative genetic modeling of regional brain volumes and cognitive performance in older male twins. *Biological Psychology, 61*, 139–155.

Christensen, H., Mackinnon, A. J., Jorm, A. F., Korten, A., Jacomb, P., Hofer, S. M., et al. (2004). The Canberra Longitudinal Study: Design, aims, methodology, outcomes and recent empirical investigations. *Aging Neuropsychology and Cognition, 11*(2–3), 169–195.

Christensen, K., Holm, N. V., McGue, M., Corder, L., & Vaupel, J. W. (1999). A Danish population-based twin study on general health in the elderly. *Journal of Aging and Health, 11*, 49–64.

Christensen, K., Petersen, I., Skytthe, A., Herskind, A. M., McGue, M., & Bingley, P. (2006). Birth weight in twins and singletons and school performance in adolescence. *British Medical Journal, 333*, 1095–1097.

Christensen, K., Vaupel, J. W., Holm, N. V., & Yashin, A. I. (1995). Mortality among twins after age-6: Fetal origins hypothesis versus twin method. *British Medical Journal, 310*, 432–436.

Collins, F. S., Lander, E. S., Rogers, J., & Waterston, R. H. (2004). Finishing the euchromatic sequence of the human genome. *Nature, 431*, 931–945.

Corder, E. H., Saunders, A. M., Strittmatter, W. J., Schmechel, D. E., Gaskell, P. C., Small, G. A., et al. (1993). Gene dose of apolipoprotein E type 4 allele and the risk of Alzheimer's disease in late onset families. *Science, 261*, 921–923.

Crawford, D. C., Akey, D. T., & Nickerson, D. A. (2005). The patterns of natural variation in human genes. *Annual Review of Genomics and Human Genetics, 6*, 287–312.

Crowe, M., Andel, R., Pedersen, N., Johansson, B., & Gatz, M. (2003). Does participation in leisure activities lead to reduced risk of Alzheimer's disease? A prospective study of Swedish twins. *Journal of Gerontology: Psychological Sciences, 58B*, P249–P255.

Deary, I. J., Hamilton, G., Hayward, C., Whalley, L. J., Powell, J., Starr, J. M., et al. (2005a). Nicastrin gene polymorphisms, cognitive ability level and cognitive ageing. *Neuroscience Letters, 373*, 110–114.

Deary, I. J., Harris, S. E., Fox, H. C., Hayward, C., Wright, A. F., Starr, J. M., et al. (2005b). KLOTHO genotype and cognitive ability in childhood and old age in the same individuals. *Neuroscience Letters, 378*, 22–27.

Deary, I. J., Whalley, W. J., St. Clair, D., Breen, G., Leper, S., Lemmon, H., et al. (2003). The influence of the e4 allele of the apolipoprotein E gene on childhood IQ, nonverbal reasoning in old age, and lifetime cognitive change. *Intelligence, 31*(1), 85–92.

Deater-Deckard, K., & Mayr, U. (2005). Cognitive change in aging: Identifying genotype–environment correlation and nonshared environment mechanisms. *Journals of Gerontology Series B—Psychological Sciences and Social Sciences, 60B*, 24–31.

de Frias, C. M., Annerbrink, K., Westberg, L., Eriksson, E., Adolfsson, R., & Nilsson, L. G. (2004). COMT gene polymorphism is associated with declarative memory in adulthood and old age. *Behavior Genetics, 34*(5), 533–539.

de Frias, C. M., Annerbrink, K., Westberg, L., Eriksson, E., Adolfsson, R., & Nilsson, L. R. (2005). Catechol O-methyltransferase Val(158)Met polymorphism is associated with cognitive performance in nondemented adults. *Journal of Cognitive Neuroscience, 17*(7), 1018–1025.

Dobzhansky, T. (1973). Nothing in biology makes sense except in light of evolution. *American Biology Teacher, 35*, 125–129.

Farrer, L. A., Cupples, L. A., Haines, J. L., Hyman, B., Kukull, W. A., Mayeux, R., et al. (1997). Effects of age, sex, and ethnicity on the association between apolipoprotein E genotype and Alzheimer disease: A meta-analysis. *JAMA, 278,* 1349–1356.

Feingold, A. (1992). Good-looking people are not what we think. *Psychological Bulletin, 111,* 304–341.

Finkel, D., & Pedersen, N. (2000). Contribution of age, genes, and environment to the relationship between perceptual speed and cognitive ability. *Psychology and Aging, 15,* 56–64.

Finkel, D., & Pedersen, N. (2004). Processing speed and longitudinal trajectories of change for cognitive abilities: The Swedish Adoption/Twin Study of Aging. *Aging Neuropsychology and Cognition, 11,* 325–345.

Finkel, D., Pedersen, N., & Harris, J. R. (2000). Genetic mediation of the associations among motor and perceptual speed and adult cognitive abilities. *Aging, Neuropsychology, and Cognition, 7,* 141–155.

Finkel, D., Pedersen, N., Reynolds, C. A., Berg, S., de Faire, U., & Svartengren, M. (2003a). Genetic and environmental influences on decline in biobehavioral markers of aging. *Behavior Genetics, 33,* 107–123.

Finkel, D., Pedersen, N. L., McGue, M., & McClearn, G. E. (1995). Heritability of cognitive abilities in adult twins: Comparison of Minnesota and Swedish data. *Behavior Genetics, 25,* 421–431.

Finkel, D., Pedersen, N. L., Plomin, R., & McClearn, G. E. (1998). Longitudinal and cross-sectional twin data on cognitive abilities in adulthood: The Swedish Adoption/Twin Study of Aging. *Developmental Psychology, 34,* 1400–1413.

Finkel, D., Reynolds, C. A., McArdle, J. J., Gatz, M., & Pedersen, N. (2003b). Latent growth curve analyses of accelerating decline in cognitive abilities in late adulthood. *Developmental Psychology, 39,* 535–550.

Finkel, D., Reynolds, C. A., McArdle, J. J., & Pedersen, N. (2005). The longitudinal relationship between processing speed and cognitive ability: Genetic and environmental influences. *Behavior Genetics, 35,* 535–549.

Fisher, R. A. (1918). The correlation between relatives on the supposition of Mendelian inheritance. *Transactions of the Royal Society of Edinburgh, 52,* 399–433.

Fraga, M. F. (2005). Epigenetic differences arise during the lifetime of monozygotic twins. *Proceedings of the National Academy of Sciences, 102,* 10604–10609.

Fraser, H. B., Khaitovich, P., Plotkin, J. B., Pääbo, S., & Eisen, M. B. (2005). Aging and gene expression in the primate brain. *PLoS Biology, 3*(9), e274.

Frederiksen, H., Gaist, D., Bathum, L., Andersen, K., McGue, M., Vaupel, J. W., et al. (2003). Angiotensin I-converting enzyme (ACE) gene polymorphism in relation to physical performance, cognition and survival: A follow-up study of elderly Danish twins. *Annals of Epidemiology, 13*(1), 57–65.

Gatz, M., Svedberg, P., Pedersen, N. L., Mortimer, J. A., Berg, S., & Johansson, B. (2001). Education and risk of Alzheimer's disease: Findings from the Study of Dementia in Swedish Twins. *Journal of Gerontology: Psychological Sciences and Social Sciences, 56B,* P292–P300.

Gauderman, W. J. (2002). Sample size requirements for matched case-control studies of gene–environment interaction. *Statistics in Medicine, 21,* 35–50.

Goldberg, T. E., Egan, M. F., Gscheidle, T., Coppola, R., Weickert, T., Kolachana, B. S., et al. (2003). Executive subprocesses in working memory—relationship to catechol-O-methyltransferase Val158Met genotype and schizophrenia. *Archives of General Psychiatry, 60*(9), 889–896.

Gottesman, I. I. (1997). Human genetics—twins: En route to QTLs for cognition. *Science, 276,* 1522–1523.

Gray, J. R., & Thompson, P. M. (2004). Neurobiology of intelligence: Science and ethics. *Nature Reviews Neuroscience, 5,* 471–482.

Grigorenko, E. L. (2005). The inherent complexities of genotype-environment interactions. *Journal of Gerontology: Social Sciences, 60B,* 53–64.

Gussekloo, J., Heijmans, B. T., Slagboom, P. E., Lagaay, A. M., Knook, D. L., & Westendorp, R. G. J. (1999). Thermolabile methylenetetrahydrofolate reductase gene and the risk of cognitive impairment in those over 85. *Journal of Neurology, Neurosurgery, and Psychiatry, 67*(4), 535–538.

Hall, J. G., & Lopez-Rangel, E. (1996). Twins and twinning. In D. L. Rimoin, J. M. Connor & R. E. Pyeritz (Eds.), *Principles and practice of medical genetics.* New York: Churchill Livingstone.

Hallman, D. M., Boerwinkle, E., Saha, N., et al. (1991). The apolipoprotein E polymorphism: A comparison of allele frequencies and effects in nine populations. *American Journal of Human Genetics, 49,* 338–349.

Hamilton, W. D. (1966). The moulding of senescence by natural selection. *Journal of Theoretical Biology, 12,* 12–45.

Harris, S. E., Wright, A. F., Hayward, C., Starr, J. M., Whalley, L. J., & Deary, I. J. (2005). The functional COMT polymorphism, Val158Met, is associated with logical memory and the personality trait intellect/imagination in a cohort of healthy 79 year olds. *Neuroscience Letters, 385*(1), 1–6.

Hedden, T., & Gabrieli, J. D. E. (2005). Healthy and pathological processes in adult development: New evidence from neuroimaging of the aging brain. *Current Opinion in Neurology, 18,* 740–747.

Hessner, M. J., Dinauer, D. M., Kwiatkowski, R., Neri, B., & Raife, T. J. (2001). Age-dependent prevalence of vascular disease-associated polymorphisms among 2689 volunteer blood donors. *Clinical Chemistry, 47*(10), 1879–1884.

Heyer, E. J., Wilson, D. A., Sahlein, D. H., Mocco, J., Williams, S. C., Sciacca, R., et al. (2005). APOE-epsilon 4 predisposes to cognitive dysfunction following uncomplicated carotid endarterectomy. *Neurology, 65*(11), 1759–1763.

Hofer, S. M., Christensen, H., Mackinnon, A. J., Korten, A. E., Jorm, A. F., Henderson, A. S., et al. (2002). Change in cognitive functioning associated with ApoE genotype in a community sample of older adults. *Psychology and Aging, 17,* 194–208.

International HapMap Consortium. (2005). A haplotype map of the human genome. *Nature, 437,* 1299–1320.

Ioannidis, J. P. A., Ntzani, E. E., Trikalinos, T. A., & Contopoulos-Ioannidis, D. G. (2001). Replication validity of genetic association studies. *Nature Genetics, 29*(3), 306–309.

Johansson, B., Hofer, S. M., Allaire, J. C., Maldonado-Molina, M. M., Piccinin, A. M., Berg, S., et al. (2004). Change in cognitive capabilities in the oldest old: The effects of proximity to death in genetically related individuals over a 6-year period. *Psychology and Aging, 19*(1), 145–156.

Johnson, W., Bouchard, T. J., McGue, M., Segal, N., Tellegen, A., Keyes, M., et al. (2006). Genetic and environmental influences on the Verbal-Perceptual-Image Rotation (VPR) model of the structure of mental abilities in the Minnesota Study of Twins Reared Apart. *Intelligence.*

Jordan, B. D., Relkin, N. R., Ravdin, L. D., Jacobs, A. R., Bennett, A., & Gandy, S. (1997). Apolipoprotein E ε4 associated with chronic traumatic brain injury in boxing. *JAMA, 278*(2), 136–140.

Kachiwala, S. J., Harris, S. E., Wright, A. F., Hayward, C., Starr, J. M., Whalley, L. J., et al. (2005). Genetic influences on oxidative stress and their association with normal cognitive ageing. *Neuroscience Letters, 386,* 116–120.

Kehoe, P., Wavrant-De Vrieze, F., Crook, R., Wu, W. S., Holmans, P., Fenton, I., et al. (1999).

A full genome scan for late onset Alzheimer's disease. *Human Molecular Genetics, 8*(2), 237–245.

Kelada, S. N., Eaton, D. L., Wang, S. S., Rothman, N. R., & Khoury, M. J. (2003). The role of genetic polymorphisms in environmental health. *Environmental Health Perspectives, 111*(8), 1055–1064.

Kendler, K. S. (2005). Psychiatric genetics—a methodologic critique. *American Journal of Psychiatry, 162*(1), 3–11.

Kendler, K. S., & Gardner, C. O. (1998). Twin studies of adult psychiatric and substance dependence disorders: Are they biased by differences in the environmental experiences of monozygotic and dizygotic twins in childhood and adolescence? *Psychological Medicine, 28*, 625–633.

Khachaturian, A. S., Corcoran, C. D., Mayer, L. S., Zandi, P. P., & Breitner, J. C. S. (2004). Apolipoprotein E epsilon 4 count affects age at onset of Alzheimer disease, but not lifetime susceptibility—the Cache County Study. *Archives of General Psychiatry, 61*(5), 518–524.

Kim, K. W., Youn, J. C., Jhoo, J. H., Lee, D. Y., Lee, K. U., Lee, J. H., et al. (2002). Apolipoprotein E epsilon 4 Allele is not associated with the cognitive impairment in community-dwelling normal elderly individuals. *International Journal of Geriatric Psychiatry, 17*(7), 635–640.

La Rue, A., & Jarvik, L. F. (1987). Cognitive function and prediction of dementia in old age. *International Journal of Aging and Human Development, 25*(2), 79–89.

Lahiri, D. K., Sambamurti, K., & Bennett, D. A. (2004). Apolipoprotein gene and its interaction with environmentally driven risk factors: Molecular, genetic, and epidemiological studies of Alzheimer's disease. *Neurobiology of Aging, 25*, 651–660.

Lehmann, D. J., Cortina-Borja, M., Warden, D. R., Smith, A. D., Sleeglers, K., Prince, J. A., et al. (2005). Large meta-analysis establishes the ACE insertion-deletion polymorphism as a marker of Alzheimer's disease. *American Journal of Epidemiology, 162*(4), 305–317.

Levy, F., McLaughlin, M., Wood, C., Hay, D., & Waldman, I. (1996). Twin–sibling differences in parental reports of ADHD, speech, reading and behaviour problems. *Journal of Child Psychology and Psychiatry, 37*(5), 569–578.

Lewis, C. M., Levinson, D. F., Wise, L. H., DeLisi, L. E., Straub, R. E., Hovatta, I., et al. (2003). Genome scan meta-analysis of schizophrenia and bipolar disorder, part II: Schizophrenia. *American Journal of Human Genetics, 7*(1), 34–48.

Loehlin, J. C. (1992). *Genes and environment in personality development.* Newbury Park, CA: Sage.

Mahley, R. W., & Rall, S. C. (2000). Apolipoprotein E: Far more than a lipid transport protein. *Annual Review of Genomics and Human Genetics, 1*, 507–537.

Malhotra, A. K., Kestler, L. J., Mazzanti, C., Bates, J. A., Goldberg, T., & Goldman, D. (2002). A functional polymorphism in the COMT gene and performance on a test of prefrontal cognition. *American Journal of Psychiatry, 159*(4), 652–654.

McArdle, J. J., Prescott, C. A., Hamagami, F., & Horn, J. L. (1998). A contemporary method for developmental-genetic analyses of age changes in intellectual abilities. *Developmental Neuropsychology, 14*, 69–114.

McClearn, G. E., Johansson, B., Berg, S., Pedersen, N. L., Ahern, F., Petrill, S. A., et al. (1997). Substantial genetic inlfuence on cognitive abilities in twins 80 or more years old. *Science, 276*, 1560–1563.

McDaniel, M. A. (2005). Big-brained people are smarter: A meta-analysis of the relationship between in vivo brain volume and intelligence. *Intelligence, 33*(4), 337–346.

McGue, M., Bouchard, T. J., Iacono, W. G., & Lykken, D. T. (1993). Behavioral genetics of cognitive ability: A lifespan perspective. In R. Plomin & G. E. McClearn (Eds.),

Nature, nurture and psychology (pp. 59–76). Washington, DC: American Psychological Association.

McGue, M., & Christensen, K. (2001). The heritability of cognitive functioning in very old adults: Evidence from Danish twins aged 75 years and older. *Psychology and Aging, 16,* 272–280.

McGue, M., & Christensen, K. (2002). The heritability of level and rate-of-change in cognitive functioning in Danish twins aged 70 years and older. *Experimental Aging Research, 28,* 435–452.

Meyer, M. R., Tschanz, J. T., Norton, M. C., Welsh-Bohmer, K. A., Steffens, D. C., Wyse, B. W., et al. (1998). APOE genotype predicts when—not whether—one is predisposed to develop Alzheimer disease. *Nature Genetics, 19*(4), 321–322.

Moffitt, T. E., Caspi, A., & Rutter, M. (2005). Strategy for investigating interactions between measured genes and measured environments. *Archives of General Psychiatry, 62,* 473–481.

Neale, M. C., Boker, S. M., Xie, G., & Maes, H. H. (1999). *Mx: Statistical modeling* (5th ed.). Box 126 MCV, Richmond VA 23298: Department of Psychiatry.

Neale, M. C., & Cardon, L. R. (1992). *Methodology for genetic studies of twins and families.* Dordrecht: Kluwer Academic.

Neale, M. C., & McArdle, J. J. (2000). Structured latent growth curves for twin data. *Twin Research, 3,* 165–177.

Newton-Cheh, C., & Hirschhorn, J. N. (2005). Genetic association studies of complex traits: Design and analysis issues. *Mutation Research, 573,* 54–69.

Oriá, R. B., Patrick, P. D., Blackman, J. A., Lima, A. A. M., & Guerrant, R. L. (2007). Role of apolipoprotein E4 in protecting children against early childhood diarrhea outcomes and implications for later development. *Medical Hypotheses, 68,* 1099–1107.

Osler, M., McGue, M., & Christensen, K. (2006). Socioeconomic position and twins' health: A life-course analysis of 1266 pairs of middle-aged Danish twins. Submitted.

Partridge, L., & Gems, D. (2002). Mechanisms of ageing: Public or private? *Nature Reviews Genetics, 3,* 165–175.

Payton, A., Gibbons, L., Davidson, Y., Ollier, W., Rabbitt, P., Worthington, J., et al. (2005). Influence of the serotonin transporter gene polymorphisms on cognitive decline and cognitive abilities in a nondemented elderly population. *Molecular Psychiatry, 10,* 1133–1139.

Pedersen, N. L., Gatz, M., Berg, S., & Johansson, B. (2004). How heritable is Alzheimer's disease late in life? Findings from Swedish twins. *Annals of Neurology, 55*(2), 180–185.

Pedersen, N. L., McClearn, G. E., Plomin, R., Nesselroade, J. R., Berg, S., & de Faire, U. (1991). The Swedish Adoption/Twin Study of Aging: An update. *Acta Geneticae Medicae et Gemellologiae, 40,* 7–20.

Pedersen, N. L., Plomin, R., Nesselroade, J. R., & McClearn, G. E. (1992). A quantitative genetic analysis of cognitive abilities during the second half of the life span. *Psychological Science, 3*(6), 346–353.

Petrill, S. A., Plomin, R., Berg, S., Johansson, B., Pedersen, N., Ahern, F., et al. (1998). The genetic and environmental relationship between general and specific cognitive abilities in twins age 80 and older. *Psychological Science, 9,* 183–189.

Peyton, A., Holland, F., Diggle, P., Rabbitt, P., Horan, M., Davidson, Y., et al. (2003). Cathepsin D exon 2 polymorphism associated with general intelligence in a healthy older population. *Molecular Psychiatry, 8,* 14–18.

Pfefferbaum, A., Sullivan, E. V., & Carmelli, D. (2004). Morphological changes in aging brain structures are differentially affected by time-linked environmental influences despite strong genetic stability. *Neurobiology of Aging, 25,* 175–183.

Pfefferbaum, A., Sullivan, E. V., Swan, G. E., & Carmelli, D. (2000). Brain structure in men

remains highly heritable in the seventh and eight decades of life. *Neurobiology of Aging*, *21*, 63–74.

Plomin, R., & Crabbe, J. (2000). DNA. *Psychological Bulletin*, *126*, 806–828.

Plomin, R., DeFries, J. C., McClearn, G. E., & McGuffin, P. (2001). *Behavioral genetics* (4th ed.). New York: W.H. Freeman.

Plomin, R., Pedersen, N., Lichtenstein, P., & McClearn, G. E. (1994). Variability and stability in cogntive abilities are largely genetic later in life. *Behavior Genetics*, *24*, 207–215.

Podewils, L. J., Guallar, E., Kuller, L. H., Fried, L. P., Lopez, O. L., Carlson, M., et al. (2005). Physical activity, APOE genotype, and dementia risk: Findings from the Cardiovascular Health Cognition Study. *American Journal of Epidemiology*, *161*(7), 639–651.

Posthuma, D., De Geus, E. J. C., Baare, W. F. C., Pol, H. E. H., Kahn, R. S., & Boomsma, D. I. (2002). The association between brain volume and intelligence is of genetic origin. *Nature Neuroscience*, *5*(2), 83–84.

Posthuma, D., De Geus, E. J. C., Bleichrodt, N., & Boomsma, D. I. (2000). Twin-singleton differences in intelligence? *Twin Research*, *3*, 83–87.

Posthuma, D., Luciano, M., de Geus, E. J. C., Wright, M. J., Slagboom, P. E., Montgomery, G. W., et al. (2005). A genomewide scan for intelligence identifies quantitative trait loci on 2q and 6p. *American Journal of Human Genetics*, *77*(2), 318–326.

Pritchard, J. K., & Cox, N. J. (2002). The allelic architecture of human disease genes: Common-disease-common variant or not? *Human Molecular Genetics*, *11*, 2417–2423.

Purcell, S. (2002). Variance components models for gene-environment interaction in twin analysis. *Twin Research*, *6*, 554–571.

Pushkar, D., Etezadi, J., Andres, D., Arbuckle, T., Schwartzman, A. E., & Chaikelson, J. (1999). Models of intelligence in late life: Comment on Hultsch et al. (1999). *Psychology and Aging*, *14*, 520–527.

Rabbitt, P., Diggle, P., Holland, F., & McInnes, L. (2004). Practice and drop-out effects during a 17-year longitudinal study of cognitive aging. *Journals of Gerontology Series B-Psychological Sciences and Social Sciences*, *59*(2), P84–P97.

Raz, N. (2000). Aging of the brain and its impact on cognitive function: Integration of structural and functional findings. In F. I. M. Craik & T. A. Salthouse (Eds.), *Handbook of aging and cognition* (2nd ed., pp. 1–90). Mahwah, NJ: Lawrence Erlbaum Associates, Inc.

Raz, N., Lindenberger, U., Rodrigue, K. M., Kennedy, K. M., Head, D., Williamson, A., et al. (2005). Regional brain changes in aging healthy adults: General trends, individual differences and modifiers. *Cerebral Cortex*, *15*(11), 1676–1689.

Reeve, C. L., & Lam, H. (2005). The psychometric paradox of practice effects due to retesting: Measurement invariance and stable ability estimates in the face of observed score changes. *Intelligence*, *33*(5), 535–549.

Resnick, S. M., Pham, D. L., Kraut, M. A., Zonderman, A. B., & Davatzikos, C. (2003). Longitudinal magnetic resonance imaging studies of older adults: A shrinking brain. *Journal of Neuroscience*, *23*(8), 3295–3301.

Reynolds, C. A., Finkel, D., Gatz, M., & Pedersen, N. L. (2002). Sources of influence on rate of cognitive change over time in Swedish twins: An application of latent growth models. *Experimental Aging Research*, *28*, 407–433.

Reynolds, C. A., Finkel, D., McArdle, J. J., Gatz, M., Berg, S., & Pedersen, N. L. (2005). Quantitative genetic analysis of latent growth curve models of cognitive abilities in adulthood. *Developmental Psychology*, *41*(1), 3–16.

Richard, F., Berr, C., Amant, C., Helbecque, N., Amouyel, P., & Alperovitch, A. (2000). Effect of the angiotensin I-converting enzyme I/D polymorphism on cognitive decline. *Neurobiology of Aging*, *21*(1), 75–80.

Ronalds, G. A., De Stavola, B. L., & Leon, D. A. (2005). The cognitive cost of being a twin:

Evidence from comparisons within families in the Aberdeen children of the 1950s cohort study. *British Medical Journal, 331*, 1306–1310.

Rowe, D. C., Clapp, M., & Wallis, J. (1987). Physical attractiveness and the personality resemblance of identical twins. *Behavior Genetics, 17*(2), 191–201.

Rutter, M., & Silberg, J. (2002). Gene–environmental interplay in relation to emotional and behavioral disturbance. *Annual Review of Psychology, 53*, 463–490.

Salthouse, T. (1996). The processing-speed theory of adult age differences in cognition. *Psychological Review, 103*, 403–428.

Salthouse, T. A. (2004). Localizing age-related individual differences in a hierarchical structure. *Intelligence, 32*, 541–561.

Salthouse, T. A. (2006). Mental exercise and mental aging: Evaluating the validity of the "use it or lose it" hypothesis. *Perspectives on Psychological Science, 1*(1), 68–87.

Salthouse, T., & Ferrer-Caja, E. (2003). What needs to be explained to account for age-related effects on multiple cognitive variables? *Psychology and Aging, 18*, 91–110.

Seeman, T. E., Huang, M. H., Bretsky, P., Crimmins, E., Launer, L., & Guralnik, J. M. (2005). Education and APE-e4 in longitudinal cognitive decline: MacArthur studies of successful aging. *Journals of Gerontology Series B—Psychological Sciences and Social Sciences, 60*(2), P74–P83.

Segal, N. (2000). *Entwined lives: Twins and what they tell us about human behavior.* New York: Plume.

Segurado, R., Detera-Wadleigh, S. D., Levinson, D. F., Lewis, C. M., Gill, M., Nurnberg, J. I., et al. (2003). Genome scan meta-analysis of schizophrenia and bipolar disorder, part III: Bipolar disorder. *American Journal of Human Genetics, 73*(1), 49–62.

Singer, T., Lindenberger, U., & Baltes, P. B. (2003). Plasticity of memory for new learning in very old age: A story of major loss? *Psychology and Aging, 18*(2), 306–317.

Small, B. J., Rosnick, C. B., Fratiglioni, L., & Bäckman, L. (2004). Apolipoprotein E and cognitive performance: A meta-analysis. *Psychology and Aging, 19*(4), 592–600.

Stewart, R., Powell, J., Prince, M., & Mann, A. (2004). ACE genotype and cognitive decline in an African-Caribbean population. *Neurobiology of Aging, 25*(10), 1369–1375.

Swan, G. E., LaRue, A., Carmelli, D., Reed, T. E., & Fabsitz, R. R. (1992). Decline in cognitive performance: Heritability and biobehavioral predictors from the National Heart, Lung, and Blood Institute Twin Study. *Archives of Neurology, 49*, 476–481.

Swan, G. E., Reed, T., Jack, L. M., Miller, B. L., Markee, T., Wolf, P. A., et al. (1999). Differential genetic influence for components of memory in aging adult twins. *Archives of Neurology, 56*, 1127–1132.

Syvänen, A. C. (2005). Toward genome-wide SNP genotyping. *Nature Genetics, 37*, s5-s10.

Thompson, P. M., Cannon, T. D., Narr, K. L., van Erp, T., Poutanen, V. P., Huttunen, M., et al. (2001). Genetic influences on brain structure. *Nature Neuroscience, 4*(12), 1253–1258.

Thomson, P. A., Harris, S. E., Starr, J. M., Whalley, L. J., Porteous, D. J., & Deary, I. J. (2005). Association between genotype at an exonic SNP in DISC1 and normal cognitive aging. *Neuroscience Letters, 389*(1), 41–45.

Toga, A. W., & Thompson, P. M. (2005). Genetics of brain structure and intelligence. *Annual Review of Neuroscience, 28*, 1–23.

Troen, A., & Rosenberg, I. (2005). Homocysteine and cognitive function. *Seminars in Vascular Medicine, 5*(2), 209–214.

Tucker, K. L., Qiao, N., Scott, T., Rosenberg, I., & Spiro, A. I. (2005). High homocysteine and low B vitamins predict cognitive decline in aging men: The Veterans Affairs Normative Study. *American Journal of Clinical Nutrition, 82*(3), 627–635.

Turic, D., Fisher, P. J., Plomin, R., & Owen, M. J. (2001). No association between apolipoprotein E polymorphisms and general cognitive ability in children. *Neuroscience Letters, 299*, 97–100.

Turkheimer, E., Haley, A., Waldron, M., D'Onofrio, B., & Gottesman, I. I. (2003). Socioeconomic status modifies heritability in young children. *Psychological Science, 14,* 623–628.

Turkheimer, E., & Waldron, M. (2000). Nonshared environment: A theoretical, methodological, and quantitative review. *Psychological Bulletin, 126,* 78–108.

Vandenberg, S. G. (1972). Assortative mating, or who marries whom. *Behavior Genetics, 2,* 127–157.

Visscher, P. M., Tynan, M., Whiteman, M. C., Pattie, A., White, I., Hayward, C., et al. (2003). Lack of association between polymorphisms in angiotensin-converting-enzyme and methylenetetrahydrofolate reductase genes and normal cognitive ageing in humans. *Neuroscience Letters, 347*(3), 175–178.

Weaver, I. C. G., Cervoni, N., Champagne, F. A., D'Alessio, A. C., Sharma, S., Seckl, J. R., et al. (2004). Epigenetic programming by maternal behavior. *Nature Neuroscience, 7,* 847–854.

Wechsler, D. (1981). *Manual for the Wechsler Adult Intelligence Scale—Revised.* New York: Psychological Corporation.

Williams, G. C. (1957). Pleiotropy, natural selection, and the evolution of senescence. *Evolution, 11,* 398–411.

Wilson, R. S., Bienias, J. L., Berry-Kravis, E., Evans, D. A., & Bennett, D. A. (2002a). The apolipoprotein E ε2 allele and decline in episodic memory. *Journal of Neurology, Neurosurgery, and Psychiatry, 73,* 672–677.

Wilson, R. S., Schneider, J. A., Barnes, L. L., Beckett, L. A., Aggarwal, N. T., Cochran, E. J., et al. (2002b). The apolipoprotein E epsilon 4 allele and decline in different cognitive systems during a 6-year period. *Archives of Neurology, 59*(7), 1154–1160.

Wright, A., Charlesworth, B., Rudan, I., Carothers, A., & Campbell, H. (2003). A polygenic basis for late-onset disease. *Trends in Genetics, 19*(2), 97–106.

Wright, J. W., & Harding, W. (1994). Brain angiotensin receptor suptypes in the control of physiological and behavioural responses. *Neuroscience and Biobehavioral Review, 18,* 21–53.

Yip, A. G., Brayne, C., Easton, D., & Rubinsztein, D. C. (2002a). Apolipoprotein E4 is only a weak predictor of dementia and cognitive decline in the general population. *Journal of Medical Genetics, 39,* 639–643.

Yip, A. G., Brayne, C., Easton, D., & Rubinsztein, D. C. (2002b). An investigation of ACE as a risk factor for dementia and cognitive decline in the general population. *Journal of Medical Genetics, 39*(6), 403–406.

York, T. P., F., M. M., Kendler, K. S., Jackson-Cook, C., Bowman, M. L., & Eaves, L. (2005). Epistatic and environmental control of genome-wide gene expression. *Twin Research, 8,* 5–15.

Zhao, J. H., Brunner, E. J., Kumari, M., Singh-Manoux, A., Hawe, E., Talmud, P. J., et al. (2005). APOE polymorphism, socioeconomic status and cognitive function in mid-life: The Whitehall II Longitudinal Study. *Social Psychiatry and Psychiatric Epidemiology, 40*(7), 557–563.

Zuccala, G., Onder, G., Marzetti, E., Lo Monaco, M. R., Cesari, M., Cocchi, A., et al. (2005). Use of angiotensin-converting enzyme inhibitors and variations in cognitive performance among patients with heart failure. *European Heart Journal, 26*(3), 226–233.

3

The Neuropsychology of the Development of Alzheimer's Disease

Marilyn S. Albert
Johns Hopkins University School of Medicine

INTRODUCTION

Dementia, particularly Alzheimer's disease (AD), was first emphasized as a major public health problem 30 years ago (Katzman 1976). This led to increased research efforts to understand the clinical presentation and diagnosis, the pathobiology and underlying cause, treatments for established disease, and, more recently, an emphasis on early diagnosis and treatment.

It is fortunate that there is considerable consensus with regard to the clinical phenotype of AD. This has led to the development of widely accepted clinical criteria for use in both clinical and research settings (American Psychiatric Association, 1994; McKhann, Drachman, Folstein, Katzman, Price, & Stadlan, 1984). Many subsequent studies have demonstrated that these criteria can be reliably applied across sites and that accuracy of diagnosis in comparison with pathological findings is high (e.g., Blacker, Albert, Bassett, Go, Harrell, & Folstein, 1994). Agreement about clinical criteria also permitted the conduct of a large number of clinical trials, ultimately leading to approval of five medications for AD, four cholinesterase inhibitors and Memantine (an NMDA antagonist, which reduces glutamate transmission). These medications offer symptomatic relief, but do not alter the rate at which patients decline over time.

This has increased the urgency of finding better treatments for AD, as the demographic shift in the population toward greater life expectancy suggests geometrically increasing numbers of AD patients in the coming

decades, unless more effective treatments can be developed. An improved understanding of the neurobiology of AD has led to optimism that disease-modifying treatments may be on the horizon (Selkoe, 2005). There is, however, concern that if disease is too far advanced, response to these treatments may be muted. This, in turn, has led to a focus on identifying patients as early as possible in the course of disease.

Since AD was first described, it has been clear that the symptoms develop gradually over many years (Alzheimer, 1907). Thus, it would seem that, by definition, there must be a prodromal phase of disease during which symptoms are evolving but the individual does not yet meet criteria for dementia. Various terms have been used to describe this prodromal phase, but the term Mild Cognitive Impairment (MCI) has gained the widest recognition (Flicker, Ferris, & Reisberg, 1991; Petersen, Smith, Waring, Ivnik, Tangalos, & Kokmen, 1999). There has been divergence, however, in how the criteria for MCI have been applied, leading to widely varying estimates of its prevalence in the population (e.g., Larrieu et al., 2002; Ritchie, Artero, & Touchon, 2001) and controversy regarding its utility as a clinical syndrome (Gautier & Touchon, 2005).

The current review will focus on the neuropsychology of AD and MCI, delineating the broad areas of consensus that exist and, where there is disagreement, outlining the primary issues to be resolved. Since the cognitive deficits in AD and MCI are the result of selective alterations in the brain, the relationship between neuropsychological deficits and neuropathological or brain imaging findings will also be discussed, where relevant. An increasing area of interest is the boundary between normal aging and MCI, as well as predictors of maintenance of cognitive function with age, thus, recent research findings in this area will also be discussed.

ALZHEIMER'S DISEASE AND RELATED DISORDERS

As noted above, the most common form of dementia is AD, accounting for approximately 70% of the cases of dementia (either alone or in combination with other pathologies). Other causes of dementia include: frontotemporal dementia (FTD), diffuse Lewy body dementia (DLBD), multi-infarct dementia (MID), the dementia of Parkinson's disease (PD) and Creutzfeldt-Jakob disease (CJD). Each of these has a characteristic clinical presentation, caused by characteristic pathological changes in the brain. Most of these dementing disorders cannot currently be definitively diagnosed during life without highly invasive procedures, such as a brain biopsy (with the exception of CJD). The clinical diagnosis is therefore considered "probable." The Appendix to this chapter provides

information about the clinical presentation of AD and the ways in which it differs from the less common forms of dementia noted above.

This chapter will focus on research in the area of AD for several reasons. First, the neuropsychological approaches to studying AD are similar to those employed in the study of the other dementing disorders. Second, the conceptual issues that are the primary focus of research today in AD are likely to represent the future direction of research that will be undertaken with regard to the other disorders.

The initial cognitive deficit in the majority of patients with AD is a gradually progressive difficulty with learning and retention of new information (generally referred to as a deficit in episodic memory). This is consistent with the fact that the earliest pathological changes of the disease are seen in medial temporal lobe regions essential for normal memory (e.g., the entorhinal cortex and hippocampus; Braak & Braak, 1998). Over time, pathological abnormalities (e.g., neurofibrillary tangles, neuritic plaques, synaptic and neuronal loss) impact more and more brain regions, until these abnormalities are seen throughout the temporal, parietal and frontal lobes. The range of neuropsychological deficits in the patients increases as a function of this expanding pathology. The Appendix contains a description of the evolution of disease in a typical case of AD. The average duration of disease, after diagnosis, is approximately 10 years. Some brain regions have minimal pathology, even in the end stages of disease (e.g., the primary motor and sensory cortices). The selective manner in which the disease begins and progresses over time is why AD is thought to represent the degeneration of a selective brain system, with multiple nodes (Braak, Del Tredici, Schultz, & Braak, 2000). Other neurodegenerative disorders share this characteristic; recent advances in the treatment for PD have capitalized on this fact (Vitek et al., 2003).

There is consensus regarding how AD is clinically diagnosed, as mentioned above. This fact, in combination with the selective system degeneration in the brain, is likely the reason why neuropsychological studies of established AD have produced generally consistent findings. These are described in detail below.

PRODROMAL AD

There is also considerable evidence to support the argument that there is a transitional phase between normal function and AD dementia. This is consistent with the fact that the pathological changes take many years to accumulate in the brain. The feasibility of studying this transitional phase is based on the fact that the clinical hallmark of AD is a progressive

decline in cognitive function. A number of research groups have therefore recruited nondemented individuals with mild cognitive impairments and followed them over time, with the goal of examining the nature of the cognitive changes that occurred during the transitional phase between normality and frank dementia. These studies have demonstrated that cognitive impairments are present 5–10 years prior to dementia and can be used to predict with significant accuracy which specific individuals are destined to develop dementia many years later (e.g., Albert, Moss, Tanzi & Jones, 2001; Tierney, Yao, Kiss, & McDowell, 2005).

Neuropsychological studies of individuals defined as neither normal nor demented demonstrate progressive declines in cognition over time, which are particularly striking in the area of episodic memory, as discussed further below. Other domains appear to be affected as well, consistent with the fact that the clinical criteria for dementia require impairment in two or more cognitive domains.

Pathological findings in nondemented cognitively impaired individuals are particularly important in this context, since it is essential to demonstrate that at least some of these nondemented individuals have the pathological features of AD. Given the difficulty of obtaining brain tissue at a time when individuals are not demented, it is not surprising that few published results are available. The largest sample comes from the Religious Order Study and included 37 individuals with a clinical diagnosis of MCI, 60 normal controls, and 83 cases of AD (Bennett et al., 2005a). Of the 37 MCI cases, 40% had a low likelihood of AD based on the neuropathological criteria for AD (known as the NIA-Reagan, NIA-R, criteria), with 60% demonstrating an intermediate or high likelihood of AD. This was in contrast to the normals, where these proportions were reversed (60% vs. 40%, respectively). Only 10% of the cases with clinically diagnosed AD had a low likelihood of AD based on pathological criteria. A report from the Mayo Clinic included 15 individuals who died with a clinical diagnosis of MCI, 28 normal controls and 23 cases of AD (Petersen et al., 2006). Most patients with MCI did not meet neuropathologic criteria for AD; the authors argued that the pathological features represented a transitional state of evolving AD. These reports contrast with the findings from Washington University where almost all of the cases met pathological criteria for AD (Morris et al., 2001). This suggests that there is likely variation in the clinical criteria used to define the cases during life. It is evident that in some sets of cognitively impaired nondemented cases, the proportion of those with a high likelihood of AD based on pathological criteria is much less than among individuals who meet clinical criteria for AD. However, a substantial number of nondemented cognitively impaired individuals do meet pathological criteria for AD. It is also important to note that many of the cases, regardless of clinical diagnosis,

had evidence of vascular disease (Bennett et al., 2005a; Petersen et al., 2006).

Taken together, these findings indicate that it is possible to identify individuals in a transitional state between normal function and AD dementia, and that such individuals have cognitive and brain changes that are consistent with a transitional phase of disease. For research purposes, it seems important to retain the distinctiveness of this phase of disease so that the characteristics of this phase and the effectiveness of interventions can be carefully studied. In clinical settings, distinguishing a transitional phase of disease also seems very important in order to provide appropriate feedback to patients. Recent research studies indicate that there is considerable variation in the clinical outcome of individuals who are said to be cognitively impaired but nondemented by whatever criteria. As prediction of outcome remains challenging, even in research settings, it seems important to communicate this lack of certainty when providing a clinical diagnosis to individual patients.

HETEROGENEITY OF MCI

A review of the literature suggests that much of the controversy surrounding the term MCI derives largely from the fact that the criteria have been implemented in a variety of ways in research settings, while at the same time the syndrome is more heterogeneous than originally suggested. The clinical criteria have changed over time in recognition of this heterogeneity. However, a number of important issues remain to be clarified.

The MCI criteria elucidated by Petersen and colleagues in 1999 implied that cases of MCI represented a fairly uniform group of individuals (Petersen, Smith, Waring, Ivnik, Tangalos, & Kokmen, 1999). These criteria were as follows:

- memory complaint, corroborated by an informant if possible
- objective memory impairment for age
- relatively preserved general cognition for age
- intact basic activities of daily living
- not demented.

Following studies demonstrating that MCI cases defined in this manner had a more variable outcome than had been previously suggested, the criteria were modified to permit clinical subtypes with variable outcomes, based on the presumed etiology underlying the disorder. Two primary subtypes were delineated, based on whether a predominant memory disorder was present or absent, called amnestic and nonamnestic MCI

(Petersen, 2004). The revised criteria also acknowledged the possibility that more than one cognitive domain might be impaired within each of these subtypes (e.g., amnestic MCI, single or multiple domain impaired). These revised criteria are conceptually similar to the term Cognitive Impairment No Dementia (CIND) introduced by the Canadian Study of Health and Aging (Davis & Rockwood, 2004) in that they encompass a broad range of cognitive deficits caused by multiple etiologies.

In this context, the original clinical criteria for MCI were clearly focused on amnestic MCI, and Petersen and colleagues were attempting to focus on individuals likely to be in the prodromal phase of AD. Their work and that of numerous other groups has since demonstrated that amnestic MCI subjects (single or multiple domain impaired) are at increased risk of progressing to a diagnosis of AD over time.

What was also unrecognized in the original reports was the importance of the source of subjects as a factor in both the severity and the nature of the population under study. In retrospect it now seems clear that the broader one casts the net of inclusion in a study, the more likely one is to include individuals with less severe underlying disease. It is therefore not surprising that studies emerging from memory clinics in tertiary care settings report the highest proportion of individuals who progress to meet criteria for AD over time (e.g., Rubin, Morris, Grant, & Vendegna, 1989); whereas studies that recruit broadly from the community (e.g., via the media) are likely to have much lower rates of "conversion" to AD on follow-up (e.g., Daly, Zaitchik, Copeland, Schmahmann, Gunther, & Albert, 2000). This does not necessarily mean that the underlying disease process is different, but rather that the investigators have captured a different range of disease severity within their study population.

An additional source of variation is introduced when studies are conducted in epidemiological settings as opposed to clinical settings. In epidemiological settings it is virtually impossible to require that each subject should have an informant (as is usually the case in clinic-based studies), as epidemiological studies seek to represent the entire range of individuals in the population. Therefore it is necessary to rely more heavily on neuropsychological testing as the marker of cognitive decline. This increases the importance of the particular cognitive tests that have been selected. The reliability and validity of each of the tests are critical, as well as the range of cognitive domains included in the test battery. For example, if tests are selected that have a ceiling effect, it is likely that fewer individuals with impairments will be found. Likewise, if a particular cognitive domain is not included in a test battery (e.g., executive function), it is not possible to determine whether the subjects would have been impaired in that domain. In order to maximize enrollment and follow-up it is also necessary to reduce the length of the evaluation in an

epidemiological setting, as opposed to a clinical setting, resulting in less detailed information than is optimal. These restrictions, if applied equally to all participants, most likely influence the absolute numbers of individuals identified in a particular category (as sensitivity will vary depending on the procedures employed), but they should not alter the relative proportion of individuals meeting criteria for various diagnostic categories, or the proportion of individuals who change status over time.

As studies of nondemented cognitively impaired individuals expanded to broader settings, it also became clear that there were substantial numbers of individuals whose memory impairment was the predominant but not sole cognitive problem that could be seen. Many individuals with prodromal AD were slightly impaired in other domains (e.g., language or executive function) in addition to memory. Likewise, individuals were seen whose primary cognitive impairment was in domains other than memory (e.g., attention or spatial skill). The recent revision of the MCI criteria (Petersen, 2004) recognizes these findings and appropriately acknowledges that multiple clinical syndromes must, by definition, have a transitional phase during which cognitive impairments are in evolution. The revised criteria now describe criteria for amnestic MCI (single and multiple domains impaired), which is thought to represent the majority of individuals who will progress to a diagnosis of AD over time. Those with nonamnestic MCI (single and multiple domains impaired) are thought to pertain to the transitional phase of other dementias (e.g., FTD, MID, DLBD) as well as psychiatric disorders (e.g., depression), though in practice these distinctions can be blurred (e.g., Fisk, Merry, & Rockwood, 2003). (See Petersen & Morris, 2005 and DeCarli, 2003 for a further discussion of these issues.)

It is therefore necessary to evaluate an MCI case who comes for clinical evaluation with the same rigor one would bring to the diagnosis of a patient with dementia. That is, to consider all potential medical, psychiatric or neurologic causes of cognitive impairment before making a diagnosis. The number of nonamnestic MCI cases that have been followed to a diagnosis of dementia is limited (e.g., Yaffe, Petersen, Linquist, Kramer, & Miller, 2006). It is therefore difficult to provide much information about which specific MCI criteria they fit the best, and the numbers of subjects with various non-AD dementias or psychiatric disorders one is likely to see within a group of MCI cases, defined broadly. There is, however, sufficient evidence to indicate that cases of depression will be included in this group. Moreover, cases of amnestic MCI who progress to AD are also likely to have neuropsychiatric symptoms (particularly dysphoria and irritability), thus making the diagnostic process challenging (Copeland, Daly, Hines, Mastromauro, Zaitchik, Gunther, & Albert, 2003; Hwang, Masterman, Ortiz, Fairbanks, & Cummings, 2004).

NEUROPSYCHOLOGICAL TESTING IN AD AND MCI

Episodic Memory

Difficulty with the acquisition of new information is generally the first and most salient symptom to emerge in patients with AD, as noted above. When clinical neuropsychological tests are used to evaluate memory in AD patients, it is clear that recall and recognition performance are impaired in both the verbal and nonverbal domain (Storandt & Hill, 1989; Wilson, Bacon, Fox, & Kaszniak, 1983).

Experimental studies have examined AD patients to determine whether the manner in which information is lost over brief delays is unique in any way to this patient group. A comparison of AD patients to amnestic patients with Korsakoff's syndrome (KS) and demented patients with Huntington's disease (HD) demonstrated that AD patients recalled significantly fewer words over a 2-minute delay than either of the other two patient groups (Moss, Albert, Butters, & Payne, 1986). Whereas the KS, HD, and normal control subjects lost an average of 10% to 15% of the verbal information between the 15-second and 2-minute delay intervals, patients with AD lost an average of 75% of the material.

Numerous studies have compared AD patients to controls and confirmed that the patients consistently showed a rapid loss of information over brief delays (e.g., Butters, Salmon, Heindel, & Granholm, 1988; Hart, Kwentus, Harkins, & Taylor, 1988). A comparison of AD patients and patients with FTD (Moss & Albert, 1988) and with progressive supranuclear palsy (PSP) (Milberg & Albert, 1989) demonstrated the severe recall deficits of the AD patients in comparison to patients with FTD and PSP. Consistent with the findings above, a comparison of a range of memory measures in a national study involving mildly impaired AD patients and controls (the CERAD study) concluded that measures of delayed recall (in the form of a saving score where measures are adjusted for the information originally acquired) are best at discrimating AD patients from controls (Welsh, Butters, Hughes, Mohs, & Heyman, 1991, 1992).

Measures of episodic memory are, however, not particularly useful in staging AD patients across levels of severity, primarily because memory is so impaired early in the course of disease. An analysis of the CERAD study data found that a combination of measures that included fluency, visuospatial ability, and recognition memory best differentiated mildly impaired patients from those with either moderate or severe levels of impairment (Welsh et al., 1992). These findings support the conclusion that in most patients with AD memory impairments precede impairments in language and spatial function.

As noted above, recently numerous research groups have recruited

nondemented individuals with MCI and followed them over time to determine the nature of the cognitive changes that occurred during pro-dromal AD. Among these studies there is considerable consensus that tests of memory are significantly different among nondemented individuals with mild memory deficits who receive a diagnosis of AD on follow-up, as compared with those who also have memory problems but do not progress to AD within a few years' time (Albert et al., 2001; Bondi et al., 1994; Chen, Ratcliff, Belle, Cauley, DeKosky, & Ganguli, 2000; Howieson et al., 2003; Jacobs, Sano, Dooneief, Marder, Bell, & Stern, 1995; Kluger, Ferris, Golomb, Mittelman, & Reisberg, 1999; Newmann, Warrington, Kennedy, & Rossor, 1994; Petersen, Smith, Ivnik, Kokmen, & Tangalos, 1994; Rubin, Morris, Grant, & Vendegna, 1989; Small, LaRue, Komo, Kaplan, & Mandelkern, 1995; Tierney et al., 1996; Tuokko, Vernon-Wilkinson, Weir, & Beattie, 1991).

There is also widespread agreement concerning the underlying cause of these memory changes in AD. Synaptic dysfunction, neuronal loss, and AD pathology first occur in medial temporal lobe regions (Hyman, VanHoesen, Damasio, & Barnes, 1984; Selkoe, 2005). This is particularly evident in the entorhinal cortex and CA1 region of the hippocampus (Gomez-Isla et al., 1996), brain regions critical for normal memory (Squire & Zola, 1996). This conclusion is supported by in vivo neuroimaging studies showing significant atrophy of these brain regions in MCI cases (for reviews see Atiya, Hyman, Albert, & Killiany, 2003; Kantarci & Jack, 2003).

Executive Function

In addition to memory problems, mildly impaired AD patients are sub-stantially impaired in a set of abilities collectively referred to as "executive functions." These include: the concurrent manipulation of information, cue-directed attention, and concept formation.

An alteration in executive function ability among AD patients was not recognized initially, as early studies did not include sensitive tests of executive function. Once investigators began to evaluate mildly impaired AD patients with sensitive tests of executive function, these impairments became apparent. For example, mildly impaired patients were shown to be impaired on a task that involved coordinating two concurrent tasks (Baddeley, Logie, Bressi, Della Sala, & Spinnler, 1986) as well as tasks requiring shifting between stimulus dimensions (Filoteo, Delis, Massman, Demadura, Butters, & Salmon, 1992; Sahakian et al., 1990). Mild-to-moderately impaired patients also demonstrate executive function defi-cits (Becker, 1988; Bondi et al., 2002; Lafleche, Stuss, Nelson, & Picton, 1990; Morris & Baddeley, 1988; Nestor, Parasuraman, & Haxby, 1991).

In order to determine whether an impairment in executive function

precedes or coexists with significant deficits in spatial and language function, a number of studies have compared very mildly impaired AD patients to controls on tasks assessing a range of cognitive domains. Grady et al. (1988) reported that deficits on tasks of memory and executive function preceded impairments in language. Lafleche and Albert (1995) attempted to characterize the specific aspect of executive function that was impaired in very mildly impaired AD patients. They assessed a broad range of executive abilities, including: set shifting and self-monitoring (i.e., the concurrent manipulation of information), cue-directed attention (e.g., the ability to use cues to direct attention), and concept formation (e.g., abstraction). Most of the tasks that revealed a significant deficit were those that required set shifting and self-monitoring. By contrast, performance on tasks that assessed cue-directed attention and verbal concept formation were not significantly impaired in the patients. Likewise, performance on the tests of confrontation naming, figure copying, and sustained attention were not impaired. Taken together, these findings suggest that selected aspects of executive function, particularly those involving set shifting and self-monitoring, are affected very early in the course of the disease.

There is, however, a lack of consensus regarding whether executive function deficits are prominent during prodromal AD. The discrepancies among studies are due, at least in part, to the fact that few studies have examined a wide variety of cognitive domains, thus limiting the types of associations that can be found.

A number of studies have reported that executive function abnormalities are evident in the prodromal stage of AD (Albert et al., 2001; Albert, Blacker, Moss, Tanzi, & McArdle, in press; Chen et al., 2000; Chen, Ratcliff, Belle, Cauley, DeKosky, & Ganguli, 2001; Grady et al., 1988; Sahakian et al., 1990, Tierney et al., 1996). Others have reported that declines in confrontation naming are more likely to be impaired among those destined to develop AD (e.g., Saxton et al., 2004). The reasons for these discrepancies remain to be resolved.

The brain abnormalities responsible for the executive function deficits seen among individuals destined to develop AD are also unclear. At least two potential neurobiological explanations have been suggested. Findings from functional imaging indicate that during prodromal AD there is dysfunction within a brain network that involves the dorsolateral prefrontal cortex and the anterior cingulate (Milham et al., 2002). Alterations in these brain regions have been associated with impairments in executive function (Bush et al., 2002). An alternative possibility is that the disruption of the cortico-cortical connections that are seen in AD, and are not specific to the frontal lobes (Morrison & Hof, 2002), may be responsible for executive dysfunction during prodromal AD.

Language

Mild-to-moderately impaired AD patients have impairments in confrontation naming and verbal fluency. Some investigators have argued that these deficits are the result of a broader impairment in semantic memory, defined as "that system which processes, stores and retrieves information about the meaning of words, concepts and facts" (Warrington, 1975).

Semantic memory abnormalities in patients with AD have been documented using a range of tasks that include category fluency (Chan, Butters, Paulsen, Salmon, Swenson, & Maloney, 1993; Hodges, Salmon, & Butters, 1992; Martin & Fedio, 1983; Troster, Salmon, McCullough, & Butters, 1989), category membership (Grossman, Robinson, Biassou, White-Devine, & D'Esposito, 1998), confrontation naming (Grossman et al., 1998; Hodges et al., 1992; Martin & Fedio, 1983), and similarity judgments (Chan et al., 1993, 1995, 1997). In addition, several studies of word priming (Glosser, Grugan, Friedman, Lee, & Grossman, 1998; Milberg, McGlinchey-Berroth, Duncan, & Higgins, 1999; Salmon, Shimamura, Butters, & Smith, 1988) have reported significant deficits in AD patients, though other studies failed to find this effect (Nebes & Brady, 1988).

Studies of semantic memory in AD patients suggest that some conceptual domains may be more impaired than others, in particular, that patients with AD have a specific impairment in the conceptual domain of "living things." For example, in studies assessing confrontation naming (Grossman et al., 1998; Silveri, Daniele, Giustolisi, & Gainotti, 1991) and picture recognition (Silveri et al., 1991), mild to moderate AD patients performed significantly worse on living things than nonliving things. Other studies have, however, failed to reveal such category-specific differences, using a variety of tasks including recognition naming (Tippett, Grossman, & Farah, 1996), category-naming fluency and drawing fluency (Mickanin, Grossman, Onishi, Auriacombe, & Clark, 1994), and category membership judgments (Grossman et al., 1998). It has been suggested that discrepant findings regarding category-specific semantic loss in AD patients relate to the fact that some brain regions are more critical for category-specific judgments than others, and the appearance of a deficit depends on the anatomic distribution of disease in the specific patients examined (Grossman et al., 1998). These issues remain unresolved.

Visuospatial Function

Visuospatial function is impaired in the course of AD. On simple copying tasks, such as drawing a clock or a triangle, mild AD patients do not differ from normal controls (Kararasch, Sinerva, Granholm, Rinne, & Laine, 2005; Rouleau, Salmon, Butters, Kennedy, & McGuire, 1992). However,

visuospatial impairments are common among mild-to-moderately impaired patients (Kurylo, Corkin, & Growdon, 1994; Rouleau, Salmon, & Butters, 1996).

When subjects are asked to draw a figure to command, such as a clock, impairments are evident among mildly impaired AD patients. However, these appear to be the result of conceptual errors, rather than visuospatial errors. Mildly impaired AD patients tend to make perseverative errors and "stimulus-bound responses" but graphic difficulties are extremely uncommon at this stage of disease (Rouleau et al., 1992). Evaluations of patients at differing levels of severity (Heinik, Solomesh, Shein, & Becker, 2002) as well as longitudinal data collected from the same individuals (Rouleau et al., 1996) indicate that performance on clock drawing to command gets progressively worse over time, and that conceptual errors are particularly sensitive to overall change in dementia severity.

The sensitivity of clock drawing to command in mild AD patients led investigators to determine whether this task might be sensitive to individuals in the prodromal phase of AD. However, a number of studies indicate that clock drawing to command is not useful for the identification of MCI cases (Powlishta et al., 2002; Siegerschmidt, Mosch, Siemen, Forstl, & Bickel, 2002).

It should be noted that some aspects of spatial skill are very well retained early in the course of AD. Mirror-tracing skill, which involves tracing a pattern (e.g., a 4- or 6-pointed star seen only in a mirror-reversed view), has been the best studied. While mild-to-moderately AD patients have poor recall or recognition of their mirror-tracing experience, they acquire and retain mirror-tracing skill and generalize it to another object as well as normal subjects (Gabrieli, Corkin, Mickel, & Growdon, 1993; Rouleau et al., 2002). This is comparable to the findings reported in the amnestic patient H.M. (Gabrieli et al., 1993).

Attention

Mild AD patients do not have impairments on a simple test of sustained attention that makes few demands on memory, such as digit span forward. However, mildly impaired patients demonstrate selective impairments on attentional tasks that are more complex. Tests of choice reaction time and cued choice reaction time are impaired in mild AD (Levinoff, Saumier, & Chertkow, 2005). Dual task performance is also impaired in mild AD patients, particularly when one or both of the tasks are not relatively automatized (Crossley, Hiscock, & Foreman, 2004; Fernandez-Duque & Black, 2006).

ADDITIONAL APPROACHES

Inference of Emotion and Beliefs

Successful social interaction depends at least in part on the ability to make inferences about the emotions and beliefs of others (Fodor, 1987). The ability to infer what another person is feeling has been studied for many years in patients with acute brain damage, such as a stroke. The data suggest that impairments in emotion perception are related to difficulty with social interactions. The ability to infer what another person believes to be true (often known as the individual's "theory of mind") has also been studied for many years, initially in children with developmental disabilities. These data also suggest that impairments in inference of belief are related to difficulty with social interaction.

Studies investigating emotion processing in patients with AD have focused primarily on the ability to identify emotions (either perceptually or by inference). Results of these studies suggest that AD patients are not impaired in processing emotional information conveyed in facial expression, vocal intonation, or gesture, but that they are impaired on tasks that require interpretation of situational information portrayed in scenes and stories (Albert, Cohen, & Koff, 1991; Allender & Kaszniak, 1989; Cadieux & Greve, 1997; Koff, Zaitchik, Montepare, & Albert, 1999).

The ability to infer beliefs in others has also been examined in several studies involving AD patients. One of these studies included both first-order tasks (where participants are asked to infer the beliefs of others) and second-order tasks (where participants are asked to infer someone's belief about someone else's belief). In this study, performance of AD patients on the first-order tasks was no different from that of healthy controls, but AD patients were impaired relative to controls on the second-order tasks (Gregory et al., 2002). One study examining only first-order tasks (Zaitchik, Koff, Brownell, Winner, & Albert, 2006) and another examining only second-order tasks (Garcia-Cuerva, Sabe, Kuzis, Tiberti, Dorrego, & Starkstein, 2001) reported similar findings.

A recent study has directly compared the ability to infer emotions with the ability to infer beliefs in patients with mild-to-moderate AD (Zaitchik et al., 2006). Parallel procedures were used to assess inference of beliefs and inference of emotion in both first-order and second-order tasks. Each task included a control condition to determine whether any impairments of the subjects are due to the mental state inference in particular (i.e., inference about an emotion or a belief), as compared with inferences about information unrelated to a mental state (e.g., inference about an object, such as a picture). Results showed that the ability to infer emotions and beliefs in first-order tasks remains largely intact in mild-to-moderate

AD patients. Patients were able to utilize mental states in the prediction, explanation, and moral evaluation of behavior. Impairment on second-order tasks involving inference of mental states was equivalent to impairment on control tasks, suggesting that patients' difficulty is secondary to their cognitive impairments.

Screening Tests

The most widely used screening tests are the Mini Mental State Exam (MMSE; Folstein, Folstein, & McHugh, 1975), the Blessed Dementia Scale (Blessed, Tomlinson, & Roth, 1968), the Short Portable Mental Status Questionnaire (Pfeiffer, 1975), the Clock Drawing Test (CDT; Watson, Arfken, & Birge, 1993) and the 7-Minute Screen (Solomon et al., 1998). These tests all take approximately 10 minutes to administer and have high test–retest reliability.

Of these, the MMSE has most commonly been used in clinical settings. Its strength is that it assesses a broad range of cognitive abilities (i.e., memory, language, spatial ability, set shifting) in a simple and straight-forward manner. In addition, the wide use of the MMSE in epidemiologic studies has yielded cut-off scores that facilitate the identification of patients with cognitive dysfunction. The other screening tests have been used in a variety of experimental settings, but epidemiologic data are limited. Finally, the extensive use of the MMSE has produced widespread familiarity with its scoring system, facilitating communication among clinicians.

Each of these tests is imperfect as a screening tool, in that they are not sensitive to early stages of disease and are impacted by the age, education and racial background of the individual (Manly et al., 1999). As a result, there is a continuing debate about whether screening for dementia is beneficial, particularly in primary care settings. The most recent con-sensus statement from the US Preventive Services Task Force did not rec-ommend screening for dementia (Boustani, Peterson, Hanson, Harris, & Lohr, 2003). They found good evidence that some screening tests have good sensitivity but only fair specificity in detecting cognitive impair-ment and dementia. In the absence of effective treatments for AD, they could not recommend screening, particularly because the feasibility of screening and treatment in routine clinical practice and the potential harms of screening (i.e., labeling the patient) are unknown. When disease-modifying agents for AD are available, the risk–benefit ratio for screening will change. The consensus recommendations may then change as well.

Neuropsychological Evaluation in Clinical Trials

All randomized controlled clinical trials in the US of medications aimed at treating patients with AD have used neuropsychological tests as one of the two primary markers of drug efficacy (the other measure is a global clinical rating). The most widely used test in these clinical trials is the Alzheimer's Disease Assessment Scale–Cognitive Subscale (ADAS–Cog; see Mohs, 1996 for a review). The primary reason the ADAS–Cog has been so widely accepted is that it was shown to be not only a valid and reliable measure of cognition in AD patients, but to also change reliably with disease severity over time. Although the FDA has not mandated its use, the inclusion in early trials accepted by the FDA resulted in the concern that use of any other test would be problematic.

Several recent clinical trials have attempted to broaden the way in which cognition is evaluated in patients with AD and MCI. The Alzheimer's Disease Cooperative Study group evaluated five types of tasks that might extend the cognitive domains assessed by the ADAS–Cog as well as the range of symptom severity covered. These tasks included: a word list learning test with delayed free recall; a recognition memory test for faces; a series of letter and digit cancellation tests; tests of praxis; and a series of maze completion tests. The test that proved to be sensitive to a broad range of dementia severity was the digit cancellation (Mohs et al., 1997). The word list learning test and a subset of maze tasks were impaired in very mild AD cases. These were therefore recommended for inclusion in future trials. An alternative approach is best represented by the test battery used by Elan in the trial of AN-1792 (the first immunotherapy trial for AD; Gilman et al., 2005). A broad neuropsychological battery was included as an adjunct to the ADAS–Cog and clinical global rating. No significant differences were found between the antibody responder and placebo groups for the ADAS–Cog or the clinical global rating of change. However, analyses of a composite score from the neuropsychological battery demonstrated improvement in the antibody responders. This finding was used to support the continuation of the development of an immunization approach to AD.

The Alzheimer's Disease Neuroimaging Initiative (ADNI) a multicenter national effort, designed as a natural history clinical trial, is focused on developing imaging measures for inclusion in clinical trials of cases of AD and MCI (Mueller et al., 2005). However, a broad range of neuropsychological measures have been included in the study, and data will therefore be available on the relationship between the cognitive and imaging measures as markers of disease progression.

These, and other data, will therefore be available to determine improved ways of assessing cognition for use in future clinical trials. This

will be particularly important when trials are routinely extended to cases of MCI.

BOUNDARY BETWEEN AGING AND MCI

There is increasing evidence that the pathology of AD can take many years, if not decades, to evolve, as noted above. This suggests that some individuals who appear normal (i.e., functionally asymptomatic) have gradually accumulating pathology. Recent reports based on autopsies of well-characterized normal individuals corroborate this hypothesis (Bennett et al., 2005b; Hulette et al., 1998; Knopman et al., 2000). For example, in the Religious Order Study mentioned above, of 60 normal individuals who had come to autopsy, approximately 60% had a low "likelihood" of AD, based on the NIA-R criteria, while 40% had an intermediate or high "likelihood" of AD.

These findings suggest that it may be possible to identify characteristic changes among normal individuals with a high likelihood of substantial underlying AD pathology during life, using existing methodologies. One potential approach is to determine whether neuropsychological performance among normal individuals can predict the time to develop mild degrees of cognitive impairment, suggestive of the incipient stages of AD.

Few studies to date have addressed this issue. One previous report (Schmitt, Davis, Wekstein, Smith, Ashford, & Markesbery, 2000) concerned normal subjects who received detailed neuropathological examinations and died shortly thereafter (Schmitt et al., 2000). Not only did these individuals have test scores that fell within the normal range, but neither they nor a collateral source had observed any functional decline in daily life. Some normal individuals were found to have AD pathology on autopsy, and the investigators reported that episodic memory performance differed between subjects with and without pathological findings. Another recent study is consistent with this report (Blacker et al., 2007). These investigators found that the likelihood of progressing from normal to MCI was considerably greater among those with lower scores on measures of episodic memory. It is noteworthy that the episodic memory tests that were significant predictors of progression from normal to MCI measured verbal learning and recall in a setting where multiple learning trials are provided, and performance can be improved if the subject takes advantage of organizational clues that are provided either implicitly or explicitly (i.e., the California Verbal Learning Test, the Selective Reminding Test, respectively). This suggests that this type of episodic memory test may be particularly beneficial for revealing mild deficits in normal individuals likely to progress to MCI. These results are also consistent

with a previous report of an association between degree of AD pathology in cognitively normal individuals and performance on tests of episodic memory (Schmitt et al., 2000). They are also consistent with the known neurobiology of AD, which involves medial temporal lobe structures essential for normal memory, as noted above.

These results differ, however, from another study that also performed autopsies on a small number of normal subjects who had been carefully examined during life. These investigators (Goldman et al., 2001) reported that there was no decline in cognitive performance for normal individuals with pathology ($n = 3$) on autopsy as compared with those lacking pathological findings ($n = 5$), based on either individual test scores or a factor score derived from the test battery as a whole. The explanation for this discrepancy may relate to the impact of the small sample size (making it difficult to identify differences between groups), as well as the individual tests examined, and the fact that neuropsychological testing was administered annually.

This area of research is likely to be greatly expanded in the coming years in anticipation of the time when disease-modifying agents become available for AD. It will then be important to intervene as early as possible in the disease, and the ideal time to intervene would be when individuals are considered normal (i.e., asymptomatic). A thorough understanding of the difference between age-related changes in memory and those related to the earliest stage of AD will be essential for progress in this area.

PREDICTORS OF MAINTENANCE OF COGNITIVE FUNCTION WITH AGE

The ideal intervention would be to delay the development of AD pathology as long as possible, since delaying the disease by even 5 years is estimated to reduce the prevalence of disease by one-half (Brookmeyer, Gray, & Kawas, 1998). Thus, studies examining factors predictive of maintenance of cognitive function have increased greatly in recent years.

Most of the work in this area involves epidemiological studies of community-dwelling individuals. All of the studies have a common design, in that individuals are selected from a representative sample of the population who are high functioning, a wide variety of factors are assessed, above and beyond cognition, and the subjects are then re-evaluated after a number of years have elapsed. The analyses have then looked either at factors predicting maintenance of cognition over time or risk of dementia in general or AD in particular.

The first of these studies (Albert et al., 1995) examined individuals who were already elderly (i.e., ages 70–80). Many subsequent reports have,

however, been based on individuals who were assessed in middle age, and were then followed into old age (Karp, Paillard-Borg, Wang, Silverstein, Winblad, & Fratiglioni, 2006). This latter approach is preferable since it reduces the likelihood that the pathological processes responsible for the cognitive decline (e.g., AD) might have already accumulated at the time of the first evaluation and thereby influenced behavior in subtle ways, even though participants appeared to be asymptomatic. Moreover, the subjects who have been evaluated vary widely in ethnic and cultural background, and live in both urban and rural settings (e.g., Albert et al., 1995; Laurin, Verreault, Lindsay, MacPherson, & Rockwood, 2001; Rovio et al., 2005; Scarmeas, Levy, Tang, Manly, & Stern, 2001; Schmand, Smit, Geerlings, & Lindeboom, 1997; Verghese et al., 2003; Weuve, Kang, Manson, Breteler, Ware, & Grodstein, 2004; Wilson et al., 2002; Wilson, Bennett, Bienias, Mendes, DeLeon, Morris, & Evans, 2003). This reduces the likelihood that factors unrelated to the variables of interest are responsible for the findings. It is also notable that these studies have used a wide range of cognitive measures as outcomes. Some have examined composite scores based on a comprehensive neuropsychological battery, while others have looked primarily at selected areas of cognition, such as memory. Thus, the results appear to be reasonably robust and to transcend one particular cognitive domain.

A panel of scientists, convened by three of the institutes at the National Institutes of Health (i.e., NIA, NINDS, NIMH), reviewed the existing literature and issued a White Paper on their findings (Hendrie et al., 2006). The review concluded that there were four independent factors (apart from genetics) that appear to be consistently predictive of maintenance of cognitive function:

- increased levels of physical activity
- increased levels of mental activity
- increased social engagement
- control of vascular risk factors.

Moreover, the data suggest that the benefit gained from each of these lifestyle interventions provides an added benefit, in that risk of cognitive decline is incrementally reduced with the addition of two or more of these factors (Karp et al., 2006).

Physical activity is generally assessed by evaluating a range of physical activities in which the participant might engage in daily life (e.g., walking, climbing stairs, etc.), and developing a measure of total kilocalories expended, adjusted for potentially confounding factors (e.g., comorbid conditions, physical limitations, smoking, etc.; Albert et al., 1995; Weuve et al., 2004). In earlier studies, mental activity was measured by

educational attainment, but in more recent studies it has been assessed by evaluating a range of mental activities in which the participant might engage (e.g., reading books, going to lectures, playing board games, etc.) and developing a measure of the total hours spent doing these activities, adjusted for potentially confounding factors (Wilson et al., 2002, 2003). Social engagement was measured by a variety of scales that assessed social factors, such as social networks, feelings of self-efficacy, feelings of self-worth, etc. (Albert et al., 1995; Karp et al., 2006). Vascular risk factors assessed include: blood pressure, cholesterol, diabetes, weight, and smoking (Elias et al., 2004).

The mechanisms by which these lifestyle factors may benefit brain function are an increasingly active area of research. These have been best studied by the use of animal models, since animal models can disentangle the issue of innate differences during life vs. differences based on experience and, at the same time, address the issue of the underlying brain mechanisms that may be involved. The study design most commonly employed has been to examine changes in brain function, as well as cognition, in groups of animals prior to and after exposure to an environmental manipulation, and compare these measures to those from animals with no environmental manipulation. The animal most commonly used in these studies has been the rodent (i.e., rats or mice), and cognitive performance has most often been assessed by measuring memory performance in the Morris Water Maze (Morris, 1984). Genetics can be controlled by dividing litter mates into experimental and control groups.

The best animal model developed to date pertains to physical activity, where a voluntary exercise paradigm has been employed. In this paradigm, a running wheel is made available to the animal for short (e.g., 4 weeks) or long periods of time (e.g., 5 months), with measurements of brain function and cognition conducted in those with exposure to the exercise paradigm vs. those without. Several consistent findings have emerged:

(1) Exercise enhances learning in the water maze in both young animals (Berchtold, Kesslak, & Cotman, 2002) and old animals (van Praag, Kemperman, & Gage, 2000).

(2) Exercise enhances mRNA expression of brain-derived neurotrophic factor (BDNF) in at least one subregion of the hippocampus (i.e., the dentate gyrus) (e.g., Berchtold et al., 2002; Farmer, Zhao, van Praag, Wodtke, Gage, & Christie, 2004).

(3) Exercise enhances neurogenesis in the hippocampus (e.g., Brown et al., 2003).

It is noteworthy that, while neurogenesis has been reported in young and

old animals in both the hippocampus and the olfactory bulb, the increase in neurogenesis following exercise occurs only in the hippocampus. Increases in BDNF expression likely serve to increase synaptic plasticity in nerve cells, while neurogenesis provides an increased supply of nerve cells in a brain region essential for normal memory. Investigators are currently examining the effects of varying factors such as frequency, duration, and age of exposure to exercise in order to determine the specific parameters of physical activity that might be most beneficial, as well as to more convincingly demonstrate a causal relationship between physical activity and cognition, rather than just an association (for reviews of these issues see Cotman & Berchtold, 2003; Dishman et al., 2006). The impact of physical exercise on animal models of Alzheimer's disease is described below.

The animal model most commonly used to mimic mental activity is the enriched environment (Hebb, 1947). In the current version of this paradigm, the enriched environment consists of an animal cage in which many objects have been placed that the animal can explore. Like the voluntary running wheel, duration of exposure can be varied, as can degree of stimulation (e.g., by changing the objects at varying frequencies and/or by altering the number of animals in the cage at the same time). Two consistent findings have emerged from this work as well: (a) an enriched environment enhances learning in the water maze (e.g., Kemperman, Kuhn, & Gage, 1997), and (b) an enriched environment enhances hippocampal neurogenesis, but not neurogenesis in the olfactory bulb (Brown et al., 2003). There are also reports of increased expression of growth factors, such as nerve growth factor (Pham et al., 1999), but these findings have been less widely replicated. The interpretation of the findings from these studies remains unclear, however, as investigators have not disentangled the overall effect of increased exercise in the enriched environment and mental enrichment. There have, in fact, been few direct comparisons of enrichment vs. exercise. One potential approach would be to determine if the benefits are additive, i.e., exposure to an enriched environment following exposure to exercise provides a greater change in the outcome measures than either intervention alone. It would also be helpful to find additional changes in the brain following both interventions than one alone (see van Praag et al., 2000 for a review of this issue). Difficulty with interpretation of the animal data increases the challenge of interpreting the human findings as well. It has been hypothesized that mentally stimulating activity may reduce risk of cognitive decline by strengthening processing skills such as working memory, permitting compensation for age-related declines, and thereby providing cognitive reserve. (The concept of cognitive reserve is discussed by Christensen and colleagues in chapter 4.) An alternative hypothesis is that mental activity

has a direct impact on AD pathology. This hypothesis has been tested in animal models and is discussed further below.

The animal models of social engagement have, to date, been limited and much less satisfactory. For example, restraining the movement of an animal for varying periods of time impairs memory performance (Conrad, Galea, Kuroda, & McEwen, 1996). It is hypothesized that this alteration is the result of increased glucocorticoid levels in the brain (glucocorticoids are adrenal steroid hormones secreted in response to stress). In addition, increasing glucocorticoid levels alters spatial memory, synaptic plasticity and hippocampal volume (e.g., Bodnoff, Humphreys, Lehman, Diamond, Rose, & Meaney, 1995). However, an animal model which establishes a firm connection between increased periods of stress, elevation of glucocorticoids, and damage to neuronal function has yet to be developed (for a review of these issues see Sapolsky, 2003).

Although there are animal models of individual vascular risk factors, such as increased blood pressure (Moore, Killianey, Rosene, Prusty, Hollander, & Moss, 2003), the association between increased vascular risks and cognitive decline has been best demonstrated through both epidemiological and clinical data in humans, rather than animal models. It has been demonstrated that older individuals with multiple vascular risks have poorer cognitive function than healthy controls (Selnes, Grega, Borowicz, Royall, McKhann, & Baumgartner, 2003), and that individuals with evidence of vascular risk factors are at greatest risk for cognitive decline (Elias et al., 2004; Grodstein, Chen, Wilson, & Manson, 2001; Pelia, White, Masaki, Petrovitch, & Launer, 2006; Qiu et al., 2006; Swan et al., 1998). Dietary patterns thought to alter vascular risks have also been associated with lowering risk for cognitive decline and dementia (Morris et al., 2003; Scarmeas, Stern, Tang, Mayeux, & Luchsinger, 2006). There is also evidence that the greater the number of vascular risks, the greater the likelihood of cognitive decline over time (Whitmer, Sidney, Selby, Johnston, & Yaffe, 2005).

Though the findings described above are quite consistent and have been replicated by numerous independent groups, the primary limitation in making specific recommendations to the general public is that the data in humans are primarily based on observational findings. There are some findings from controlled clinical trials, but these are limited. Small clinical trials have been conducted in the area of physical activity and these results have been encouraging. For example, it has been shown that exposing older individuals to a 6-month program of aerobic activity enhances performance on neuropsychological tasks (e.g., attention and executive functions), as well as increasing brain activation during a functional MRI task requiring complex attention (Erickson et al., 2006). Likewise, there have been a number of controlled clinical trials looking at

the effect of lowering blood pressure on cognitive decline, but the results have been mixed (McGuinness, Todd, Passmore, & Bullock, 2006), and no trials have examined more than one vascular risk factor at a time. Much more work needs to be done in this area before firm guidelines can be provided to the general public about the nature and type of lifestyle changes that are most likely to reduce the risk for cognitive decline.

A better understanding of the role of genetics would also be beneficial. As noted above, it is clear that genetic factors influence learning ability in general. For example, from studies of identical twins reared together vs. those reared apart, it appears that genetic factors account for approximately 50% of an older individual's memory performance (Finkel & McGue, 1998; Johansson, Whitfield, Pedersen, Hofer, Ahern, & McClearn, 1999; McClearn et al., 1997) (see chapter 2 by McGue & Johnson on Genetics of Cognitive Aging for a review). Thus, it is important to know if lifestyle factors can modify genetic risk for cognitive decline. Animal models have again been used to help address this issue. Several relevant studies have been conducted using transgenic mice, containing genetic mutations that increase risk for AD. These mice produce plaques, similar to those seen in AD, which contain the amyloid beta (Aβ) protein. Moreover, as the animals age, they develop memory problems above and beyond those seen by their litter mates without the genetic mutations.

Several studies have now examined whether exposure to an enriched environment or voluntary exercise improves memory in these transgenic animals and alters amyloid load. Those studies that have examined cognition consistently find that memory performance is improved in the mice exposed to the environmental manipulation. However, studies differ with regard to whether amyloid burden also decreases; some report reduced levels of Aβ (Adlard, Perreau, Pop, & Cotman, 2005; Lazarov et al., 2005), some report that levels of Aβ are stable (Arendash, Garcia, Costa, Cracchiolo, Wefes, & Potter, 2004), and some report increased amounts of Aβ (Jankowsky et al., 2005). Much work remains to be done to identify the methodological differences that contribute to these varying results.

In addition, the relationship between lifestyle factors and severity of AD pathology has been examined in a small number of recent studies. The findings suggest that level of education modifies the association of amyloid load with cognitive performance (Bennett et al., 2005b); a similar finding has also been reported for social network size as a modifier of the association between AD pathology and cognition (Bennett, Schneider, Tang, Arnold, & Wilson, 2006). These findings also need to be expanded in order to be fully understood.

APPENDIX

Typical Clinical Presentation of AD

Clinical Vignette

A 75-year-old female, married for almost 50 years, began having evidence of gradual cognitive decline. She had increasing difficulty remembering recent events. For example, from one week to the next she might forget a conversation she had with her daughter over the phone, she was increasingly likely to forget appointments with friends, and might forget to buy some of the items at the store that she needed to get. Over time, the memory problems became more pronounced, so that she might forget conversations from one day to the next, rather than one week to the next, and began asking the same questions over and over within a short period of time. She could, however, still remember important personal and political events from the past. In addition, multistepped tasks, such as cooking or balancing the checkbook, became problematic. For example, she had been an excellent cook, and on occasion would forget an essential ingredient in a recipe she knew well, or overcook one item in a meal, while another was underdone. In casual social situations she seemed unchanged, but she seemed less interested in spending time with family and friends, and when at community events was less likely to be actively engaged.

As these problems became gradually worse, her family realized that something was wrong and brought her for evaluation. Her neurological examination was unremarkable. She had a snout reflex and decreased ankle jerks, but no focal signs or symptoms. On mental status testing, she received a score of 25 on the Mini Mental State Examination (MMSE), losing 2 points on recall of the three items, losing 2 points on orientation, and 1 point on spelling WORLD backwards.

Formal neuropsychological testing showed impaired recall of a story after a delay, and impaired list learning and retention. She was impaired on Trails B of the Trail Making Test (which requires one to alternately connect numbers and letters in sequence); she took much longer than normal to complete the task, and made two errors. Her verbal fluency was decreased both for generation of words based on letters (e.g., F, A, S) and categories (e.g., animals). Her confrontation naming ability, as assessed by the Boston Naming Test, was slightly low. Trails A of the Trail Making Task (which only requires one to connect numbers in sequence) was, however, within normal limits, as was digit span forward (the ability to repeat a series of numbers in the order they were given).

A magnetic resonance imaging (MRI) scan showed atrophy, but no

evidence of strokes or other structural lesion. Laboratory tests performed to examine potential metabolic problems were within normal limits. She was taking medication for hypertension and hypercholesterolemia, both of which appeared to be well treated.

Over the course of the next 6 years, the cognitive problems became progressively worse. Her memory impairment was so severe that she no longer remembered getting married or recognized her children or grand-children. She developed progressive difficulty with language; over time she had more and more difficulty finding words in conversation. She was able to read but comprehension was gradually impaired. Her social inter-action was limited, as she was increasingly fearful outside the home and became agitated in group situations with a lot of activity.

On postmortem, she received a diagnosis of definite AD. She had wide-spread neuronal loss, and evidence of neuritic plaques and neurofibrillary tangles throughout the temporal, parietal and frontal lobes. She also had a couple of lacunar infarcts and other evidence of small vessel disease.

Clinical Issues

Cognitive Presentation

This clinical presentation typifies the vast majority of patients with AD. It is a disorder whose initial feature is gradually progressive difficulty with learning and retention of new information. This difficulty with epi-sodic memory is evident in day-to-day activities where retention over a delay is needed (such as remembering conversations and appointments), and on memory tasks that require an individual to learn something new (e.g., a story or a word list) and then retain it over a delay (Welsh et al., 1991). Once the disease is well established, impairments are evident on episodic memory tasks that assess both verbal and nonverbal information (Storandt & Hill, 1989).

Problems with executive function are also common in most patients early in the course of disease. Multistep tasks that require switching from one aspect of a task to another, such as preparing a meal, are particularly prone to difficulty. Neuropsychological tasks that emphasize set forma-tion and set switching are, likewise, most sensitive impairments in the early phase of disease. The Trail Making Test is a good example of this, particularly because it requires the individual to switch from one over-learned series to another (i.e., switching from numbers to letters, both of which must be connected in order).

The typical AD patient then develops problems with language. There are subtle problems with naming and verbal fluency early in disease. Some investigators have argued that this is because of an underlying

problem with semantic networks (Chan et al., 1993), an issue that is discussed further above. During the middle phase of disease, it is the language problems that become progressively worse. The patient has increasing difficulty finding the words to express themselves and understanding complex ideas or sentences. Interestingly, reading is generally preserved till late in the disease, but this is often accomplished with little understanding of what is being read.

Spatial abilities also experience the greatest decline in the middle stages of disease in patients with a typical presentation. As a consequence, tasks that involve copying two-dimensional figures are generally preserved in mildly impaired patients. It has been reported that tasks that involve a spatial component are impaired in mild AD, but this is usually because they make other types of cognitive demands as well. For example, clock copying is generally preserved in mildly impaired patients, whereas clock drawing to command, which requires planning and organization, as well as spatial ability, is not (Rouleau et al., 1996).

Sustained attention is well preserved in mild-to-moderately impaired AD patients. If a task is simple enough that the patient can keep the instructions in mind (e.g., as in digit span where one is asked to repeat a series of numbers in order), then it is generally performed within the normal range. This finding is so consistent, that impairments in attention in an otherwise mildly impaired patient are used as a marker that the patient has a disorder other than AD, such as dementia with Lewy bodies (McKeith, 2006) or delirium (Kramer & Reifler, 1992).

It should be noted that the symptoms of a small number of AD patients present and evolve in a different manner. In one group of patients onset is characterized by gradually progressive difficulty with spatial ability. Any task that requires spatial skill will be impaired. There is difficulty with episodic memory but in the early stage of disease there tends to be less loss of information over a delay than retention over a delay than is the case in the typical patient (Albert, Duffy, & McAnulty, 1990), leading to less memory impairment in daily life. For a second group of patients, the initial symptoms consist of gradually progressive difficulty with language ability, including problems with naming, comprehension, repetition, and reading. Both of these unusual presentations tend to occur in early onset cases and are, in fact, rare among patients over the age of 65.

Cognitive History

While cognitive testing is important in confirming the diagnosis of AD, a good cognitive history is essential. Since the patient's self-report may be unreliable, it is important to obtain a cognitive history from one or more

family members (or equivalent caregivers). The history needs to elicit information about three issues:

- the initial symptoms
- the time of onset
- the nature of progression.

Determining the initial symptoms will provide essential information regarding the diagnosis. For example, an early symptom of frontotemporal dementia (FTD) is often a change in personality (e.g., inappropriate behavior), while the most common early symptom of Alzheimer's disease is a gradually progressive decline in the ability to learn new information. Several years after the disease has begun, which is when most patients' conditions are actually diagnosed, the cognitive symptoms of the two disorders may be very similar, so that information regarding the initial symptoms may be critical to accurate diagnosis.

Establishing the time of onset will provide important clues regarding the nature of the disorder, because some diseases are well known for their particularly rapid rate of decline (e.g., Creutzfeldt-Jakob disease). It will also enable the clinician to give the family some tentative feedback regarding the course of the illness. If the point at which the disorder began is known, the rate of decline can be determined by seeing how long it has taken the patient to reach the present level of function. While estimates of the rate of progression can be only roughly approximated, it is extremely helpful for the family to have an estimate in making plans for the future.

Determining whether the initial symptoms came on suddenly or gradually also aids in diagnosis. If the onset of illness is gradual and insidious, as in Alzheimer's disease, it is often only in retrospect that the family realizes that a decline has occurred. In contrast, a series of small strokes, even if not evident on CT, generally produce a history of sudden onset and stepwise progression. There may, for example, be an incident (e.g., a fall or a period of confusion) that marks the beginning of the disorder. Delirium generally has an acute onset as well, although if they are the result of a condition such as drug toxicity, this may not be the case. The manner in which the symptoms have progressed over time also provides important diagnostic information. A stepwise deterioration, characterized by sudden exacerbations of symptoms, is most typical of multi-infarct dementia. However, a physical illness in a patient with Alzheimer's disease (e.g., pneumonia, a hip fracture, etc.) can cause a rapid decline in cognitive function. The sudden worsening of symptoms in a psychiatric patient (e.g., depression) also can produce an abrupt decrease in mental status. Careful questioning is therefore necessary to determine the underlying cause of a stepwise decline in function.

Neurological Examination, Laboratory, and Imaging Findings

The neurological examination is generally unremarkable in the early stage of AD. Thus it is most useful for identifying whether signs and symptoms of disorders other than AD are present (e.g., Parkinson's disease, Creutzfeldt-Jakob disease, Huntington's disease, etc.). Laboratory findings are also used to identify causes of cognitive decline that are unrelated to a neurodegenerative process (e.g., thyroid, liver or kidney disease, B12 deficiency, etc.). Likewise, in the clinical setting, imaging findings are generally used to determine whether other diseases, beside AD, are the cause of the patient's cognitive decline (e.g., strokes, tumors, etc.). In the United States, positron emission tomography (PET) is approved for reimbursement only for the differential diagnosis of AD vs. FTD. Thus, physicians are only supposed to request reimbursement from Medicare for a PET scan if FTD is suspected.

Diagnostic Criteria for AD

The clinical diagnostic criteria for AD encapsulate the description above. They require that the patient has a gradually progressive decline in two or more domains of cognition (with memory predominant), of sufficient severity to impair social and occupational function. As noted above, these criteria (American Psychiatric Association, 1994; McKhann et al., 1984) have been widely accepted for a number of decades. This uniformity of approach has greatly helped research into the underlying cause of the disease because it has meant that similar patient populations are likely to be included in studies regardless of their location around the world.

REFERENCES

Adlard, P., Perreau, V., Pop, V., & Cotman, C. (2005). Voluntary exercise decreases amyloid in a transgenic model of Alzheimer's disease. *Journal of Neuroscience, 25*, 4217–4221.

Albert, M., Blacker, D., Moss, M., Tanzi, R., & McArdle, J. (in press). Longitudinal change in cognitive performance among individuals with mild cognitive impairment. *Neuropsychology.*

Albert, M., Cohen, C., & Koff, E. (1991). Perception of affect in patients with dementia of the Alzheimer type. *Archives of Neurology, 48*, 791–795.

Albert, M., Duffy, F., & McAnulty, G. (1990). Electrophysiological comparisons between two groups of patients with Alzheimer's disease. *Archives of Neurology, 47*, 857–863.

Albert, M., Jones, K., Savage, C., Berkman, L., Seeman, T., Blazer, D. et al. (1995). Predictors of cognitive change in older persons: MacArthur Studies of Successful Aging. *Psychology and Aging, 10*, 578–589.

Albert, M., Moss, M., Tanzi, R., & Jones, K. (2001). Preclinical prediction of AD using neuropsychological tests. *Journal of the International Neuropsychological Society, 7*, 631–639.

Allender, J., & Kaszniak, A. W. (1989). Processing of emotional cues in patients with dementia of the Alzheimer's type. *International Journal of Neuroscience, 46*, 47–155.

Alzheimer, A. (1907) Uber eine eigenartige Erkrankugn der Hirnrinde. *Allgemeine Zeitschrift für Psychiatrie und psychisch-gerichtliche Medizin, 64*, 146–148.

American Psychiatric Association (1994). *Diagnostic and Statistical Manual* (4th ed.). Washington, DC: American Psychiatric Association.

Arendash, G., Garcia, M., Costa, D., Cracchiolo, J., Wefes, I., & Potter, H. (2004). Environmental enrichment improves cognition in aged Alzheimer's trangenic mice despite stable β amyloid deposition. *NeuroReport, 15*, 1751–1754.

Atiya, M., Hyman, B. T., Albert, M., & Killiany, R. (2003). Structural magnetic resonance imaging in established and prodromal Alzheimer's disease: A review. *Alzheimer Disease and Associated Disorders, 17*, 177–195.

Baddeley, A., Logie, R., Bressi, S., Della Sala, S., & Spinnler, H. (1986). Dementia and working memory. *Quarterly Journal of Experimental Psychology, 38*, 603–618.

Becker, J. T. (1988). Working memory and secondary memory deficits in Alzheimer's disease. *Journal of Clinical and Experimental Neuropsychology, 10*, 739–753.

Bennett, D., Schneider, J., Bienias, J., et al. (2005a). Mild cognitive impairment is related to Alzheimer pathology and cerebral infarctions. *Neurology, 64*, 834–841.

Bennett, D., Schneider, J., Tang, Y., Arnold, S., & Wilson, R. (2006). The effect of social networks on the relation between Alzheimer's disease pathology and level of cognitive function in old people: A longitudinal cohort study. *Lancet Neurology, 5*, 406–412.

Bennett, D., Schneider, J., Wilson, R., Bienias, J., & Arnold, S. (2005b) Education modifies the association of amyloid but not tangles with cognitive function. *Neurology, 65*, 953–955.

Berchtold, N., Kesslak, J., & Cotman, C. (2002). Hippocampal brain-derived neurotrophic factor gene regulation by exercise and the medial septum. *Journal of Neuroscience Research, 68*, 511–521.

Blacker, D., Albert, M., Bassett, S., Go, R., Harrell, E., & Folstein, M. (1994). Reliabiity and validity of NINCDS-ADRA criteria for Alzheimer's disease. The National Institute of Mental Health Genetics Initiative. *Archives of Neurology, 51*, 1198–1204.

Blacker, D., Lee, H., Muzikansky, A., Martin, E., Tanzi, R., McArdle, M., et al. (2007). Neuropsychological measures in normal individuals that predict subsequent cognitive decline. *Archives of Neurology, 64*, 862–871.

Blessed, G., Tomlinson, B. E., & Roth, M. (1968). The association between quantitative measures of dementia and of senile changes in the cerebral gray matter of elderly subjects. *British Journal of Psychiatry, 114*, 797–811.

Bodnoff, S., Humphreys, A., Lehman, J., Diamond, D., Rose, G., & Meaney, M. (1995). Enduring effects of chronic corticosterone treatment on spatial learning, synaptic plasticity, and hippocampal physiology in young and mid-aged rats. *Journal of Neuroscience, 66*, 235–240.

Bondi, M., Monsch, A., Galasko, D., Butters, N., Salmon, D., & Delis, D. (1994). Preclinical cognitive markers of dementia of the Alzheimer type. *Neuropsychology, 8*, 374–384.

Bondi, M., Serody, A., Chan, A., Eberson-Shumate, S., Delis, D., Hansen, L., et al. (2002). Cognitive and neuropathologic correlates of Stroop Color-Word Test performance in Alzheimer's disease. *Neuropsychology, 16*, 335–343.

Boustani, M., Peterson, B., Hanson, L., Harris, R., & Lohr, K. (2003). Screening for dementia in primary care: A summary of the evidence for the U.S. Preventive Services Task Force. *Annals of Internal Medicine, 138*, 927–937.

Braak, H., & Braak, E. (1998). Evolution of neuronal changes in the course of Alzheimer's disease. *Journal of Neural Transmission, Supplement, 53*, 127–140.

Braak, H., Del Tredici, K., Schultz, C., & Braak, E. (2000). Vulnerability of select neuronal types in Alzheimer's disease. *Annals of the New York Academy of Science, 924*, 53–61.

Brookmeyer, R., Gray, S., & Kawas, C. (1998). Projections of Alzheimer's disease in the

United States and the public health impact of delaying disease onset. *American Journal of Public Health, 88*, 1337–1342.

Brown, J., Cooper-Kuhn, C., Kemperman, G., van Praag, H., Winkler, J., Gage, F., et al. (2003). Enriched environment and physical activity stimulate hippocampal but not olfactory bulb neurogenesis. *European Journal of Neuroscience, 17*, 2042–2046.

Bush, G., Vogt, B. A., Holmes, J., Dale, A., Greve, D., Jenike, M., et al. (2002). Dorsal anterior cingulate cortex: A role in reward-based decision making. *Proceedings of the National Academy of Science, 99*, 523–528.

Butters, N., Salmon, D., Heindel, W., & Granholm, E. (1988). Episodic, semantic and procedural memory: Some comparisons of Alzheimer and Huntington disease patients. In: R. D. Terry (Ed.), *Aging and the brain* (pp. 63–87). New York: Raven Press.

Cadieux, N., & Greve, K. (1997). Emotion processing in Alzheimer's disease. *Journal of the International Neuropsychology Society, 3*, 411–419.

Chan, A. S., Butters, N., Paulsen, J. S., Salmon, D. P., Swenson, M., & Maloney, L. (1993). An assessment of the semantic network in patients with AD. *Journal of Cognitive Neuroscience, 5*, 254–61.

Chan, A. S., Butters, N., Salmon, D. P., Johnson, S., Paulsen, J., & Swenson, M. (1995). Comparison of the semantic networks in patients with dementia and amnesia. *Neuropsychology, 9*, 177–186.

Chan, A. S., Butters, N., & Salmon, D. P. (1997). The deterioration of semantic networks in patients with Alzheimer's disease: A cross-sectional study. *Neuropsychologia, 35*, 241–248.

Chen, P., Ratcliff, G., Belle, S., Cauley, J., DeKosky, S., & Ganguli, M. (2000). Cognitive tests that best discriminate between presymptomatic AD and those who remain nondemented. *Neurology, 55*, 1847–1853.

Chen, P., Ratcliff, G., Belle, S., Cauley, J., DeKosky, S., & Ganguli, M. (2001). Patterns of cognitive decline in presymptomatic Alzheimer disease: A prospective community study. *Archives of General Psychiatry, 58*, 853–858.

Conrad, C., Galea, L., Kuroda, Y., & McEwen, B. (1996). Chronic stress impairs rat spatial memory on the Y maze, and this effect is blocked by tianeptine pretreatment. *Behavioral Neuroscience, 110*, 1321–1334.

Copeland, M., Daly, E., Hines, V., Mastromauro, C., Zaitchik, D., Gunther, J., et al. (2003). Psychiatric symptomology and prodromal AD. *Alzheimer's Disease and Associated Disorders, 17*, 1–8.

Cotman, C., & Berchtold, N. (2003). Exercise: A behavioral intervention to enhance brain health and plasticity. *Trends in Neuroscience, 25*, 295–301.

Crossley, M., Hiscock, M., & Foreman, J. (2004). Dual-task performance in early stage dementia: Differential effects of automatic and effortful processing. *Journal of Clinical and Experimental Neuropsychology, 26*, 332–346.

Daly, E., Zaitchik, D., Copeland, M., Schmahmann, J., Gunther, J., & Albert, M. (2000). Predicting "conversion" to AD using standardized clinical information. *Archives of Neurology, 57*, 675–80.

Davis, H., & Rockwood, K. (2004). Conceptualization of mild cognitive impairment: A review. *International Journal of Geriatric Psychiatry, 19*, 313–319.

DeCarli, C. (2003). Mild cognitive impairment: prevalence, prognosis, aetiology and treatment. *Lancet Neurology, 2*, 15–21.

Dishman, R., Berthoud, H., Booth, F., Cotman, C., Edgerton, V., Fleshner, M., et al. (2006). Neurobiology of exercise. *Obesity, 14*, 345–356.

Elias, M., Sullivan, L., Agostino, R., Elias, P., Beiser, A., Au, R., et al. (2004). Framingham stroke risk profile and lowered cognitive performance. *Stroke, 35*, 404–409.

Erickson, K., Colcombe, S., Wadnwa, R., Bherer, L., Peterson, M., Scalf, P., et al. (2006)

Training-induced functional activation changes in dual-task processing: An fMRI study. *Cerebral Cortex, 17,* 192–204.

Farmer, J., Zhao, X., van Praag, H., Wodtke, K., Gage, F., & Christie, B. (2004). Effects of voluntary exercise on synaptic plasticity and gene expression in the dentate gyrus of adult male Sprague-Dawley rats in vivo. *Neuroscience, 124,* 71–79.

Fernandez-Duque, D., & Black, S. (2006) Attentional networks in normal aging and Alzheimer's disease. *Neuropsychology, 20,* 133–143.

Filoteo, J., Delis, D., Massman, P., Demadura, T., Butters, N., & Salmon, D. (1992). Directed and divided attention in Alzheimer's disease: Impairment in shifting attention to global and local stimuli. *Journal of Clinical and Experimental Neuropsychology, 14,* 871–883.

Finkel, D., & McGue, M. (1998). Age differences in the nature and origin of individual differences in memory: A behavior genetic analysis. *International Journal of Aging and Human Development, 47,* 217–239.

Fisk, J., Merry, H., & Rockwood, K. (2003). Variations in case definition affect prevalence but not outcomes of mild cognitive impairment. *Neurology, 61,* 1179–84.

Flicker, C., Ferris, S., & Reisberg, B. (1991). Mild cognitive impairment in the elderly: Predictors of dementia. *Neurology, 41,* 1006–1009.

Fodor, J. (1987). *Psychosemantics: The problem of meaning in the philosophy of mind.* Cambridge, MA: Bradford Books/MIT Press.

Folstein, M., Folstein, S., & McHugh, P. (1975). "Mini-mental state". A practical method for grading the cognitive state of patients for the clinician. *Journal of Psychiatric Research, 12,* 189–198.

Gabrieli, J., Corkin, S., & Mickel, S., Growdon, J. (1993). Intact acquisition and long-term retention of mirror tracking skill in Alzheimer's disease and global amnesia. *Behavioral Neuroscience, 107,* 899–910.

Garcia-Cuerva, A., Sabe, L., Kuzis, G., Tiberti, C., Dorrego, F., & Starkstein, S. (2001). Theory of mind and pragmatic abilities in dementia. *Neuropsychiatry, Neuropsychology, and Behavioral Neurology, 14,* 153–158.

Gautier, S., & Touchon, J. (2000). Mild cognitive impairment is not a clinical entity and should not be treated. *Archives of Neurol*ogy, *62,* 1164–1166.

Gilman, S., Koller, M., Black, R., Jenkins, L., Griffith, S., Fox, N., et al. (2005). Clinical effects of Aβ immunization (AN1792) in patients with AD in an interrupted trial. *Neurology, 64,* 1553–1562.

Glosser, G., Grugan, P.K., Friedman, R.B., Lee, J.H., & Grossman, M. (1998). Lexical, semantic, and associative priming in Alzheimer's disease. *Neuropsychology, 2,* 218–224.

Goldman, W., Price, J., Storandt, M., Grant, E., McKeel, D., Rubin, E., et al. (2001). Absence of cognitive impairment or decline in preclinical Alzheimer's disease. *Neurology, 56,* 361–367.

Gomez-Isla, T., Price, J. L., McKeel, D. W., Morris, J.C., Growdon, J. H., & Hyman, B. T. (1996). Profound loss of layer II entorhinal cortex neurons occurs in very mild Alzheimer's disease. *Journal of Neuroscience, 16,* 4491–4500.

Grady, C. L., Haxby, J. V., Horwitz, B., et al. (1988). Longitudinal study of the early neuropsychological and cerebral metabolic changes in dementia of the Alzheimer type. *Journal of Clinical and Experimental Neuropsychology, 10,* 576–596.

Gregory, C., Lough, S., Stone, V., Erzinclioglu, S., Martin, L., Baron-Cohen, S., et al. (2002). Theory of mind in patients with frontal variant frontotemporal dementia and Alzheimer's disease: theoretical and practical implications. *Brain, 125,* 752–764.

Grodstein, F., Chen, J., Wilson, R., & Manson, J. (2001). Type 2 diabetes and cognitive function in community-dwelling elderly women. *Diabetes Care, 24,* 1060–1065.

Grossman, M., Robinson, K., Biassou, N., White-Devine, T., & D'Esposito, M. (1998).

Semantic memory in AD: Representativeness, ontologic category, and material. *Neuropsychology, 12,* 34–42.

Hart, R. P., Kwentus, J. A., Harkins, S. W., & Taylor, J. R. (1988). Rate of forgetting in mild Alzheimer's type dementia. *Brain and Cognition, 7,* 31–38.

Hebb, D. O. (1947). The effects of early on problem-solving at maturity. *American Psychologist, 22,* 306–307.

Heinik, J., Solomesh, I., Shein, V., & Becker, D. (2002). Clock drawing test in mild and moderate dementia of the Alzheimer's type: A comparative and correlation study. *Journal of Geriatric Psychiatry, 17,* 480–485.

Hendrie, H., Albert, M., Butters, M., Gao, S., Knopman, D., Launer, L., et al. (2006). The NIH cognitive and emotional health project: Report of the critical evaluation study committee. *Alzheimer's and Dementia, 2,* 12–32.

Hodges, J., Salmon, D., & Butters, N. (1992). Semantic memory impairment in AD: Failure of access or degraded knowledge? *Neuropsychologia, 30,* 301–14.

Howieson, D., Camicioli, R., Quinn, J., Silbert, L., Care, B., Moore, M., et al. (2003). Natural history of cognitive decline in the oldest old. *Neurology, 60,* 1489–1494.

Hulette, C., Welsh-Bohmer, K., Murray, M., Saunders, A., Mash, D., & McIntyre, L. (1998). Neuropathological and neuropsychological changes in 'normal' aging: Evidence for pre-clinical Alzheimer disease in cognitively normal individuals. *Journal of Neuropathology and Experimental Neurology, 57,* 1168–1174.

Hwang, T., Masterman, D., Ortiz, F., Fairbanks, L., & Cummings, J. (2004). Mild cognitive impairment is associated with characteristic neuropsychiatric symptoms. *Alzheimer's Disease and Associated Disorders, 18,* 17–21.

Hyman, B. T., VanHoesen, G., Damasio, A., & Barnes, C. (1984). Alzheimer's disease: Cell specific pathology isolates the hippocampal formation. *Science, 225,* 1168–1170.

Jacobs, D., Sano, M., Dooneief, G., Marder, K., Bell, K., & Stern, Y. (1995). Neuropsychological detection and characterization of preclinical Alzheimer's disease. *Neurology, 45,* 957–962.

Jankowsky, J., Melnikova, T., Fadale, D., Xu, G., Slunt, H., Gonzales, V., et al. (2005). Environmental enrichment mitigates cognitive deficits in a mouse model of Alzheimer's disease. *Journal of Neuroscience, 25,* 5217–5224.

Johansson, B., Whitfield, K., Pedersen, N., Hofer, S., Ahern, F., & McClearn, G. (1999). Origins of individual differences in episodic memory in the oldest-old: A population-based study of identical and same-sect fraternal twins aged 80 and older. *Journals of Gerontology, Series B: Psychological Sciences and Social Sciences, 54,* 173–179.

Kantarci, K., & Jack, C. R. (2003) Neuroimaging in Alzheimer disease: An evidence-based review. *Neuroimaging Clinics of North America, 13,* 197–209.

Kararasch, M., Sinerva, E., Granholm, P., Rinne, J., & Laine, M. (2005). CERAD test performance in amnestic mild cognitive impairment and Alzheimer's disease. *Acta Neurologica Scandinavica, 111,* 172–179.

Karp, A., Paillard-Borg, S., Wang, H., Silverstein, M., Winblad, B., & Fratiglioni, L. (2006). Mental, physical and social components in leisure activities equally contribute to decrease dementia risk. *Dementia and Geriatric Cognitive Disorders, 21,* 65–73.

Katzman, R. (1976) The prevalence and malignancy of Alzheimer disease. A major killer. *Archives of Neurology, 33,* 217–218.

Kemperman, G., Kuhn, H., & Gage, F. (1997). More hippocampal neurons in adult mice living in an enriched environment. *Nature, 386,* 493–495.

Kluger, A., Ferris, S., Golomb, J., Mittelman, M., & Reisberg, B. (1999). Neuropsychological performance of decline in dementia in non-demented elderly. *Journal of Geriatric Psychiatry and Neurology, 12,* 168–179.

Knopman, D., Parisi, J., Salviati, A., Floriach-Robert, M., Boeve, B., Ivnik, R. J., et al. (2000).

Neuopathology of cognitively normal elderly. *Journal of Neuropathology and Experimental Neurology, 62*, 1087–1095.

Koff, E., Zaitchik, D., Montepare, J., & Albert, M. (1999). Processing of emotion through the visual and auditory domains by patients with Alzheimer's disease, *Journal of the International Neuropsychological Society, 5*, 32–40.

Kramer, S., & Reifler, B. (1992). Depression, dementia and reversible dementia. *Clinics in Geriatric Medicine, 8*, 289–297.

Kurylo, D., Corkin, S., & Growdon, J. (1994). Perceptual organization in Alzheimer's disease. *Psychology and Aging, 9*, 562–567.

Lafleche, G., & Albert, M. (1995). Executive function deficits in mild Alzheimer's disease. *Neuropsychology, 9*, 313–320.

Lafleche, G. C., Stuss, D. T., Nelson, R. F., & Picton, T. W. (1990). Memory scanning and structured learning in Alzheimer's disease and Parkinson's disease. *Canadian Journal of Aging, 9*, 120–134.

Larrieu, S., Letenneur, L., Orgogozo, J., et al. (2002). Incidence and outcome of mild cognitive impairment: A population-based prospective cohort. *Neurology, 59*, 1594–1599.

Laurin, D.,Verreault, R., Lindsay, J., MacPherson, K., & Rockwood, K. (2001). Physical activity and risk of cognitive impairment and dementia in elderly persons. *Archives of Neurology, 58*, 498–504.

Lazarov, O., Robinson, J., Tang, Y.-P., Hairston, I., Korade-Mirnics, Z., Lee, V., et al. (2005). Environmental enrichment reduces Aβ levels and amyloid deposition in transgenic mice. *Cell, 120*, 701–713.

Levinoff, E., Saumier, D., & Chertkow, H. (2005). Focused attention deficits in patients' Alzheimer's disease and mild cognitive impairment. *Brain and Cognition, 57*, 127–130.

McClearn, G., Johansson, B., Berg, S., Pedersen, N., Ahern, F., Petrill, S., et al. (1997). Substantial genetic influence on cognitive abilities in twins 80 or more years old. *Science, 276*, 1560–1563.

McGuinness, B., Todd, S., Passmore, P., & Bullock, R. (2006). The effects of blood pressure lowering on development of cognitive impairment and dementia in patients without apparent prior cerebrovascular disease. *Cochrane Database System Review, 2*, CD004034.

McKeith, I. (2006). Consensus guidelines for the clinical and pathologic diagnosis of dementia with Lewy bodies (DLB): Report of the consortium on DLB International Workshop. *Journal of Alzheimer's Disease, 9*, 417–423.

McKhann, G., Drachman, D., Folstein, M. F., Katzman, R., Price, D., & Stadlan, E. (1984). Clinical diagnosis of Alzheimer's disease: Report of the NINCDS-ADRDA work group under the auspices of Department of Health and Human Services Task Force. *Neurology, 34*, 939–944.

Manly, J., Jacobs, D., Sano, M., Bell, K., Merchant, C., Small, S., et al. (1999). Effect of literacy on neuropsychological test performance in nondemented, education-matched elders. *Journal of the International Neuropsychological Society, 5*, 191–202.

Martin, A., & Fedio, P. (1983). Word production and comprehension in Alzheimer's disease: The breakdown of semantic knowledge. *Brain and Language, 39*, 124–141.

Mickanin, J., Grossman, M., Onishi, K., Auriacombe, S., & Clark, C. (1994). Verbal and nonverbal fluency in patients with probable Alzheimer's disease. *Neuropsychology, 8*, 385–394.

Milberg, W., & Albert, M. (1989). Cognitive differences between patients with PSP and Alzheimer's disease. *Journal of Clinical and Experimental Neuropsychology, 11*, 605–614.

Milberg, W. P., McGlinchey-Berroth, R., Duncan, K. M., & Higgins, J. (1999). Alterations in the dynamics of semantic activation in Alzheimer's disease: Evidence for the gain/decay hypothesis of a disorder of semantic memory. *Journal of the International Neuropsychological Society, 5*, 641–658.

Milham, M. P., Erickson, K., Banich, M. T., Kramer, A. F., Webb, A., Wszalek, T., et al. (2002). Attentional control in the aging brain: Insights from an fMRI study of the Stroop task. *Brain and Cognition, 49,* 277–296.

Mohs, R. (1996) The Alzheimer's Disease Assessment Scale. *International Psychogeriatrics, 8,* 195–203.

Mohs, R., Knopman, D., Petersen, R., Ferris, S., Ernesto, C., Grundman, M., et al. (1997). Development of cognitive instruments for use in clinical trials of antidementia drugs: Additions to the Alzheimer's Disease Assessment Scale that broaden its scope. *Alzheimer's Disease and Associated Disorders, 11,* S13–21.

Moore, T., Killiany, R., Rosene, D., Prusty, S., Hollander, W., & Moss, M. (2003) Hypertension-induced changes in monoamine receptors in the prefrontal cortex of rhesus monkeys. *Neuroscience, 120,* 177–189.

Morris, J., Storandt, M., Miller, J., McKeel, D., Price, J., et al. (2001) Mild cognitive impairment represents early-stage Alzheimer's disease. *Archives of Neurology, 58,* 397–405.

Morris, M., Evans, D., Bienias, J., Tangney, C., Bennett, D., Wilson, R., et al. (2003). Consumption of fish and n-3 fatty acids and risk of incident Alzheimer disease. *Archives of Neurology, 60,* 940–946.

Morris, R. (1984). Developments of a water-maze procedure for studying spatial learning in the rat. *Journal of Neuroscience, 11,* 47–60.

Morris, R. G., & Baddeley, A. D. (1988). Primary and working memory functioning in Alzheimer-type dementia. *Journal of Clinical and Experimental Neuropsychology, 10,* 276–279.

Morrison, J., & Hof, P. (2002). Selective vulnerability of corticocortical and hippocampal circuits in aging and Alzheimer's disease. *Progress in Brain Research, 136,* 467–486.

Moss, M. B., & Albert, M. S. (1988). Alzheimer's disease and other dementing disorders. In M. S. Albert & M. B. Moss (Eds.), *Geriatric neuropsychology* (pp. 145–178). New York: Guilford Press.

Moss, M. B., Albert, M. S., Butters, N., & Payne, M. (1986). Differential patterns of memory loss among patients with Alzheimer's disease, Huntington's disease and Alcoholic Korsakoff's Syndrome. *Archives of Neurology, 43,* 239–246.

Mueller, S., Weiner, M., Thal, L., Petersen, R., Jack, C., Jagust, W., et al. (2005) The Alzheimer's Disease Neuroimaging Initiative. *Neuroimaging Clinics of North America, 15,* 869–877.

Nebes, R. D., & Brady, C. B. (1988) Integrity of semantic fields in Alzheimer's disease. *Cortex, 24,* 291–299.

Nestor, P. G., Parasuraman, R., & Haxby, J. V. (1991). Speed of information processing and attention in early Alzheimer's dementia. *Developmental Neuropsychology, 7,* 243–236.

Newmann, S., Warrington, E., Kennedy, A., & Rossor, M. (1994) The earliest cognitive change in a person with familial Alzheimer's disease: Presymptomatic neuropsychological features in a pedigree with familial Alzheimer's disease confirmed at necropsy. *Journal of Neurology, Neurosurgery, and Psychiatry, 57,* 967–972.

Pelia, R., White, L., Masaki, K., Petrovitch, H., & Launer, L. (2006). Reducing risk of dementia: Efficacy of long-term treatment of hypertension. *Stroke, 37,* 1165–1170.

Petersen, R. (2004). Mild cognitive impairment. *Journal of Internal Medicine, 256,* 183–194.

Petersen, R., & Morris, J. (2005). Mild cognitive impairment as a clinical entity and treatment target. *Archives of Neurology, 62,* 1160–1163.

Petersen, R., Parisi, J., Dickson, D., Johnson, K., Knopman, D., Boeve, B., et al. (2006). Neuropathologic features of amnestic mild cognitive impairment. *Archives of Neurology, 63,* 665–672.

Petersen, R., Smith, G., Ivnik, R., Kokmen, E., & Tangalos, E. (1994). Memory function in very early Alzheimer's disease. *Neurology, 44,* 867–872.

Petersen, R., Smith, G., Waring, S., Ivnik, R., Tangalos, E., & Kokmen, E. (1999). Mild

cognitive impairment: Clinical characterization and outcome. *Archives of Neurology, 56,* 303–308.

Pfeiffer, E. (1975). A short portable mental status questionnaire for the assessment of organic brain deficit in elderly patients. *Journal of the American Geriatric Society, 23,* 433–441.

Pham, T., Ickes, B., Albeck, D., Soderstrom, S., Granholm, A., & Mohammed, A. (1999). Changes in brain nerve growth factor levels and nerve growth factor receptors in rats exposed to environmental enrichment for one year. *Neuroscience, 94,* 279–286.

Powlishta, K., Von Dras, D., Stamford, A., Carr, D., Tsering, C., Miller, J., et al. (2002). The clock drawing test is a poor screen for very mild dementia. *Neurology, 59,* 898–903.

Qiu, C., Winblad, B., & Fratiglioni, L. (2006) Cerebrovascular disease, APOE epsilon4 allele and cognitive decline in a cognitively normal population. *Neurology Research, 28,* 650–656.

Ritchie, K., Artero, S., & Touchon, J. (2001) Classification criteria for mild cognitive impairment: A population-based validation study. *Neurology, 56,* 37–42.

Rouleau, I., Salmon, D., & Butters, N. (1996). Longitudinal analysis of clock drawing in Alzheimer's disease patients. *Brain and Cognition, 31,* 7–34.

Rouleau, I., Salmon, D., Butters, N., Kennedy, C., & McGuire, K. (1992) Quantitative and qualitative analyses of clock drawings in Alzheimer's and Huntington's disease. *Brain and Cognition, 18,* 70–87.

Rouleau, I., Salmon, D., & Virbancic, M. (2002). Learning, retention and generalization of mirror tracking skill in Alzheimer's disease. *Journal of Clinical and Experimental Neuropsychology, 24,* 239–250.

Rovio, S., Kareholt, I., Helkala, E., Viitanen, M., Winblad, B., Tuomilehto J., et al. (2005). Leisure-time physical activity at midlife and risk of dementia and Alzheimer's disease. *Lancet Neurology, 4,* 705–711.

Rubin, E., Morris, J., Grant, E., & Vendegna, T. (1989) Very mild senile dementia of the Alzheimer type. I. Clinical assessment. *Archives of Neurology, 46,* 379–382.

Sahakian, B., Downes, J., Eagger, S., Evenden, J., Levy, R., Philpot, M., et al. (1990) Sparing of attentional relative to mnemonic function in a subgroup of patients with dementia of the Alzheimer type. *Neuropsychologia, 28,* 1197–1213.

Salmon, D. P., Shimamura, A. P., Butters, N., & Smith, S. (1988) Lexical and semantic priming deficits in patients with Alzheimer's disease. *Journal of Clinical and Experimental Neuropsychology, 10,* 477–494.

Sapolsky, R. (2003). Stress and plasticity in the limbic system. *Neurochemical Research, 28,* 1735–1742.

Saxton, J., Lopez, O., Ratcliff, G., Dulberg, C., Fried, L., Carlson, M., et al. (2004) Preclinical Alzheimer's disease: Neuropsychological test performance 1.5 to 8 years prior to onset. *Neurology, 63,* 2341–2347.

Scarmeas, N., Levy, G., Tang, M., Manly, J., & Stern, Y. (2001). Influence of leisure activity on the incidence of Alzheimer's disease. *Neurology, 57,* 2236–2242.

Scarmeas, N., Stern, Y., Tang, M-X., Mayeux, R., & Luchsinger, J. (2006). Mediterranean diet and risk for Alzheimer's disease. *Annals of Neurology, 59,* 912–921.

Schmand, B., Smit, J., Geerlings, M., & Lindeboom, J. (1997). The effects of intelligence and education on the development of dementia. A test of the brain reserve hypothesis. *Psychological Medicine, 27,* 1337–1344.

Schmitt, F., Davis, D., Wekstein, D., Smith, C., Ashford, J., & Markesbery, W. (2000). 'Preclinical' AD revisited: Neuropathology of cognitively normal older adults. *Neurology, 55,* 370–376.

Selkoe, D. (2005). Defining molecular targets to prevent Alzheimer disease. *Archives of Neurology, 62,* 192–195.

Selnes, O., Grega, M., Borowicz, L., Royall, R., McKhann, G., & Baumgartner, W. (2003). Cognitive changes with coronary artery disease: A prospective study of coronary

artery bypass graft patients and nonsurgical controls. *Annals of Thoracic Surgery, 75,* 1377–1384.

Siegerschmidt, E., Mosch, E., Siemen, M., Forstl, H., & Bickel, H. (2002). The clock drawing test and questionable dementia: Reliability and validity. *International Journal of Geriatric Psychiatry, 17,* 1048–1054.

Silveri, M. C., Daniele, A., Giustolisi, L., & Gainotti, G. (1991). Dissociation between living and nonliving things in dementia of the Alzheimer type. *Neurology, 41,* 545–546.

Small, G., LaRue, A., Komo, S., Kaplan, A., & Mandelkern, M. (1995). Predictors of cognitive change in middle-aged and older adults with memory loss. *American Journal of Psychiatry, 152,* 1757–1764.

Solomon, P., Hirschoff, A., Kelly, B., Relin, M., Brush, M., DeVeaux, R., et al. (1998). A 7-minute neurocognitive screening battery highly sensitive to Alzheimer's disease. *Archives of Neurology, 55,* 349–355.

Squire, L. R., & Zola, S. M. (1996). Structure and function of declarative and nondeclarative memory systems. *Proceedings of the National Academy of Sciences, 93,* 13515–13522.

Storandt, M., & Hill, R. D. (1989). Very mild senile dementia of the Alzheimer type. II. Psychometric test performance. *Archives of Neurology, 46,* 383–386.

Swan, G., DeCarli, C., Miller, B., Reed, T., Wolf, P., Jack, L., et al. (1998). Association of midlife blood pressure to late-life cognitive decline and brain morphology. *Neurology, 51,* 986–993.

Tierney, M., Szalai, J., Snow, W., Fisher, R., Nores, A., Nadon, G., et al. (1996). Prediction of probable Alzheimer's disease in memory-impaired patients: A prospective longitudinal study. *Neurology, 46,* 661–665.

Tierney, M., Yao, C., Kiss, A., & McDowell, I. (2005). Neuropsychological tests accurately predict incident Alzheimer's disease after 5 and 10 years. *Neurology, 64,* 1853–1859.

Tippett, L.J., Grossman, M., & Farah, M. J. (1996). The semantic memory impairment of Alzheimer's disease: Category specific? *Cortex, 32,* 143–153.

Troster, A., Salmon, D., McCullough, D., & Butters, N. (1989). A comparison of the category fluency deficits associated with Alzheimer's and Huntington's disease. *Brain and Language, 37,* 500–513.

Tuokko, H., Vernon-Wilkinson, J., Weir, J., & Beattie, W. (1991) Cued recall and early identification of dementia. *Journal of Clinical and Experimental Neuropsychology, 13,* 871–879.

van Praag, H., Kemperman, G., & Gage, F. (2000). Neural consequences of environmental enrichment. *Nature Reviews, 1,* 191–197.

Verghese, J., Lipton, R., Katz, M., Hall, C., Derby, C., Kuslansky, G., et al. (2003). Leisure activities and the risk of dementia in the elderly. *New England Journal of Medicine, 348,* 2508–2516.

Vitek, J., Bakay, R., Freeman, A., Evatt, M., Green, J., McDonald, W., et al. (2003). Randomized trial of pallidotomy versus medical therapy for Parkinson's disease. *Annals of Neurology, 53,* 558–569.

Warrington, E. K. (1975). The selective impairment of semantic memory. *Quarterly Journal of Experimental Psychology, 27,* 635–657.

Watson, Y., Arfken, C., & Birge, S. (1993). Clock completion: An objective screening test for dementia. *Journal of the American Geriatric Society, 41,* 1235–1240.

Welsh, K., Butters, N., Hughes, J., Mohs, R., & Heyman, A. (1991). Detection of abnormal memory decline in mild cases of Alzheimer's disease using CERAD neuropsychological measures. *Archives of Neurology, 48,* 278–281.

Welsh, K., Butters, N., Hughes, J., Mohs, R., & Heyman, A. (1992). Detection and staging in Alzheimer's disease: Use of the neuro psychological measures developed for the consortium to establish a registry for Alzheimer's disease. *Archives of Neurology, 49,* 448–452.

Weuve, J., Kang, J., Manson, J., Breteler, M., Ware, J., & Grodstein, F. (2004). Physical activity,

including walking, and cognitive function in older women. *Journal of the American Medical Association, 292,* 1454–1461.

Whitmer, R., Sidney, S., Selby, J., Johnston, S., & Yaffe, K. (2005). Midlife cardiovascular risk factors and risk of dementia in late life. *Neurology, 64,* 277–281.

Wilson, R., Bacon, L., Fox, P., & Kaszniak, A. (1983). Primary memory and secondary memory in dementia of the Alzheimer type. *Journal of Clinical Neuropsychology, 5,* 337–344.

Wilson, R., Bennett, D., Bienias, J., Mendes DeLeon, C., Morris, M., & Evans, D. (2003). Cognitive activity and cognitive decline in a biracial community population. *Neurology, 61,* 812–816.

Wilson, R., Mendes DeLeon, C., Barnes, L., Schneider, J., Bienias, J., Evans, D., et al. (2002). Participation in cognitively stimulating activities and risk of incident Alzheimer's disease. *Journal of the American Medical Association, 287,* 742–748.

Yaffe, K., Petersen, R., Linquist, K., Kramer, J., & Miller, B. (2006). Subtype of mild cognitive impairment and progression to dementia and death. *Dementia and Geriatric Cognitive Disorders, 22,* 312–319.

Zaitchik, D., Koff, E., Brownell, H., Winner, E., & Albert, M. (2006). Inference of belief and emotions in patients with Alzheimer's disease. *Neuropsychology, 20,* 11–20.

4

Intelligence, Education, and the Brain Reserve Hypothesis

Helen Christensen
Kaarin J. Anstey
Liana S. Leach
Andrew J. Mackinnon
The Australian National University

SYNOPSIS

The brain reserve hypothesis (BRH) is an influential hypothesis in neurology and cognitive science. It has proved difficult to advance empirically, largely because there are different conceptualizations, and because the notion of reserve varies. In this chapter, we describe a number of empirical strategies that have been used by researchers to investigate the hypothesis. We argue that these strategies largely provide supporting evidence rather than critical tests of the hypothesis. A systematic review of research studies is then undertaken to investigate both the supporting evidence and direct tests of the hypothesis.

Seventy-three papers from a variety of sources were included. We summarize the findings with respect to four broad areas:

- the relationship between intelligence, education, occupation and measures of head size, brain volume or specific brain volumes of a variety of regions of interest
- the association between intelligence/education and brain atrophy
- the effect of age and dementia on the relationship between various brain indices and intelligence or education
- a review of studies directly testing the "true brain reserve hypothesis."

A number of relationships are clearly supported between indices of the brain (such as head size and brain volume) and intellectual functioning in

133

young people. These relationships, based on cross-sectional data, include: a consistent, small to moderate sized relationship between head size or brain volume and intelligence and education; with a roughly equivalent association found for both performance and verbal intelligence, and for men and women. The association is present for specialized brain structures such as the hippocampus, and becomes weaker with increased age of the sample. We identify gaps in the research literature, especially with respect to longitudinal change in brain volume (atrophy) and measures of reserve, and a paucity of research papers directly addressing the true brain reserve hypothesis.

Finally, we suggest that for the BRH to progress, there needs to be specification of the brain injury, the proposed buffer (reserve), the biological mechanisms giving rise to reserve, and the predicted outcome. We identify multiple versions of the brain reserve hypothesis. Future areas of investigation will focus on the mechanisms by which reserve emerges from the brain, the way in which brain structure or function gives rise to *g* and whether dementia or "normal" aging are associated with different types of reserve.

INTRODUCTION

> Players sustaining injury during the course of the match and not in a condition to continue, even if temporary, shall be substituted or replaced at the next stoppage in play. A team shall be comprised of a minimum number of 15 athletes and seven substitutes. A team can substitute up to two front row players and five other players. Substitutions may only be made when the ball is dead and with the permission of the referee.
>
> (Official International Rugby Board website, *http://www.irb.com*, accessed 25 February 2006)

Background

Research into the relationship between the size and physical structure of the brain and cognitive capacity has accelerated rapidly over the last 20 years. More than 40 review papers examine correlations between cognitive abilities and a range of brain indices including head size, brain shape, brain volume, and volume of various locations or regions of interest. Encompassing diverse theoretical perspectives, these reviews can be classified into five types. The first type comprises comparative reviews of studies investigating brain size in a variety of animals including humans. The second investigates the relationship between intelligence and brain structure in (mostly) young volunteer samples. These reviews include studies attempting to identify the biological basis of intelligence and

studies with a focus on gender differences in brain size and intellectual performance. A third set of studies details relationships between intelligence, the brain, and racial groupings. Reviews in the fourth group focus on the way in which age is associated with changes in both the brain and intelligence, and the effect of Alzheimer's disease (AD) on pathology and brain atrophy. A fifth class of reviews concerns the relationship between brain structure and cognitive abilities from the perspective of the brain reserve hypothesis (BRH). A number of these reviews and landmark studies are listed in Table 4.1.

Although these reviews address related questions and summarize similar literature, little synthesis across these areas of discourse is apparent. For example, findings from reviews addressing the potential biological basis of *g* are highly relevant to an understanding of the biological basis of brain aging. However, these topics are rarely reviewed in the neuroscience literature relevant to the BRH. Research into the psychology of individual differences in intelligence is rarely integrated with research from neurology, cognitive science, or aging. The aim of the present chapter is to draw together literature from these traditions using a framework derived from recent formulations of the BRH.

Definitions and Development of the Brain Reserve Hypothesis

The BRH is a ubiquitous, highly influential, and frequently invoked concept applied in neuropsychology, neuropsychiatry, neurology, and cognitive aging. Historically, the hypothesis began with concrete anatomical views of reserve (bigger brain, more neurons, greater reserve) but recently, with the advent of functional neuroimaging, views of reserve as dynamic network capabilities are emerging (Stern et al., 2005). We start here with the original conceptions of the reserve hypothesis. Briefly stated, the hypothesis is that high premorbid intelligence, education, an active, stimulating lifestyle, or a physically larger brain provide reserve capacity which protects the individual from the negative effects of aging and disease on brain function (Cohen, 2000; Satz et al., 1993). More recently, genetic makeup, including the presence of apolipoprotein (APOE) ε4 allele (Bunce, in press), has been explicitly proposed as a contributor to reserve. The BRH was originally introduced to explain the substantial dissociation observed between brain damage and cognitive and functional performance.

As early as the 1930s, Rothschild (1937) noted a lack of clear correspondence between brain structure and cognitive performance. Classic studies (Roth, Tomlinson, & Blessed, 1966; Tomlinson, Blessed, & Roth, 1970) supported a threshold mechanism underpinning the development of functional incapacity. On autopsy, these investigators reported a broad

TABLE 4.1
Reviews and Landmark Studies

Type of Review	Purpose of the Research
Comparative studies of brain size	**Studies of brain–body sizes in animals provide an understanding of the nature of intelligence**
Passingham (1975)	This paper examines the use of the neocortex medulla volume as a measure of responsiveness to novel objects. It considers indices of brain development and notes that a comparison of the size of the brain is not helpful between species, and that the brain–body ratio will often advantage smaller animals.
Passingham, Stephan, and Kotter (2002)	It has been claimed that our frontal lobes, and in particular the prefrontal cortex, may be relatively more enlarged in the human brain relative to other animals. The ratio of frontal cortex to brain size in humans is greater than in monkeys and gibbons, but not greater than the great apes at 38%. The prefrontal cortex is about twice as large as expected, based on the size of the entire neocortex.
Gibson (2002)	Examines models for the evolution of human intelligence with respect to roles of brain size and mental ability.
Marino (2005)	Examines brain–body ratios in animals reporting that "various measures of brain size are positively correlated with feeding innovation, tool use and learning, social complexity, behaviour repertoire in mammals, and unpredictability of the environment in hominids . . ." (p. 5306). Large brains confer an advantage when responding to variable, unpredictable, and novel ecological demands through enhanced behavioral flexibility, learning, and innovation.
Roth and Dicke (2005)	Brain properties assumed to correlate with intelligence include the size of the brain, the cortex, the prefrontal cortex, and the degree of encephalization. However, the number of cortical neurons and conduction velocity correlate better.
Brain and intelligence relationships	**An attempt to establish the biological basis of g in humans**
Van Valen (1974)	Reviewed eight previous studies of the relationship between head size and IQ tests or school grades. A correlation of 0.30 was reported between brain size and intelligence. Examined three explanations: an artifact, mediation by a secondary factor (such as nutrition), or a true effect.
Lynn (1999)	A theoretical review of sex differences in intelligence and brain size, which explores explanations for the relatively smaller brain size of women and the lack of difference in intelligence between men and women. Proposes that IQ differences do emerge after 14 years of age, and this can be accounted for by differential developmental rates between the sexes.

Vernon, Wickett, Bazana, and Stelmack (2000)	Reported the association between head size and intelligence as 0.19 and the association between in vivo head size and intelligence as 0.33.
Nguyen and McDaniel (2000)	Examined the relationship between head and three subcategories of external head measurement and reported correlations between 0.17 to 0.26. Head size and intelligence were correlated 0.37 based on 14 correlations.
Ree and Carretta (2002)	This paper focuses on the potential biological substrate of g. A series of physiological correlates of g are summarized. These include brain size, brain myelination, brain electrical potential, speed of neural processing, brain glucose metabolism rate.
Kaplan and Robson (2002)	A paper examining the evolution of the large human brain.
Gignac, Vernon, and Wickett (2003)	Examined brain size and intelligence and reported an overall association of 0.37.
McDaniel (2005)	This review focused on in vivo measures of full brain volume and measures of intelligence in 37 samples. Measures of general intelligence were correlated. The uncorrected estimate for the relationship was 0.29 and the corrected estimate was 0.33.

Brain, intelligence, and race — An attempt to establish the biological basis of g in humans and to interpret differences in cognitive ability

Miller (1991)	Racial differences in intelligence arose from cold climates.
Lynn (1991)	Presents evidence that there are racial differences in intelligence and suggests that selection pressures favored enhanced intelligence. Evidence is presented of brain size differences. This paper also summarizes 16 studies on head size and intelligence.
Rushton and Ankney (1996)	The established relationship between brain size and intelligence is reported to be about 0.40. Head perimeter measures are estimated at 0.20. Head size is significantly correlated with IQ within families. IQ at birth correlates with IQ age 7. Racial differences remain even after corrections are made for head size and other variables.
Kamin and Omari (1998)	Racial differences in head circumference and shape are reviewed.
Rushton and Jensen (2005)	The "culture only" and the "hereditarian" models of the causes of cognitive differences between black and white populations are assessed. Thirty years of research is summarized.

The aging brain — Reviews address the biological basis of cognitive aging effects

Almkvist and Winblad (1999)	Examines the evidence for early markers of AD. Reports that AD patients have atrophy, particularly in the medial temporal lobes, and atrophy in the hippocampus.
Buckner (2004)	This paper describes the brain mechanisms underlying memory loss in older adults and those with AD. It concludes that functional imaging studies suggest "increased areas of brain recruitment" which reflect compensation. The BRH is discussed.

(Continued)

TABLE 4.1
(Continued)

Type of Review	Purpose of the Research
Raz et al. (2005)	Although not a review, the study summarizes brain changes in aging in health adults. The study found non-uniform changes in brain structure with greatest shrinkage in caudate, cerebellum, hippocampus, and tertiary association areas. Longitudinal changes were noted for the cerebellum, prefrontal white matter, visual cortex, and inferior temporal cortex.
Cerebral reserve capacity	**Studies of the brain reserve hypothesis**
Satz (1993)	Earliest review putting forward a theory of brain reserve capacity. Provides a review of relevant literature with respect to a range of indices of reserve, and with respect to injury, disease, and aging.
Schofield (1999)	A review of the reserve hypothesis as it relates to AD.
Stern (2002)	This review describes passive and active models of reserve, and distinguishes between optimization and compensation.
Fein and Di Sclafani (2004)	Provides a brief and useful overview of the brain reserve hypothesis, including a brief discussion of early evidence, functional and brain imaging studies, and the relationship between AD and intelligence and education. The theory is then discussed with reference to alcoholism and drug addiction.
Scarmeas and Stern (2004)	A review of epidemiological evidence examining the association between education, intelligence, and occupation and risk for AD.
Whalley, Deary, Appleton, and Starr (2004)	Reviews structural and functional brain imaging studies and describes plausible neural substrates of cognitive reserve.
Valenzuela and Sachdev (2006)	A review of evidence of BRH on incident dementia. The review focuses on 22 longitudinal cohort studies of the incidence of dementia.

distribution of senile plaques that were only modestly related to pre-death cognitive impairment. Frank cognitive impairment was present only above a certain threshold of plaque density. Katzman et al. (1988), in a study of 137 nursing home residents, found that 10 individuals with high levels of neocortical plaques at autopsy demonstrated pre-death cognitive performance within the limits of nondemented subjects. The brains of these individuals were characterized by a greater number of neurons and greater weight, relative to the poorer functioning individuals. Katzman et al. concluded that these individuals may have had AD but were cognitively intact because of a greater neuronal reserve associated with their larger brains. Mortimer (1997) also described the results of prospective studies showing that older, nondemented individuals met neuropathological criteria for AD, but did not show clinical expressions of the disease.

Other similar findings followed, including major studies such as that of Mori et al. (1997) who examined associations between premorbid brain volume and brain atrophy on the one hand, and intelligence, language ability, and memory deficits on the other, in patients with AD. Premorbid brain size was positively correlated with intelligence and negatively with the amount of brain atrophy. Brain atrophy, but not brain size, was associated with memory and language deficits in AD. Premorbid brain volume was seen to be a determinant of reserve capacity, with cognitive impairment only obvious once a threshold of damage was reached. However, the differential results for intelligence, compared to memory and language ability in this study, suggested that reserve might be more beneficial for specific cognitive abilities. Graves, Mortimer, Larson, Wendow, and Bowen (1996) in a study of 1985 Japanese Americans aged 65 years or older also noted that those with a small premorbid brain were associated with an earlier onset or a more rapid clinical progression of the disease than those with a larger premorbid brain. In a follow-up study, Graves et al. (2001) reported that head circumference (lowest tertile of head circumference) predicted incidence of dementia in this cohort. Smaller head size, when combined with APOE ε4, was associated with accelerated development of AD. In these clinical studies of dementia patients, large premorbid brain size or some other neurological feature was commonly argued to be the protective factor against decline in intellectual abilities and risk of dementia.

Other research work has focused on the relationship between educational level, as a measure of reserve, and brain structure. Individuals with higher education or premorbid intelligence have been reported to exhibit pathological indicators of greater disease severity (Stern, Alexander, Prohovnik, & Mayeux, 1992). The inference is made that higher levels of education and/or premorbid intelligence create a buffer

such that substantially more brain impairment is required before intellectual function is reduced to a level that is clinically defined as impaired. In this sense, education and intelligence have also been seen as reserve constructs, usually conceptualized as proxies for a brain process that permits functional tolerance of greater brain insult (see Scarmeas, Albert, Manly, & Stern, 2006).

The risk of AD and the incidence of dementia are reported to increase with low educational levels (Valenzuela & Sachdev, 2006), although debate continues about whether low education is associated with greater brain pathology or whether diagnostic status is more quickly reached because low premorbid levels of cognitive functioning are associated with low educational level. Functional magnetic resonance imaging (fMRI) studies by Cabeza and Nyberg (2000), focusing on well-functioning older adults, suggest that age-related decline in neural activity is compensated in adults who perform highly through the use of functional reserve as well as plasticity in neurocognitive networks. In this formulation, the reserve (intelligence, for example) is associated with the capacity to activate additional functional neurological areas.

Limitations of the Brain Reserve Hypothesis

The fact that the BRH is not a single entity, but rather a suite of hypotheses, presents difficulties. Major problems include differing conceptions of what constitutes reserve, how reserve might be represented biologically, the mechanism by which reserve acts to buffer the effects of various brain processes, and the conditions under which reserve might operate (for example, whether the hypothesis is valid for AD, vascular dementia, head injury, or normal aging). The most advanced discussion of different models to date has been provided by Stern (2002), who distinguished passive and active reserve models. In passive models, reserve usually refers to the capacity to replace damaged brain areas. For example, individuals with larger reserve (bigger brains) have greater capacity to replace compromised brain areas, and this supports the maintenance of high functioning. As noted above, because bigger brains are associated with higher education or intelligence, education or intelligence is often used as a proxy measure of reserve. Models within this category include those described by Katzman (1993) and Satz et al. (1993) as neurological brain reserve, and by Mortimer (1997) as neuronal reserve (p. 449). Stern noted that "in passive models, reserve is defined in terms of the amount of damage that can be sustained before reaching a threshold for clinical expression" (p. 449). In active models, the reserve is functional, such as the capacity to harness existing brain capability to compensate for tissue loss or brain damage. An active model may specify the nature of the

reserve (compensatory strategies), the mechanism (recruitment of or activation of broader brain areas to undertake a task), and the outcome—unimpaired cognitive functioning. In the context of these models, education or intelligence may be proxy measures for superior compensatory strategies.

The absence of an explicit operationalization of brain burden is a particular problem for the hypotheses. The original studies in this area examined brains at autopsy, measuring senile plaques and neurofibrillary tangles. More recent studies have used indices that can be measured in vivo to assess the extent of pathological processes or age-related brain changes. These have included measures such cerebrospinal fluid (CSF) volume as an index of brain size and brain atrophy (brain volume as a function of intracranial space). Atrophy can be inferred in cross-sectional studies by comparing brain to skull size, or it can be assessed over time in longitudinal studies. Measures of CSF and brain volume (as a function of intracranial space) are indirect measures of brain burden, may not reflect disease processes, and are agnostic to the nature of the mechanisms involved. Other examples of indices of brain pathology include white matter hyperintensities (WMH; actual numbers, or proportion as a function of brain volume), and reduced brain perfusion or glucose metabolism. There is often little articulation of the biological mechanisms that provide reserve in the face of these pathological or normal aging processes. That is, the way in which the reserve is reflected biologically (through greater functional flexibility, for example) is not explicated in most accounts.

An additional complication for the BRH is the broadening of the use of the concept of brain reserve—originally developed with respect to dementia—to describe mechanisms of normal aging and other types of brain pathology or insult, such as alcoholism and brain injury. The broad applicability of the BRH is enunciated by Stern (2002) who notes:

> The concept of reserve should be relevant to any situation where the brain sustains injury. In addition, it will be argued that the concept of reserve should be extended to encompass variation in healthy individuals' performance, particularly when they must perform at their maximum capacity.
>
> (p. 448)

Strategies used to Investigate the Brain Reserve Hypothesis

It is clear that a fully developed BRH requires four features:

- explicit specification of the brain insult/deterioration (sometimes called the brain burden)

- delineation of the nature of the reserve (bigger brain, higher education)
- specification of the mechanism by which the reserve delivers unimpaired performance (substitution, better brain recruitment)
- the expected outcome from such processes.

A brief overview of research testing the hypothesis indicates that such specification is rarely achieved. Most strategies to investigate the BRH investigate only subcomponents of BRH models, providing evidence consistent with one part of the underlying concept behind the BRH or evidence that is ambiguous. Only rarely is the full model tested. This requires, at minimum, a measure of reserve (either direct or proxy), a measure of brain damage/impairment (usually a biological measure of brain burden), and a measure of cognitive outcome. Table 4.2 outlines a number of methodologies that have been used by researchers to evaluate the BRH. Major limitations of the first three of these strategies in attempting to test versions of the BRH have been described in the literature (see, for example, Deary, 2001; Staff, Murray, Deary, & Whalley, 2004; Stern, 2002). For example, the first three strategies do not directly test whether education, intelligence, or a bigger brain (as measures of reserve) regulate the relationship between brain burden and cognitive outcomes. Strategy 1 involves cross-sectional data, where education or intelligence is correlated with indices of brain size (such as brain volume (BV) or intracranial volume (ICV)). There is no measure of cognitive performance. Strategy 2 investigates the same associations as Strategy 1 but uses longitudinal data to measure atrophy, or infers atrophy based on the ratio of brain size to skull size.[1] No cognitive data are investigated. Strategy 3 attempts to establish that the rate of development of atrophy is retarded with advancing age in those with high education and intelligence. This approach requires examining the effect of age in addition to measures of atrophy or cognitive change and education, but again these strategies provide no opportunity to test the hypothesis given that cognitive outcomes are not measured. Thus, these three approaches provide supporting evidence for the BRH, but do not constitute tests of it. Finding an

---

[1]Estimates of change must assume that the size of the cranium reflects the size of the brain in young adulthood. Based on available data, ICV is assumed to be about 93% of its size at adulthood at 6 years of age (Wolf et al., 2003) with BV reaching adult dimensions and then declining in the sixth and seventh decades of life (Caviness et al., 1996). At older ages, atrophy represents an estimate of the loss of BV from peak brain size. Atrophy can be measured longitudinally (shrinkage between two time periods) or estimated cross-sectionally using the difference between ICV and BV adjusted for head size. The amount of cerebrospinal fluid (CSF) has also been used to estimate atrophy.

association between brain size and intelligence provides some support for the use of intelligence as a proxy measure of brain size, or support for the speculation that those with higher intelligence may have greater reserve because of larger brain size, but it does not test the hypothesis that brain size acts as a buffer to allow individuals to maintain cognitive performance at previous levels. Such a demonstration would require evidence that those with more brain tissue or higher education (reserve) have better cognitive outcomes in the face of brain damage, injury, or disease.

Another set of strategies (not shown in Table 4.2) examines the association between education and cognitive decline, using cross-sectional associations, longitudinal change, or acceleration models using age as an additional variable. The hypothesis that education protects against cognitive decline has some support from the literature (Anstey & Christensen, 2000; Hultsch, Hertzog, Small, & Dixon, 1999; Kramer, Bherer, Colcombe, Dong, & Greenough, 2004; Schaie, 1984; Valenzuela & Sachdev, 2006; Wilson, Gilley, Bennett, Beckett, & Evans, 2000) but does not by itself constitute a test of the BRH, as no measure of brain capacity/insult/ deterioration or damage is investigated.[2] This hypothesis is not discussed further in this chapter.

A final strategy (Strategy 4 in Table 4.2) attempts to demonstrate that the relationship between atrophy and cognitive decline is a direct function of reserve capacity, often operationalized as education level. Three components of the BRH are present: a measure of reserve (for example, intelligence, education, or a large brain), a measure of brain deterioration (for example, atrophy or amyloid load), and an outcome to indicate some buffering—i.e., measures of cognitive deterioration. We contend that Strategy 4 is the only rigorous test of the BRH. It involves an explicit test of the role of reserve (for example, education) in mediating the effect of brain atrophy on cognitive performance or change in performance.

In the following sections of this chapter, we review the relationship between various brain structures and measures of reserve, including intelligence, education, and brain size. As noted above, these relationships provide supporting evidence for the BRH, but do not formally test it. We later describe studies that directly test versions of the brain reserve hypothesis.

---

[2]Cross-sectional estimates of deterioration, based on contrasting the results of contemporaneously administered tests of premorbid intelligence (such as the National Adult Reading Test) and current levels of fluid intelligence, have been found to be valid when compared against actual cognitive change (Deary, 2001).

TABLE 4.2
Research Investigating the Brain Reserve Hypothesis (BRH)

Strategy Type	Description	Expectation	Comment
1	Examination of the relationship between education/intelligence and brain size/structure as a measure of brain reserve.	Greater education/intelligence is associated with greater brain volume, or larger brain structures.	This strategy investigates whether there are biological differences in brain structure between those with greater reserve. From the perspective of the true BRH, this strategy informs about the possible mechanisms provided by intelligence or education that give rise to reserve.
2	Examination of the relationship between education/intelligence/brain size and *change* in brain volume (e.g., atrophy) or structure.	Higher education/intelligence/ brain size is associated with less brain atrophy.	This strategy examines whether bigger/smarter brains show less change in brain structure over time or with age. Brain atrophy is a measure of brain aging. Intelligence/education/brain size is seen as a measure of reserve.
3	Examination of differences in the relationship between education/intelligence/brain size and *change* in brain volume as a function of age.	The rate of the development of atrophy is greater in those with less reserve.	Atrophy is seen as a measure of brain aging. Intelligence and education are proxies for reserve. This tests whether reserve is more important in the face of greater brain aging. It also tests whether the *rate* of atrophy is reduced in those with higher reserve.
4	Education or intelligence mediates the relationship between cognitive function and the degree of brain biological change/pathology. In the passive version, additional biological resources exist to overcome injury. In the active version, resources are recruited to compensate	Those with greater reserve (education, intelligence, etc.) will have adequate cognitive functioning despite evidence of brain atrophy or brain aging.	Requires measures of reserve, brain injury, and cognitive capacity/decline.

Studies of Head Circumference, Brain Size, Brain Region, and Intelligence

A number of reviews have shown small to moderate positive associations between brain size or head size, and intelligence. A variety of indicators of brain size have been used, including head circumference (which remains constant throughout life at the completion of growth), ICV (the space inside the cranium, which reaches a maximum at around 7 years of age and then remains constant through life; Wolf, Kruggel, Hensel, Wahlund, Arendt, & Gertz, 2003), or BV (the amount of brain tissue within the head), which reaches adult dimensions by puberty (Caviness, Kennedy, Richelme, Rademacher, & Filipek, 1996) and begins to decline in the third decade.

One review of 17 studies (Rushton & Ankney, 1996) found that mental ability and head measures had an average correlation of 0.21 (ranging from 0.08 to 0.35), a figure similar to a second review of 14 studies where the correlation between head circumference and intelligence ranged from 0.08 to 0.22, with an n-weighted mean partial correlation (controlling for height) of 0.10 (Johnson, 1991). In a large study of healthy older individuals ($n = 818$), head circumference was reported to be related to performance on tests of intelligence, global cognitive functioning (measured by the Mini Mental State Examination, MMSE; Folstein, Folstein, & McHugh, 1975), and speed of information processing (Stroop Color Word Task; Stroop, 1935), but not memory (Word Learning Task; Tisserand, Bosma, Van Boxtel, & Jolles, 2001). The correlation between head circumference and memory recall was −0.09. Reviews by Van Valen (1974) and Lynn (1999) shown in Table 4.1 report consistent findings, with reported aggregated correlations of approximately 0.3 with head size and cognition from 8 and 16 studies, respectively.

Willerman, Schultz, Rutledge, and Bigler (1991) undertook the first in vivo investigation of the association. Using magnetic resonance imaging (MRI) to estimate brain size, they reported a correlation of 0.35 between BV and intelligence from a sample of college students selected for high or low SAT performance. McDaniel (2005), in a more recent meta-analysis, reported correlations between brain volume (as assessed by MRI) and intelligence ranging between 0.33 to 0.37.

More recently, the "bigger is better" hypothesis has been introduced to explain relationships between specific cognitive abilities and specific neuroanatomical regions. For example, an assumption in much of the neuropsychiatry and neuropsychology literature has been that larger hippocampi are associated with better episodic memory performance, although this has recently been questioned due to lack of support in a meta-analysis (Van Petten, 2004). Van Petten reported that in young

adults smaller volumes may be advantageous. In contrast, smaller hippocampal volumes have been found to be predictive of memory decline in studies of older samples in whom brain atrophy has already commenced (Anstey & Maller, 2003; Mungas et al., 2005). In younger populations, studies of taxi drivers (known to have extensive acquired spatial knowledge) have shown increased size of the posterior hippocampus, suggesting that brain structure can change with experience (Maguire et al., 2000).

Education, Intelligence, Socioeconomic Status, and Brain Reserve

Both education and intelligence have been used as proxy measures of brain reserve. Education and intelligence are highly correlated, their causal relationship is ambiguous, and their association varies as a function of the type of intelligence (verbal, performance, full scale) or education measure (schooling, continuing education, etc.). Years of schooling may more likely reflect innate abilities, while continuing education may reflect curiosity, motivation, or opportunity. Satz (1993), in a review of functional reserve theory, proposed that intelligence is a more valid direct measure of cerebral reserve than is education, the latter argued to be determined as much by environmental circumstances as innate reserve. More recent studies provide weak support. Schmand, Smit, Geerlings, and Lindeboom (1997), in the Amsterdam Study of the Elderly, examined the association of both education and intelligence with the incidence of dementia. Intelligence predicted dementia onset more accurately than did education. Ivanovic et al. (2004) reported that intelligence had a stronger association with brain volume and head circumference than did a measure of socioeconomic status. Correlations between socioeconomic status (SES) and BV, head circumference, and corpus callosum were largely nonsignificant for both males and females. Intelligence (measured as Full Scale Intelligence Quotient, FSIQ, using the Wechsler Adult Intelligence Scale—Revised, WAIS-R) correlated moderately strongly with both head circumference and brain volume.

Specific Brain Regions in relation to Intelligence and Education

Although the relationship between intelligence and brain volume is relatively well established, there is little knowledge but much speculation about which sections of the brain might be more likely to be correlated with intelligence or education. Speculation arises from outcomes of comparative studies of the ratio of prefrontal cortex to the neocortex, and from more recent studies indicating that certain areas of the brain correlate with intelligence, and are more heritable than other areas. Given evidence on

the larger size of the prefrontal cortex against the neocortex, there may be some argument for these associations to be greater in that area if reserve is located in this section of the brain. According to Passingham, Stephan, and Kotter (2002), frontal gray matter might offer the strongest associations. Thompson et al. (2001) reported some of the first data on the heritability of brain structure based on a sample of 40 twins. These authors found that the overall volume of the brain itself and certain brain structures including the corpus callosum and the ventricles were "somewhat genetically influenced" (p. 1253), whereas other structures such as gyral patterns were less heritable. Using MRI to make three-dimensional maps of gray matter, these researchers correlated g with brain areas, estimating the genetic contribution to individual differences in gray matter volume. They reported that frontal and language-related cortices were under "significant genetic control." The heritability of brain size did not vary markedly by hemisphere. Differences in frontal gray matter were significantly linked with differences in intellectual function. They found the strongest associations with g were with total gray matter volume (effect size, ES = 1.73) and in frontal areas (ES = 1.95), and weaker associations in temporal (ES = 0.23), parietal (ES = 0.41), and occipital (ES = 0.15) areas. As noted by Plomin and Kosslyn (2001) the analyses undertaken by Thompson et al. were relative ones, in that the associations are partial regressions which estimate the associations between each brain area and g independently of other brain regions (p. 1154). These estimates are thus likely to underestimate the extent to which gray matter volume correlates with g, in the sense that gray matter volumes in different brain regions are likely to be intercorrelated.

One of the most comprehensive investigations of associations between intelligence and specific brain areas has been undertaken by Haier, Jung, Yeo, Head, and Alkire (2004). These authors used voxel-based morphometry to estimate volumes of gray matter. Data were collected from a younger (mean age = 27) and an older sample (mean age = 59), although these samples were later collapsed. Using nearly 60 regions of interest, the authors found significant relationships between FSIQ, measured by the Wechsler Adult Intelligence Score (WAIS), and gray matter for the following Brodmann areas (BA): 10, 46, and 9 in the frontal lobes, BA 21, 37, 22, and 42 in the temporal lobes, BA 43 and 3 in the parietal lobes, and BA 19 in the occipital lobe. These associations were corrected for multiple comparisons. The authors note that these findings support earlier findings of the view of the importance of the frontal lobes for intelligence. No tests of significance for differential magnitude of the volume–IQ relationships were reported.

Sex Differences in relation to Brain, IQ, and Reserve

Sex differences in the structure and functioning of the brain have also given rise to speculation about sex differences in the association of intelligence/education and brain structure. The mechanisms by which sex differences in brain volumes arise are not understood but possibly involve estrogen (Spratt, 2000). Estrogen has a neuroprotective and neurotrophic effect that has been documented in animal models and supported by clinical studies. Ankney (1992) reported that autopsy data showed that men's brains were on average 100 g heavier than those of women, even when body size was taken into account. There is some controversy over this finding, given that women and men apparently have the same levels of intelligence, and that intelligence is related to brain size. A number of explanations for the association have been offered, including the suggestions that (a) intelligence tests are biased in favor of women, (b) women have more efficient brains, and (c) since men are better spatially, more brain matter is required for spatial compared to verbal functioning. Heilman, Nadeau, and Beversdorf (2003) noted: "Whereas men's brains are larger than women's, the cerebral cortex of women's brains is as thick as men's suggesting that the size may be related to men having more white matter than women" (p. 347).

More recently, Gur et al. (1999) reported that, in men, increased cranial volume is associated with a proportional increase in gray matter and white matter, whereas in women, the increase in white matter as a function of cranial volume is lower (see p. 4068). There is reportedly a higher proportion of gray matter in women compared to men. Sex differences in the human corpus callosum have been widely reported (Shin et al., 2005) although the "functional significance of these differences" requires further investigation (Ozer, Kayalioglu, & Erturk, 2005). All these findings suggest the possibility that correlations might be stronger between intelligence and gray matter for women.

In one review, McDaniel (2005) reported that the positive correlation of BV with intelligence was larger for female compared to male samples. The study reported a correlation of 0.40 for women (based on 12 samples) and a correlation of 0.34 for men (based on 17 samples). Earlier reports are mixed. Akgun, Okuyan, Baytan, and Topbas (2003) reported a significant positive association between intelligence and cranial capacity in male subjects ($r = 0.31$) compared to female subjects ($r = 0.20$) in a sample of 89 men and 56 women. There were strong significant correlations for left-handed women and men ($r = 0.78$; 8 males and females each) and speculation that left-handed women have larger hippocampi. This speculation is supported by recent results from the PATH Through Life Study of 478 adults aged 60 to 64 that showed left-handed women do have larger hippocampi

than right-handed women, although handedness was not associated with hippocampal volume in men (Anstey et al., 2004).

Gur et al. (1999) suggested that differences in anatomy between men and women may provide the neural substrate for differences in cognition. These authors reported a significant positive correlation between ICV and verbal performance for women but not for men. Ankney (1992) also describes an interesting study by Andreasen et al. (1993) in which MRI estimates of brain volume for men and women were examined. Brain volume correlated more highly with performance intelligence (PIQ) than with verbal intelligence (VIQ) for men, but the opposite pattern was found for women. No formal tests of differences in the magnitude of these IQ volume correlations were reported. Similarly, Wickett, Vernon, and Lee (1994, p. 835) used MRI to measure brain volume in 40 women and found that it correlated 0.44 with VIQ but only 0.28 with PIQ, although this difference was not significant (Hotelling's t(37) = 1.212, NS).

Type of Intelligence Tests in relation to Brain Volume and Head Circumference

Some discussion has focused on which type of intelligence test correlates most strongly with brain volume or head circumference, although Wickett et al. (2000) noted: "This aspect has been almost completely ignored in the literature" (p. 1096). Work by Jensen (1994) suggests that tests correlate with head size to the extent they are g-loaded. However, findings are mixed. Raz et al. (1993) found that the correlation ($r = 0.43$) between the Cattell Culture-Fair Test (Cattell & Cattell, 1960) and BV was stronger than the correlation between Vocabulary scores and BV ($r = 0.10$). However, Wickett et al. reported that brain volume was correlated about 0.3 with both Verbal (VIQ) and Performance (PIQ). These investigators also correlated factor scores derived from a large battery with brain volume. Brain volume correlated positively with g (their factor 1), PIQ, VIQ, and memory, but not with spatial ability ($r = -0.14$, NS). In an analysis of the vector of correlations, Wickett et al. also found that the "higher a test's g loading, the more highly it correlated with brain volume" (p. 1117). These authors concluded that tests measuring crystallized ability correlate with brain volume only to the extent that they also correlate with other cognitive abilities, namely g.

WMH and Brain Reserve

Another avenue of investigation has been the relationship between measures of pathology such as WMH, and measures of cognitive function. Recent studies have found no or only weak associations between

cognitive performance and white matter hyperintensities. Staff et al. (2004) found that measures of brain pathology did not correlate with cognitive ability or intelligence, occupational status, or education (see Staff et al., 2004). Gunning-Dixon and Raz (2000) undertook a meta-analysis of the relationship between WMH and psychometric intelligence. They reported that while WMHs correlate with measures of processing speed, immediate and delayed memory, executive functions, and indices of global cognitive function (measured by brief screening tests), there were no significant associations with intelligence (measured by psychometric intelligence tests) in the studies they reviewed. Seven studies examined PIQ and four examined VIQ. The average correlation between both WMH and VIQ, and between white matter hyperintensities and PIQ was 0.09 and not significant.

The Present Review

The present chapter provides a systematic review of the relationships between education, occupation, and intelligence on the one hand, and specific measures of brain structure, shrinkage, or pathology on the other, taking into account age and dementia status. Four areas of investigation are covered:

(1) The relationship between intelligence, education, and occupation (as measures of reserve) and measures of head size, brain volume, or the volume of a variety of regions of interest. This line of investigation essentially reflects research described in Table 4.1 as Strategy 1 research, and it provides supportive evidence for the BRH.

(2) The association between intelligence, education, and occupation (as reserve) and brain *atrophy* is investigated. This reflects Strategy 2 type research, again providing potential supporting evidence for the BRH.

(3) The effect of age on the relationship between brain indices and intelligence or education (Strategy 3) is also investigated.

(4) Empirical studies directly testing the "true brain reserve hypothesis" (Strategy 4) are summarized.

For each question, we present a brief summary of the literature to date, and the results of our meta-analysis.

Studies for the review were selected irrespective of the source of the literature, the date of the study, the use of scanning technologies, the theoretical position of the researcher, or the research question addressed. To compensate for the lack of research papers specifically addressing the effect of age on the relationship between intelligence and brain indices,

we compiled data from all available studies and reported the strength of relationship as a function of the stated age of the sample.

METHODOLOGY

Literature Search

A search of the literature using the databases PubMed, PsycInfo (via Ovid), and Web of Science was conducted to identify studies reporting on the association between brain structures and mental reserve (education, intelligence, SES, or occupation). Each search was limited to articles published in English between 1965 and August 2005 and was restricted to human subjects. A total of 2911 unique articles were identified.

Keywords used in the PubMed search were: Brain: brain [with MeSH terms], head [without MeSH terms], intracranial; Brain indices: size, circumference, volume*, cavity, vault, atrophy, white matter hyperintensities; Mental reserve: educat*, occupation*, mental activity, reserve, intell*, IQ. MeSH terms are a controlled vocabulary that PubMed uses to index articles. These terms help to identify articles that may use different terminology, but are still relevant to the search. Keywords used in the PsycInfo search were: Brain and brain indices: explode "cerebral atrophy.sh," explode "brain size.sh," intracranial AND size, volume$, cavity, vault, atrophy, white matter hyperintensities; Mental reserve: educat$, occupation$, mental activity, reserve, intell$, IQ. The explode term in PsycInfo retrieves all results within a particular subject heading; again this allows for a broader search with fewer restrictions on terminology. Keywords used in the Web of Science search were: Brain: brain, head, intracranial; Brain indices: size, circumference, volume*, cavity, vault, atrophy, white matter hyperintensities; Mental reserve: educat*, occupation*, mental activity, reserve, intell*, IQ. The asterisks and dollar symbols (*, $) are wildcards which capture variations based on the word stem.

Study Selection

Selection of the relevant studies from the 2911 abstracts identified was conducted in two stages. The first stage involved screening the titles and abstracts according to a set of criteria. Studies were included if they contained (a) a measure of both brain reserve and brain structure, (b) reported data on the association between these two factors, and (c) were original full-text contributions. Studies were excluded if the intelligence measure used was not a standard intelligence test, if the sample size was smaller than five, or if the sample members had a concurrent mental illness such

as depression, systemic illness, or a major lesion or abnormality (e.g., head injury). Samples with AD or other forms of dementia were included in the review. Nonclinical control groups within a clinical study with sample sizes of at least 30 were also included as a separate sample. Where it could be discerned that from the information available a study did not meet the inclusion criteria, it was excluded. To ensure that relevant studies were not rejected erroneously, this initial screening process erred on the side of over-inclusion. The second stage of study selection involved obtaining and examining the full-text of the remaining 417 articles and applying the exclusion criteria with greater rigor. After this process, the final number of studies meeting the inclusion criteria was 73 (a list of references to research papers included in the review are available directly from the authors: Helen.Christensen@anu.edu.au).

We also hand-searched a number of published reviews of head circumference and brain reserve for missed papers. A small number of additional studies were found. For example, a paper by Gur et al. (1999) on sex differences in brain size was not captured by our search (it reported correlations of about 0.39–0.40 with intelligence and gray matter). A paper retrieved for our research was also excluded somewhat paradoxically because it included too many data points, through the contribution of correlations of between 60 brain regions and FSIQ (Haier et al., 2004). It proved too difficult to collapse categories to match with the broad brain regions of interest organized through scoping of the areas examined in the literature. However, relevant findings from these papers are provided in the literature review.

Data Extraction

A coding sheet was designed to extract data from the 73 included studies. Recorded information included: study details; method of structural brain measurement; method of intelligence/education/SES/occupation measurement; MRI details and sample characteristics. Statistical data reporting on the association between brain structures and mental reserve were also recorded. A second coder checked all the information against the original articles for any errors or omissions. Approximately 30 coding errors (< 1% of total information captured) were found, including cases where information was coded as missing, but was in fact available. In addition to this, 15 relevant relationships between brain structures and mental reserve were missed in the original coding (3% of total relationships recorded). Psychometric tests were coded according to whether they assessed General Intelligence (IQ), PIQ, or VIQ. FSIQ included the full score on the Stanford Binet (Thorndike, Hagen, & Sattler, 1986) or the full WAIS. VIQ included scores from the National Adult Reading Test (NART; Nelson &

O'Connell, 1978), Spot the Word Test (Baddeley, Emslie, & Nimmo-Smith, 1993), and any verbal subtests of the WAIS (Wechsler, 1955). PIQ included the Raven's Progressive Matrices (Raven, Court, & Raven, 1976) and performance subtests of the WAIS.

Database Summary

Data from the coding sheets were entered into a database using SPSS version 12. Sixty-two studies contained one relevant sample, seven studies recorded data for both males and females (generating information for two samples), and four studies had information recorded for both the whole sample as well as by gender (generating information for three samples). The database therefore contained a total of 88 study comparisons, one for each sample studied. One in three coding lines was checked for data entry errors. Approximately 45 data entry errors were found and corrected (< 2% of the data coded).

Sample Characteristics

The database indicated that 70 of the studies were cross-sectional, while only three were longitudinal. Brain structures were most often measured using MRI scans (73%), followed by computed tomography (CT) scans (16%), head circumference measures (7%), or other methods (4%). When MRI tracings were used, most studies reported reliability ratings above 0.80 (54%), mostly using semi-automated methods (63%), with volumes normed for head size (37%) or body size (24%). Most studies did not report results by gender (68%). A range of samples was used: representative (22%), volunteer (39%), clinical (21%), control groups assembled to compare outcomes with clinical patients (9%), or not specified (9%). Fifty-four of the studies (70%) included participants with no diagnosis and nine (12%) used patients with AD. There were also samples of mild cognitive impairment ($n = 1$), mixed dementia ($n = 7$), twins ($n = 1$), and other ($n = 5$). Study sample size varied from 10 to 1869 (mean = 153). The age of participants ranged from 16 to 81 (mean = 55.2).

Based on the type of data provided in the research paper, two databases were established. One consisted of correlations between brain measures and reserve (the correlation database). The other consisted of mean values taken from various groups provided in the paper (i.e, groups of high and low education and their mean levels of BV, for example)—the mean group database. Sixty-two studies reported correlations (or data on the significance/lack of significance of correlations) between various brain structures and measures of reserve (with both variables in these cases continuous). Frequently, a single study examined more than one region of

interest. Consequently, a total of 410 correlations were extracted from the 62 studies. The second database (the mean group database) contained 16 samples that reported grouped data (means and standard deviations/percentages) to examine the association between brain structures and mental reserve (either one or both variables in these cases was categorical). A total of 44 group differences were examined. Five samples contained both correlations and grouped data, and so were included in both databases. Findings from the categorical database are not reported in the body of this report, but are available on request from the authors.[3] Thus, all tables in this review report data from the correlation database.

Justification for Region of Interest Classifications

The classification of regions of interest was determined on the basis of commonly used classifications of brain tissue and brain regions that have been studied in relation to brain morphology and aging. Proportions of tissue types (gray matter and white matter), lobar volumes, CSF, and ventricular size can be used to generate estimates of atrophy when used as ratios to ICV. ICV is used as a proxy of premorbid brain size. WMHs are a nonspecific marker of neurodegeneration associated with brain aging and dementia. Amyloid plaques represent neuropathology associated with AD.

Statistical Analyses

The method proposed by Hunter and Schmidt (1990) for aggregating correlations was used to estimate mean effects of the strength of relationship between brain structure and mental reserve. This method of meta-analysis implements a random effects model, assuming that the observed effect sizes have been sampled from a (conceptual) population of studies. Thus this model incorporates within- and between-study sources of variation in estimating homogeneity of effects and confidence intervals. In a small number of studies, no information was available about sample size. For these studies, sample size was imputed using the harmonic mean

---

[3]The findings concur with those from the correlation database, with intelligence associated with greater brain volume, and the associations being weaker for education and SES (see, for example, Reynolds, Johnston, Dodge, DeKosky, & Ganguli, 1999). White matter hyperintensities correlated with education in one study of a clinical group (see Hirono et al., 2000). Five studies focused on atrophy. These studies found no relationship between measures of education and the amount of brain atrophy for those in normal samples (Golomb, de Leon, Kluger, George, Tarshish, & Ferris, 1993; LaFosse, Mednick, Praestholm, Vestergaard, Parnas, & Schulsinger, 1994; O'Brien, Desmond, Ames, Schweitzer, & Tress, 1997) and pathological samples (Launer, Scheltens, Lindeboom, Barkhof, Weinstein, & Jonker, 1995; Meyer, Rauch, Rauch, & Haque, 2000).

of available sample sizes. The heterogeneity of effect sizes was evaluated to determine whether the correlations of studies in the meta-analysis could be regarded as measuring a common effect. Given the noninde-pendence of correlations (multiple correlations from the same study), no secondary analyses were undertaken of these correlations.

RESULTS

Intelligence, Education, and Occupation as Correlates of Brain Size and Brain Pathology

Our review first evaluated the relationship between intelligence, educa-tion, and/or occupation on the one hand and brain size or brain pathology on the other. Based on the literature reviewed earlier, we expected to find the following: (a) a small to moderate association between intelligence/ education and brain size, with this being stronger for intelligence rather than for education; (b) following Thompson et al. (2001), strong associ-ations between specific areas of the brain, such as the frontal lobes, and intelligence; and (c) variations in the magnitude of the correlations between tests of verbal and performance intelligence, but with the possi-bility that these associations may be mediated by the extent to which the test loaded on g.

Table 4.3 shows the pooled means from relevant studies reporting associations between intelligence, education, and occupation, and the various measures of brain structure for both normal (*N) and pathological samples (*P). The means were weighted according to the sample size of the studies. The pooled means were tested for hetereogeneity (columns 5, 10, 15). The significance column summarizes reported significance or non-significance of the association for all studies where this information was available. The data from Table 4.3 indicate that there is a moderate associ-ation between intelligence and head circumference (average weighted correlation $r = 0.18$) and ICV ($r = 0.20$). Only two studies reported associ-ations between head circumference and education ($r = 0.19$) and between head circumference and occupation ($r = 0.19$), and these results were both significant. Three observations of the association between ICV and educa-tion in clinical samples were available ($r = 0.17$).

Head circumference comparisons showed significant heterogeneity. However, perusal of the actual studies did not suggest that heterogeneity was related to the type of intelligence test, age, or sample type. (Study details available on request.)

Although no formal analyses were undertaken, brain volume measures were associated with stronger correlations than were circumference or

TABLE 4.3

Pooled Means of Studies Reporting Associations between Intelligence, Education, and Occupation, and Various Measures of Brain Structure for both Normal (*N) and Pathological (*P) Samples

Type of Structure	Intelligence					Education					Occupation					Significance %
	Mean (weighted)	SE	95% CI	Heterogeneity χ^2 (sig)	N	Mean (weighted)	SE	95% CI	Heterogeneity χ^2 (sig)	N	Mean (weighted)	SE	95% CI	Heterogeneity χ^2 (sig)	N	
Head Circumference	.28 (.18)	.03	.13–.23	52.38 (.001)	22	.18 (.19)	.02	.15–.23	2.21 (.138)	2	.18 (.19)	.06	.07–.31	.75 (.385)	2	44 (.38, n=14)
Brain ICV *N	.20 (.20)	.08	.05–.35	2.39 (.122)	2											50 (.20, n=2)
Brain ICV *P						.11 (.17)	.10	-.03–.37	4.08 (.130)	3	.10 (.10)	.04	.03–.17	.23 (.63)	2	25 (.10, n=2)
Whole Brain Volume *N	.35 (.34)	.03	.29–.39	74.94 (.001)	41	.06		-.09–.21		1						67 (.30, n=14)
Whole Brain Volume *P	.43 (.43)	.03	.37–.50	1.19 (.552)	3	-.06		-.28–.17		1						60
Grey Matter Volume *N	.16 (.17)	.06	.05–.29	13.68 (.057)	8											38 (.33, n=3)
Grey Matter Volume *P																0
Cortical Matter Volume	.37 (.39)	.10	.19–.59	10.45 (.015)	4											50 (.38, n=2)
Subcortical Matter Volume	.10 (.10)	.04	.02–.17	.11 (.739)	2											0 (.10, n=1)
White Matter Volume	.24 (.19)	.04	.12–.27	4.64 (.704)	8	.26 (.26)	.03	.21–.32	.12 (.731)	2						20 (.28, n=3)
Hemispheric Volume																0
Left Hemispheric Volume	.21 (.21)	.07	.07–.35	7.97 (.158)	6											22 (.21, n=2)
Right Hemispheric Volume	.21 (.20)	.06	.08–.33	6.37 (.272)	6											22 (.22, n=2)
Cerebral Hemispheric Volume	.36 (.35)	.03	.29–.41	26.49 (.089)	19											84 (.36, n=15)
CSF *N	.16 (.13)	.08	-.03–.28	13.24 (.021)	6											58 (.15, n=2)
CSF *P																33
Lateral Ventricles Whole *N	.07 (.06)	.03	-.01–.12	.59 (.898)	4	.15		.00–.29		1						13 (.08, n=4)
Lateral Ventricles Whole *P																0
Right Lateral Ventricle	.03 (.03)	.02	-.01–.06	.22 (.898)	3											0 (.03, n=1)
Left Lateral Ventricle	.08 (.08)	.01	.06–.09	.03 (.985)	3											0 (.08, n=1)
Enlarged Perivascular Spaces	.04 (.04)	.10	-.16–.24	9.09 (.011)	3											33 (.04, n=1)
Frontal Cortex Whole	.22 (.22)	.02	.18–.26	.37 (.830)	3	.07		-.08–.22		1						58 (.15, n=2)
Left Frontal Cortex	.23 (.23)	.00	.22–.23	.01 (.942)	2	.37		.03–.63		1						33 (.30, n=2)
Right Frontal Cortex	.21 (.21)	.03	.14–.27	.42 (.515)	2	.30		-.05–.58		1						0 (.25, n=2)
Prefrontal Cortex						.21 (.21)	.08	.06–.36	.85 (.357)	2						0
Parietal Lobe	.18 (.18)	.03	.12–.25	.85 (.655)	3											33 (.18, n=1)
Occipital Lobe	.11 (.11)	.02	.07–.15	.38 (.823)	3											0 (.11, n=1)

Structure	r	SE	95% CI	Q (p)	N	r	SE	95% CI	Q (p)	N	r	95% CI	Q (p)	Significance
Temporal Lobe	.25 (.25)	.02	.20—.30	.55 (.761)	3									50 (.25, n=1)
Left Temporal Lobe	.23 (.22)	.05	.13—.31	4.65 (.325)	5									25 (.23, n=2)
Right Temporal Lobe	.35 (.33)	.05	.23—.44	7.02 (.135)	5									38 (.34, n=2)
Corpus collusum *N	.17 (.14)	.03	.08—.21	28.72 (.190)	24									22 (.21, n=6)
Corpus collusum *P	.66 (.66)	.05	.56—.76	.63 (.731)	3	.10 (.10)				8				68 (.66, n=1)
Hippocampus *N	.27 (.25)	.03	.19—.32	11.98 (.286)	11	.08		–.05—.25	17.06 (.017)	8				44 (.28, n=3)
Hippocampus *P						.07				1				0 (.07, n=1)
Cerebellum	.24 (.22)	.07	.09—.35	14.42 (.013)	6			–.22—.35		1				50 (.25, n=3)
Cingulate *P	–.19		–.48—.13		1									0 (—.19, n=1)
Other structure *N	.11 (.11)	.02	.07—.15	90.83 (<.001)	50	.14 (.11)	.04	.03—.19	11.21 (.130)	8	.13 (13)			20 (.16, n=16)
Other structure *P	–.09 (—.07)	.05	–.18—.03	71.07 (<.001)	23	.18 (.17)	.04	.09—.26	7.01 (.536)		.02	.08—.18	.46 (.927)	36 (.06, n=6)
White matter lesions *N	–.08 (—.10)	.04	–.18—.03	48.51 (<.001)	21									32 (—.04, n=4)
White matter lesions *P	–.04 (—.04)	.03	–.10—.02	.67 (.710)	3	–.05		–.27—.18		1				0 (—.04, n=1)
Amyloid *P	–.31 (—.31)	.10	–.51—.10	.82 (.366)	2									50 (—.31, n=1)

Note. The percentage of studies reporting significant associations is provided in the Significance column. N refers to the number of observations for each structure. These include both the number of observations of correlations plus the number of observations of significance. *N = normal sample; *P = pathological sample.

intracranial measures. The average weighted correlation was .34 for normal samples and 0.43 for one clinical sample (Yeo, Turkheimer, Raz, & Bigler, 1987).

Based on these few available observations, and not tested directly, the correlation with brain volume appeared to be weaker for education and occupation than for intelligence. There was also significant heterogeneity in the studies contributing to the correlation between whole brain volume and measures of intelligence. Again, there was no clear basis for the heterogeneity that we could discern based on inspection of the outcome studies. (Study details available on request.)

Brain Subvolumes as Correlates of Intelligence and Education

Gray matter, white matter, cortical and subcortical brain volumes, and hemispheric volumes all correlated positively with intelligence in pooled analyses (Table 4.3). Weighted correlations ranged from $r = 0.10$ for subcortical matter to $r = 0.39$ for cortical matter. The correlations between intelligence and indices of CSF, including the ventricular spaces, were smaller (for example, mean weighted $r = 0.06$, lateral ventricles). There were no data available on the association of CSF with education or occupation. The strongest correlations were with cortical matter volume ($r = 0.37$), cerebral hemisphere volume ($r = 0.36$), and right temporal lobe volume ($r = 0.33$). Compared to whole brain volume, correlations were lower for gray matter, white matter, subcortical regions, frontal cortex, and most other cortices with the exception of the right temporal lobe. These differences were not formally tested. Correlations with hippocampal volumes were moderate (0.27), while correlations with the corpus callosum were low for normal samples ($r = 0.17$).

There is little evidence regarding brain subvolumes in samples with pathology. The data on brain volumes for the clinical samples are drawn from 12 studies (Fukui & Kertesz, 2000; Gutzmann, Klimitz, & Avdaloff, 1982; Hirono, Kitagaki, Kazui, Hashimoto, & Mori, 2000; Kidron et al., 1997; Minagar, Sevush, & Bertran, 2000; Mori et al., 1997; Neary et al., 1986; Schofield, Mosesson, Stern, & Mayeux, 1995; Wolf et al., 2003; Wu, Schenkenberg, Wing, & Osborn, 1981; Yamauchi et al., 1993; Yasuda et al., 1998). The average correlation between intelligence and corpus callosum volume was high ($r = .66$, $n = 3$), particularly when judged against the average correlation for the normal samples ($r = .17$).

For those with brain pathology (mild cognitive impairment or AD), reports of the association between education and brain size were less frequent.

Relationship to Type of Cognitive Test

Table 4.4 examines associations between specific regions of interest as a function of intelligence test type. The most interesting question here is whether PIQ or VIQ tests show greater correlations with brain volumes. For whole brain volume the average weighted correlation was 0.41 ($n = 16$) for general intelligence tests, 0.31 for verbal tests ($n = 23$) and 0.31 for PIQ ($n = 10$).

Although the confidence intervals for these observations overlapped those for brain volume, there was a consistent pattern across almost all areas showing that FSIQ correlated more strongly than verbal intelligence. The effect was evident in those areas that correlated highly with intelligence overall, including gray matter volume, white matter volume, left temporal lobe, right temporal lobe, and hippocampus.

Relationships to Measures of Pathology

We found no significant association between intelligence and WMH, or education and WMH (Table 4.4). Based on the few available observations, there did not appear to be a relationship between reserve (operationalized in terms of intelligence or education) and WMH in individuals with AD or other forms of dementia.

Sex Differences in the Relationship between Brain Volumes and IQ, Education, and Occupation

Table 4.5 examines sex differences in the relationship between reserve constructs and structural brain measures where data were reported separately for men and women. Our first analysis (not shown) simply aggregated weighted correlations across all the available data points. For men, based on 99 observations, intelligence correlated with brain structures 0.26 (SD = 0.19), for education 0.22 (based on 12 observations, SD = 0.17), and for SES 0.17 (based on 8 observations, SD = 0.11). For women, these correlations were 0.23 (based on 46 observations, SD = 0.20) for intelligence, and 0.07 for SES ($n = 8$, SD = 0.17). Because the distribution of regions of interest (ROI) differed between the genders, this initial aggregated analysis was very approximate. Table 4.5 displays the outcomes using data points derived from the exact tests that were administered to both of the samples. Overall, these results suggest little difference between men and women. There is a suggestion of slightly stronger relationships in women for the cerebral volume measures, and weaker relationships for women compared to men for the corpus callosum (Table 4.5).

TABLE 4.4
Associations between Specific Regions of Interest as a Function of Intelligence Test Type

Type of Structure	General Intelligence					Verbal Intelligence					Performance Intelligence				
	Mean (weighted)	SE	95% CI	Heterogeneity χ² (sig)	N	Mean (weighted)	SE	95% CI	Heterogeneity χ² (sig)	N	Mean (weighted)	SE	95% CI	Heterogeneity χ² (sig)	N
Head Circumference	.26 (.18)	.07	.05–.31	22.72 (.002)	8	.24 (.16)	.03	.10–.21	13.35 (.038)	7	.34 (.32)	.05	.23–.41	6.97 (.323)	7
Brain ICV						.30		.11–.47		1	.09		–.11–.28		1
Whole Brain Volume *N	.41 (.41)	.04	.34–.49	27.78 (.023)	16	.32 (.31)	.04	.23–.39	26.75 (.013)	14	.32 (.31)	.03	.24–.37	7.40 (.596)	10
Whole Brain Volume *P	.47		.27–.63		1	.67		.07–.91		1	.55		–.12–.88		1
Grey Matter Volume	.22 (.24)	.09	.05–.42	2.30 (.130)	2	.14 (.14)	.08	–.03–.30	6.93 (.074)	4	.45 (.17)	.12	–.07–.41	3.66 (.056)	2
Cortical Matter Volume	.24		–.24–.63		1	.18		–.06–.40		1	.53 (.59)	.06	.48–.70	1.37 (.242)	2
Subcortical Matter	.04		–.42–.49		1						.15		–.33–.57		1
White Matter Volume	.26 (.22)	.05	.13–.31	1.00 (.607)	3	.11 (.12)	.00	.11–.12	.00 (.957)	2	.31 (.23)	.08	.08–.38	2.71 (.258)	3
Hemispheric Volume															
Left Hemispheric Volume	.23 (.23)	.11	.02–.44	2.08 (.149)	2	.27 (.26)	.13	.01–.52	3.12 (.077)	2	.13 (.12)	.11	–.09–.34	1.96 (.162)	2
Right Hemispheric	.21 (.21)	.11	–.01–.43	2.19 (.139)	2	.24 (.24)	.13	–.01–.49	2.93 (.087)	2	.16 (.16)	.08	.01–.32	1.06 (.302)	2
Cerebral Hemispheric Volume	.37 (.37)	.01	.36–.38	.02 (.990)	3	.36 (.36)	.01	.35–.37	.017 (.895)	2	.38 (.35)	.05	.27–.44	23.90 (.013)	12
CSF	.19 (.16)	.15	–.13–.45	5.23 (.022)	2	.12 (.11)	.06	–.02–.23	.93 (.334)	2	.16 (.12)	.17	–.22–.45	6.95 (.008)	2
Lateral Ventricles Whole	.20		–.28–.60		1						.03 (.04)	.02	.00–.08	.16 (.922)	3
Right Lateral Ventricle	.02		–.22–.26		1	–.01		–.25–.23		1	.07		–.17–.31		1
Left Lateral Ventricle	.08		–.16–.31		1	.06		–.18–.30		1	.09		–.15–.32		1
Enlarged Perivascular						.16	.03	.11–.22	.32 (.570)	2	–.21		–.39–		2
Frontal Cortex Whole	.25		.05–.43		1	.17		–.04–.36		1	.24		.03–.43		1
Left Frontal Cortex						.23		.03–.41		1	.22		.02–.40		1
Right Frontal Cortex						.16		–.04–.35		1	.25		.05–.43		1
Prefrontal Cortex															
Parietal Lobe	.20		–.01–.39		1	.11		–.10–.31		1	.24		.03–.43		1
Occipital Lobe	.12		–.09–.32		1	.06		–.15–.26		1	.15		–.06–.35		1
Temporal Lobe	.28		.08–.46		1	.19		–.02–.38		1	.28		.08–.46		1
Left Temporal Lobe	.33		.10–.53		1	.21 (.19)	.06	.07–.32	3.44 (.179)	3	.20		–.04–.42		1
Right Temporal Lobe	.46		.25–.63		1	.33 (.31)	.07	.17–.46	5.24 (.073)	3	.30		.06–.50		1

Corpus Callosum *N	.18 (.15)	.05	.05–.25	9.70 (.287)	9	.11 (.11)	.04	.02–.19	6.06 (.533)	8	.23 (.19)	.07	.05–.33	11.89	7
Corpus Callosum *P	.76		.25–.94		1	.67		.07–.91		1	.55		–.12–.88		1
Hippocampus	.36 (.36)	.03	.32–.41	.46 (.795)	3	.23 (.20)	.07	.07–.34	6.81 (.078)	4	.25 (.24)	.02	.20–.29	.79 (.851)	4
Cerebellum	.27 (.24)	.12	–.00–.48	5.22 (.022)	2	.21 (.18)	.12	–.06–.42	4.96 (.026)	2	.26 (.24)	.11	.03–.44	3.83 (.050)	2
Cingulate *P						–.19		–.48–.13		1					
Other Structure *N	.12 (.08)	.04	–.00–.16	15.58 (.049)	9	.16 (.10)	.03	.04–.16	20.50 (.083)	14	.16 (.15)	.03	.09–.21	34.99	21
Other Structure *P	–.17 (–.17)	.07	–.31–	30.30 (.001)	11	.04 (.00)	.10	–.16–.24	11.14 (.025)	5	–.03 (.01)	.10	–.18–.21	20.71	7
White Matter Lesions *N	–.04 (–.07)	.11	–.27–.14	17.53 (.002)	5	–.00 (–.01)	.03	–.07–.06	5.26 (.628)	8	–.19 (–	.05	–.31–.12	12.54	8
White Matter Lesions *P	–.04		–.26–.19		1	.03		–.20–.25		1	–.11		–.33–.12		1
Amyloid															
Amyloid *P	–.45		–.77–.04		1	–.16		–.59–.35		1					

Note. The percentage of studies reporting significant associations is provided in the Significance column. N refers to the number of observations for each structure. These include both the number of observations of correlations plus the number of observations of significance. *N = normal sample; *P = pathological sample.

TABLE 4.5
Sex Differences in Relationship between Reserve Constructs and Structural Brain Measures where Data Reported Separately for Men and Women

Type of Structure	Intelligence					Education					Occupation				
	Mean (weighted)	SE	95% CI	Heterogeneity χ² (sig)	N	Mean (weighted)	SE	95% CI	Heterogeneity χ² (sig)	N	Mean (weighted)	SE	95% CI	Heterogeneity χ² (sig)	N
Head Circumference															
M	.28 (.26)	.05	.17–.35	16.59 (.084)	11						.10		–.20–.37		1
F	.34 (.35)	.04	.28–.43	5.29 (.625)	8						.27		–.01–.51		1
Whole Brain Volume															
M	.39 (.38)	.04	.32–.45	56.36 (<.001)	24						.05		–.24–.33		1
F	.36 (.36)	.02	.33–.39	.77 (.993)	44						.15		–.14–.41		1
Cerebral Hemisphere Volume															
M	.39 (.36)	.09	.19–.53	8.52 (.074)	5										
F	.50 (.50)	.09	.33–.66	6.06 (.048)	3										
Lateral Ventricles Whole															
M	.10 (.09)	.03	.02–.15	.32 (.853)	3										
F	–.01		–.31–.29		1										
Corpus Callosum															
M	.29 (.26)	.03	.20–.33	8.02 (.784)	13						.26 (.26)	.05	.17–.34	1.73 (.631)	4
F	.02 (.02)	.03	–.04–.08	5.17 (.879)	11						–.05 (–.05)	.09	–.23–.13	6.40 (.094)	4
Other Structure															
M	.17 (.14)	.04	.07–.22	42.42 (<.001)	17	.16 (.12)	.06	.01–.24	10.34 (.066)	6	.11 (.11)	.02	.08–.14	08 (.823)	2
F	.12 (.13)	.16	.01–.24	13.05 (.110)	9						.16 (.16)	.04	.08–.23	.30 (.581)	2

Note. N = number of studies included; M = males; F = females.

Summary

Findings from Tables 4.4 and 4.5 can now be summarized to address the two main research questions outlined in Strategy 1: (1) Do people with higher intelligence have bigger brains? (2) What clues do these findings provide about the nature of the brain processes from which reserve emerges? The answers are relatively clear: higher intelligence is associated with larger whole brain volume and larger intracranial volume. These associations are of greater magnitude for cortical volume and temporal lobes compared to subcortical areas. The associations are stronger for brain volume compared to intracranial volume. Cortical volume has the strongest association with intelligence, perhaps providing some clue as to where intelligence is "located." One interesting finding is that the presence of WMH does not correlate with intelligence.

The Association between Reserve Capacity and Brain Atrophy

In this section, we investigate the relationship between reserve capacity (measured as intelligence, education, or brain size) and brain shrinkage or atrophy. Atrophy may be examined longitudinally (by measuring shrinkage between two observations taken at two time points) or estimated using cross-sectional data by calculating the difference between ICV and brain volume adjusted for head size. The amount of CSF relative to brain volume has also been used to estimate atrophy, as it increases as brain volume decreases. Most studies addressing this issue recruit participants from older age groups and most infer atrophy rather than measure it. The relevant measures of reserve are measures that reflect the person's level of competence earlier in life—these include measures of premorbid intelligence (such as the NART) or a measure of crystallized intelligence, measures of ICV (reflecting peak brain size and early adult intelligence), and education (as this reflects achievement early in life). The use of measures of current intelligence is less interpretable in this context because these measures reflect current brain burden as much as premorbid ability.

The view that higher education, intelligence, and larger brains are associated with reduced atrophy at older ages has little evidence to support it at this stage, at least in normal samples. Raz et al. (2005) failed to confirm that bigger brains at pretest were associated with less atrophy using measures taken over five years:

> We tested the hypothesis that having larger brain volumes at baseline may ameliorate longitudinal brain shrinkage. Of the 12 regions of interest, only two evidenced significant though relatively small correlations between the initial level and the magnitude of change, and it was in the direction opposite

to the predicted direction, i.e. smaller initial volumes were associated with lesser decline.

(Raz et al. 2005, p. 1681)

The correlations were −0.35 for visual cortex and −0.32 for the cerebellum. Measures of intelligence, occupation, and education as reserve have also been investigated with atrophy as an outcome variable. Raz et al. (1993) failed to find a relationship between levels of education and atrophy in a cross-sectional analysis.

Education has been found to be associated with greater CSF volume—a marker of cortical atrophy—in one cross-sectional study of 320 elderly normal people (Coffey, Saxton, Ratcliff, Bryan, & Lucke, 1999). In this study, education was found to be associated with greater CSF volume, indicating greater atrophy. This finding may represent a type 1 error, however, because education failed to associate significantly with other measures of brain structure, including cerebral hemisphere volume, frontal region area, and temporal parietal region. Other studies have reported no association between CSF and education (Kidron et al., 1997; Mori et al., 1997) in cross-sectional analyses.

Atrophy and Measures of Reserve

The relationships between atrophy and measures of intelligence are reported in Table 4.6, as a function of sample type. There was no significant overall association between measures of atrophy and measures of reserve for normal samples ($r = .01$, $n = 2$). This indicates that atrophy was no greater in the less well educated. In the pathological samples, however, atrophy was negatively associated with intelligence ($r = -0.48$, $n = 6$), indicating greater atrophy in those with lower intelligence. Total BV as a ratio of ICV was negatively associated with intelligence ($r = -.35$, $n = 4$). For education, in a pathological group, the mean weighted r was 0.27 but this was nonsignificant.

Summary

Higher intelligence did not protect against brain atrophy in normal samples (both when atrophy was inferred from brain volume as a function of ICV and when atrophy was measured using two time points). However, in clinical samples, lower intelligence was associated with greater atrophy.[4] A major limitation in interpreting these findings is the

---

[4]Two studies (Launer et al., 1995; Meyer et al. 2000) which contributed group mean data rather than correlations found no relationship between brain atrophy and educational level in clinical samples. (The categorical database contains group mean data from a number of studies—see pp. 153–154.)

TABLE 4.6

Relationships between Atrophy and Measures of Intelligence as a Function of Sample Type

Type of structure	Intelligence					Education					Occupation					Significance %
	Mean (weighted)	SE	95% CI	Heterogeneity χ^2 (sig)	N	Mean (weighted)	SE	95% CI	Heterogeneity χ^2 (sig)	N	Mean (weighted)	SE	95% CI	Heterogeneity χ^2 (sig)	N	
Atrophy*N	.01 (.01)	.04	−.06–.08	.98 (.322)	2											0 (.01, n=1)
Atrophy*P	−.51 (−.48)	.08	−.63–.33	16.63 (.005)	6	.27 (.18)	.19	−.19–.54	8.54 (.004)	2						68 (−.24, n=4)
Total brain	−.35 (−.35)	.01	−.36–.34	.05 (.997)	4											80 (−.35, n=1)
Volume/ICV*N																

contamination of the measure of reserve (intelligence) with current levels of functioning.

Rate of Change in Atrophy as a Function of Intelligence and Education (Strategy 3)

Strategy 3 attempts to examine whether the *rate* (rather than the amount) of atrophy is greater in those with less education. Research focusing on this outcome was scant. Only three of the studies included in the review examined longitudinal change, so the number of studies capable of examining rates of change in atrophy were very limited. We therefore drew on results from cross-sectional studies that reported age-linked outcomes, to gain an insight into the relationship between reserve (IQ, education, SES) and various brain structure changes over the lifespan. We acknowledge limitations in using cross-sectional results to make inferences about longitudinal change (see Hofer & Sliwinski, 2001). We also acknowledge that the BRH makes no specific predictions as to whether the correlation between education and brain structures increases or decreases with age. Nevertheless, the issue is of interest. Should associations between reserve and brain structure remain strong across the lifespan? Would these associations be expected to increase, or remain stable? Would there be a shift in the correlations between different brain regions, as the brain develops with age? For example, would shrinking frontal lobes be likely to be more weakly associated with *g* than shrinkage of other regions? These questions have rarely been addressed.

One study (MacLullich, Ferguson, Deary, Seckl, Starr, & Wardlaw, 2002) examined brain structure and intelligence relationships in a group of older people aged 65 to 70 years. Correlations between the NART and hippocampal, frontal, and temporal lobe volumes were in the order of 0.07 to 0.23 (left frontal lobe). For Raven's Progressive Matrices, the correlations with volumes of specific areas ranged from 0.22 to 0.32 and were mostly significant. The correlations between NART and Raven's scores and ICV were 0.30 and 0.39 respectively. A second relevant study, Haier et al. (2004), suggested that correlations of these measures with different regions of interest may vary with age. Using data previously described in this chapter and work undertaken by others examining the relationship between IQ and volume in children, these authors suggest:

> Taken together, the relationship between frontal brain regions and IQ across different ages appears to progress from anterior cingulate (pediatric cohort), to medial frontal (young cohort), to more dorsolateral frontal regions (older cohort). We suspect that the progression observed across these cohorts is

likely to be modulated by accelerated brain volume loss across the life span preferentially affecting frontal gray matter.

(Haier et al., 2004, p. 431)

These observations raise the possibility that intelligence measures will correlate differentially at older ages (i.e., correlations should be stronger in the dorsolateral frontal regions compared to medial frontal areas).

The Age of the Sample and Brain Associations

Figure 4.1(a) illustrates the relationship between age of the sample and the magnitude of the correlation with reserve measure (education, intelligence, occupation, SES). The data points and regression lines are shown in black for the normal samples and in gray for the pathological samples. The correlations become weaker with age in the normal samples, but not the pathological sample.[5] The raw correlation for all observations is −0.36 ($p<0.001$).

The distribution of the regions of interest used in the normal and pathological samples differed substantially. Figure 4.1(b) repeats the analysis using aggregated data (one observation per brain structure per study). The data points and regression lines are shown in black for the normal samples and in gray for the pathological samples. Correlating the 123 effects with age produces a coefficient of −0.220, and $p = 0.014$.

Empirical Studies explicitly Testing the True BRH

Research papers specifically addressing the true BRH are rare. These studies require that the study has measures of reserve (usually premorbid intelligence or education), a measure of brain burden such as brain atrophy or brain structure impairment, and a measure of change in cognitive capacity. These studies are also required to demonstrate that the reserve is responsible for regulating the relationship between the brain injury or burden and cognitive decline. Both brain atrophy and cognitive change may be estimated rather than measured. We scrutinized our set of papers for those that evaluated all three components of the BRH needed for the comprehensive test. Earlier studies, such as the important cross-sectional study of Mori et al. (1997), examined relationships between brain size and

---

[5]A second analysis classified 53 samples on the basis of the mean age of the sample into four categories based on quartiles: 16.4 years to 27.0 years; 28 years and above to less than 60 years; above 60 years to 70 years, and then older than 70 years. The mean average correlation between the brain measures and measures of reserve for these four age groups were: $r = 0.22$ ($n = 135$) (young); $r = 0.20$ ($n = 90$) (adult); $r = −0.04$ ($n = 54$) (young old); and $r = .00$ ($n = 331$) (old old), respectively.

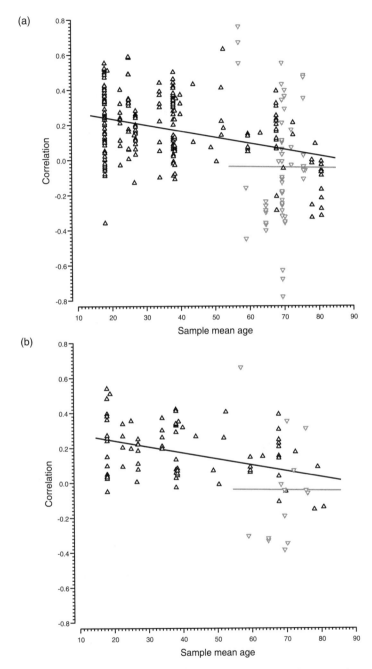

FIG. 4.1. Scatterplots and lines of best fit of correlations and age: (a) all reported correlations; (b) aggregated by ROI within studies (△—normal samples; ▽—pathological samples). Correlations are between measures of reserve and brain ROI.

brain atrophy, but did not directly test whether brain size regulated the relationship between cognitive performance and brain atrophy. Moreover, these early studies did not have longitudinal measures of cognitive decline.

We identified five studies of the true brain reserve hypothesis. Staff et al. (2004) noted that: "Testing the cognitive reserve hypothesis is difficult, because it demands a set of measured variables that are rarely available in a single cohort" (p. 1192). In their study of the true brain reserve hypothesis, Staff et al. used test measures collected 70 years earlier to control for cognitive decline, two measures of brain aging—a WMH score from MRI and a measure of brain atrophy—and measures of occupational and educational status as indicators of brain reserve. Cognitive performance at age 79 was measured by Raven's Progressive Matrices and the Auditory Verbal Learning Test (RVLT; Rey, 1958).To quote Staff et al.:

> We formulated tests of the reserve hypothesis as follows: if the cerebral reserve hypothesis is correct, then the measure of reserve should account for significant variance in cognitive outcomes in old age after adjusting for variance contributed by childhood mental ability and burden.
>
> (p. 1192)

Ninety volunteers participated. In the testing of the active version of the brain reserve hypothesis, measures of reserve were education and occupation, with WHMs and brain atrophy serving as measures of brain burden. Using ANCOVA, the investigators examined the effect of occupation/education on verbal memory and fluid intelligence (separately) taking account of IQ scores from early in life and measures of brain burden (WMH) and atrophy. They found that occupation and education significantly predicted cognitive outcomes when brain atrophy was used as a measure of brain burden. For occupation this effect was significant for both memory and performance measures. For education, the effect was significant only for verbal memory. The researchers concluded that education and occupation "accumulate reserve." One limitation of the research is that cognitive performance at age 11 is used to estimate premorbid intelligence. This represents a problem if intelligence measured before peak levels is not an accurate measure of premorbid IQ.

A second study, Dufouil, Alperovitch, and Tzourio (2003), examined the relationship between WMH and cognitive performance over a 4-year period, using a large epidemiological sample of 1394 individuals. Participants with severe WMH performed worse than others on tests of attention and speed, including Digit Symbol Substitution, Trail Making Test, Raven's Progressive Matrices and the Finger Tapping Test. A significant interaction effect with years of education was found, such that high

education was associated with less impaired performance for MMSE, Raven's Progressive Matrices and Word Fluency. This protective effect did not hold for speed tasks. The authors conclude that education "modulates" the effects of WMH, but attempt no explanation for the differential effect of education on various measures of cognition.

More recently, Bennett and associates (Bennett, Schneider, Wilson, Bienias, & Arnold, 2005; Bennett et al., 2003) investigated the relationships between education, cognitive function (a composite measure of global performance based on 19 cognitive tests), and autopsy measures of neuritic and diffuse plaques and neurofibrillary tangles. Directly testing the reserve hypothesis by examining the interaction effect of education and pathology in predicting cognitive performance, these researchers found that education protected against the negative cognitive effects of neuritic plaques and diffuse plaques, but not neurofibrillary tangles. The strongest protective effects were for speed, followed by semantic memory, and weakest for episodic memory. These findings are displayed in Figure 4.2. In a follow-up study, the same sample was reinvestigated using a less biased stain (modified Bielschowsky silver stain), confirming that education did not modify the effect of neurofibrillary tangles.

In a further published study, Bennett, Schneider, Tang, Arnold, and Wilson (2006), using a similar methodology, reported that social networks, as measured through structured interview, modified the relationship between cognition and the presence of neurofibrillary tangles and a measure of "global Alzheimer's disease pathology" (p. 409). The importance of an engaged or active lifestyle in maintaining cognitive functioning has been widely examined in cognitive aging research, and alteration of brain structure as a function of complex environments (including social factors) in animals is well documented (Lewis, 2004). The Bennett et al. (2006) study raises the possibility that social networks may be markers of a form of reserve.

A final approach to studying reserve is worth mentioning here. It attempts to understand and map the brain networks that may underpin cognitive reserve. This work focuses on understanding possible brain mechanisms that give rise to cognitive reserve, rather than directly testing the brain reserve hypothesis. For example, Stern et al. (2005) identified a pattern of brain functioning (using positron emission tomography) that was associated with high demand memory activity in young adults. The right hippocampus, posterior insula, thalamus, and right and left operculum were most activated. Young adults with higher NART and VIQ scores showed increased activation, suggesting to Stern et al. that it might be the mechanism underlying improved reserve. Older, high reserve participants, however, had decreased activation of these areas, suggesting to Stern that they make different (compensatory) use of such networks.

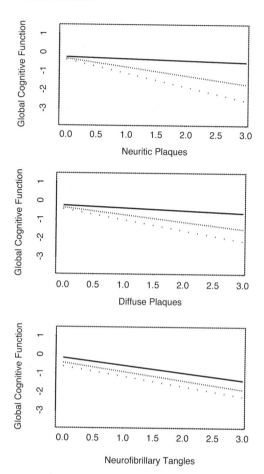

FIG. 4.2. Predicted relation between a measure of neuritic plaques (top), diffuse plaques (middle), and neurofibrillary tangles (bottom) and the global cognitive score proximate to death for participants with 22 years of education (90th percentile; solid line), 18 years of education (50th percentile; dashed line), and 15 years of education (10th percentile; dotted line). Reproduced with permission from Bennett et al. (2003). Education modifies the relation of AD pathology to level of cognitive function in older persons. *Neurology, 60*(12), 1909–1915.

DISCUSSION

The Relationship between Brain Structure and Intelligence

Our review of the empirical literature clearly supports the existence of relationships between indices of the brain (such as head size and brain

volume) and intellectual functioning. These include: a consistent, small to moderate sized relationship between head size or brain volume and intelligence and education; a consistent, small to moderate sized association for both performance and verbal intelligence, and for men and women. The association is present for specialized brain structures such as the hippocampus, and becomes weaker with age of the sample. The evidence is consistent with the idea that brain volume is positively associated with increased g and that brain volume (and head size) is associated with intellectual capacity in young adults.

The Relationship between Brain Size and Brain Atrophy

Our investigation of the relationship between brain structure and brain atrophy revealed gaps in the research literature, especially with respect to longitudinal change in brain volume and measures of reserve. The available data extracted from our search suggest that atrophy is not associated with either smaller brain size or greater education in most samples. We conclude that the evidence clearly indicates no protection in nonimpaired elderly samples, but that the mixed findings for individuals with pathology are worthy of further research. A host of other risk factors are associated with brain atrophy, including smoking, harmful levels of alcohol consumption, hypertension, genetic factors, brain injury, environmental toxins, viruses, and nutrition. Analysis of the interaction of these risk factors with indices of reserve may be another approach to evaluating the BRH. These types of analyses may cast light on the etiology of brain atrophy. Localization of the effects of risk factors is becoming possible through the use of emerging neuroimaging techniques such as voxel-based morphometry. For example, recent analysis of the PATH Through Life Study (Chen, Wen, Anstey, & Sachdev, 2006) has shown sex-specific and location-specific effects of hypertension on gray matter in frontal cortex. This study also found that men had less gray matter in the right superior, bilateral medial frontal, left superior temporal, and left precentral gyri, related to hypertension. Advances in the BRH will result when findings such as these are evaluated in the context of IQ, education, and aging.

The Relationship between Age and the Correlation of Reserve and Brain Structure

An interesting finding from the present review was the weakening of the association between brain measures and measures of reserve with age. This effect was strong and present for almost all sets of observations (an exception was gray matter). One interpretation of this finding is that brain

volume is influenced by disease or lifestyle factors to a greater degree than by education, intelligence, or other reserve at older ages. Strong potential lifestyle or disease processes include vascular disease and alcohol or drug use.

Findings from the True Brain Reserve Hypothesis

We identified only five papers which provided direct tests of the brain reserve hypothesis, namely: Staff et al. (2004), Dufouil et al. (2003), Bennett et al. (2005, 2003), and Bennett et al. (2006). These studies used relevant designs and included measures of brain burden, reserve, and cognitive outcomes. In these investigations, there was support for education modifying the effects of brain atrophy or amyloid deposition. The effect of education in modifying WMH was less clear, as the findings were inconsistent. There may be other studies directly testing the hypothesis that the systematic review failed to uncover. However, these five studies point to emerging evidence for education and premorbid intelligence providing reserve in the face of brain aging.

Limitations of the Review

Although the review conducted here attempted to systematically evaluate variants of the BRH and associated literature, it must be considered in the light of its limitations. These stem largely from the difficulty in integrating a diverse literature that, for the most part, does not explicitly test the BRH in a well-articulated fashion. Most scientific papers focus on reporting relationships among key variables. The expense of neuroimaging data means that studies of this type are often limited in their scope. Most of the studies reviewed were not undertaken with the purpose of evaluating the BRH, hence limitations, for the most part, stem from the questions we asked of them, some of which had not been articulated at the time the studies were conducted. We also acknowledge that relevant literature may have been overlooked. That said, it is clear that the distribution of research is focussed on cross-sectional studies of younger individuals. There has been intense interest in the investigation of relationships between brain function and intelligence in young people, with little investigation at older ages. There is also a focus on the effects of intelligence rather than on education, occupation, or social connectedness. Investigations of brain structure and *rates* of change in brain structures as a function of premorbid intelligence and education were not identified in the review. Very few studies have addressed the BRH directly, although this is changing rapidly. Specific weaknesses of the literature and the review are considered below.

Influences on the Magnitude of Correlations and Nonindependence of the Observations

Correlations in samples of older subjects may be reduced because of restrictions in the range of test scores, or reduced variability of scores in individuals with pathology. The unreliability of test instruments and measures may also reduce observed correlations. From a statistical perspective, lack of independence existed at study level, between and within regions of interest. Fifteen of the 88 samples in the current study were nonindependent. Most samples contributed more than one observation to the review as more than one ROI (for example, temporal lobe, overall brain volume) was examined. Some studies contributed more than one measure of a region of interest (for example, three different measures of temporal lobe structure or three measures of head size—perimeter, height, width—were reported). These interdependencies represent difficulties for secondary analysis of meta-analysis data since these higher order analyses assume independence of observations. The best methods to overcome these multiple levels of dependency are not clear, particularly given the information available from studies. In this review, where possible, regions of interest were aggregated within studies to provide one observation per study for some analyses and tests of homogeneity and confidence intervals were provided. Secondary analyses of correlational data were avoided. We were thus unable to say whether the magnitude of correlations were significantly different between different groups or regions.

Adjustments for Head Size and Brain Volume

Although researchers routinely correct for head size and brain volume, the method of adjustment may introduce bias into the results. The field requires methodological contributions to address some of the inherent problems that researchers face when attempting to compare brain subvolumes between individuals with different premorbid or current brain size. At present there are mixed results from empirical work investigating adjusting for height and weight. Passingham (1975) claimed that correlations are reduced if cranial capacity is adjusted for height. Ivanovic et al. (2004) failed to find any difference in adjustment for body size. At best, researchers can be aware of the issues and the potential biases that their correction methods may introduce into their results.

Sample Sizes: Use of a Variety of Samples Recruited from Different Sources

Both the source of sampling and the sampling procedure may influence the results found in individual studies and explain inconsistent results. Our review was also hampered in some instances by the nonindependence of observations. In some areas we were forced to rely heavily on a few articles that provided detailed results. Another factor impacting on our conclusions is the small sample size of many studies, particularly those of clinical groups.

Publication Bias

As with any field of research, it is likely that significant results are reported, while nonsignificant associations of particular interest to the BRH (e.g., education and brain size) are not reported in the literature. This means that our review may overestimate the actual effect sizes studied.

Specific Problems in the Review

Like all meta-analyses, our review aggregated and summarized datasets. As a result we accorded equal status to data derived from papers varying in quality. Clearly, the inherent faults of all studies are preserved in their inclusion in the meta-analysis. This includes factors such as the inclusion of dementia or incipient dementia patients in normal samples, type of adjustment for head size or body size, whether adjustments were made for education or sex, and so on.

THE STATUS OF THE BRAIN RESERVE HYPOTHESIS

One of the major findings of our investigations was that the BRH is not a single entity and that a testable reserve hypothesis must specify and measure the protective factor, describe how it might be represented biologically or functionally (so that it is credible and can be measured), measure brain burden, and then provide evidence of improved cognitive outcomes. We were only able to locate five major studies which directly tested versions of the "true brain hypothesis."

In reviewing this literature, we were struck by the lack of clarity concerning the concept of reserve. In other areas of health research, the concept of reserve implies that there is additional capacity that can be called upon in moments of need or emergency. For example, in pulmonary reserve, capacity is available to be harnessed to *increase* the person's

resources if needed. The construct of reserve, in the present context, however, generally refers to the capacity to provide a buffer in order to maintain the person at their characteristic level of functioning rather than operating as a resource that will provide increased emergency capacity. Reserve is often viewed metaphorically in hydraulic or mechanical terms as a reservoir, a vat of capacity, which becomes depleted with brain aging and wear and tear. A better metaphor to describe various brain reserve hypotheses may be to consider reserve in the context of a sporting team— perhaps a team of rugby union players. The team loses a player through injury, and a reserve comes into place to fill the vacancy: the size of the team is not increased, but the replacement allows the team to continue to play on an equal footing. Buffering may be passive, as a biological resource to be drawn upon as brain damage occurs. In this case the buffering can be seen to be the ability of the team to bring in a reserve. Buffering processes can also be seen to be compensatory or active, allowing the person to operate competently at a functional level despite the effects of damage or pathology. Continuing the sport analogy, a team without reserves which plays strategically can still succeed (an example of active buffering through compensation). In this case, strategic game play rather than the addition of a player is the buffer. The analogy of the rugby team extends to more realistic and complex scenarios. For example, a key player(s) may be lost (the goal kicker, two of the front row forwards), and despite both active and passive buffering through the addition of a reserve and very clever strategy, the team may not be able to compensate for its specific or localized loss.

Application of the rugby metaphor is helpful in illustrating why the area is difficult to progress and what is needed. Table 4.7 outlines the components required to articulate a testable BRH. These are the nature of the brain insult, the buffer, the mechanism, and the expected outcome. The table also articulates the type of BRH (passive or active) and whether the hypothesis is testable. Multiple factors may be at work: there may be many simultaneous biological injuries, multiple reserves, numerous mechanisms, and various outcomes. This is illustrated for one particular model (Model 1). In this model, WMHs develop with an aging brain. The buffer (or reserve) is hypothesized to be a bigger brain, capable of contributing uninjured brain matter to replace the injured or degraded areas (the equivalent of sending in the reserves on the rugby field). A bigger brain endows the person with a buffer, despite the buildup of WMH. In contrast, those with smaller brains will show signs of cognitive aging. This model represents a testable model of the buffering hypothesis if measures of WMH, brain size, and cognitive decline are available.

To keep the rugby analogy alive, there may be a limit to how many reserves are available. Presumably at some point WMH saturation

TABLE 4.7
Components Required to Articulate a Testable BRH

Model	Type of Brain Injury	The Buffer (Reserve)	The Mechanism	The Outcome	Type	Testability
1	Presence of WMH	Bigger brain	Provides areas of uninjured brain	No change in cognitive capacity relative to others	PASSIVE	Yes.
2	Presence of WMH	Intelligence	Provides a more networked brain	No change	PASSIVE	Yes (requires that intelligence is associated with a more networked brain).
3	Loss of brain matter with age	Education	Increases the arborization of dendrites	No change in cognitive capacity relative to others	PASSIVE	Yes (even better if a measure of arborization of dendrites is possible).
4	Loss of brain matter with age	Intelligence	Provides a more networked brain: with more areas with specialization Provides greater recruitment of brain areas	No change	PASSIVE	Yes (even better if a more networked brain can be assessed). The type of model originally proposed by Mori et al. (1997).
5	Loss of hippocampal volume	Intelligence	Allows the recruitment of strategies to compensate for hippocampal loss	No change	ACTIVE	Yes (requires the demonstration of compensatory strategies in more able adults and that these strategies produce change).
6	Loss of brain matter or presence of WMH	Brain size (ICV)	Not specified	No support for ICV as a buffer for cognitive decline	PASSIVE	Yes (tested by Staff, 2004 in a normal sample).

(Continued)

TABLE 4.7
(Continued)

Model	Type of Brain Injury	The Buffer (Reserve)	The Mechanism	The Outcome	Type	Testability
7	Loss of brain matter	Occupation Education	Not specified	Support for education and occupation as buffer for memory and fluid IQ decline	PASSIVE	Yes (tested by Staff et al., 2004 in a normal sample).
8	Presence of WMH	Education	Not specified	Support for education as a buffer of cognitive decline over four years	Not clear	Yes (tested by Dufouil et al., 2003 in a normal sample).
9	Autopsy-based pathology including senile plaques, neurofibrillary tangles, Lewy bodies, white matter rarefaction	Education	Not specified	No evidence	Not clear	Yes.

becomes critical, even in those with large brains. As in rugby—once the reserves have been expended—the play is likely to deteriorate without further player replacement. Although Model 1 is testable, issues remain. For example, what is the saturation point? How many reserves are allowed? Who determines how many players are allowed on the field at any one point? A second major difficulty is that the hypothesis essentially predicts lack of change (i.e., a non-effect) (see The Outcome, Table 4.7). In rugby it may be possible to compare previous match statistics to determine whether deterioration has occurred. Analogously, cognitive outcomes can be kept longitudinally.

Advances in the Brain Reserve Hypothesis

A number of potential and actual models described in the literature are articulated in Table 4.7. Identifying these components also helps us to identify the questions that should be asked, as well as the perspective to categorize areas of research. Major areas of investigation will be "the mechanism" or the way in which reserve produces the buffer, the way in which the buffer emerges from the brain and whether the mechanisms underlying reserve in dementia differ from those in normal aging. These are addressed below.

Understanding how Reserve Processes might Work

An important question to consider is how reserve processes might regulate cognitive performance. A variety of biological and psychological models have been proposed, including greater dendritic field size in those with higher education (Kramer et al., 2004); increases in phosphocreatine (Valenzuela & Sachdev, 2001); or greater synaptic density and more complex neurocortical interneuronal connections. Other models describe functional compensatory recruitment of brain areas and networks (Staff et al., 2004). For example, Cabeza and Nyberg (2000) found greater recruitment of brain areas in better performing young adults. Rosen et al. (2002) noted that older adults with high memory scores showed significant recruitment of frontal regions, compared to low scoring older adults. "Increasing recruitment may operate to maintain a high level of performance in older adults in the presence of detrimental physiological changes" (Buckner, 2004, p. 204). More recently, Stern et al. (2005) have referred to compensatory, perhaps altered, networks in older adults as a manifestation of reserve.

Understanding how the Structure and Function of the Brain gives Rise to g

Understanding the brain structures which support intelligence may provide some insight into the mechanisms by which reserve works. A variety of structures have been proposed to give rise to g, including brain size and volume, brain myelination (Waxman, 1992), brain electrical potentials supported by studies reporting correlations between average evoked potential and measure of g (Ree & Carretta, 2002), speed of processing, and brain glucose metabolism rate. Plomin and Kosslyn (2001) argue that because g is heritable, it is of interest to examine the heritability of various brain structures. They asked whether the heritability of gray matter follows a similar developmental course to that for the heritability of g. They report that heritability increases almost linearly from infancy (about 20%) to childhood (about 40%) to old age (about 60%):

> Although it is possible that a single fundamental brain characteristic such as frontal gray matter volume is responsible for g, it seems more likely that many brain processes are involved. However, so far the pickings are slim other than brain volume measures. For example, although EEG alpha peak frequency, EEG coherence (which has been taken as a measure of brain interconnectivity) and peripheral nerve conduction velocity are all highly heritable, these measures do not relate to g. Thus g does not seem to involve speedier brains.
>
> (Plomin & Kosslyn, 2001, p. 1155)

The increased heritability of g with age has been supported in a recent meta-analysis (Lee, 2003), although there is recognition of the importance of methodological factors in producing biased estimates. (For a more comprehensive review of this area see McGue & Johnson, chapter 2.) Recent papers point to two areas of significant gene linkage to general intelligence, one on chromosome 2 and one on 6, and other potential areas such as chromosome 14 (Posthuma et al., 2005). Lee (2003) suggests that genes may constitute a type of reserve.

Understanding how the Brain Ages

At this stage, our understanding of brain changes in older age and their link to cognitive processes is limited. There is recognition that aging associated with dementia may involve a qualitatively different pattern of brain changes than those associated with normal aging. Buckner (2004) reviewed a number of potential candidates that may produce declines in age-related executive function, including damage to white matter, which is common. Reporting findings by Ylikoski, Erkinjuntti, Raininko, Sarna,

Sulkava, and Tilvis (1995), Buckner notes that as many as 65% of individuals over age 75 have these deficits. DeCarli et al. (2005) report that as many as 30% of people over the age of 80 have a least one brain insult. The prevalence of the condition, together with the association of WMH with cognitive performance, makes this a possibility. (Note, however, that the present review did not find associations of WMH with intelligence.) A second factor may be brain atrophy, particularly of frontal areas. A third possibility is depletion of dopamine. The mechanisms responsible for the development of medial lobe dysfunction and dementia may differ. Candidates responsible for the development of dementia include the buildup of amyloid and tau. Neurofibrillary tangles appear in the medial temporal lobe and spread outwards (Buckner, 2004). Structures in the medial temporal lobe shrink in both normal and pathological aging and the question of whether AD represents a faster development of a normal aging process is not resolved. However, there is clear evidence that some very old individuals do not show signs of AD. Evidence from studies of genetic mutations suggests that there may be dissociations between these two systems (frontal striatal vs. medial temporal). Clearly, these findings suggest that the injuries in normal aging and dementia may differ. The mechanism through which reserve may operate may also differ as a result.

CONCLUDING REMARKS

The present review confirms that, in general, the current approach to investigating BRHs requires more sophistication, and there are signs that progress is being made. Brain reserve hypotheses are now being described and classified (see, for example, Stern, 2002). Exceptionally good long-term longitudinal studies which record measures of cognitive performance in young adulthood and describe cognitive performance decades later, which include measures of brain function and structure, even autopsy data, allow direct tests of the true BRH. Notable studies are those of Staff et al. (2004) with the Aberdeen Study, and Bennett et al. (2003, 2005) with the Religious Order's Study. There are behavioral and genetic studies that attempt to seek the basis of g and of reserve (see, for example Stern et al., 2005; Thompson et al., 2001). As this work continues, researchers must be aware of which components of which BRH they are investigating and how it fits with the full picture. They might ask which part of the game am I investigating: the individual players, the game play, the strategies used by the team, the quality and number of the reserve players, the match outcomes, or the whole dynamic match from start to finish.

REFERENCES

Akgun, A., Okuyan, M., Baytan, S. H., & Topbas, M. (2003). Relationships between nonverbal IQ and brain size in right and left-handed men and women. *International Journal of Neuroscience, 113*(7), 893–902.

Almkvist, O., & Winblad, B. (1999). Early diagnosis of Alzheimer dementia based on clinical and biological factors. *European Archives of Psychiatry and Clinical Neurosciences, 249*(9), S3–S9.

Andreasen, N. C., Flaum, M., Swayze, V., Oleary, D. S., Alliger, R., Cohen, G., et al. (1993). Intelligence and brain structure in normal individuals. *American Journal of Psychiatry, 150*(1), 130–134.

Ankney, C. D. (1992). The brain size/IQ debate. *Nature, 360*(6402), 292.

Anstey, K., & Christensen, H. (2000). Education, activity, health, blood pressure and apolipoprotein e as predictors of cognitive change in old age: A review. *Gerontology, 46*(3), 163–177.

Anstey, K. J., & Maller, J. J. (2003). The role of volumetric MRI in understanding mild cognitive impairment and similar classifications. *Aging & Mental Health, 7*(4), 238–250.

Anstey, K. J., Maller, J. J., Meslin, C., Christensen, H., Jorm, A. F., Wen, W., et al. (2004). Hippocampal and amygdalar volumes in relation to handedness in adults aged 60–64. *Neuroreport, 15*(18), 2825–2829.

Baddeley, A., Emslie, H., & Nimmo-Smith, I. (1993). The Spot-the-Word test: A robust estimate of verbal intelligence based on lexical decision. *British Journal of Clinical Psychology, 32*(Pt 1), 55–65.

Bennett, D. A., Schneider, J. A., Tang, Y., Arnold, S. E., & Wilson, R. S. (2006). The effect of social networks on the relation between Alzheimer's disease pathology and level of cognitive function in old people: A longitudinal cohort study. *Lancet Neurology, 5*(5), 406–412.

Bennett, D. A., Schneider, J. A., Wilson, R. S., Bienias, J. L., & Arnold, S. E. (2005). Education modifies the association of amyloid but not tangles with cognitive function. *Neurology, 65*(6), 953–955.

Bennett, D. A., Wilson, R. S., Schneider, J. A., Evans, D. A., Mendes de Leon, C. F., Arnold, S. E., et al. (2003). Education modifies the relation of ad pathology to level of cognitive function in older persons. *Neurology, 60*(12), 1909–1915.

Buckner, R. L. (2004). Memory and executive function in aging and AD: Multiple factors that cause decline and reserve factors that compensate. *Neuron, 44*(1), 195–208.

Bunce, D. (in press). APOE and cognitive function in non-demented old age: A genetic basis for brain or cognitive reserve? In E.M. Welsh (Ed.), *Progress in Alzheimer's disease research.* New York: Nova Science Publishers.

Cabeza, R., & Nyberg, L. (2000). Imaging cognition II: An empirical review of 275 PET and FMRI studies. *Journal of Cognitive Neuroscience, 12*(1), 1–47.

Cattell, R. B., & Cattell, A. K. S. (1960). *Handbook for the individual or group culture fair intelligence test.* Champaign, IL: APT.

Caviness, V. S., Jr., Kennedy, D. N., Richelme, C., Rademacher, J., & Filipek, P. A. (1996). The human brain age 7–11 years: A volumetric analysis based on magnetic resonance images. *Cerebral Cortex, 6*(5), 726–736.

Chen, X., Wen, W., Anstey, K. J., & Sachdev, P. S. (2006). Effects of cerebrovascular risk factors on gray matter volume in adults aged 60–64 years: A voxel-based morphometric study. *Psychiatry Research, 147*(2–3), 105–114.

Coffey, C. E., Saxton, J. A., Ratcliff, G., Bryan, R. N., & Lucke, J. F. (1999). Relation of education to brain size in normal aging—implications for the reserve hypothesis. *Neurology, 53*(1), 189–196.

Cohen, C. I. (2000). Relation of education to brain size in normal aging. *Neurology, 54*(5), 1207–1208.

Deary, I. J. (2001). Individual differences in cognition: British contributions over a century. *British Journal of Psychology, 92,* 217–237.

DeCarli,C., Massaro, J., Harvey, D., Hald, J., Tullberg, M., Au, R., et al. (2005). Measures of brain morphology and infarction in the Framingham heart study: Establishing what is normal. *Neurobiology of Aging, 26*(4), 491–510.

Dufouil, C., Alperovitch, A., & Tzourio, C. (2003). Influence of education on the relationship between white matter lesions and cognition. *Neurology, 60*(5), 831–836.

Fein, G., & Di Sclafani, V. (2004). Cerebral reserve capacity: Implications for alcohol and drug abuse. *Alcohol, 32*(1), 63–67.

Folstein, M. F., Folstein, S. E., & McHugh, P. R. (1975). "Mini-mental state". A practical method for grading the cognitive state of patients for the clinician. *Journal of Psychiatric Research, 12*(3), 189–198.

Fukui, T., & Kertesz, A. (2000). Volumetric study of lobar atrophy in Pick Complex and Alzheimer's disease. *Journal of Neurological Sciences, 174*(2), 111–121.

Gibson, K. R. (2002). Evolution of human intelligence: The roles of brain size and mental construction. *Brain, Behavior & Evolution, 59*(1–2), 10–20.

Gignac, G., Vernon, P. A., & Wickett, J. C. (2003). Factors influencing the relationship between brain size and intelligence. In H. Nyborg (Ed.), *The scientific study of general intelligence: Tribute to Arthur R. Jensen* (Vol. 93–106). New York: Pergamon.

Golomb, J., de Leon, M. J., Kluger, A., George, A. E., Tarshish, C., & Ferris, S. H. (1993). Hippocampal atrophy in normal aging. An association with recent memory impairment. *Archives of Neurology, 50*(9), 967–973.

Graves, A.B, Mortimer, J. A., Bowen, J. D., McCormick, W. C., McCurry, S. M., Schellenberg, G. D., et al. (2001). Head circumference and incident Alzheimer's disease: Modification by apolipoprotein e. *Neurology, 57*(8), 1453–1460.

Graves, A. B., Mortimer, J. A., Larson, E. B., Wenzlow, A., & Bowen, J. D. (1996). Head circumference as a measure of cognitive reserve. Association with severity of impairment in Alzheimer's disease. *British Journal of Psychiatry, 169*(1), 86–92.

Gunning-Dixon, F. M., & Raz, N. (2000). The cognitive correlates of white matter abnormalities in normal aging: A quantitative review. *Neuropsychology, 14*(2), 224–232.

Gur, R. C., Turetsky, B. I., Matsui, M., Yan, M., Bilker, W., Hughett, P., et al. (1999). Sex differences in brain gray and white matter in healthy young adults: Correlations with cognitive performance. *Journal of Neuroscience, 19*(10), 4065–4072.

Gutzmann, H., Klimitz, H., & Avdaloff, W. (1982). Correlations between psychopathology, psychological test results and computerized tomography changes in senile dementia. *Archives of Gerontology & Geriatrics, 1*(3), 241–259.

Haier, R. J., Jung, R. E., Yeo, R. A., Head, K., & Alkire, M. T. (2004). Structural brain variation and general intelligence. *Neuroimage, 23*(1), 425–433.

Heilman, K. M., Nadeau, S. E., & Beversdorf, D. O. (2003). Creative innovation: Possible brain mechanisms. *Neurocase, 9*(5), 369–379.

Hirono, N., Kitagaki, H., Kazui, H., Hashimoto, M., & Mori, E. (2000). Impact of white matter changes on clinical manifestation of Alzheimer's disease—a quantitative study. *Stroke, 31*(9), 2182–2188.

Hofer, S. M., & Sliwinski, M. J. (2001). Understanding ageing. An evaluation of research designs for assessing the interdependence of ageing-related changes. *Gerontology, 47*(6), 341–352.

Hultsch, D. F., Hertzog, C., Small, B. J., & Dixon, R. A. (1999). Use it or lose it: Engaged lifestyle as a buffer of cognitive decline in aging? *Psychology and Aging, 14*(2), 245–263.

Hunter, J. E., & Schmidt, F. L. (1990). *Methods of meta-analysis: Correcting error and bias in research findings*. Newbury Park, CA: Sage.

Ivanovic, D. M., Leiva, B. P., Castro, C. G., Olivares, M. G., Jansana, J. M. M., Castro, V. G., et al. (2004). Brain development parameters and intelligence in Chilean high school graduates. *Intelligence, 32*(5), 461–479.

Ivanovic, D. M., Leiva, B. P., Perez, H. T., Olivares, M. G., Diaz, N. S., Urrutia, M. S. C., et al. (2004). Head size and intelligence, learning, nutritional status and brain development head, IQ, learning, nutrition and brain. *Neuropsychologia, 42*(8), 1118–1131.

Jensen, A. R. (1994). Psychometric g—related to differences in head size. *Personality and Individual Differences, 17*(5), 597–606.

Johnson, F. W. (1991). Biological factors and psychometric intelligence: A review. *Genetic, Social,and General Psychology Monographs, 117*(3), 313–357.

Kamin, L. J., & Omari, S. (1998). Race, head size, and intelligence. *South African Journal of Psychology, 28*(3), 119–128.

Kaplan, H. S., & Robson, A. J. (2002). The emergence of humans: The coevolution of intelligence and longevity with intergenerational transfers. *Proceedings of the National Academy of Sciences USA, 99*(15), 10221–10226.

Katzman, R. (1993). Education and the prevalence of dementia and Alzheimer's disease. *Neurology, 43*(1), 13–20.

Katzman, R., Terry, R., DeTeresa, R., Brown, T., Davies, P., Fuld, P., et al. (1988). Clinical, pathological, and neurochemical changes in dementia: A subgroup with preserved mental status and numerous neocortical plaques. *Annals of Neurology, 23*(2), 138–144.

Kidron, D., Black, S. E., Stanchev, P., Buck, B., Szalai, J. P., Parker, J., et al. (1997). Quantitative MR volumetry in Alzheimer's disease—topographic markers and the effects of sex and education. *Neurology, 49*(6), 1504–1512.

Kramer, A. F., Bherer, L., Colcombe, S. J., Dong, W., & Greenough, W. T. (2004). Environmental influences on cognitive and brain plasticity during aging. *Journals of Gerontology Series A: Biological Sciences and Medical Sciences, 59*(9), M940–957.

LaFosse, J. M., Mednick, S. A., Praestholm, J., Vestergaard, A., Parnas, J., & Schulsinger, F. (1994). The influence of parental socioeconomic status on CT studies of schizophrenia. *Schizophrenia Research, 11*(3), 285–290.

Launer, L. J., Scheltens, P., Lindeboom, J., Barkhof, F., Weinstein, H., & Jonker, C. (1995). Medial temporal lobe atrophy in an open population of very old persons: Cognitive, brain atrophy, and sociomedical correlates. *Neurology, 45*(4), 747–752.

Lee, J. H. (2003). Genetic evidence for cognitive reserve: Variations in memory and related cognitive functions. *Journal of Clinical and Experimental Neuropsychology, 25*(5), 594–613.

Lewis, M.H. (2004). Environmental complexity and central nervous system development and function. *Mental Retardation and Developmental Disabilities Research Reviews, 10*(2), 91–95.

Lynn, R. (1991). The evolution of racial-differences in intelligence. *Mankind Quarterly, 32*(1–2), 99–121.

Lynn, R. (1999). Sex differences in intelligence and brain size: A developmental theory. *Intelligence, 27*(1), 1–12.

MacLullich, A. M. J., Ferguson, K. J., Deary, I. J., Seckl, J. R., Starr, J. M., & Wardlaw, J. M. (2002). Intracranial capacity and brain volumes are associated with cognition in healthy elderly men. *Neurology, 59*(2), 169–174.

Maguire, E. A., Gadian, D. G., Johnsrude, I. S., Good, C. D., Ashburner, J., Frackowiak, R. S., et al. (2000). Navigation-related structural change in the hippocampi of taxi drivers. *Proceedings of the National Academy of Sciences USA, 97*(8), 4398–4403.

Marino, L. (2005). Big brains do matter in new environments. *Proceedings of the National Academy of Sciences USA, 102*(15), 5306–5307.

McDaniel, M. A. (2005). Big-brained people are smarter: A meta-analysis of the relationship between in vivo brain volume and intelligence. *Intelligence, 33*(4), 337–346.

Meyer, J. S., Rauch, G., Rauch, R. A., & Haque, A. (2000). Risk factors for cerebral hypoperfusion, mild cognitive impairment, and dementia. *Neurobiology of Aging, 21*(2), 161–169.

Miller, E. M. (1991). Climate and intelligence. *Mankind Quarterly, 32*(1–2), 127–132.

Minagar, A., Sevush, S., & Bertran, A. (2000). Cerebral ventricles are smaller in Hispanic than non-Hispanic patients with Alzheimer's disease. *Neurology, 55*(3), 446–448.

Mori, E., Hirono, N., Yamashita, H., Imamura, T., Ikejiri, Y., Ikeda, M., et al. (1997). Premorbid brain size as a determinant of reserve capacity against intellectual decline in Alzheimer's disease. *American Journal of Psychiatry, 154*(1), 18–24.

Mortimer, J. A. (1997). Brain reserve and the clinical expression of Alzheimer's Disease. *Geriatrics, 52* (Suppl. 2), 50–53.

Mungas, D., Harvey, D., Reed, B. R., Jagust, W. J., DeCarli, C., Beckett, L., et al. (2005). Longitudinal volumetric MRI change and rate of cognitive decline. *Neurology, 65*(4), 565–571.

Neary, D., Snowden, J. S., Mann, D. M., Bowen, D. M., Sims, N. R., Northen, B., et al. (1986). Alzheimer's disease: A correlative study. *Journal of Neurology, Neurosurgery & Psychiatry, 49*(3), 229–237.

Nelson, H. E., & O'Connell, A. (1978). Dementia: The estimation of premorbid intelligence levels using the New Adult Reading Test. *Cortex, 14*(2), 234–244.

Nguyen, N. T., & McDaniel, M. A. (2000). Brain size and intelligence: A meta-analysis. *First Annual Conference of the International Society of Intelligence Research.* Cleveland, OH.

O'Brien, J. T., Desmond, P., Ames, D., Schweitzer, I., & Tress, B. (1997). Magnetic resonance imaging correlates of memory impairment in the healthy elderly: Association with medial temporal lobe atrophy but not white matter lesions. *International Journal of Geriatric Psychiatry, 12*(3), 369–374.

Ozer, M. A., Kayalioglu, G., & Erturk, M. (2005). Topographic anatomy of the fornix as a guide for the transcallosal-interforniceal approach with a special emphasis on sex differences. *Neurologia Medico- Chirurgica (Tokyo), 45*(12), 607–612.

Passingham, R. E. (1975). The brain and intelligence. *Brain Behavior and Evolution, 11*(1), 1–15.

Passingham, R. E. (1979). Brain size and intelligence in man. *Brain Behavior and Evolution, 16*(4), 253–270.

Passingham, R. E., Stephan, K. E., & Kotter, R. (2002). The anatomical basis of functional localization in the cortex. *Nature Reviews Neuroscience, 3*(8), 606–616.

Plomin, R., & Kosslyn, S. M. (2001). Genes, brain and cognition. *Nature Neuroscience, 4*(12), 1153–1154.

Posthuma, D., Luciano, M., Geus, E. J., Wright, M. J., Slagboom, P. E., Montgomery, G. W., et al. (2005). A genomewide scan for intelligence identifies quantitative trait loci on 2q and 6p. *American Journal of Human Genetics, 77*(2), 318–326.

Raven, J. C., Court, J. H., & Raven, J. (1976). *Manual for Raven's progressive matrices.* London: H.K. Lewis.

Raz, N., Lindenberger, U., Rodrigue, K. M., Kennedy, K. M., Head, D., Williamson, A., et al. (2005). Regional brain changes in aging healthy adults: General trends, individual differences and modifiers. *Cerebral Cortex, 15*(11), 1676–1689.

Raz, N., Torres, I. J., Spencer, W. D., Millman, D., Baertschi, J. C., & Sarpel, G. (1993). Neuroanatomical correlates of age-sensitive and age-invariant cognitive-abilities—an in-vivo MRI investigation. *Intelligence, 17*(3), 407–422.

Ree, M. J., & Carretta, T. R. (2002). g2k. *Human Performance, 15*(1–2), 3–23.

Rey, A. (1958). *L'examin cinique en psychologie.* Paris: Presses Universitaire de France

Reynolds, M. D., Johnston, J. M., Dodge, H. H., DeKosky, S. T., & Ganguli, M. (1999). Small

head size is related to low Mini-Mental State Examination scores in a community sample of nondemented older adults. *Neurology, 53*(1), 228–229.

Rosen, A. C., Prull, M. W., O'Hara, R., Race, E. A., Desmond, J. E., Glover, G. H., et al. (2002). Variable effects of aging on frontal lobe contributions to memory. *Neuroreport, 13*(18), 2425–2428.

Roth, G., & Dicke, U. (2005). Evolution of the brain and intelligence. *Trends in Cognitive Sciences, 9*(5), 250–257.

Roth, M., Tomlinson, B. E., & Blessed, G. (1966). Correlation between scores for dementia and counts of 'senile plaques' in cerebral grey matter of elderly subjects. *Nature, 209*(18), 109–110.

Rothschild, D. (1937). Pathological changes in senile psychosis and their psychobiological significance. *American Journal of Psychiatry, 93*, 757–788.

Rushton, J., & Ankney, C. (1996). Brain size and cognitive ability: Correlations with age, sex, social class, and race. *Psychonomic Bulletin & Review, 3*(1), 21–36.

Rushton, J. P., & Jensen, A. R. (2005). Thirty years of research on race differences in cognitive ability. *Psychology Public Policy and Law, 11*(2), 235–294.

Satz, P. (1993). Brain reserve capacity on symptom onset after brain injury: A formulation and review of evidence for threshold theory. *Neuropsychology, 7*(3), 273–295.

Satz, P., Morgenstern, H., Miller, E. N., Selnes, O. A., McArthur, J. C., Cohen, B. A., et al. (1993). Low education as a possible risk factor for cognitive abnormalities in HIV-1: Findings from the multicenter AIDS cohort study (MACS). *Journal of Acquired Immune Deficiency Syndromes, 6*(5), 503–511.

Scarmeas, N., Albert, S. M., Manly, J. J., & Stern, Y. (2006). Education and rates of cognitive decline in incident Alzheimer's disease. *Journal of Neurology, Neurosurgery & Psychiatry, 77*(3), 308–316.

Scarmeas, N., & Stern, Y. (2004). Cognitive reserve: Implications for diagnosis and prevention of Alzheimer's disease. *Current Neurology and Neuroscience Reports, 4*(5), 374–380.

Schaie, K. (1984). Midlife influences upon intellectual functioning in old age. *International Journal of Behavioral Development, 7*(4), 463–478.

Schmand, B., Smit, J. H., Geerlings, M. I., & Lindeboom, J. (1997). The effects of intelligence and education on the development of dementia. A test of the brain reserve hypothesis. *Psychological Medicine, 27*(6), 1337–1344.

Schofield, P. (1999). Alzheimer's disease and brain reserve. *Australasian Journal on Ageing, 18*(1), 10–14.

Schofield, P. W., Mosesson, R. E., Stern, Y., & Mayeux, R. (1995). The age at onset of Alzheimer's disease and an intracranial area measurement—a relationship. *Archives of Neurology, 52*(1), 95–98.

Shin, Y. W., Kim, D. J., Ha, T. H., Park, H. J., Moon, W. J., Chung, E. C., et al. (2005). Sex differences in the human corpus callosum: Diffusion tensor imaging study. *Neuroreport, 16*(8), 795–798.

Spratt, D. (2000). Sex differences in the brain. *Journal of Neuroendocrinology, 12*(7), 597–598.

Staff, R. T., Murray, A. D., Deary, I. J., & Whalley, L. J. (2004). What provides cerebral reserve? *Brain, 127*(5), 1191–1199.

Stern, Y. (2002). What is cognitive reserve? Theory and research application of the reserve concept. *Journal of the International Neuropsychological Society, 8*(3), 448–460.

Stern, Y., Alexander, G. E., Prohovnik, I., & Mayeux, R. (1992). Inverse relationship between education and parietotemporal perfusion deficit in Alzheimer's disease. *Annals of Neurology, 32*(3), 371–375.

Stern, Y., Habeck, C., Moeller, J., Scarmeas, N., Anderson, K. E., Hilton, H. J., et al. (2005). Brain networks associated with cognitive reserve in healthy young and old adults. *Cerebral Cortex, 15*(4), 394–402.

Stroop, J. R. (1935). Studies of interference in serial verbal reactions. *Journal of Experimental Psychology, 18,* 643–622.

Thompson, P. M., Cannon, T. D., Narr, K. L., van Erp, T., Poutanen, V. P., Huttunen, M., et al. (2001). Genetic influences on brain structure. *Nature Neuroscience, 4*(12), 1253–1258.

Thorndike, R. L., Hagen, E. P., & Sattler, J. M. (1986). *Standford-Binet Intelligence Scale* (4th ed.). Chicago: Riverside Publishing Co.

Tisserand, D. J., Bosma, H., Van Boxtel, M. P., & Jolles, J. (2001). Head size and cognitive ability in nondemented older adults are related. *Neurology, 56*(7), 969–971.

Tomlinson, B. E., Blessed, G., & Roth, M. (1970). Observations on the brains of demented old people. *Journal of the Neurological Sciences, 11*(3), 205–242.

Valenzuela, M. J., & Sachdev, P. (2001). Magnetic resonance spectroscopy in AD. *Neurology, 56*(5), 592–598.

Valenzuela, M. J., & Sachdev, P. (2006). Brain reserve and dementia: A systematic review. *Psychological Medicine, 36*(4), 441–454.

Van Petten, C. (2004). Relationship between hippocampal volume and memory ability in health individuals across the lifespan: Review and meta-analysis. *Neuropsychologia, 42,* 1394–1413.

Van Valen, L. (1974). Brain size and intelligence in man. *American Journal of Physical Anthropology, 40*(3), 417–423.

Vernon, P. A., Wickett, J. C., Bazana, P., & Stelmack, R. M. (2000). The neuropsychology and psychophysiology of human intelligence. In R.J. Sternberg (Ed.), *Handbook of intelligence.* New York: Cambridge University Press.

Waxman, S. G. (1992). Molecular organization and pathology of axons. In A. K. Asbury, G. M. McKhann, & W. L. McDonald (Eds.), *Diseases of the nervous system: Clinical neurobiology* (pp. 25–43). Philadelphia: Saunders.

Wechsler, D. (1955). *WAIS manual.* New York: The Psychological Corporation.

Whalley, L. J., Deary, I. J., Appleton, C. L., & Starr, J. M. (2004). Cognitive reserve and the neurobiology of cognitive aging. *Ageing Research Review, 3*(4), 369–382.

Wickett, J. C., Vernon, P. A., & Lee, D. H. (1994). In vivo brain size, head perimeter, and intelligence in a sample of healthy adult females. *Personality & Individual Differences, 16*(6), 831–838.

Wickett, J. C., Vernon, P. A., & Lee, D. H. (2000). Relationships between factors of intelligence and brain volume. *Personality & Individual Differences, 29*(6), 1095–1122.

Willerman, L., Schultz, R., Rutledge, J., & Bigler, E. D. (1991). In vivo brain size and intelligence. *Intelligence, 15*(2), 223–228.

Wilson, R. S., Gilley, D. W., Bennett, D. A., Beckett, L. A., & Evans, D. A. (2000). Person-specific paths of cognitive decline in Alzheimer's disease and their relation to age. *Psychology and Aging, 15*(1), 18–28.

Wolf, H., Kruggel, F., Hensel, A., Wahlund, L. O., Arendt, T., & Gertz, H. J. (2003). The relationship between head size and intracranial volume in elderly subjects. *Brain Research, 973*(1), 74–80.

Wu, S., Schenkenberg, T., Wing, S. D., & Osborn, A. G. (1981). Cognitive correlates of diffuse cerebral atrophy determined by computed tomography. *Neurology, 31*(9), 1180–1184.

Yamauchi, H., Fukuyama, H., Harada, K., Nabatame, H., Ogawa, M., Ouchi, Y., et al. (1993). Callosal atrophy parallels decreased cortical oxygen metabolism and neuropsychological impairment in Alzheimer's disease. *Archives of Neurology, 50*(10), 1070–1074.

Yasuda, M., Mori, E., Kitagaki, H., Yamashita, H., Hirono, N., Shimada, K., et al. (1998). Apolipoprotein e epsilon 4 allele and whole brain atrophy in late-onset Alzheimer's disease. *American Journal of Psychiatry, 155*(6), 779–784.

Yeo, R. A., Turkheimer, E., Raz, N., & Bigler, E. D. (1987). Volumetric asymmetries of the human brain: Intellectual correlates. *Brain & Cognition, 6*(1), 15–23.

Ylikoski, A., Erkinjuntti, T., Raininko, R., Sarna, S., Sulkava, R., & Tilvis, R. (1995). White matter hyperintensities on MRI in the neurologically nondiseased elderly. Analysis of cohorts of consecutive subjects aged 55 to 85 years living at home. *Stroke, 26*(7), 1171–1177.

5

Attention

Arthur F. Kramer
University of Illinois

David J. Madden
Duke University Medical Center

INTRODUCTION

In the past decade a number of critical reviews of the literature on attention and aging have been published (e.g., Kramer & Kray, 2006; Madden & Whiting, 2004; Madden, Whiting, & Huettel, 2005a). Indeed, excellent chapters on aging and attention have appeared in the last two versions of this handbook (Hartley, 1992; McDowd & Shaw, 2000). Given the availability of these review chapters, some of which have been published in the past few years, how will we offer a novel perspective on this large and ever expanding literature? We plan to cover the central theoretical issues and recent empirical studies within this research domain, that is, the manner in which aging influences the control and expression of attention from both a selective and divided attention perspective. Our focus will be on behavioral studies of attention and aging, but we will also include recent neuroimaging studies that provide insights into changes in attentional processes across the adult lifespan. We will also discuss a number of issues not traditionally included in reviews of the attention and aging literature, for example: (a) whether expertise, often acquired in specific professions over several decades, can moderate age-related decline in attentional processes; (b) the extent to which practice or training on tasks that entail selective and/or divided attention have similar effects for younger and older adults; (c) the implications of age-related changes in attentional processes for extra-laboratory settings and tasks. Finally, we will conclude our chapter with suggestions for the future of

the study of aging and attention, in particular the interaction of attention with other fields of inquiry.

Before beginning our review we believe it important to briefly define some of the aspects of attention that will serve as the focus of our chapter. In general, *selective attention* refers to the ability to both focus on information of relevance to the organism and inhibit or ignore information which is task-irrelevant. It is important to note, however, that selective attention is a dynamic set of processes since relevance is often contextually defined and what is relevant at one time can quickly become irrelevant depending on the task and environment. *Divided attention* entails the ability to concurrently attend and process information from different locations in the auditory, visual, or somatosensory environment (or from multimodal environments) or concurrently perform or switch among different skills or tasks. A good example is that when driving an automobile this involves scanning for other vehicles and pedestrians, lane tracking and manual control of the vehicle, and all too often performing tasks that are not relevant to driving such as speaking on a cellular telephone, fiddling with the global position satellite navigation system, and in the near future dictating or listening to electronic mail.

When examining both selective and divided attention it is important to consider that these processes, in turn, may be influenced in either a goal-directed manner, a stimulus-driven manner, or both (Connor, Egeth, Yantis 2004; Egeth & Yantis, 1997; Yantis, 2005). *Goal-directed* or *top-down attention* refers to an individual's ability to intentionally and selectively process information in the environment. Central to the definition of goal-directed attention is that this form of attentional control relies on an observer's expectancies about events in the environment, knowledge of and experience with similar environments, and the ability to develop and maintain an attentional set for particular kinds of environmental events. In contrast, *stimulus-driven* or *bottom-up attention* entails the control of attention by characteristics of the environment, independently of an observer's intentions, expectancies, or experience. For example, there is a substantial body of literature that has attempted to explicate the features of the environment, such as the sudden appearance of new and sometimes novel objects and stimuli that have a unique feature in the current environment, that engender stimulus driven or bottom-up attention (sometimes also called attentional capture). Indeed, it is often the case that goal-directed and stimulus-driven attentional processes interact (in either a cooperative or competitive fashion) to determine the focus of attention (see Figure 5.1). Many models of attention devote considerable discussion to how goal-directed and stimulus-driven processes jointly determine the current and future focus of attention (Chun & Wolfe, 2001; Duncan, 2004; Quinlan, 2003; Wolfe, 1994; Wolfe & Horowitz, 2004).

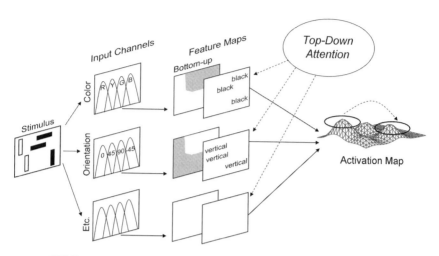

FIG. 5.1. Interaction of top-down and bottom-up visual processing (modified from Wolfe, 1994).

Cognitive Neuroscience of Aging and Attention

The age-related changes in brain structure and function relevant to cognitive aging are discussed by Dennis and Cabeza (chapter 1). Throughout this review we will mention briefly findings from neuroimaging studies bearing directly on age-related changes in attention (Kramer, Fabiani, & Colcombe, 2006c; Madden et al., 2005a; Salthouse & Madden, 2008). Research on this topic is still developing (though rapidly) and little definitive evidence is available, but several broad themes have emerged.

First, the brain structures mediating cognitive abilities are distributed widely, although individual components or modules may be highly localized (Duncan, 2004; LaBerge, 2000; Mesulam, 1990). For visual information processing, activation within a frontoparietal network modulates the attentional influences on visual cortical regions (Freiwald & Kanwisher, 2004; Kastner & Ungerleider, 2000). For example, Kastner, Pinsk, De Weerd, Desimone, and Ungerleider (1999) reported that covert attention to a peripheral spatial location leads to increased brain activation in a frontoparietal network, but critically activation was also increased in a visual processing (extrastriate) region; this latter activation was increased further when the stimulus was presented. More generally, spatial attention appears to increase the level of baseline activity in visual cortical regions, consistent with an enhancement of relevant (target) information (Gandhi, Heeger, & Boynton, 1999; Somers, Dale, Seiffert, & Tootell, 1999). Gazzaley, Cooney, Rissman, and D'Esposito (2005) have proposed

that, when an appropriate neutral baseline is also included (e.g., passive viewing), the top-down suppression of task-irrelevant activation in visual association cortex (as distinct from enhancement) can also be observed.

A second critical theme is that a variety of age-related structural and functional changes occur that affect the quality of bottom-up processing for older adults. It has been frequently observed that age-related declines in the volume and integrity of both gray and white matter exhibit an anterior to posterior gradient. That is, the age-related declines are often more pronounced in prefrontal regions with relative sparing of visual and other sensory cortical regions (Head et al., 2004; Raz et al., 2005; Salat et al., 2005). While recognizing this general trend it is also important to appreciate that age-related changes occur in widely distributed networks that are not limited to the frontal lobe (Greenwood, 2000; Tisserand & Jolles, 2003). For example, within the visual pathways, there is degradation of fibers in the optic nerve (Sandell & Peters, 2001) and thinning of gray matter near the primary visual cortex (Salat et al., 2004), which are bound to affect the quality of the visual signal. The blood-oxygen-level dependent (BOLD) signal measured by functional magnetic resonance imaging (fMRI) is noisier for older adults than for younger adults (Gazzaley & D'Esposito, 2005; Huettel, Singerman, & McCarthy, 2001), and there is indication that an age-related decline occurs in either the amplitude (Buckner, Snyder, Sanders, Raichle, & Morris, 2000) or spatial extent (Huettel et al., 2001) of activation in primary visual cortex.

Third, it is important to consider the relation of cognitive performance to neural measures of structure and function. Although this may seem an intuitively obvious recommendation from the perspective of cognitive aging, it is only recently that researchers have given this issue significant emphasis. Initially, as neuroimaging techniques were being developed, so little was known regarding age-related changes in the relevant measures that any demonstration of an age-related change in brain structure or function was valuable. Currently, many neuroimaging studies of age-related change are incorporating analyses of the pattern of correlation between the brain variables and behavioral variables. As in behavioral studies, such correlational analyses cannot always identify causality, but such analyses can go a long way towards identifying the relative importance of individual variables and their pattern of shared and unique variance.

MODELS OF COGNITIVE AGING AND ATTENTION

General Slowing and Processing Speed

Age-related slowing is a well-established empirical phenomenon that has had substantial impact on theories of cognitive aging. Some of the earliest studies to use reaction time (RT) as a measure of age-related changes in attention noted the difficulty in distinguishing the specific effects of attention from more general effects related to processing speed (PS). Botwinick, Brinley, and Birren (1957), for example, stated:

> On the basis of increased reaction time with age, one might expect proportional increases of the latencies in other processes. This may be expected whether the processes involve time required to organize responses or develop expectancies, or whether they involve time required to recover and reorganize from overestimated expectancies.
>
> (p. 304)

Subsequent research has demonstrated that slowing is not associated specifically with either early (sensory) or later (response) stages of information processing, but instead has pervasive effects throughout many of the components comprising cognitive performance (Birren & Fisher, 1995; Madden, 2001; Salthouse, 1985, 1996, 2000). Before interpreting the results of a particular experiment as representing an age-related change in attention, it is therefore necessary to determine whether this interpretation can be distinguished empirically from an interpretation based on processing speed. In other words, is a deficit in attention different from simply performing the task more slowly? This has been a surprisingly difficult question to answer in research on cognitive aging. Consider, for example, one of the most widely investigated forms of attention—capacity. A strong case can be made that speed is a fundamental property of the information-processing architecture, and in this sense speed is isomorphic with what is usually termed attentional capacity (Kail & Salthouse, 1994; Salthouse, 1988). Indeed, assuming that cognitive functions such as attention are represented in the brain as widely distributed neural networks, the efficiency of the network would at some level depend on the speed of communication among the constituents.

The evidence for a prominent role of processing speed is derived from *within-context* and *out-of-context* measures of speed (Salthouse, 1990b). Analyses of within-context measures use the dependent variable of primary interest (usually RT), in the context of a particular task, to distinguish the age-related changes in some cognitive construct (e.g., attention) from processing speed. Analyses of out-of-context measures of

processing speed depend on identifying some measure, typically a psychometric measure of digit-symbol substitution, or simple RT, that is separate from the dependent variable within the primary task representing attention.

For within-context analyses conducted in the general linear model framework, a first step in demonstrating this distinction is isolating an Age × Task condition interaction, indicating that the change in RT associated with the independent variable (task condition) varies as a function of age to a greater extent than would be expected by chance. This necessary first step is typically not sufficient, however, because interactions may occur in mean RT even though the age-related changes in RT are related systematically across task conditions. The most well-known illustration of this issue is the Brinley plot, in which the older adults' mean RTs in each task condition are plotted on the y-axis, as a function of the corresponding means for younger adults, on the x-axis (see Figure 5.2; Brinley, 1965). This type of plot typically yields a highly linear (or at least monotonic) function that is consistent across a wide range of cognitive tasks (but cf. Hale, Myerson, Faust, & Fristoe, 1995; Lima, Hale, & Myerson, 1991). The implication of the Brinley plot is that older adults' RT performance is monotonically increased relative to that of younger adults regardless of

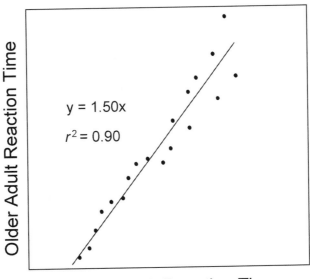

$$y = 1.50x$$

$$r^2 = 0.90$$

FIG. 5.2. Brinley plot. Each data point is the mean reaction time in one task condition, for older adults, plotted as a function of the mean RT in the corresponding task condition for younger adults.

the task conditions designed to elicit task-specific age differences. This systematic relation between younger and older adults' task condition RT values can hold even when an Age × Task condition interaction is statistically significant (Salthouse, 1985).

The value of Brinley plots in interpreting age differences is widely debated. One view is that the slope of the Brinley function is a measure of the relative processing speed of younger and older adults, and that the slope measure can be interpreted in a similar manner across its application to a variety of tasks (Myerson, Adams, Hale, & Jenkins, 2003). Alternatively, the slope is viewed as a mathematical property of the comparison of two sets of task condition means (i.e., one set for younger adults and one for older adults), which are each samples drawn from a complete RT distribution for a particular task. According to this view, the Brinley function is a plot of the sampled quantiles from each of these distributions against each other (i.e., a quantile-quantile plot), in which case the meaning of the slope is dependent on the underlying theoretical model of the task (Ratcliff, Spieler, & McKoon, 2004).

Analytic procedures are available for separating the effects of age from the systematic relations expressed in the Brinley plot, however, and these should be explored before concluding that the age differences in a particular data set are related to attention rather than speed (Faust, Balota, Spieler, & Ferraro, 1999; Madden, Pierce, & Allen, 1992; Salthouse & Kersten, 1993). These procedures typically involve transforming the younger adult RT values in a manner that reflects the degree of age-related slowing as defined by the Brinley plot. As a result of the transformation, the younger adult values are matched to those of the older adults on the basis of the degree of general slowing (GS) implied by the Brinley plot. Thus, if the age difference in a task-specific measure of attention, such as a change in RT between informatively cued and noncued task conditions, remains significant statistically following the transformation, then there is additional evidence that the age difference is to some extent independent of processing speed. These transformations, however, typically retain the assumption that the appropriate level of analysis is the measure of central tendency for individual participants (e.g., mean RT), within the task conditions. Another approach to identifying the degree of task specificity in age-related slowing is to test the fit of a formal model of the task-related changes in performance. This latter approach often entails the consideration of RT and accuracy concurrently, as well as the analysis of the complete distribution of RTs rather than just mean RTs for individuals (Ratcliff, 2002; Ratcliff, Thapar, & McKoon, 2001; Spaniol, Madden, & Voss, 2006; Thapar, Ratcliff, & McKoon, 2003).

Analyses of out-of-context measures often rely on hierarchical regression procedures to distinguish the age-related variance associated with

performance in the primary task (e.g., in a primary task measuring attention) from the age-related variance in the separate measure of processing speed. Specifically, the processing speed measure is entered before age in a stepwise regression model predicting primary task performance. Thus, the additional variance in the primary task associated with age, relative to a model in which age is the only predictor, can be determined. As a further step, the degree to which the processing speed measure attenuates (i.e., reduces) the initial age-related variance can be estimated, as an index of the degree to which speed mediates age differences in primary task performance. These analytic procedures have been developed by Salthouse and colleagues (Salthouse, 1993b, 1996). Related techniques involve the application of path analysis to assess specified models of the age–speed relation (Salthouse, Kausler, & Saults, 1988), and RT distribution analysis, in which RT at the faster end of the distribution can be used as the measure of processing speed (Salthouse, 1993a, 1998). Across many studies, it is often the case that a substantial portion, 75% or more, of the age-related variance in the primary task is shared with the measure of processing speed, and thus the age-related variance that can be attributed uniquely to other cognitive operations such as attention is relatively small. However, as Salthouse, Atkinson, and Berish (2003) have noted, the interpretation of these types of analyses is complicated when there is a high degree of correlation between the primary task measure (e.g., attention) and the potential mediator (e.g., speed). In this case, when the variables represent nearly the same dimension of variation, the regression procedures may have the effect of essentially partialling a variable from itself.

In assessing the relative contribution of processing speed and attention to cognitive performance, it is useful to recognize that the theoretical alternatives are not mutually exclusive. That is, the demonstration that processing speed contributes to a cognitive task does not necessarily mean that there is no effect of attention, only that the unique contribution of attention must be demonstrated empirically. Similarly, a significant effect of attention or other cognitive component does not disprove the substantial contribution of general age-related slowing to cognitive performance. Within any cognitive task, there are likely to be both speed-related and attention-related components to be disentangled. When assessing the relative contributions of attention and speed, it is important to not rely entirely on a "straw-person" depiction of general slowing as comprising a single factor influencing cognitive performance. There may be several types of speed-related changes that all have general effects throughout the sequence of information-processing stages. Finally, there is continued development of different methodologies for separating the general and specific components of age-related cognitive changes.

Schmiedek and Li (2004), for example, have proposed that stepwise regression and related methods are biased towards the general slowing interpretation. These authors have developed a nested factor model that attempts to minimize this bias by reducing the linear dependency among parameter estimates.

Identifying the contribution of processing speed would be more straightforward if the aspect of central nervous system functioning that mediates speed could be defined precisely. Birren emphasized that an age-related slowing of information processing was a fundamental property of the central nervous system, although the precise physiological basis of this property is not known (Birren, 1965, 1974). As we noted previously in this section, the neural networks defining attention and other cognitive functions are distributed widely in the brain, and thus speed of processing is likely to be a widely distributed property of the brain as well, in terms of the efficiency of communication among these networks. The network functioning will also be affected by any number of regionally specific changes, however, in the volume of gray matter structures and white matter pathways, and in the regional activation of gray matter.

Research to date has not completely characterized the interaction of these variables as determinants of age-related changes in speed. Although, for example, decline in fluid intelligence measures and decline in cortical volume share age-related variance, it is not clear whether the volumetric changes specifically mediate the age-related changes in speed (Raz, 2000, 2005; Salthouse & Madden, 2008; Schretlen et al., 2000; Tisserand, Visser, van Boxtel, & Jolles, 2000). Several authors have proposed that local disconnections within distributed neural networks, caused by age-related decline in the integrity of white matter pathways connecting cortical regions, lead to age-related changes in cognitive performance (Bartzokis et al., 2004; O'Sullivan et al., 2001; Peters & Sethares, 2002). The brain regions exhibiting an age difference in the correlation between white matter integrity and speed, however, may not be the same as those exhibiting an age-related decline in white matter integrity (Madden, Whiting, Provenzale, & Huettel, 2004). Similarly, little is known regarding the relation between cortical activation and processing speed, in relation to age. In general, increases in activation across task conditions are associated with increases in RT, but the specific regions that are active may differ as a function of age group (Madden et al., 1997, 1999). Within task conditions, increasing activation tends to be associated with faster responses, but again the particular regions exhibiting this relation vary across age (Madden et al., 2004c). There is in addition evidence that, in the case of working memory retrieval, the relation between cortical activation and response speed differs qualitatively between younger and older

adults, with higher levels of activation leading to faster responding for older adults but leading to slower responding for younger adults (Rypma & D'Esposito, 2000).

Resource Model

Processing speed is a fundamental cognitive resource, but research has also been concerned with attentional resources that can be distinguished from speed. Much of this research is based on theoretical constructs derived from Kahneman's (1973) proposal that the concept of attention has an energetic or effortful dimension. This proposal connects intuitively to the phenomenology of attention—our impression that we are devoting effort to processing some aspects of the environment rather than others. That is, one aspect of attention is the allocation of limited capacity to task performance. Many of the types of age-related declines in cognitive performance that are observed empirically could, in theory, be the result of an age-related decline in either the amount of attentional capacity available, or in the ability to allocate attention effectively (Hoyer & Plude, 1982; Madden, 1990a). Age-related decline in memory encoding and retrieval processes, for example, can be conceptualized as the result of a decline in attentional resources (Craik & Byrd, 1982). In the context of visual search tasks, age-related decline in processing resources has been proposed as a determinant of age-related increase in the interference from adjacent display items (McCarley, Mounts, & Kramer, 2004b) and age-related decrease in the ability to segregate small groups of targets (Watson, Maylor, & Manson, 2002). But the concept of attentional resources is also applied more widely, as a cause of age-related decline in other "activities of daily living," such as gait and motor control (Melzer & Oddsson, 2004; Sparrow, Bradshaw, Lamoureux, & Tirosh, 2002).

Researchers have most often developed resource models in the context of dual-task paradigms, under the assumption that performing two tasks concurrently requires the allocation of limited processing resources (attention), and thus performance declines in dual-task conditions, relative to a single-task baseline, will be an index of attentional capacity demands. Influential studies in this regard were those of Wright (1981), Macht and Buschke (1983), and Craik and McDowd (1987), all of whom reported that age-related decline in short-term memory tasks was more pronounced under dual-task conditions than under single-task conditions, consistent with a deficit in either the amount or allocation of attentional resources. Several studies have replicated the age-related increase in dual-task effects and have attempted to determine whether these effects are associated more closely with particular task domains or stages of information processing. Riby, Perfect, and Stollery (2004) proposed that age-related

dual-task effects are significant in episodic memory retrieval but not in semantic memory retrieval. Age differences in dual-task costs have also been observed during memory encoding, but whether the age-related increase in dual-task interference is differentially greater at encoding or retrieval is difficult to ascertain, due to possible age differences in the way in which attention is allocated between tasks (Whiting, 2003; Whiting & Smith, 1997).

Other investigations have focused more specifically on whether age-related dual-task effects can be distinguished empirically from age-related slowing. As noted previously, the theoretical constructs of attention and speed may be essentially the same, in which case RT measures of general slowing may be reflecting the same attentional resource as dual-task effects. But a distinction between dual-task effects and speed, if viable, would be important as a means of defining operationally one form of attentional capacity or effort that is subjected to the dual-task allocation. McDowd and Craik (1988) observed that age differences in dual-task performance can be well fit by a Brinley plot function, which implies that it is difficult to distinguish an interpretation based on effort from one based on speed. It is possible that some properties of secondary-task performance, such as the change in secondary-task RT in relation to the temporal interval between primary- and secondary-task events, may be diagnostic of age-related changes in attentional capacity as distinct from processing speed (Madden, 1986, 1987). An important issue in the interpretation of dual-task effects is that they may represent uncontrolled differences in emphasis between the primary and secondary tasks. In addition, a fundamental problem is that the hypothesized theoretical construct of resources is rarely measured independently of the age differences in performance that the construct is intended to explain (Salthouse, 1988). Taking a more empirical approach, Verhaeghen, Steitz, Sliwinski, and Cerella (2003) conducted a meta-analysis of published dual-task studies of aging and reported that the effect of aging on dual-task RT measures was greater than predicted by a general slowing model. The specific dual-task effect was independent of task complexity, however, and appeared to represent the addition of a single processing stage. Verhaeghen et al. do not speculate as to what this processing stage might be, but one possibility is the coordination of a more complex response in the dual-task case (Hartley, 2001).

The concept of attentional capacity has a central role in the characterization of age differences in selective attention developed by Maylor and Lavie (1998). This characterization, in turn, depends on the perceptual load theory of Lavie and colleagues (Lavie, 1995; Lavie, Hirst, de Fockert, & Viding, 2004; Lavie & Tsal, 1994). According to perceptual load theory, the allocation of selective attention is successful in excluding irrelevant

information only when the processing demands of the relevant information approach the limits of available capacity. As a result, distracting effects, such as those provided by irrelevant, response-incompatible display items, will be greater under conditions of low perceptual load (e.g., small number of display items) than under conditions of higher load. This theory is a useful context in which to examine age-related attentional changes, because it predicts greater task-related effects (e.g., response competition) under conditions of overall lower RT (i.e., lower perceptual load). Thus, age-related effects would also be expected to be most visible under lower perceptual load conditions. Virtually all theories of cognitive aging, however, especially generalized slowing, lead to the prediction of an age-related increase in task-related effects as RT increases.

Maylor and Lavie (1998) used perceptual load theory to characterize the relation between age-related deficits in inhibitory functioning and the capacity demands of visual search. These authors found that, as predicted by perceptual load theory, when the search task required participants to ignore a peripheral distractor, the magnitude of the distraction (in terms of response slowing) for response-incompatible distractors, relative to neutral distractors, decreased as the number of items in the display (perceptual load) increased. This perceptual load effect was more pronounced for younger adults than for older adults and appeared to represent age-related declines in both selective attention and attentional capacity. At the lower values of display size (i.e., lower perceptual load), the interference from the response-incompatible distractor was greater for older adults than for younger adults, reflecting an age-related decline in selective attention (inhibitory control). The age difference in attentional capacity was expressed as a more rapid improvement in attentional selectivity, as a function of increasing display size, for older adults than for younger adults. That is, the older adults' processing limits were reached with a relatively smaller number of display items.

Following up the Maylor and Lavie (1998) proposal, Madden and Langley (2003) replicated the effects of perceptual load on selective attention but found that the age differences were evident primarily under data-limited conditions, when display duration was brief and the error rate was relatively high. Under these conditions, the interference from a response-incompatible distractor was greater for older adults than for younger adults, and this age difference was evident only at the lower display sizes, as reported by Maylor and Lavie. The Madden and Langley findings differed from those of Maylor and Lavie, however, in that the increase in display size necessary to eliminate distractor interference was the same for the two age groups. This result suggests that the age difference in selective attention was not attributable to an attentional capacity limitation as proposed by Maylor and Lavie. In addition, Madden and

Langley found that under resource-limited viewing conditions (i.e., longer display duration and lower error rates) the disruptive influence of the distractor was not due entirely to response competition but also included a more general inhibitory function, arising from internal recognition responses to display items. Both the general and response-specific forms of inhibition, under resource-limited viewing conditions, were similar in magnitude for younger and older adults. Thus, whether an age-related decrease in attentional capacity occurs, and whether this decrease interacts with attentional selectivity, depends on several variables including task difficulty, the structure of the display, and display duration.

Context Model

Braver and colleagues have developed a model in which age-related changes in attention are the result of a decline in a more fundamental ability, the use of context (Braver & Barch, 2002; Braver et al., 2001; Braver & West, chapter 7). In this model, context is the more fundamental variable because it is assumed to control or bias functioning in multiple cognitive domains, especially attention and memory. By context, Braver et al. mean the active subset of representations within working memory that govern how other representations are used. Thus, context includes the observer's understanding of task instructions and intended actions, as well as specific prior events and processing results. The context model does not directly address the issues of age-related slowing or attentional resources, but, as noted below, the model does include some predictions that allow it to be distinguished from a generalized slowing model.

The two fundamental characteristics of the context model are that it is both formal (i.e., can be implemented computationally) and neurobiological (i.e., is defined in terms of neurobiological functioning). The formal aspect is based on parallel distributed processing (i.e., neural network) modeling techniques, which allow predictions to be simulated computationally (Rumelhart & McClelland, 1986). In simulating the context model, Braver and colleagues have used the AX-CPT task, in which participants respond to a probe (X) but only when it follows a cue (A). Thus, participants must withhold a response to an X probe not preceded by an A cue (BX trials) as well as to trials on which the cue is followed by a nonprobe letter (AY). In this task, the cue serves as a context for the probe, and relying on the context will reduce the tendency to respond incorrectly on BX trials, but it will increase the errors on AY trials. The computer simulation of this task assumes that a context module serves as an indirect pathway that modulates processing in a direct stimulus–response pathway. In simulating a reduced efficiency of the context

module, Braver et al. (2001) found that the primary results were slowing and less accurate performance on BX trials, as predicted by the model. A simulated deficit in context actually improved performance on the AY trials, however, because errors on these latter trials are context-based.

Braver et al. (2001) have followed up these simulations with empirical tests of the model, and have found that in comparisons of younger and older adults' performance in the AX-CPT task, the older adults' performance fits the predictions associated with a context deficit. In particular, under a high context demand (interference) condition, the older adults exhibited a higher number of BX errors than younger adults, while also exhibiting a lower number of AY errors. In addition, the RT data in a standard (noninterference) condition indicated that responses were slower on AY trials than on BX trials for younger adults but not for older adults, and in fact RT on the AY trials was comparable for the two age groups. This latter finding cannot be easily accommodated within a generalized slowing model but is consistent with the context model.

The neurobiological aspect of the context model is the hypothesis that the maintenance and representation of context are functions of dorsolateral prefrontal cortex. Regulation of context is a gating mechanism that is mediated by dopaminergic projections to this prefrontal area. Thus, impairment in this dopaminergic gating mechanism is responsible for age-related deficits in context processing. This model captures the general trends that have been described as the "frontal lobe theory of aging," that is, the proposal that age-related cognitive changes are the result of structural and functional changes specific to prefrontal brain regions (Perfect, 1997; West, 1996; but cf. Greenwood, 2000; Rubin, 1999; Salthouse, Fristoe, & Rhee, 1996). For example, Bäckman et al. (2000) reported that, in hierarchical regression analyses, nearly all of the age-related variance in episodic memory and perceptual speed performance could be accounted for by individual differences in dopaminergic neurotransmission (D_2 receptor binding for the caudate and putamen). More direct evidence comes from functional neuroimaging studies of the AX-CPT task, which suggest that increased reliance on context leads to increased left dorsolateral prefrontal activation for younger adults, but to a decrease in activation in this region for older adults (Braver & Barch, 2002).

Li and colleagues (Li, 2005; Li, Lindenberger, & Sikström, 2001) have developed a model similar in spirit to that of Braver and colleagues. The Li et al. model also emphasizes the computational approach and proposes that dopaminergic neurotransmission is a primary mechanism of age-related changes in cognitive function. One difference between the models is that the Li et al. model is concerned with the dopaminergic system in general, rather than with its specific role in prefrontal cortical functioning.

In addition, Li et al. propose that age-related reduction in cognitive performance occurs as a result of a reduction in the signal-to-noise ratio of cortical representation, rather than the use of context.

In the Li model, the function relating the strength of an input signal to a neuron's firing rate is expressed computationally as an S-shaped logistic function with a negative bias. Reducing the gain parameter of this function flattens the firing rate so that the simulated neuron is less responsive. Age-related decline in dopaminergic modulation is simulated by sampling values of gain from a distribution with a lower mean for older adults than for younger adults. The result of the lowered gain is an increase in the temporal variability of an individual neuron's response to an identical input signal. In the simulation, neural networks comprised of these individual units with lowered gain will consequently yield activation patterns that are less differentiable than those with higher levels of gain. These activation patterns correspond to the internal representation of information, and in this manner the age-related decrease in gain would lead to a higher level of neural noise. At the behavioral level, the increased noise would lead to a decrease in the availability of the context-specific information necessary for learning and memory, and presumably to an increase in the time required to discriminate perceptual representations within information-processing stages.

Neural Noise

As Li (2005) noted, the concept of a decreased signal to noise ratio of cortical activation has actually been discussed previously as a potential mechanism of age-related cognitive change, notably by Crossman and Szafran (1956) and Welford (1981). In these discussions an age-related increase in neural noise was postulated as a causal mechanism of age-related decline in attentional and cognitive performance. The neural noise construct has heuristic value because age-related slowing is an observed phenomenon (i.e., a dependent variable) as well as an explanatory construct, and neural noise provides an underlying mechanism for age-related slowing. In addition to the computational evidence provided by Li and colleagues, there is empirical evidence for the noise construct, deriving from the correlation between sensory functioning and higher order cognitive abilities. Most notably, measures of visual and auditory sensory functioning tend to share nearly 90% of the age-related variance in a wide variety of cognitive tests representing speed, reasoning, knowledge, memory, and fluency (Baltes & Lindenberger, 1997; Lindenberger & Baltes, 1994; Salthouse, Hancock, Meinz, & Hambrick, 1996b). This pattern of results suggests that age-related changes in sensory functioning, perceptual speed, and cognitive performance all derive from a "common

cause" that is most likely a general decline in the efficiency of central nervous system functioning.

In spite of the evidence leading to the concept of neural noise, this concept, like that of attentional resources, has been difficult to define operationally. Salthouse and Lichty (1985) addressed this difficulty by examining age differences in visual classification tasks, in which the stimuli were either distorted or embedded in extraneous noise. As would be expected, either increasing the amount of background noise or decreasing the intactness of the stimuli led to an overall increase in classification RTs and lowered thresholds of tolerance for distortion and noise. Surprisingly, however, Salthouse and Lichty found that there were no detectable age differences in the noise and distortion thresholds, and an age difference would be expected if an age-related increase in neural noise contributed to task performance. The classification task, however, involved only two relatively simple target items, "+" and "x." Cremer and Zeef (1987) followed up this approach using a more complex, picture identification task, in which the target pictures were presented at varying levels of completeness. Cremer and Zeef proposed that older adults' accuracy-completeness functions differed from those of younger adults in a manner (increased intercept) that was consistent with an age-related increase in neural noise as discussed by Salthouse and Lichty.

Neural noise has also been invoked as an explanatory construct in several other cognitive tasks. Allen and colleagues have proposed that neural noise is a determinant of age-related changes in short-term memory (Allen, 1990; Allen & Coyne, 1988; Allen, Madden, Weber, & Crozier, 1992b). Age differences in some forms of visual search and discrimination also support the hypothesis of an age-related increase in neural noise. Allen, Madden, Groth, and Crozier (1992a) interpreted the age-related changes in RT for a two-choice letter identification task in terms of internal perceptual noise. These authors found that the decrease in search RT associated with redundant targets in the display (i.e., repetition of the target items) was similar for younger and older adults when no other display items were present, but that the redundant targets' effect was disproportionately greater for older adults when nontarget letters were present in the display. According to Allen et al., the additional, redundant targets were differentially helpful to older adults by reducing the noise introduced by additional nontarget letters. Bucur, Madden, and Allen (2005) also reported a disproportionately greater improvement in RT for redundant visual dimensions in a letter identification task. These authors performed analyses of the complete distribution of RTs from individual trials, which allowed them to demonstrate that the features of the relevant target were coactivated (i.e., lead to a summed output rather than to separate outputs), for both younger and older adults. The Bucur et al. find-

ings suggest that the age-related increase in neural noise is not completely pervasive, in that some attentional processes, such as coactivation, may operate to offset the noise effects.

AGING AND ATTENTION

Attentional Selection and Search

Selective attention, as noted previously, refers to the ability to focus on relevant information and inhibit irrelevant information. Age-related changes in selectivity have been investigated extensively, and the results in this area are a fundamental part of current views of aging and attention. Rabbitt's (1965a, 1965b, 1968) pioneering studies of visual search and discrimination tasks, for example, promoted the hypothesis of an age-related decline in the ability to ignore irrelevant information, that is, a decline in selective attention. Researchers have subsequently refined this hypothesis and have developed empirical tests of a wide variety of related predictions. Much of this work has been reviewed previously (Hartley, 1992; Madden & Whiting, 2004; McDowd & Shaw, 2000). For the present purposes, we will limit our discussion to several topics related to the interpretation of age differences in selective attention: (a) selection based on particular stimulus dimensions; (b) the time course of attentional allocation; (c) the separation of attentional enhancement and inhibition effects; and (d) the spatial distribution of attention.

Selection by Display Dimensions

Age-related deficits do not occur invariably in visual selective attention tasks, but rather occur in relation to particular task demands. Farkas and Hoyer (1980) used a card-sorting version of search (as did Rabbitt, 1965b) and proposed that older adults were differentially slowed by distractor items that were similar to the target (e.g., a vertical target among vertical distractors), as compared to distractors that were dissimilar to the target (e.g., a vertical target among horizontal distractors). This age difference remained when the location of the target was constant, allowing selective filtering of the target. Thus, according to Farkas and Hoyer, it was not the presence of irrelevant information per se but the ability to make use of the perceptual organization in the display that was responsible for the age-related slowing in search performance. Expressing a similar theme, Gilmore, Tobias, and Royer (1985) found that older adults were not as successful as younger adults in using the featural similarity among nontargets to improve search performance.

Comparison across studies of selective attention can be problematic because the dependent variable of interest is in some instances mean RT and in other instances interpretation focuses on the increase in RT as a function of the number of display items (i.e., search rate). In general, however, results suggest that older adults are able to exhibit significant improvements in the rate of search when provided with additional information regarding the color or location of the target, or the homogeneity of distractor features (Humphrey & Kramer, 1997; Madden, 1983; Madden, Pierce, & Allen, 1996; Plude & Hoyer, 1986; Plude & Doussard-Roosevelt, 1989; Nebes & Madden, 1983). Because older adults exhibit an increased slowing relative to younger adults, comparable improvements in the absolute magnitude of performance measures for the two age groups may (depending on the dependent variable of interest) be expressed as somewhat smaller proportional improvements for older adults. Thus, whether an age-related decline exists in selective attention to the spatial features of visual displays is a matter of perspective. The most important determinants of search performance—the degree of featural similarity among nontargets (increasing which helps performance; Duncan & Humphreys, 1989) and the degree of featural similarity between targets and distractors (increasing which hurts performance)—appear to operate consistently throughout adulthood.

As noted previously, the distinction between top-down and bottom-up components of selective attention is central to current models of visual search performance. The top-down versus bottom-up categorization is also important for understanding age effects because of evidence that at least some executive control processes—those related to the planning, updating, and coordinating of cognitive operations—are differentially vulnerable to age-related decline (Verhaeghen & Cerella, 2002; Wecker, Kramer, Hallam, & Delis, 2005; Wecker, Kramer, Wisniewski, Delis, & Kaplan, 2000; West, 1996; West & Bowry, 2005). Top-down guidance of selective attention would intuitively appear to be a prototypical form of executive processing and thus a likely candidate for age-related decline. Consistent with this account, there is evidence that older adults are less efficient than younger adults in using top-down attention, at least for displays comprised of moving items (Folk & Lincourt, 1996; Watson & Maylor, 2002; but cf. Kramer, Martin-Emerson, Larish, & Anderson, 1996). In the more typical case of search through stationary items, however, top-down attentional effects are often comparable for younger and older adults. Whiting, Madden, Pierce, and Allen (2005) demonstrated that even during a highly efficient search (i.e., RT × Display Size slopes near zero), older adults were as successful as younger adults in preparing for a visual target to have a particular, color, size, or orientation. Using a more complex search task, Madden, Whiting, Cabeza, and Huettel (2004a)

found that both older and younger adults exhibited substantial changes in search performance based on the likelihood that a color singleton (e.g., a red letter among gray letters) corresponded to the predefined target. The ability to inhibit display items presented in a preview set (i.e., visual marking) also appears to be a form of top-down attentional selection that is preserved for older adults, as long as the display items are not moving (Kramer & Atchley, 2000).

Top-down attentional effects can be distinguished further into an explicit component, representing the observer's knowledge of task-relevant information, and an implicit component, representing the accumulation of that information across successive trials. For younger adults, this distinction has been explored extensively in visual search studies of repetition priming, in which the measure of interest is the improvement in performance across repetitions of the search target (Kristjansson, Wang, & Nakayama, 2002; Maljkovic & Nakayama, 1994; Wolfe, Butcher, Lee, & Hyle, 2003). The age constancy in top-down attention discussed in the previous paragraph refers primarily to the explicit component. The implicit component, however, has also exhibited an age-related preservation. The improvement in search performance associated with the repetition priming of display features appears to be generally comparable for younger and older adults (McCarley, Kramer, Colcombe, & Scialfa, 2004; Schmitter-Edgecombe & Nissley, 2002). In these latter experiments, the interpretation of repetition priming based on implicit top-down attention is related closely to accounts of repetition priming observed in measures of implicit learning and memory (Howard, Howard, Dennis, Yankovich, & Vaidya, 2004; Light & La Voie, 1993; Light & Singh, 1987). It is likely that similar cognitive mechanisms are involved in each case, with differences being related to the behavioral goals: either the identification of a different search target on each trial, in the case of visual search tasks, or the learning of episodic (context-dependent) information across trials, in the case of implicit memory tasks.

Madden, Whiting, Spaniol, and Bucur (2005b) compared the explicit and implicit components of top-down attentional guidance directly, in terms of the RT difference between search for completely predictable target features and the repetition priming of unpredictable target features. Their results were consistent with those of Schmitter-Edgecombe and Nissley (2002) and McCarley et al. (2004a) in that repetition priming effects were similar for younger and older adults. The stimulus representation created by that priming, however, when based specifically on the inhibition of distractor features, appeared to be less complete for older adults than for younger adults. In addition, older adults appeared to place greater emphasis on the explicit component of top-down selective attention, perhaps in compensation for the lower signal-to-noise ratio in the

representation of display features. Thus, although age differences in top-down selective attention exist, they do not follow a simple path of decline as might be expected from the hypothesis of an age-related deficit in executive functioning.

Little is known regarding neural changes accompanying age-related changes in selective attention, although neuroimaging studies suggest that selectivity involves different forms of brain activation for younger and older adults. Madden et al. (1997) reported that, when attention was divided among different display locations during visual search, older adults exhibited greater activation in a frontoparietal network, and less activation in visual cortical regions, than younger adults. Older adults may rely more heavily on the frontoparietal network during search performance than do younger adults, to compensate for the age-related decline in the bottom-up processing mediated by sensory cortical regions (see also Dennis & Cabeza, chapter 1). Such compensation may be expressed alternatively by increasing the level of activation in visual processing regions, rather than by recruiting the frontoparietal network (Madden et al., 2002). The age-related changes do appear to relate specifically to the top-down guidance of attentional selection. Madden et al. (2007) reported that the use of a unique display item (color singleton) during search performance was correlated with activation in the frontoparietal network for older adults, but was correlated with visual cortical (fusiform) activation for younger adults. This age difference in the activation–performance correlation, however, only held when there was a predictable relation between the color singleton and the search target, that is, when search depended on top-down attentional control (see Figure 5.3). The role of other attentional networks, especially those involving frontostriatal and other subcortical pathways, is likely to be important but is currently not well defined (Bäckman et al., 2000; Hicks & Birren, 1970; Madden et al., 2004c; Rubin, 1999).

Time Course of Attentional Allocation

Even if older adults are successful in attending selectively to relevant visual features, it is possible that, given age-related slowing, the time course of developing an appropriate attentional set is more extended for older adults. The available evidence for this hypothesis, however, is mixed. As predicted by this account, Botwinick et al. (1957) reported that simple RT to a tone following a variable preparatory interval, signaled by a simultaneous auditory and visual signal, across 1–6 seconds, was disproportionately greater for older adults following the shorter interval, 1 s. This finding may not reflect preparation entirely but may also include an age difference in the psychological refractory period (PRP)

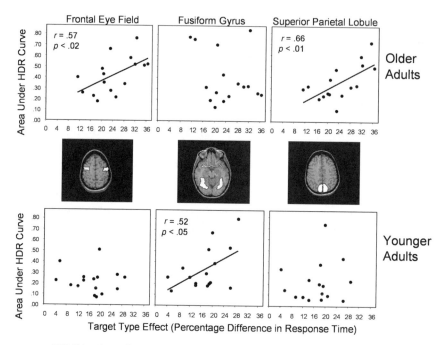

FIG. 5.3. Age-related difference in the activation of frontoparietal activation during top-down visual search (from Madden et al., 2007). Area
under the HDR curve refers to the measure of activation, defined by the
area of the hemodynamic response (HDR) curve. The target type effect
refers to a behavioral measure of visual search performance, the percentage
change in reaction time for target letter identification when the target is a
color singleton, relative to when one of the nontarget items is a color
singleton.

effect. Madden (1990b) varied the time course of the availability of a visual cue over a much shorter interval, 50–183 ms before display onset, in a
two-choice letter discrimination task. The cue was peripheral (a bar
marker located adjacent to one display location) and was always a valid
indicator of target location. When the target letter was not accompanied
by any distractor letters, the effect of the cue on RT was minimal for both
younger and older adults. When the target was accompanied by distractor letters, however, there was a decrease in RT across the cue-display
interval that was more pronounced for younger adults than for older
adults. This latter effect, which remained significant following a transformation for general age-related slowing, suggests an age-related deficit
in bottom-up processing: The presence of the distractor letters was more
disruptive of attentional allocation to the cue for older adults. Lincourt,
Folk, and Hoyer (1997) reported that peripherally presented invalid cues

led to an age-related increase in RT for single-target displays with spatially unpredictable targets. This effect was due primarily to older adults' RT to invalid peripheral cues remaining constant across stimulus onset asynchronies (SOAs) of 100–300 ms, whereas the younger adults' RTs decreased. In this set of task conditions, mean RTs conformed to a linear Brinley plot function; however, this is consistent with a generalized slowing effect.

In contrast, Greenwood, Parasuraman, and Haxby (1993) found some evidence for an age-related increase in the RT effects of central cues (both the benefit for valid cues and cost for invalid cues), relative to peripheral cues. In the Greenwood et al. study, though, as in several others that varied the cue-display SOA (Hartley, Kieley, & Slabach, 1990; Madden, 1986; Nissen & Corkin, 1985), the overall pattern and time course of cuing effects were similar for younger and older adults, which suggests that in these tasks some aspect of attentional allocation is spared from age-related slowing. Given the variety of tasks and time course values employed, additional evidence on this issue would be valuable.

Attentional Enhancement and Inhibition

The characterization of age differences in search and discrimination as a "decline in selective attention" provides little information about the nature of this decline, because selectivity comprises both the enhancement of relevant information and inhibition of irrelevant information. Investigations of younger adults' performance, using psychophysical techniques, have demonstrated that both threshold-level visual detection, and the contextual integration between a target and surrounding items, are improved by attending selectively to a specific display location (Cameron, Tai, & Carrasco, 2002; Freeman, Sagi, & Driver, 2001). Relatively few studies of adult age differences, however, have been designed in a manner that allows the separation of effects associated specifically with the attentional enhancement of relevant information. One approach, addressing primarily the enhancement aspect, is to examine the improvement in search performance associated with the presence of additional, redundant items. In general, the presence of redundant but target-relevant information facilitates target identification in a similar manner for younger and older adults, suggesting some preservation of the enhancement component (Allen, Weber, & Madden, 1994; Bucur et al., 2005).

Age-related change in the inhibition of irrelevant information, in contrast, has been a prominent theme of many behavioral studies of aging and attention. Rabbitt (1965a, 1965b, 1968) emphasized the declining ability to ignore irrelevant information as a determinant of age differences in visual search performance. Rabbitt's definition of this ability, however,

referred to the use of the minimal cues necessary to distinguish classes of items and did not include a specifically inhibitory component. This latter component is a fundamental aspect of an influential theory developed by Hasher, Zacks, and colleagues (Hasher & Zacks, 1988; Hasher, Zacks, & May, 1999; Zacks, Hasher, & Li, 2000). Although this theory has been developed primarily within the memory domain, the theory employs inhibition as an attentional mechanism responsible for age-related deficits in cognitive tasks. In a reading with distraction task, for example, older adults were differentially penalized by the occurrence of irrelevant information, especially if that information was related conceptually to the target information and was not spatially predictable (Carlson, Hasher, Zacks, & Connelly, 1995; Connelly, Hasher, & Zacks, 1991). These and related findings, such as an age-related increase in Stroop interference (Brink & McDowd, 1999; Hartley, 1993; Spieler, Balota, & Faust, 1996), support the proposal that a decline in the ability to inhibit irrelevant information may have an influence across a wide range of attention and memory tasks.

The role of inhibition as a mechanism of age-related cognitive decline has been discussed extensively (Burke, 1997; Maylor, Schlaghecken, & Watson, 2005; McDowd, 1997; Zacks & Hasher, 1997). Inhibition does appear to have an important role in age-related effects associated with some tasks, especially those involving context-dependent (episodic) memory, but not in other tasks, especially those involving context-independent (semantic) memory or predictable spatial location of target items. In addition, the appeal of inhibition is that it may serve as a unitary theoretical construct that can account for a variety of empirical phenomena, but, like the related concepts of processing resources and neural noise, it is difficult to distinguish the specific effects of inhibition from other related effects. In a meta-analysis of Stroop research, for example, Verhaeghen and De Meersman (1998) proposed that the data representing age differences in Stroop interference fall predominantly along a Brinley function, suggesting a substantial contribution of generalized age-related slowing to the observed effects. Persad, Abeles, Zacks, and Denburg (2002), however, reported that there was a significant contribution of inhibition to age-related variance in measures of attention and verbal list-learning after individual differences in perceptual speed were controlled statistically. Salthouse et al. (2003) noted a more fundamental problem with the inhibition construct. When these authors examined the psychometric properties of several widely used inhibitory measures, the construct of inhibition was low in both convergent validity (the degree to which the variables were related to each other, taking into account their relations to other constructs) and in discriminant validity (the degree to which the variables were related to the inhibition construct specifically,

rather than to other constructs). It is likely that inhibition is not a unitary construct, and that the most accurate characterization of age-related changes in inhibition will recognize different forms of inhibition, perhaps mediated by different cortical pathways (Kramer, Humphrey, Larish, Logan, & Strayer, 1994; Maylor et al., 2005; Sweeney, Rosano, Berman, & Luna, 2001).

Three neuroimaging studies have focused specifically on age-related changes in attentional inhibition, though none of the tasks involved visual search. Milham et al. (2002) directly compared younger and older adults' fMRI activation during a Stroop task. Activation of a medial prefrontal region (anterior cingulate) was associated with both congruent and incongruent information for older adults, but younger adults only exhibited this activation when the task required the inhibition of incongruent information.

Nielson, Langenecker, and Garavan (2002) examined participants' ability to inhibit responses to repeated targets in a go/no-go task. Comparisons of the activation patterns among four age groups spanning 18–78 years indicated that the ability to inhibit responses declined with age and was associated with prefrontal activation that was more bilateral for older adults than for younger adults. Nielson et al. interpreted this age-related increase in prefrontal activation as compensatory, based on increases in prefrontal activation being associated with the older and least accurate participants.

Finally, Gazzaley et al. (2005) sought to separate attentional enhancement and inhibition (suppression) effects in a working memory task. Participants viewed a series of faces and scenes with instructions to ignore one type of stimulus and to remember the other for a subsequent memory test. For the scene stimuli, relative to a passive viewing condition, the younger adults exhibited both enhancement and suppression of the fMRI signal in a scene-relevant brain region (parahippocampal gyrus), for the attend and ignore conditions, respectively. But for older adults only the enhancement of activation in the attend-scene condition was significant, and the degree of age-related decline in the degree of parahippocampal suppression was related to the degree of impairment in memory for the faces. Direct comparison between the age groups in activation change measures for the attend and ignore conditions, relative to passive viewing, indicating an age-related decline in the degree of suppression of activation in the ignore condition, but a comparable level of activation for the two age groups in the attend condition. Gazzaley et al. view these findings as an age-related deficit in top-down suppression of irrelevant information during memory encoding.

Spatial Distribution of Attention

Investigations of the various forms of selective attention and its time course typically assume that the spatial distribution of attention remains constant across the task manipulations. Does this distribution differ as a function of adult age? The evidence is not as yet complete. Independently of the age issue, theoretical formulations of attention vary substantially in their characterization of the spatial properties of attention. In recent models, attention has been described in terms of a spatially limited spotlight that traverses the display at a constant rate (Shulman, Remington, & McLean, 1979; Tsal, 1983), a variable-width spotlight (Eriksen & Yeh, 1985; Jonides, 1980), a spatially distributed gradient (Henderson, 1991; LaBerge & Brown, 1989), and a row of spatially fixed spotlights that light up sequentially (Sperling & Weichselgartner, 1995).

Hartley and McKenzie (1991) reported evidence that older adults maintained a more spatially limited (i.e., narrower) spatial distribution of attention than younger adults. These authors used a paradigm introduced by LaBerge (1983), in which participants view two briefly shown displays (e.g., letter strings) sequentially, but respond only to the second display, when the first display contains a predefined feature (e.g., a target letter in the central position). Variation in the SOA between displays allows inferences regarding changes in the spatial distribution of attention. Hartley and McKenzie found that, when the task required focused attention to the center of the first display, older adults exhibited a greater increase in error rate for second-display targets, as a function of the eccentricity of these targets. That is, older adults appeared to maintain a more narrowly focused distribution of attention and thus tended to miss targets outside of this focus. Madden and Gottlob (1997) also used a variant of the LaBerge paradigm but measured RT flanker effects within the second display. Under some conditions (unpredictable location for second-display targets), the flanker effects were actually smaller for older adults than for younger adults, again indicating that older adults were maintaining a more narrow focus of spatial attention. Using a visual masking paradigm, Atchley and Hoffman (2004) reported that forcing participants to increase the breadth of attentional focus was more detrimental to the performance of older adults than that of younger adults. Atchley and Hoffman concluded that older adults were maintaining a more narrow focus of attention as a way of enhancing a more impoverished stimulus representation.

Other findings are less consistent with the concept of an age-related narrowing of attentional focus. Hartley, Kieley, and McKenzie (1992) found no interaction between age group and variables leading to change in width of attentional focus. Madden (1992) investigated the effects of peripheral cuing in a visual search task and proposed that increasing the

validity of the peripheral cue led to an increase in the concentration of attention at the cued location, in a similar manner for younger and older adults. McCalley, Bouwhuis, and Juola (1995) used different types of spatial cues, such as a ring with a noncued center versus a filled circle cue. The results suggested qualitative differences between younger and older adults in the spatial distribution of attention, but Cornelissen and Kooijman (2000) proposed that analysis of the McCalley et al. data was consistent with a general slowing model.

Greenwood and Parasuraman (1999) developed an elegant methodology for measuring observers' ability to adjust the scale of attentional focus. These authors used cues that varied in size and thus could comprise a single display item, a column of items, or the whole display. Greenwood and Parasuraman also compared different groups of older adults, 63–74 years of age and 76–84 years of age, to younger adults. Their findings suggest that age-related change in the scaling of attentional focus does occur but is determined by the type of search task (feature vs. conjunction) and cue-display SOA. A general theme of their results was that older adults, especially those in the oldest group, were less efficient at adjusting the scale of attentional focus to match that of the cue, which in turn contributes to a slowing in the disengagement of attention from a nontarget location. Verhaeghen and colleagues have described a related concept, an age-related decline in the ability to switch the focus of attention, although the focus in this instance refers to the contents of working memory rather than contents of a visual display (Verhaeghen & Basak, 2005; Verhaeghen, Cerella, Bopp, & Basak, 2005).

The assumption that spatial attention is defined by a single, limited focus may not be accurate in all perceptual tasks. When the distance between relevant display features is equated, the role of those features in comprising an identifiable object is an important determinant of attentional effects, and these object-based (as opposed to space-based) effects are comparable for younger and older adults (Kramer & Weber, 1999). Multiple foci of spatial attention are also possible. Hahn and Kramer (1995) compared younger and older adults' performance in a task that required the comparison of two target letters in spatially noncontiguous locations. Response-incompatible distractor letters, located between the targets, slowed performance for both age groups, but only when presented as onset stimuli. When the distractors were presented as nononset stimuli (by the removal of lines from figure-8 characters), the distractors did not disrupt performance for either age group. Thus, older adults were as successful as younger adults in "splitting the beam" of attention across different display locations.

Similarly, older adults are capable of tracking multiple items that move in complex paths in a dynamic display (Trick, Perl, & Sethi, 2005). Mul-

tiple object tracking is difficult to reconcile with the assumption of a spatially limited focus of attention, because the tracking would be difficult if not impossible if attention were limited in this manner. Trick et al. found that the maximum number of objects successfully tracked was less for older adults than for younger adults, which may represent either an age-related decline related specifically to multiple object tracking, or a decline in the working memory storage of items prior to their report. This age difference in multiple object tracking may in addition be related to the age-related decline in the top-down selection of moving display items (Folk & Lincourt, 1996; Watson & Maylor, 2002).

Task Switching and Multitask Performance

Two different paradigms, task switching and dual or multitask performance, have served an important role in enhancing our understanding of age-related changes in attentional control and more specifically in the allocation of attention to multiple tasks or skills. These two classic paradigms are similar in that they both entail coordinating processes necessary for the rapid and accurate performance of multiple tasks and skills. Both paradigms also represent skills that can be performed in well-controlled laboratory settings as well as in the real world (e.g. skills that entail driving, working in a busy office, playing games such as tennis, bridge and many others). However, the task-switching and dual-task paradigms differ in that task switching entails the rapid switching between different tasks or skills, often with overlapping stimuli and responses, while dual-task performance entails the attempt at concurrent performance of different tasks. As will be seen below, different theories have been proposed to account for age-related differences and similarities in performance in these two paradigms.

Aging and Task Switching

The task-switching paradigm involves rapid switching between two or more RT tasks (e.g., Allport, Styles, & Hsieh, 1994; Jersild, 1927; Rogers & Monsell, 1995). It is assumed that the comparison among three different conditions in this paradigm (trials in task-homogeneous blocks, switch trials in task-heterogeneous blocks, and nonswitch trials in task-heterogeneous blocks) enable the separation of distinct attentional control components and their interactions. In task-homogeneous blocks, participants perform the same task on every trial, while in task-heterogeneous blocks two (or more) tasks are intermixed. Task-heterogeneous blocks consist of two types of trials: switch and nonswitch, in which the present task is either different from or the same as the preceding trial,

respectively. Switch and nonswitch trials can occur in either a predictable or an unpredictable sequence. When the trial sequence is not predictable, the particular task to be performed next is cued exogenously (i.e., with a an external cue such as a color, geometric shape, or verbal label). With a predictable sequence of switch and nonswitch trials, the cuing is endogenous, in that participants keep track of when to perform each task. Tasks that have been used in task-switching paradigms are often relatively simple discrimination tasks that entail distinguishing between numbers on the basis of their value or numerosity, geometric shapes, colors, words, or semantic categories. Responses can be either univalent, in which separate responses are mapped to each task, or bivalent, in which the same responses are mapped to two or more tasks.

The difference between RTs on switch trials and nonswitch trials within task-heterogeneous blocks has been termed *specific* or *local switch costs* (Meiran, 1996; Rogers & Monsell, 1995). Specific switch costs appear to reflect the effectiveness of attentional control processes responsible for the activation of the currently relevant task set and the deactivation of the task set that was relevant on the previous trial. In contrast, *general* or *global switch costs* are defined as the difference in RTs between task-heterogeneous blocks and task-homogeneous blocks. General switch costs appear to reflect the efficiency of maintaining multiple task sets in working memory, as well as the selection of the task to be performed next (Kray & Lindenberger, 2000; Mayr, 2001).

Theoretical Issues in Task Switching. There are two different classes of theories that attempt to explain performance decrements (i.e., switch costs) during changes in task or response sets. One class of theories emphasizes the role of active preparation while the other class of theories emphasizes passive or active interference from previously active task sets. The preparation theories focus on the active preparation for task performance. These processes allow the individual to prepare in advance by reconfiguring his or her internal task state. In contrast, interference theories generally rely on passive decay of the previous task set from working or long-term memory. Interference effects from previous task sets are largest soon after the task has been performed.

Preparatory Processes. Rogers and Monsell (1995; see also Monsell, 2003) distinguished between two types of preparation, exogenous or stimulus triggered preparation and endogenous or active preparation. Endogenous preparation is under the intentional control of the participant, whereas exogenous preparation occurs automatically, in response to the presentation of a task cue or imperative stimulus. In a series of what have now become classic studies, Rogers and Monsell observed that the

increased RTs associated with performing two tasks, as compared to a single task, could be reduced with cue–target intervals of several hundred ms. Thus, participants could intentionally reduce switch costs through active preparation. Interestingly, even with long cue–target intervals switch costs often were not completely abolished. Rogers and Monsell suggested, on the basis of these data, that the remaining or residual switch costs could only be reduced upon the presentation of the imperative stimulus. Thus, at least some proportion of the switch cost could not be eliminated with advance preparation but could only be reduced through exogenous preparation elicited in an automatic fashion by the appearance of the imperative stimulus.

De Jong (2000) has argued that such residual switch costs can be accounted for by a failure to prepare on a subset of trials. Indeed, he has suggested, in his "failure to engage" model, that switch costs reflect a mixture of trials on which subjects are fully prepared and trials on which subjects fail to prepare for the subsequent trial. De Jong (2000, 2001) proposed that successful advanced preparation requires both (a) an explicit goal or intention to prepare for subsequent trials; and (b) the retrieval and execution of this goal at the appropriate time. Failure of either of these processes will lead to a switch cost. Successful preparation for a task switch has been found to be more likely with highly motivated subjects, short trial blocks, and sufficient preparatory time.

Task Set Inertia.   Allport and colleagues have argued that the reduction with increasing lag in performance costs observed when individuals switch between tasks is a consequence of decreased interference, as a result of decay of the previous task set from working memory, rather than as a result of the failure to fully prepare for the subsequent task (Allport et al., 1994; Allport & Wylie, 1999; see also Mayr & Keele, 2000). In support of this "task set inertia" (TSI) theory, Allport et al. found that providing additional time between a participant's response and the next stimulus leads to a reduction in switch cost. However, the results obtained by several other investigators suggest a potential problem with TSI theory as a complete account for switch costs.

Meiran (1996) for example, systematically and orthogonally manipulated two different time periods between a participant's response and the subsequent stimulus. The response–cue interval (RCI) is the time between a participant's response and the cue which indicates which task will be performed next. The cue–target interval (CTI) is the amount of time between the cue indicating the task to be performed next and the stimulus for that task. Meiran reasoned that varying the RCI while holding the CTI constant would provide a measure of the decay of TSI since subjects would not know which task to prepare for next until they received the

cue. On the other hand, varying the CTI while holding the time between the subject's response and the task stimulus (response–stimulus interval or RSI) constant would allow for an assessment of the ability of the subject to actively prepare for the next task. Meiran's results (see also Meiran, Gotler, & Perlman, 2001) indicated that switch costs were reduced when either or both of these intervals were manipulated, suggesting a role for both active preparation and task set inertia decay in switching between tasks.

Aging and Task Switch Costs.   Previous studies of task switching and aging have found significant general and specific switch costs for both younger and older adults (e.g., Kray, Li, & Lindenberger, 2002) that were present even after extensive practice and when preparation time was relatively long (but see Kramer, Hahn, & Gopher, 1999b). Research has also shown that age-related differences in specific switch costs are often moderate to absent when effects of general slowing are taken into account (Brinley, 1965; Kramer et al., 1999b; Kray & Lindenberger, 2000; Mayr & Kliegl, 2000; Salthouse, Fristoe, McGuthry, & Hambrick, 1998). However, when age differences in specific switch costs are observed, the switch costs for older adults are larger than those for younger adults (Kramer et al., 1999b; Kray et al., 2002; Mayr, 2001).

Age effects in general switch costs are usually found to be larger than age effects in specific switch costs (Kray & Lindenberger, 2000; Mayr, 2001) and are often still observed following correction for general slowing. Kray and Lindenberger attributed this difference in the magnitude of age-related general and specific switch costs to the impairments of working memory associated with aging. In their study, task-heterogeneous blocks required the participants to keep track of the task sequence and remember twice as many stimulus–response (S–R) associations than task-homogeneous blocks did. Therefore, the demands on working memory in task-heterogeneous blocks were larger than those in task-homogeneous blocks. Kramer et al.'s (1999b) findings support this explanation by showing that in situations where working memory load was low, older adults were capable of learning to switch between tasks as effectively as younger adults. However, under high working memory load, older adults were unable to capitalize on practice to improve switch performance to levels exhibited by younger adults.

Mayr (2001) suggested that age-related differences in working-memory capacity could not, in and of themselves, account for all of the age-related difference in switch costs. He examined this issue by minimizing the requirement to maintain the sequential structure of task switches in working memory through the use of cues and equal number of S–R rules employed in task-homogeneous and task-heterogeneous blocks. Large

age-related differences in general switch costs were found under conditions of reduced working memory, but they were present only in situations in which the stimulus was ambiguous and there was response
overlap between tasks (see also Hahn et al., 2004). The switch costs were
interpreted in terms of an age-related impairment in the ability to internally differentiate among task sets. Keele and Rafal (2002), in a study that
assessed switch costs in frontal lobe patients, also eliminated the difference in working memory demands between task-homogeneous and task-
heterogeneous blocks by using cues and an equal number of S–R rules in
both types of trial blocks. Patients with lesions in the left frontal lobe
showed larger general switch costs than the other groups, whereas specific switch costs did not differ among groups. Their results suggest that
general switch costs, unlike specific switch costs, are related to frontal
lobe functioning and therefore can be more affected by aging than specific
switch costs.

Some experiments, however, have found that age differences are not
always larger for general than for specific switch costs (Kray et al., 2002;
Salthouse et al., 1998). Kray et al. (2002) used the same tasks as the Kray
and Lindenberger (2000) study did but, in contrast to the previous study,
the participants were provided with cues on a trial-by-trial basis. Age-
related differences in general and specific switch costs were equal, mostly
due to large age effects in specific switch costs. Thus, it is possible that the
pattern of age differences found in the other studies holds only for certain
situations placing high demands on task control. Cues reduce those
demands and, as a result, reduce the difference in age effects between
general and specific switch costs. Interestingly, a similar study by Mayr
(2001), which was mentioned earlier, also used external cues but found
age-related differences to be larger for general than for specific switch
costs. Thus, although, for the most part, larger general than specific switch
costs have been observed for older than for younger adults, possibly as a
result of the demands of maintaining multiple task sets in memory, the
circumstances under which age differences in specific switch costs are
reliably observed remain to be elucidated.

What do we know about age differences in preparatory versus task set
inertia (TSI; and related processes) components of task-switching costs?
The studies reviewed above suggest that at least under some conditions
older adults appear as capable as younger adults in disengaging from one
task set and switching to another task set. However, older adults do
appear to have particular difficulties with univalent responses and high
memory loads. Are these difficulties the result of preparatory failures or
increased TSI? Several studies have been conducted to address this
question.

Cepeda, Kramer, and Gonzalez de Sather (2001) conducted a study in

which 152 participants, ranging from 7 to 82 years of age, were asked to switch between two different tasks. One task required the determination of the value of the individual digit (e.g., 7777—greater or less than 5?), whereas the other task required the determination of the number of digits in the display (e.g., 1111111—greater or less than 5?). In an effort to relate the switch costs to the constructs of preparation and TSI, the researchers systematically manipulated the cue–target interval (CTI) and the response–cue interval (RCI).

Overall, switch costs were well portrayed by a U-shaped function with costs highest for children and older adults. Interestingly, however, all participants were able to capitalize on the extra preparatory time available at the longer CTI (i.e., 1200 ms versus 100 ms for the short CTI). Indeed, the benefits of additional preparatory time were larger for the children and older adults than they were for the younger adults. Switch costs were also reduced with longer RCIs for all adults, suggesting decreased TSI with additional time between responses and subsequent task cues. An examination of the interaction of CTI and RCI is also quite interesting. For younger adults, the benefits of longer RCIs were only observed at short (i.e., 100 ms) CTIs. These data suggest that, for younger adults, TSI becomes less of a factor when individuals have a sufficient amount of time to prepare for a new task. However, a different pattern of results was observed for the older adults. That is, older adults showed benefits of longer RCIs for both short and long CTIs. Such data suggest that increased preparation for a new task (i.e., via increased CTI) was not sufficient to fully overcome the effects of TSI for older adults.

A similar pattern of relatively intact preparation but more substantial costs for older than for younger adults, attributed to TSI, was reported in a study conducted by Meiran et al. (2001), with different tasks. Additional support for an age-related change in TSI (i.e., more extended TSI for older than for younger adults) was reported in an interesting study conducted by Mayr and Liebscher (2001). In their study, younger and older adults were told that they would switch between two tasks for the first 40 trials of a 120-trial block. Following the first 40 trials participants were informed that they would perform only a single task for the 80 remaining trials in the block. Participants also received explicit cues on each trial as to which task would be performed. Despite these instructions and explicit trial-to-trial cues, older adults showed a switch cost, relative to a single task block, for 70 trials following the transition from task switching to single task performance. The transition or fade-out costs occurred for only 10 trials for the younger adults. Thus, these data, when viewed along with the results of the studies discussed above, suggest that TSI can be a substantial problem for older adults.

Given the age-related deficiencies in general switch costs and TSI

discussed above, one might wonder whether there are any situations in which switch costs could be similar for older and younger adults? The tentative answer would appear to be yes. Bojko, Kramer, and Peterson (2004) examined switch costs for tasks that required eye movements to simple visual stimuli, rather than manual responses, to examine whether age differences in switch costs could be reduced or eliminated with very well practiced responses. Younger and older adults performed two different eye movement tasks, both separately and in task-heterogeneous (i.e. switching) blocks: a prosaccade task involved making an eye movement towards a visual stimulus as soon as it appears; an antisaccade task involved making an eye movement in the opposite direction of a suddenly appearing visual stimulus. Both general and specific switch costs were observed with these tasks. However, there were no age differences in either type of switch cost. The authors attributed the age equivalence to the well-practiced nature of eye movements.

Neuroimaging techniques may prove useful in elucidating the neural or cognitive mechanisms that underlie potential age differences in task switching (Kramer et al., 2006c). Although there is a multitude of neuroimaging studies on task switching (see, for example, Brass & von Cramon, 2004; Braver, Reynolds, & Donaldson, 2003; Dreher & Grafman, 2003; Sylvester et al., 2003), only one has been conducted to examine aging and task switching specifically. DiGirolamo et al. (2001) examined age differences in brain activation, in a blocked fMRI design, as younger and older adults performed two different numerical judgment tasks: judging the value of a number to be greater or less than 5, versus judging whether there are fewer or more than 5 numbers in the display. The magnitude of fMRI activation was compared across three conditions: a fixation control, single task blocks, and switching blocks. The younger adults exhibited substantial changes in activation between the single task and switching conditions in dorsolateral and medial frontal cortex. For the older adults, however, activation was apparently near ceiling in the single task conditions. They showed a substantial increase in activation from the fixation to the single task conditions in dorsolateral and medial frontal cortex with no further changes in activation from the single task to the switching blocks.

The pattern of fMRI results obtained in the DiGirolamo et al. (2001) study is consistent with a recent model proposed by Reuter-Lorenz and Mikels (2006). The compensation-related utilization of neural circuits (CRUNCH) model suggests that, with declining neural efficiency, additional neural circuitry is required at lower levels of task demands. Compensation can take several forms, including bilateral recruitment of homologous brain regions or recruitment of different brain regions for older as compared to younger adults. One possibility consistent with the

CRUNCH model is that older adults will show additional recruitment at lower levels of task difficulty than good performing younger adults, thereby showing smaller increases in activation in more difficult conditions (see also Madden et al., 2002). These predictions are generally consistent with the smaller increase in activation in the dorsolateral and medial frontal cortex from the single task to the switch trials for the older than for the younger adults in the DiGirolamo et al. (2001) study.

In a similar study, Smith et al. (2001), using positron emission tomography, examined differences in brain activation in the Operation Span task between younger and older adults. The Operation Span task required that subjects complete a series of equations and remember a word or other item presented at the end of each of multiple equations. Thus, the Operation Span task might be considered a form of task switching, because participants first complete several equations and then recall the words, in the correct serial order, associated with the multiple equations. Older adults and lower performing younger adults showed increased activation in a number of left prefrontal regions, including the dorsolateral prefrontal cortex, when performing in the combined task (i.e., the Operation Span task) compared to performance on the constituent tasks. Higher performing younger adults did not show these prefrontal effects. Thus, in both of these studies older adults may be recruiting additional brain regions, and particularly those regions associated with attentional control, to either perform a difficult single task (DiGirolamo et al., 2001) or to perform both components of the Operation Span task (Smith et al. 2001).

Relationship of Switching to Other Constructs.   As discussed previously, there are several different models of the task-switching paradigm, some of which emphasize active preparatory processes and others of which focus on the influence of previous experiences on the need to switch task sets (i.e., task set inertia). An important question with respect to the nature of task switching is how this construct relates to other processes that are necessary for task performance. In addition, if a switching construct can be defined, how is it related to aging and cognitive change? A few studies have addressed these issues.

Salthouse et al. (1998) examined a set of three different task-switching tasks under conditions that stressed speeded responding. An exploratory factor analysis of the data from 100 adults indicated independent factors for task switching and speeded responding. Across several different experiments with younger and older adults, Kramer et al. (1999b) regressed single task RTs on switch RTs and then correlated the residuals across tasks and experimental sessions. Approximately 75% of the residual correlations across multiple studies were significant. Thus, these data, like those reported by Salthouse et al. (1998), suggest that the

processes that underlie task switching are distinct, at least in part, from those required to perform individual tasks (see also Miyake, Friedman, Emerson, Witzki, Howerter, & Wager, 2000).

Given the distinctiveness of the task-switching construct we can now ask whether age-related variance in task switching is at least partially independent of age-related variance in other cognitive constructs. At present, the answer to this question is somewhat equivocal. Cepeda et al. (2001) performed a series of hierarchical regression analyses to examine whether age-related variance in task switching was independent of age-related variance in other constructs including perceptual speed, working memory, and performance on nonswitch trials in task-switching paradigms. They found that 53% of the age-related variance in switching was independent of age-related variance in these other constructs. Across several experiments, Kramer et al. (1999b) reported that approximately 50% of the age-related variance in switching performance was independent of the age-related variance in nonswitching performance. However, in a study of 161 adults from 18 to 80 years of age Salthouse et al. (1998) found that the majority of age-related variance in task switching could be accounted for by other variables, most notably perceptual speed.

To summarize the literature on aging and task switching, it is now fairly well established that older adults have more difficulty than younger adults in maintaining multiple tasks in memory, particularly when these tasks have incompatible or ambiguous stimulus–response mappings. Older adults also appear to have more difficulty with TSI, although in some cases performance difficulties in task switching may also be attributable to less efficient preparatory processes. Given the studies described above it is clear that additional research will be necessary to determine the extent to which age-related variance in task switching is distinct from that of other constructs. The nature of the switching tasks (i.e., given factors such as specific and general switch costs as well as contributions from preparatory and task set inertia processes) and the health, age, and training of participants may also be important in examining the relationship between age and the task switching.

Aging and Multitask Processing

As discussed previously, age-related differences in the ability to perform multiple tasks concurrently are of interest both from the perspective of the development of theories of cognitive aging as well as from the applied perspective of understanding complex coordinative behavior like that experienced in real-world tasks. Given that we have already discussed several aspects of the aging and multitask processing literature, we concentrate, in the present section, on relatively recent research that has

employed a classic dual-task paradigm, the psychological refractory period (PRP) task.

In the PRP paradigm two tasks are performed on the same trial. The trial usually begins with a warning signal. The stimulus for Task 1 is then presented. After a variable amount of time the stimulus for Task 2 is presented. The time between the onsets of the two tasks, termed stimulus onset asynchrony (SOA), varies in duration. Importantly, the subjects are usually instructed to respond to Task 1 first and then respond to the second task. Mean RTs and error rates are measured in both tasks. A typical finding is an increase in RT in Task 2 when the SOA between the two tasks is decreased, which is referred to as the PRP effect. On the other hand, the RT observed in Task 1 is usually unaffected when subjects follow the instructions to give the first task the higher priority.

Two different classes of models have been proposed to account for the PRP effect, that is, the elevated Task 2 RT when the two tasks are presented with a brief SOA. Bottleneck models suggest that information processing takes place via several discrete stages: usually an early perceptual stage, a later central processing stage, and a final response selection and execution stage. Some of the stages can be performed in parallel with those of another task, while other stages cannot. The PRP effects are the result of bottlenecks that occur when two tasks concurrently require a serial stage (i.e., a stage of processing that is only available to one task at a time). Although bottlenecks have been suggested to occur at different stages, the general consensus is that the central stage usually serves as the bottleneck (Pashler, 1994). Meyer and Kieras (1997) proposed the executive process interactive control (EPIC) model to account for PRP (and other) effects. In this model there is no immutable bottleneck. Instead, strategies determine where and if a bottleneck in processing occurs. That is, individuals can strategically set and release bottlenecks to ensure efficient task coordination.

Studies have attempted to examine age-related differences in PRP task performance within the context of both of these classes of models. Hartley and Little (1999) reported that once age-related slowing is controlled statistically, older adults show a larger PRP effect than younger adults, at short SOAs, with a larger PRP difference being observed when the two tasks require manual responses (see also Allen, Smith, Vires-Collins, & Sperry, 1998; Hartley, 2001). As a result of this observation, Hartley concluded that the age-related deficit observed in the PRP task is localized to the response generation stage. Glass et al. (2000) examined age differences in a set of PRP tasks within the context of the EPIC model. The model was fit to the PRP data obtained at different SOAs for younger and older adults. As a result of the model fitting, Glass and colleagues concluded

that age-related deficits were the result of three different factors: (a) general slowing; (b) process-specific slowing, more specifically in perceptual identification; and (c) the use of more cautious task coordination strategies by the older adults. However, despite the fact that older adults were more cautious than the young, task strategies were otherwise quite similar for the two age groups.

Although the extensive research of Hartley and colleagues suggests that older adults often show larger dual-task deficits when both tasks require manual responses (Hartley, 2001; Hartley & Little, 1999), exceptions have been noted (Allen, Lien, Murphy, Sanders, Judge, & McCann, 2002; Bherer, Kramer, Peterson, Colcombe, Erickson, & Becic, 2006), which suggests that older adults' dual-task deficits in some conditions may be partly explained by age-related differences in the use of task coordination strategies as proposed by Glass et al. (2000). However, another possibility is that, as a result of older adults' lifetime of experience with some tasks, it is easier for them to complete some components of the PRP paradigm in parallel. Indeed, some researchers have obtained data consistent with this automaticity hypothesis in a "locus of slack analysis" of PRP data. This type of analysis assumes, within the context of bottleneck models, that the central stage of Task 2 is postponed until the central processing stage is completed for Task 1. Thus, the central bottleneck creates a delay—a period of cognitive slack—between the perceptual and central stages for Task 2 at short SOAs. However, at longer SOAs there is no period of cognitive slack. Thus, within this theoretical framework variables that influence the perceptual stage should produce effects that are underadditive with SOA. That is, increases in processing duration of pre-bottleneck stages should be absorbed into the cognitive slack. On the other hand, variables that influence the duration of central processing should be additive with SOA.

Lien, Allen, Ruthruff, Grabbe, McCann, and Remington (2006; see also Allen et al., 2002) examined whether lexical tasks would be more amenable to parallel processing for older than for younger adults, given older adults' lifetime of experience with the linguistic domain. Older and younger adults performed visual and auditory discrimination tasks for Task 1 and a lexical decision task (with word frequency manipulated) for Task 2. Consistent with the automaticity hypothesis, older but not younger adults showed an underadditive effect of SOA and word frequency. Thus, it would appear that increased automaticity of lexical processing with age engendered an absorption of slack effect in the PRP task. Interestingly, when Task 2 was changed to an object size discrimination task both younger and older adults showed additive performance between Task 2 difficulty and SOA. The data obtained by Lien et al. suggest that under limited conditions, particularly when high levels of

practice occur during the lifetime, older adults may display very efficient dual-task processing.

Maquestiaux, Hartley, and Bertsch (2004) examined the influence of several days of practice on an auditory-verbal and visual-manual PRP task performed by younger and older adults. Practice was effective in reducing the PRP effect for both younger and older adults. However, the difference between the two age groups increased with practice. Interestingly, when the complexity of stimulus–response mappings was reduced, for either Task 1 or Task 2, older adults showed a substantial reduction in the PRP effect while younger adults did not. Maquestiaux et al. interpreted these data to suggest that older adults might require an additional stage to switch between one task and the other (i.e., a stage that entails loading the stimulus–response mappings of the subsequent task into working memory) following a bottleneck, and that a reduction in stimulus–response complexity diminishes the duration of this stage for older adults. This extra switch cost, especially with the increased working memory load incurred with more complex stimulus–response mappings, is consistent with the aging and task switching literature (Kramer et al., 1999b).

Bherer et al. (2006) also investigated the influence of practice on age-related differences in the magnitude of the PRP effect with an auditory and a visual task. However, Bherer and colleagues, unlike Maquestiaux et al. (2004), used individualized adaptive feedback and task prioritization instructions to train participants on the PRP task. This training approach has previously been found to reduce age-related differences in dual-task performance costs and also to enhance transfer to untrained tasks (Kramer et al., 1999b; Kramer, Larish, & Strayer, 1995). Bherer et al. found that dual-task performance improvements, following five sessions of training, was equivalent for younger and older adults for RTs and larger for the older adults for accuracy, although the accuracy effect is likely due, in part, to ceiling effects for the younger adults. Nevertheless, the observation of similar training benefits for younger and older adults in the Bherer et al. but not in the Maquestiaux et al. study suggests that specific training strategies merit additional attention in future experiments. Finally, Bherer et al. also examined transfer effects from trained to untrained PRP tasks. Significant transfer effects were found both to a new set of auditory/visual and visual/visual tasks. This is a particularly interesting observation given that transfer is often quite poor in cognitive training studies (Ball, Owsley, Sloane, Roenker, & Bruni, 2002).

At present we are aware of only a single study that has examined changes in patterns of brain activation, for younger and older adults, over the course of dual-task training. Erickson et al. (2007) conducted a dual-task training study with younger and older adults to investigate

whether performance improvements change the magnitude or pattern of fMRI activation, thereby suggesting plasticity retention in old age. Younger and older adults were randomized to a training or a wait list control group. All subjects participated in two fMRI sessions approximately two weeks apart. The training group subjects also received five 1-hour behavioral training sessions, with individualized adaptive feedback, between the two fMRI sessions. Several interesting results were obtained. First, like the Bherer et al. study, older and younger training subjects showed substantial and equivalent improvements in performance. Such improvements were not found for the control subjects. Second, both younger and older adults showed an increased asymmetry in patterns of activation in the ventral lateral prefrontal cortex for the dual-task trials with training and an age-related convergence in activation in the dorsal lateral prefrontal cortex (i.e. decreased activation for old and increased activation for young adults with training). These changes in activation, particularly in left ventral lateral prefrontal cortex, may signify increased reliance on verbal or inner speech strategies during dual-task performance, with training. Finally, changes in patterns of brain activation in ventral lateral prefrontal cortex and dorsal lateral prefrontal cortex, brain regions previously associated with multitask processing (Herath, Klingberg, Young, Amunts, & Roland, 2001; Szameitat, Schubert, Muller, & Von Cramon, 2002), were strongly correlated with improvements in performance.

The results of the Erickson et al. study are interesting both because they begin to define the brain regions which support dual-task processing for older adults and also because they suggest that, at least under some conditions, patterns of increased brain asymmetry are associated with better performance in younger and older adults (see also Colcombe, Kramer, Erickson, & Scalf, 2005). Clearly, however, additional research, with multiple neuroimaging techniques that provide high spatial and temporal precision, is necessary to explore both age-related differences in dual-task processing over the course of practice, as well as the associated changes in the brain.

AGING, ATTENTION, AND EXPERIENCE

Over the years there have been a number of reviews of studies that have examined whether substantial experience in work, sport, or leisure activities can serve to reduce age-related declines on basic perceptual, cognitive, or motor processes or aid in the development of domain general or specific strategies that can compensate for the influence of aging on complex skills or their component processes (Kramer & Morrow, in press;

Salthouse, 1990a, 2006). In the present section we review several studies that have examined the influence of real-world experience on attentional processes and skills.

Hoyer and colleagues (Clancy & Hoyer, 1994; Dollinger & Hoyer, 1996; Hoyer & Ingolfsdottir, 2003) conducted a number of studies to examine whether real-world experience of medical technologists can reduce age-related deficits in visual search and identification processes. In these studies, young (average age = 25 years) and middle-aged (average age = 49 years) medical technologists' visual search performance was compared to that of age-matched young and middle-aged control participants. Importantly, the young and middle-aged technologists were matched for years of professional experience, something that is very difficult to achieve in most studies of age and expertise.

In each of the studies visual search performance for predefined targets was compared across these four groups for both domain relevant (e.g., searching photomicrographs for specific strains of bacteria) and domain irrelevant (e.g., searching for particular letters in letter arrays or particular objects in sets of varied objects) search tasks. In general, search rates and accuracies were higher for the medical technologists than nontechnologists, particularly for the middle-aged participants. Consistent with the specificity of expertise effects reported in other studies, the diminished age effect for the medical technologists was much greater for the domain relevant than the domain irrelevant search tasks. Finally, domain relevant context served to further reduce, and in some cases ameliorate, age differences in performance for the medical technologists.

These data suggest that expertise or experience can indeed reduce age-related performance differences, at least on tasks that resemble those performed in the course of professional activities. Whether this occurs as a function of knowledge-based compensation, automatization of component task processes, or a combination of these factors is an interesting and important question for future research.

Tsang and Shaner (1998; see also Tsang & Voss, 1996) examined whether piloting expertise would reduce commonly observed age-related decrements in multitask processing. Such a proposal appears plausible given the inherent multitask nature of piloting an aircraft. Ninety participants between the ages of 20 and 79 years, half of whom were pilots, were asked to perform a variety of different single and dual tasks. Age × Expertise interactions were observed for a number of the dual-task conditions with smaller dual-task decrements (i.e., [dual task performance – single task performance] single task performance) being observed for the older pilots than for the older nonpilots. Age × Expertise interactions were not obtained for any of the single tasks. Thus, these data suggest a specificity of expertise effects on the skills most related to piloting rather than a

general effect on the performance of psychomotor and cognitive tasks. It is important to point out, however, that not all dual-task combinations produced Age × Expertise effects.

In a recent study, Kramer, Cassavaugh, Horrey, Becic, and Mayhugh (2006a) examined the ability of young and older drivers to avoid potential forward and side object collisions in a simulated driving task. Participants drove in a series of challenging scenarios both with and without collision alert devices (i.e., simulated forward and side radar that signals a potential collision). A very surprising observation was that older adults responded just as quickly as younger adults to potential collisions (and had an equivalent number of collisions). This was true both in a relatively easy driving scenario and in a scenario with unpredictable crosswinds and a secondary task that required reading written information from an in-vehicle liquid crystal display. Interestingly, the same older drivers who responded just as quickly as younger drivers in the collision avoidance task were approximately 35% slower on auditory and visual simple and choice RT tasks in the laboratory. Older drivers also performed poorly on the secondary task which was unrelated to driving. These data suggest that, at least under some driving conditions, decades of experience may enable older drivers to prioritize driving-related and unrelated tasks to maximize driving safety. However, the increasing accident rates associated with aging suggest that effective compensation is not possible in all situations (Evans, 2004). Clearly, the limits of effective experience-related compensation related to attentional control is an important topic for future research on aging and driving.

This brief review of the literature on aging and experience in particular domains of relevance to attentional control skills suggests that experience may indeed be useful in reducing age-related decrements in tasks that are similar to those on which experience has been acquired. However, as suggested by the studies discussed above, generalization of skills is quite narrow. It is also important to point out that experience-based sparing is not always observed (Salthouse, 2006) and the sparing that is observed may be the result of selective attrition of older professionals. However, the experience-based sparing that has been observed suggests the necessity for additional studies, ideally over several decades, to more fully explicate the role and nature of experience-based sparing of cognition.

ATTENTION OUTSIDE THE LABORATORY

The great majority of the studies described above have focused on explicating, in well-controlled laboratory settings, the mechanisms that underlie changes in attentional control across the adult lifespan. While

this is a worthy endeavor it is also important to understand age-related differences beyond the laboratory door, that is, in real-world environments with a degree of complexity that far surpasses that in laboratory studies.

The main focus of studies of aging and attentional control outside of the laboratory has been in the domain of automobile driving. This is likely attributable to the fact that accident rates increase over the age of 65 as do the number of fatalities (Evans, 2004). Driving also entails a number of attentional processes including multitasking, visual search, change detection, and attentional capture. In the following paragraphs we briefly describe a small subset of articles on aging, driving, and attention to illustrate some of the important scientific questions that have been addressed.

An important focus of aging, attention, and driving research has been pursued by Ball, Owsley, and their colleagues with the design and validation of their useful field of view (UFOV) task as a predictor of accident rates. The UFOV task includes several subtasks that entail (a) the rapid localization of targets at varying distances from fovea, with and without distractors; and (b) the separate and concurrent performance of a foveal discrimination task with the peripheral task (Ball & Owsley, 2000; Clay, Wadley, Edwards, Roth, Roenker, & Ball, 2005). In essence, the UFOV provides a measure of the ability to divide attention between the fovea and periphery of the visual field in the search of task-relevant information, often among distractors.

Over the past decade or so a number of studies with older adults have found that constricted UFOVs are predictive of state and self-reported accident rates (Ball et al., 1993), as well as poorer driving performance in on-road driving and simulator studies (Duchek et al., 1998; Roenker et al., 2003). Indeed, poor UFOV performance predicts driving performance and accidents after removing the variance accounted for by visual sensory function and general measures of mental function (Clay et al., 2005).

Other studies have found that performance in the change detection task, which involves detecting changes to objects in the visual field in either static (e.g., photographs) or dynamic (e.g., simulated driving) situations, is predictive of driving performance and driving-related behaviors. Hoffman et al. (2005) compared the extent to which a change detection task with photographs of driving scenes and the UFOV task was predictive of a composite measure of simulator driving performance and state reported accident history over the past three years. Change detection performance was the strongest predictor of simulator performance. This may be because the change detection task appears to require visuospatial memory and comparison processes, as well as attention, all of which are likely required for efficient scanning of the environment during driving (Mitroff, Simons, & Levin, 2004; Pringle, Irwin, Kramer, & Atchley, 2001; Pringle, Kramer, & Irwin, 2004). Two subscales of the UFOV, selective and

divided attention, also accounted for significant variance in simulator performance. Interestingly, neither test significantly predicted accident rates over the past three years. This may be due to the use of a diverse sample of older drivers rather than oversampling of drivers for high accident rates as has been done in a number of previous studies of the UFOV.

Caird, Edwards, Creaser, and Horrey (2005) used the flicker version of the change detection task (i.e., alternating between two different versions of driving scenes with an interspersed gray screen) to examine age differences in the detection of driving critical information such as pedestrians and other vehicles during turns. Older adults performed significantly more poorly on the task than did young and middle-aged drivers. Finally, McCarley et al. (2004a) found that hands-free cell phone conversations during change detection resulted in substantially higher RT and more misses of driving-critical changes, relative to a single task change detection condition. The additional task of listening to a radio broadcast, however, did not have this pronounced effect on change detection. The cell-phone dual-task deficit was substantially larger for older adults and, perhaps most importantly, older adults' change detection performance did not differ for driving-relevant and -irrelevant changes when on the cell phone.

The research discussed above is just a subset of the rapidly expanding literature on aging and driving, much of which addresses the role of attentional control in driving safety and performance. Future research will likely examine whether other attentional phenomena that have been examined in the laboratory are useful in understanding age-related differences in driving performance and safety.

A number of recent studies have also been examining whether interventions designed to enhance the cognitive vitality of older adults influence attentional processes. For example, Kramer et al. (1999a) examined changes in a number of aspects of attentional control as a function of a 6-month aerobic fitness program (see Colcombe & Kramer, 2003; Heyn, Abreu, & Ottenbacher, 2004, meta-analyses of this expanding literature). Older adults who participated in aerobic fitness training showed substantial improvements in task switching, inhibitory function, and focused attention over the 6-month fitness training period, whereas control subjects who participated in a toning and stretching control program did not improve. Although a complete discussion of the fitness training literature, with older humans and nonhuman animals, is beyond the scope of the present chapter (but see Cotman & Berchtold, 2002; Kramer, Bherer, Colcombe, Dong, & Greenough, 2004), improvements in aerobic fitness have been found to enable a number of structural and functional brain changes in animals including the increased production of neuroprotective growth factors, increases in capillaries, increased neuronal connections, and even

selective increases in new neurons. Animal studies have found, in turn, that these brain changes are related to improvements in learning and memory.

Recently, human studies have also examined changes in brain structure and function in response to fitness interventions. For example, Colcombe et al. (2004) found, using event-related fMRI, that the neural circuits in the frontal lobes supporting focused attention in the face of distractors become more asymmetrically activated, like that of younger adults, with increased fitness levels of older adults. That is, increased attentional control engendered by improvements in aerobic fitness is reflected in an increased asymmetry in the dorsolateral frontal cortex. A similar pattern of performance and brain changes has been observed for the Sternberg memory search task in response to improvements in aerobic fitness for older adults (Kramer, Colcombe, Erickson, & Scalf, 2006b). Changes in brain structure have also been observed, in both cross-sectional and longitudinal studies, as a function of differences or improvements in the aerobic fitness of older adults (Colcombe et al., 2003; Kramer et al., 2006b). In these cases, increases in the volume of gray and white matter, in prefrontal and temporal brain regions, have been observed as a function of fitness differences and changes. Changes in the timing of different cognitive and brain processes have also been observed in response to fitness differences (Hillman, Kramer, Belopolsky, & Smith, 2006).

Increasingly, other extra-laboratory interventions are also examining changes in attentional control of older participants. For example, Carlson, Colcombe, Kramer, Mielke, and Fried (2006a) examined changes in a variety of cognitive processes of older adults who participated in a year-long program called Experience Corps. This program involved training older adults to provide literacy support, library support, and conflict resolution support in kindergarten through third grade in the inner city schools in Baltimore, MD. The older adult participants were randomized to a wait list control or to the Experience Corps program which required that they spend at least 15 hours per week in the schools for the academic year.

The Experience Corps program is unique in that it provides a meaningful and multimodal intervention program for older adults. That is, the intervention entails increases in social interactions, intellectual and emotional challenges, and increased physical activities for the participants. The multitude of changes observed for the Experience Corps participants is beyond the scope of this chapter. However, significant improvements in attentional control skills were observed for the program participants as were changes in brain function in an attentional control task, measured by fMRI, in a small subset of the participants (Carlson et al., 2006b).

In summary, although there is still much to be learned about changes in

basic attentional processes, and the brain regions that support them, across the adult lifespan there is also an acknowledgement and increasing interest in examining whether our laboratory results can be "scaled up" to more realistic and complex tasks and environments. Clearly, initial studies of attention and aging beyond the laboratory door suggest that basic research can, under some circumstances, provide important insights into complex real-world behaviors and that studying attention in extra-laboratory environments can also feed back into the laboratory. We look forward to following further developments in theoretically motivated applied aging

CONCLUSIONS AND FUTURE DIRECTIONS

We have endeavored in the present chapter to provide an up-to-date but necessarily selective review of important theoretical and applied topics in the study of aging and attention. Clearly, one focus of this research has been the understanding of selective and divided attention, both within the context of models of aging and cognition as well as within models of attention. As illustrated above, we are beginning to understand the qualitative and quantitative changes in attentional mechanisms across the adult lifespan and the relationship of such changes to general slowing. Recent research has also begun to integrate behavioral and neuroscience approaches to the study of aging (see Dennis & Cabeza, chapter 1). Indeed, the study of morphological and neurochemical changes in the brain during normal aging has enriched our understanding of aging and attention. We anticipate that the rapid development of neuroimaging techniques, particularly multimodal imaging (i.e., the integration of different neuroimaging techniques), will continue to enhance our understanding of attentional changes across the adult lifespan (Kramer et al., 2006c).

Genes, Attention, and Aging

The study of the relationship between allelic variation, aging, and attention is a research area that we anticipate will develop quickly in the next several years (Goldberg & Weinberger, 2004; Greenwood & Parasuraman, 2003). This relatively new field of study, termed allelic association, is an outcome of the sequencing of the human genome. The main goal of allelic association studies is to examine individual differences in the strength of association between variants of candidate genes and a cognitive phenotype. Variation in alleles (i.e., the nucleotides adenine, cytosine, guanine, and thymine that form the basis of DNA) result from the substitution of

one nucleotide for another. These substitutions are referred to as a single nucleotide polymorphism (SNP).

In many cases candidate genes are selected for study because they influence neurotransmitter systems implicated in the cognitive processes of interest. For example, on the basis of the literature that has examined the association between brain networks implicated in attention and their neurochemical innervation, Parasuraman, Greenwood, Kumar, and Fossella (2005) hypothesized that SNPs of nicotinic acetylcholine receptors, and in particular in the CHRNA4 gene, might serve to modulate visuospatial attention. They tested this hypothesis by examining the relationship between individual differences in alleles on the CHRNA4 gene and costs and benefits in RT on a cued attention task with valid and invalid spatial cues. The number of C alleles for the C1545T SNP on the CHRNA4 gene were positively related to RT benefits and negatively related to RT costs on the spatial attention task. Interestingly, performance on a working memory task, presumably not supported in large part by nicotinic acetylcholine receptors, was not related to the SNPs on the CHRNA4 gene. Thus, such data suggest that theoretically based examination of allelic associations has the potential to further enhance our understanding of important genetic moderators of cognitive processes such as attention. Indeed, other recent studies have suggested that fitness training effects on attentional control processes may be moderated by the number of ε4 alleles on the APOE gene (Rovio et al., 2005; Schuit, Feskens, Launer, & Kromhout, 2001).

Clearly, further study of the association between genetic variation and cognition (and functional neural networks as revealed by fMRI) over the adult lifespan has the potential to explicate mechanisms underlying individual differences in cognitive aging. However, it is important to point out that there are limitations, at present, to the technique. For example, given the uneven distribution of different alleles on genes of interest it is often necessary to obtain fairly large samples in allelic association studies. Given the complexity of most cognitive processes it is also unlikely that a single gene will control a majority of the variance in any task-relevant process. Therefore, the study of the influence of multiple genes and environmental factors will likely be required in study of individual differences in cognitive processes and aging in future studies.

Aging and Attentional Vitality

As already briefly described there have been several studies exploring the extent to which work or leisure experiences or specific interventions modify the efficiency of attentional processes of older adults. In general, many

of these studies have found narrow transfer of trained skills to similar tasks. Indeed, a large randomized cognitive training trial found that while older adults improved on trained abilities and retained the trained skills relatively little transfer was observed to other laboratory and real-world tasks (Ball et al., 2002).

However, there are some exceptions. For example, fitness training appears to enhance a number of different attentional control processes. This could be the result of relatively broad effects of fitness training on brain structure and function as suggested by the animal literature (Kramer & Hillman, 2006). An additional possibility, that is not inconsistent with the former explanation, is that improved fitness may free resources devoted to bodily functions such as postural control that can be devoted to attentional and cognitive processes (Li, Lindenberger, Freund, & Baltes, 2001). Future research will be needed to further examine these potential explanations.

It is also conceivable that training in rich and integrative tasks and environments may serve to develop attentional control skills that may be transferred to other tasks and contexts. Such an approach is not the norm in the aging literature, in which training is usually confined to laboratory tasks that are focused on narrow abilities (Ball et al., 2002). Preliminary data from the Experience Corps project described above tentatively support the hypothesis that training in rich and integrative tasks and environments may lead to broader transfer (Carlson et al., 2006b). This hypothesis is also consistent with a recent study by Green and Bavelier (2003) who found that training in an action video game enhanced a number of attentional abilities of young adults. Whether similar results will be observed with older adults is an interesting question for future studies.

A growing body of literature on the benefits of nutritional compounds such as foods that are high in antioxidants, polyphenols, and omega–3 fatty acids for brain health and cognition also suggest that we should consider nutrition as an important component of healthy aging (Lau, Shukitt-Hale, & Joseph, 2005; Martin, Youdim, Szprengiel, Shukitt-Hale, & Joseph, 2002). Indeed, multimodal interventions that combine cognitive training, fitness training, appropriate diets, and social interaction offer great promise for enhancing attentional control and, more broadly, cognitive and brain function of older adults.

ACKNOWLEDGMENTS

Preparation of this chapter was supported by research grants R37 AG002163, R01 AG11622, R37 AG25667, and R01 AG25032 from the National Institute on Aging.

REFERENCES

Allen, P. A. (1990). Influence of processing variability on adult age differences in memory distribution of order information. *Cognitive Development, 5*, 177–192.

Allen, P. A., & Coyne, A. C. (1988). Age differences in primary organization or processing variability? Part II: Evidence for processing variability. *Experimental Aging Research, 14*, 151–157.

Allen, P. A., Lien, M. C., Murphy, M. D., Sanders, R. E., Judge, K. S., & McCann, R. S. (2002). Age differences in overlapping-task performance: Evidence for efficient parallel processing in older adults. *Psychology and Aging, 17*, 505–519.

Allen, P. A., Madden, D. J., Groth, K. E., & Crozier, L. C. (1992a). Impact of age, redundancy, and perceptual noise on visual search. *Journal of Gerontology, 47*, 69–74.

Allen, P. A., Madden, D. J., Weber, T., & Crozier, L. C. (1992b). Age differences in short-term memory: Organization or internal noise? *Journal of Gerontology, 47*, 281–288.

Allen, P. A., Smith, A. F., Vires-Collins, H., & Sperry, S. (1998). The psychological refractory period: Evidence for age differences in attentional time-sharing. *Psychology and Aging, 13*, 218–229.

Allen, P. A., Weber, T. A., & Madden, D. J. (1994). Adult age differences in attention: Filtering or selection? *Journal of Gerontology, 49*, 213–222.

Allport, A., Styles, E. A., & Hsieh, S. (1994). Shifting intentional set: Exploring the dynamic control of tasks. In C. Umilta & M. Moscovitch (Eds.), *Attention and performance XV* (pp. 421–452). Cambridge, MA: MIT Press.

Allport, A., & Wylie, G. (1999). Task-switching: Positive and negative priming of task-set. In G. W. Humphreys, J. Duncan & A. M. Treisman (Eds.), *Attention, space and action: Studies in cognitive neuroscience*. Oxford: Oxford University Press.

Atchley, P., & Hoffman, L. (2004). Aging and visual masking: Sensory and attentional factors. *Psychology and Aging, 19*, 57–67.

Bäckman, L., Ginovart, N., Dixon, R. A., Wahlin, T. B., Wahlin, A., Halldin, C., et al. (2000). Age-related cognitive deficits mediated by changes in the striatal dopamine system. *American Journal of Psychiatry, 157*, 635–637.

Ball, K., Berch, D. B., Helmers, K. F., Jobe, J. B., Leveck, M. D., Marsiske, M., et al. (2002). Effects of cognitive training interventions with older adults: A randomized controlled trial. *Journal of the American Medical Association, 288*, 2271–2281.

Ball, K., & Owsley, C. (2000). Increasing mobility and reducing accidents of older drivers. In K. W. Schaie & M. Pietrucho (Eds.), *Mobility and transportation in the elderly* (pp. 213–277). New York: Springer.

Ball, K., Owsley, C., Sloane, M. E., Roenker, D. L., & Bruni, J. R. (1993). Visual attention problems as a predictor of vehicle crashes in older drivers. *Investigative Ophthalmology & Visual Science, 34*, 3110–3123.

Baltes, P. B., & Lindenberger, U. (1997). Emergence of a powerful connection between sensory and cognitive functions across the adult life span: A new window to the study of cognitive aging? *Psychology and Aging, 12*, 12–21.

Bartzokis, G., Sultzer, D., Lu, P. H., Nuechterlein, K. H., Mintz, J., & Cummings, J. L. (2004). Heterogeneous age-related breakdown of white matter structural integrity: Implications for cortical "disconnection" in aging and Alzheimer's disease. *Neurobiology of Aging, 25*, 843–851.

Bherer, L., Kramer, A. F., Peterson, M. S., Colcombe, S., Erickson, K., & Becic, E. (2006). Training effects on dual-task performance: Are there age-related differences in plasticity of attentional control? *Psychology and Aging, 20*, 695–709.

Birren, J. E. (1965). Age changes in speed of behavior: Its central nature and physiological

correlates. In A. T. Welford & J. E. Birren (Eds.), *Behavior, aging, and the nervous system.* Springfield, IL: Thomas.

Birren, J. E. (1974). Translations in gerontology—from lab to life: Psychophysiology and speed of response. *American Psychologist, 29,* 808–815.

Birren, J. E., & Fisher, L. M. (1995). Aging and speed of behavior: Possible consequences for psychological functioning. *Annual Review of Psychology, 46,* 329–353.

Bojko, A., Kramer, A. F., & Peterson, M. S. (2004). Age equivalence in switch costs for prosaccade and antisaccade tasks. *Psychology and Aging, 19,* 226–234.

Botwinick, J., Brinley, J. F., & Birren, J. E. (1957). Set in relation to age. *Journal of Gerontology, 12,* 300–305.

Brass, M., & von Cramon, D. Y. (2004). Decomposing components of task preparation with functional magnetic resonance imaging. *Journal of Cognitive Neuroscience, 16,* 609–620.

Braver, T. S., & Barch, D. M. (2002). A theory of cognitive control, aging cognition, and neuromodulation. *Neuroscience and Biobehavioral Reviews, 26,* 809–817.

Braver, T. S., Barch, D. M., Keys, B. A., Carter, C. S., Cohen, J. D., Kaye, J. A., et al. (2001). Context processing in older adults: Evidence for a theory relating cognitive control to neurobiology in healthy aging. *Journal of Experimental Psychology: General, 130,* 746–763.

Braver, T. S., Reynolds, J. R., & Donaldson, D. I. (2003). Neural mechanisms of transient and sustained cognitive control during task switching. *Neuron, 39,* 713–726.

Brink, J. M., & McDowd, J. M. (1999). Aging and selective attention: An issue of complexity or multiple mechanisms? *Journal of Gerontology: Psychological Sciences, 54B,* 30–33.

Brinley, J. F. (1965). Cognitive sets, speed and accuracy of performance in the elderly. In A. T. Welford & J. E. Birren (Eds.), *Behavior, aging, and the nervous system* (pp. 114–149). Springfield, IL: Thomas.

Buckner, R. L., Snyder, A. Z., Sanders, A. L., Raichle, M. E., & Morris, J. C. (2000). Functional brain imaging of young, nondemented, and demented older adults. *Journal of Cognitive Neuroscience, 24–34.*

Bucur, B., Madden, D. J., & Allen, P. A. (2005). Age-related differences in the processing of redundant visual dimensions. *Psychology and Aging, 20,* 435–446.

Burke, D. M. (1997). Language, aging, and inhibitory deficits: Evaluation of a theory. *Journal of Gerontology: Psychological Sciences, 52B,* 254–264.

Caird, J. K., Edwards, C. J., Creaser, J. I., & Horrey, W. J. (2005). Older driver failures of attention at intersections: Using change blindness methods to assess turn decision accuracy. *Human Factors, 47,* 235–249.

Cameron, E. L., Tai, J. C., & Carrasco, M. (2002). Covert attention affects the psychometric function of contrast sensitivity. *Vision Research, 42,* 949–967.

Carlson, M. C., Hasher, L., Zacks, R. T., & Connelly, S. L. (1995). Aging, distraction, and the benefits of predictable location. *Psychology and Aging, 10,* 427–436.

Carlson, M. C., Colcombe, S. J., Kramer, A. F., Mielke, M., & Fried, L. P. (2006a, April). *Exploring effects of Experience Corps on neurocognitive function.* Paper presented at the Cognitive Aging Conference, Atlanta, Georgia.

Carlson, M. C., Saczynski, J. S., Rebok, G. W., McGill, S., Tielsch, J., Seeman, T., et al. (2006b). *Experience Corps: Effects of a pilot trial of a senior service program on executive and memory functions in older adults.* Manuscript submitted for publication.

Cepeda, N. J., Kramer, A. F., & Gonzalez de Sather, J. C. (2001). Changes in executive control across the life span: Examination of task-switching performance. *Developmental Psychology, 37,* 715–730.

Chun, M. M., & Wolfe, J. M. (2001). Visual attention. In G. E. Bruce (Ed.), *Blackwell handbook of perception* (pp. 272–310). Malden, MA: Blackwell.

Clancy, S. M., & Hoyer, W. J. (1994). Age and skill in visual search. *Developmental Psychology, 30,* 545–552.

Clay, O. J., Wadley, V. G., Edwards, J. D., Roth, D. L., Roenker, D. L., & Ball, K. K. (2005). Cumulative meta-analysis of the relationship between useful field of view and driving performance in older adults: Current and future implications. *Optometry and Vision Science, 82,* 724–731.

Colcombe, S., & Kramer, A. F. (2003). Fitness effects on the cognitive function of older adults: A meta-analytic study. *Psychological Science, 14,* 125–130.

Colcombe, S. J., Erickson, K. I., Raz, N., Webb, A. G., Cohen, N. J., McAuley, E., et al. (2003). Aerobic fitness reduces brain tissue loss in aging humans. *Journal of Gerontology: Medical Sciences, 58A,* M176–180.

Colcombe, S. J., Kramer, A. F., Erickson, K. I., & Scalf, P. (2005). The implications of cortical recruitment and brain morphology for individual differences in inhibitory function in aging humans. *Psychology and Aging, 20,* 363–375.

Colcombe, S. J., Kramer, A. F., Erickson, K. I., Scalf, P., McAuley, E., Cohen, N. J., et al. (2004). Cardiovascular fitness, cortical plasticity, and aging. *Proceedings of the National Academy of Sciences of the United States of America, 101,* 3316–3321.

Connelly, S. L., Hasher, L., & Zacks, R. T. (1991). Age and reading: The impact of distraction. *Psychology and Aging, 6,* 533–541.

Connor, C. E., Egeth, H. E., & Yantis, S. (2004). Visual attention: Bottom-up versus top-down. *Current Biology, 14,* 850–852.

Cornelissen, F. W., & Kooijman, A. C. (2000). Does age change the distribution of visual attention? A comment on McCalley, Bouwhuis, and Juola (1995). *Journal of Gerontology: Psychological Sciences, 55B,* P187–190.

Cotman, C. W., & Berchtold, N. C. (2002). Exercise: A behavioral intervention to enhance brain health and plasticity. *Trends in Neurosciences, 25,* 295–301.

Craik, F. I. M., & Byrd, M. (1982). Aging and cognitive deficits: The role of attentional resources. In F. I. M. Craik & S. E. Trehub (Eds.), *Aging and cognitive processes* (pp. 191–211). New York: Plenum.

Craik, F. I. M., & McDowd, J. M. (1987). Age differences in recall and recognition. *Journal of Experimental Psychology: Learning, Memory, and Cognition., 13,* 474–479.

Cremer, R., & Zeef, E. J. (1987). What kind of noise increases with age? *Journal of Gerontology, 42,* 515–518.

Crossman, E. R., & Szafran, J. (1956). Changes with age in the speed of information-intake and discrimination. *Experientia, 128–134.*

De Jong, R. (2000). An intention-activation account of residual switch costs. In S. Monsell & J. Driver (Eds.), *Attention and performance XVIII: Control and cognitive processes* (pp. 357–376). Cambridge, MA: MIT Press.

De Jong, R. (2001). Adult age differences in goal activation and goal maintenance. *European Journal of Cognitive Psychology, 13,* 71–89.

DiGirolamo, G. J., Kramer, A. F., Barad, V., Cepeda, N. J., Weissman, D. H., Milham, M. P., et al. (2001). General and task-specific frontal lobe recruitment in older adults during executive processes: A fMRI investigation of task-switching. *Neuroreport, 12,* 2065–2071.

Dollinger, S. M. C., & Hoyer, W. J. (1996). Age and skill differences in the processing demands of visual inspection. *Applied Cognitive Psychology, 10,* 225–239.

Dreher, J. C., & Grafman, J. (2003). Dissociating the roles of the rostral anterior cingulate and the lateral prefrontal cortices in performing two tasks simultaneously or successively. *Cerebral Cortex, 13,* 329–339.

Duchek, J. M., Hunt, L., Ball, K., Buckles, U., & Morris, J. C. (1998). Attention and driving performance in Alzheimer's disease. *Journals of Gerontology: Series B: Psychological Sciences and Social Sciences, 53B*(2), 130–141.

Duncan, J. (2004). Selective attention in distributed brain systems. In M. I. Posner (Ed.), *Cognitive neuroscience of attention* (pp. 105–113). New York: Guilford Press.

Duncan, J., & Humphreys, G. W. (1989). Visual search and stimulus similarity. *Psychological Review, 96*, 433–458.

Egeth, H. E., & Yantis, S. (1997). Visual attention: Control, representation, and time course. *Annual Review of Psychology, 48*, 269–297.

Erickson, K. I., Colcombe, S. J., Wadhwa, R., Bherer, L., Peterson, M. S., Scalf, P. E., et al. (2007). Training-induced plasticity in older adults: Effects of training on hemispheric asymmetry. *Neurobiology of Aging, 28*, 272–283.

Eriksen, C. W., & Yeh, Y.-Y. (1985). Allocation of attention in the visual field. *Journal of Experimental Psychology: Human Perception and Performance, 11*, 583–597.

Evans, L. (2004). *Traffic safety*. Bloomfield Hills, MI: Science Serving Society.

Farkas, M. S., & Hoyer, W. J. (1980). Processing consequences of perceptual grouping in selective attention. *Journal of Gerontology, 35*, 207–216.

Faust, M. E., Balota, D. A., Spieler, D. H., & Ferraro, F. R. (1999). Individual differences in information processing rate and amount: Implications for group differences in response latency. *Psychological Bulletin, 125*, 777–799.

Folk, C. L., & Lincourt, A. E. (1996). The effects of age on guided conjunction search. *Experimental Aging Research, 22*, 99–118.

Freeman, E., Sagi, D., & Driver, J. (2001). Lateral interactions between targets and flankers in low-level vision depend on attention to flankers. *Nature Neuroscience, 4*, 1032–1036.

Freiwald, W. A., & Kanwisher, N. G. (2004). Visual selective attention: Insights from brain imaging and neurophysiology. In M. S. Gazzaniga (Ed.), *The cognitive neurosciences III* (pp. 575–588). Cambridge, MA: MIT Press.

Gandhi, S. P., Heeger, D. J., & Boynton, G. M. (1999). Spatial attention affects brain activity in human primary visual cortex. *Proceedings of the National Academy of Sciences of the United States of America, 96*, 3314–3319.

Gazzaley, A., Cooney, J. W., Rissman, J., & D'Esposito, M. (2005). Top-down suppression deficit underlies working memory impairment in normal aging. *Nature Neuroscience, 8*, 1298–1300.

Gazzaley, A., & D'Esposito, M. (2005). Bold functional MRI and cognitive aging. In R. Cabeza, L. Nyberg & D. Park (Eds.), *Cognitive neuroscience of aging: Linking cognitive and cerebral aging* (pp. 107–131). New York: Oxford University Press.

Gilmore, G. C., Tobias, T. R., & Royer, F. L. (1985). Aging and similarity grouping in visual search. *Journal of Gerontology, 40*, 586–592.

Glass, J. M., Schumacher, E. H., Lauber, E. J., Zurbriggen, E. L., Gmeindl, L., Kieras, D. E., et al. (2000). Aging and the psychological refractory period: Task-coordination strategies in young and old adults. *Psychology and Aging, 15*, 571–595.

Goldberg, T. E., & Weinberger, D. R. (2004). Genes and the parsing of cognitive processes. *Trends in Cognitive Sciences, 8*, 325–335.

Green, C. S., & Bavelier, D. (2003). Action video game modifies visual selective attention. *Nature, 423*, 534–537.

Greenwood, P. M. (2000). The frontal aging hypothesis evaluated. *Journal of the International Neuropsychological Society, 6*, 705–726.

Greenwood, P. M., & Parasuraman, R. (1999). Scale of attentional focus in visual search. *Perception & Psychophysics, 61*, 837–859.

Greenwood, P. M., & Parasuraman, R. (2003). Normal genetic variation, cognition, and aging. *Behavioral and Cognitive Neuroscience Reviews, 2*, 278–306.

Greenwood, P. M., Parasuraman, R., & Haxby, J. V. (1993). Changes in visuospatial attention over the adult lifespan. *Neuropsychologia, 31*, 471–485.

Hahn, S., Andersen, G. J., & Kramer, A. F. (2004). Age influences multi-set dimensional set switching. *Aging, Neuropsychology, and Cognition, 11*, 25–36.

Hahn, S., & Kramer, A. F. (1995). Attentional flexibility and aging: You don't need to be 20 years of age to split the beam. *Psychology and Aging, 10,* 597–609.

Hale, S., Myerson, J., Faust, M., & Fristoe, N. (1995). Converging evidence for domain-specific slowing from multiple nonlexical tasks and multiple analytic methods. *Journal of Gerontology: Psychological Sciences, 50,* 202–211.

Hartley, A. A. (1992). Attention. In F. I. M. Craik & T. A. Salthouse (Eds.), *The handbook of aging and cognition* (pp. 3–50). Hillsdale, NJ: Lawrence Erlbaum Associates, Inc.

Hartley, A. A. (1993). Evidence for the selective preservation of spatial selective attention in old age. *Psychology and Aging, 8,* 371–379.

Hartley, A. A. (2001). Age differences in dual-task interference are localized to response-generation processes. *Psychology and Aging, 16,* 47–54.

Hartley, A. A., Kieley, J., & McKenzie, C. R. M. (1992). Allocation of visual attention in younger and older adults. *Perception & Psychophysics, 52,* 175–185.

Hartley, A. A., Kieley, J. M., & Slabach, E. H. (1990). Age differences and similarities in the effects of cues and prompts. *Journal of Experimental Psychology: Human Perception and Performance, 16,* 523–537.

Hartley, A. A., & Little, D. M. (1999). Age-related differences and similarities in dual-task interference. *Journal of Experimental Psychology: General, 128,* 416–449.

Hartley, A. A., & McKenzie, C. R. (1991). Attentional and perceptual contributions to the identification of extrafoveal stimuli: Adult age comparisons. *Journal of Gerontology, 46,* 202–206.

Hasher, L., & Zacks, R. T. (1988). Working memory, comprehension, and aging: A review and a new review. In G. H. Bower (Ed.), *The psychology of learning and motivation* (Vol. 22, pp. 193–225). Orlando: Academic Press.

Hasher, L., Zacks, R. T., & May, C. P. (1999). Inhibitory control, circadian arousal, and age. In D. Gopher & A. Koriat (Eds.), *Attention and performance XVII: Cognitive regulation of performance: Interaction of theory and application* (pp. 653–675). Cambridge, MA: MIT Press.

Head, D., Buckner, R. L., Shimony, J. S., Williams, L. E., Akbudak, E., Conturo, T. E., et al. (2004). Differential vulnerability of anterior white matter in nondemented aging with minimal acceleration in dementia of the alzheimer type: Evidence from diffusion tensor imaging. *Cerebral Cortex, 14,* 410–423.

Henderson, J. M. (1991). Stimulus discrimination following covert attentional orienting to an exogenous cue. *Journal of Experimental Psychology: Human Perception and Performance, 17,* 91–106.

Herath, P., Klingberg, T., Young, J., Amunts, K., & Roland, P. (2001). Neural correlates of dual task interference can be dissociated from those of divided attention: An fMRI study. *Cerebral Cortex, 11,* 796–805.

Heyn, P., Abreu, B. C., & Ottenbacher, K. J. (2004). The effects of exercise training on elderly persons with cognitive impairment and dementia: A meta-analysis. *Archives of Physical Medicine and Rehabilitation, 85*(10), 1694–1704.

Hicks, L. H., & Birren, J. E. (1970). Aging, brain damage, and psychomotor slowing. *Psychological Bulletin, 74,* 377–396.

Hillman, C. H., Kramer, A. F., Belopolsky, A. V., & Smith, D. P. (2006). A cross-sectional examination of age and physical activity on performance and event-related brain potentials in a task switching paradigm. *International Journal of Psychophysiology, 59,* 30–39.

Howard, J. H., Jr., Howard, D. V., Dennis, N. A., Yankovich, H., & Vaidya, C. J. (2004). Implicit spatial contextual learning in healthy aging. *Neuropsychology, 18,* 124–134.

Hoyer, W. J., & Ingolfsdottir, D. (2003). Age, skill, and contextual cuing in target detection. *Psychology and Aging, 18,* 210–218.

Hoyer, W. J., & Plude, D. J. (1982). Aging and the allocation of attentional resources in visual information-processing. In R. Sekuler, D. Kline, & K. Dismukes (Eds.), *Aging and human visual function* (pp. 245–263). New York: Liss.

Huettel, S. A., Singerman, J. D., & McCarthy, G. (2001). The effects of aging upon the hemodynamic response measured by functional MRI. *Neuroimage, 13*, 161–175.

Humphrey, D. G., & Kramer, A. F. (1997). Age differences in visual search for feature, conjunction, and triple-conjunction targets. *Psychology and Aging, 12*, 704–717.

Jersild, A. T. (1927). Mental set and shift. *Archives of Psychology*, whole no. 89.

Jonides, J. (1980). Towards a model of the mind's eye's movement. *Canadian Journal of Psychology, 34*, 103–112.

Kahneman, D. (1973). *Attention and effort*. Englewood Cliffs, NJ: Prentice-Hall.

Kail, R., & Salthouse, T. A. (1994). Processing speed as a mental capacity. *Acta Psychologica, 86*, 199–225.

Kastner, S., Pinsk, M. A., De Weerd, P., Desimone, R., & Ungerleider, L. G. (1999). Increased activity in human visual cortex during directed attention in the absence of visual stimulation. *Neuron, 22*, 751–761.

Kastner, S., & Ungerleider, L. G. (2000). Mechanisms of visual attention in the human cortex. *Annual Review of Neuroscience, 23*, 315–341.

Keele, S. W., & Rafal, R. (2002). Deficits of task set in patients with left prefrontal cortex lesions. In J. Driver & S. Monsell (Eds.), *Attention and performance XVIII* (pp. 577–627). Cambridge, MA: MIT Press.

Kramer, A. F., & Atchley, P. (2000). Age-related effects in the marking of old objects in visual search. *Psychology and Aging, 15*, 286–296.

Kramer, A. F., Bherer, L., Colcombe, S. J., Dong, W., & Greenough, W. T. (2004). Environmental influences on cognitive and brain plasticity during aging. *Journal of Gerontology: Medical Sciences, 59*, M940–957.

Kramer, A. F., Cassavaugh, N., Horrey, W. J., Becic, E., & Mayhugh, J. (2006a). *Influence of age and proximity warning devices on collision avoidance in simulated driving*. Manuscript submitted for publication.

Kramer, A. F., Colcombe, S. J., Erickson, K. I., & Scalf, P. (2006b, April). *Fitness training and the brain: From molecules to minds*. Paper presented at the 2006 Cognitive Aging Conference, Atlanta, Georgia.

Kramer, A. F., Fabiani, M., & Colcombe, S. (2006c). Contributions of cognitive neuroscience to the understanding of behavior and aging. In J. E. Birren & K. W. Schaie (Eds.), *Handbook of the psychology of aging* (6th ed., pp. 57–84). London: Elsevier.

Kramer, A. F., Hahn, S., Cohen, N. J., Banich, M. T., McAuley, E., Harrison, C. R., et al. (1999a). Ageing, fitness and neurocognitive function. *Nature, 400*, 418–419.

Kramer, A. F., Hahn, S., & Gopher, D. (1999b). Task coordination and aging: Explorations of executive control processes in the task switching paradigm. *Acta Psychologica, 101*, 339–378.

Kramer, A. F., & Hillman, C. H. (2006). Aging, physical activity, and neurocognitive function. In E. Acevedo & P. Ekekakis (Eds.), *Psychobiology of physical activity* (pp. 45–60). Champaign, IL: Human Kinetics.

Kramer, A. F., Humphrey, D. G., Larish, J. F., Logan, G. D., & Strayer, D. L. (1994). Aging and inhibition: Beyond a unitary view of inhibitory processing in attention. *Psychology and Aging, 9*, 491–512.

Kramer, A. F., & Kray, J. (2006). Aging and attention. In F. I. M. Craik & E. Bialystock (Eds.), *Lifespan cognition: Mechanisms of change* (pp. 57–69). Oxford: Oxford University Press.

Kramer, A. F., Larish, J. F., & Strayer, D. L. (1995). Training for attentional control in dual task

settings: A comparison of young and old adults. *Journal of Experimental Psychology: Applied, 1*, 50–76.

Kramer, A. F., Martin-Emerson, R., Larish, J. F., & Anderson, G. J. (1996). Aging and filtering by movement in visual search. *Journal of Gerontology: Psychological Sciences, 51B*, P201–216.

Kramer, A. F., & Morrow, D. (in press). Cognitive training and expertise. In D. Park & N. Schwartz (Eds.), *Cognitive aging: A primer*. Philadelphia, PA: Psychology Press.

Kramer, A. F., & Weber, T. A. (1999). Object-based attentional selection and aging. *Psychology and Aging, 14*, 99–107.

Kray, J., Li, K. Z., & Lindenberger, U. (2002). Age-related changes in task-switching components: The role of task uncertainty. *Brain and Cognition, 49*, 363–381.

Kray, J., & Lindenberger, U. (2000). Adult age differences in task switching. *Psychology and Aging, 15*, 126–147.

Kristjansson, A., Wang, D., & Nakayama, K. (2002). The role of priming in conjunctive visual search. *Cognition, 85*, 37–52.

LaBerge, D. (1983). Spatial extent of attention to letters and words. *Journal of Experimental Psychology: Human Perception and Performance, 9*, 371–379.

LaBerge, D. (2000). Networks of attention. In M. S. Gazzaniga (Ed.), *The new cognitive neurosciences* (2nd ed., pp. 711–723). Cambridge, MA: MIT Press.

LaBerge, D., & Brown, V. (1989). Theory of attentional operations in shape identification. *Psychological Review, 96*, 101–124.

Lau, F. C., Shukitt-Hale, B., & Joseph, J. A. (2005). The beneficial effects of fruit polyphenols on brain aging. *Neurobiology of Aging, 26* (Suppl. 1), 128–132.

Lavie, N. (1995). Perceptual load as a necessary condition for selective attention. *Journal of Experimental Psychology: Human Perception and Performance, 21*, 451–468.

Lavie, N., Hirst, A., de Fockert, J. W., & Viding, E. (2004). Load theory of selective attention and cognitive control. *Journal of Experimental Psychology: General, 133*, 339–354.

Lavie, N., & Tsal, Y. (1994). Perceptual load as a major determinant of the locus of selection in visual attention. *Perception & Psychophysics, 56*, 183–197.

Li, K. Z. H., Lindenberger, U., Freund, A. M., & Baltes, P. B. (2001a). Walking while memorizing: Age-related differences in compensatory behavior. *Psychological Science, 12*, 230–237.

Li, S.-C. (2005). Neurocomputational perspectives linking neuromodulation, processing noise, representational distinctiveness, and cognitive aging. In R. Cabeza, L. Nyberg, & D. Park (Eds.), *Cognitive neuroscience of aging: Linking cognitive and cerebral aging* (pp. 354–379). New York: Oxford University Press.

Li, S.-C., Lindenberger, U., & Sikström, S. (2001b). Aging cognition: From neuromodulation to representation. *Trends in Cognitive Sciences, 5*, 479–486.

Lien, M. C., Allen, P. A., Ruthruff, E., Grabbe, J., McCann, R. S., & Remington, R. W. (2006). Visual word recognition without central attention: Evidence for greater automaticity with advancing age. *Psychology and Aging, 21*, 431–447.

Light, L. L., & La Voie, D. (1993). Direct and indirect measures of memory in old age. In P. Graf & M. E. J. Masson (Eds.), *Implicit memory: New directions in cognition, development, and neuropsychology* (pp. 207–230). Hillsdale, NJ: Lawrence Erlbaum Associates, Inc.

Light, L. L., & Singh, A. (1987). Implicit and explicit memory in young and older adults. *Journal of Experimental Psychology. Learning, Memory, and Cognition, 13*, 531–541.

Lima, S. D., Hale, S., & Myerson, J. (1991). How general is general slowing? Evidence from the lexical domain. *Psychology and Aging, 6*, 416–425.

Lincourt, A. E., Folk, C. L., & Hoyer, W. J. (1997). Effects of aging on voluntary and involuntary shifts of attention. *Aging, Neuropsychology, and Cognition, 4*, 290–303.

Lindenberger, U., & Baltes, P. B. (1994). Sensory functioning and intelligence in old age: A strong connection. *Psychology and Aging, 9*, 339–355.

Macht, M. L., & Buschke, H. (1983). Age differences in cognitive effort in recall. *Journal of Gerontology, 38,* 695–700.

Madden, D. J. (1983). Aging and distraction by highly familiar stimuli during visual search. *Developmental Psychology, 19,* 499–507.

Madden, D. J. (1986). Adult age differences in the attentional capacity demands of visual search. *Cognitive Development, 1,* 335–363.

Madden, D. J. (1987). Aging, attention, and the use of meaning during visual search. *Cognitive Development, 2,* 201–216.

Madden, D. J. (1990a). Adult age differences in attentional selectivity and capacity. *European Journal of Cognitive Psychology, 2,* 229–252.

Madden, D. J. (1990b). Adult age differences in the time course of visual attention. *Journal of Gerontology, 45*(1), P9–16.

Madden, D. J. (1992). Selective attention and visual search: Revision of an allocation model and application to age differences. *Journal of Experimental Psychology: Human Perception and Performance, 18,* 821–836.

Madden, D. J. (2001). Speed and timing of behavioral processes. In J. E. Birren & K. W. Schaie (Eds.), *Handbook of the psychology of aging* (5th ed., pp. 288–312). San Diego, CA: Academic Press.

Madden, D. J., & Gottlob, L. R. (1997). Adult age differences in strategic and dynamic components of focusing visual attention. *Aging, Neuropsychology, and Cognition, 4,* 185–210.

Madden, D. J., Gottlob, L. R., Denny, L. L., Turkington, T. G., Provenzale, J. M., Hawk, T. C., et al. (1999). Aging and recognition memory: Changes in regional cerebral blood flow associated with components of reaction time distributions. *Journal of Cognitive Neuroscience, 11,* 511–520.

Madden, D. J., & Langley, L. K. (2003). Age-related changes in selective attention and perceptual load during visual search. *Psychology and Aging, 18,* 54–67.

Madden, D. J., Pierce, T. W., & Allen, P. A. (1992). Adult age differences in attentional allocation during memory search. *Psychology and Aging, 7,* 594–601.

Madden, D. J., Pierce, T. W., & Allen, P. A. (1996). Adult age differences in the use of distractor homogeneity during visual search. *Psychology and Aging, 11,* 454–474.

Madden, D. J., Spaniol, J., Whiting, W. L., Bucur, B., Provenzale, J. M., Cabeza, R., et al. (2007). Adult age differences in the functional neuroanatomy of visual attention: A combined fMRI and DTI study. *Neurobiology of Aging, 28,* 459–476.

Madden, D. J., Turkington, T. G., Provenzale, J. M., Denny, L. L., Langley, L. K., Hawk, T. C., et al. (2002). Aging and attentional guidance during visual search: Functional neuroanatomy by positron emission tomography. *Psychology and Aging, 17,* 24–43.

Madden, D. J., Turkington, T. G., Provenzale, J. M., Hawk, T. C., Hoffman, J. M., & Coleman, R. E. (1997). Selective and divided visual attention: Age-related changes in regional cerebral blood flow measured by $H_2^{15}O$ PET. *Human Brain Mapping, 5,* 389–409.

Madden, D. J., & Whiting, W. L. (2004). Age-related changes in visual attention. In P. T. Costa & I. C. Siegler (Eds.), *Recent advances in psychology and aging* (pp. 41–88). Amsterdam: Elsevier.

Madden, D. J., Whiting, W. L., Cabeza, R., & Huettel, S. A. (2004a). Age-related preservation of top-down attentional guidance during visual search. *Psychology and Aging, 19,* 304–309.

Madden, D. J., Whiting, W. L., & Huettel, S. A. (2005a). Age-related changes in neural activity during visual perception and attention. In R. Cabeza, L. Nyberg, & D. Park (Eds.), *Cognitive neuroscience of aging: Linking cognitive and cerebral aging* (pp. 157–185). New York: Oxford University Press.

Madden, D. J., Whiting, W. L., Huettel, S. A., White, L. E., MacFall, J. R., & Provenzale, J. M.

(2004b). Diffusion tensor imaging of adult age differences in cerebral white matter: Relation to response time. *Neuroimage, 21*, 1174–1181.

Madden, D. J., Whiting, W. L., Provenzale, J. M., & Huettel, S. A. (2004c). Age-related changes in neural activity during visual target detection measured by fMRI. *Cerebral Cortex, 14*, 143–155.

Madden, D. J., Whiting, W. L., Spaniol, J., & Bucur, B. (2005b). Adult age differences in the implicit and explicit components of top-down attentional guidance during visual search. *Psychology and Aging, 20*, 317–329.

Maljkovic, V., & Nakayama, K. (1994). Priming of pop-out: I. Role of features. *Memory & Cognition, 22*, 657–672.

Maquestiaux, F., Hartley, A. A., & Bertsch, J. (2004). Can practice overcome age-related differences in the psychological refractory period effect? *Psychology and Aging, 19*, 649–667.

Martin, A., Youdim, K., Szprengiel, A., Shukitt-Hale, B., & Joseph, J. (2002). Roles of vitamins E and C on neurodegenerative diseases and cognitive performance. *Nutrition Reviews, 60*, 308–326.

Maylor, E. A., & Lavie, N. (1998). The influence of perceptual load on age differences in selective attention. *Psychology and Aging, 13*, 563–573.

Maylor, E. A., Schlaghecken, F., & Watson, D. G. (2005). Aging and inhibitory processes in memory, attentional, and motor tasks. In R. W. Engle, G. Sedek, U. v. Hecker, & D. N. McIntosh (Eds.), *Cognitive limitations in aging and psychopathology* (pp. 313–345). Cambridge: Cambridge University Press.

Mayr, U. (2001). Age differences in the selection of mental sets: The role of inhibition, stimulus ambiguity, and response-set overlap. *Psychology and Aging, 16*, 96–109.

Mayr, U., & Keele, S. W. (2000). Changing internal constraints on action: The role of backward inhibition. *Journal of Experimental Psychology: General, 129*, 4–26.

Mayr, U., & Kliegl, R. (2000). Task-set switching and long-term memory retrieval. *Journal of Experimental Psychology: Learning, Memory, and Cognition, 26*, 1124–1140.

Mayr, U., & Liebscher, T. (2001). Is there an age deficit in the selection of mental sets? *European Journal of Cognitive Psychology, 13*, 47–69.

McCalley, L. T., Bouwhuis, D. G., & Juola, J. F. (1995). Age changes in the distribution of visual attention. *Journal of Gerontology: Psychological Sciences, 50B*, 316–331.

McCarley, J. S., Kramer, A. F., Colcombe, A. M., & Scialfa, C. T. (2004a). Priming of pop-out in visual search: A comparison of young and old adults. *Aging, Neuropsychology, and Cognition, 11*, 80–88.

McCarley, J. S., Mounts, J. R., & Kramer, A. F. (2004b). Age-related differences in localized attentional interference. *Psychology and Aging, 19*, 203–210.

McDowd, J. M. (1997). Inhibition in attention and aging. *Journal of Gerontology: Psychological Sciences, 52B*, P265–273.

McDowd, J. M., & Craik, F. I. (1988). Effects of aging and task difficulty on divided attention performance. *Journal of Experimental Psychology: Human Perception and Performance, 14*, 267–280.

McDowd, J. M., & Shaw, R. J. (2000). Attention and aging: A functional perspective. In F. I. M. Craik & T. A. Salthouse (Eds.), *The handbook of aging and cognition* (2nd ed., pp. 221–292). Hillsdale, NJ: Lawrence Erlbaum Associates, Inc.

Meiran, N. (1996). Reconfiguration of processing mode prior to task performance. *Journal of Experimental Psychology: Learning, Memory, and Cognition, 22*, 1423–1442.

Meiran, N., Gotler, A., & Perlman, A. (2001). Old age is associated with a pattern of relatively intact and relatively impaired task-set switching abilities. *Journal of Gerontology: Psychological Sciences, 56B*, P88–P102.

Melzer, I., & Oddsson, L. I. (2004). The effect of a cognitive task on voluntary step execution

in healthy elderly and young individuals. *Journal of the American Geriatrics Society, 52,* 1255–1262.

Mesulam, M. M. (1990). Large-scale neurocognitive networks and distributed processing for attention, language, and memory. *Annals of Neurology, 28,* 597–613.

Meyer, D. E., & Kieras, D. E. (1997). A computational theory of executive cognitive processes and multiple-task performance: Part 1. Basic mechanisms. *Psychological Review, 104,* 3–65.

Milham, M. P., Erickson, K. I., Banich, M. T., Kramer, A. F., Webb, A., Wszalek, T., et al. (2002). Attentional control in the aging brain: Insights from an fMRI study of the Stroop task. *Brain and Cognition, 49,* 277–296.

Mitroff, S. R., Simons, D. J., & Levin, D. T. (2004). Nothing compares 2 views: Change blindness can occur despite preserved access to the changed information. *Perception & Psychophysics, 66,* 1268–1281.

Miyake, A., Friedman, N. P., Emerson, M. J., Witzki, A. H., Howerter, A., & Wager, T. D. (2000). The unity and diversity of executive functions and their contributions to complex "frontal lobe" tasks: A latent variable analysis. *Cognitive Psychology, 41,* 49–100.

Monsell, S. (2003). Task switching. *Trends in Cognitive Sciences, 7,* 134–140.

Myerson, J., Adams, D. R., Hale, S., & Jenkins, L. (2003). Analysis of group differences in processing speed: Brinley plots, q-q plots, and other conspiracies. *Psychonomic Bulletin & Review, 10,* 224–237.

Nebes, R. D., & Madden, D. J. (1983). The use of focused attention in visual search by young and old adults. *Experimental Aging Research, 9,* 139–143.

Nielson, K. A., Langenecker, S. A., & Garavan, H. (2002). Differences in the functional neuroanatomy of inhibitory control across the adult life span. *Psychology and Aging, 17,* 56–71.

Nissen, M. J., & Corkin, S. (1985). Effectiveness of attentional cueing in older and younger adults. *Journal of Gerontology, 40,* 185–191.

O'Sullivan, M., Jones, D. K., Summers, P. E., Morris, R. G., Williams, S. C., & Markus, H. S. (2001). Evidence for cortical "disconnection" as a mechanism of age-related cognitive decline. *Neurology, 57,* 632–638.

Parasuraman, R., Greenwood, P. M., Kumar, R., & Fossella, J. (2005). Beyond heritability: Neurotransmitter genes differentially modulate visuospatial attention and working memory. *Psychological Science, 16,* 200–207.

Pashler, H. (1994). Dual-task interference in simple tasks: Data and theory. *Psychological Bulletin, 116,* 220–244.

Perfect, T. (1997). Memory aging as frontal lobe dysfunction. In M. A. Conway (Ed.), *Cognitive models of memory* (pp. 315–339). Cambridge, MA: MIT Press.

Persad, C. C., Abeles, N., Zacks, R. T., & Denburg, N. L. (2002). Inhibitory changes after age 60 and their relationship to measures of attention and memory. *Journal of Gerontology: Psychological Sciences, 57,* 223–232.

Peters, A., & Sethares, C. (2002). Aging and the myelinated fibers in prefrontal cortex and corpus callosum of the monkey. *Journal of Comparative Neurology, 442,* 277–291.

Plude, D. J., & Doussard-Roosevelt, J. A. (1989). Aging, selective attention, and feature integration. *Psychology and Aging, 4,* 98–105.

Plude, D. J., & Hoyer, W. J. (1986). Age and the selectivity of visual information processing. *Psychology and Aging, 1,* 4–10.

Pringle, H. L., Irwin, D. E., Kramer, A. F., & Atchley, P. (2001). The role of attentional breadth in perceptual change detection. *Psychonomic Bulletin & Review, 8,* 89–95.

Pringle, H. L., Kramer, A. F., & Irwin, D. E. (2004). Individual differences in the visual representation of scenes. In D. T. Levin (Ed.), *Thinking and seeing: Visual metacognition in children and adults* (pp. 165–186). Westport, CT: Greenwood.

Quinlan, P. T. (2003). Visual feature integration theory: Past, present, and future. *Psychological Bulletin, 129,* 643–673.

Rabbitt, P. (1965a). An age-decrement in the ability to ignore irrelevant information. *Journal of Gerontology, 20,* 233–238.

Rabbitt, P. (1965b). Age and discrimination between complex stimuli. In A. T. Welford & J. E. Birren (Eds.), *Behavior, aging, and the nervous system* (pp. 35–53). Springfield, IL: Charles C. Thomas.

Rabbitt, P. (1968). Age and the use of structure in transmitted information. In G. A. Talland (Ed.), *Human aging and behavior* (pp. 75–92). New York: Academic Press.

Ratcliff, R. (2002). A diffusion model account of response time and accuracy in a brightness discrimination task: Fitting real data and failing to fit fake but plausible data. *Psychonomic Bulletin & Review, 9,* 278–291.

Ratcliff, R., Spieler, D., & McKoon, G. (2004). Analysis of group differences in processing speed: Where are the models of processing? *Psychonomic Bulletin & Review, 11,* 755–769.

Ratcliff, R., Thapar, A., & McKoon, G. (2001). The effects of aging on reaction time in a signal detection task. *Psychology and Aging, 16,* 323–341.

Raz, N. (2000). Aging of the brain and its impact on cognitive performance: Integration of structural and functional findings. In F. I. M. Craik & T. A. Salthouse (Eds.), *The handbook of aging and cognition* (2nd ed., pp. 1–90). Mahwah, NJ: Lawrence Erlbaum Associates, Inc.

Raz, N. (2005). The aging brain observed in vivo: Differential changes and their modifiers. In R. Cabeza, L. Nyberg, & D. Park (Eds.), *Cognitive neuroscience of aging: Linking cognitive and cerebral aging* (pp. 19–57). New York: Oxford University Press.

Raz, N., Lindenberger, U., Rodrigue, K. M., Kennedy, K. M., Head, D., Williamson, A., et al. (2005). Regional brain changes in aging healthy adults: General trends, individual differences and modifiers. *Cerebral Cortex, 15,* 1676–1689.

Reuter-Lorenz, P. A., & Mikels, J.A. (2006). The aging mind and brain: Implications of enduring plasticity for behavioral and cultural change. In P. Baltes, P. A. Reuter-Lorenz, & F. Roesler (Eds.), *Lifespan development and the brain: The perspective of biocultural co-constructivism* (pp. 255–276). Cambridge: Cambridge University Press.

Riby, L., Perfect, T., & Stollery, B. (2004). Evidence for disproportionate dual-task costs in older adults for episodic but not semantic memory. *Quarterly Journal of Experimental Psychology, 57A,* 241–267.

Roenker, D. L., Gissell, G. M., Ball, K. K., Wadley, V. G., & Edwards, J. D. (2003). Speed-of-processing and driving simulator training result in improved driving performance. *Human Factors, 45*(2), 218–233.

Rogers, R. D., & Monsell, S. (1995). Costs of a predictable switch between simple cognitive tasks. *Journal of Experimental Psychology: General, 124,* 207–231.

Rovio, S., Kareholt, I., Helkala, E. L., Viitanen, M., Winblad, B., Tuomilehto, J., et al. (2005). Leisure-time physical activity at midlife and the risk of dementia and Alzheimer's disease. *Lancet Neurology, 4,* 705–711.

Rubin, D. C. (1999). Frontal-striatal circuits in cognitive aging: Evidence for caudate involvement. *Aging, Neuropsychology, and Cognition, 6,* 241–259.

Rumelhart, D. E., & McClelland, J. L. (1986). *Parallel distributed processing: Explorations in the microstructure of cognition.* Cambridge, MA: MIT Press.

Rypma, B., & D'Esposito, M. (2000). Isolating the neural mechanisms of age-related changes in human working memory. *Nature Neuroscience, 3,* 509–515.

Salat, D. H., Buckner, R. L., Snyder, A. Z., Greve, D. N., Desikan, R. S., Busa, E., et al. (2004). Thinning of the cerebral cortex in aging. *Cerebral Cortex, 14,* 721–730.

Salat, D. H., Tuch, D. S., Greve, D. N., van der Kouwe, A. J., Hevelone, N. D., Zaleta, A. K., et al. (2005). Age-related alterations in white matter microstructure measured by diffusion tensor imaging. *Neurobiology of Aging, 26,* 1215–1227.

Salthouse, T. A. (1985). Speed of behavior and its implications for cognition. In J. E. Birren & K. W. Schaie (Eds.), *Handbook of the psychology of aging* (2nd ed., pp. 400–426). New York: Van Nostrand Reinhold.

Salthouse, T. A. (1988). Resource-reduction interpretations of cognitive aging. *Developmental Review, 8,* 238–272.

Salthouse, T. A. (1990a). Influence of experience on age differences in cognitive functioning. *Human Factors, 32,* 551–569.

Salthouse, T. A. (1990b). Working memory as a processing resource in cognitive aging. *Developmental Review, 10,* 101–124.

Salthouse, T. A. (1993a). Attentional blocks are not responsible for age-related slowing. *Journal of Gerontology: Psychological Sciences, 48B,* 263–270.

Salthouse, T. A. (1993b). Speed mediation of adult age differences in cognition. *Developmental Psychology, 29,* 722–738.

Salthouse, T. A. (1996). The processing-speed theory of adult age differences in cognition. *Psychological Review, 103,* 403–428.

Salthouse, T. A. (1998). Relation of successive percentiles of reaction time distribution to cognitive variables and adult age. *Intelligence, 26,* 153–166.

Salthouse, T. A. (2000). Aging and measures of processing speed. *Biological Psychology, 54,* 35–54.

Salthouse, T. A. (2006). Mental exercise and mental aging: Evaluating the validity of the use it or lose it hypothesis. *Perspectives in Psychological Science.*

Salthouse, T. A., Atkinson, T. M., & Berish, D. E. (2003). Executive functioning as a potential mediator of age-related cognitive decline in normal adults. *Journal of Experimental Psychology: General, 132*(4), 566–594.

Salthouse, T. A., Fristoe, N., McGuthry, K. E., & Hambrick, D. Z. (1998). Relation of task switching to speed, age, and fluid intelligence. *Psychology and Aging, 13,* 445–461.

Salthouse, T. A., Fristoe, N., & Rhee, S. H. (1996a). How localized are age-related effects on neuropsychological measures? *Neuropsychology, 10,* 272–285.

Salthouse, T. A., Hancock, H. E., Meinz, E. J., & Hambrick, D. Z. (1996b). Interrelations of age, visual acuity, and cognitive functioning. *Journal of Gerontology: Psychological Sciences, 51B,* 317–330.

Salthouse, T. A., Kausler, D. H., & Saults, J. S. (1988). Utilization of path-analytic procedures to investigate the role of processing resources in cognitive aging. *Psychology and Aging, 3,* 158–166.

Salthouse, T. A., & Kersten, A. W. (1993). Decomposing adult age differences in symbol arithmetic. *Memory & Cognition, 21,* 699–710.

Salthouse, T. A., & Lichty, W. (1985). Tests of the neural noise hypothesis of age-related cognitive change. *Journal of Gerontology, 40,* 443–450.

Salthouse, T. A., & Madden, D. J. (2008). Information processing speed and aging. In J. DeLuca & J. Kalmar (Eds.), *Information processing speed in clinical populations* (pp. 221–241). New York: Psychology Press.

Sandell, J. H., & Peters, A. (2001). Effects of age on nerve fibers in the rhesus monkey optic nerve. *Journal of Comparative Neurology, 429,* 541–553.

Schmiedek, F., & Li, S.-C. (2004). Toward an alternative representation for disentangling age-associated differences in general and specific cognitive abilities. *Psychology and Aging, 19,* 40–56.

Schmitter-Edgecombe, M., & Nissley, H. M. (2002). Effects of aging on implicit covariation learning. *Aging, Neuropsychology, and Cognition, 9,* 61–75.

Schretlen, D., Pearlson, G. D., Anthony, J. C., Aylward, E. H., Augustine, A. M., Davis, A. et al. (2000). Elucidating the contributions of processing speed, executive ability, and frontal

lobe volume to normal age-related differences in fluid intelligence. *Journal of the International Neuropsychological Society, 6*, 52–61.

Schuit, A. J., Feskens, E. J., Launer, L. J., & Kromhout, D. (2001). Physical activity and cognitive decline, the role of the apolipoprotein e4 allele. *Medicine and Science in Sports and Exercise, 33*, 772–777.

Shulman, G. L., Remington, R. W., & McLean, J. P. (1979). Moving attention through visual space. *Journal of Experimental Psychology: Human Perception and Performance, 5*, 522–526.

Smith, E. E., Geva, A., Jonides, J., Miller, A., Reuter-Lorenz, P., & Koeppe, R. A. (2001). The neural basis of task-switching in working memory: Effects of performance and aging. *Proceedings of the National Academy of Sciences of the United States of America, 98*, 2095–2100.

Somers, D. C., Dale, A. M., Seiffert, A. E., & Tootell, R. B. (1999). Functional fMRI reveals spatially specific attentional modulation in human primary visual cortex. *Proceedings of the National Academy of Sciences of the United States of America, 96*, 1663–1668.

Spaniol, J., Madden, D. J., & Voss, A. (2006). A diffusion model analysis of adult age differences in episodic and semantic long-term memory retrieval. *Journal of Experimental Psychology: Learning, Memory, and Cognition, 32*, 101–117.

Sparrow, W. A., Bradshaw, E. J., Lamoureux, E., & Tirosh, O. (2002). Ageing effects on the attention demands of walking. *Human Movement Science, 21*, 961–972.

Sperling, G., & Weichselgartner, E. (1995). Episodic theory of the dynamics of spatial attention. *Psychological Review, 102*, 503–532.

Spieler, D. H., Balota, D. A., & Faust, M. E. (1996). Stroop performance in healthy younger and older adults and in individuals with dementia of the Alzheimer's type. *Journal of Experimental Psychology: Human Perception and Performance, 22*, 461–479.

Sweeney, J. A., Rosano, C., Berman, R. A., & Luna, B. (2001). Inhibitory control of attention declines more than working memory during normal aging. *Neurobiology of Aging, 22*, 39–47.

Sylvester, C. Y., Wager, T. D., Lacey, S. C., Hernandez, L., Nichols, T. E., Smith, E. E., et al. (2003). Switching attention and resolving interference: fMRI measures of executive functions. *Neuropsychologia, 41*, 357–370.

Szameitat, A. J., Schubert, T., Muller, K., & Von Cramon, D. Y. (2002). Localization of executive functions in dual-task performance with fMRI. *Journal of Cognitive Neuroscience, 14*, 1184–1199.

Thapar, A., Ratcliff, R., & McKoon, G. (2003). A diffusion model analysis of the effects of aging on letter discrimination. *Psychology and Aging, 18*, 415–429.

Tisserand, D. J., & Jolles, J. (2003). On the involvement of prefrontal networks in cognitive ageing. *Cortex, 39*, 1107–1128.

Tisserand, D. J., Visser, P. J., van Boxtel, M. P., & Jolles, J. (2000). The relation between global and limbic brain volumes on MRI and cognitive performance in healthy individuals across the age range. *Neurobiology of Aging, 21*, 569–576.

Trick, L. M., Perl, T., & Sethi, N. (2005). Age-related differences in multiple-object tracking. *Journal of Gerontology: Psychological Science, 60B*, 102–105.

Tsal, Y. (1983). Movements of attention across the visual field. *Journal of Experimental Psychology: Human Perception and Performance, 9*, 523–530.

Tsang, P. S., & Shaner, T. L. (1998). Age, attention, expertise, and time-sharing performance. *Psychology and Aging, 13*, 323–347.

Tsang, P. S., & Voss, D. T. (1996). Boundaries of cognitive performance as a function of age and flight experience. *International Journal of Aviation Psychology, 6*, 359–377.

Verhaeghen, P., & Basak, C. (2005). Ageing and switching of the focus of attention in working memory: Results from a modified n-back task. *Quarterly Journal of Experimental Psychology, 58A*, 134–154.

Verhaeghen, P., & Cerella, J. (2002). Aging, executive control, and attention: A review of meta-analyses. *Neuroscience and Biobehavioral Reviews, 26*, 849–857.

Verhaeghen, P., Cerella, J., Bopp, K. L., & Basak, C. (2005). Aging and varieties of cognitive control: A review of meta-analyses on resistance to interference, coordination, and task switching, and an experimental exploration of age-sensitivity in the newly identified process of focus switching. In R. W. Engle, G. Sedek, U. v. Hecker, & D. N. McIntosh (Eds.), *Cognitive limitations in aging and psychopathology* (pp. 160–189). Cambridge: Cambridge University Press.

Verhaeghen, P., & De Meersman, L. (1998). Aging and the Stroop effect: A meta-analysis. *Psychology and Aging, 13*, 120–126.

Verhaeghen, P., Steitz, D. W., Sliwinski, M. J., & Cerella, J. (2003). Aging and dual-task performance: A meta-analysis. *Psychology and Aging, 18*, 443–460.

Watson, D. G., & Maylor, E. A. (2002). Aging and visual marking: Selective deficits for moving stimuli. *Psychology and Aging, 17*, 321–339.

Watson, D. G., Maylor, E. A., & Manson, N. J. (2002). Aging and enumeration: A selective deficit for the subitization of targets among distractors. *Psychology and Aging, 17*, 496–504.

Wecker, N. S., Kramer, J. H., Hallam, B. J., & Delis, D. C. (2005). Mental flexibility: Age effects on switching. *Neuropsychology, 19*, 345–352.

Wecker, N. S., Kramer, J. H., Wisniewski, A., Delis, D. C., & Kaplan, E. (2000). Age effects on executive ability. *Neuropsychology, 14*, 409–414.

Welford, A. T. (1981). Signal, noise, performance, and age. *Human Factors, 23*, 97–109.

West, R. L. (1996). An application of prefrontal cortex function theory to cognitive aging. *Psychological Bulletin, 120*, 272–292.

West, R. L., & Bowry, R. (2005). The aging of cognitive control. In R. W. Engle, G. Sedek, U. von Hecker, & D. N. McIntosh (Eds.), *Cognitive limitations in aging and psychopathology* (pp. 97–121). Cambridge: Cambridge University Press.

Whiting, W. L. (2003). Adult age differences in divided attention: Effects of elaboration during memory encoding. *Aging, Neuropsychology, and Cognition, 10*, 141–157.

Whiting, W. L., Madden, D. J., Pierce, T. W., & Allen, P. A. (2005). Searching from the top down: Ageing and attentional guidance during singleton detection. *Quarterly Journal of Experimental Psychology, 58A*, 72–97.

Whiting, W. L., & Smith, A. D. (1997). Differential age-related processing limitations in recall and recognition tasks. *Psychology and Aging, 12*, 216–224.

Wolfe, J. M. (1994). Guided search 2.0: A revised model of visual search. *Psychonomic Bulletin & Review, 1*(2), 202–238.

Wolfe, J. M., Butcher, S. J., Lee, C., & Hyle, M. (2003). Changing your mind: On the contributions of top-down and bottom-up guidance in visual search for feature singletons. *Journal of Experimental Psychology. Human Perception and Performance, 29*, 483–502.

Wolfe, J. M., & Horowitz, T. S. (2004). What attributes guide the deployment of visual attention and how do they do it? *Nature Reviews. Neuroscience, 5*(6), 495–501.

Wright, R. E. (1981). Aging, divided attention, and processing capacity. *Journal of Gerontology, 36*, 605–614.

Yantis, S. (2005). How visual salience wins the battle for awareness. *Nature Neuroscience, 8*, 975–977.

Zacks, R., & Hasher, L. (1997). Cognitive gerontology and attentional inhibition: A reply to Burke and McDowd. *Journal of Gerontology: Psychological Sciences, 52*, 274–283.

Zacks, R. T., Hasher, L., & Li, K. Z. H. (2000). Human memory. In F. I. M. Craik & T. A. Salthouse (Eds.), *The handbook of aging and cognition* (2nd ed., pp. 293–357). Mahwah, NJ: Lawrence Erlbaum Associates, Inc.

New Considerations in Aging and Memory

The Glass May Be Half Full

Mark A. McDaniel
Washington University in St. Louis

Gilles O. Einstein
Furman University

Larry L. Jacoby
Washington University in St. Louis

Previous reviews of memory and aging, including those in prior volumes of *The Handbook of Aging and Cognition,* have critically examined the well-documented age-related declines in memory. These reviews provide superb coverage of the range of memory paradigms and tasks for which older adults demonstrate declines in memory performance relative to younger adults and highlight the contemporary theoretical approaches to explaining age-related memory decline (e.g., Craik & Jennings, 1992; Kausler, 1994; Light, 1991; Smith, 1996; Zacks, Hasher, & Li, 2000). For a number of reasons, in this chapter we instead plumb different themes. Specifically, we examine recent work indicating that variables other than purely cognitive ones may account for at least some of the age-related decline. Next, we explore and evaluate research suggesting memory processes that are preserved in older adults, as well as factors such as individual differences that may help sustain memory performance in older adults. Continuing in this vein, in the final section we consider the value of interventions ranging from training regimens to physical activity to "brain-specific" supplements for improving or maintaining memory with age.

We adopted this approach primarily because much has been written about age-related memory decline, and we were not certain that we would have much to add to the excellent reviews cited above. Moreover, there is a growing research literature that has not yet been pieced together

that scientifically explores a range of interventions and treatments for age-related decline in memory. In parallel, as demographics in the United States and throughout the world change such that the population is increasingly represented by older adults, products, courses, nutritional supplements, and advice columns directed at "fixing" memory decline proliferate. We believe that assembling the scientific literature on this topic is useful, as it provides a basis for more reasonable and rational input to these public concerns. Thus, we are hopeful that this chapter will both stimulate basic researchers in the area and hold interest for researchers and gerontologists focusing on a range of applied issues pertaining to aging and memory.

MODERATING INFLUENCES ON AGING AND MEMORY

As noted above and as pointed out in many reviews on aging and memory (e.g., Zacks, Hasher, & Li, 2000), there is ample evidence that there are age-related memory declines and that these declines occur on a variety of memory tasks (e.g., Park, Lautenschlager, Hedden, Davidson, Smith, & Smith, 2002). Perhaps the dominant explanation for this decline is that there are biological changes in the brain that occur with age (Prull, Gabrieli, & Bunge, 2000; Raz, 2000; West, 1996; Woodruff-Pak, 1997; see Dennis & Cabeza, chapter 1), and these compromise the effectiveness of neuronal functioning and hence cognitive processing. These biological changes include general shrinkage of neurons, losses in myelination, reduced dendritic branching, reduced cerebral blood flow, and decreased availability of certain neurotransmitters. The thinking is that these physiological changes impact basic cognitive mechanisms such as processing speed (Salthouse, 1991), processing capacity (Craik, 1986), and/or inhibitory processes (Hasher & Zacks, 1988).

Whereas this view of compromised cognitive processing likely explains at least some of the age-related decline in memory, following the suggestions of Zacks et al. (2000) and Hess (2005), we believe it is important to consider cognitive processing in relation to other changes (e.g., social, motivational, health) that also occur with age (cf. Baltes & Baltes, 1990). In recent years, there is growing evidence that developmental changes in factors such as circadian rhythms, health, motivation, emotional outlook, and goals can moderate cognitive functioning (see, for example, Carstensen & Mikels, 2005; see Hess, 2005, for an excellent review). In this section we consider the influence of two of these moderating variables on memory performance. Specifically, we evaluate the extent to which deficits in sensory function and negative beliefs about aging (at least in western cultures) can affect memory performance.

Effortfulness Hypothesis: Age-related Memory Deficits May Sometimes Result from Compensation for Sensory Deficits

We first consider the possibility that some age-related "memory" deficits may not reflect declines in memory per se. In designing research and interpreting results, cognitive psychologists have tended to overlook the well-demonstrated effects of aging on sensory processes (Schneider & Pichora-Fuller, 2000). Recently, McCoy, Tun, Cox, Colangelo, Stewart, and Wingfield (2005) and Wingfield, Tun, and McCoy (2005) have proposed the effortfulness hypothesis and presented compelling evidence that some of the memory deficits of some older adults may be due to encoding limitations that arise from shifting resources to compensate for sensory problems.

This relationship was first noticed by Rabbitt (1968) in a study in which he auditorally presented items and compared recall of the early items in the list depending on whether the later items were presented in clear or masked fashion. He consistently found (with both digits and prose passages) that memory for the early information was poorer when the later items were presented through a noise mask relative to when they were presented clearly. Rabbitt's interpretation was that subjects in the noise condition compensated for the degraded stimulus by devoting resources to the processing of the speech, and this interfered with rehearsing the earlier items.

As applied to aging, the effortfulness hypothesis starts with the observation that many older adults suffer hearing loss. This age-related hearing deficit tends to be particularly pronounced for high frequency sounds, which is a range of sounds that is important for the faithful perception of speech. Interestingly, most older adults with mild to moderate hearing loss do not use hearing aids and for those who do, hearing aids tend to be less than completely effective in correcting the deficit (Schneider & Pichora-Fuller, 2000). In addition, everyday speech often occurs in noisy contexts and this exacerbates the accuracy of speech perception especially for older adults (Tun, 1998). The effortfulness hypothesis assumes that people with hearing loss can use central processing resources in the service of perceptual processing in order to successfully identify items from a degraded sensory trace. With this extra effort devoted to perceptual processing, however, there will be fewer resources available for rehearsing, elaborating, and/or organizing the information, and thus this information will be less memorable.

To examine this hypothesis, McCoy et al. (2005) tested older adults with mild to moderate hearing loss and those with good hearing (hereafter referred to as the better hearing group). These groups were matched on age, education, and vocabulary. The subjects were auditorally

presented lists of items and told to listen to them carefully as they would occasionally be stopped and prompted to recall the immediately preceding three items. Their results showed nearly perfect recall for the last item in both the hearing loss ($M = 98.2\%$) and better hearing ($M = 99.5\%$) groups, indicating that both groups could, through one means or another, correctly perceive the items. Interestingly, and consistent with the effortfulness hypothesis, recall of the first two items was much lower in the hearing loss group ($M = 80.2\%$) relative to the better hearing group ($M = 94.8\%$). Given the high recall of the last item, it seems likely that hearing loss subjects were able to identify the prior two items in the list but that the poor memory for these items was due to the effort that was devoted to identifying the items—effort that compensated for the hearing loss and led to successful identification but compromised rehearsal and maintenance of the prior items.

It is important to note that this pattern occurred only with essentially unrelated lists of words. With word lists that had medium and high levels of approximation to the English language, recall was near ceiling for all items and not significantly different between the hearing loss and better hearing groups. The explanation here is that the linguistic constraints imposed by the context in the lists with reasonable approximations to the English language greatly improved word perception without drawing extensively on central processing resources. Thus, the finding of hearing-related memory differences only in situations in which word perception is difficult is entirely consistent with the effortfulness hypothesis.

Tun, McCoy, Cox, and Wingfield (2006) provided more direct evidence that those with hearing loss expend greater resources when processing and encoding spoken words. They did so by asking younger and older subjects, who either had good hearing or hearing loss, to learn and later recall lists of auditorally presented words. They also varied whether subjects performed an additional visual distraction task (visually tracking a moving dot on a computer monitor) during encoding and retrieval. The results were consistent with the view that hearing-impaired people need to devote extensive resources to compensate for sensory deficits. When encoding the spoken words, hearing-impaired subjects were more disrupted than nonimpaired subjects in maintaining their tracking of the visual target (relative to when they performed only the visual tracking task). Interestingly, this pattern occurred for both younger and older subjects. As might be expected if the quality of the encoding of hearing-impaired subjects suffers because of the additional resources devoted to perceiving the words, retrieval of the hearing-impaired subjects also exacted greater costs on the visual tracking task.

In summary, this research is intriguing in showing that some of the age-related declines in memory may sometimes actually result from sensory

deficits that tend to occur with age. It is interesting to consider the range of situations in which this type of compensation could contribute to age-related memory declines and what we typically interpret as the result of central losses in cognitive resources (e.g., Craik, 1986). We agree with Schneider and Pichora-Fuller's (2000) view that cognitive researchers have in the past tended to ignore age-related sensory deficits, and we echo their recommendation as well as that of Wingfield et al. (2005) to consider the interdependence of sensory deficits and cognitive processing.

Stereotype Threat and Aging Effects

Over the past 10 to 15 years, researchers have made an increasingly strong case that part of the typically observed age-related memory decline is due to the beliefs that older adults have about the effects of aging on memory. If, for example, we believe that memory declines with age and that we have little power to overcome this inevitable effect of aging, then as we get older we may take less active and strategic approaches to learning information.

According to Hertzog and Hultsch (2000), most studies, although not all, indicate that older adults are sensitive to typically found age-related memory losses as they believe that their memories have declined with age. Relative to younger adults, older adults believe not only that they have poorer memory but also that they have reduced control over their memory (Berry & West, 1993; Gilewski, Zelinski, & Schaie, 1990; Hultsch, Hertzog, & Dixon, 1987; West, Dennehy-Basile, & Norris, 1996). This pattern is reinforced in longitudinal research as well. In one study in which older adults were sampled three times over a 6-year period, they rated their memory efficacy and their perceived control over memory as declining significantly even over this relatively brief period (McDonald-Miszczack, Hertzog, & Hultsch, 1995). Moreover, beliefs about one's own memory abilities are correlated with actual memory performance (Cavanaugh & Poon, 1989) and with the use of strategies (Hertzog, McGuire, & Lineweaver, 1998). Although these relations suggest that the self-efficacy beliefs of older adults can affect their memory performance, because of the correlational nature of this research it may be that it is the poorer memory of older adults that leads to lower self-efficacy ratings.

One approach to evaluating the extent to which negative stereotypes can influence memory performance is to compare younger and older adults across cultures that vary in terms of their view of aging. Toward that end, Levy and Langer (1994) examined whether the belief systems of older adults in cultures with positive or negative stereotypes actually affect their memory performance. On the basis of past research they assumed that there were negative stereotypes about aging in the typical

American culture but positive stereotypes in the mainland China culture. These assumptions about attitudinal differences were confirmed in the research with measures of attitudes toward aging. Interestingly, relative to people from mainland China, older as well as younger subjects from the American culture had significantly more negative attitudes about aging.

Levy and Langer (1994) also developed a memory composite score based on four different measures of memory (including immediate and delayed recall of dot patterns and cued recall of activities that had been associated with pictures of faces). The intriguing result from their research was that there was a culture effect for older adults but not younger adults. Specifically, for older adults memory was highest in the Chinese culture and lowest in the American culture whereas for younger adults memory did not vary across the cultures. Also, there was a large and significant age difference favoring younger adults in the American culture but the difference was small and not significant in the Chinese culture. It should be noted, however, that Yoon, Hasher, Feinberg, Rahhal, and Winocur (2000), when comparing younger and older Anglophone and Chinese Canadians, failed to find convincing support for the view that positive cultural attitudes about aging affect memory performance. In fact, their younger Anglophone and Chinese Canadians significantly outperformed their older counterparts on all four memory tests. Also, Hedden, Park, Nisbett, Ji, Jing, and Jiao (2002) did not find differences between older adults from China and the United States on visuospatial perceptual speed and working memory tasks. Generally, however, there has been relatively little research contrasting memory across cultures varying in their attitudes about aging (although see Park & Gutchess, 2006, for another approach to studying age-related processing differences across cultures).

Stronger support for the view that aging stereotypes can affect the memory performance of older adults comes from research showing that emphasizing that the experiment is designed to test memory disproportionally hurts the memory of older adults (Rahhal, Hasher, & Colcombe, 2001). The idea here is that strong memory instructions can activate negative age-related stereotypes in older adults. Younger and older subjects in the Rahhal et al. experiment were presented with obscure trivia items (e.g. "it takes six hours to boil an ostrich egg"), and after each item they were told whether the item was actually true. Later, the items were presented again, and subjects were asked to indicate which were true and which were false. One half of the subjects were given memory-emphasis instructions in which they were *repeatedly* told that the purpose of the study was to test their *memory*. The others were given memory-neutral instructions that focused on the learning of facts and the acquisition of knowledge. In both experiments there were significant age differences in the memory-

emphasis condition but not in the memory-neutral condition. Thus, when the memory nature of the task was emphasized, which is arguably typical of memory testing situations, there were strong age differences. On the other hand, when negative stereotypes associated with aging and memory were not activated with instructions, there were no age differences.

In a more recent set of experiments, Chasteen, Bhattacharyya, Horhota, Tam, and Hasher (2005) presented older and younger subjects with a set of behavioral descriptions, and subjects were told to use these either to form an impression of a person or to learn them for a memory test. There was better memory for the impression instructions than for the memory instructions and better memory for younger subjects relative to older ones. Importantly, however, impression instructions did not reduce the magnitude of the age differences on either recall or recognition tests. Although at first blush these results seem to conflict with those of Rahhal et al. (2001), Chasteen et al. measured negative stereotype activation during the experiment and found equally strong negative stereotype activation for older adults in both the memory and impression formation conditions. They also found that stereotype activation completely mediated the relation between age and memory performance. Indeed, their conclusion was that because aging stereotypes have such a powerful effect in memory studies, it is difficult to remove the stereotype threat with more neutral impression formation instructions.

A related approach to examining the relation between aging stereotypes and memory performance has been to implicitly or explicitly prime negative aging stereotypes. Levy (1996) implicitly primed positive or negative aging stereotypes of older adults by rapidly presenting (too fast for conscious awareness) words related either to "senility" or "wise" themes. The implicit primes affected the memory performance of older adults but not of younger adults. In particular, relative to performance measured prior to the priming manipulation, positive primes tended to improve memory and negative primes tended to decrease memory. Stein, Blanchard-Fields, and Hertzog (2002) also found that negative implicit primes can reduce the performance of older adults on at least some memory tasks. This general pattern of results was extended by Hess, Hinson, and Statham (2004). In two experiments, they explicitly or implicitly activated positive or negative aging stereotypes and presented subjects with a list of categorized items to learn for a free recall test. Consistent with the results of Levy, they found that positive primes reduced age differences in memory performance and that negative primes increased age differences. They also found that the effects of priming on memory were greatest under implicit priming conditions.

Although the research just described showed muted effects of

stereotype priming with explicit cues, other research shows that direct and strong explicit information that either reinforces or contradicts the aging stereotype can influence age-related differences in memory. Hess, Auman, Colcombe, and Rahhal (2003) had younger or older subjects read either no articles or one of two types of newspaper-like articles about recent evidence concerning aging and memory. The theme for one set was negative and reinforced the idea of age-related memory declines whereas the theme for the other set was positive and indicated that older adults have the ability to perform well on memory tests. They found that reading negative information about aging and memory significantly decreased free recall for older subjects (but not for younger subjects) relative to those who read either no information or positive information. Moreover this negative effect on memory of reading information confirming the negative stereotype of aging was more pronounced for subjects who indicated that they highly valued memory ability.

All in all, the research supports the general view that stereotypes about aging can affect memory performance in the laboratory. There is evidence that (1) age differences are more pronounced in cultures in which there are negative aging stereotypes; (2) de-emphasizing the memory nature of a task improves memory for older adults; (3) implicitly priming negative aging stereotypes decreases memory of older adults; and (4) explicitly reminding subjects about the negative effects of aging interferes with the memory performance of older adults.

In reviewing this research, one is struck both by the strength of some of the effects (e.g., the elimination of age differences with memory-neutral instructions, Rahhal et al., 2001; and when testing participants from mainland China, Levy & Langer, 1994) and also by a good deal of inconsistencies across studies (e.g., the failure to attenuate age differences with memory-neutral instructions, Chasteen et al., 2005; and when testing Chinese Canadians, Yoon et al., 2000). Consider also the research on implicit priming of positive and negative stereotypes. In the Levy (1996) research, although there was a significant interaction between type of prime (positive or negative) and memory performance before and after the priming intervention on four of the five memory tasks, positive primes significantly improved memory on only one of the memory tasks. Also, in the Stein et al. (2002) experiment, positive primes did not improve performance on either of the two memory tasks. Thus, we believe there is a lot more to learn both about the robustness of these effects and the situations that are especially sensitive to stereotype effects. It seems likely that the magnitude of the effects involving activation of aging stereotypes depends on a number of factors including characteristics of the individual as well as the nature of the memory test (cf., Jenkins, 1979). As an example, Hess et al. (2004) found that stereotype threat had a stronger

effect on those older adults who highly valued their memory ability. To the extent that stereotype threat compromises working memory resources, it may have a greater effect on those tasks that depend more on controlled processes than on automatic processes. Thus, further research should explore not only the kinds of testing situations that activate the negative aging stereotype but also the kinds of personality characteristics and cognitive processes that are most susceptible to activation of stereotypes.

An important general implication of this research is that testing conditions can affect the extent to which negative stereotypes are activated. Thus, we need to be concerned about how testing environments differentially affect the psychological attitudes of younger and older adults and consequently the magnitude of the age-related differences that are observed (see Hess, 2005). As Rahhal et al. (2001) indicate, we need to carefully evaluate the wording of instructions as well as consider other aspects of the experimental context such as: "laboratory names, advertisements for recruiting participants, consent forms, and other materials in the laboratory may also contain triggers that could affect experimental findings" (p. 705). Another implication is that one mechanism by which training procedures can or do affect memory performance is by enhancing a sense of self-efficacy in memory situations (see Floyd & Scoggin, 1997).

Further research on stereotype threat will also help us adjudicate among several interesting theoretical interpretations of the underlying processes by which activating stereotypes interfere with the performance older adults. One theoretical view is based on Steele and Aronson's (1995) finding that African Americans performed more poorly than their white peers on an intelligence test when they were told it was a measure of intelligence but not when the test was presented as unrelated to intelligence. According to Steele (1997), defining the test as an intelligence test created a threat and concern in terms of possibly confirming negative social stereotypes about their group. This threat affected anxiety and/or disruptive thoughts which in turn reduced the capacity available for performing the task. As applied to aging, within this view, aspects of the experimental situation that activate the negative aging stereotype could lead to off-task thoughts and compromised working memory capacity (see Schmader & Johns, 2003, for evidence of reduced working memory capacity when activating a relevant stereotype for women and Latinos). A related but different idea is based on Bandura's (1997) theory of self-efficacy. Specifically, when people are put in situations in which they do not believe they can perform well, they will have reduced effort and motivation for the task. Consistent with this view, West, Bagwell, and Dark-Freudeman's (2005; see also West, Welch, & Thorn, 2001) results

suggest that older adults will maintain their effort and improve their memory performance when they get feedback indicating that they are making progress toward their goal but seem to abandon this effort with more negative feedback. Generally, the idea is that when older adults in western cultures are given a task that is explicitly a memory task, they are less likely to engage active, effortful, and strategic processing, and this is likely to ensure poor memory in most situations.

A third theoretical view is based on Bargh and Chartrand's (1999) theory that the perception of social stereotypes can automatically trigger behavioral tendencies related to that stereotype. For example, Holland, Hendricks, and Aarts (2006) found that introducing the citrus scent of an all-purpose cleaner into a laboratory led subjects to unconsciously keep their table cleaner when eating a crumbly cookie. In terms of aging, Bargh, Chen, and Burrows (1996) found that implicitly priming subjects with items that were characteristic of the aging stereotype caused them to walk more slowly down a hallway relative to controlled subjects. Within this view, the negative effects on memory of stereotype activation are direct and can occur unconsciously. Results showing that implicit priming can affect memory performance are consistent with this view (Levy, 1996).

In summary, given the compelling evidence for age-related declines in brain functioning briefly outlined earlier in this chapter, it seems clear that some of the observed memory deficits in older adults are due to basic biological effects. But there also seems to be tantalizing evidence that, at least under some conditions, stereotypes about aging also contribute to age-related cognitive declines. It would seem important to continue to explore the extent to which these kinds of social factors can account for age differences in memory. Thus, we believe that our understanding of aging effects on memory will benefit from research that examines the conditions under which negative aging stereotypes modulate age differences in memory performance as well as research that tests the theoretical perspectives just presented. We now turn to an examination of selected memory tasks and processes for which age-related decline may be minimized.

PROSPECTIVE MEMORY

We begin with prospective memory—remembering to perform an intended action at an appropriate moment in the future. Prospective memory is ubiquitous in our everyday lives and none less so for older adults. Minimal reflection underscores the importance of prospective memory tasks for maintaining the fabric of older adults' lives. These tasks range from remembering to send a grandchild a birthday card to

remembering to pay bills, to remembering health-related intentions (taking medication, medical appointments). Experimental work on prospective memory has emerged only in the last 25 years, with research on prospective memory and aging increasing substantially within the past decade. This literature has already yielded complicated patterns of age-related results, and these patterns have recently been reviewed (Henry, Macleod, Phillips, & Crawford, 2004; McDaniel & Einstein, in press, 2007a). Here, we briefly highlight a prominent theme on prospective memory and aging reflected in this literature, and then turn to a more detailed treatment of the latest findings in this area that suggest spared memory processes in older adults.

An important distinction with regard to age-related effects on prospective memory is between *time-based* prospective memory and *event-based* prospective memory. In time-based tasks, the intended action is appropriately executed at a particular time of day (a doctor's appointment) or after the passage of a particular amount of time (taking cookies out of the oven in 10 minutes). Time-based *laboratory* prospective memory tasks typically produce age-related deficits, whereas time-based *naturalistic* tasks do not (see Henry's et al., 2004, meta-analytic review). Clearly, in some naturalistic time-based studies, older adults used external memory aids to support prospective remembering (e.g., Moscovitch, 1982), as they ordinarily might in their everyday lives. However, Kvavilashvili and Fisher (2007) reported no age-related declines in a naturalistic time-based task when participants were explicitly discouraged from using external memory aids. We return to this surprising result at the conclusion of this section after considering the implications of findings on event-based tasks.

In event-based prospective memory tasks, the intended action is executed when a particular environmental event is present. Examples are remembering to give a message to a neighbor when you see her and remembering to buy an anti-inflamatory medication when you pass the drug store. A substantial number of laboratory studies of event-based prospective memory report significant age-related declines in event-based prospective memory (e.g., d'Ydewalle, Luwel, & Brunfaut, 1999; Maylor, 1996; Park, Hertzog, Kidder, Morrell, & Mayhorn, 1997; see Henry et al., 2004, for a complete review). These age-related declines for laboratory event-based prospective memory (and time-based prospective memory) tasks are generally consistent with a seminal theoretical approach of Craik (1986). Craik suggested that prospective memory requires more self-initiated retrieval than any retrospective memory task (because in prospective memory one has to remember to remember). He suggested further that self-initiated retrieval processes decline with age. Consequently, this view anticipates that prospective memory should be especially at risk for older adults, more so than for any other type of episodic memory task.

However, this strong position has not received support in Henry et al.'s (2004) direct meta-analytic comparisons of aging and prospective versus retrospective memory. They found that the age-related impairment in prospective memory was of significantly less magnitude than the age-related deficit in free recall and only slightly (and nonsignificantly) greater than the age-related deficit in recognition. On subsequent reflection, considering event-based prospective memory, it is likely that the environmental event (indicating the appropriateness for performing the intended action) serves as a memory cue to support retrieval of the intended action, thereby mitigating the degree of self-initiated retrieval required (Einstein & McDaniel, 1990). Generally, then, the magnitude of age-related decline in prospective memory is likely not as extreme as initial theoretical approaches suggested.

Moreover, a convincing number of laboratory experiments have reported no significant age-related decline in event-based prospective memory (Cherry & LeCompte, 1999; Einstein & McDaniel, 1990; Einstein, Holland, McDaniel, & Guynn, 1992; Einstein, McDaniel, Richardson, & Cunfer, 1995; Marsh, Hicks, Cook, & Mayhorn, 2007; Vogels, Dekker, Brouwer, & de Jong, 2002). These converging findings suggest that further theoretical development is needed to fully understand the processes underlying prospective memory and the impact of aging on such processes. This is the issue which is most central to the themes of the present chapter and to which we now turn. At the conclusion of this section, we briefly offer some possibilities for why age-related declines in event-based prospective memory are found in some laboratory paradigms but not others. For a more comprehensive discussion of this issue see McDaniel and Einstein (2007a).

Intact Prospective Memory in Older Adults

Event-based Prospective Memory

One contemporary explanation of intact prospective memory performance in older adults rests on a view by Smith (2003; see also Smith & Bayen, 2006) that shifts the emphasis of highly demanding processes in prospective memory from self-initiated retrieval to preparatory attentional processes. The assumption is that prospective remembering requires attentional resources to monitor the environment for the presence of signals indicating the moment to perform the intended action. The idea is that as a person moves from one event to the next (e.g., a trial in an experiment), he or she evaluates whether the event is the appropriate marker for initiating the intended action. Because of presumed reduced attentional resources in older adults, this view anticipates age-related decline in at least some components of the prospective memory context, with the particular decline depending on the resource allocation policies that older adults adopt. If older adults choose to maintain performance on their ongoing tasks, then their limited attentional resources will not be sufficient to effectively monitor and prospective memory will decline relative to younger adults (Smith & Bayen, 2006). On the other hand, in some cases older adults may prefer to allocate their resources to maintain prospective memory performance. However, this would presumably place demands on their limited attentional resources which would disproportionately (relative to younger adults) reduce performance on the ongoing activity in which the prospective memory task is embedded. Except for one study that we will summarize in a moment, existing experiments have not been designed to be sensitive to a possible age-related exaggeration of costs on the ongoing activity.

An alternative framework is that prospective memory relies on memory processes that are spared with aging. McDaniel and Einstein (2000; 2007a) suggested that in event-based prospective memory tasks in which the critical features of the target event are processed as part of the ongoing activity (see Einstein & McDaniel, 2005; Einstein et al., 2005, for details), retrieval can be relatively spontaneous. Based on Moscovitch's (1994) proposal that the cognitive system supports reflexive, obligatory associative retrieval in the presence of an associated cue, the idea here is that when a prospective memory target event is processed it can stimulate spontaneous retrieval of the intended action (McDaniel & Einstein, 2000; see also, Guynn, McDaniel, & Einstein, 1998). With regard to aging, on this view, older adults do not show event-based prospective memory decline because reflexive associative retrieval is spared with age. Further, because retrieval is reflexive, attentional processes are not devoted to prospective remembering, and therefore older adults would not show exaggerated costs to the ongoing task to maintain high levels of prospective memory.

Before considering recent results pertinent to the above debate, two central points should be emphasized. First, it is critical to note that this reflexive associative aspect of automatic retrieval is theoretically different from the automatic retrieval mediated by familiarity (cf. Zacks et al., 2000) and underscored in age-related patterns in recognition experiments reported by Jacoby and colleagues (that we discuss in a subsequent section of this chapter). Second, though some theorists have hinted that a reflexive associative retrieval process might be spared in older adults (in support of episodic memory; e.g., Naveh-Benjamin, 2000; Zacks et al., 2000), direct evidence for this notion is exceedingly difficult to come by. This is because explicit retrospective memory tasks always allow the contribution of controlled associative processes, thereby obscuring the dynamics of putative reflexive processes. Prospective memory is an exciting paradigm in this regard because it has the trappings of a prototypical associative memory task—the cued recall task (McDaniel & Einstein, 1993). In the cued recall paradigm, the subject is given a list of paired items that includes a cue item and an item to be remembered (e.g., "Train—BLACK"). Then at test, the subject is provided with the cue ("Train") and prompted to try to remember the target item. In a parallel fashion, in a prospective memory task, a person pairs a particular anticipated event (e.g., encounter of a colleague) with an intended action (give a message). Later the individual encounters the cue event and must remember the associated intention, but without an explicit agent requesting retrieval. Consequently, the possibility is allowed that retrieval is not mediated by strategic processes (either stimulated by retrospective-memory instructions or by attentional monitoring).

An experiment reported in McDaniel, Einstein, and Rendell (in press) examined both prospective memory performance and the costs to the ongoing task for younger and older adults. Participants were presented with the ongoing task of making a category judgment about presented words. This ongoing activity involved presentation of a word and a category label, and participants were required to decide as quickly as possible whether the word was a category coordinate. For the prospective memory task, following typical laboratory procedures, participants were instructed to try to remember to perform a particular action (e.g., press a designated key) whenever a particular target work appeared (e.g., "dormitory"). To gauge baseline response accuracy and latency to the category judgment task, in a control block participants only performed the category judgment task. With younger adults, Einstein et al. (2005, Experiment 1) demonstrated that response latencies for category judgments were sensitive to costs incurred by the prospective memory task when participants were explicitly encouraged to concentrate on the prospective memory task. Of interest in the McDaniel et al. study was whether younger and especially older participants showed a cost to the category judgment task when the prospective memory task was not emphasized as particularly important (in the instructions). Also, of interest was whether older adults would maintain levels of prospective memory performance at levels evidenced by younger adults.

Older adults were as likely as younger adults to perform the prospective memory task (no significant age difference), and prospective memory performance was relatively high (older and younger adults remembered to respond about 75% of the time). Of central importance, in supporting this level of prospective memory performance, no significant costs to the category judgment task were incurred (either in terms of accuracy or response latency) for either younger or older adults. A similar finding of no age-related decline in prospective memory and no cost to ongoing activity was observed in another experiment using a face-processing ongoing activity (McDaniel et al., in press, Experiment 1). This pattern is consistent with the theoretical interpretation that event-based prospective memory can be supported by relatively spontaneous memory processes (e.g., reflexive retrieval of the intended activity) and, accordingly, older adults will be spared in prospective memory, presumably because reflexive retrieval components remain intact with age.

More direct evidence for sparing of reflexive retrieval in older adults was recently reported in a modification of the usual prospective memory paradigm. In the initial phase of the experiment, Einstein, Arnold, Bishop, and Scullin (2006) gave groups of younger and older participants instructions and practice on an image-rating ongoing task. In the next phase, participants received instructions and practice for the prospective memory task. Participants were asked to press a designated key on the computer keyboard whenever they saw either of two target words *in the context of the image-rating task.* In the next phase, participants were told that they would return to these tasks later and that they would first perform a lexical decision task. Participants were instructed to suspend all previous task demands, and to focus exclusively on responding as quickly and accurately as possible on this task. Critically, each prospective memory target and also matched control items were presented during this lexical decision task.

Even though there was no intention to perform the prospective memory task during lexical decision, reflexive retrieval processes might stimulate retrieval of the intended action and doing so would plausibly interfere with responding on the lexical decision task. Consistent with this reasoning, there was significant slowing to the prospective memory targets relative to the control items. Moreover, this slowing was at least as large in older adults (a slowing of 44 ms) as for younger adults (a slowing of 17 ms; see also Einstein et al., 2005, Experiment 5). These initial results suggest that reflexive retrieval of intention-related information when presented with specific prospective memory target events is robust in older adults. More generally, the laboratory study of prospective memory, under appropriate conditions (see Einstein & McDaniel, 2005; Einstein et al., 2005; McDaniel & Einstein, 2007b), might well provide an additional tool to established procedures (see section below on process dissociation) by which researchers can begin to thoroughly investigate and understand spontaneous retrieval processes in younger and older adults.

It should be noted that when there are a number of different target events (as can be the case in laboratory tasks), thereby increasing retrospective memory demands (e.g., four to six unrelated target words), age-related declines in prospective memory performance are observed (Einstein et al., 1992; Smith & Bayen, 2006). Also, with a nonfocal target event, which is a target event that is not part of the information being considered by the person in their ongoing activity (e.g., the target is a grocery store, for stopping to buy bread, located a bit off the road, and the ongoing activity is traveling in rush hour traffic and thus attending closely to the other cars; see Einstein & McDaniel, 2005), then prospective retrieval may require more resource demanding processes, with age decrements in prospective memory emerging (e.g., Maylor, 1996; Park et al., 1997) or age-related exaggeration of costs to the cover task occurring (McDaniel et al., in press).

Time-based Prospective Memory

We now return to the apparently puzzling result noted earlier concerning the absence of age-related decline in naturalistic time-based prospective memory tasks. Age-related sparing of spontaneous retrieval may play an intriguing role in these findings. The premise is that outside of the laboratory, between the formation of the intention and the time to perform the intention, there are chance encounters with cues that stimulate retrieval of the time-based intention (Kvavilashvili & Fisher, 2007). As an example, a week before your mother's birthday you decide to call her on Monday between 11 am and 1 pm (when she'll be home for lunch). During the week, you might encounter someone talking about a birthday, see a gift being wrapped at a store, or simply look at the telephone. These chance encounters could remind you that you intend to call your mother on her birthday, which in turn may promote more spontaneous retrieval of the intention with subsequent cues.

Kvavilashvili and Fisher (2007) recently reported data supporting this possibility. Young and older adults were given a typical semi-naturalistic time-based prospective memory task (participants were instructed in the laboratory on a Monday that they were to try to remember to call the experimenter the next Sunday at an appointed time). The typical pattern in a naturalistic setting was obtained: 81% of the older adults remembered to telephone on time, whereas 68% of the younger adults telephoned on time. The novel twist was that during the retention interval, participants made an entry in diaries whenever the intended action (a reminder) came to mind. For both younger and older adults, reminders occurred significantly more frequently in the presence of a chance external cue relative to an incidental internal thought or to a self-initiated, plan-related thought. External cues included things like seeing a telephone, hearing a telephone ring, or even the word "memory" being spoken. Apparently, for both young and older adults, reminders can spontaneously activate the intention, perhaps fostering rehearsal of the prospective memory task or the opportunity to associate additional cues with the intended action, and these factors may further sensitize the individual to encounters with cues as the interval between intention formation and the time to perform the intention progresses. If so, time-based prospective memory in everyday contexts may not necessarily rely on high levels of self-initiated processing and correspondingly robust age-related declines (cf. Einstein et al., 1995).

Habitual Prospective Memory

Habitual prospective memory tasks have received little attention with regard to aging (or for younger adults for that matter), but are prevalent in daily activity. In habitual prospective memory tasks, the intended activity is one that is performed on a regular basis. Older adults are faced with a number of important habitual prospective memory tasks, such as taking medications, remembering to monitor physical status (e.g., diabetics), and paying bills. As the task becomes habitual, forgetting may be minimized (see Einstein, McDaniel, Smith, & Shaw, 1998). However, habitual tasks may introduce a new challenge of remembering whether the intended activity was actually performed on a particular day or a particular time. Misremembering having performed the activity on a particular day, for instance, could result in omission of the activity that particular day (e.g., pertinent to older adults, undermedicating); misremembering that the activity was not performed on a particular day could result in repetitions of the activity (e.g., overmedicating). Essentially, these prospective memory failures are failures in output monitoring, and given that older adults are disadvantaged at source memory in general (see the Zacks et al., 2000, review), one might expect age-related increases in these kinds of errors in habitual prospective memory.

In an attempt to approximate a laboratory habitual task, Einstein et al. (1998) instructed participants to perform the same prospective memory task within each of 11 episodes (ongoing activities). Errors of commission that were related to self-reports that the participant remembered performing the intended action during a particular episode did not differ across young and older participants. Interpretation of these data is not clear-cut, though, because of reliance on self-reports. More definitive were the repetition errors in individual episodes, which could only occur if participants had faulty output monitoring (either did not remember executing the task or misassociated the execution of the intention with another episode). When the demands of the ongoing activity were not excessive, older adults displayed a relatively low number of repetition errors that were no greater than those committed by younger adults.

Marsh et al. (2007) directly examined possible age differences in output monitoring by instructing participants to initiate one intended action ("Action A") on the first time they remembered to perform the prospective memory task and to initiate a different action ("Action B") for the second time (second successful trial). The age differences can be summarized straightforwardly. On the second appearance of the target cue, younger adults were more likely (than older adults) to respond with Action B (indicating they believed they had responded upon the initial occurrence of the target cue), whereas older adults were more likely (than younger adults) to respond with Action A (indicating they believed they did not respond on the initial occurrence of the target). Critically, these patterns were obtained whether or not participants in fact responded on the first occurrence of the target so that the results indicated an age difference in response bias. Consequently, depending on the type of output monitoring error assessed, either the younger or the older participants performed more poorly. In the situation where participants correctly responded with Action A, older adults tended to more often forget they had performed the task (as indicated by repeating Action A on the second occurrence of the target). In contrast, when participants forgot to perform the task initially, younger adults tended to more often erroneously "remember" that they had performed the task initially (responding with Action B). The available results then do not indicate global age-related decline in output monitoring of prospective memory tasks.

Einstein et al. (1998) did find in their habitual task that under highly demanding ongoing activities (participants had to perform a secondary task in conjunction with the ongoing task), older adults produced substantially more repetition errors than younger adults (who still evidenced very few repetition errors). In a subsequent experiment we, along with Grit Ramuschkat (described in McDaniel & Einstein, 2007c), instructed older adults to execute the prospective memory task with an unusual or distinct motor movement ("while pressing a designated key on the keyboard, put your other hand on your head"). Using this distinct motor movement, repetition errors for older adults dropped to the low level evidenced by young adults. Thus, the preliminary evidence does not indicate immutable age-related decline in output monitoring in prospective memory. Even with demanding ongoing activity, age-related disadvantages in output monitoring appear to be remedied by engaging in distinctive motor sequences for execution (though see Marsh et al., 2007, Experiment 2, for the absence of a benefit for older adults in their paradigm, when the motor sequence required adults to turn in the chair to speak the prospective memory response to the experimenter).

DISTINCTIVE PROCESSING IN OLDER ADULTS

The just mentioned finding raises the more general issue of whether older adults' retrospective memory (recall, recognition) can be improved with distinctiveness—i.e., whether older adults show spared capabilities for distinctive processing of target information (processing that identifies unique or distinguishing features of stimuli) and effective use of distinct features at retrieval (see Hunt & Worthen, 2006). Surprisingly little research has been directed at this question within paradigms producing effects typically related to distinctive processing (see Smith, 2006). One such effect is the bizarreness effect, and the other is the isolation or von Restorff effect.

The Bizarreness Effect

In the bizarreness paradigm, people typically are instructed to form mental images (though sometimes other encoding tasks are used) of the referents of common sentences (e.g., *The MAID wiped the AMMONIA off the TABLE*) and of bizarre sentences *(e.g., The MAID licked the AMMONIA off the TABLE).* After study, participants are given a free recall test for the target nouns (typically capitalized during presentation). In a host of experiments with younger adult participants, the consistent finding is that the nouns presented in the bizarre sentences are recalled significantly better than when the nouns are presented in the common sentences (see Worthen, 2006, for a recent review). One notable limitation is that the effect appears reliably in within-list but not between-list manipulations (Einstein & McDaniel, 1987; McDaniel & Einstein, 1986, 1993, 2000). This limitation converges on explanations of the effect that appeal to distinctive processing at encoding and at retrieval as underlying the effect (see McDaniel, Dornburg, & Guynn, 2005).

Only two recent studies (as far as we know) have examined whether older adults display the distinctiveness effects found in the bizarreness paradigm. Following the standard paradigm, Geraci, McDaniel, and Roediger (2006, Experiment 2) had younger and older adults form mental images of the referents of bizarre and common sentences (intermixed in the list), followed by a free recall test for the target nouns. Three measures of free recall were derived: the proportion of nouns recalled; the proportion of sentences for which at least one noun was recalled; and the proportion of sentences for which all three nouns were recalled. Table 6.1 displays the results as a function of age group and sentence type. As can be seen, for all measures older adults showed an increase in recall of bizarre versus common items (significantly so) and this increase was proportionally similar to that evidenced with younger adults

TABLE 6.1
The Bizarreness Effect in Younger and Older Adults

	Geraci et al. (2006)		Black et al. (2004)			
			Exp 1		Exp 2	
Words Recalled	Younger	Older	Younger	Older	Younger	Older
Bizarre	.47	.23	.41	.18	.35	.21
Common	.33	.15	.31	.13	.28	.18
Sentences Recalled (1-word measure)						
Bizarre	.61	.41	.52	.30	.50	.35
Common	.42	.28	.37	.21	.38	.28
Sentences Recalled (3-word measure)						
Bizarre	.29	.09				
Common	.20	.04				

(there was no significant interaction between age group and sentence type).

Black, McCown, Lookadoo, Leonard, Kelley, and Spence (2004) also employed the standard paradigm, but across two experiments varied the intentionality of the learning task (Experiment 1 used incidental learning, as in Geraci et al.; Experiment 2 included incidental and intentional learning conditions). Table 6.1 (right-hand columns) shows that in both experiments, older and younger adults recalled bizarre items better than common items. Again, the bizarreness effect did not interact with age. Therefore the available, albeit limited, data suggest that distinctive processing as revealed in the bizarreness paradigm appears to be generally intact for older adults.

Aging and the Consistency Effect

Bizarre sentences are odd because they violate our knowledge about the world and the normal course of events. For instance, *a maid licking ammonia off a table* is inconsistent with our expectation of what maids and people in general ordinarily do. An effect similar to the bizarreness effect is found with young adults' memory for items that are inconsistent with expectations. These items are remembered better than items consistent with expectations (Friedman, 1979), presumably because they are processed in terms of their distinctiveness relative to the expected setting. A series of experiments by Mäntylä and Backman (1992) examined this inconsistency effect (note that the effect is sometimes referred to as the "consistency" effect) with younger and older adults. A room arranged as a typical office was shown to participants to study in preparation for answering some questions about the office. Many objects in the room were consistent with a normal office setting (telephone, typewriter), whereas other objects were inconsistent with an office setting (hand mixer). After viewing the room, participants were taken to a different room and given a recognition memory test in which they had to determine which objects (verbal labels or photographs depending on the experiment) had been in the office (old) and which had not been present (new).

When recognition was tested immediately with a verbal test (Experiment 1), performance was in general not significantly different for older and younger adults, and most importantly older adults displayed recognition gains for inconsistent items (relative to consistent items) comparable to those observed for younger adults. When recognition was tested after a 2-week delay with a visual test (Experiment 2), though there was a general age-related decline in recognition, older (and younger) adults again displayed an inconsistency effect and the effect was nominally more pronounced than for younger adults. As well, both younger and older adults showed an inconsistency effect in free recall and in remembering the location in the room in which the object was placed, though the effect was somewhat but not significantly moderated for older adults. Thus, across a range of memory measures and retention intervals, older adults were able to encode features of objects that were unique relative to their normal occurrence (i.e., presence of the object and its location in an atypical setting) and use that information to enhance memory generally to the same extent as younger adults.

It is noteworthy that this spared processing for older adults was limited to precisely the dimensions on which the objects were distinctive. Token recognition tests were constructed in which either the objects themselves or photographs of target objects (depending on the experiment) were replaced by another particular instance of that object (a black telephone replaced by a white telephone of a different style). Younger but not older adults showed a significant inconsistency effect. Here, the particular inconsistent objects themselves were not unusual, just their placement in the office setting, and it was precisely this latter distinctive information for which older adults gained mnemonic benefit.

The Isolation Effect

In the isolation paradigm, participants study a list of items in which one item is different along some dimension from the remainder of list items, which are all similar to each other along that dimension. The typical effect is that people show superior memory for an unusual or incongruent item relative to when that identical item is presented in a control list in which the item is not incongruent to the other list items (see Hunt, 1995, for details). Just two experiments have examined the isolation effect in younger and older adults, with apparently discrepant findings.

Geraci et al. (2006, Experiment 1) isolated the item along a conceptual dimension. The isolate was the only item from its category presented in the list. As an example, the word, *table*, might be presented in a list of types of fish. In a control list, the target item (*table*) was not isolated. Here, all the words were from different semantic categories. Retention was assessed by a cued recall test in which category labels were presented as cues. Both younger and older adults showed an isolation effect, which did not interact with age.

By contrast, Cimbalo and Brink (1982) isolated the item along the physical dimension of size. A target consonant was either presented in a larger or the same size as the other consonants in the list. Participants were required to recall the consonants in the order of original presentation. In general, younger but not older participants showed the isolation effect. However, the requirement for serial recall may have itself disadvantaged older adults (Friedman, 1966), thereby reducing their resources for processing the distinct features of the isolate. Indeed, Cimbalo and Brink (1982) found that with a slower 3-second presentation rate (and when the isolate appeared late in the list) older adults showed nearly double the recall of isolated items ($M = .29$) than nonisolated items ($M = .15$). This proportion increase was nearly identical to that found with younger adults under these conditions ($M = .61$ vs. .33 for isolated and nonisolated items, respectively).

Thus, the evidence, though sparse, tends toward the conclusion that older adults can generally notice and encode differences against a background of similarity and exploit that distinctive information at retrieval, at least under conditions that do not place undue demands on older adults or provide insufficient study time (for divergence on this conclusion see Smith, 2006; Smith, Lozito, & Bayen, 2005). The similar findings accruing from the bizarreness and consistency-effect paradigms further converge on the notion that distinctive processing may be relatively intact in older adults in general

INDIVIDUAL DIFFERENCES IN OLDER ADULTS

One aspect of age-related memory decline is the higher variability in older adults' memory performances relative to younger adults (but see Salthouse, 2003, indicating that age-related memory decline need not be accompanied by age-related increases in variability). As shown in Figure

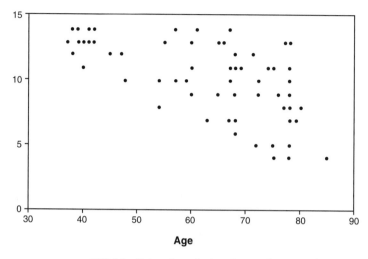

FIG. 6.1. Delayed recall of stories as a function of age.

6.1 with text recall, younger adults' scores are clumped near the top of the recall scale. Relative to this, one finds older adults who perform as well as younger adults, older adults who perform substantially less well than younger adults, and a distribution of older adults between these extremes. Though this variability has long been appreciated, much less is known about the particular individual factors that distinguish or mediate the relatively spared memory performances seen in a segment of the older adult population, as opposed to the significant decline in memory performances well documented when older adults are considered as a group. One general idea has been that health, and more specifically undetected Alzheimer's disease, is a factor in the relatively large variability of memory performance in older adults (see Zacks et al., 2000). Research conducted primarily since the Zacks et al. review represents intriguing progress at identifying more particular factors and suggests that specific neurocognitive aspects may play substantial roles in older adults' memory performances and the sparing of memory functioning with age.

Neuropsychological Findings

One prominent view is that declining frontal lobe functioning may underlie older adults' memory difficulties (Balota, Cortese, Duchek, Adams, Roediger, McDermott et al., 1999; Mather, Johnson, & De Leonardis, 1999; Moscovitch & Winocur, 1995; West, 1996). Leverage on this view can be provided by evaluating older adults' frontal-lobe functioning through a battery of neuropsychological measures. Because a battery developed by Glisky and her colleagues has been prominent in recent work that we review below, we briefly describe that battery. The battery was developed from a factor-analytic examination of a number of tests assumed to reflect frontal functioning and other psychometric and cognitive/memory tests. In an exploratory factor analysis, Glisky, Polster, and Routhieaux (1995) identified five tests that robustly loaded on a single factor and did not significantly load on any other factor. All of these tests were those that presumably were sensitive to frontal functioning (Wisconsin Card Sort, word fluency, mental arithmetic, mental control, and backward digit span), and consequently this factor was considered a frontal factor. Confirmatory factor analysis from a separate and larger group of older adults converged on this frontal factor (Glisky, Rubin, & Davidson, 2001). A composite score of the five tests for an individual participant can thus be used to index frontal functioning and thereby assess the degree to which it relates to older adults' memory performance. Providing some validity to the score, some of the tests have been investigated in neuroimaging studies and have been associated with prefrontal activation (see Chan & McDermott, in press, for more details). Further, a composite score on four other tests identified as a medial temporal factor can be used to discount the interpretation that differences in memory ascribed to frontal scores represent some sort of general cognitive or neurocognitive difference across individuals (see Glisky et al., 2001, for details). The following sections indicate that this frontal battery captures an individual difference that is highly predictive of older adults' source memory, word list memory, and memory for complex materials.

Source Memory

An increasingly large literature exists on memory for the source of an event—the when, where, and how of an event—and age-related changes in memory for source. For instance, studies with younger and older adults have examined the spatial location in which an item was presented ("where"; see Chalfonte & Johnson, 1996; Glisky et al., 2001, Experiment 2), and the "how" in which an event occurred: memory for perceptual modality (Durso & Johnson, 1980; Belli, Lindsay, Gales, & McCarthy, 1994), memory for type font (Naveh-Benjamin & Craik, 1995), and memory for particular speakers who presented the items (e.g, Glisky et al., 1995). Zacks et al. (2000) provide a thorough entrée to this literature, and appropriately note that though the particulars of the age-related effects are complex, age-related deficits are generally found, with elimination of those effects being very rare (the honesty and character of a source may be well retained in older adults, Rahhal, May, & Hasher, 2002, though see

Siedlecki, Salthouse, & Berish, 2005, for age-related deficits even for these source attributes).

When frontal functioning of older adults is examined, however, some interesting dissociations emerge. Older adults' performances on source memory tasks have been related to frontal functioning, with those adults with higher frontal functioning showing better source memory than those with lower frontal functioning (Craik, Morris, Morris, & Loewen, 1990; Glisky et al., 1995; Henkel, Johnson, De Leonardis, 1998; Parkin, Walter, & Hunkin, 1995). More remarkably, older adults characterized as high in frontal functioning are not necessarily disadvantaged in source memory relative to younger adults. In two experiments, Glisky et al. (2001) found that high frontal older adults (as determined by the frontal battery described above) performed as well as young adults in remembering source information. Extending the typical procedure, in one experiment a large number of different voices was associated with either of two sentences, with the source information being the sentences (a particular voice was considered the item). In the other experiment, Glisky et al. moved beyond verbal materials and presented photographs of different kinds of chairs located in one of two rooms; the source information was the room in which a particular chair was located. In contrast to the high frontal older adults, low frontal older adults showed impairments in source memory relative to the younger adults, performing no better than chance on the source recognition tasks. This sparing of source memory for high frontal older adults appears not to be accounted for in terms of generally superior cognitive function. These older adults scored comparably (did not score higher) on the Mini Mental State Examination, vocabulary, and the medial temporal factor composite relative to the low-frontal older adults.

Veridical and False Memory for Word Lists

Older adults' frontal functioning (assessed by the Glisky et al., 1995, 2001, battery for all of the experiments reviewed below) has subsequently been found to be highly related to age-related decline in recall of word lists. Butler, McDaniel, Dornburg, Price, and Roediger (2004) examined free recall using the Deese-Roediger-McDermott (DRM) word lists that produce the false memory effects discussed in a previous section, thereby allowing examination of both veridical recall and false recall across younger and older adults. The usual finding is an age-related deficiency in both veridical recall (lower recall for older adults) and in false recall (higher false recall for older adults; see Roediger & McDaniel, 2007). As shown in the top panel of Table 6.2, Butler et al. replicated this finding when the entire group of older adults was compared to the younger

TABLE 6.2
Veridical (List Items) and False Recall (Critical Nonpresented Items) for Younger Adults and
Older Adults

				Frontal Status[a]	
	Item Type	Younger	Older	High	Low
Butler et al. (2004)[b]	List	.61	.52	.57	.46
	Critical	.31	.42	.32	.52
Roediger, Geraci, & Meade[c] Test 1[d]	List	.44	.43	.45	.41
	Critical	.17	.26	.15	.36
Roediger, Geraci, & Meade[c] Test 2[d]	List	.42	.44	.45	.43
	Critical	.18	.32	.16	.47

[a] Older adults decomposed by frontal status; [b] free recall of DRM lists; [c] reported in Roediger and McDaniel (2007); [d] cued recall of categorized lists.

adults. However, when the frontal status of the older adults was considered, only the low-frontal older adults exhibited the deficiencies in veridical and false recall. High frontal older adults' recall performance was indistinguishable from that of younger adults. As in Glisky et al. (2001), the high and low frontal older adults did not differ significantly on the medial temporal composite score, as well as other measures of cognitive functioning.

A similar pattern has been obtained using a categorized list technique to examine age differences in false recall. In this technique items from several categorized lists are presented for study, but the more frequent category members are not included in the list. False memory errors are evidenced when these nonpresented category members are recalled later on (Smith, Ward, Tindell, Sifonis, & Wilkenfeld, 2000). In several experiments with older and younger adults, on successive cued-recall tests (cues are the category labels) older adults overall showed slight declines in veridical recall of category members (relative to younger adults), and robust exaggeration of false recall (Meade & Roediger, 2006). Again, however, when older adults' frontal status was considered (see Roediger & McDaniel, 2007), these age-related exaggerations in false memory were restricted to the low-frontal older adults. High-frontal older adults were performing a percentage or two better than younger adults (see the lower panel of Table 6.2).

Further convergence with the theme that frontal status is a potent individual difference factor in age-related memory processes was found in two additional experiments examining older adults' performance on DRM lists. Post-hoc examination of frontal status for the older adults in an experiment varying modality of list presentation (Gallo & Roediger,

2003) showed a benefit of visual list presentation compared to auditory presentation for high-frontal older adults (as found with younger adults) but not for low-frontal older adults (see Smith et al., 2005, for report of these data). Thomas and McDaniel (2007) investigated false recognition in the DRM paradigm in both a standard list presentation condition and a sentence elaboration condition designed to foster conceptual distinctive processing of the list items relative to the critical lure (which would not be elaborated). (In the sentence elaboration condition the list item was always presented as the last word in the sentence.) High-frontal older adults were not as able to discriminate the critical lure from list items as were young adults ($d' = -.29$ and .36, respectively) but were significantly advantaged relative to low-frontal older adults ($d' = -.83$). Importantly, both young and high-frontal older adults showed substantial reductions in false recognition (and comparable improvements in d') in the sentence elaboration condition, whereas low-frontal older adults evidenced a decline from their performance in the standard word list condition ($d' = -1.29$).

The implication from both of the above findings is that age-related deficits in distinctive processing, if found, appear to be limited to low-frontal functioning older adults. Consistent with this implication is an analysis of the older adults' performances as a function of frontal status in the Geraci et al. (2006) isolation-effect experiment. Older adults with high-frontal scores displayed a significant isolation effect, whereas older adults with low-frontal scores did not show a memory advantage for the isolated items relative to the nonisolated items.

In summary, these findings from different word list paradigms suggest a provocative modification to the idea that aging is associated with declines in (word-list) memory. The "aging effect" for recall of at least thematic word lists (DRM and categorized lists) is borne entirely by presumably low-frontal functioning older adults, as are effects related to distinctive processing of presented items relative to critical nonpresented items. At this juncture, it is worth noting several points that will be critical to fully consider in subsequent work before this provisional conclusion merits acceptance. First, further work is needed to securely tie the nature of this individual difference factor to frontal functioning. Second, the initial work described above provides no information about the extent to which younger adults vary in frontal functioning and whether any such variation would be related to memory performances. Younger adults may also vary in frontal functioning, with memory performance being associated with that variation in frontal functioning (see Chan & McDermott, in press, for just such a finding). Thus, age differences in memory between younger and older adults who are relatively equivalent in frontal functioning are possible. Accordingly, higher frontal functioning older adults may exhibit equivalent memory performance to younger adults on average, but still decline in memory relative to the highest functioning younger adults. With these cautionary notes in mind, we move to similar research using more complex verbal materials and visual material.

Memory Illusions with Complex Material

A now classic false memory paradigm is one in which people observe a visual event such as a traffic accident or crime, following which subsequent descriptions or questions about the event can change people's memory for the original visual event (Loftus, Miller & Burns, 1978). Only a handful of studies have examined this misinformation effect with older adults, and the results are mixed. Three experiments reported that older adults exhibited a greater misinformation effect than did younger adults (Cohen & Faulkner, 1989, Experiment 2, using a 3-min film involving a kidnapping as the target event; Mitchell, Johnson, & Mather, 2003, using a 5-min video of a home burglary and police chase; Roediger & Geraci, 2007, using a slide sequence of a crime). On the other hand, several other studies have found no differences in older and younger adults in the magnitude of the misinformation effect (Coxon & Valentine, 1997, using a 3-min video of a baby being abducted; Gabbert, Memon, & Allan, 2003, with the misinformation of a 1.5-min video originating from a co-witness), and one study even found a reduced misinformation effect for older relative to younger adults (Marche, Jordan, & Owre, 2002, using a slide sequence of a theft, and a 3-week delay before misleading information).

For present purposes, of interest is a recent experiment conducted by Roediger and Geraci (2007, Experiment 2) that selected older adults who had been pretested as high or low frontal (using Glisky et al.'s, 1995, battery). After viewing a slide sequence of a crime, participants read a narrative (from another observer, according to the cover story) that contained details either inconsistent (incorrect) or consistent (correct) with the slide sequence. Moreover, there was also a neutral condition in which some details were referred to in generic terms (for a "hammer" presented in the slide, the narrative would mention a "tool"). After reading the narrative, participants were given a source-monitoring test on which they judged the source in which an object appeared.

The misinformation effect is revealed when participants given inconsistent information more often judge an inconsistent item (e.g. "screwdriver") as appearing in the slide sequence than when participants are given consistent or neutral information. With either of these baselines (consistent, neutral), low-frontal older adults showed an augmented misinformation effect relative to high-frontal older adults. For instance, relative to the neutral baseline, with an inconsistent narrative, low frontals showed a .29 increase in source errors and high frontals showed a .13 increase in source errors. In a companion experiment, younger adults showed a .14 increase in source errors (relative to the neutral baseline). This initial result suggests that as with false memories elicited in word-list paradigms, age-related exaggerations in the misinformation effect may be associated with individual differences in older adults' frontal status.

Finally, another interesting angle to investigating older adults' memory of complex events such as a crime involves the effectiveness of the Cognitive Interview for eliciting older adults' recall. The Cognitive Interview is a procedure to stimulate greater recall by instructions encouraging contextual reinstatement, the use of multiple retrieval paths, and repeated recall (Geiselman, Fisher, MacKinnon, & Holland, 1985). Only two published studies have investigated the Cognitive Interview's effectiveness with older adults for recalling visually presented events. Mello and Fisher (1996) reported that the Cognitive Interview, relative to a standard police interview, increased the older adults' correct recall of robbery a half hour after viewing the filmed robbery. However, Mello and Fisher also reported increased incorrect recall as a function of the Cognitive Interview, thereby resulting in slightly lower recall accuracy with the Cognitive Interview for older adults. With parallel materials, McMahon (2000) found a similar trend in increased correct and incorrect recall for older adults with the Cognitive Interview (relative to a multiple recall procedure), although significant differences were not obtained, with McMahon noting that there was considerable variability in the older adults' recall performances.

Dornburg and McDaniel (2006) examined the efficacy of the Cognitive Interview with older adults using a text recall paradigm and a 3-week retention interval. To gain some leverage on the previously reported variability in older adults' performances, Dornburg and McDaniel assessed their participants' frontal status (all adults were older). As reported above, the Cognitive Interview produced gains in both correct and incorrect recall relative to multiple recall under standard instructions. Interestingly, for incorrect recall, frontal status significantly interacted with recall instructions such that with the Cognitive Interview incorrect recall increased as frontal status declined, but with the standard instructions there was no relation to frontal status. (For correct recall there was no significant relation between frontal status and recall.) Thus, frontal status may be an important individual difference factor in the effectiveness of the Cognitive Interview in older adults for increasing net accurate recall of complex events.

Personality Factors

Interest is emerging regarding possible relations between stable personality characteristics during adulthood and age-related changes in memory functioning. One candidate characteristic is neuroticism, which might be characterized as "proneness to psychological distress" (Wilson, Evans, Bienias, Mendes de Leon, Schneider, & Bennett, 2003). The theoretical connection to memory is that the functional and structural integrity of the hippocampus is negatively affected by stress (Sapolsky, 2000), with hippocampal function mediating episodic memory. In a 6-year study described in more detail below conducted with the Victoria Longitudinal Study data, no relation was found between neuroticism and changes in memory function (recall of facts, recall of words, recall of prose, working memory; Hultsch, Hertzog, Small, & Dixon, 1999).

On the other hand, two other large-scale correlational studies have reported a significant relation between neuroticism and memory performances in older adults. In a sample of 326 World War II veterans (mean age = 65), neuroticism was modestly but significantly related to digit-span performance with lower neuroticism associated with higher digit span (Arbuckle, Gold, Andres, Schwartzman, & Chaikelson, 1992; as well, extraversion was positively related to free recall). A longitudinal study of personality and cognitive function tested 704 older Swedish men and women (mean age = 64) on as many as three occasions at approximately 3-year intervals (Wetherell, Reynolds, Gatz, & Pederson, 2002). Individuals diagnosed with dementia during the study were excluded. Only a few memory measures were included, but neuroticism was significantly related to memory performance on a test requiring associative pairing of studied names and faces (lower neuroticism associated with better memory). No relation between neuroticism and digit span was detected, however, and neuroticism was not related to accelerated rates of memory decline (or general cognitive function) over the course of the study.

Perhaps the most dramatic findings come from a recent study using data from the Religious Orders Study, which examined changes in episodic memory (composite of seven tests), semantic memory (four tests), working memory (four tests), and other cognitive functioning over about a 5-year interval (on average; Wilson, Bennett, Bienias, Aggarwal, Mendes de Leon, Morris et al., 2002). In contrast to the earlier studies, striking relations emerged between neuroticism and episodic memory decline. Individuals low in neuroticism (tenth percentile) showed minimal episodic memory decline, whereas those high in neuroticism showed a rate of decline that was over 10 times that seen at the low end of the neuroticism scale. Further, this decline was limited to episodic memory. Finally, clinical symptoms of Alzheimer's disease (AD) were twice as likely to emerge during the time period for individuals high in neuroticism relative to those low in neuroticism. These findings fit with the notion that prolonged stress (as indexed by high levels of neuroticism) may have deleterious neurophysiological effects that are particularly damaging to episodic memory systems and thereby contribute to age-related decline in memory. Because there was no relation between neuroticism and neurological pathology associated with AD (determined at autopsy), one possibility is that prolonged stress reduces the tolerance of the system to pathology in terms of maintaining memory function. Given these results and the associated theoretical underpinnings, research on neuroticism (perhaps as a proxy for prolonged stress) and its relation to age-related memory decline could be a promising direction for individual difference approaches.

FORMS OF MEMORY: AGE DIFFERENCES IN COGNITIVE CONTROL

In this section, we further describe memory deficits that arise from age-related decline in frontal lobe function and relate those deficits to dual-process models that distinguish between cognitively controlled and automatic influences of memory. We then further relate decline in frontal lobe function to cognitive control by considering different forms of cognitive control that decline with aging.

A tendency of older adults to unknowingly repeat stories can be understood in terms of a dual-process model of memory (Jacoby, 1999). By that model, repetition of a story has two effects, one of which is to "strengthen" or increase the familiarity of a story, making it more likely to be repeated. This automatic, habit-like influence of memory is opposed by "recollection," a more consciously controlled use of memory that allows unwanted repetition to be avoided by recollecting the specific prior telling of a story. These two forms or uses of memory are illustrated by an experiment (Jacoby, 1999) whose results demonstrate that older adults are vulnerable to an ironic effect of repetition.

In a first phase of that experiment, young and older adults (aged 65 and over) were visually presented with a list of words to be read aloud. Words in this list were presented 1, 2, or 3 times, with repetition intended to mimic prior tellings of a story. Next, participants heard a list of words that they were told to remember for a subsequent memory test. For that test, participants were instructed to respond "yes" only if a word had been *heard* earlier and were correctly warned that the test would also include words that had been read earlier and should be rejected.

Results showed that younger adults' false recognition of earlier read items declined with increasing repetition. However, for older adults, the opposite pattern held, as repeated reading had the ironic effect of *increasing* the probability of falsely recognizing earlier read items as having been heard. Thus, older adults were less able to counter an increase in the familiarity of a repeated item with a specific memory (recollection) of its prior occurrence, making them vulnerable to false memories. Younger adults forced to respond quickly also showed an ironic effect of repetition, exhibiting more false memories for repeated items. This elevation in false memories with repetition for younger adults, who presumably have intact recollection, suggests that recollection, in addition to being vulnerable to aging, may be slower than the more automatic processes that support familiarity.

Accepting an earlier read word as being one that was earlier heard qualifies as an example of false memory. The ironic effects of repetitions show that older adults are more prone to false memory as are young adults who are required to respond rapidly. Similar ironic effects of repetition have been found for the DRM task (Benjamin, 2001; Budson, Daffner, Desikan, & Schacter, 2000; Watson, McDermott, & Balota, 2004). Light, Patterson, Chung, and Healy (2004) also observed an ironic effect of repetition in an associative learning task. In their experiment, pairs of words were studied and then intact pairs (both words studied together) were intermixed with rearranged pairs (both words studied but with different partners) for a test of recognition memory. Results showed that repetition of pairs during study had the ironic effect of increasing false alarms to rearranged pairs for older adults tested with or without response deadlines and for younger adults tested with a short deadline.

Findings of ironic effects of repetition provide support for a distinction between automatic and cognitively controlled forms or uses of memory, and suggest that automatic influences of memory are relatively age invariant. Dual-process models that distinguish between recollection and automatic influences of memory have been used to show that automatic influences in recognition memory (see Yonelinas, 2002 for a review) and cued-recall (e.g., Jacoby, Debner, & Hay, 2001) tasks remain constant through old age. Schmitter-Edgecombe (1999) used an inclusion/exclusion procedure to gain estimates of recollection and automatic influences of memory. For the exclusion task, automatic influences of memory would be a source of errors just as in the ironic effects experiments, whereas automatic influences would facilitate performance on the inclusion task. Results from her experiment showed that both aging and dividing attention during study reduced the probability of recollection but left automatic influences of memory invariant. Howard, Bessette-Symons, Zhang, and Hoyer (2006) reached a similar conclusion by modeling receiver operating characteristic curves of recognition memory for pictures. They found that aging selectively impairs recollection. Although small age differences in automatic influences are sometimes found (e.g., Healy, Light, & Chung, 2005), there is general agreement that age-related decline in cognitively controlled use of memory is much larger than is change in automatic influences of memory.

MODES OF COGNITIVE CONTROL: UNDERPINNINGS OF AGE-RELATED MEMORY DECLINE UNDER INTERFERENCE

The ironic effects of memory illustrate the general finding that age-related differences in memory are largest under conditions of high interference, conditions that rely heavily on cognitive (executive) control of responding. Earlier we reviewed evidence to show false memory in the DRM paradigm is larger for older adults who show diminished executive control as measured by tests of frontal lobe function. Similarly, ironic effects of memory could be described as interference effects that reflect poor cognitive control that results from decline in frontal lobe functions. However, recent research suggests that there are multiple forms of cognitive control. An account of older adults' lessened ability to cope with interference appeals to age-related decline in inhibitory processes (e.g., Hasher & Zacks, 1988). Other accounts postulate age differences in ability to recollect particular events (e.g., Jacoby et al., 2001) and age differences in source memory (e.g., Glisky, et al., 2001).

Inhibitory functions can be further fractionated as means of cognitive control. Friedman and Miyake (2004) used a latent variable analysis to examine relations among sets of tasks thought to measure different inhibitory functions. Results from their analyses suggested that prepotent response inhibition and distractor interference were closely related (and thus may not represent different functions). Stroop interference is an example of a task that requires inhibition of a prepotent response whereas a flanker task is one that requires ignoring distraction. Both distractor interference and inhibition of a prepotent response were unrelated to resistance to proactive interference. Subsequent structural equation modeling examined the contribution of the different forms of inhibition to other cognitive tasks. Among the findings was that reading span recall, a measure of working memory, was related to resistance to proactive interference (cf. Lustig, May, & Hasher, 2001). Recent developments of the inhibition-deficit account of age differences in interference effects (Hasher, Zacks, & May, 1999) agree with Friedman and Miyake (2004) in proposing multiple inhibitory functions, all of which presumably involve the frontal lobes.

The ironic effects of repetition revealed by older adults might reflect a deficit in source memory, which has been related to frontal lobe functions (e.g., Glisky et al., 2001). However, Jacoby, Shimizu, Velanova, and Rhodes (2005) have argued that it is important to distinguish between ways that source memory can serve as a means of cognitive control. They likened cognitive control to quality control in manufacturing, noting that quality control can be improved either by increasing the precision of production techniques or by increasing the number of inspectors on the line who reject defective products. For cognitive control, the contrast is between gaining control by restricting memory access (source-constrained retrieval) compared to relying on a post-access process (source monitoring) that serves to edit out inappropriate responses. Source-constrained retrieval serves to restrict the potential responses that are brought to mind whereas source monitoring assesses the adequacy of a response after it comes to mind. Age differences in source memory are commonly found (see above) and have generally been interpreted as resulting from a deficit in source monitoring. However, Jacoby et al. developed new procedures to show that poor performance on a source-memory task can reflect age-related differences in source-constrained retrieval. Their results suggest that, in part, the poorer memory performance of older adults results from their engaging in more superficial processing of potential cues for retrieval than do young adults. Braver, Gray, and Burgess (2007) proposed mechanisms of cognitive control for working memory that are similar to those proposed by Jacoby et al. for source memory, and support their proposal by providing evidence of different neural bases for the two modes of cognitive control.

OLDER ADULTS' RELIANCE ON AUTOMATIC MEMORY PROCESSES

Rather than identifying different forms of executive control with different tasks, as done by latent-variable techniques, Jacoby, Bishara, Hessels, and Toth (2005) used a multinomial model to separate the contribution of different forms of cognitive control within a task. The general procedure for their experiments involved presenting pairs of related words for study (e.g., "knee bone") with memory then tested by providing participants with a cue word along with a fragment of the response word ("knee b_n_"). The critical manipulation involved presenting a prime word just prior to presentation of the recall cue (word+fragment) pair. This prime was either the same as the target word (a *valid* prime: "bone"), an alternative to the target word (an *invalid* prime: "bend"), or a neutral nonword stimulus (a *baseline* prime: "&&&&").

Results revealed that older adults were much more likely than young adults to show false memory by mistakenly reporting an invalid prime as earlier studied. The multinomial model that was fit to the results included a parameter (termed "capture") that indexed an inhibition deficit for older as compared to young adults. A recollection parameter in the model was made equal for young and older adults by allowing older adults more time to study. A third parameter, which measured processes similar to those involved in source memory, revealed age differences with older adults being more likely to misattribute the familiarity of a response to its prior study.

Evidence of different forms or modes of cognitive control is important for better specifying individual differences in cognitive control and for relating individual difference to brain differences as well as for devising effective training procedures. Jacoby et al. (2005) suggested that the automatic influences of memory shown by older adults in combination with reduced cognitive control make older adults more susceptible to memory scams. That suggestion vilifies automatic influences as does the suggestion that automatic influences of memory are responsible for older adults' unwanted repetition of stories, described in the context of ironic effects of repetition. However, automatic influences of memory typically serve to facilitate performance. Reliance on automatic influences in the form of habits often frees one from the necessity of recollecting particular prior events. For example, one can avoid searching for one's keys by routinely placing the keys in a particular location. In this vein, Pearman and Storandt (2004) have shown that memory complaints are better predicted by personality measures, including a measure of conscientiousness, than by performance on objective tests of memory performance. Those who are well organized can rely on automatic influences of memory, largely avoiding negative consequences of decline in cognitive control—so long as they are not in nonroutine situations, faced with high interference.

THE VALUE OF INTERVENTION AND TRAINING REGIMENS

Training Memory

Can training memory eliminate age differences in memory performance? Do effects of memory training transfer widely to memory tasks that were not used for training? Unfortunately, the answer to these questions as revealed by most investigations of training effects is "no," however, there are some intriguing exceptions to this trend noted in the following review.

Training Memory Strategies

The most common means of training memory performance has been to teach older adults memory strategies. For example, Ball et al. (2002) taught older adults strategies for remembering lists of words and other materials, and gave them exercises and performance feedback in memory tasks. Training did produce improvements in memory performance and effects were durable for over 2 years. However, effects of training showed little transfer to tasks that were not used for training. Verhaeghen, Marcoen, and Goossens (1992) reported a meta-analysis of 33 separate studies that were conducted to examine whether age-related memory loss can be reduced with mnemonic training. Training gains were found to be larger for older individuals who were trained with mnemonic techniques as compared to older control participants.

Clearly, older adults can benefit from mnemonic training. However, they do not benefit more than do younger adults. Kliegl and colleagues (e.g., Baltes & Kliegl, 1992) examined effects of training by using a "testing-the-limits" methodology. They found that age differences in mnemonic performance using the method of loci *increased* from pretraining performance to posttest performance that followed several weeks of training. Older adults did show dramatic improvement in word recall after extensive training, but young adults showed even larger improvements.

Training Executive Control: Time Sharing

In contrast to results from experiments that employed mnemonic training, Kramer and his colleagues (Kramer, Larish, & Strayer, 1995; Kramer, Larish, Weber, & Bardell, 1999) used a variable priority training procedure and did find that training *decreased* age differences in performance. In their experiments, participants were required to concurrently engage in two tasks, a pattern learning task and a tracking task. Participants in a fixed priority condition were instructed to treat the two tasks as being equally important, whereas those in a variable priority condition were required to constantly vary their priorities between the two tasks. Variable priority training led to faster acquisition and better performance doing the tasks together than did fixed priority training. Individuals trained with variable priority also showed better transfer to untrained tasks and better retention of time-sharing skills over a 2-month interval. Further, variable priority training substantially reduced age differences in the efficiency of dual-task performance.

Time-sharing relies on executive processes. Given the importance of age differences in executive processing, described earlier, it is surprising that more training research has not been aimed at diminishing age differences in executive processes. Priority training in dual-task performance also involves training under conditions of high interference, conditions under which older adults are maximally disadvantaged.

Retrieval Practice Strategies

A training procedure that is very effective is to teach older adults to use retrieval practice to enhance their memory performance. Use of retrieval practice is a strategy that can be widely applied and retrieval practice often enhances memory performance more than further study (e.g., Roediger & Karpicke, 2006). Training by means of retrieval practice is effective even for people whose memory performance is very badly impaired (Camp, Foss, O'Hanlon, & Stevens, 1996).

Bishara and Jacoby (2006) examined the effects of retrieval practice on the memory performance of young and older adults. In their Experiment 1, pairs of words were presented to be read three times in one condition whereas in another condition word pairs were read once followed by two retrievals of the right-hand member of pairs given the left-hand member as a cue. Performance on a subsequent cued-recall test showed that retrieval practice was more beneficial than was repeated reading, and equally so for young and older adults.

A second experiment was analogous to the ironic effects of repetition experiments (Jacoby, 1999) and was designed to determine whether retrieval practice had its effect by enhancing recollection or, instead, by means of an increase in automatic influences of memory. In the first phase of Experiment 2, pairs were read three times or presented once followed by two trials of retrieval practice just as in Experiment 1. Next, a second list of pairs was presented for study with each pair in this second list (List 2) being read once. Memory for List 2 was tested by means of a cued-recall test. The relationship between lists was such that responses that were presented and retrieved (e.g., knee-bend) in Phase 1 served as competitors for the target responses presented in List 2 (e.g., knee-bone). Increased automaticity produced by retrieval practice would result in increased interference from Phase 1 responses (e.g., "bend" intruding when "bone" was intended to be recalled). Results showed an effect of retrieval practice that was similar to the ironic effects of repetition. For older adults, practice retrieving a competitor reduced the accuracy of recall of a subsequent list, showing increased interference that reflected an automatic influence of memory. In contrast, retrieval practice of a competitor did not produce increased interference for young adults. Presumably, for young adults, retrieval practice resulted in increased recollection which was used to successfully oppose the increased automatic influences produced by retrieval practice.

Training Cognitively Controlled Uses of Memory

Age differences in the effects of retrieval practice highlight the importance of distinguishing between cognitively controlled and automatic influences of memory when designing a training program. Procedures that enhance automatic influences of memory provide an effective means of improving memory performance so long as the conditions of test are compatible with those of retrieval practice, but can result in increased interference and heavier need for ability to recollect if retrieval conditions are changed. Returning to the earlier example of finding one's keys, routinely placing one's keys in a particular location can improve one's ability to later find the keys when one puts them in that location. However, if one inadvertently placed the keys elsewhere on a particular occasion, an ability to recollect is needed to overcome the interference effects created by typically placing the keys in the favored location.

The finding of ironic effects encourages attempts to design training procedures to enhance older adults' ability to recollect particular events. Most training procedures have not distinguished between cognitively controlled and automatic forms of memory. Also, the focus of training procedures has typically been on encoding processes with the assumption being that the poorer memory performance of older adults reflects their less effective processing during study. However, a focus on interference effects implicates retrieval processes as being as important as are encoding processes. In that vein, results found by Dornburg and McDaniel (2006) that show the efficacy of the Cognitive Interview procedures for improving memory performance of older adults demonstrate the importance of retrieval processes, as do results reported by Jacoby et al. (2005). Deficient retrieval processing likely plays a role in the heightened interference effects observed for older adults.

Jennings and Jacoby (2003) devised a procedure for training the memory performance of older adults under conditions of high interference with the goal of improving older adults' cognitively controlled use of memory. Their procedure required participants to respond differentially to words that were remembered as having been presented in a study list and foils that were made familiar by having been repeated in the test list. During training, the difficulty of distinguishing between the two types of words was gradually increased by increasing the spacing of repetitions of foils in the test list. Participants responded and were given feedback at a particular level of spacing until they met an accuracy criterion, and then spacing was increased and participants again responded with feedback until they met an accuracy criterion, and so on. Increasing the spacing of foils served to increase the difficulty of recollecting that the foil had been earlier presented in the test list rather than during study. The recollection performance of older adults improved dramatically with training. It is also interesting to note that the older adults were not instructed on particular strategies for improving recollection, but instead developed them on their own. Jennings, Webster, Kleykamp, and Dagenbach (2005) replicated the results reported by Jennings and Jacoby and showed that the effects of training transferred to several other tasks, including working memory, self-ordered pointing, and digit-symbol substitution. This transfer to untrained tasks is remarkable against the backdrop of the common finding of a lack transfer between memory tasks.

Experiments currently underway in Jacoby's laboratory are aimed at training recollection by means of training older adults to cope with proactive interference in cued recall. The rationale underlying the procedure is similar to that underlying the Jennings and Jacoby procedure in that avoiding proactive interference requires reliance on recollection as a basis for accurate responding. Preliminary results are encouraging in showing that even minimal training is sufficient to substantially reduce the large effects of proactive interference shown by older adults.

Our attempts to train memory differ from those of most others by being inspired by theoretical advances in distinguishing between cognitively controlled and automatic influences of memory. Traditionally, attempts at training have been motivated by applied concerns and been largely isolated from research aimed at understanding age differences in memory performance. In contrast, we believe that attempts at training can serve as a valuable tool for purposes of theory as well as for applied purposes. We encourage others to attempt to train older adults' memory performance under conditions of high interference, the conditions under which largest age differences in memory are observed.

Practical Considerations in Training

We end this section by considering some practical concerns for investigating effects of memory training. Perhaps the major obstacle for research on memory training is that such research is incredibly time consuming and expensive, particularly when training extends across a large number of sessions as is probably necessary to produce substantial effects of training. The possibility of using the web to investigate effects of memory training might help to solve this problem. More older adults are becoming computer savvy and spending time on the internet, making research of this sort possible. A second problem is that most memory training research has attempted to train older adults' memory performance by asking them to remember lists of unrelated words. Remembering word lists is incredibly boring and does not result in learning that is useful in its own right. To solve that problem, we are currently initiating experiments that are aimed at training memory by teaching older adults about birdwatching. Birdwatching is a popular hobby, identifying birds places a heavy burden on memory (see section below), and birdwatching can involve long walks, the sort of physical exercise that has been shown to enhance cognitive functioning (see Physical Exercise section below). Perhaps a nutritious snack while birdwatching would also be helpful (see Brain-specific Nutrients section below), as would practice in prospective memory for spotting a particular family of birds.

General Mental Activity

A popularized idea is that age-related memory decline can be forestalled or mitigated by daily engagement in demanding, engaging, or challenging mental activity. Although no published experimental research has evaluated this assertion, there are several large-scale correlational studies addressing the topic. One set of studies has focused on a sample from a 30-year longitudinal study begun in the early 1960s (Kohn & Schooler, 1983). The most recent additions to the study included a set of standard cognitive measures which included a word-list free recall task and a semantic memory task (vocabulary test). The structural equation models combined all of the cognitive measures with other measures of intellectual functioning to create one latent variable (Schooler, Mulatu, & Oates, 1999). Thus, the results do not specifically isolate the memory tasks from the other measures, so that the summary of this set of findings should be viewed as relating to general cognitive or intellectual functioning and not just memory per se.

One study from this data base analyzed the complexity of people's work (as defined by their jobs) and its relation to cognitive functioning in older adult workers (Schooler et al., 1999). Complexity of work was gauged by job activities rather than by career occupation; work rating high in complexity included problem solving about personnel and about unpredictable factors, generating original ideas, and setting up new equipment and machines. The structural equation modeling techniques revealed bidirectional associations of work complexity and cognitive functioning in male and female older adults. As might be expected, higher cognitive functioning produced more involvement in complex work. But there was also a significant path indicating that engagement in complex work produced higher levels of cognitive functioning in older adults, and nonchallenging work produced a decrease in older adults' cognitive functioning (similar findings have been obtained in Japan, Poland, and Ukraine; see Schooler et al. for review). Of special interest in this study was that the cohort had aged since an earlier analysis (the sample now ranged from 41 to 83 years), and the impact of complex work on cognitive functioning was almost twice as great in an older group of workers than a younger group of workers. Thus, for older adults especially, demanding and intellectually challenging work seemed an important determinant of cognitive functioning.

Using the same longitudinal data base, Schooler and Mulatu (2001) extended their analysis to the relation between the degree of intellectual complexity in leisure activities and cognitive functioning (measured as described above) in older adults. In parallel with the findings on work complexity, the structural equation modeling results revealed that complex leisure activity impacted the current level of cognitive functioning. A reciprocal effect also emerged showing an even stronger impact of cognitive functioning on the complexity of leisure activity. One optimistic interpretation of this pattern is the existence of a cyclical pathway in which higher levels of cognitive functioning lead to more complex leisure activity which itself raises (or maintains) the level of cognitive functioning as the individual ages.

Another study with Canadian World War II veterans (mean age was 64.8 years) focused on memory functioning per se. Arbuckle et al. (1992) found an indirect association between habitual level of intellectual activities (including involvement in social, recreational, family, intellectual, and occupational activities previously rated with respect to the amount of intellectual effort required) and memory performance on word-list recall, cued recall, story recognition, and digit span. Current intelligence level was the most robust predictor of the memory performances, with habitual level of intellectual activity related to current intelligence. Because level of intellectual activity was not a direct predictor of memory performance, the authors suggested that intellectual activity may facilitate older adults' memory through "generalized transfer mechanisms, such as learning to learn" (p. 32).

Hultsch et al. (1999) more directly focused on the degree to which intellectually engaging leisure activities would buffer older adults against memory decline per se. Over a 6-year period, older adults' memory performance on a variety of memory tasks (recall of facts, recall of words, recall of prose, and working memory) was assessed, along with the adults' involvement in a variety of physical activities (walking, jogging), social activities (visiting a friend or attending a party), hobbies/home-maintenance activities (repairing mechanical items), and challenging intellectual activities (learning a new language, playing bridge). The last variable was isolated as a measure of intellectual engagement, with the first three contextual variables combined into an index of "active lifestyle." Interestingly, general engagement in leisure activities (active lifestyle) showed little relation to maintenance of memory functioning over the 6-year study period. Only the intellectual engagement variable was significantly related to memory over the course of the study. Specifically, higher levels of intellectual engagement and smaller decreases in intellectual engagement (over the 6 years) were related to less decline in working memory (working memory was itself significantly related to the other memory measures). These results are consistent with the idea that intellectually engaging activities can attenuate longitudinally related memory decline in older adults.

A critical point, however, is that Hultsch et al. (1999) also found that the data were just as well accounted for with a model in which memory/cognitive decline fostered reduction in intellectually engaging activities. This underscores the inability of correlational studies to unambiguously establish causal relations between engagement in intellectually challenging work/leisure activity and attenuation of age-related memory decline. Another critical distinction that can be blurred in interpreting the training and mental activity results is whether effects of mental engagement slow the rate of age-related memory decline or raise the level of memory performance for older adults without slowing rate of decline. Along these lines, a recent review by Salthouse (2006) focusing more generally on mental performance (rather than memory) found little evidence for the conjecture that mentally engaging activity can attenuate the *rate* of cognitive decline associated with age, i.e., attenuate the slope of the function relating age and mental performance (but see the Hultsch et al., 1999, and Schooler et al., 1999, results above). Even if mental activity (or training) were to increase levels of cognitive performance for older adults without attenuating the rate of decline, positive benefits would accrue because poor performance levels would still be reached later in life. At this point, descriptive (correlational) results are suggestive that memory in older adults might be improved by engagement in intellectual activity, and such results appear to justify the initiation of experimental research that directly evaluates potential causal effects of engagement in intellectual activity on both the rate of age-related memory decline and absolute levels of memory functioning.

Brain-specific Nutrients

Notwithstanding the orientation discussed at the beginning of the chapter that social expectations and cultural factors play a role in age-related memory decline, as we noted initially, evidence continues to mount that age is associated with biological decline across a wide array of neurophysiological and neurochemical dimensions. As noted earlier, these include general shrinkage of neurons, loss in myelination, loss of functional synapses, reduced blood flow (thereby reducing oxygenation and metabolic potential), and decreased availability of certain neurotransmitters. Such age-related biological deterioration is presumably related to decreased memory and cognitive functioning in older adults. This premise raises the possibility that nutritional supplements that are particularly important for brain health or neuronal function could reduce or repair the neurological biological decline and consequently moderate age-related memory loss. Epidemiological studies have provided some, albeit limited, data on the relation between intake of various candidate nutrients from foods (e.g., antioxidant nutrients, n-3 fatty acids) and age-related memory decline.

Beyond good nutrition, however, is the idea that some nutrients are especially useful for maintaining neuron health and function and that systematic regimens of such nutrients through supplements could improve memory function. This idea has stimulated a number (a perhaps surprising number to the readers of the mainstream aging and memory literature) of double-blind placebo controlled experiments in the last 15 years on the effects of various "brain-specific" nutrients on memory and cognition in older adults (see McDaniel, Maier, & Einstein, 2002, for a detailed review, and Gold, Cahill, & Wenk, 2002, for a review of work with *Ginkgo biloba*). Most of these experiments have focused on older adults with pathological memory decline, perhaps because these groups have a more urgent need for neurotrophic treatments and demonstrate a salient memory loss. Far fewer experiments have focused on the present topic— normally aging older adults—and at best these studies have produced mixed results (see Gold et al., 2002; McDaniel et al., 2002, for details). There are several preliminary patterns, however, that suggest certain conditions under which brain-specific nutrient supplements may benefit older adults' memory performance, and it is these that we describe next.

In a 12-week treatment experiment, Wesnes, Ward, McGinty, and Petrini (2000) administered a compound of ginkgo and ginseng or a placebo pill to adults between the ages of 38 and 66. (Ginkgo's positive neural effects appear to include protection of neurons from oxidative stress, enhancement of the acetylcholine system, and increased glucose utilization in frontal and parietal areas.) Memory was tested prior to treatment (see Table 6.3 for the primary memory indices), during the 12-week treatment period, and 2 weeks post treatment. On testing days, the entire memory battery was repeated at various appointed times throughout the day. In general, after 4 weeks of treatment the ginkgo– ginseng group showed significantly greater improvement on the memory tests than did the placebo control group. This beneficial effect of the ginkgo–ginseng treatment was sustained through the 2-week post-treatment memory testing. But a tantalizing qualification of these results due to time of day of testing is evident on close examination. As is highlighted in Table 6.3, by the end of treatment, at the 7:30 am testing time,

TABLE 6.3
Performance of Ginkgo–Ginseng and Placebo Groups in Wesnes, Ward, McGinty, & Petrini (2000), as summarized in McDaniel, Maier, & Einstein (2002)

		Group			
		Placebo		Ginkgo–Ginseng	
Memory test	Week	7:30 a.m	2:30 p.m.	7:30 a.m.	2:30 p.m.
Spatial working memory	0	85.95	76.35	86.00	72.32
	12	6.77	5.72	4.76	10.78
	14	5.27	4.87	5.23	13.12
Numeric working memory	0	91.80	89.42	92.20	86.94
	12	1.53	4.90	1.93	5.17
	14	1.23	−0.31	2.99	3.55
Immediate word recall	0	34.94	31.07	35.52	29.90
	12	2.41	−1.95	1.97	0.89
	14	2.60	−0.31	3.33	1.28
Delayed word recall	0	20.76	9.08	22.90	8.06
	12	4.18	0.46	3.72	3.12
	14	4.06	−0.57	3.39	5.05
Word recognition	0	56.17	49.96	55.10	46.07
	12	2.07	−0.84	0.15	2.92
	14	0.92	−2.15	0.98	2.05
Picture recognition	0	75.92	70.52	74.10	68.28
	12	1.55	4.42	3.28	1.69
	14	3.45	−0.29	2.54	2.60

Note. For Week 0 (predosing baseline), the table shows the percentage correct on each test. For Weeks 12 and 14, the table shows the change from the baseline score, Week 14 was 2 weeks after treatment was discontinued.

there was little if any advantage for the ginkgo–ginseng treatment. Indeed, the placebo group displayed slightly more improvement (relative to baseline) than did the ginkgo–ginseng group. The most pronounced benefit of the ginko–ginseng treatment occurred at a later 2:30 pm testing time (note this was the case even 2 weeks after treatment was terminated).

This pattern remains unexplained but an appeal to the cognitive aging literature suggests two interesting possibilities (McDaniel et al., 2002). One rests on increasing evidence showing that memory and cognitive processes are influenced by circadian arousal patterns. Pertinent here is that older adults' peak times of functioning are early to mid-morning, with memory performance declining in the afternoon (e.g., see Intons-Peterson, Rocchi, West, McLellan, & Hackney, 1998; May, Hasher, & Stoltzfus, 1993; refer to Zacks et al., 2000, for a review). Accordingly, one interpretation of the Wesnes et al. (2000) finding is that brain-specific nutrients (in this case ginkgo/ginseng) might benefit memory for older adults at times when their circadian arousal is low, times when these adults are especially vulnerable to less efficient cognitive functioning. Another possibility relates to the Wesnes et al. procedure of administering the memory battery four times on the testing days, such that the 2:30 pm tests were preceded by three prior testing sessions for the day. It is not unreasonable to assume that relatively high proactive interference was present by the 2:30 pm testing times, thereby increasing the challenges on at least some of the memory tests in the battery. Perhaps effects of ginkgo–ginseng (and perhaps more generally brain-specific nutrients) are most prominent in memory situations with high interference, situations that are especially challenging for aging adults (see preceding section on age effects for memory under high interference).

Another parameter that may be important for whether brain-specific nutrient supplements produce memory benefits is the relative level of memory decline for the older adults taking the supplements. One supplement of note is phosphatidylserine (PS) which is a phospholipid thought to be especially vital to the neuronal membrane. The animal studies suggest that PS is especially important with regard to maintaining neuron structure and health, sustaining functionality of receptor sites on the neuron, and activating a particular kinase that plays a critical role in learning and memory (see McDaniel et al., 2002, for details)—all aspects of neurophysiology that likely decline with age. For these reasons, researchers have been interested in the possible influence of PS supplements on older adults' memory performance.

One double-blind placebo controlled study examined a 12-week treatment of PS in adults over the age of 50, who did not exhibit history or existence of brain dysfunction, neurological disorder, or use of drugs that might produce cognitive deterioration (Crook, Tinkleberg, Yesavage, Petrie, Nunzi, & Massari, 1991). Prior to the study and at systematic intervals throughout the study, memory was tested with a number of tasks. However, only the results for five primary memory measures were completely reported: learning of face–name associations; delayed recall of the face–name associations; memory for faces; recall of telephone numbers; and recall of misplaced objects. At the end of the treatment period, the only significant advantage of the PS-treated group relative to the control was for face memory. Consequently, the researchers examined the subgroup of participants who scored the most poorly at baseline on the memory tests. For this subgroup, at the conclusion of treatment, PS produced benefits relative to controls (from the subgroup) on all of the primary memory tests and for text recall.

In the next section, we review findings with exercise and cognitive functioning that are perhaps related to the restricted finding with the PS treatment. To foreshadow, exercise seems to most benefit the more impaired older adults (as indexed by age). Though speculative, the idea is that brain-specific nutritional supplements (and exercise interventions) may be useful for countering memory decline observed in the more impaired segment of the healthy aging population. As well, supplements may offer mnemonic benefits for older adults in general, when the memory situation especially disadvantages older adults (nonoptimal time of day, heavy interference). We emphasize that these ideas are based on very limited experimental data, but they may suggest fruitful avenues for extending the presently scarce and equivocal research findings on brain-specific supplements and memory effects in normally aging older adults.

Physical Exercise

Research clearly shows that balanced exercise programs can slow down normal age-related physical declines in cardiovascular efficiency, maximal oxygen consumption (the body's maximum capacity to transfer oxygen throughout the body during exercise), and muscle mass (American College of Sports Medicine, 1998). Of central interest to cognitive aging researchers, however, is the extent to which exercise attenuates the effects of aging on brain structure, neuronal functioning, and cognitive processes. In recent years, a great deal of research has addressed these issues. On the whole, the results are very encouraging and a variety of methods indicate that exercise can significantly ameliorate age-related cognitive declines (see Kramer & Madden, chapter 5, for benefits of exercise on attentional control). In this section, after briefly reviewing the changes in the brain that occur with exercise, we present correlational and experimental research examining the relation between exercise and cognitive functioning.

Effects on the Brain

One general mechanism by which aerobic fitness could affect cognitive functioning is through increasing blood flow which in turn enhances oxygenation of the brain. The research supports this view as cardiovascular exercise has been shown to increase the stroke volume of the heart and oxygen transportation in the brain (National Institute on Aging, 1996). Research with animals shows that exercise improves both cognitive and brain functioning (see Kramer, Erickson, & Colcombe, 2006, for a review). These benefits include new capillary development in older rats (Black, Isaacs, Anderson, Alcantara, & Greenough, 1990), neurogenesis in older mice (Van Praag, Shubert, Zhao, & Gage, 2005), increases in levels of the neurotransmitters serotonin and acetylcholine (Blomstrand, Perret, Parry-Billings, & Newsholme, 1989; Fordyce & Farrar, 1991), increases in the density of dopamine receptor sites in older rats (Fordyce & Farrar), and increases in brain-derived neurotrophic factor (which is related to general health of neurons and possibly neurogenesis, Black et al., 1990). Exercise has also been found to significantly reduce levels of amyloid plaques in the brains of knockout mice who produce a lot of plaques (Adlard, Perreau, Pop, & Cotman, 2005). Brain imaging studies with humans have shown that people who have participated in a fairly modest 6-month exercise intervention program (involving brisk walking) show increased activity (relative to controls) in the frontal and parietal lobes when performing a task that involved selectively processing a target and ignoring misleading flankers (Colcombe et al., 2004). In another study, this type of short-term exercise intervention produced increases in brain volume in the frontal lobe and the superior temporal lobe (Kramer, Colcombe, Erickson, & Paige, 2006). Thus the evidence is in agreement with the view that exercise causes changes in the brain that could support cognitive functioning (see Kramer, Erickson, & Colcombe, 2006).

Correlational Studies

Most large-scale studies with humans show a positive correlation between self-reported measures of exercise (e.g., hiking, walking, participating in racquet sports) and changes in cognitive ability (Larson et al., 2006; Weuve, Kang, Manson, Breteler, Ware, & Grodstein, 2004; Yaffe, Barnes, Nevitt, Lui, & Covinsky, 2001, but see Wilson et al., 2002, for an exception). As one example, Yaffe et al. followed 5925 older women (over 65) and found that higher levels of self-reported exercise were associated with less cognitive decline over a 6–8 year period on the Mini Mental State Examination. As another example, Weuve et al. cognitively assessed 16,353 women, who were over 70, initially and then on average 1.8 years later. The assessment included the Telephone Interview for Cognitive Status (highly correlated with the Mini Mental State Examination, MMSE), delayed recall of a word list, immediate and delayed recall of paragraphs, backward digit span, and category fluency. They also developed a measure of physical activity that was based on the level of metabolic activity in the activities reported and the number of hours per week spent performing them. This was a long-term measure based on their reported level of activity every two years over the past 8–15 years. After controlling for many variables (e.g., health problems), the results indicated that higher levels of physical activity were associated with higher cognitive performance and with less decline in cognitive performance over the testing interval between baseline and subsequent testing.

Experimental Interventions

The above research suggests that aerobic fitness attenuates age-related cognitive declines. Nonetheless, the correlational nature of these studies leaves open the possibility that it is cognitive declines that cause reductions in exercise. Despite the limitation of examining the effects of shorter durations of exercise, experimental research on physical interventions is important in addressing the nature of the relation between physical activity and cognitive functioning. Although the evidence is mixed, there are a number of studies that demonstrate at least selective benefits of aerobic exercise on cognitive functioning (Colcombe & Kramer, 2003).

As an example, consider the research of Kramer et al. (1999). They randomly assigned half of their 124 participants, who ranged in age from 60 to 75, to an aerobic conditioning (walking) group and the others to a toning group (designed to improve muscle flexibility but not cardiorespiratory fitness). Both groups met with trained exercise leaders 3 days a week over a 6-month period for 40–60 minutes each session. In the toning group, participants mainly stretched all of the large muscle groups in the lower and upper body. In the aerobic group, participants started off with short 15-minute light intensity walking workouts. The duration and intensity of the workouts increased to the point that participants were walking 40 minutes at a moderate pace by the end of the 6 months. Participants were also tested on a number of cognitive tests both before and after the exercise intervention.

The results showed that walking training was effective in the sense that the aerobic group had significantly higher cardiorespiratory fitness (measured by maximal oxygen consumption) at the end of the 6-month period. Interestingly, participants in the aerobic group demonstrated selective benefits on the cognitive measures such that there were significant improvements in the tasks thought to involve executive control processes and frontal lobe regions but no improvement in other tasks. For example, at the end of training subjects who engaged in aerobic exercise were significantly faster (relative to subjects who toned) in their speed of task switching. The toning group actually got slower from the pretest to the posttest (by 22 milliseconds) whereas the walking group lowered its average response time by 537 milliseconds. By contrast, there were no effects of aerobic training on tasks or measures that were assumed to not tap executive control processes (e.g., speed of responding on nonswitch trials). Also, the improvements in cognitive functioning were reliable for both the younger and more senior older adults.

In a meta-analysis designed to explore patterns among the group of studies showing mixed benefits of physical exercise interventions, Colcombe and Kramer (2003) included 18 studies that had been published between 1966 and 2001. They examined the benefits of exercise interventions on tasks that were coded to engage executive processing, controlled processing, visuospatial processing, or speed of responding. The results showed that exercise subjects improved significantly more than control subjects on all four types of cognitive tests. Moreover, consistent with Kramer et al.'s (1999) results described above, the beneficial effects of exercise were significantly larger for executive tasks than for the other tasks. Beneficial exercise effects were also more pronounced for mid- and old-older participants (66–80 years old) than for young-older participants (55–65 years old), for females, for exercise interventions lasting more than 30 minutes, and when the exercise intervention included both aerobic and resistance training.

In summary, there is now impressive evidence that exercise helps offset age-related declines in brain structure, brain functioning, and cognitive functioning. Whereas this pattern appears clear when examining a variety of different kinds of data, there is still a host of unresolved questions addressing issues such as the most effective exercise regimens, the time period over which the effects endure, and the type of individuals who benefit most from exercise (see Kramer et al., 2006, for more information about these and other issues). Given that the frontal lobes seem to be most compromised by normal aging (e.g., West, 1996; see also section on Individual Differences), a particularly encouraging result is that physical exercise appears to especially affect the frontal lobes and cognitive processes thought to be subserved by the frontal lobes. Thus, those functions that are most at risk from normal aging emerge as those that benefit most from physical exercise.

SUMMARY

In summary, our approach in writing this chapter has been to focus on four themes that evaluate the possibility that aging may not compromise all memory processes and that there may be ways to compensate for those that are affected. One theme is that what appear to be fundamental age-related declines in memory may result in part from redeploying central processes to help offset age-associated sensory deficits and/or failing to deploy available resources because of negative stereotypes. Not inconsistent with this, another theme is that there are strong suggestions that there are memory-related processes that are relatively spared with normal aging. Since the last edition of the handbook, there is now more established support for sparing of familiarity based memory processes, and there is preliminary but tantalizing evidence suggesting relatively intact spontaneous retrieval and some types of distinctive processing.

A third theme is that specifiable individual differences can serve to identify segments of the aging population that reveal little if any decline relative to average younger adult memory functioning. At this stage, individual differences in frontal processes (as assessed by neuro-psychological batteries) have received the most attention in experimental studies, and additional research is needed to explore other factors. These three themes taken in concert raise the provocative, but as of yet untested, possibility that there may be more widespread sparing of memory functioning with normal aging than typically thought. This may seem especially possible in light of other moderating influences that have been identified in other reviews (e.g., the influence of circadian rhythms, Hasher, Goldstein, & May, 2005; Zacks et al., 2000).

The fourth theme is that even for older individuals who display the typical age-related decline in many memory tasks and processes, research in the past decade has focused on a variety of promising interventions to elevate older adult memory functioning. These interventions include training programs aimed at specific kinds of decline such as controlled processes in the use of recollective memory. Additionally, more broad-based approaches focus on increasing physical and mental activity, with the research on physical activity providing fairly convincing positive effects on older adults' cognitive and memory functioning. Finally, there is a less known (in the experimental memory arena) approach that specific nutrient intakes could forestall or ameliorate biological decline in brain tissue and neurochemicals. This approach is much less developed, but with appropriate sophistication might prove fruitful.

We close by noting that much of the work reviewed herein is relatively new and does not yet represent mature literatures. Certainly, some of these preliminary findings will be further refined, and some may even be reversed. Yet from a broader perspective, we believe that the four themes highlighted in this chapter provide an exciting, invigorating agenda for the next era of work in memory and aging.

ACKNOWLEDGMENTS

Preparation of this chapter was supported in part (MAM's contribution) by National Institute of Aging Grant AG 17481. We thank Mary Derbish for assistance with technical aspects of the manuscript preparation. Correspondence concerning the chapter should be addressed to Mark A. McDaniel, Department of Psychology, Washington University, One Brookings Dr., St. Louis, MO 63130–4899.

REFERENCES

Adlard, P., Perreau, V., Pop, V., & Cotman, C. (2005). Voluntary exercise decreases amyloid load in a transgenic model of Alzheimer's Disease. *Journal of Neuroscience, 25,* 4217–4221.

American College of Sports Medicine (1998). ACSM position stand on exercise and physical activity for older adults. *Medicine & Science in Sports & Exercise, 30,* 992–1008.

Arbuckle, T. Y., Gold, D. P., Andres, D., Schwartzman, A., & Chaikelson, J. (1992). The role of psychosocial context, age, and intelligence in memory performance of older men. *Psychology and Aging, 7,* 25–36.

Ball, K., Berch, D. B., Helmers, K. F., Jobe, J. B., Leveck, M. D., Marsiske, M., et al. (2002). Effects of cognitive training interventions with older adults. *Journal of the American Medical Association, 288,* 2271–2281.

Balota, D. A., Cortese, M. J., Duchek, J. M., Adams, D., Roediger, H. L., McDermott, K. B., et al. (1999). Veridical and false memories in healthy older adults and in dementia of the Alzheimer's type. *Cognitive Neuropsychology, 16,* 361–384.

Baltes, P. B., & Baltes, M. M. (1990). *Successful aging: Perspectives from the behavioral sciences.* Cambridge: Cambridge University Press.

Baltes, P. B., & Kliegl, R. (1992). Further testing of limits of cognitive plasticity: Negative age differences in a mnemonic skill are robust. *Developmental Psychology, 28,* 121–125.

Bandura, A. (1997). *Self-efficacy: The exercise of control.* New York: Freeman.

Bargh, J.A., & Chartrand, T. L. (1999). The unbearable automaticity of being. *American Psychologist, 54,* 462–479.

Bargh, J. A., Chen, M., & Burrows, L. (1996). Automaticity of social behavior: Direct effects of trait construct and stereotype activation on action. *Journal of Personality and Social Psychology, 71,* 230–244.

Belli, R. F., Lindsay, D. S., Gales, M. S., & McCarthy, T. T. (1994). Memory impairment and source misattribution in postevent misinformation experiments with short retention intervals. *Memory & Cognition, 22*(1), 40–54.

Benjamin, A. S. (2001). On the dual effects of repetition on false recognition. *Journal of Experimental Psychology: Learning and Memory & Cognition, 27,* 941–947.

Berry, J. M., & West, R. L. (1993). Cognitive self-efficacy in relation to personal self-matery and goal setting across the life span. *International Journal of Behavioral Development, 16,* 351–379.

Bishara, A. J., & Jacoby, L. L. (2006). Aging, spaced retrieval, and inflexible memory performance. Manuscript submitted for publication.

Black, J. E., Isaacs, K. R., Anderson, B. J., Alcantara, A. A., & Greenough, W. T. (1990). Learning causes synaptogenesis, whereas motor activity causes angiogenesis, in cerebellar cortex of adult rats. *Proceedings of the National Academy of Sciences USA, 87,* 5568–5572.

Black, S. R., McCown, S., Lookadoo, R. L., Leonard, R. C. Kelley, M., & Spence. S. A. (2004, April). *Aging, distinctiveness, and the bizarreness effect.* Poster presented at the Tenth Cognitive Aging Conference, Atlanta, Georgia.

Blomstrand, E., Perret, D., Parry-Billings, M., & Nesholme, E. A. (1998). Effect of sustained exercise on plasma amino acid concentrations on 5-hydroxytryptamine metabolism in six different brain regions in the rat. *Acta Physiologica Scandinavica, 136,* 473–481.

Braver, T. S., Gray, J. R., & Burgess, G. C. (2007). Explaining the many varieties of working memory variation: Dual mechanisms of cognitive control. In A. R. A. Conway, C. Jarrold, M. Kane, A. Miyake, & J. Towse (Eds.), *Variation in working memory.* New York: Oxford University Press.

Budson, A. E., Daffner, K. R., Desikan, R., & Schacter, D. L. (2000). When false recognition is unopposed by true recognition: Gist-based memory distortion in Alzheimer's disease. *Neuropsychology, 14,* 277–287.

Butler, K. M., McDaniel, M. A., Dornburg, C. C., Price, A. L., & Roediger, H. L. (2004). Age differences in veridical and false recall are not inevitable: The role of frontal lobe function. *Psychonomic Bulletin & Review, 11*, 921–925.

Camp, C. J., Foss, J. W., O'Hanlon, A. M., & Stevens, A. B. (1996). Memory interventions for persons with dementia. *Applied Cognitive Psychology, 10*, 193–210.

Carstensen, L. L., & Mikels, J. A. (2005). At the intersection of emotion and cognition. *Current Directions in Psychological Science, 14*, 117–121.

Cavanaugh, J. C., & Poon, L. W. (1989). Metamemorial predictors of memory performance in young and older adults. *Psychology and Aging, 4*, 365–368.

Chalfonte, B. L., & Johnson, M. K. (1996). Feature memory and binding in young and older adults. *Memory & Cognition, 24*, 403–416.

Chan, J. C. K., & McDermott, K. B. (in press). The effects of frontal lobe functioning and age on veridical and false recall. *Psychonomic Bulletin & Review.*

Chasteen, A. L., Bhattacharyya, S., Horhota, M., Tam, R., & Hasher, L. (2005). How feelings of stereotype threat influence older adults' memory performance. *Experimental Aging Research, 31*, 235–260.

Cherry, K. E., & LeCompte, D. C. (1999). Age and individual differences influence prospective memory. *Psychology and Aging, 14*, 60–76.

Cimbalo, R. S., & Brink, L. (1982). Aging and the von Restorff isolation effect in short-term memory. *Journal of General Psychology, 106*, 69–76.

Cohen, G., & Faulkner, D. (1989). Age differences in source forgetting: Effects on reality monitoring and on eyewitness testimony. *Psychology and Aging, 4*, 10–17.

Colcombe, S. J., & Kramer, A. F. (2003). Fitness effects on the cognitive function of older adults: A meta-analytic study. *Psychological Science, 14*, 125–130.

Colcombe, S. J., Kramer, A. F., Erickson, K. I., Scalf, P., McAuley, E., Cohen, N. J., et al. (2004). Cardiovascular fitness, cortical plasticity, and aging. *Proceedings of the National Academy of Sciences USA, 101*, 3316–3321.

Coxon, P., & Valentine, T. (1997). The effects of the age of eyewitnesses on the accuracy and suggestibility of their testimony. *Applied Cognitive Psychology, 11*, 415–430.

Craik, F. I. M. (1986). A functional account of age differences in memory. In F. Klix & H. Hagendorf (Eds.), *Human memory and cognitive capabilities: Mechanisms and performances* (pp. 409–422). Amsterdam: North-Holland.

Craik, F. I. M., & Jennings, J. M. (1992). Human memory. In F. I. M. Craik & T. A. Salthouse (Eds.), *The handbook of aging and cognition* (pp. 51–110). Hillsdale, NJ: Lawrence Erlbaum Associates, Inc.

Craik, F. I. M., Morris, L. W., Morris, R. G., & Loewen, E. R. (1990). Relations between source amnesia and frontal lobe functioning in older adults. *Psychology and Aging, 5*, 148–151

Crook, T. H., Tinkleberg, J., Yesavage, J., Petrie, W., Nunzi, M.G., & Massari, D. C. (1991) Effects of phosphatidylserine in age-associated memory impairment. *Neurology, 41*, 644–649.

Dornburg, C. C., & McDaniel, M. A. (2006). The cognitive interview enhances long-term free recall of older adults. *Psychology and Aging, 21*, 196–200.

Durso, F. T., & Johnson, M. K. (1980). The effects of orienting tasks on recognition, recall, and modality confusion of pictures and words. *Journal of Verbal Learning & Verbal Behavior, 19*, 416–429.

d'Ydewalle, G., Luwel, K., & Brunfaut, E. (1999). The importance of on-going concurrent activities as a function of age in time- and event- based prospective memory. *European Journal of Cognitive Psychology, 11*, 219–237.

Einstein, G. O., Arnold, K., Bishop, R. B., & Scullin, M. (2006, March). *Prospective memory: Evidence for spontaneous retrieval processes in older adults.* Paper presented at the meeting of the Southeastern Psychological Association, Atlanta, GA.

Einstein, G. O., Holland, L. J., McDaniel, M. A. & Guynn, M. J. (1992). Age-related deficits in prospective memory: The influence of task complexity. *Psychology and Aging, 7*, 471–478.

Einstein, G. O., & McDaniel, M. A. (1987). Distinctiveness and the mnemonic benefits of bizarre imagery. In M. A. McDaniel and M. Pressley (Eds.), *Imagery and related mnemonic processes: Theories, individual differences and applications.* (pp. 78–102). New York: Springer-Verlag.

Einstein, G. O., & McDaniel, M. A. (1990). Normal aging and prospective memory. *Journal of Experimental Psychology: Learning, Memory, and Cognition, 16*, 717–726.

Einstein, G. O., & McDaniel, M. A. (2005). Prospective memory: Multiple retrieval processes. *Current Directions in Psychological Science, 14*, 286–290.

Einstein, G. O., McDaniel, M. A., Richardson, S. L., Guynn, M. J., & Cunfer, A. R. (1995). Aging and prospective memory: Examining the influences of self-initiated retrieval processes. *Journal of Experimental Psychology: Learning, Memory, and Cognition, 21*, 996–1007.

Einstein, G. O., McDaniel, M. A., Smith, R. E., & Shaw, P. (1998). Habitual prospective memory and aging: Remember intentions and forgetting actions. *Psychological Science, 9*, 284–288.

Einstein, G. O., McDaniel, M. A., Thomas, R., Mayfield, S., Shank, H., Morrisette, N., et al. (2005). Multiple processes in prospective memory retrieval factors determining monitoring versus spontaneous retrieval. *Journal of Experimental Psychology: General, 134*, 327–342.

Floyd, M., & Scoggin, F. (1997). Effects of memory training on the subjective memory functioning and mental health of older adults: A meta-analysis. *Psychology and Aging, 12*, 150–161.

Fordyce, D. E., & Farrar, R. P. (1991). Enhancement of spatial learning in F344 rats by physical activity and related learning-associated alterations in hippocampal and cortical cholinergic functioning. *Behavioral Brain Research, 46*, 123–133.

Friedman, H. (1966). Memory organization in the aged. *Journal of Genetic Psychology, 109*, 3–8.

Friedman, H. (1979). Framing pictures: The role of knowledge in automatized encoding and memory for gist. *Journal of Experimental Psychology: General, 108*, 316–355.

Friedman, N. O., & Miyake, A. (2004). The relations among inhibition and interference control functions: A latent-variable analysis. *Journal of Experimental Psychology: General, 133*, 101–135.

Gabbert, F., Memon, A., & Allan, K (2003). Memory conformity: Can eyewitnesses influence each other's memories for an event? *Applied Cognitive Psychology, 17*, 533–543.

Gallo, D. A., & Roediger, H. L. (2003). The effects of associations and aging on illusory recollections. *Memory and Cognition, 31*, 1036–1044.

Geraci, L., McDaniel, M. A., & Roediger, H. L. (2006). *Aging and memory for distinctive events: The influence of frontal functioning and type of distinctiveness.* Unpublished manuscript, Washington University in St Louis.

Geiselman, R. E., Fisher, R. P., MacKinnon, D. P., & Holland, H. L. (1985). Eyewitness memory enhancement in the police interview: Cognitive retrieval mnemonics versus hypnosis. *Journal of Applied Psychology, 70*, 401–412.

Gilewski, M. J., Zelinski, E. M., & Schaie, K. W. (1990). The Memory Functioning Questionnaire for assessment of memory complaints in adulthood and old age. *Psychology and Aging, 5*, 482–490.

Glisky, E. L., Polster, M. R., & Routhieaux, B. C. (1995). Double dissociation between item and source memory. *Neuropsychology, 9*, 229–235.

Glisky, E. L., Rubin, S. R., & Davidson, P. S. R. (2001). Source memory in older adults: An encoding or retrieval problem? *Journal of Experimental Psychology: Learning, Memory, and Cognition, 27*, 1131–1146.

Gold, P. E., Cahill, L., & Wenk, G. L. (2002). Ginko biloba: A cognitive enhancer? *Psychological Science in the Public Interest, 3*, 2–11.

Guynn, M. J., McDaniel, M. A., & Einstein, G. O. (1998). Prospective memory: When reminders fail. *Memory & Cognition, 26*, 287–298.

Hasher, L., Goldstein, D., & May, C. P. (2005). It's about time: Circadian rhythms, memory, and aging. In C. Izawa & N. Ohta (Eds.), *Human learning and memory: Advances in theory and application*. Mahwah, NJ: Lawrence Erlbaum Associates, Inc.

Hasher, L., & Zacks, R. T. (1988). Working memory, comprehension and aging: A review and a new view. In G. H. Bower (Ed.), *The psychology of learning and motivation* (Vol. 22, pp. 193–225). San Diego, CA: Academic Press.

Hasher, L., & Zacks, R. T. (1999). Working memory, comprehension, and aging. A review and a new view. In G. H. Bower (Ed.), *The psychology of learning and motivation* (Vol. 22, pp. 193–226). New York: Academic Press.

Healy, M. R., Light, L. L., & Chung, C. (2005). Dual-process models of associative recognition in young and older adults: Evidence from receiver operating characteristics. *Journal of Experimental Psychology: Learning, Memory & Cognition, 31*, 768–788.

Hedden, T., Park, D. C., Nisbett, R., Ji, L. J., Jing, Q., & Jiao, S. (2002). Cultural variation in verbal versus spatial neurospsychological function across the life span. *Neuropsychology, 16*, 65–73.

Henkel, L., Johnson, M. K., & De Leonardis, D. (1998). Aging and source monitoring: Cognitive proecesses and neuropsychological correlates. *Journal of Experimental Psychology: General, 127*, 251–268.

Henry, J. D., MacLeod, M. S., Phillips, H., & Crawford, J. R. (2004). A meta-analytic review of prospective memory and aging. *Psychology and Aging, 19*, 27–39.

Hertzog, C., & Hultsch, D. F. (2000). Metacognition in adulthood and old age. In F. I. M. Craik & T. A. Salthouse (Eds.), *The handbook of aging and cognition* (pp. 417–466). Mahwah, NJ: Lawrence Erlbaum Associates, Inc.

Hertzog, C., McGuire, C. L., & Lineweaver, T. T. (1998). Aging, attributions, perceived control, and strategy use in a free recall task. *Aging, Neuropsychology, and Cognition, 5*, 85–106.

Hess, T. M. (2005). Memory and aging in context. *Psychological Bulletin, 131*, 383–406.

Hess, T. M., Auman, C., Colcombe, S. J., & Rahhal, T. A. (2003). The impact of stereotype threat on age differences in memory performance. *Journal of Gerontolgy: Psychological Sciences, 58B*, P3–P11.

Hess, T. M., Hinson, J. T., & Statham. J. A (2004). Implicit and explicit stereotype activation effects on memory: Do age and awareness moderate the impact of priming? *Psychology and Aging, 19*, 495–505.

Holland, R.W., Hendricks, M., & Aarts, H. (2005). Smells like clean spirit: Nonconscious effects of scent on cognition and behavior. *Psychological Science, 16*, 689–693.

Howard, M.W., Bessette-Symons, B., Zhang, Y., & Hoyer, W. (2006). Aging selectively impairs recollection in recognition memory for pictures: Evidence from modeling and receiver operating characteristic curves. *Psychology and Aging, 21*, 96–106.

Hultsch, D. F., Hertzog, C., & Dixon, R. A. (1987). Age differences in metamemory: Resolving the inconsistencies [special issue]. *Canadian Journal of Psychology, 41*, 193–208.

Hultsch, D. F., Hertzog, C., Small, B. J., & Dixon, R. A. (1999). Use it or lose it: Engaged lifestyle as a buffer of cognitive decline in aging? *Psychology and Aging, 14*, 245–263.

Hunt, R. R. (1995). The subtlety of distinctiveness: What von Restorff really did. *Psychonomic Bulletin & Review, 2*, 105–112.

Hunt, R. R., & Worthen, J. B. (Eds.). (2006). *Distinctiveness and memory*. New York: Oxford University Press.

Intons-Peterson, M. J., Rocchi, P., West, T., McLellan, K., & Hackney, A. (1998). Aging, optimal testing times, and negative priming: Correction. *Journal of Experimental Psychology: Learning, Memory, & Cognition, 24*, 362–376.

Jacoby, L.L. (1999). Ironic effects of repetition: Measuring age-related differences in memory. *Journal of Experimental Psychology: Learning, Memory and Cognition, 25*, 3–22.

Jacoby, L. L., Bishara, A. J., Hessels, S., & Toth, J. P. (2005). Aging, subjective experience, and cognitive control: Dramatic false remembering by older adults. *Journal of Experimental Psychology: General, 134*, 131–148.

Jacoby, L. L., Debner, J. A., & Hay, J. F. (2001). Proactive interference, accessibility bias, and process dissociations: Valid subjective reports of memory. *Journal of Experimental Psychology: Learning, Memory, and Cognition, 27*, 686–700.

Jacoby, L. L., Shimizu, Y., Velanova, K., & Rhodes, M. G. (2005). Age differences in depth of retrieval: Memory for foils. *Journal of Memory and Language: Metamemory, 52*, 493–504.

Jenkins, J. J. (1979). Four points to remember: A tetrahedral model of memory experiments. In L. S. Cermak & F. I. M. Craik (Eds.), *Levels of processing in human memory* (pp. 429–446). Hillsdale, NJ: Lawrence Erlbaum Associates, Inc.

Jennings, J., & Jacoby, L. L. (2003). Improving memory in older adults: Training recollection. *Neuropsychological Rehabilitation, 13*, 417–440.

Jennings, J. M., Webster, L. M., Kleykamp, B. A., & Dagenbach, D. (2005). Recollection training and transfer effects in older adults: Successful use of a repetition-lag procedure. *Aging, Neuropsychology and Cognition, 12*, 278–298.

Kausler, D. H. (1994). *Learning and memory in normal aging.* San Diego, CA: Academic Press.

Kohn, M. L., & Schooler, C. (with Miller, J., Miller, K., Schoenbach, C., & Schoenberg, R.). (1983). *Work and personality: An inquiry into the impact of social stratification.* Norwood, NJ: Ablex.

Kramer, A. F., Colcombe, S. J., Erickson, K. I., & Paige, P. (2006). Fitness training and the brain: From molecules to minds. *Proceedings of the 2006 Cognitive Aging Conference.* Atlanta, Georgia.

Kramer, A. F., Erickson, K. I., & Colcombe, S. (2006). Exercise, cognition and the aging brain. *Journal of Applied Physiology, 101*, 1237–1242.

Kramer, A. F., Hahn, S., Cohen, N. J., Banich, M. T., McAuley, E., Harrison, C. R., et al. (1999). Aging, fitness and neurocognitive function. *Nature, 400*, 418–419.

Kramer, A. F., Hahn, S., McAuley, E., Cohen, N. J., Banich, M. T., Harrison, C., et al. (1999). Exercise, aging and cognition: Healthy body, healthy mind? In A. D. Fisk & W. Rogers (Eds.), *Human factors interventions for the health care of older adults.* Hillsdale, NJ: Lawrence Erlbaum Associates, Inc.

Kramer, A. F., Larish, J., & Strayer, D. L. (1995). Training for attentional control in dual-task settings: A comparison of young and old adults. *Journal of Experimental Psychology: Applied, 1*, 50–76.

Kramer, A. F., Larish, J., Weber, T., & Bardell, L. (1999). Training for executive control: Task coordination strategies and aging. In D. Gopher & A. Koriat (Eds.), *Attention and performance XVIII.* Cambridge, MA: MIT Press.

Kvavilashvili, L., & Fisher, L. (2007). Is time-based prospective remembering mediated by self-initiated rehearsals? Effects of incidental cues, ongoing activity, age and motivation. *Journal of Experimental Psychology: General, 136*, 112–132.

Larson, E. B., Wang, L., Bowen, J. D., McCormick, W. C., Teri, L., Crane, P. et al. (2006). Exercise is associated with reduced risk for incident dementia among persons 65 years of age or older. *Annals of Internal Medicine, 144*, 73–81.

Levy, B. (1996). Improving memory in old age through implicit self-stereotyping. *Journal of Personality and Social Psychology, 71*, 1092–1107.

Levy, B., & Langer, E. (1994). Aging free from negative stereotypes: Successful memory in China and among the American deaf. *Journal of Personality and Social Psychology, 66*, 989–997.

Light, L. L. (1991). Memory and aging: Four hypotheses in search of data. *Annual Review of Psychology, 42*, 333–376.

Light, L. L., Patterson, M. M., Chung, C., & Healy, M. R. (2004). Effects of repetition and response deadline on associative recognition in young and older adults. *Memory & Cognition, 32*, 1182–1193.

Loftus, E. F., Miller, D. G., & Burns, H. J. (1978). Semantic integration of verbal information into a visual memory. *Journal of Experimental Psychology: Learning, Memory & Cognition, 4*, 19–31.

Lustig, C., May, C., & Hasher, L. (2001). Working memory span and the role of proactive interference. *Journal of Experimental Psychology: General, 130*, 199–207.

Mäntylä, T., & Backman, L. (1992). Encoding variability and age-related retrieval failures. *Psychology and Aging, 5*, 545–550.

Marche, T., Jordan, J., & Owre, K. (2002). Younger adults can be more suggestible than older adults: The influence of learning difference on misinformation reporting. *Canadian Journal on Aging, 21*, 85–93.

Marsh, R. L., Hicks, J. L., Cook, G. I., & Mayhorn, C. B. (2007). Comparing older and younger adults in an event-based prospective memory paradigm containing an output monitoring component. *Aging, Neuropsychology, and Cognition, 14*, 168–188.

Mather, M., Johnson, M., & De Leonardis, D. (1999). Stereotype reliance in source monitoring: Age differences and neuropsychological test correlates. *Cognitive Neuropsychology* [special issue: The cognitive neuropsychology of false memories], *16*, 437–458.

May, C. P., Hasher, L., & Stoltzfus, E. R. (1993). Optimal time of day and the magnitude of age differences in memory. *Psychological Science, 4*, 326–330.

Maylor, E. A. (1996). Age-related impairment in an event-based prospective memory task. *Psychology and Aging, 11*, 74–78.

McCoy, S. L., Tun, P. A., Cox, L. C., Colangelo, M., Stewart, R. A., & Wingfield, A. (2005). Hearing loss and perceptual effort: Downstream effects on older adults' memory for speech. *Quarterly Journal of Experimental Psychology, 58A*, 22–33.

McDaniel, M. A., Dornburg, C. C., & Guynn, M. J. (2005). Disentangling encoding versus retrieval explanations for the bizarreness effect: Implications for distinctiveness. *Memory and Cognition, 33*, 270–279.

McDaniel, M. A., & Einstein, G. O. (1986). Bizarre imagery as an effective memory aid: The importance of distinctiveness. *Journal of Experimental Psychology: Learning, Memory and Cognition, 12*, 54–65.

McDaniel, M. A., & Einstein, G. O. (1993). The importance of cue familiarity and cue distinctiveness in prospective memory. *Memory, 1*, 23–41.

McDaniel, M. A., & Einstein, G. O. (2000). Strategic and automatic processes in prospective memory retrieval: A multiprocess framework. *Applied Cognitive Psychology, 14*, S127–S144.

McDaniel, M. A., & Einstein, G. O. (in press). Prospective memory and aging: Old issues and new questions. In S. M. Hofer & D. F. Alwin (Eds.), *The handbook on cognitive aging: Interdisciplinary perspectives.* Thousand Oaks, CA: Sage.

McDaniel, M. A., & Einstein, G. O. (2007a). *Prospective memory.* Thousand Oaks, CA: Sage.

McDaniel, M. A., & Einstein, G. O. (2007b). Spontaneous retrieval in prospective memory. In J. S. Nairne (Ed.), *The foundations of remembering: Essays in honor of Henry L. Roediger III,* (pp. 225–240). New York: Psychology Press.

McDaniel, M. A., & Einstein, G. O. (2007c). Prospective memory components most at risk for older adults and implications for medication adherence. In D. C. Park & L. Liu (Eds.), *Medical adherence and aging: Social and cognitive perspectives* (pp. 49–75). Washington, DC: American Psychological Association.

McDaniel, M. A., Einstein, G. O., DeLosh, E. L., May, D., & Brady, P. (1995). The bizarreness effect: It's not surprising, it's complex. *Journal of Experimental Psychology: Learning, Memory and Cognition, 21*, 422–435.

McDaniel, M. A., Einstein, G. O., & Rendell, P. G. (in press). The puzzle of inconsistent age-related declines in prospective memory: A multiprocess explanation. In M. Kliegel, M. A. McDaniel, & G. O. Einstein (Eds.), *Prospective memory: Cognitive, neuroscience, developmental, and applied perspectives.* Mahwah, NJ: Lawrence Erlbaum Associates, Inc.

McDaniel, M. A., Maier, S. F., & Einstein, G. O. (2002). "Brain-specific" nutrients: A memory cure? *Psychological Science in the Public Interest, 3*, 12–38.

McDonald-Miszczak, L., Hertzog, C., & Hultsch, D. F. (1995). Stability and accuracy of metamemory in adulthood and aging: A longitudinal analysis. *Psychology and Aging, 10*, 553–564.

McMahon, M. (2000). The effect of the enhanced cognitive interview on recall and confidence in elderly adults. *Psychiatry, Psychology and Law, 7*, 9–32.

Meade, M., L., & Roediger, H. L., III. (2006). The effect of forced recall on illusory recollection in younger and older adults. *American Journal of Psychology, 119*, 433–462.

Mello, E.W., & Fisher, R. P. (1996). Enhancing older adult eyewitness memory with the cognitive interview. *Applied Cognitive Psychology, 10*, 403–417.

Mitchell, K. J., Johnson, M. K., & Mather, M. (2003). Source monitoring and suggestibility to misinformation: Adult age-related differences. *Applied Cognitive Psychology, 16*, 635–650.

Moscovitch, M. (1982). A neuropsychological approach to memory and perception in normal and pathological aging. In F. I. M. Craik and S. Trehub (Eds.), *Advances in the study of communication and affect: Aging and cognitive processes* (pp. 55–78). New York: Plenum.

Moscovitch, M. (1994). Memory and working with memory: Evaluation of a component process model and comparisons with other models. In D. L. Schacter and E. Tulving (Eds.), *Memory systems* (pp. 269–310). Cambridge, MA: MIT Press.

Moscovitch, M., & Winocur, G. (1995). Frontal lobes, memory, and aging. In J. Grafman, K. J. Holyoak, & F. Boller (Eds.), *Structure and functions of the human prefrontal cortex* (pp. 119–150). New York: New York Academy of Sciences.

National Institute on Aging (1996). *Exercise can boost cardiac fitness in conditioned and out-of-shape older people.* Washington, DC: National Institutes of Health.

Naveh-Benjamin, M. (2000). Adult age differences in memory performance: Tests of an associative deficit hypothesis. *Journal of Experimental Psychology: Learning, Memory and Cognition, 26*, 1170–1187.

Naveh-Benjamin, M., & Craik, F. I. M. (1995). Memory for context and its use in item memory: Comparisons of younger and older persons. *Psychology & Aging, 10*, 284–293.

Park, D., & Gutchess, A. (2006). The cognitive neuroscience of aging and culture. *Current Directions in Psychological Science, 15*, 105–108.

Park, D. C., Hertzog, C., Kidder, D. P., Morrell, R. W., & Mayhorn, C. B. (1997). Effect of age on event-based and time-based prospective memory. *Psychology and Aging, 12*, 314–327.

Park, D. C., Lautenschlager, G., Hedden, T., Davidson, N. S., Smith, A. D., & Smith, P. K. (2002). Models of visuospatial and verbal memory across the adult life span. *Psychology and Aging, 17*, 299–320.

Parkin, A. J., Walter, B. M., & Hunkin, N. M. (1995). Relationships between normal aging, frontal lobe function, and memory for temporal and spatial information. *Neuropsychology, 9*, 304–312.

Pearman, A., & Storandt, M. (2004). Predictors of subjective memory in older adults. *Psychological Sciences and Social Sciences, 59B*, 4–6.

Prull, M. W., Gabrieli, J. D. E., & Bunge, S. A. (2000). Age-related changes in memory: A cognitive neuroscience perspective. In F. I. M. Craik & T. A. Salthouse (Eds.), *The handbook of aging and cognition* (pp. 91–153). Mahwah, NJ: Lawrence Erlbaum Associates, Inc.

Rabbitt, P.M. A. (1968). Channel capacity, intelligibility and immediate memory. *Quarterly Journal of Experimental Psychology, 20,* 241–248.

Rahhal, T. A., Hasher, L., & Colcombe, S. J. (2001). Instructional manipulations and age differences in memory: Now you see them, now you don't. *Psychology and Aging, 16,* 697–706.

Rahhal, T. A., May, C. P., & Hasher, L. (2002). Truth and character: Sources that older adults can remember. *Psychological Science, 13,* 101–105.

Raz, N. (2000). Aging of the brain and its impact on cognitive performance: Integration of structural and functional findings. In F. I. M. Craik & T. A. Salthouse (Eds.), *The handbook of aging and cognition* (pp. 1–90). Mahwah, NJ: Lawrence Erlbaum Associates, Inc.

Roediger, H. L., & Geraci, L. (2007). Aging and the misinformation effect: A neuropsychological analysis. *Journal of Experimental Psychology: Learning, Memory, and Cognition, 33,* 321–334.

Roediger, H. L., & Karpicke, J. D. (2006). Test-enhanced learning: Taking memory tests improves long-term retention. *Psychological Science, 17,* 249–255.

Roediger, H. L. III., & McDaniel, M. A. (2007). Illusory recollection in older adults: Testing Mark Twain's conjecture. In M. Gary & H. Hayne (Eds.), *Do justice and let the sky fall: Elizabeth F. Loftus and her contributions to science, law and academic freedom* (pp. 105–136). Mahwah, NJ: Lawrence Erlbaum Associates, Inc.

Salthouse, T. A. (1991). *Theoretical perspectives on cognitive aging.* Hillsdale, NJ: Lawrence Erlbaum Associates, Inc.

Salthouse, T. A. (2003). Memory aging from 18 to 80. *Alzheimer Disease and Associated Disorders, 17,* 162–167.

Salthouse, T. A. (2006). Mental exercise and mental aging: Evaluating the validity of the "use it or lose it" hypothesis. *Perspectives on Psychological Science, 1,* 68–87.

Sapolsky, R. M. (2000). Glucocorticoids and hippocampal atrophy in neuropsychiatric disorders. *Archives of General Psychiatry, 57,* 925–935.

Schmader, T., & Johns, M. (2003). Converging evidence that stereotype threat reduces working memory capacity. *Journal of Personality and Social Psychology, 85,* 440–452.

Schmitter-Edgecombe, M. (1999). Effects of divided attention and time course on automatic and controlled components of memory in older adults. *Psychology and Aging, 14,* 331–345.

Schneider, B. A., & Pichora-Fuller, M. K. (2000). Implications of perceptual deterioration for cognitive aging research. In F. I. M. Craik & T. A. Salthouse (Eds.), *The handbook of aging and cognition* (pp. 155–219). Mahwah, NJ: Lawrence Erlbaum Associates, Inc.

Schooler, C., & Mulatu, M. S. (2001). The reciprocal effects of leisure time activities and intellectual functioning in older people: A longitudinal analysis. *Psychology and Aging, 16,* 466–482.

Schooler, C., Mulatu, M. S., & Oates, G. (1999). The continuing effects of substantively complex work on the intellectual functioning of older workers. *Psychology and Aging, 14,* 483–506.

Siedlecki, K. L., Salthouse, T. A., & Berish, D. E. (2005). Is there anything special about the aging of source memory? *Psychology and Aging, 20,* 19–32.

Smith, A. D. (1996). Memory. In J. E. Birren & K. W. Schaie (Eds.), *Handbook of the psychology of aging* (4th ed., pp. 236–250). San Diego, CA: Academic Press.

Smith, R. E. (2003). The cost of remembering to remember in event-based prospective memory: Investigating the capacity demands of delayed intention performance. *Journal of Experimental Psychology: Learning, Memory, and Cognition, 29,* 347–361.

Smith, R. E. (2006). Adult age differences in episodic memory: Item-specific, relational, and distinctive processing. In R. R. Hunt & J. Worthen (Eds.), *Distinctiveness and memory* (pp. 259–287). New York: Oxford University Press.

Smith, R. E., & Bayen, U. J. (2006). The source of adult age differences in event-based prospective memory: A multinomial modeling approach. *Journal of Experimental Psychology: Learning, Memory, and Cognition, 32,* 623–635.

Smith, R. E., Lozito, J., & Bayen, U. J. (2005). Adult age differences in distinctive processing: The modality effect in false recall. *Psychology and Aging, 20,* 486–492.

Smith, S. M., Ward, T. B., Tindell, D. R., Sifonis, C. M., & Wilkenfeld, M. J. (2000). Category structure and created memories. *Memory & Cognition, 28,* 386–395.

Steele, C. M. (1997). A threat in the air: How stereotypes shape intellectual identify and performance. *American Psycholgist, 52,* 613–629.

Steele, C. M., & Aronson, J. (1995). Contending with a stereotype: African-American intellectual test performance and stereotype threat. *Journal of Personality and Social Psychology, 69,* 797–811.

Stein, R., Blanchard-Fields, F., & Hertzog, C. (2002). The effects of age-stereotype priming on memory performance in older adults. *Experimental Aging Research, 28,* 169–181.

Thomas, A. K., & McDaniel, M. A. (2007). Not all older adults are equal: How cognitive functioning mediates the use of distinctive processing in reducing memory illusions. Manuscript under review.

Tun, P. A. (1998). Fast noisy speech: Age differences in processing rapid speech with background noise. *Psychology and Aging, 17,* 453–467.

Tun, P. A., McCoy, S., Cox, C., & Wingfield, A. (2006, April). *Divided attention costs for memory for speech depend on both age and hearing ability.* Cognitive Aging Conference, Atlanta, GA.

Van Praag, H., Shubert, T., Zhao, C., & Gage, F. H. (2005). Exercise enhances learning and hippocampal neurogenesis in aged mice. *Journal of Neuroscience, 25,* 8680–8685.

Verhaeghen, P., Marcoen, A., & Goossens, L. (1993). Fact and fiction about memory aging: A quantitative interrogation of research findings. *Journal of Gerontology: Psychological Service, 48,* P157–P171.

Vogels, W. W. A., Dekker, M. R., Brouwer, W. H., & de Jong, R. (2002). Age-related changes in event-related prospective memory performance: A comparison of four prospective memory tasks. *Brain & Cognition, 49,* 341–362.

Watson, J. M., McDermott, K. B., & Balota, D. A. (2004). Attempting to avoid false memories in the Deese-Roediger-McDermott paradigm: Assessing the combined influence of practice and warnings in young and old adults. *Memory & Cognition, 32,* 135–141.

Wesnes, K. A., Ward, T., McGinty, A., & Petrini, O. (2000). The memory enhancing effects of a ginkgo biloba/panax ginseng combination in healthy middle-aged volunteers. *Psychopharmacology, 152,* 353–361.

West, R. L. (1996). An application of prefrontal cortex function theory to cognitive aging. *Psychological Bulletin, 120,* 272–292.

West, R. L., Bagwell, D. K., & Dark-Freudeman, A. (2005). Memory and goal setting: The response of older and younger adults to positive and negative feedback. *Psychology and Aging, 20,* 195–201.

West, R. L., Dennehy-Basile, D., & Norris, M. P. (1996). Memory self evaluation: The effects of age and experience. *Aging, Neuropsychology, and Cognition, 3,* 67–83.

West, R. L., Welch, D. C., & Thorn, R. M. (2001). Effects of goal setting and feedback on memory performance and beliefs among older and younger adults. *Psychology and Aging, 16,* 240–250.

Wetherell, J. L., Reynolds, C. A., Gatz, M.U., & Pedersen, N. L. (2002). Anxiety, cognitive performance, and cognitive decline in normal aging. *Journals of Gerontology: Series B: Psychological Sciences and Social Sciences, 57B,* P246–P255.

Weuve, J., Kang, J. H., Manson, J. E., Breteler, M.M.B., Ware, J. H., & Grodstein, F. (2004). Physical activity including walking and cognitive function in older women. *Journal of the American Medical Association, 292,* 1454–1461.

Wilson, R. S., Bennett, D. A., Bienias, J. L., Aggarwal, N. T., Mendes de Leon, C. F., Morris, M.

C., et al. (2002). Cognitive activity and incident AD in a population-based sample of older persons. *Neurology, 59*, 1910–1914.

Wilson, R S., Evans, D. A., Bienias, J. L., Mendes de Leon, C. F., Schneider, J. A. & Bennett, D. A. (2003). Proneness to psychological distress is associated with risk of Alzheimer's Disease. *Neurology, 61*, 1479–1485.

Wingfield, A., Tun, P. A., & McCoy, S. L. (2005). Hearing loss in older adulthood: What it is and how it interacts with cognitive performance. *Current Directions in Psychological Science, 14*, 144–148.

Woodruff-Pak, D. S. (1997). *The neuropsychology of aging*. Malden, MA: Blackwell.

Worthen, J. B. (2006). Resolution of discrepant memory strengths: An explanation of the effects of bizarreness on memory. In R. R. Hunt & J. Worthen (Eds.), *Distinctiveness and memory* (pp. 259–287). New York: Oxford University Press.

Yaffe, K., Barnes, D., Nevitt, M., Lui, L. Y., & Covinsky, K. (2001). A prospective study of physical activity and cognitive decline in elderly women. *Archives of Internal Medicine, 161*, 703–708.

Yonelinas, A. P. (2002). The nature of recollection and familiarity: A review of 30 years of research. *Journal of Memory and Language, 46*, 441–517.

Yoon, C., Hasher, L., Feinberg, F., Rahhal, T. A., & Winocur, G. (2000). Cross-cultural differences in memory: The role of culture-based stereotypes about aging. *Psychology and Aging, 15*, 694–704.

Zacks, R. T., Hasher, L., & Li, K. Z. H. (2000). Human memory. In F. I. M. Craik & T. A. Salthouse (Eds.), *The handbook of aging and cognition* (2nd ed., pp. 293–357). Mahwah, NJ: Lawrence Erlbaum Associates, Inc.

7

Working Memory, Executive Control, and Aging

Todd S. Braver
Washington University in St. Louis

Robert West
Iowa State University

INTRODUCTION

Research on cognitive aging seems to have three primary goals: first, to determine the extent to which the diversity of observed behavioral changes that occur with advancing age can be potentially explained by a small set of fundamental cognitive mechanisms or "primitives"; second, to thoroughly and explicitly specify the nature of these mechanisms, potentially by drawing links to underlying neurobiology or to more formalized descriptions of how such underlying mechanisms might bring about observable behavioral changes; and third, to use the knowledge gained in the pursuit of the first two goals to develop effective interventions that can minimize (or ideally, reverse) the effects of cognitive aging.

Studies of working memory (WM) and executive control in older adults provide a clear example of these three goals in action, and the potential tension that often arises between them. In particular, over the last decade there has been increasing interest in the role of working memory and executive control as fundamental causes of age-related cognitive change. However, at the same time this research has often been plagued by failures of specification. In particular, it has been difficult to define exactly which cognitive and behavioral processes fall under the purview of working memory and executive control, and thus should be affected by age-related declines in these domains. This definitional imprecision has led to controversy and confusion in the field, with researchers adopting different operational criteria for what constitutes a working memory or executive control task or measure, and with a mixture of results regarding the extent to which such measures either account for age-related variance or differentiate from other mechanistic constructs (e.g., processing speed).

In the current chapter, we review recent research in the area with a focus that is unashamedly influenced by our own theoretical perspective. Specifically, we describe an emerging theoretical framework, that in our view provides a productive middle-ground, incorporating both: (a) increased specificity in terms of the particular mechanisms of working memory and executive control affected by advancing age; and (b) clear linkages to both underlying neurophysiology and to observable behavioral effects across a range of cognitive domains. Thus, our goal for the chapter is to lay out an explicit account of age-related changes in working memory and executive control that both clearly specifies what types of empirical phenomena should be explainable under this account as well as what classes of data should not fall within its purview. This theoretical account, which we refer to as *the goal maintenance account*, will then serve as a reference point, from which to review and evaluate the recent literature on working memory and executive control in adults. Critically, we will aim to determine the extent to which this growing literature can be integrated under the goal maintenance account. In the final section, we discuss emerging trends and future research directions that may provide a better test of the theory, or point to ways in which it should be extended or refined. Before describing the goal maintenance theory, we begin by discussing first the historical trends and research approaches prominent in cognitive aging studies of working memory and executive control.

HISTORICAL TRENDS IN THE STUDY OF WORKING MEMORY AND EXECUTIVE FUNCTION

The dominant theoretical influence on working memory research over the past two decades has been the model of Baddeley and colleagues (Baddeley, 1986, 2003). This model gained prominence by suggesting that short-term storage of information was utilized primarily in the service of complex cognitive tasks. Thus, the short-term storage system serves as a temporary workspace from which to keep task-relevant information in a highly accessible form for inspection and computation. This tight integration of the storage and processing components of the WM system provides functionality in higher cognitive domains, such as planning, problem solving, and reasoning. At the same time, the Baddeley model postulates a structural distinction between the storage buffers and executive control components, which suggests that the two can be studied independently. The model potentially serves as an attractive basis for cognitive aging research, in that one might postulate age-related reductions in relatively circumscribed mechanisms—i.e., the function of the WM storage buffers—as a source for more global impairments in higher cognitive function. Thus, one research strategy is to determine how well reductions in WM storage capacity can account for more general age-related cognitive impairment (Salthouse, 1990). However, a problem with this strategy is that the tasks which seem to best tap into the function of WM storage buffers, the so-called simple or passive span measures (such as digit span), show minimal age differences (Bopp & Verhaeghen, 2005; Craik, 1977; Zacks, Hasher, & Li, 2000)

An alternative strategy has been to examine age differences, and their relationship to cognitive performance, with span tasks that require the coordination of short-term storage with the processing capacity of the executive controller. These so-called complex span tasks (such as reading span), do show robust and reliable age differences (Babcock & Salthouse, 1990; Bopp & Verhaeghen, 2005). More importantly, a great deal of research has provided evidence that at least some of the age-related deficits in different cognitive domains such as reasoning and language are mediated by performance on complex span tasks (Hartley, 1986; Light & Anderson, 1985; Salthouse, 2005a; Stine & Wingfield, 1990). Nevertheless, there have been many areas of contention and conflicting findings, such as the degree of reduction in span size, and the extent to which span effects, rather than other constructs such as processing speed, serve as the true mediator of age-related variance in these cognitive domains (Salthouse, 1994; Zacks et al., 2000).

A more serious problem concerns how age differences in complex span measures are interpreted in terms of WM theory. The most natural interpretation is that span effects reflect an age-related decline in WM capacity that relates to the interaction of storage and control mechanisms. Yet, more recently the WM literature has been moving toward the view that individual and group differences in complex span measures primarily reflect executive processes rather than the storage capacity of the buffers. This view can be seen most clearly in the work of Engle and colleagues, who have suggested that complex WM span tasks correlate with performance in other cognitive domains because of the dependence of these tasks on control processes—that they term "executive attention"—rather than because of their demands on short-term storage capacity (Engle, 2002). Thus, under such a view, age deficits in complex WM span tasks may primarily reflect a decline in executive control abilities (e.g., management of proactive interference, as discussed below under Working Memory), rather than a decline in storage capacity per se. Moreover, a somewhat radical implication of this view is that it is unnecessary, and maybe even not preferable, to utilize WM span tasks at all when measuring age-related cognitive decline in executive control processes. Nevertheless, such age-related declines in executive control may be the main source of impaired performance among older adults in WM tasks.

The recent theoretical developments in WM research just discussed have also prompted a clear shift in the cognitive aging literature, in which there appears to be a greater emphasis on older adult performance in executive control tasks that have no obvious WM storage component, and conversely in focusing primarily on the executive control components of WM tasks. The focus of the current review will reflect this emerging emphasis in the literature, by focusing on a range of domains of executive control that are enjoying new or renewed research attention. In addition to the variety of domains of executive control that are currently being studied in cognitive aging research, there are also a variety of research approaches being used. We next discuss these distinct research traditions in terms of their similarity and differences in analytic strategy and theoretical perspective.

APPROACHES TO THE STUDY OF EXECUTIVE FUNCTION AND WORKING MEMORY

Efforts to understand the effects of aging on executive functions and working memory, and to identify the impact of these effects on other aspects of cognition, have incorporated a variety of analytic strategies. Rather than trying to provide an exhaustive review of the diverse methodologies that have been applied in this domain of research, we have chosen to focus on three general approaches that have had the widest influence. These include *cross-sectional covariation* studies, wherein the central question is whether age-related variation in measures of executive function or working memory covaries with age-related change in other measures of cognition and functional status (Salthouse, Atkinson, & Berish, 2003); studies of *neurocognition*, that seek to define the functional anatomical or biochemical bases of age-related decline in executive functions or working memory (Cabeza, Nyberg, & Park, 2005); and studies utilizing *process analysis* that are designed to elucidate the cognitive processes that give rise to age-related decline on the performance of various measures of executive function or working memory (e.g., Fristoe, Salthouse, & Woodard, 1997).

Studies incorporating the cross-sectional covariation approach have been designed to address two fundamentally different questions: (1) to what degree are age-related differences in various domains of cognition mediated by age-related declines in executive functions or working memory (Royall, Palmer, Chiodo, & Polk, 2004; Salthouse, Mitchell, Skovronek, & Babcock, 1989); (2) what types of processes account for age-related differences in measures of executive function or working memory (Salthouse, 2005b). Early work related to the first question was designed to determine whether there was in fact a relationship between measures of executive function and measures of cognition (Craik, Morris, Morris, & Loewen, 1990; Parkin & Walter, 1992). Following these early findings, later work using mediated regression, growth curve analysis, and structural equation modeling has demonstrated that age-related declines in episodic memory, activities of daily living, and other measures are mediated by individual differences in executive functions (Royall et al., 2004; Salthouse et al., 2003; Troyer, Graves, & Cullum, 1994).

Probably the most influential proponent of the cross-sectional covariation approach has been Salthouse, who has addressed both of these questions using a variety of analytic methods, most recently including structural equation modeling (Salthouse, 2000; Salthouse et al., 2003). As Salthouse suggests, the strength of the cross-sectional covariation approach is that it typically involves psychometrically robust design features, such as the characterization of the relative amount of age-related variance captured by a particular construct (e.g., executive function) in relationship to other competing constructs (e.g., perceptual speed, reasoning), and the extent to which a particular construct can account for age-related variance even after controlling for other factors that are not of theoretical interest. The cross-sectional covariation approach may be limited by a typical reliance on multiple standardized psychometric measures that are potentially less sensitive indices of executive function constructs. Additionally, the approach is vulnerable to statistical misestimation due to the confounding effects of general (rather than covarying) population-level rates of age-related change (Hofer & Sliwinski, 2001). Finally, as discussed below, the psychometric-based measurement approach of individual difference analyses is somewhat in tension with the process-based approach, which aims to fractionate executive control measures into those which most selectively and sensitively index the constructs and mechanisms of age-related cognitive change (Salthouse, 2006).

The neurocognitive approach can be seen as evolving from two lines of scientific inquiry. The first is rooted in neuropsychology and is characterized by incorporation of experimental tasks widely used in the experimental neuropsychological literature (e.g., Wisconsin Card Sorting Test (WCST), self-ordered pointing (SOPT), trail making, verbal fluency, etc.) to determine what type of neuropsychological profile best characterizes the performance of older adults. Out of this work a fairly clear consensus has arisen that the effects of aging are somewhat greater on cognitive processes supported by the prefrontal cortex (PFC) than on cognitive processes more heavily dependent on posterior cortex (Hartley, 1993; Moscovitch, 1992; West, 1996). More recent work has focused on further distinctions in cognitive aging that can be inferred from differing cognitive profiles associated with different types of frontal lesions (e.g., anterior vs. posterior, left vs. right, lateral vs. medial). For example, there has been some recent suggestion that older adults' cognitive deficits correspond better to a neuropsychological profile associated with lateral vs. medial frontal damage (MacPherson, Phillips, & Della Sala, 2002). A strength of this approach is that it enables a researcher to pick tasks on the basis of evidence that the tasks are dependent on the integrity of particular brain regions. On the other hand, one limitation is that many of the tasks in current usage have reasonably high sensitivity, but not great selectivity, such that behavioral impairments are associated with damage to a number of brain regions and systems. For instance, poor performance on the WCST, which is often associated with damage to the PFC (Demakis, 2003; Stuss et al., 2000), is not always differentially diagnostic of frontal versus posterior pathology (Anderson, Damasio, Jones, & Tranel, 1991).

The second trend in neurocognitive research involves directly assaying the neurobiological effects of aging in the human brain using noninvasive methods. In this approach the goal is to determine the extent to which age-related neurobiological changes can be tightly linked to cognitive changes. One common method is to examine correlations between cognitive function and neuroanatomical or neurochemical markers that are sensitive to age. For example, anatomical brain-imaging studies have demonstrated that declines in gray matter volume in prefrontal cortex are associated with cognitive impairments in tasks such as the WCST and Tower of Hanoi (Gunning-Dixon & Raz, 2003; Raz, Gunning-Dixon, Head, Dupuis, & Acker, 1998), while studies of neurochemical markers have demonstrated that dopamine receptor binding accounts for most of the age-related variance in tasks such as self-ordered pointing and trail making (Bäckman & Farde, 2005).

Most recently, advances in functional brain imaging have made it possible to directly measure anatomically localized brain activation patterns in older adults that arise during the performance of cognitive tasks, rather than relying on more indirect correlational measures. For example, studies using functional MRI (fMRI) to examine the effects of aging on patterns of neural recruitment associated with working memory and executive functions have revealed some of the most provocative findings to emerge from the literature incorporating the neurocognitive approach (Cabeza, 2002; Reuter-Lorenz & Sylvester, 2005). One strength of this approach is that it has the potential for illuminating whether older adults show the same types of brain–behavior relationships observed in younger adults. Recent findings have suggested that they may not—instead demonstrating patterns of activation that may represent compensation for a reduced ability to meet the demands of cognitively challenging tasks, or alternatively, may reflect an age-related shift in cognitive strategy (Reuter-Lorenz & Sylvester, 2005; Rypma & D'Esposito, 2000).

The final research approach utilizes cognitive task analysis as a means of more narrowly localizing the processes that give rise to age-related differences in paradigms wherein efficient task performance is determined by multiple factors. The WCST represents an excellent example of such a paradigm (Milner, 1963). In this task individuals are required to sort a series of cards into categories defined by the color, number, or form of stimuli presented on the cards based on a rule that must be abstracted from yes/no feedback that is provided by the experimenter following each sort. The pattern of age-related performance differences in the WCST occur in a variety of measures, and thus could be consistent with a number of interpretations regarding cognitive impairment, such as a decline in category abstraction, an increase in the tendency to perseverate on a category once it becomes irrelevant, or a decline in the ability to utilize feedback (Rhodes, 2004). The task analysis approach attempts to determine which explanation may best account for group differences in task performance, through modification of the basic paradigm. For example, this approach has been used very successfully in developmental studies of children performing variants of the WCST (Diamond, 1998; Jacques & Zelazo, 2001). Similarly, in work with older adults, Fristoe et al. (1997) had individuals perform a modified WCST wherein they indicated with a verbal response what category was being applied on the current sort. This allowed the investigators to consider the consistency of participants' expressed intentions and actions, and to examine possible age-related differences in the use of feedback. The findings of this study revealed that the degree of consistency between intention and action was lower in older adults than in younger adults, and that older adults were less likely to maintain a category after positive reinforcement than were younger adults and more likely to maintain a category after negative reinforcement than were younger adults (Fristoe et al., 1997; Hartman, Bolton, & Fehnel, 2001). Furthermore, 77% of the age-related variance in a composite index of task performance was accounted for by controlling for individual differences in feedback usage.

The strength of the task analysis approach is that it provides a means of getting at the core cognitive processes in individual tasks that are associated with age-related decline, such that these processes might be shown to generalize across various different paradigms. Moreover, because this approach respects the maxim that "no task is process pure," researchers adopting it are prompted to search for more sophisticated ways to measure performance in a way that better isolates the process of interest. An example of such measurement approaches are recent trends to using process dissociation analysis and other mathematical modeling methods, such as ex-Gaussian estimation of reaction time distributions, to provide better estimates of the cognitive process of interest (Jennings & Jacoby, 1993; Spieler, 2001). Weaknesses of the task analysis approach are that it may serve to identify processes that are quite task specific and therefore fail to capture a significant portion of age-related variance in cognitive function. Furthermore, by typically focusing on single rather than multiple tasks (in contrast to the cross-sectional covariation approach) the process analysis approach makes it difficult to assess the convergent validity of the cognitive processes under study.

All three of the approaches to cognitive aging research—cross-sectional covariation, neurocognitive, and process analysis—have made invaluable contributions to our understanding of the nature and mechanisms of age-related change in working memory and executive control function. In the next section we describe a theoretical framework that we believe may further help to synthesize the growing literature in this domain, both in terms of what particular executive processes are expected to be impacted with advancing age and, conversely, what processes might be spared.

A THEORETICAL FRAMEWORK FOR UNDERSTANDING AGE-RELATED CHANGES IN EXECUTIVE CONTROL

The theoretical framework that has motivated much of our recent work, and around which we have structured this review, is known as the goal maintenance account. This account is based on a synthesis of findings arising from both young adult and aging research using the three research approaches described above. The first set of findings arises from process-based and individual differences research, and suggests that a common feature of many executive control tasks is that they rely on internal representations of task-set or behavioral goals. This is clearly the case in well-established paradigms such as the Stroop task, WCST, and dual-task coordination. Moreover, individual differences studies have demonstrated that the links between working memory capacity, general fluid intelligence, and performance on a wide range of executive control tasks appear to be mediated by the construct of "executive attention," which is the component present in complex WM span tasks that is not mediated by short-term memory storage (Engle, Tuholski, Laughlin, & Conway, 1999; Kane & Engle, 2002). It is important to note that executive attention, as conceived by Engle, Kane and colleagues, is a latent construct rather than a specific observable measure of task performance. This conception is very consistent with the process analysis perspective since it suggests that core executive processes might not map in a straightforward one-to-one way to particular measures of performance in executive task paradigms. Nevertheless, Engle, Kane, and colleagues suggest that the executive attention component is most strongly taxed in complex WM tasks when there is a high potential for proactive interference from previous trials (Kane & Engle, 2000). These interference effects can be best avoided by actively maintaining only goal-relevant information in WM. Thus, executive attention refers to the ability to actively maintain goals and to use goal maintenance to suppress contextually inappropriate response tendencies. Conversely, failures of executive attention can be thought of as instances of "goal neglect" (Kane & Engle, 2003).

This "goal neglect" view of executive control impairment is similar to the one arising out of the experimental literature on PFC function, in which damage to this brain region seems to commonly produce an executive control impairment that is also well characterized as goal neglect (Duncan, Emslie, Williams, Johnson, & Freer, 1996). Indeed, Duncan, like Engle and colleagues, has suggested that reduced efficacy of lateral PFC function is a common mechanism that underlies the increased tendency towards goal neglect in frontal patients and the less severe goal neglect problems that are faced by healthy individuals with lower levels of general fluid intelligence (Duncan, 1995). The third perspective arises out of neuropsychologically and neurobiologically based aging research and, as described in the previous section, emphasizes the similarity of neuropsychological profile between healthy older adults and patients with damage to the frontal lobes (Hartley, 1993; Moscovitch & Winocur, 1992; West, 1996). This neuropsychological similarity has been confirmed by a rapidly growing neurobiological literature demonstrating that aging is marked by preferential changes to prefrontal cortex structure and physiology (Cabeza et al., 2005). These changes involve reductions in gray and white matter volume, neuronal density, metabolic activity, and neurochemical modulation, particularly by the neurotransmitter dopamine (Raz, 2000).

The goal maintenance theory of PFC function nicely synthesizes these three perspectives on cognitive aging and executive control[1] (Braver & Barch, 2002; Braver, Cohen, & Barch, 2002). According to this theory, lateral PFC plays a critical role in control functions because of three interrelated properties of this region (Braver et al., 2002; Miller & Cohen, 2001): (1) the representational coding scheme of lateral PFC is one that conveys information about the prior temporal context and/or internal behavioral

---

[1]This framework is also known variously as the context processing (Braver et al., 2001) and guided activation theory (Miller & Cohen, 2001), but for purposes of this chapter we will refer to it as goal maintenance theory.

goals (i.e., the desired outcomes of action and perception); (2) these representations can be actively maintained over time in a highly accessible form (i.e., storage of information via sustained neuronal activity patterns); (3) the output of this region is an activation signal that biases the flow of ongoing processing in other brain regions, such as those responsible for perception, action selection, memory retrieval, and emotional evaluation. Additionally, in goal maintenance theory the neurotransmitter dopamine plays a key modulatory role over lateral PFC function by regulating the way that goal representations are maintained and updated. Specifically, dopamine activation may serve to regulate the access of afferent inputs to lateral PFC, thus serving the function of both insulating actively maintained goal information from the disruptive effects of noise during intervals when such information needs to be sustained, while at the same time allowing for appropriate updating of goal information when the situation dictates (Braver & Barch, 2002; Braver & Cohen, 2000).

According to goal maintenance theory, a fundamental function of lateral PFC is to serve as a source of cognitive control, utilizing actively maintained goal representations as a stable top-down bias exerted on posterior and subcortical brain systems engaged in task-specific processing. The top-down biasing role of PFC is a critical one, that serves to modulate the outcome of competition for processing in local task-specific networks, similar to the well-established biased competition account of attentional control put forward by Desimone and Duncan (1995). When there is a high degree of competition in task-specific pathways, active goal representations can serve as a critical attentional template that enables the most goal-relevant of different potential perceptual targets or dimensions to have priority in processing. Additionally, having an active goal representation regarding the desired targets of action is critical under situations when current internal states or environmental conditions are associated with dominant, but contextually inappropriate (i.e., goal-incongruent), action tendencies. The Stroop task provides an elegant example of both types of situation. In the Stroop there are both multiple perceptual dimensions that compete for attention (i.e., word and color) as well as a dominant but inappropriate response tendency to read the name of the word. In such a situation, representations of task-context or behavioral goals can serve to appropriately bias the attention and response selection systems by enhancing color-naming processes and suppressing and inhibiting word-reading processes and the action tendencies associated with them.

Goal maintenance theory also provides a unique and unifying view of how lateral PFC function contributes to working memory. The theory diverges from the classic Baddeley model by suggesting that active maintenance is a critical, "embedded" characteristic of a cognitive control mechanism, rather than postulating a strict segregation of storage and control functions (although recent formulations of the Baddeley model have somewhat revised this view, e.g., Baddeley, 2003). Thus, lateral PFC representations can be viewed as the subset of representations within working memory that are specifically engaged in the service of cognitive control. In contrast, the theory also makes clear that activation of lateral PFC is not obligatory for maintenance of information in working memory tasks, as there may be other available mechanisms that can enable short-term storage, for example, the phonological-articulatory rehearsal mechanisms typically ascribed to the phonological loop. Instead, the role of PFC-mediated goal representations in working memory tasks may be to help transform actively maintained representations into a plan for how to optimally prepare and respond to upcoming stimuli. For example, in a typical working memory task like the Sternberg item recognition paradigm (Sternberg, 1966), a goal representation may take the items "A, B" presented as a memory set, and transform this information into a representation of the form "if the probe item is A or B, press the target button, otherwise press the nontarget button." By activating and then maintaining such goal representations over the delay interval the cognitive system can optimally prepare for the upcoming probe. Nevertheless, it is clear that whereas this process of goal representation can optimize performance in many working memory tasks, it is not necessary for reasonably successful performance. As such, the theory makes clear that the extent to which working memory tasks depend upon the efficacy of the lateral PFC function may be highly variable and dependent on many task factors.

Finally, goal maintenance theory also clarifies the relationship between attention, working memory, and inhibition, and the role of lateral PFC in these domains. In particular, whereas performance in working memory tasks may be influenced by the degree to which the biasing effects of goal representations can be maintained over time, tasks requiring attentional or inhibitory control may depend upon goal representations to selectively enhance the processing of task-relevant perceptual dimensions and/or suppress the processing of task-irrelevant perceptual dimensions or action tendencies. Importantly, in situations of behavioral inhibition, the top-down biasing effects of goal representations may have a suppressive effect through indirect mechanisms. This is again in accord with biased competition theory (Desimone & Duncan, 1995), which suggests that there is local competition for representation at all levels of the pathway from sensation to action and that this local competition takes the form of mutually inhibitory interactions. Thus, a source of top-down excitatory bias arising from lateral PFC goal representations can alter the outcome of such competitions in favor of goal-relevant percepts and actions, even when goal-irrelevant competitors may have been otherwise dominant.

The goal maintenance account has been applied to the study of cognitive aging, by postulating that age-related declines in lateral PFC and dopamine function result in a specific impairment in the ability of older adults to actively represent and maintain goal information over time (Braver & Barch, 2002; Braver et al., 2001). Because of the role of such goal information in working memory, attention, and inhibition, an impairment in goal representation and maintenance is predicted to produce specific decrements in cognitive task situations that are most demanding of such goal maintenance functions. In particular, according to the goal mainten-ance account as described above, older adults should show the most dif-ficulty under situations in which: (a) goal representations need to be maintained over time in working memory, to bias task-appropriate responding; (b) goal representations are needed as an attentional template to enhance processing of otherwise weak perceptual features or actions; and (c) goal representations must be used as a top-down bias to suppress or inhibit otherwise dominant, but goal-incongruent perceptual features or dimension or response tendencies. As such, the model makes strong testable predictions regarding the nature of executive control and work-ing memory impairments in cognitive aging. Nevertheless, a practical difficulty, which we will return to at the conclusion of the chapter, is that of determining, purely through task analysis, whether a particular execu-tive control paradigm actually satisfies these conditions.

Over the last decade, research has accelerated in a number of relevant areas that provide a growing empirical database from which to evaluate the explanatory success of the goal maintenance account. In the following sections, we review and examine this database, focusing on the domains of working memory, strategic control of memory, response inhibition, task management, and context processing. In the final section of the review, we discuss recent theoretical and empirical developments in understanding age-related changes in executive control function, focus-ing on recent attempts to further explicate and fractionate components and dimensions of executive control that are not within the primary scope of the standard goal maintenance account.

WORKING MEMORY

Studies on the effects of aging on short-term and working memory have a rich tradition in the cognitive aging literature. A host of the salient findings in this area of inquiry have been expertly reviewed in previous editions of this handbook (Craik & Jennings, 1992; Zacks et al., 2000). Investigations of the effects of aging on short-term storage have sought to determine whether age-related declines might be greater for primary or secondary memory and whether the effects of aging are greater on processing or storage aspects of working memory in the verbal or spatial domain. As described earlier, the outcomes of recent population-based and meta-analytic studies reveal that there are several unresolved issues related to these questions. In particular, the results of these studies call into question the degree to which deficits in short-term storage per se, as measured by passive span tasks (e.g., forward digit span), are a prominent feature of age-related working memory decline. Conversely, the working memory tasks that do show the most robust age differences are the complex span tasks, which require the integration of short-term storage with executive control processes (e.g., manipulation of stored content as in backward digit span, or coordination with other complex cognitive computations such as mental arithmetic in operation span; Bopp & Verhaeghen, 2005; Myerson, Emery, White, & Hale, 2003). Consequently, current research on aging in working memory has tended to focus on the executive control components of working memory tasks as a primary source of age differences.

We examine evidence from three lines of research emerging from the literature in the last several years that illustrate recent developments in our understanding of the effect of aging on working memory in terms of the role of executive processes. Importantly, many of the relevant findings are anticipated by goal maintenance theory. These include: (a) increased susceptibility to interference as a critical factor in understanding age-related differences in working memory (Lustig, May, & Hasher, 2001); (b) age-related declines in the ability to control the focus of attention within working memory (Oberauer, 2001); and (c) strong age-related memory impairments occurring in task conditions that require the binding of arbitrary stimulus features together in working memory (Chalfonte & Johnson, 1996).

The idea that aging is associated with an increased susceptibility to proactive and retroactive interference has a long history in the cognitive aging literature, but has most recently been explored as an account of age-related declines in the efficiency of working memory (Bowles & Salthouse, 2003; Hasher, Chung, May, & Foong, 2002; Hedden & Park, 2001; Hedden & Park, 2003; May, Hasher, & Kane, 1999; Oberauer & Kliegl, 2001). The impact of increased susceptibility to proactive interference in older adults has been examined using a variety of methodologies. An elegant demonstration of the influence of proactive interference on age-related differences in working memory was reported in a study utilizing standard measures of simple and complex span (May, et al., 1999a). The fundamental logic incorporated in the study was that there is typically a confound between memory load and proactive interference in the typical administration of span tasks, in that the total amount of information processed across the task increases with list length. This is because standard testing begins with short list lengths and then moves to longer list lengths. To break this confound, May et al. (1999a) administered the reading span and backward digit span tasks in descending order, thereby minimizing proactive interference at the longest list lengths. Across two experiments, ascending administration revealed the typical pattern of age-related differences. In contrast, descending administration served to eliminate age-related differences in these span tasks (Lustig et al., 2001; May, Zacks, Hasher, & Multhaup, 1999b). In a replication of the original finding, Lustig et al. (2001) demonstrated that the relationship between working memory span and prose recall was eliminated in older adults, but not younger adults, with descending administration of list length. Other work reveals a potential neural locus for the age-related increase in the susceptibility to proactive interference in working memory (Jonides, Marshuetz, Smith, Reuter-Lorenz, Koeppe, & Hartley, 2000). In this study an increase in proactive interference was associated with a decline in the efficiency with which older adults recruited left lateral prefrontal cortex. Taken together these results are fully consistent with the idea that older adults' reduced ability to maintain goal representations in working memory leads to a greater vulnerability to proactive interference effects, and that such effects may strongly contribute to the observed age-related reductions in working memory capacity on complex span tasks.

Data from studies utilizing the cross-sectional covariation approach (McCabe & Hartman, 2003; Salthouse, 1992, 1994) might also provide indirect evidence for age-related increases in the influence of interference on working memory. For instance, one recent study found that age-related variance in reading span was accounted for by variance in speed of processing and simple word span (McCabe & Hartman, 2003). Based on the findings presented in the previous paragraph it could be assumed that proactive interference (unless properly controlled) represents one source of age-related variance in simple word span, thereby contributing to the relationship between reading span and word span (Lustig et al., 2001). The relationship between speed of processing and interference may be less obvious until one considers recent work demonstrating that an increased susceptibility to distraction contributes to age-related differences in commonly used measures of speed of processing (Lustig, Hasher, & Tonev, 2006). Given these findings, it seems possible that shared age-related variance in speed of processing, simple span, and complex span may arise from an increased susceptibility to interference and distraction (Hasher & Zacks, 1988). Nevertheless, the demonstration that susceptibility to interference and distraction/inhibition may reflect somewhat distinct constructs (Friedman & Miyake, 2004) suggests that further research is required in order to provide a full account of the influence of an age-related increase in susceptibility to interference on working memory.

The embedded process model of working memory (Cowan, 1988, 1995, 1999) has served as the backdrop for a number of studies examining the effects of aging in this domain. Within this model the contents of working memory reflect both currently activated long-term memory representations as well as information that is in the more narrow focus of attention (Cowan, 1999). The focus of attention serves as a region of direct access that represents the information most relevant to the immediate processing demands of the current task (Oberauer, 2002). Whereas activated long-term memory is thought to be time limited rather than capacity limited, the focus of attention is thought to be severely capacity limited (but not time limited), and may have a capacity of only a single conceptual unit (Cowan, 1999; McElree, 2001). Thus, the conceptualization of the focus of attention in working memory as postulated by the embedded process model seems very close to the conceptualization of actively maintained goal representations within the goal maintenance account.

Recent studies have sought to characterize the effects of aging on component processes that are thought to underlie efficient working memory in the embedded process model. Various studies have demonstrated that aging is associated with a decline in efficiency with which individuals can refresh (Johnson, Mitchell, Raye, & Greene, 2004; Johnson, Reeder, Raye, & Mitchell, 2002) or update (Verhaeghen & Basak, 2005) the focus of attention in addition to an accelerated loss of accessibility to the contents of activated long-term memory (Verhaeghen & Basak, 2005). The most comprehensive investigation of the effects of aging within the context of the embedded process model is represented in a series of studies conducted by Oberauer and colleagues (Oberauer, 2001, 2005b; Oberauer, Demmrich, Mayr, & Kliegl, 2001). This line of research has revealed age-related equivalence in relation to a number of variables including the effect of variation in memory load within the activated portion of long-term memory (Oberauer et al., 2001), the time required to remove information from the focus of attention (Oberauer, 2001), and the time required to move information from activated long-term memory back into the focus of attention (Oberauer, 2005b). In contrast, other processes reveal quite dramatic age-related differences. Older adults require a much greater amount of time to access information in the activated portion of long-term memory than do younger adults, and also show a diminished likelihood of successfully switching information into the focus of attention (Oberauer et al., 2001; Verhaeghen, Cerella, Bopp, & Basak, 2005). The influence of recently activated but task irrelevant information also appears to be greater for older than younger adults. For instance, older adults require significantly more time to reject a lure from a task irrelevant memory set in short-term recognition paradigms (e.g., the Sternberg task) than do younger adults (Oberauer, 2001, 2005a).

Together, the findings of this line of research demonstrate that the effects of aging can be localized to a limited set of working memory processes within the context of the embedded process model, rather than there being a general or pervasive effect of aging on working memory processes. Specifically, these deficits may relate to the ability to utilize the focus of attention when required, and to utilize this mechanism as a means of suppressing interference from activated items outside the focus. Likewise, the goal maintenance account suggests that aging will primarily affect working memory processes dependent upon active goal representation and maintenance and the utilization of such mechanisms in an attentional and inhibitory fashion, rather than basic short-term storage per se.

The binding deficit hypothesis of aging is predicated on the idea that older adults exhibit a specific disruption in the ability to bind together the various elements of a representation within working memory, such that the bound representation can be stored as a durable memory trace (Chalfonte & Johnson, 1996; Mitchell, Johnson, Raye, Mather, & D'Esposito, 2000b). Support for this hypothesis has been provided in a number of studies wherein the investigators contrasted the effects of aging on memory for the individual features of a representation (e.g., location, color, identity) with memory for conjunctions of features (e.g., location+identity). The primary finding from studies designed to assess the efficacy of the binding hypothesis is that there are typically not age-related differences when individuals encode, and are tested on, information related to the specific features of a stimulus. Instead, age-related differences are observed when memory is assessed for conjunctions of features, with these differences expressed as a decrease in target discrimination and an increase in response time to reject conjunction lures (Chalfonte & Johnson, 1996). The age-related decline in the efficiency of binding is observed when encoding is either incidental or intentional, with the deficit being somewhat greater with intentional encoding (Chalfonte & Johnson, 1996; Mitchell, et al., 2000b). Moreover, the effect is not the result of differences in memory load for feature and conjunction conditions (Mitchell et al., 2000). Neuroimaging studies have suggested that the age-related decline in the efficiency of binding in working memory is associated with a failure on the part of older adults to recruit left anterior hippocampus and right rostral prefrontal cortex in feature conjunction relative to single feature encoding conditions (Mitchell, Johnson, Raye, & D'Esposito, 2000a). The linkage of age-related binding changes to goal representation and maintenance has not been made directly, but a plausible interpretation is that binding depends on the top-down biasing effects of goal representations in lateral prefrontal cortex that constrain how different features are integrated together as a memory trace (i.e., in the hippocampus). If this goal-based top-down biasing process is impaired in older adults, then feature binding will not be constrained in a goal-directed manner, which should impair subsequent retrieval. Moreover, as discussed at the end of the chapter, binding operations may be similar to the concept of integration, and thus might represent a distinct executive control process impacted by aging.

STRATEGIC CONTROL OF MEMORY

The idea that control processes play an important role in efficient memory is one that has a rich history in the cognitive aging literature (Craik & Jennings, 1992; Hasher & Zacks, 1979). Many of the findings related to this issue have been thoroughly reviewed in chapters in earlier editions of this volume (Moscovitch & Winocur, 1992; Prull, Gabrieli, & Bunge, 2000; Zacks et al., 2000). In this section, we review recent work examining how distinct forms of memory disruption in older adults might preferentially reflect the contribution of age-related declines in executive processes associated with goal maintenance. We focus on work in both episodic and prospective memory. Whereas episodic memory refers to the encoding and retrieval of items and associations, prospective memory refers to the formation, storage, retrieval, and implementation of goals and intentions (see also McDaniel, Jacoby, & Einstein, chapter 6).

Episodic Memory

Some of the key findings from the older literature are that the effects of age are typically increased when: retrieval of specific contextual details is required relative to when retrieval is limited to item level information (Spencer & Raz, 1995); episodic memory is probed with free recall rather than recognition (Craik & Jennings, 1992); and when the processing demands of retrieval are increased (Anderson, Craik, & Naveh-Benjamin, 1998). In the present review we highlight evidence from three more recent lines of research that have focused on the specific contributions of frontal lobe function to episodic memory in older adults (Glisky, Polster, & Routhieaux, 1995), goal neglect vs. recollection in older adult retrieval deficits (Jacoby, Bishara, Hessels, & Toth, 2005), and age-related binding deficits in episodic as well as working memory (Mitchell et al., 2000b; Naveh-Benjamin, 2000).

The first line of research examines the degree to which individual differences in measures of executive or frontal lobe function account for age-related differences in episodic memory. One of the more compelling examples of research in this line of inquiry is found in the work of Elizabeth Glisky and colleagues (Davidson & Glisky, 2002; Glisky et al., 1995). In these studies, individual differences in frontal lobe status (as measured by a standard neuropsychological battery) were found to account for age-related differences in source memory and recollection, but be largely unrelated to memory for item level information or familiarity. Other work in this line of research demonstrated an interaction between the effects of divided attention, and individual differences in frontal (executive) and medial temporal lobe function that seems consistent with goal maintenance theory. Specifically, individuals with low frontal function but high medial temporal function recalled a significant number of additional items once dual task demands were removed, after performing the initial recall under divided attention (Fernandes, Davidson, Glisky, & Moscovitch, 2004). This finding leads to the suggestion that these individuals may have been unable to maintain controlled retrieval processes in the face of divided attention even though the items were clearly accessible in memory. The influence of executive function also extends to the effects of aging on false memories in addition to veridical memory (Butler, McDaniel, Dornburg, Price, & Roediger, 2004). In the Butler et al. (2004) study, older adults that showed high levels of frontal function (using the Glisky battery) demonstrated levels of false recall comparable with younger adults in a Deese Roediger McDermott (DRM) paradigm. However, low frontal adults showed significantly increased levels of false recall.

The work of Larry Jacoby and colleagues provides a second line of research demonstrating the contribution of age-related declines in executive function to poor episodic memory in older adults (Hay & Jacoby, 1999; Jennings & Jacoby, 1993, 2003). Studies by this group have consistently demonstrated that disruptions of episodic memory in older adults arise from age-related declines in recollection or controlled memory processes. Conversely, aging has relatively little if any effect on more automatic aspects of episodic memory, including familiarity and accessibility bias. While compelling in demonstrating a reliable effect of aging on controlled processes underlying episodic memory, the early work of this group does not directly support the goal maintenance theory. However, findings from a more recent study do converge with the idea that a disruption of goal maintenance may contribute to age-related declines in episodic memory (Jacoby et al., 2005). In this study the investigators sought to examine predictions related to disruptions of goal maintenance and recollection failure in a cued recall task involving a high degree of proactive interference due to misleading primes. Under such task conditions, disruptions of episodic memory can result either from capture errors (representing goal neglect) where a primed but irrelevant response is selected, or from a failure of recollection. Across a series of experiments designed to test a formal multinomial model, Jacoby et al. (2005) demonstrated that the responses of older adults were much more likely to reflect capture errors than those of younger adults, revealing a clear disruption of goal maintenance.

The third line of research follows from the binding deficit account of age-related declines in working memory that was discussed above (Mitchell et al., 2000b). One of the fundamental predictions derived from this hypothesis is that the reduced ability of older adults to bind elements of a representation in working memory should lead to age-related differences in other domains of cognition including episodic memory (Mitchell et al., 2000b). This prediction has been realized in the associative deficit hypothesis of aging, that postulates disruptions of episodic memory in older adults as primarily due to declines in the ability to form novel associations between elements of a representation (Naveh-Benjamin, 2000; Naveh-Benjamin, Hussain, Guez, & Bar-On, 2003). Across a series of studies Naveh-Benjamin and colleagues have observed robust age-related declines in the ability to retrieve associative information in the context of no or minimal declines in the ability to retrieve item information (Naveh-Benjamin, 2000; Naveh-Benjamin, Guez, Kilb, & Reedy, 2004; Naveh-Benjamin et al., 2003). A potential neural basis of the age-related decline in associative binding was explored in a recent computational modeling study (Li, Naveh-Benjamin, & Lindenberger, 2005). In this study, reducing the gain parameter of model units (which reduced the differentiation of internal representations in response to fine gradations in inputs) produced an associative memory deficit similar to that reported by Naveh-Benjamin (2000). The manipulation of the gain parameter to model age-related differences in associative memory is fundamentally similar to work directly related to goal maintenance theory, in which gain-related disruptions of the dopamine system in prefrontal cortex are the source of goal-representation and maintenance deficits that occur in aging (Braver et al., 2001) and psychopathology (Braver, Barch, & Cohen, 1999). As such, the associative deficit and related binding hypotheses are very compatible with the idea that age-related deficits in these functions are due to reduced distinctiveness in prefrontal goal representations that are needed to appropriately structure associative traces in memory systems such as the hippocampus.

Prospective Memory

Prospective memory situations arise when goals and intentions are not immediately attainable in the environment, and thus must be stored in memory for later retrieval. Some examples include delivering a message to a colleague that one will see at a meeting later in the day, and remembering to check food in the oven in 30 minutes. These examples demonstrate the major classes of prospective memory (i.e., event based and time based; Brandimonte, Einstein, & McDaniel, 1996; Shum, Valentine, & Cutmore, 1999) that have been considered in empirical studies, although the greatest emphasis has been related to the processes underlying event-based prospective memory. The prominent role of goal representations in prospective memory tasks suggests that this would be a domain strongly sensitive to age-related impairments, according to the goal maintenance account. Indeed, much of the early experimental research on prospective memory was done in the context of cognitive aging (Dobbs & Rule, 1987; Einstein & McDaniel, 1990). Surprisingly, however, early findings seemed to suggest—contrary to the goal maintenance account—that prospective memory may be somewhat immune to the effect of aging (Einstein & McDaniel, 1990; Moscovitch, 1982). In the last decade, research on prospective memory has greatly increased, leading to a substantial rise in the number of published studies on the topic. When taken together, this larger literature has clearly revealed a pronounced age-related deficit in the efficiency of prospective memory, as demonstrated by a recent comprehensive meta-analysis (Henry, MacLeod, Phillips, & Crawford, 2004).

A fundamental conceptual distinction in the prospective memory literature is that the realization of delayed intentions is supported by both prospective and retrospective components (McDaniel & Einstein, 1992). The prospective component is thought to reflect processes that underlie the detection or recognition of a prospective cue when the relevant stimulus is encountered in the environment or the appropriate time arrives. In contrast, the retrospective component is thought to reflect processes that underlie the retrieval of the relevant intention from memory. This basic distinction represents the foundation of a number of theories designed to account for the processes underlying prospective memory. For instance, within the "noticing plus search" and more recently "discrepancy attribution and search theories," the prospective component of prospective memory is thought to be supported by processes that are relatively automatic or spontaneous, while the retrospective component is thought to be supported by relatively more controlled or attention-demanding processes (Einstein & McDaniel, 1996; Einstein et al., 2005; McDaniel, Guynn, Einstein, & Breneiser, 2004). This account is directly opposite to the one put forward in strategic monitoring views of prospective memory (Guynn, 2003; Smith, 2003; Smith & Bayen, 2004), which postulates that the prospective component is supported by processes that require the allocation of working memory capacity or controlled attention to support the detection of prospective memory cues. Conversely, in this account the processes underlying the retrospective component may (Smith & Bayen, 2004) or may not (West, Bowry, & Krompinger, 2006) require the allocation of working memory capacity.

This distinction between prospective and retrospective components of prospective memory has served as the basis for a number of studies designed to examine the effects of aging on the two components. Much of this research was motivated by the consistent finding that age-related differences in prospective memory persist even when variation in the ability to explicitly recall the demands of the prospective memory task at the end of the testing session is taken into account (Salthouse, Berish, & Siedlecki, 2004; West & Craik, 2001). One means of examining the effects of aging on the different components of prospective memory is to use experimental manipulations that involve multiple prospective cue–intention pairings (Mäntylä, 1994). This enables a determination of whether prospective memory errors result from failures of cue detection (i.e., prospective cues are ignored in favor of a primary ongoing task response; *the prospective component*) or failures of intention retrieval (i.e., prospective cues elicit the wrong prospective response or individuals are unable to recall the intention after detecting the prospective cue; *the retrospective component*, West & Craik, 2001). Two important findings have emerged from studies including multiple prospective cue–intention associations. First, it is clear that dissociable factors underlie the prospective and retrospective components of prospective memory (Cohen, West, & Craik, 2001; West & Craik, 2001). Second, across these studies the effects of aging have been consistently greater on the prospective component than on the retrospective component (West & Craik, 2001), even when the retrospective demands of the task are relatively high (Cohen et al., 2001). Evidence from a recent study incorporating a mathematical model of the processes underlying prospective memory is consistent with these findings (Smith & Bayen, 2006). In this study, Smith and Bayen demonstrated that older adults were less likely to recruit preparatory attentional processes that support the detection of prospective cues than were younger adults, and that aging had little if any effect on retrospective processes underlying prospective memory.

The finding that older adults are less likely than younger adults to recruit the preparatory attentional processes that underlie the prospective component of prospective memory (Smith & Bayen, 2006; West & Bowry, 2005) leads to the prediction that age-related declines in executive functions or working memory capacity may account for disruptions of prospective memory observed in older adults. The efficacy of this prediction has been tested in studies using two methodologies. One approach has been to examine the effects of dividing attention or increasing the working memory demands of the ongoing activity on the relationship between aging and prospective memory. The second approach has been to determine whether or not individual differences in measures of working memory capacity or executive functions account for age-related variance in prospective memory.

Evidence for the effects of divided attention and variation in the ongoing task demands on the effect of aging on prospective memory is somewhat mixed in existing studies. In the typical prospective memory paradigm where the intention can be realized as soon as the prospective cue is detected, Einstein, McDaniel, and colleagues have demonstrated that the effects of divided attention can in some instances be similar for older and younger adults, and in other instances may be greater in magnitude for older than younger adults (Einstein, McDaniel, Manzi, Cochran, & Baker, 2000; Einstein, Smith, McDaniel, & Shaw, 1997). Logie, Maylor, Della Sala, & Smith (2004) report data suggesting a greater effect of divided attention in older adults than in younger adults. Other data indicate that the impact of divided attention on prospective memory in older adults may be particularly pronounced when individuals are required to actively maintain the intention over a short delay before it can be realized (Einstein et al., 2000; McDaniel, Einstein, Stout, & Morgan, 2003), or when the need for output monitoring is introduced into the task (Marsh, Hicks, Cook, & Mayhorn, 2007). Also, divided attention may serve to increase the number of false prospective responses when output monitoring is required (Einstein, McDaniel, Smith, & Shaw, 1998). Like studies examining the influence of divided attention, work considering the effect of varying the working memory demands of the ongoing activity on age-related differences in prospective memory has produced mixed results. In a study where the working memory demands of the ongoing activity varied between two and three items, there was a tendency for the effects of aging on prospective memory to increase with memory load (Kidder, Park, Hertzog, & Morrell, 1997).

Evidence from a number of studies indicates that age-related differences in working memory capacity and executive functions partially mediate the effects of aging on prospective memory (McDaniel, Glisky, Rubin, Guynn, & Routhieaux, 1999). Across studies, measures of these constructs have accounted for 30% to 100% of the age-related variance in prospective memory (Kliegel, Martin, & Moor, 2003; Salthouse et al., 2004; West & Craik, 2001). The degree of mediation appears to be sensitive to the demands of the prospective memory task (Martin, Kliegel, & McDaniel, 2003) and whether or not realization of the intention follows detection of the prospective cue or must be postponed for some period of time (Einstein et al., 2000). Based on the available evidence it seems likely that working memory capacity and executive functions influence the prospective rather than retrospective component of prospective memory, although this idea has not been formally tested.

The evidence reviewed in the previous paragraphs clearly demonstrates that there are robust age-related declines in the efficiency of the processes underlying successful prospective memory, and that these covary with individual differences in working memory capacity and executive functions. These findings motivate the question of whether age-related differences in prospective memory might be accounted for within the goal maintenance theory. Three sets of findings appear to offer an affirmative answer to this question. The first set of findings is related to the transient nature of failures of prospective memory, reflecting the tendency for the same or a similar prospective memory cue to variably elicit a prospective response over the course of task performance. Maylor (1993, 1998) sought to quantify this phenomenon by estimating the probability of forgetting (i.e., the probability of a prospective miss following a prospective hit) and recovery (i.e., the probability of a prospective hit following a prospective miss). For individuals who could recall the requirements of the prospective memory task, Maylor found that forgetting was more frequent in older than in younger adults and that recovery was less frequent in older than in younger adults. This finding could be seen as consistent with goal maintenance theory if one assumes that the fidelity of the prospective cue–intention association becomes degraded over time, thereby leading to instances of forgetting. Thus, transient lapses in prospective memory represent a form of goal neglect, due to age-related impairments in the ability to keep the prospective goal maintained at a high level of accessibility (Vogels, Dekker, Brouwer, & de Jong, 2002; West & Craik, 1999).

A second set of findings is related to the increased tendency of older adults to make false alarms to prospective memory lures (i.e., stimuli that are perceptually similar to prospective cues but require an ongoing activity response) relative to younger adults (Vogels et al., 2002; West & Covell, 2001; West & Craik, 1999). Similar to the increased rate of forgetting in older adults, this finding is consistent with the idea that an age-related impairment in goal representation and maintenance results in a degraded representation of the prospective cue–intention association, leading to prospective false alarms. Finally, the third finding that age-related differences in prospective memory are particularly pronounced when individuals are required to actively maintain the intention for as little as 5 seconds before it can be realized (Einstein et al., 2000; McDaniel et al., 2003) is consistent with other evidence indicating that older adults have difficulty maintaining goal-related contextual information for brief periods of time in order to guide task performance (Braver et al., 2001; Braver, Satpute, Rush, Racine, & Barch, 2005).

INHIBITION OF PREPOTENT RESPONSES

The ability to inhibit a prepotent response tendency has been recognized as an important executive function in a variety of domains including neuropsychology (Luria, 1966), developmental psychology (Bjorklund & Harnishfeger, 1995; Hasher & Zacks, 1988), and the study of individual differences (Engle, Conway, Tuholski, & Shisler, 1995; Kane & Engle, 2003). A number of structurally diverse tasks have been used to examine the factors that influence the inhibition of prepotent responses. However, these paradigms all possess the common feature that successful task performance requires suppressing a dominant response tendency that is incongruent with current internally represented goals, in order to produce an alternative response that is goal congruent, but weaker in strength. In the current review we consider evidence from three paradigms (Stroop task, antisaccade task, and stop-signal task) wherein age-related differences in the ability to inhibit a prepotent response tendency have been observed, with special attention given to whether or not the extant pattern of age-related differences is consistent with predictions derived from goal maintenance theory.

The Stroop task (Stroop, 1935) is the best-known of a larger class of Stimulus–Stimulus/Stimulus–Response compatibility tasks (Kornblum, 1992), and has been used extensively in the aging literature to examine response inhibition. The classic finding of interference in naming the color of incongruent color words (i.e., RED presented in blue) relative to color naming when stimuli are congruent (i.e., RED presented in red) or neutral (i.e., do not contain a color word, such as %%% presented in red) has been repeatedly found to be enhanced in older adults (Verhaeghen & De Meersman, 1998; West, 1999). Moreover, large sample studies within an elderly population have found that the interference effect accelerates in an exponential fashion from the sixth to eighth decades (Uttl & Graf, 1997; van Boxtel, ten Tusscher, Metsemakers, Willems, & Jolles, 2001).

Although the primary accounts of age-related increases in Stroop interference tend to focus on changes in inhibitory processing (Spieler, Balota, & Faust, 1996) or executive functions such as attentional control (Hartley, 1993) and maintenance of task context and goals (West & Baylis, 1998), other work has called into question whether these effects can be explained by nonexecutive factors. For example, a number of studies, primarily using cross-sectional covariation and meta-analytic techniques, have suggested that increased Stroop effects in older adults can be explained by global or generalized changes in speed of processing (Shilling, Chetwynd, & Rabbitt, 2002; Verhaeghen & De Meersman, 1998), by sensory components such as age-related impairments in low-level visual processing (van Boxtel et al., 2001), or by noncognitive factors such as circadian rhythms (which are different for younger and older adults;. May & Hasher, 1998). Moreover, the magnitude of Stroop interference is well known to be sensitive to task practice (MacLeod & Dunbar, 1988), which raises the possibility that age-related changes in the rate of learning (over the course of a task session) might also account for some of the data. There is some indication that practice effects in the Stroop task occur through different mechanisms in younger and older adults (Dulaney & Rogers, 1994), even though the overall amount of practice-related reduction in Stroop interference is similar for both age groups (Davidson, Zacks, & Williams, 2003). Finally, recent work has suggested that the magnitude of age-related changes in interference effects is strongly moderated by bilingualism, with bilingual older adults showing very similar patterns of interference to monolingual younger adults that were further minimized with task practice (albeit in a Simon rather than Stroop variant of the stimulus–response interference task; Bialystok, Craik, Klein, & Viswanathan, 2004; Craik & Bialystok, 2005).

The mixed literature on the mechanisms underlying increased Stroop interference effects in older adults indicates that task performance measures might reflect a mixture of a number of component processes rather than purely an index of inhibitory control. This interpretation is supported by studies using mathematical or computational modeling approaches that indicate how attentional, inhibitory, or executive processes might contribute to performance on congruent and neutral trials, in addition to incongruent ones (Cohen, Dunbar, & McClelland, 1990; Lindsay & Jacoby, 1994; Melara & Algom, 2003; Spieler et al., 1996). Consequently, it is likely that increased understanding of the role of executive control processes in mediating age effects in the Stroop task will be most advanced by studies utilizing a process analysis approach. We next describe a number of studies of this type that have provided support for goal maintenance theory.

A series of studies conducted by West and colleagues has demonstrated that manipulations of task context substantially increase the prominence of age-related Stroop interference effects. In one study, blocks varied in the proportion of congruent versus incongruent trials (West & Baylis, 1998). Age-related differences in the interference effect were significant when incongruent trials were frequent, and were not significant when incongruent trials were infrequent. These findings suggest that older adults struggled to actively maintain task goals in a high state of accessibility when this was needed for task performance. Likewise, in related work, older adults showed a dramatically increased rate of intrusion errors (naming the word rather than the ink color), consistent with the idea that they suffered from repeated instances of goal neglect or goal failure (West, 1999). In an event-related potential (ERP) study of this phenomenon, intrusion errors were associated with a change in brain waves over lateral PFC sites prior to the onset of the Stroop stimuli (West & Alain, 2000a), further supporting the notion of lateral PFC involvement in the generation of goal neglect phenomena in older adults. In more recent work, task context was manipulated by comparing blocked versions of color naming and word reading against blocks where the two tasks were cued on a trial-by-trial basis (West, 2004). Under such conditions the number of intrusion errors was four to five times greater in older adults relative to younger adults. Analyses of ERP data from this study suggested that the effect resulted from decline in the ability of older adults to recruit a PFC-centered neural system that supports the implementation of cognitive control (West, 2004; West & Moore, 2005). Importantly, these effects, although occurring in the context of a task-switching paradigm (discussed at length in a subsequent section), appeared to be independent of switching demands (West & Schwarb, 2006). Thus, the data clearly indicate that an age-related decline in the processes underlying goal maintenance supported by the lateral PFC may be an important contributor to age-related declines in performance of the Stroop task.

The antisaccade and anticue tasks have also been used to examine the effects of aging on the susceptibility to prepotent inhibition (Butler, Zacks, & Henderson, 1999; De Jong, 2001). The antisaccade requires that eye movements be generated in the direction opposite to a cued location; in the anticue task, a target decision has to be made regarding a stimulus presented in the anticued location. Antisaccade performance requires the suppression of an automatic tendency to attentionally orient towards abrupt visual cues (which is measured in prosaccade conditions), and has been well established to depend on the integrity of the lateral PFC (Funahashi, Chafee, & Goldman-Rakic, 1993; Guitton, Buchtel, & Douglas, 1985). Studies examining the effects of aging on performance of the antisaccade task have revealed several robust findings. Saccade errors are more frequent in older adults than in younger adults in the antisaccade condition, while error rates are similar for younger and older adults in the prosaccade condition (a condition for which few errors are made). Saccade onset latency is often slower for older than younger adults and this difference is typically greater for correct antisaccades than for correct prosaccades (Munoz, Broughton, Goldring, & Armstrong, 1998), although the age by condition interaction is not always observed (Butler et al., 1999). In studies of the anticue task that have manipulated cue–target intervals (Nieuwenhuis, Ridderinkhof, de Jong, Kok, & van der Molen, 2000), older adults show significantly slower rises to asymptote in terms of both error rates and saccade response latencies (presumably due to the need to correct an initial incorrect prosaccade). These effects do not appear to be generalized changes in speed of eye movement control, as age-related differences are minimal on prosaccade trials.

Evidence from a growing number of studies supports the idea that a deficit in goal maintenance may contribute to the effects on aging on performance of the antisaccade task. For instance, Eenshuistra, Ridderinkhof, and van der Molen (2004) found that the age-related increase in the number of antisaccade errors was greater under dual-task than single-task conditions, when the secondary task involved a working memory load. Other findings have led to the interpretation that some older adults may rely on onset of the target stimulus as an exogenous cue to initiate a (pro)saccade to the target rather than utilizing an endogenous representation of task context (i.e., the goal to make an antisaccade) to initiate an antisaccade following the cue (De Jong, 2001; Nieuwenhuis, Broerse, Nielen, & de Jong, 2004; Nieuwenhuis et al., 2000). Supporting this idea, Nieuwenhuis et al. (2000) observed that filling all possible target locations with stimuli at the onset of the target greatly reduced age-related differences in the asymptote of accuracy in the anticue condition. This finding indicates that age-related differences in context processing may, at least in some instances, reflect a strategic reduction in older adults' tendency to utilize a representation of task context to support efficient behavior, potentially as a compensatory mechanism for degraded task goal representation. This is supported by the failure of older adults to reach the same level as younger adults even in the filled location condition.

In the stop-signal task, an intermittent cue signals the requirement to withhold or stop the execution of an already ongoing response to a simple primary task (Logan & Cowan, 1984). The primary measure of interest is the stopping time, which is typically calculated from the probability of successful response suppression as a function of the stop-signal delay (the interval from stimulus onset to the presentation of the stop signal). The effects of aging on response inhibition in the stop-signal task have been examined in relatively few studies, but these have led to some evidence of age-related impairment. Data from studies utilizing a lifespan approach demonstrate that stop-signal response times increase in later adulthood and that this effect may be essentially linear from the twenties to the eighties (Bedard, Nichols, Barbosa, Schachar, Logan, & Tannock, 2002; Kramer, Humphrey, Larish, Logan, & Strayer, 1994; Williams, Ponesse, Schachar, Logan, & Tannock, 1999). The effect of aging on the probability of withholding a response is less clear. Several studies have reported that the probability of stopping is similar for younger and older adults (Bedard et al., 2002; Kramer et al., 1994; Williams et al., 1999). In contrast, May and Hasher reported that the likelihood of stopping was reduced in older adults relative to younger adults (May & Hasher, 1998), although this was moderated by circadian rhythm (i.e., time-of-day) effects.

A recent study examined age-related changes in stop-signal inhibition compared to other tasks with inhibitory demands (e.g., Stroop, and AX-CPT, described later), after careful control for global processing speed effects (Rush, Barch, & Braver, 2006). Although significant age effects were found, they tended to be small relative to other inhibitory measures. These findings suggest that the stop-signal task may index age-related changes in the ability to activate response suppression processes based on cued activation of a task goal. However, it may be that the task is not optimal for examining goal maintenance impairments in older adults. In particular, because the primary measure is the speed of engaging response suppression processes once cued to do so, the dependence of the task on strongly maintained goal representations may be minimal. It may be interesting for future studies to examine task manipulations that increase the demands on goal maintenance processes, for example by pre-cuing participants when a stop-signal trial is likely to occur. In a brain imaging study of this type conducted in younger adults, this manipulation reliably increased pre-target activation within lateral PFC (Hester, Murphy, Foxe, Foxe, Javitt, & Garavan, 2004).

TASK MANAGEMENT

A central notion of many theories of executive control is that specialized mechanisms are required to enable flexible coordination and switching between different tasks that need to be completed. These control mechanisms—internal representations of "task sets" or "task rules" and processes that can rapidly update such representations when needed—are thought to be distinct from the task-specific representations and processes themselves, and as such serve a managerial function in coordinating task flow. It has long been thought that a primary source of cognitive impairment in aging is a loss of the ability to successfully manage and coordinate multiple task demands (Craik & Byrd, 1982). Classically, task coordination processes have been studied in aging research using dual-task or divided attention paradigms (Craik, Govoni, Naveh-Benjamin, & Anderson, 1996; Craik & McDowd, 1987; McDowd & Craik, 1988). In such paradigms, performance in dual-task and divided attention conditions is contrasted against performance in single task and full attention conditions, to identify age-related effects. The robust findings of age-related declines in these domains have been reviewed in detail in previous and current editions of this handbook (Hartley, 1992; McDowd & Shaw, 2000; Kramer & Madden, chapter 5), and have been quantitatively confirmed in a rigorous manner through meta-analyses (Verhaeghen, Steitz, Sliwinski, & Cerella, 2003) and structural equation modeling (Salthouse & Miles,

2002). These latter studies confirm that dual-task slowing in older adults is not accounted for by generalized slowing and that a coherent dual-task latent construct can be defined that has both convergent and divergent validity in its relationship to cognitive aging.

Yet even with these findings, dual-task and divided attention paradigms have acknowledged limitations in their ability to provide a fine-grained analysis of the nature of age-related impairments in task-management processes. As a consequence, there has been a recent shift in focus to potentially more informative paradigms for understanding the nature of task-set representation, coordination, and updating. Two paradigms of particular interest have been the psychological refractory period (PRP) paradigm and task switching. Studies of these tasks appear to provide rather direct support for the goal maintenance account.

Task Switching

Task-switching paradigms are similar to classic dual-task paradigms in that participants have more than one task to perform within a block of trials, but differ in that only one task is performed at a time, such that task changes occur on a trial-to-trial basis in either a predictable or unpredictable sequence. Thus, task-switching paradigms offer a window into both how task sets or task rules are internally represented, and how such representations become updated when needed. Task-switching studies have a long history of study in both the young adult (Jersild, 1927; Spector & Biederman, 1976) and aging literatures (Brinley, 1965), but it is only recently that the paradigm has become an active area of focused research (Allport, Styles, & Hsieh, 1994; Meiran, 1996; Rogers & Monsell, 1995). Current task-switching studies focus on the processes and task factors that produce "switching costs" (the reduction in performance that occurs on trials where the task has switched from the previous trial) and "mixing costs" (the reduction in performance that occurs even on nontask-switch trials presented within a task-switching block relative to the same trials presented in a single-task block). A number of findings have been observed in task-switching studies with older adults that provide information regarding how task-management processes are impacted by advancing age, and which have implications for goal maintenance theory.

One of the most intriguing findings in the literature on task switching and aging is that older adults show consistent and large age-related increases in mixing costs and less robust age-related differences in switching costs (Verhaeghen et al., 2005). This pattern was first rigorously investigated and reported in studies by Kray and Lindenberger (2000) and Mayr (2001). Kray and Lindenberger examined task switching using an alternating runs paradigm (i.e., tasks follow a predictable AABBAABB sequence) in which task preparation time was manipulated by varying the interval between the response and next stimulus (response-to-stimulus interval, RSI). The results were very clear in illustrating that mixing costs (also termed global switching costs) were significantly higher in older adults and remained so even after extensive practice and with long preparation times. In contrast, after controlling for practice, preparation, and generalized slowing, local switch costs were not greater in older adults. In a follow-up study, Mayr (2001) demonstrated that the same pattern of age-differential effects for mixing but not switching effects could be obtained in a task-cuing paradigm (but for contrasting results see Kray, Li, & Lindenberger, 2002). The task-cuing paradigm allows sequences of task switches to be unpredictably structured, thus removing potential age confounds related to predictive expectancies and micropractice effects (i.e., learning due to short runs of same-task repetitions).

Since these original reports, the general finding of strong age-related increases in mixing costs, along with weak or absent age effects in switching costs, has been replicated numerous times, including in large sample and lifespan studies, and thus appears to be highly reliable (Reimers & Maylor, 2005). For example, in a meta-analysis of task-switching studies, Verhaeghen and Cerella (2002) found that after taking generalized age-related slowing into account, older adults showed clear evidence of increased mixing costs but no effect in switching costs. Other task-switching studies have been useful in providing important additional constraints on the nature of the mixing cost effect in older adults. For example, mixing cost effects are influenced by whether the tasks being intermixed have overlapping and bivalent stimulus and response features (e.g., the same response or feature could be present when performing either task; Mayr, 2001), which can lead to response incongruencies (i.e., when the stimulus is associated with two different responses, depending on the task being performed; Rubin & Meiran, 2005). The presence of these factors also appears to contribute strongly to age differences in mixing cost, indicating that the problem for older adults may be in utilizing task-set representations as a means of minimizing task cross-talk or interference (Mayr, 2001; Meiran, Gotler, & Perlman, 2001). De Jong (2001) demonstrated that the mixing cost effect could be removed when older adults were placed under strict response deadlines. This suggests that without such pressures older adults will tend to keep both task sets at an equivalent level of activation, rather than prioritize one over the other in a context-appropriate manner. Such behavior can be seen as a form of goal neglect, which minimizes control demands, but increases overall mixing costs.

The minimal effect of aging on local switch costs at first seems somewhat surprising from the standpoint of executive control theories of cognitive aging. In particular, a hope of early task-switching research was that local switch costs could provide a direct index of the efficacy of control processes in selecting and updating task-set representations (Monsell, 2003). Specifically, most theories of executive control in aging, including the goal maintenance account, would postulate that task-set selection and management is a core executive process that declines with increasing age. However, it is now becoming clear that local switch costs, similar to Stroop interference effects, represent a complex mixture of factors of which only some may be related to task-set representation. In particular, recent research has suggested that switch costs can be influenced by cue repetitions (Logan & Bundesen, 2003), response repetitions (Meiran, 2000), target-evoked associations (Allport & Wylie, 2000), and higher order sequential effects (Brown, Reynolds, & Braver, 2006).

The complexity of local switch costs can also be seen in the fact that when long preparatory intervals are provided, as in cueing paradigms, switching costs are significantly reduced, but not eliminated (i.e., leaving a so-called residual switch cost; Monsell, 2003). Interestingly, older adults show similar benefits of preparation to younger adults, but have larger residual switch costs (De Jong, 2001; Meiran et al., 2001). This is consistent with the interpretation that older adults do utilize task cues to engage in general task preparation, but they are less able to use such information to appropriately select the currently relevant task set and deselect the currently irrelevant set. Such an effect would be fully consistent with the goal maintenance account, which suggests that task goal updating as well as maintenance processes occur less robustly in older adults.

Evidence from ERP and brain imaging studies provide further support for this account, and for the role of lateral PFC in local and global switch costs. Although lateral PFC appears to be reliably engaged following cues that enable preparation for the upcoming task, PFC activation appears to be similar regardless of whether the cue indicates a task-switch or task-repeat trial will be occurring (Brass & von Cramon, 2004; Braver, Reynolds, & Donaldson, 2003; Ruge, Brass, Koch, Rubin, Meiran, & von Cramon, 2005; West, 2004). Conversely, mixing costs do appear to be associated with sustained activation within anterior regions of lateral PFC (Braver et al., 2003), suggesting that performance of multitask blocks is dependent on active task goal maintenance. Although there have been very few brain imaging and ERP studies of task switching in older adults to date, the available evidence is consistent with the hypothesis that older adults fail to increase activation of lateral PFC during task-switching blocks (DiGirolamo et al., 2001), and show reduced activity following task cues (West, 2004). Together, these findings give credence to the idea that age-related impairments in global mixing costs may be a valid indicator of specific goal (i.e., task-set) representation and maintenance problems in lateral PFC that are present during mixed-task conditions, but which occur on both task-switch and task-repeat trials. In contrast, local switch costs may be a more complex measure of task-maintenance processes due to the multifactorial nature of this measure. Indeed as Mayr (2001, p.106) suggests, global mixing costs "may actually be a more fundamental and less ambiguous indicator of executive control demands in set-selection situations than local costs."

PRP Studies

The other approach most recently used to understand age effects on dual-task coordination is the psychological refractory period (PRP) paradigm (Welford, 1952). The key aspect of the PRP paradigm is an explicit manipulation of the temporal overlap between two tasks by varying the stimulus onset asynchrony (SOA) for the second task (T2) relative to the first (T1). Often a critical variable is the size of the PRP effect, which is the slowing of response latency on T2 (but not T1) for short SOAs relative to long SOAs. The PRP effect is thought to measure the degree of interference caused by dual-task coordination, but with more precision, since in the baseline long SOA condition both tasks are still performed, but sequentially and without overlap (since at long SOAs the T1 response will be given before the T2 stimulus is presented). Thus, the magnitude of overlap interference can be dissociated from more general difficulty effects related to having to complete two different tasks within a short time window (Pashler, 1994). A theoretical advantage of the PRP paradigm for aging research is that it provides a means of refining explanations of dual-task interference effects in older adults. In particular, whereas classic accounts of age-related dual-task interference effects typically postulate a reduction in "general processing resources," PRP studies have focused on the more specific question of whether PRP interference reflects a time-sharing deficit at a particular processing stage, or a reduced ability of older adults to update task goals in a rapidly sequential manner.

Findings of enhanced PRP effects in older adults were first reported by Allen, Smith, Vires-Collins, and Sperry (1998) and Hartley and Little (1999). Allen et al. (1998) suggested that the results indicated older adults had a selective impairment in time-sharing ability. Hartley and Little (1999) carried out an extensive series of studies that attempted to determine whether enhanced PRP effects in older adults could be interpreted as general reduced capacity, generalized slowing, or a more specific impairment in time sharing. The results appeared inconsistent with a general reduced capacity account, but were consistent with age-related slowing particularly at the response selection stage of processing. In later work, Glass et al. (2000) observed similar results, which were interpreted within the context of the EPIC computational model of adaptive executive control (Meyer & Kieras, 1997). In trying to fit older adult PRP data to the model, the investigators found that in addition to generalized slowing effects, increased slowing of certain specific processes and changes to time-sharing parameters were required in the model. The latter parameters specifically referred to the time required to "lock" and "unlock" T2 processing at the bottleneck stage after T1 had passed through this stage. This locking process may be similar to a mechanism of rapid task goal activation and updating. In later studies, additional findings were also observed, such as selectively enhanced PRP effects in older adults when both tasks required the same type of motor response (Hartley, 2001), or when the T2 stimulus was especially salient and so caused an attentional capture effect (Hein & Schubert, 2004). Thus, in both cases, age-related PRP effects appeared to be a reduced ability to manage cross-task interference, either at the perceptual or response level.

Most recently, investigators have used the PRP paradigm to examine whether dual-task coordination can be improved in older adults with extensive practice. Maquestiaux, Hartley, and Bertsch (2004) found that practice substantially reduced the magnitude of PRP effects, but to a lesser degree in older adults than younger adults. Thus, practice actually amplified the magnitude of age-related PRP effects. To account for this finding, Maquestiaux et al. (2004) suggested that in addition to generalized slowing, older adults had additional difficulty in switching to T2 processing after T1 completion—an effect that was predicted to be present especially in tasks with complex S–R mapping rules (as they had used in training) that would presumably be more difficult for older adults to maintain in working memory during T1 processing (see also Glass et al. 2000). Consistent with this account, when the practiced participants transferred to either a novel T1 or a T2 that was less complex than the practiced one, age-related PRP effects decreased. Bherer, Kramer, Peterson, Colcombe, Erickson, and Becic (2005) found that practice did lead to equivalent dual-task improvements in older adults compared to younger adults, and that these practice effects were both maintained over time and transferred to novel task conditions. However, in this study, training did not reduce the larger age-related effects in "task-set costs," a measure conceptually similar to mixing costs in task switching (i.e., the cost of performing the T1 or T2 task within dual-task vs. single-task conditions).

When taken together, the findings of the PRP studies suggest that age-related enhancements in PRP effects are similar to those observed in task-switching paradigms. Thus, if successful dual-task coordination in PRP studies reflects rapid switching between tasks rather than true time sharing or dividing attentional resources, as most current theoretical models predict (Logan & Gordon, 2001; Pashler, 1994), then older adult deficits in such situations may not reflect poorer time sharing per se, but rather a reduced ability to appropriately select the task-relevant goal representation during T1 and then rapidly update this representation when initiating T2 performance. As such, older adults may tend to keep both task sets at an equal level of activation, leading to an increased vulnerability to cross-task interference and task-set costs. Although no neuroimaging studies have been conducted to examine PRP-type dual-task processing in older adults, recent work in younger adults is consistent with this hypothesis. In particular, lateral PFC regions appear to be the source of PRP-type bottleneck effects, and show evidence of sequential updating from T1 to T2 (Dux, Ivanoff, Asplund, & Marois, 2006). Moreover, these regions appear to be the only ones that show increased activity following extensive dual-task training (Erickson et al., 2007). Thus, a promising direction for future research would be to conduct aging studies of these effects, to determine whether older adults show altered dynamics of lateral PFC activity, and how these dynamics might be impacted by dual-task training.

CONTEXT PROCESSING

A recent area of research that has attempted to directly test the ideas of the goal maintenance theory comes from studies that have examined context processing functions. In particular, the AX-CPT paradigm has been designed to directly probe the utilization of contextual cue information in terms of goal-based biasing functions related to active maintenance in working memory, attentional enhancement, and response inhibition (Braver et al., 2002). The AX-CPT is a variant of the classic Continuous Performance Test (CPT; Rosvold, Mirsky, Sarason, Bransome, & Beck, 1956) that requires utilization and maintenance of contextual cue information to guide responding to subsequent ambiguous probes. The task is structured such that context cues serve to update task goals (i.e., in the form of relevant S–R mappings) and create goal-based expectancies that both direct attention towards target features and responses, and enable suppression of probe-evoked interference. These effects can be measured on two types of lure trials, AY and BX, relative to an internal baseline control trial BY. The AY measure provides an index of the strength of context-induced attentional expectancies, whereas the BX measure provides an index of interference due to context failures. Finally, manipulation of the cue–target interval provides an index of the active maintenance of context over a delay.

The AX-CPT has been extensively examined across a number of both behavioral (Braver et al., 1999; Braver & Cohen, 2001; MacDonald, Goghari, Hicks, Flory, Carter, & Manuck, 2005; Servan-Schreiber, Cohen, & Steingard, 1996) and brain imaging studies (Barch, Braver, Nystrom, Forman, Noll, & Cohen, 1997; Barch et al., 2001; Braver & Bongiolatti, 2002; MacDonald & Carter, 2003; Perlstein, Dixit, Carter, Noll, & Cohen, 2003). The typical finding is that younger adults show high degrees of context-induced attentional expectancy (poor AY performance) and a low incidence of interference due to context failure (good BX performance). In functional neuroimaging studies these trial-type and delay effects have been found to be associated with task-related activation in lateral PFC. These findings are consistent with the idea that a common underlying mechanism—active prefrontal goal representations—tends to lead to both successful BX inhibition and AY cue-invalidity errors, and that these tendencies are sustained over delays via the active maintenance of such goal information.

Braver et al. (2001) conducted the first study of the AX-CPT with older adults, demonstrating that they showed a reversed pattern to young adults, with low levels of context-induced attentional expectancy and high levels of context-failure interference. An especially surprising aspect to the latter finding was that older adults not only showed few errors on AY trials, but also faster reaction times than young adults—an effect which was statistically significant after controlling for generalized response slowing. Moreover, these age effects were found to be specific to context processing, as manipulations of context processing difficulty (by filling the cue–probe delay interval with distractors) amplified age-related performance differences, but manipulations of general task difficulty had no impact.

A number of subsequent studies have provided further support for context processing deficits in older adults, due to impairments in goal representation and maintenance (Braver et al., 2005; Haarmann, Ashling, Davelaar, & Usher, 2005; Rush et al., 2006). For example, these studies have demonstrated correlations between AX-CPT impairments in older adults and performance declines in other more standard neuropsychological tasks of executive control domains that should also depend on context processing, such as stop-signal inhibition, Stroop, trail making, verbal fluency, and semantic anomaly judgments. Importantly though, it has also been shown that while AX-CPT measures might tap into similar executive control constructs, such as inhibition, they also appear to account for more age-related variance than these standard measures. Thus, BX trial performance was more significantly correlated with age than equivalent inhibitory measures in the go/no-go, stop-signal, and Stroop tasks (Rush et al., 2006). This suggests that goal representation and maintenance may be a more fundamental construct for understanding cognitive aging than other related executive control constructs. However, as we discuss further at the end of the chapter, there is still a great demand for further work examining the psychometric properties of the AX-CPT task (e.g., reliability), and in establishing the psychometric validity of the context processing construct more generally.

In a recent study, Braver et al. (2005) found evidence that there may be age-related dissociations within the context processing construct, between the representation/updating and maintenance functions. In particular, within a young-old group (65–75 years old), the age-related changes on AY and BX trials were not affected by delay manipulations, whereas in an older group (> 75 years old), context processing impairments were greater with a long delay (when maintenance functions would be most taxed). Moreover, both types of context processing impairment were found to be further exacerbated in a sample of older adults with very mild dementia of the Alzheimer's type (DAT), suggesting that deterioration of goal representation and maintenance mechanisms in lateral PFC may contribute to early stages of cognitive decline in this disease.

A key idea of goal maintenance theory is that impairments in the use of context information in older adults are caused by changes in lateral PFC (and/or DA) function. This idea is also supported by neuroimaging studies of the AX-CPT demonstrating a reduction in delay-related lateral PFC activity in older adults (Braver & Barch, 2002). In a follow-up event-related fMRI study, it was shown that the activation changes were specifically due to reduced cue-related activation of lateral PFC, even though tonic (i.e., nonspecific) activity in this region was increased among older adults (Paxton, Barch, Racine, & Braver, in press). This finding is supported by work using ERPs and a trial-by-trial cueing version of the Stroop task (West, 2004). Older adults were found to have reduced cue-related activity in frontal and occipital sites particularly after a delay, a finding that was interpreted as a reduced ability to maintain task cue information as a contextual goal representation that can bias task-specific perceptual processing areas. A related study found that older adults had reduced frontal pre-stimulus ERP activity during a Stroop-like interference task with a long preparatory interval (West & Schwarb, 2006).

RECENT DEVELOPMENTS

Perhaps one of the most significant developments in the study of executive functions over the last decade is the movement toward fractionation of the various cognitive processes related to executive control and their associated functional neuroanatomy (Miyake, Friedman, Emerson,

Witzki, Howerter, & Wager, 2000; Ridderinkhof, van den Wildenberg, Segalowitz, & Carter, 2004; Smith & Jonides, 1999; Stuss et al., 2002; Stuss, Shallice, Alexander, & Picton, 1995). In this section, we discuss the emerging trends in the literature, and how these already, or might in the future, influence our understanding of the aging of executive control.

The research enterprise aimed towards fractionation of executive control was originally motivated by three streams of evidence: (1) an uneven pattern of spared and impaired performance on measures of executive function in patients with focal and diffuse damage to the prefrontal cortex (Luria, 1966; Stuss & Benson, 1986); (2) broadly distributed activation within the prefrontal cortex of healthy young adults during performance of executive function tasks (Braver & Ruge, 2006; Cabeza & Nyberg, 2000; Duncan & Owen, 2000); and (3) potential differences in the developmental trajectory of executive functions (Casey, Tottenham, Liston, & Durston, 2005; Diamond, 2002; Zelazo, Craik, & Booth, 2004). In two important review papers, Stuss et al. (1995) and later Smith and Jonides (1999) described a set of executive or supervisory processes that are dependent on the functional integrity of the prefrontal cortex. These include activation of relevant information, inhibition of irrelevant information, scheduling processes in complex tasks, planning a sequence of subtasks to accomplish some goal, updating the contents of working memory, coding the time and place of information in working memory, the implementation of if-then logical processes, and monitoring action outcomes.

Empirical support for the conceptual and neuroanatomical fractionation of executive processes has been provided in studies using a variety of methodologies. In a series of studies of patients with focal lesions to the prefrontal cortex, Stuss and colleagues (Stuss et al., 2002; Stuss, Bisschop, Alexander, Levine, Katz, & Izukawa, 2001; Stuss, Floden, Alexander, Levine, & Katz, 2001; Stuss et al., 2000) have demonstrated that damage to circumscribed regions within the left and right dorsolateral, inferior medial, and superior medial prefrontal cortex can be associated with disruption of processes supporting activation, monitoring, inhibition, and initiation, respectively. Likewise, work examining individual differences has revealed that distinct constructs reflecting shifting, updating, inhibition, and resistance to interference can be identified in intact individuals (Friedman & Miyake, 2004; Miyake et al., 2000). Furthermore, this work demonstrates that the various executive functions may be differentially related to performance on more complex measures of executive function and working memory including the WCST, the Tower of Hanoi, random number generation, and complex span tasks (Miyake et al., 2000). Lastly, functional neuroimaging and computational studies have probably provided the most explicit attempts at, and evidence for, fractionation and dissociation of executive functions (Botvinick, Braver, Barch, Carter, & Cohen, 2001; Braver & Ruge, 2006; De Pisapia, Repovs, & Braver, in press; Frank & Claus, 2006). Within this literature, three specific types of executive processes have been emerging as possibly contributing distinct functional and anatomical mechanisms over that provided by the basic goal maintenance and biasing functions of lateral PFC. These are performance/error monitoring, affect–cognition interactions in executive control, and integration. We next discuss each of these functions in turn, in terms of recent research developments and implications for cognitive aging. Lastly, we discuss ideas relating to the dynamics of executive control that may be independent of structural/functional dissociations, but still have significant implications for cognitive aging research.

Error/Performance Monitoring

In the last ten years, there has been intense interest in the executive control literature regarding the cognitive processes and functional neuroanatomy underlying performance monitoring (Ridderinkhof et al., 2004). This interest was sparked by the discovery of a specific ERP brain wave component sensitive to error monitoring and detection, known as the error-related negativity (ERN) or error negativity (Ne) (Falkenstein, Hohnsbein, Hoormann, & Blanke, 1991; Gehring, Goss, Coles, Meyer, & Donchin, 1993). Subsequent research suggested that this brain wave is generated within the anterior cingulate cortex (ACC; Carter, Braver, Barch, Botvinick, Noll, & Cohen, 1998; Dehaene, Posner, & Tucker, 1994). More recent work has suggested that the ACC and ERN-like brain waves are activated not only by error commission itself, but also by the occurrence of response conflict (i.e., coactivation of competing response tendencies) in situations where such conflict tends to accompany errors (Yeung, Cohen, & Botvinick, 2004), or conversely by explicit error feedback under situations where error accompanying response conflict tends not to be present (Holroyd & Coles, 2002). Computational and experimental studies have suggested that the ERN and ACC activity might serve as a neural signal that enables the system to learn about task situations requiring a high degree of cognitive control over responding, to prevent errors and to regulate the systems, such as lateral PFC, that implement such control (Botvinick et al., 2001; Brown & Braver, 2005; Holroyd & Coles, 2002; Kerns, Cohen, MacDonald, Cho, Stenger, & Carter, 2004). In particular, the ACC and lateral PFC may form a control circuit that facilitates goal-directed action in a variety of tasks, by continually adjusting to the imposed control demands of the particular situation (Botvinick et al., 2001).

The basic research on ERN/conflict monitoring and ACC–PFC

interactions in cognitive control regulation has motivated investigation of such effects in older adults. Studies examining the effects of aging on the ERN have consistently demonstrated that the amplitude of this modulation is attenuated in older adults. The effect of aging appears to be relatively general and has been observed in a variety of difficult cognitive tasks for which errors are frequently committed, including mental rotation (Band & Kok, 2000), four-alternative forced choice (Falkenstein, Hoormann, & Hohnsbein, 2001), probabilistic learning (Nieuwenhuis et al., 2002), source memory (Mathewson, Dywan, & Segalowitz, 2005), and picture-word matching (Mathalon, Bennett, Askari, Gray, Rosenbloom, & Ford, 2003). Likewise, studies of conflict detection in interference tasks, such as the Stroop, have observed attenuated ERP activity arising from medial frontal regions in high-conflict (incongruent) trials (West, 2004; West & Alain, 2000b; West & Schwarb, 2006). A promising discovery within the context of the goal maintenance theory comes from findings of a computational study examining the mechanisms underlying age-related declines in the amplitude of the ERN (Nieuwenhuis et al., 2002). In this study the effects of aging on the ERN in the flanker task and a probabilistic learning task were captured by a reduction in the magnitude of a dopamine-mediated error feedback signal from the basal ganglia to the anterior cingulate.

Related work has suggested that age-related changes in Stroop interference might also be due to ACC and conflict monitoring impairments, as well as declines in the goal-maintenance functions supported by lateral PFC (Milham et al., 2002; West & Schwarb, 2006). The primary account of ACC–PFC interactions suggests that detection of high-conflict situations in the ACC leads to a subsequent adjustment in cognitive control via increased goal maintenance in lateral PFC (Botvinick et al., 2001; Cohen, Botvinick, & Carter, 2000). Thus, impaired goal maintenance in older adults might be due to a disruption of this dynamic, via age-related alterations of either lateral PFC or ACC mechanisms. Consistent with this hypothesis, West and Baylis (1998) observed that older adults were less efficient than younger adults at modulating the magnitude of the Stroop effect in response to variation in task context as might be expected if aging has a negative impact on the conflict monitor supported by ACC. Thus, aging may be associated not only with impairments in goal maintenance via changes in lateral PFC function, but also with disrupted regulation of cognitive control that may arise out of a change in ACC function as well (that is potentially DA mediated) which alters the nature of the interaction between ACC and PFC.

Affect–Cognition Interactions in Executive Control

Interest in the potentially dissociable role of affective processes in executive control was first launched by work on "somatic marker" theory (Bechara, Damasio, Tranel, & Damasio, 1997; Damasio, 1994), which postulated that affective bodily signals are explicitly (though nonconsciously) represented within ventromedial (VM) regions of PFC, and used as an additional source of top-down bias on decision making. The independence of such VM-PFC biasing signals from more cognitive biasing signals in lateral PFC was supported by a double dissociation finding (Bechara, Damasio, Tranel, & Anderson, 1998), in which VM-PFC patients exhibited normal performance on a working memory task, but never developed predictive bodily reactions to poor upcoming choices in a gambling task (and thus tended to persist in making such poor choices throughout the session). Patients with dorsolateral (DL) PFC lesions showed the opposite pattern. This work also supported the accumulated findings from many neuropsychological case studies demonstrating a general pattern of risky decision-making behavior in patients with VM-PFC damage (Bechara, Damasio, & Damasio, 2000). In subsequent years there has been an explosion of functional neuroimaging studies of gambling and related decision-making tasks (Fellows, 2004; Krawczyk, 2002), including the original Iowa Gambling Task just discussed (Fukui, Murai, Fukuyama, Hayashi, & Hanakawa, 2005; Northoff et al., 2006).

These studies support the involvement of VM and orbital PFC in responding to negative and positive feedback information that signal behavioral changes are needed (O'Doherty, Critchley, Deichmann, & Dolan, 2003; O'Doherty, Kringelbach, Rolls, Hornak, & Andrews, 2001). However, the independence of VM and DL-PFC regions is not so clear-cut, as other studies have shown that regulation of the emotional response to affectively valenced stimuli appears to involve DL-PFC regions, interacting with both VM-PFC (or more ventral ACC regions) and the amygdala (Clark, Manes, Antoun, Sahakian, & Robbins, 2003; Fellows & Farah, 2005; Manes et al., 2002; Ochsner, Bunge, Gross, & Gabrieli, 2002).

There is a growing literature on both affect-dependent decision making and VM-PFC function in healthy aging, but this has also been mixed with regard to the extent of age-related changes in these functions. In a direct comparison of executive functions supported by DL-PFC vs. VM-PFC, MacPherson et al. (2002) found consistent aging effects on measures of DL-PFC function (e.g., WCST), but no clear age-related change in the tasks used to measure VM-PFC function (e.g., Iowa Gambling task). These behavioral findings are consistent with other similar studies (Wood, Busemeyer, Koling, Cox, & Davis, 2005) and with older behavioral evidence showing conservative rather than risky decision-making behavior in older adults (Botwinick, 1969). Moreover, they are consistent with neuroanatomical investigations examining gray matter volume with MRI that indicate stronger effects of aging (in terms of volume reduction) for lateral PFC than for medial and orbital PFC (Convit et al., 2001; Raz, 2000). Yet the findings are not unequivocal, as more recent work with the Iowa task and other gambling-type paradigms have demonstrated that older adults show slower learning curves from negative feedback and a higher tolerance for risk (Deakin, Aitken, Robbins, & Sahakian, 2004; Denburg, Tranel, & Bechara, 2005). An imaging study in this kind of paradigm also revealed age-related changes in activation of both PFC and reward-related subcortical structures, such as the ventral striatum (Marschner, Mell, Wartenburger, Villringer, Reischies, & Heekeren, 2005).

A different literature on emotion–cognition interactions in older adults has also produced mixed results with regard to whether aging changes the nature of bidirectional regulation across these domains. There is now a relatively well-established literature on emotional control and the so-called "positivity bias" in older adults (Carstensen & Mikels, 2005). This research suggests that, compared to young adults, older adults are able to exert equivalent or better control over their emotions, and as such show a reduced impact of negative (vs. positive) information on memory and attention (Mather & Carstensen, 2005). This research is interesting, especially in light of the recent literature from younger adults, suggesting that control over emotional responses (especially for negative information) appears to depend on lateral (rather than medial) PFC function (Ochsner & Gross, 2005). One approach to reconciling this discrepancy has been put forward by Mather and Carstensen (2005), who suggest that older adults prioritize emotional regulation goals over other cognitive ones, thus improving emotional control but at the expense of cognitive control. A recent study (Mather & Knight, 2005) has supported this finding, in demonstrating that: (a) age-related positivity biases were found only in older adults with good cognitive control function (as indexed by a neuropsychological battery); and (b) reducing cognitive control resources via divided attention abolished the age-related positivity bias.

When taken together, these results suggest that even if VM regions of PFC are not directly impacted by age, older adults may show some level of impairments in gambling and reward-related decision-making domains and a qualitative shift in emotion regulation. These behavioral phenomena may reflect an altered input from lateral PFC regions. In particular, interaction between lateral and VM PFC regions may reflect important emotion–cognition dynamics that adjust affect and decision-making biases in response to actively maintained goal representations. Older adults may show a shift in how these biases are implemented and maintained, although further research is clearly required.

Integration

A third domain of executive control garnering recent attention in the basic cognitive neuroscience literature is that of integration (Prabhakaran, Narayanan, Zhao, & Gabrieli, 2000). Recent studies have suggested that the anterior-most regions of PFC might be selectively engaged by specific executive processes related to the integration of higher order goal information actively maintained in working memory with other internally represented information (De Pisapia, Slomski, & Braver, 2006; Koechlin, Basso, Pietrini, Panzer, & Grafman, 1999; Ramnani & Owen, 2004). For example, one study found that anterior PFC was not engaged by processing of a subtask (semantic classification) or working memory, but was engaged when the subtask had to be integrated with information previously stored in working memory to achieve the correct result (Braver & Bongiolatti, 2002). Integration operations may also be a critical component of tasks involving feature binding within working memory. As discussed previously, these tasks also engage anterior PFC regions (Mitchell et al., 2000b). A similar effect was observed in a study that found selective anterior PFC actvity under conditions requiring the integration of verbal and spatial information in working memory (Prabhakaran et al., 2000). Some theorists have suggested that these forms of integration are a key element of goal-subgoal coordination that occurs in many planning and reasoning tasks (Christoff & Gabrieli, 2000). For example, in reasoning tasks such as analogy verification and matrix reasoning, a number of different dimensions of stimuli have to be simultaneously (or sequentially) considered in order to determine whether a match on a desired dimension is present. Anterior PFC activity is selectively engaged in analogy and reasoning tasks that require relational integration (Bunge, Wendelken, Badre, & Wagner, 2005; Christoff et al., 2001). Moreover, activity in this region was found to increase parametrically with the number of dimensions needing to be considered in a set of stimuli (Kroger, Sabb, Fales, Bookheimer, Cohen, & Holyoak, 2002).

In cognitive aging research, age differences in reasoning and higher order thinking and planning tasks are well established (Phillips, MacLeod, & Kliegel, 2005; Salthouse, 2005a). It has been commonly assumed that such declines reflect a generalized loss of cognitive resources or impaired executive control function. However, it is possible that age-related changes in reasoning and higher order cognition could be due in part to the preferential dependence of certain types of these tasks on integration processes dependent on anterior PFC function. Although to date there have been no studies directly examining this question, the notion of relational integration seems similar to the construct of coordinative complexity developed by Mayr and Kliegl (1993). In a series of studies, coordinative complexity was found to lead to very large interactive slowing effects in older adults, suggesting that such tasks tap into a selectively age-impaired control mechanism (Verhaeghen, Kliegl, & Mayr, 1997). In another related study, Viskontas, Morrison, Holyoak, Hummel, and Knowlton (2004) examined relational integration complexity in analogy verification, and found that age-related impairments were increased as integration complexity increased. Moreover, these effects were exacerbated when irrelevant information had to be suppressed from relational comparisons, especially at high levels of complexity. A fruitful direction for future research would be to draw on the advances and task paradigms developed in the basic cognitive neuroscience literature on anterior PFC and integration processes. Such studies could help determine whether age-related impairments in reasoning, planning, and higher cognition tasks are reflective of a selective reduction in integration mechanisms, due to changes in anterior PFC function.

Temporal Dynamics of Executive Control

A final domain of recent work in executive control relevant to cognitive aging research concerns dynamic rather than structural dissociations in control mechanisms. A series of research studies, carried out by West and colleagues, has examined age-related changes related to transient fluctuations of executive control during task performance (West, 2001). Importantly, in this work it was observed that both older and younger adults experienced periodic and transient episodes of goal neglect during the performance of different executive tasks, such as Stroop, prospective memory and N-back working memory. What primarily differentiated older from younger adults was not the number of episodes of reduced control, but their longer duration (e.g., measured by number of consecutive intrusion errors). Subsequent studies have extended and refined the well-established finding of age-related increases in performance variability (Hultsch et al., chapter 10), by observing that such variability is particularly present under conditions of high control demands (West, Murphy, Armilio, Craik, & Stuss, 2002). Likewise, modeling of reaction time distributions in older adults indicated that age-related variability effects were independent of general slowing, and appeared to be due to relatively transient periods of poor (slower) performance rather than a generalized increase in variability.

A second recent theme of research on the dynamics of cognitive control in aging has been put forward by Braver and colleagues as part of the Dual Mechanisms of Control (DMC) account (Braver, Gray, & Burgess, 2007). The DMC account suggests that cognitive control can occur in two distinct modes: reactive and proactive. Proactive control involves sustained active maintenance of goal representations and anticipatory biasing of attention and action systems prior to the onset of imperative events. In contrast, reactive control involves transient, stimulus-driven reactivation of goal information only in situations where such information is critical to avoid inappropriate performance. An important aspect of the DMC model is that cognitive control is flexible, such that transitions between transient and sustained goal activation can occur within individuals, in relationship to changing task conditions or internal states. According to the model, older adults may have a reduced tendency to use proactive control, but a relatively spared or even enhanced tendency to engage in reactive control.

This idea was recently tested in an event-related fMRI study of the AX-CPT task, in which it was found that older adults showed reduced cue-related activation of lateral PFC, but increased activation in lateral PFC and other regions during probe periods, especially for high interference BX trials (Paxton et al., in press). Critically, however, these age-related changes in AX-CPT activation were not fixed, but instead were significantly impacted by strategic training in the use of proactive control in AX-CPT performance (i.e., by improving predictive cue utilization). Following training, behavioral results indicated a pattern of performance in older adults that was more similar to that of young adults (Paxton, Barch, Storandt, & Braver, 2006), and was accompanied by both an increase in cue-related activation and a decrease in probe-related activation of lateral PFC (Braver, Locke, Paxton, & Barch, in preparation). Thus, the results suggested that older adults could in fact rely upon the neural mechanisms of proactive control, but only following explicit training.

These findings suggest that altered PFC function in older adults may not be a static phenomenon, but may interact with the dynamics of task processing and cognitive demands on goal activation and maintenance. The recent work suggesting that these dynamic changes in older adult cognitive control might be amenable to training provides a promising potential for future research.

SUMMARY AND FUTURE DIRECTIONS

In this chapter, we have examined the literature on changes in executive control that occur with advancing age. The older literature on executive functions in aging typically occurred within the context of other cognitive domains, such as working memory, attention, and episodic memory (McDowd & Shaw, 2000; Zacks et al., 2000). More recently, however, aging effects on executive control are being studied as a primary focus of research. This shift has arisen in part from a realization that even in domains such as working memory and episodic memory, age-related deficits may be primarily due to impaired executive control, rather than the mechanisms of storage per se.

We considered a number of domains of executive control in which age-related effects are prominent, including working memory, strategic control of episodic and prospective memory, response inhibition, task management, and context processing. In each of these domains, aging effects have been investigated using a variety of approaches, including cross-sectional covariation, neurocognitive methods, and process-based task analysis. We situated this review within the context of a theoretical framework known as goal maintenance theory, which postulates that older adults suffer from a primary impairment in internally representing, updating, and maintaining task-related goals. These cognitive changes are directly linked to an underlying neurobiological change in the function of lateral PFC in its interaction with the mid-brain dopamine system, as both of these neural substrates are well established to exhibit prominent changes with advancing age. The goal maintenance framework provides an organizing account of the data that appears to explain the nature of older adult deficits in a range of executive control domains and tasks. Nevertheless, theoretical and experimental investigations of executive control in aging utilizing the goal maintenance framework are still at an early stage, and much work remains to be done to better establish the validity and explanatory power of the theory.

One important direction for future research is to better establish the boundary conditions of the goal maintenance framework as a predictive and explanatory tool in studying cognitive aging. In particular, it will be necessary to better determine which tasks and performance measures are most sensitive to age-related goal maintenance deficits. Such determinations are often difficult to make in practice, as many of the executive control tasks commonly used in the literature are complex, such that obvious performance measures may reflect multiple processes in addition to goal maintenance. Interference costs in the Stroop task and switch costs in task-switching paradigms provide good examples of this point. As we described, systematic studies of these measures reveal that they are multifactorial in nature, and thus may not provide transparent indices of goal maintenance impairments in older adults. In this regard, process-based task analyses may help to better design paradigms that provide performance measures in such paradigms that are more sensitive and specific with regard to goal maintenance effects. A potentially more powerful approach may be to utilize computational and mathematical modeling techniques to better extract estimates of goal maintenance processes within complex executive control tasks. Another exciting alternative is to use neurocognitive techniques, such as ERP or fMRI, to directly index activation within lateral PFC and other brain regions during performance of executive control tasks. In this way, estimates of neural activity may serve as something analogous to a latent construct that can form the basis for age-related comparisons across multiple tasks. Of course, such work will need to establish the validity of these activity measures through analyses of brain–behavior relationships. But it may be the case that activity within lateral PFC of older adults serves as a better indicator of age-related cognitive impairment than specific behavioral measures themselves.

A critical further goal of this work will be to try to identify multiple indices of the goal maintenance construct (via brain-based or behavior-based process estimates) across task domains, in order to more rigorously establish that such a coherent construct can be formed and utilized to understand cognitive aging more broadly. In this endeavor, the psychometrically rigorous approaches advocated by Salthouse and others (Salthouse, 2001, 2005b, 2006) will become invaluable. In particular, if and when a coherent goal maintenance construct can be established, it can form the basis for the types of cross-sectional (and longitudinal) covariation studies that are so powerful and useful within aging research. The key questions that need to be answered concern whether the goal maintenance construct can explain significant amounts of age-related variation relative to other potential constructs (e.g., processing speed), and the degree to which the goal maintenance construct is distinct from other constructs that may also impact cognitive aging. In this regard, the recent work examining error/performance monitoring, emotion–cognition interactions, and integration are potentially very informative, as they are suggestive of other dimensions of executive control and associated neural mechanisms that may be independent of goal maintenance, but may also show interesting interactions.

The final recent development that was discussed in this chapter suggests that it is equally important to consider the temporal dynamics of executive control in terms of the role of goal maintenance. In particular, recent work suggests that older adults may not have a static impairment in the ability to represent and maintain goals, but rather that the dynamics of this process become dysregulated with advancing age. Thus, it may be the case that older adults suffer from greater fluctuations in the activation level of maintained goals, or show a reduced tendency to engage and maintain goal representations in a proactive fashion. However, initial work examining these processes suggests that such changes in goal maintenance dynamics may not be a fixed impairment in older adults, but could be potentially amenable to direct training and instruction (Erickson et al., 2007; Paxton et al., 2006). Such work, though currently only in its infancy, may provide a path towards arguably the most important goal of cognitive aging research—to translate improved understanding of the fundamental age-related cognitive impairments into effective interventions that can minimize or, ideally, reverse them.

REFERENCES

Allen, P. A., Smith, A. F., Vires-Collins, H., & Sperry, S. (1998). The psychological refractory period: Evidence for age differences in attentional time-sharing. *Psychology and Aging*, 13(2), 218–229.

Allport, A., Styles, E. A., & Hsieh, S. (1994). Shifting intentional set: Exploring the dynamic control of tasks. In C. Umilta & M. Moscovitch (Eds.), *Attention and performance XV* (pp. 421–452). Cambridge, MA: MIT Press.

Allport, A., & Wylie, G. (2000). Task-switching, stimulus-response bindings, and negative priming. In S. Monsell & J. S. Driver (Eds.), *Attention and performance XVIII: Control of cognitive processes* (pp. 35–70). Cambridge, MA: MIT Press.

Anderson, N. D., Craik, F. I. M., & Naveh-Benjamin, M. (1998). The attentional demands of encoding and retrieval in younger and older adults: 1. Evidence from divided attention costs. *Psychology and Aging*, 13(3), 405–423.

Anderson, S. W., Damasio, H., Jones, D. R., & Tranel, D. (1991). Wisconsin card sorting test performance as a measure of frontal lobe damage. *Journal of Clinical and Experimental Neuropsychology*, 13(6), 909–922.

Babcock, R. L., & Salthouse, T. A. (1990). Effects of increased processing demands on age differences in working memory. *Psychology and Aging*, 5(3), 421–428.

Bäckman, L., & Farde, L. (2005). The role of dopamine systems in cognitive aging. In R. Cabeza, L. Nyberg, & D. Park (Eds.), *Cognitive neuroscience of aging: Linking cognitive and cerebral aging* (pp. 58–84). New York: Oxford University Press.

Baddeley, A. (1986). *Working memory.* Oxford: Oxford University Press.

Baddeley, A. (2003). Working memory: Looking back and looking forward. *Nature Reviews Neuroscience*, 4(10), 829–839.

Band, G. P., & Kok, A. (2000). Age effects on response monitoring in a mental-rotation task. *Biological Psychology*, 51(2–3), 201–221.

Barch, D. M., Braver, T. S., Nystrom, L. E., Forman, S. D., Noll, D. C., & Cohen, J. D. (1997). Dissociating working memory from task difficulty in human prefrontal cortex. *Neuropsychologia*, 35(10), 1373–1380.

Barch, D. M., Carter, C. S., Braver, T. S., Sabb, F. W., MacDonald, A., 3rd, Noll, D. C., et al. (2001). Selective deficits in prefrontal cortex function in medication-naive patients with schizophrenia. *Archives of General Psychiatry*, 58(3), 280–288.

Bechara, A., Damasio, H., & Damasio, A. R. (2000). Emotion, decision making and the orbitofrontal cortex. *Cerebral Cortex*, 10, 295–307.

Bechara, A., Damasio, H., Tranel, D., & Anderson, S. W. (1998). Dissociation of working memory from decision making within the human prefrontal cortex. *Journal of Neuroscience*, 18(1), 428–437.

Bechara, A., Damasio, H., Tranel, D., & Damasio, A. R. (1997). Deciding advantageously before knowing the advantageous strategy. *Science*, 275, 1293–1295.

Bedard, A. C., Nichols, S., Barbosa, J. A., Schachar, R., Logan, G. D., & Tannock, R. (2002). The development of selective inhibitory control across the life span. *Developmental Neuropsychology*, 21(1), 93–111.

Bherer, L., Kramer, A. F., Peterson, M. S., Colcombe, S., Erickson, K., & Becic, E. (2005).

Training effects on dual-task performance: Are there age-related differences in plasticity of attentional control? *Psychology and Aging, 20*(4), 695–709.

Bialystok, E., Craik, F. I. M., Klein, R., & Viswanathan, M. (2004). Bilingualism, aging, and cognitive control: Evidence from the Simon task. *Psychology and Aging, 19*(2), 290–303.

Bjorklund, D. F., & Harnishfeger, K. K. (1995). The evolution of inhibition mechanisms and their role in human cognition and behavior. In F. N. Dempster & C. J. Brainerd (Eds.), *Interference and inhibition in cognition.* San Diego: Academic Press.

Bopp, K. L., & Verhaeghen, P. (2005). Aging and verbal memory span: A meta-analysis. *Journal of Gerontology Series B: Psychological Sciences and Social Sciences, 60*(5), P223–233.

Botvinick, M. M., Braver, T. S., Barch, D. M., Carter, C. S., & Cohen, J. D. (2001). Conflict monitoring and cognitive control. *Psychological Review, 108*(3), 624–652.

Botwinick, J. (1969). Disinclination to venture versus cautiousness in responding: Age differences. *Journal of Genetic Psychology, 115,* 55–62.

Bowles, R. P., & Salthouse, T. A. (2003). Assessing the age-related effects of proactive interference on working memory tasks using the Rasch model. *Psychology and Aging, 18*(3), 608–615.

Brandimonte, M., Einstein, G., & McDaniel, M. (Eds.). (1996). *Prospective memory: Theory and applications.* Hillsdale, NJ: Lawrence Erlbaum Associates, Inc.

Brass, M., & von Cramon, D. Y. (2004). Decomposing components of task preparation with functional magnetic resonance imaging. *Journal of Cognitive Neuroscience, 16*(4), 609–620.

Braver, T. S., & Barch, D. M. (2002). A theory of cognitive control, aging cognition, and neuromodulation. *Neuroscience and Biobehavioral Reviews, 26,* 809–817.

Braver, T. S., Barch, D. M., & Cohen, J. D. (1999). Cognition and control in schizophrenia: A computational model of dopamine and prefrontal function. *Biological Psychiatry, 46,* 312–328.

Braver, T. S., Barch, D. M., Keys, B. A., Carter, C. S., Cohen, J. D., Kaye, J. A., et al. (2001). Context processing in older adults: Evidence for a theory relating cognitive control to neurobiology in healthy aging. *Journal of Experimental Psychology: General, 130,* 746–763.

Braver, T. S., & Bongiolatti, S. R. (2002). The role of frontopolar cortex in subgoal processing during working memory. *Neuroimage, 15*(3), 523–536.

Braver, T. S., & Cohen, J. D. (2000). On the control of control: The role of dopamine in regulating prefrontal function and working memory. In S. Monsell & J. Driver (Eds.), *Attention and performance XVIII* (pp. 713–738). Cambridge, MA: MIT Press.

Braver, T. S., & Cohen, J. D. (2001). Working memory, cognitive control, and the prefrontal cortex: Computational and empirical studies. *Cognitive Processing, 2,* 25–55.

Braver, T. S., Cohen, J. D., & Barch, D. M. (2002). The role of the prefrontal cortex in normal and disordered cognitive control: A cognitive neuroscience perspective. In D. T. Stuss & R. T. Knight (Eds.), *Principles of frontal lobe function* (pp. 428–448). Oxford: Oxford University Press.

Braver, T. S., Gray, J. R., & Burgess, G. C. (2007). Explaining the many varieties of working memory variation: Dual mechanisms of cognitive control. In A. Conway, C. Jarrold, M. Kane, A. Miyake, & J. Towse (Eds.), *Variation in working memory* (pp. 76–106). Oxford: Oxford University Press.

Braver, T. S., Locke, H. S., Paxton, J. L., & Barch, D. M. (in preparation). Flexible neural mechanisms of cognitive control in human prefrontal cortex.

Braver, T. S., Reynolds, J. R., & Donaldson, D. I. (2003). Neural mechanisms of transient and sustained cognitive control during task switching. *Neuron, 39*(4), 713–726.

Braver, T. S., & Ruge, H. (2006). Functional neuroimaging of executive functions. In R. Cabeza & A. Kingstone (Eds.), *Functional neuroimaging of cognition* (pp. 307–347). Cambridge, MA: MIT Press.

Braver, T. S., Satpute, A. B., Rush, B. K., Racine, C. A., & Barch, D. M. (2005). Context processing and context maintenance in healthy aging and early-stage dementia of the Alzheimer's type. *Psychology and Aging, 20,* 33–46.

Brinley, J. F. (1965). Cognitive sets, speed and accuracy of performance in the elderly. In A. T. Welford & J. E. Birren (Eds.), *Behavior, aging, and the nervous system* (pp. 114–149). Springfield: Charles C. Thomas.

Brown, J. W., & Braver, T. S. (2005). Learned predictions of error likelihood in the anterior cingulate cortex. *Science, 307,* 1118–1121.

Brown, J. W., Reynolds, J. R., & Braver, T. S. (2006). A computational model of fractionated conflict-control mechanisms in task-switching. *Cognitive Psychology.*

Bunge, S. A., Wendelken, C., Badre, D., & Wagner, A. D. (2005). Analogical reasoning and prefrontal cortex: Evidence for separable retrieval and integration mechanisms. *Cerebral Cortex, 15*(3), 239–249.

Butler, K. M., McDaniel, M. A., Dornburg, C. C., Price, A. L., & Roediger, H. L., 3rd. (2004). Age differences in veridical and false recall are not inevitable: The role of frontal lobe function. *Psychonomic Bulletin & Review, 11*(5), 921–925.

Butler, K. M., Zacks, R. T., & Henderson, J. M. (1999). Suppression of reflexive saccades in younger and older adults: age comparisons on an antisaccade task. *Memory and Cognition, 27*(4), 584–591.

Cabeza, R. (2002). Hemispheric asymmetry reduction in older adults: The HAROLD model. *Psychology and Aging, 17*(1), 85–100.

Cabeza, R., & Nyberg, L. (2000). Imaging cognition II: An empirical review of 275 PET and fMRI studies. *Journal of Cognitive Neuroscience, 12,* 1–47.

Cabeza, R., Nyberg, L., & Park, D. (2005). *Cognitive neuroscience of aging: Linking cognitive and cerebral aging.* New York: Oxford University Press.

Carstensen, L. L., & Mikels, J. A. (2005). At the intersection of emotion and cognition: Aging and the positivity effect. *Current Directions in Psychological Science, 14,* 117–121.

Carter, C. S., Braver, T. S., Barch, D. M., Botvinick, M. M., Noll, D., & Cohen, J. D. (1998). Anterior cingulate cortex, error detection, and the online monitoring of performance. *Science, 280*(5364), 747–749.

Casey, B. J., Tottenham, N., Liston, C., & Durston, S. (2005). Imaging the developing brain: What have we learned about cognitive development? *Trends in Cognitive Sciences, 9*(3), 104–110.

Chalfonte, B. L., & Johnson, M. K. (1996). Feature memory and binding in young and older adults. *Memory and Cognition, 24*(4), 403–416.

Christoff, K., & Gabrieli, J. D. (2000). The frontopolar cortex and human cognition: Evidence for a rostrocaudal hierarchical organization within the human prefrontal cortex. *Psychobiology, 28,* 168–186.

Christoff, K., Prabhakaran, V., Dorfman, J., Zhao, Z., Kroger, J. K., Holyoak, K. J., et al. (2001). Rostrolateral prefrontal cortex involvement in relational integration during reasoning. *Neuroimage, 14*(5), 1136–4119.

Clark, L., Manes, F., Antoun, N., Sahakian, B. J., & Robbins, T. W. (2003). The contributions of lesion laterality and lesion volume to decision-making impairment following frontal lobe damage. *Neuropsychologia, 41*(11), 1474–1483.

Cohen, A., West, R., & Craik, F. I. M. (2001). Modulation of the prospective and retrospective components of memory for intentions in younger and older adults. *Aging Neuropsychology and Cognition, 8*(1), 1–13.

Cohen, J. D., Botvinick, M., & Carter, C. S. (2000). Anterior cingulate and prefrontal cortex: Who's in control? *Nature Neuroscience, 3*(5), 421–423.

Cohen, J. D., Dunbar, K., & McClelland, J. L. (1990). On the control of automatic processes: A parallel distributed processing account of the Stroop effect. *Psychological Review, 97*(3), 332–361.

Convit, A., Wolf, O. T., de Leon, M. J., Patalinjug, M., Kandil, E., Caraos, C., et al. (2001). Volumetric analysis of the pre-frontal regions: Findings in aging and schizophrenia. *Psychiatry Research: Neuroimaging, 107*(2), 61–73.

Cowan, N. (1988). Evolving conceptions of memory storage, selective attention, and their mutual constraints within the human information-processing system. *Psychological Bulletin, 104*, 163–191.

Cowan, N. (1995). *Attention and memory*. Oxford: Oxford University Press.

Cowan, N. (1999). An embedded-process model of working memory. In A. Miyake & P. Shah (Eds.), *Models of working memory* (pp. 62–101). Cambridge: Cambridge University Press.

Craik, F. I. M. (1977). Age differences in human memory. In J. E. Birren & K. W. Schaie (Eds.), *Handbook of the psychology of aging* (pp. 384–420). New York: Van Nostrand Reinhold.

Craik, F. I. M., & Bialystok, E. (2005). Intelligence and executive control: Evidence from aging and bilingualism. *Cortex, 41*(2), 222–224.

Craik, F. I. M., & Byrd, M. (1982). Aging and cognitive deficits: The role of attentional resources. In F. I. M. Craik & S. Trehub (Eds.), *Aging & cognitive processes: Advances in the study of communication and affect* (Vol. 8, pp. 191–211). New York: Plenum Press.

Craik, F. I. M., Govoni, R., Naveh-Benjamin, M., & Anderson, N. D. (1996). The effects of divided attention on encoding and retrieval processes in human memory. *Journal of Experimental Psychology: General, 2*, 159–180.

Craik, F. I. M., & Jennings, J. M. (1992). Human memory. In F. I. M. Craik & T. A. Salthouse (Eds.), *The handbook of aging and cognition* (pp. 51–110). Hillsdale, NJ: Lawrence Erlbaum Associates, Inc.

Craik, F. I. M., & McDowd, J. M. (1987). Age differences in recall and recognition. *Journal of Experimental Psychology: Learning, Memory and Cognition, 13*, 474–479.

Craik, F. I. M., Morris, L. W., Morris, R. G., & Loewen, E. R. (1990). Relations between source amnesia and frontal lobe functioning in older adults. *Psychology and Aging, 5*(1), 148–151.

Damasio, A. R. (1994). *Descartes' error: Emotion, reason and the human brain*. New York: Grosset/Putnam.

Davidson, D. J., Zacks, R. T., & Williams, C. C. (2003). Stroop interference, practice, and aging. *Aging, Neuropsychology, and Cognition, 10*, 85–98.

Davidson, P. S., & Glisky, E. L. (2002). Neuropsychological correlates of recollection and familiarity in normal aging. *Cognitive, Affective, & Behavioral Neuroscience, 2*(2), 174–186.

Deakin, J., Aitken, M., Robbins, T., & Sahakian, B. J. (2004). Risk taking during decision-making in normal volunteers changes with age. *Journal of the International Neuropsychological Society, 10*(4), 590–598.

Dehaene, S., Posner, M. I., & Tucker, D. M. (1994). Localization of a neural system for error detection and compensation. *Psychological Science, 5*(5), 303–306.

De Jong, R. (2001). Adult age differences in goal activation and goal maintenance. *European Journal of Cognitive Psychology, 13*(1/2), 71–89.

Demakis, G. J. (2003). A meta-analytic review of the sensitivity of the Wisconsin Card Sorting Test to frontal and lateralized frontal brain damage. *Neuropsychology, 17*(2), 255–264.

Denburg, N. L., Tranel, D., & Bechara, A. (2005). The ability to decide advantageously declines prematurely in some normal older persons. *Neuropsychologia, 43*(7), 1099–1106.

De Pisapia, N., Repovs, G., & Braver, T. S. (in press). Computational models of attention and cognitive control. In R. Sun (Ed.), *Handbook on computational cognitive modelling*. Cambridge: Cambridge University Press.

De Pisapia, N., Slomski, J. A., & Braver, T. S. (2006). Functional specializations in lateral prefrontal cortex associated with the integration and segregation of information in working memory. *Cerebral Cortex*.

Desimone, R., & Duncan, J. (1995). Neural mechanisms of selective visual attention. *Annual Review of Neuroscience, 18*, 193–222.

Diamond, A. (1998). Evidence for the importance of dopamine for prefrontal cortex functions earlyl in life. In A. C. Roberts, T. W. Robbins, & L. Weiskrantz (Eds.), *The prefrontal cortex: Executive and cognitive functions* (pp. 144–164). Oxford: Oxford University Press.

Diamond, A. (2002). Normal development of prefrontal cortex from birth to young adulthood: Cognitive functions, anatomy, and biochemistry. In D. T. Stuss & R. T. Knight (Eds.), *Principles of frontal lobe function* (pp. 466–503). Oxford: Oxford University Press.

DiGirolamo, G. J., Kramer, A. F., Barad, V., Cepeda, N. J., Weissman, D. H., Milham, M. P., et al. (2001). General and task-specific frontal lobe recruitment in older adults during executive processes: A fMRI investigation of task-switching. *NeuroReport, 12*(9), 2065–2071.

Dobbs, A. R., & Rule, B. G. (1987). Prospective memory and self-reports of memory abilities in older adults. *Canadian Journal of Psychology, 41*(2), 209–222.

Dulaney, C. L., & Rogers, W. A. (1994). Mechanisms underlying reduction in Stroop interference with practice for young and older adults. *Journal of Experimental Psychology: Learning, Memory and Cognition, 20*, 470–484.

Duncan, J. (1995). Attention, intelligence, and the frontal lobes. In M. Gazzaniga (Ed.), *The cognitive neurosciences* (pp. 721–733). Cambridge, MA: MIT Press.

Duncan, J., Emslie, H., Williams, P., Johnson, R., & Freer, C. (1996). Intelligence and the frontal lobe: The organization of goal-directed behavior. *Cognitive Psychology, 30*, 257–303.

Duncan, J., & Owen, A. M. (2000). Common regions of the human frontal lobe recruited by diverse cognitive demands. *Trends in Neurosciences, 23*(10), 475–483.

Dux, P. E., Ivanoff, J., Asplund, C. L., & Marois, R. (2006). Isolation of a central bottleneck of information processing with time-resolved fMRI. *Neuron, 52*, 1109–1120.

Eenshuistra, R. M., Ridderinkhof, K. R., & van der Molen, M. W. (2004). Age-related changes in antisaccade task performance: Inhibitory control or working-memory engagement? *Brain and Cognition, 56*(2), 177–188.

Einstein, G. O., & McDaniel, M. A. (1990). Normal aging and prospective memory. *Journal of Experimental Psychology: Learning, Memory, and Cognition, 16*(4), 717–726.

Einstein, G. O., & McDaniel, M. A. (1996). Retrieval processes in prospective memory: Theoretical approaches and some new empirical findings. In M. Brandimonte, G. O. Einstein, & M. A. McDaniel (Eds.), *Prospective memory: Theory and applications* (pp. 115–142). Mahwah, NJ: Lawrence Erlbaum Associates, Inc.

Einstein, G. O., McDaniel, M. A., Manzi, M., Cochran, B., & Baker, M. (2000). Prospective memory and aging: Forgetting intentions over short delays. *Psychology and Aging, 15*(4), 1–13.

Einstein, G. O., McDaniel, M. A., Smith, R. E., & Shaw, P. (1998). Habitual prospective memory and aging: Remembering intentions and forgetting actions. *Psychological Science, 9*(4), 284–288.

Einstein, G. O., McDaniel, M. A., Thomas, R., Mayfield, S., Shank, H., Morrisette, N., et al. (2005). Multiple processes in prospective memory retrieval: Factors determining monitoring versus spontaneous retrieval. *Journal of Experimental Psychology: General, 134*(3), 327–342.

Einstein, G. O., Smith, R. E., McDaniel, M. A., & Shaw, P. (1997). Aging and prospective memory: The influence of increased task demands at encoding and retrieval. *Psychology and Aging, 12*(3), 479–488.

Engle, R. W. (2002). Working memory capacity as executive attention. *Current Directions in Psychological Science, 11*, 19–23.

Engle, R. W., Conway, A. R. A., Tuholski, S. W., & Shisler, R. J. (1995). A resource account of inhibition. *Psychological Science, 6*, 122–125.

Engle, R. W., Tuholski, S. W., Laughlin, J. E., & Conway, A. R. A. (1999). Working memory, short-term memory, and general fluid intelligence: A latent-variable approach. *Journal of Experimental Psychology: General, 128*, 309–331.

Erickson, K. I., Colcombe, S. J., Wadhwa, R., Bherer, L., Peterson, M. S., Scalf, P. E., et al. (2007). Training-induced functional activation changes in dual-task processing: An FMRI study. *Cerebral Cortex, 17*(1), 192–204.

Falkenstein, M., Hohnsbein, J., Hoormann, J., & Blanke, L. (1991). Effects of crossmodal divided attention on late ERP components. II. Error processing in choice reaction tasks. *Electroencephalography and Clinical Neurophysiology, 78*(6), 447–455.

Falkenstein, M., Hoormann, J., & Hohnsbein, J. (2001). Changes of error-related ERPs with age. *Experimental Brain Research, 138*(2), 258–262.

Fellows, L. K. (2004). The cognitive neuroscience of human decision making: A review and conceptual framework. *Behavioral and Cognitive Neuroscience Reviews, 3*(3), 159–172.

Fellows, L. K., & Farah, M. J. (2005). Different underlying impairments in decision-making following ventromedial and dorsolateral frontal lobe damage in humans. *Cerebral Cortex, 15*(1), 58–63.

Fernandes, M. A., Davidson, P. S., Glisky, E. L., & Moscovitch, M. (2004). Contribution of frontal and temporal lobe function to memory interference from divided attention at retrieval. *Neuropsychology, 18*(3), 514–525.

Frank, M. J., & Claus, E. D. (2006). Anatomy of a decision: Striato-orbitofrontal interactions in reinforcement learning, decision making, and reversal. *Psychological Review, 113*(2), 300–326.

Friedman, N. P., & Miyake, A. (2004). The relations among inhibition and interference control functions: A latent-variable analysis. *Journal of Experimental Psychology: General, 133*(1), 101–135.

Fristoe, N. M., Salthouse, T. A., & Woodard, J. L. (1997). Examination of age-related deficits on the Wisconsin Card Sorting Test. *Neuropsychology, 11*(3), 428–436.

Fukui, H., Murai, T., Fukuyama, H., Hayashi, T., & Hanakawa, T. (2005). Functional activity related to risk anticipation during performance of the Iowa Gambling Task. *Neuroimage, 24*(1), 253–259.

Funahashi, S., Chafee, M. V., & Goldman-Rakic, P. S. (1993). Prefrontal neuronal activity in rhesus monkeys performing a delayed anti-saccade task. *Nature, 365*, 753–755.

Gehring, W. J., Goss, B., Coles, M. G. H., Meyer, D. E., & Donchin, E. (1993). A neural system for error detection and compensation. *Psychological Science, 4*, 385–390.

Glass, J. M., Schumacher, E. H., Lauber, E. J., Zurbriggen, E. L., Gmeindl, L., Kieras, D. E., et al. (2000). Aging and the psychological refractory period: Task-coordination strategies in young and old adults. *Psychology and Aging, 15*(4), 571–595.

Glisky, E. L., Polster, M. R., & Routhieaux, B. C. (1995). Double dissociation between item and source memory. *Psychology and Aging, 9*, 229–235.

Guitton, D., Buchtel, H. A., & Douglas, R. M. (1985). Frontal lobe lesions in man cause difficulties in suppressing reflexive glances and in generating goal-directed saccades. *Experimental Brain Research, 58*, 455–472.

Gunning-Dixon, F. M., & Raz, N. (2003). Neuroanatomical correlates of selected executive functions in middle-aged and older adults: A prospective MRI study. *Neuropsychologia, 41*(14), 1929–1941.

Guynn, M. J. (2003). A two-process model of strategic monitoring in event-based prospective memory: Activation/retrieval mode and checking. *International Journal of Psychology, 38*, 245–256.

Haarmann, H. J., Ashling, G. E., Davelaar, E. J., & Usher, M. (2005). Age-related declines in context maintenance and semantic short-term memory. *Quarterly Journal of Experimental Psychology: Section A, 58*(1), 34–53.

Hartley, A. A. (1992). Attention. In F. I. M. Craik & T. Salthouse (Eds.), *The handbook of aging and cognition* (pp. 3–49). Hillsdale, NJ: Lawrence Erlbaum Associates, Inc.

Hartley, A. A. (1993). Evidence for the selective preservation of spatial selective attention in old age. *Psychology and Aging, 8*(3), 371–379.

Hartley, A. A. (2001). Age differences in dual-task interference are localized to response-generation processes. *Psychology and Aging, 16*(1), 47–54.

Hartley, A. A., & Little, D. M. (1999). Age-related differences and similarities in dual-task interference. *Journal of Experimental Psychology: General, 128*(4), 416–449.

Hartley, J. T. (1986). Reader and text variables as determinants of discourse memory in adulthood. *Psychology and Aging, 1*, 150–158.

Hartman, M., Bolton, E., & Fehnel, S. E. (2001). Accounting for age differences on the Wisconsin Card Sorting Test: Decreased working memory, not inflexibility. *Psychology and Aging, 16*(3), 385–399.

Hasher, L., Chung, C., May, C. P., & Foong, N. (2002). Age, time of testing, and proactive interference. *Canadian Journal of Experimental Psychology, 56*(3), 200–207.

Hasher, L., & Zacks, R. T. (1979). Automatic and effortful processes in memory. *Journal of Experimental Psychology, 108*(3), 356–388.

Hasher, L., & Zacks, R. T. (1988). Working memory, comprehension, and aging: A review and a new view. *The Psychology of Learning and Motivation, 22*, 193–225.

Hay, J. F., & Jacoby, L. L. (1999). Separating habit and recollection in young and older adults: Effects of elaborative processing and distinctiveness. *Psychology and Aging, 14*(1), 122–134.

Hedden, T., & Park, D. (2001). Aging and interference in verbal working memory. *Psychology and Aging, 16*(4), 666–681.

Hedden, T., & Park, D. C. (2003). Contributions of source and inhibitory mechanisms to age-related retroactive interference in verbal working memory. *Journal of Experimental Psychology: General, 132*(1), 93–112.

Hein, G., & Schubert, T. (2004). Aging and input processing in dual-task situations. *Psychology and Aging, 19*(3), 416–432.

Henry, J. D., MacLeod, M. S., Phillips, L. H., & Crawford, J. R. (2004). A meta-analytic review of prospective memory and aging. *Psychology and Aging, 19*(1), 27–39.

Hester, R. L., Murphy, K., Foxe, J. J., Foxe, D. M., Javitt, D. C., & Garavan, H. (2004). Predicting success: Patterns of cortical activation and deactivation prior to response inhibition. *Journal of Cognitive Neuroscience, 16*(5), 776–785.

Hofer, S. M., & Sliwinski, M. J. (2001). Understanding ageing. An evaluation of research designs for assessing the interdependence of ageing-related changes. *Gerontology, 47*(6), 341–352.

Holroyd, C. B., & Coles, M. G. (2002). The neural basis of human error processing: Reinforcement learning, dopamine, and the error-related negativity. *Psychological Review, 109*(4), 679–709.

Jacoby, L. L., Bishara, A. J., Hessels, S., & Toth, J. P. (2005). Aging, subjective experience, and cognitive control: Dramatic false remembering by older adults. *Journal of Experimental Psychology: General, 134*(2), 131–148.

Jacques, S., & Zelazo, P. D. (2001). The Flexible Item Selection Task (FIST): A measure of executive function in preschoolers. *Developmental Neuropsychology, 20*(3), 573–591.

Jennings, J. M., & Jacoby, L. L. (1993). Automatic versus intentional uses of memory: Aging, attention, and control. *Psychology and Aging, 8*(2), 283–293.

Jennings, J. M., & Jacoby, L. L. (2003). Improving memory in older adults: Training recollection. *Neuropsychological Rehabilitation, 13*, 417–440.

Jersild, A. T. (1927). Mental set and shift. *Archives of Psychology, 89*.

Johnson, M. K., Mitchell, K. J., Raye, C. L., & Greene, E. J. (2004). An age-related deficit in prefrontal cortical function associated with refreshing information. *Psychological Science*, 15(2), 127–132.

Johnson, M. K., Reeder, J. A., Raye, C. L., & Mitchell, K. J. (2002). Second thoughts versus second looks: An age-related deficit in reflectively refreshing just-activated information. *Psychological Science*, 13(1), 64–67.

Jonides, J., Marshuetz, C., Smith, E. E., Reuter-Lorenz, P. A., Koeppe, R. A., & Hartley, A. (2000). Age differences in behavior and PET activation reveal differences in interference resolution in verbal working memory. *Journal of Cognitive Neuroscience*, 12, 188–196.

Kane, M. J., & Engle, R. W. (2000). Working-memory capacity, proactive interference, and divided attention: Limits on long-term memory retrieval. *Journal of Experimental Psychology: Learning, Memory, and Cognition*, 26(2), 336–358.

Kane, M. J., & Engle, R. W. (2002). The role of prefrontal cortex in working-memory capacity, executive attention and general fluid intelligence: An individual-differences perspective. *Psychonomic Bulletin and Review*, 9, 637–671.

Kane, M. J., & Engle, R. W. (2003). Working-memory capacity and the control of attention: The contributions of goal neglect, response competition, and task set to Stroop interference. *Journal of Experimental Psychology: General*, 132(1), 47–70.

Kerns, J. G., Cohen, J. D., MacDonald, A. W., 3rd, Cho, R. Y., Stenger, V. A., & Carter, C. S. (2004). Anterior cingulate conflict monitoring and adjustments in control. *Science*, 303(5660), 1023–1026.

Kidder, D. P., Park, D. C., Hertzog, C., & Morrell, R. W. (1997). Prospective memory and aging: The effects of working memory and prospective memory task load. *Aging, Neuropsychology, and Cognition*, 4(93–112).

Kliegel, M., Martin, M., & Moor, C. (2003). Prospective memory and ageing: Is task importance relevant? *International Journal of Psychology*, 38, 207–214.

Koechlin, E., Basso, G., Pietrini, P., Panzer, S., & Grafman, J. (1999). The role of the anterior prefrontal cortex in human cognition. *Nature*, 399, 148–151.

Kornblum, S. (1992). Dimensional overlap and dimensional relevance in stimulus-response and stimulus-stimulus compatibility. In G. E. Stelmach & J. Requin (Eds.), *Tutorials in motor behavior II* (pp. 743–777). Amsterdam: Elsevier.

Kramer, A. F., Humphrey, D. G., Larish, J. F., Logan, G. D., & Strayer, D. L. (1994). Aging and inhibition: Beyond a unitary view of inhibitory processing in attention. *Psychology and Aging*, 9(4), 491–512.

Krawczyk, D. C. (2002). Contributions of the prefrontal cortex to the neural basis of human decision making. *Neuroscience and Biobehavioral Reviews*, 26(6), 631–664.

Kray, J., Li, K. Z., & Lindenberger, U. (2002). Age-related changes in task-switching components: The role of task uncertainty. *Brain and Cognition*, 49(3), 363–381.

Kray, J., & Lindenberger, U. (2000). Adult age differences in task switching. *Psychology and Aging*, 15(1), 126–147.

Kroger, J. K., Sabb, F. W., Fales, C. L., Bookheimer, S. Y., Cohen, M. S., & Holyoak, K. J. (2002). Recruitment of anterior dorsolateral prefrontal cortex in human reasoning: A parametric study of relational complexity. *Cerebral Cortex*, 12(5), 477–485.

Li, S. C., Naveh-Benjamin, M., & Lindenberger, U. (2005). Aging neuromodulation impairs associative binding: A neurocomputational account. *Psychological Science*, 16(6), 445–450.

Light, L. L., & Anderson, P. A. (1985). Working-memory capacity, age, and memory for discourse. *Journal of Gerontology*, 40(6), 737–747.

Lindsay, D. S., & Jacoby, L. L. (1994). Stroop process dissociations: The relationship between facilitation and interference. *Journal of Experimental Psychology: Human Perception & Performance*, 20(2), 219–234.

Logan, G. D., & Bundesen, C. (2003). Clever homunculus: Is there an endogenous act of control in the explicit task cuing procedure? *Journal of Experimental Psychology: Human Perception and Performance, 29,* 575–599.

Logan, G. D., & Cowan, W. B. (1984). On the ability to inhibit thought and action: A theory of an act of control. *Psychological Review, 91*(3), 295–327.

Logan, G. D., & Gordon, R. D. (2001). Executive control of visual attention in dual-task situations. *Psychological Review, 108*(2), 393–434.

Logie, R. H., Maylor, E. A., Della Sala, S., & Smith, G. (2004). Working memory in event- and time-based prospective memory tasks: Effects of secondary demand and age. *European Journal of Cognitive Psychology, 16,* 441–456.

Luria, A. R. (1966). *Higher cortical functions in man.* London: Tavistock.

Lustig, C., Hasher, L., & Tonev, S. T. (2006). Distraction as a determinant of processing speed. *Psychonomic Bulletin and Review, 13,* 619–625.

Lustig, C., May, C. P., & Hasher, L. (2001). Working memory span and the role of proactive interference. *Journal of Experimental Psychology: General, 130*(2), 199–207.

MacDonald, A. W., 3rd, & Carter, C. S. (2003). Event-related FMRI study of context processing in dorsolateral prefrontal cortex of patients with schizophrenia. *Journal of Abnormal Psychology, 112*(4), 689–697.

MacDonald, A. W., 3rd, Goghari, V. M., Hicks, B. M., Flory, J. D., Carter, C. S., & Manuck, S. B. (2005). A convergent-divergent approach to context processing, general intellectual functioning, and the genetic liability to schizophrenia. *Neuropsychology, 19*(6), 814–821.

MacLeod, C. M., & Dunbar, K. (1988). Training and Stroop-like interference: Evidence for a continuum of automaticity. *Journal of Experimental Psychology, 14,* 126–135.

MacPherson, S. E., Phillips, L. H., & Della Sala, S. (2002). Age, executive function, and social decision making: A dorsolateral prefrontal theory of cognitive aging. *Psychology and Aging, 17*(4), 598–609.

Manes, F., Sahakian, B., Clark, L., Rogers, R., Antoun, N., Aitken, M., et al. (2002). Decision-making processes following damage to the prefrontal cortex. *Brain, 125*(Pt 3), 624–639.

Mäntylä, T. (1994). Remembering to remember: Adult age differences in prospective memory. *Journal of Gerontology, 49*(6), P276–282.

Maquestiaux, F., Hartley, A. A., & Bertsch, J. (2004). Can practice overcome age-related differences in the psychological refractory period effect? *Psychology and Aging, 19*(4), 649–667.

Marschner, A., Mell, T., Wartenburger, I., Villringer, A., Reischies, F. M., & Heekeren, H. R. (2005). Reward-based decision-making and aging. *Brain Research Bulletin, 67*(5), 382–390.

Marsh, R. L., Hicks, J. L., Cook, G. I., & Mayhorn, C. B. (2007). Comparing younger and older adults in an event-based prospective memory paradigm containing an output monitoring component. *Aging, Neuropsychology, and Cognition, 14,* 168–188.

Martin, M., Kliegel, M., & McDaniel, M. A. (2003). The involvement of executive functions in prospective memory performance of adults. *International Journal of Psychology, 38,* 193–206.

Mathalon, D. H., Bennett, A., Askari, N., Gray, E. M., Rosenbloom, M. J., & Ford, J. M. (2003). Response-monitoring dysfunction in aging and Alzheimer's disease: An event-related potential study. *Neurobiology of Aging, 24*(5), 675–685.

Mather, M., & Carstensen, L. L. (2005). Aging and motivated cognition: The positivity effect in attention and memory. *Trends in Cognitive Sciences, 9*(10), 496–502.

Mather, M., & Knight, M. (2005). Goal-directed memory: The role of cognitive control in older adults' emotional memory. *Psychology and Aging, 20*(4), 554–570.

Mathewson, K. J., Dywan, J., & Segalowitz, S. J. (2005). Brain bases of error-related ERPs as influenced by age and task. *Biological Psychology, 70*(2), 88–104.

May, C. P., & Hasher, L. (1998). Synchrony effects in inhibitory control over thought and action. *Journal of Experimental Psychology: Human Perception and Performance, 24,* 363–379.

May, C. P., Hasher, L., & Kane, M. J. (1999a). The role of interference in memory span. *Memory and Cognition, 27*(5), 759–767.

May, C. P., Zacks, R. T., Hasher, L., & Multhaup, K. S. (1999b). Inhibition in the processing of garden-path sentences. *Psychology and Aging, 14*(2), 304–313.

Maylor, E. A. (1993). Aging and forgetting in prospective and retrospective memory tasks. *Psychology and Aging, 8*(3), 420–428.

Maylor, E. A. (1998). Changes in event-based prospective memory across adulthood. *Aging, Neuropsychology, and Cognition, 5*, 107–128.

Mayr, U. (2001). Age differences in the selection of mental sets: The role of inhibition, stimulus ambiguity, and response-set overlap. *Psychology and Aging, 16*(1), 96–109.

Mayr, U., & Kliegl, R. (1993). Sequential and coordinative complexity: Age-based processing limitations in figural transformations. *Journal of Experimental Psychology: Learning, Memory, and Cognition, 19*(6), 1297–1320.

McCabe, J., & Hartman, M. (2003). Examining the locus of age effects on complex span tasks. *Psychology and Aging, 18*(3), 562–572.

McDaniel, M. A., & Einstein, G. O. (1992). Aging and prospective memory: Basic findings and practical applications. *Advances in Learning and Behavioral Disabilities, 7*, 87–105.

McDaniel, M. A., Einstein, G. O., Stout, A. C., & Morgan, Z. (2003). Aging and maintaining intentions over delays: Do it or lose it. *Psychology and Aging, 18*(4), 823–835.

McDaniel, M. A., Glisky, E. L., Rubin, S. R., Guynn, M. J., & Routhieaux, B. C. (1999). Prospective memory: A neuropsychological study. *Neuropsychology, 13*(1), 103–110.

McDaniel, M. A., Guynn, M. J., Einstein, G. O., & Breneiser, J. (2004). Cue-focused and reflexive-associative processes in prospective memory retrieval. *Journal of Experimental Psychology: Learning, Memory, and Cognition, 30*(3), 605–614.

McDowd, J. M., & Craik, F. I. M. (1988). Effects of aging and task difficulty on divided attention performance. *Journal of Experimental Psychology: Human Perception and Performance, 14*(2), 267–280.

McDowd, J. M., & Shaw, R. J. (2000). Attention and aging: A functional perspective. In F. I. M. Craik & T. A. Salthouse (Eds.), *The handbook of aging and cognition* (2nd ed., pp. 221–292). Mahwah, NJ: Lawrence Erlbaum Associates, Inc.

McElree, B. (2001). Working memory and focal attention. *Journal of Experimental Psychology: Learning, Memory and Cognition, 27*(3), 817–835.

Meiran, N. (1996). Reconfiguration of processing mode prior to task performance. *Journal of Experimental Psychology: Learning, Memory, and Cognition, 22*(6), 1423–1442.

Meiran, N. (2000). Modeling cognitive control in task-switching. *Psychological Research, 63*, 234–249.

Meiran, N., Gotler, A., & Perlman, A. (2001). Old age is associated with a pattern of relatively intact and relatively impaired task-set switching abilities. *Journals of Gerontology: Series B: Psychological Sciences & Social Sciences, 56B*, P88–P102.

Melara, R. D., & Algom, D. (2003). Driven by information: A tectonic theory of Stroop effects. *Psychological Review, 110*(3), 422–471.

Meyer, D. E., & Kieras, D. E. (1997). A computational theory of executive cognitive processes and multiple-task performance: Part 2. Accounts of psychological refractory-period phenomena. *Psychological Review, 104*(4), 749–791.

Milham, M. P., Erickson, K. I., Banich, M. T., Kramer, A. F., Webb, A., Wszalek, T., et al. (2002). Attentional control in the aging brain: Insights from an fMRI study of the Stroop task. *Brain and Cognition, 49*(3), 277–296.

Miller, E. K., & Cohen, J. D. (2001). An integrative theory of prefrontal cortex function. *Annual Review of Neuroscience, 21*, 167–202.

Milner, B. (1963). Effects of different brain lesions on card sorting. *Archives of Neurology, 9*, 90–100.

Mitchell, K. J., Johnson, M. K., Raye, C. L., & D'Esposito, M. (2000a). fMRI evidence of age-related hippocampal dysfunction in feature binding in working memory. *Cognitive Brain Research, 10*(1–2), 197–206.

Mitchell, K. J., Johnson, M. K., Raye, C. L., Mather, M., & D'Esposito, M. (2000b). Aging and reflective processes of working memory. *Psychology and Aging, 15*(3), 527–541.

Miyake, A., Friedman, N. P., Emerson, M. J., Witzki, A. H., Howerter, A., & Wager, T. D. (2000). The unity and diversity of executive functions and their contributions to complex "frontal lobe" tasks: A latent variable analysis. *Cognitive Psychology, 41*, 49–100.

Monsell, S. (2003). Task switching. *Trends in Cognitive Sciences, 7*, 134–140.

Moscovitch, M. (1982). A neuropsychological approach to memory and perception in normal and pathological aging. In F. I. M. Craik & S. Trehub (Eds.), *Aging and cognitive processes* (pp. 55–78). New York: Plenum.

Moscovitch, M. (1992). Memory and working-with-memory: A component process model based on modules and central systems. *Journal of Cognitive Neuroscience, 4*, 257–267.

Moscovitch, M., & Winocur, G. (1992). The neuropsychology of memory and aging. In F. I. M. Craik & T. A. Salthouse (Eds.), *The handbook of aging and cognition*. Hillsdale, NJ: Lawrence Erlbaum Associates, Inc.

Munoz, D. P., Broughton, J. R., Goldring, J. E., & Armstrong, I. T. (1998). Age-related performance of human subjects on saccadic eye movement tasks. *Experimental Brain Research, 121*(4), 391–400.

Myerson, J., Emery, L., White, D. A., & Hale, S. (2003). Effects of age, domain, and processing demands on memory span: Evidence for differential decline. *Aging, Neuropsychology, and Cognition, 10*, 20–27.

Naveh-Benjamin, M. (2000). Adult age differences in memory performance: Tests of an associative deficit hypothesis. *Journal of Experimental Psychology: Learning, Memory, and Cognition, 26*(5), 1170–1187.

Naveh-Benjamin, M., Guez, J., Kilb, A., & Reedy, S. (2004). The associative memory deficit of older adults: Further support using face-name associations. *Psychology and Aging, 19*(3), 541–546.

Naveh-Benjamin, M., Hussain, Z., Guez, J., & Bar-On, M. (2003). Adult age differences in episodic memory: Further support for an associative-deficit hypothesis. *Journal of Experimental Psychology: Learning, Memory, and Cognition, 29*(5), 826–837.

Nieuwenhuis, S., Broerse, A., Nielen, M. M., & de Jong, R. (2004). A goal activation approach to the study of executive function: An application to antisaccade tasks. *Brain Cognition, 56*(2), 198–214.

Nieuwenhuis, S., Ridderinkhof, K. R., de Jong, R., Kok, A., & van der Molen, M. W. (2000). Inhibitory inefficiency and failures of intention activation: Age-related decline in the control of saccadic eye movements. *Psychology and Aging, 15*(4), 635–647.

Nieuwenhuis, S., Ridderinkhof, K. R., Talsma, D., Coles, M. G. H., Holroyd, C. B., Kok, A., et al. (2002). A computational account of altered error processing in older age: Dopamine and the error-related negativity. *Cognitive, Affective and Behavioral Neuroscience, 2*, 19–36.

Northoff, G., Grimm, S., Boeker, H., Schmidt, C., Bermpohl, F., Heinzel, A., et al. (2006). Affective judgment and beneficial decision making: Ventromedial prefrontal activity correlates with performance in the Iowa Gambling Task. *Human Brain Mapping, 27*(7), 572–587.

Oberauer, K. (2001). Removing irrelevant information from working memory: A cognitive aging study with the modified Sternberg task. *Journal of Experimental Psychology: Learning, Memory, and Cognition, 27*(4), 948–957.

Oberauer, K. (2002). Access to information in working memory: Exploring the focus of attention. *Journal of Experimental Psychology: Learning, Memory, and Cognition, 28*(3), 411–421.

Oberauer, K. (2005a). Binding and inhibition in working memory: Individual and age differences in short-term recognition. *Journal of Experimental Psychology: General, 134*(3), 368–387.

Oberauer, K. (2005b). Control of the contents of working memory—a comparison of two paradigms and two age groups. *Journal of Experimental Psychology: Learning, Memory, and Cognition, 31*(4), 714–728.

Oberauer, K., Demmrich, A., Mayr, U., & Kliegl, R. (2001). Dissociating retention and access in working memory: An age-comparative study of mental arithmetic. *Memory and Cognition, 29*(1), 18–33.

Oberauer, K., & Kliegl, R. (2001). Beyond resources: Formal models of complexity effects and age differences in working memory. *European Journal of Cognitive Psychology, 13*(1/2), 187–215.

Ochsner, K. N., Bunge, S. A., Gross, J. J., & Gabrieli, J. D. (2002). Rethinking feelings: An fMRI study of the cognitive regulation of emotion. *Journal of Cognitive Neuroscience, 14*(8), 1215–1229.

Ochsner, K. N., & Gross, J. J. (2005). The cognitive control of emotion. *Trends in Cognitive Sciences, 9*(5), 242–249.

O'Doherty, J., Critchley, H., Deichmann, R., & Dolan, R. J. (2003). Dissociating valence of outcome from behavioral control in human orbital and ventral prefrontal cortices. *Journal of Neuroscience, 23*(21), 7931–7939.

O'Doherty, J., Kringelbach, M. L., Rolls, E. T., Hornak, J., & Andrews, C. (2001). Abstract reward and punishment representations in the human orbitofrontal cortex. *Nature Neuroscience, 4*(1), 95–102.

Parkin, A. J., & Walter, B. M. (1992). Recollective experience, normal aging, and frontal dysfunction. *Psychology and Aging, 7*, 290–298.

Pashler, H. (1994). Dual-task interference in simple tasks: Data and theory. *Psychological Bulletin, 116(2)*, 220–244.

Paxton, J. L., Barch, D. M., Racine, C. A., & Braver, T. S. (in press). Cognitive control, goal maintenance, and prefrontal function in healthy aging. *Cerebral Cortex.*

Paxton, J. L., Barch, D. M., Storandt, M., & Braver, T. S. (2006). Effects of environmental support and strategy training on older adults' use of context. *Psychology and Aging, 21*(3), 499–509.

Perlstein, W. M., Dixit, N. K., Carter, C. S., Noll, D. C., & Cohen, J. D. (2003). Prefrontal cortex dysfunction mediates deficits in working memory and prepotent responding in schizophrenia. *Biological Psychiatry, 53*(1), 25–38.

Phillips, L. H., MacLeod, M., & Kliegl, M. (2005). Adult aging and cognitive planning. In G. Ward & R. Morris (Eds.), *The cognitive psychology of planning* (pp. 111–139). Hove, UK: Psychology Press.

Prabhakaran, V., Narayanan, K., Zhao, Z., & Gabrieli, J. D. (2000). Integration of diverse information in working memory within the frontal lobe. *Nature Neuroscience, 3*(1), 85–90.

Prull, M. W., Gabrieli, J. D. E., & Bunge, S. A. (2000). Age-related changes in memory: A cognitive neuroscience perspective. In F. I. M. Craik & T. A. Salthouse (Eds.), *The handbook of aging and cognition* (2nd ed., pp. 91–153). Mahwah, NJ: Lawrence Erlbaum Associates, Inc.

Ramnani, N., & Owen, A. M. (2004). Anterior prefrontal cortex: Insights into function from anatomy and neuroimaging. *Nature Reviews Neuroscience, 5*(3), 184–194.

Raz, N. (2000). Aging of the brain and its impact on cognitive performance: Integration of structural and functional findings. In F. I. M. Craik & T. A. Salthouse (Eds.), *The handbook of aging and cognition* (2nd ed.). Mahwah, NJ: Lawrence Erlbaum Associates, Inc.

Raz, N., Gunning-Dixon, F. M., Head, D., Dupuis, J. H., & Acker, J. D. (1998). Neuroanatomical correlates of cognitive aging: Evidence from structural magnetic resonance imaging. *Neuropsychology, 12*(1), 95–114.

Reimers, S., & Maylor, E. A. (2005). Task switching across the life span: Effects of age on general and specific switch costs. *Developmental Psychology, 41*(4), 661–671.

Reuter-Lorenz, P., & Sylvester, C.-Y. C. (2005). The cognitive neuroscience of working memory and aging. In R. Cabeza, L. Nyberg & D. Park (Eds.), *Cognitive neuroscience of aging: Linking cognitive and cerebral aging* (pp. 186–217). New York: Oxford University Press.

Rhodes, M. G. (2004). Age-related differences in performance on the Wisconsin card sorting test: A meta-analytic review. *Psychology and Aging, 19*(3), 482–494.

Ridderinkhof, K. R., van den Wildenberg, W. P., Segalowitz, S. J., & Carter, C. S. (2004). Neurocognitive mechanisms of cognitive control: The role of prefrontal cortex in action selection, response inhibition, performance monitoring, and reward-based learning. *Brain and Cognition, 56*(2), 129–140.

Rogers, R. D., & Monsell, S. (1995). Costs of a predictable switch between simple cognitive tasks. *Journal of Experimental Psychology: General, 124*(2), 207–231.

Rosvold, H. E., Mirsky, A. F., Sarason, I., Bransome, E. D., & Beck, L. H. (1956). A continuous performance test of brain damage. *Journal of Consulting Psychology, 20*(5), 343–350.

Royall, D. R., Palmer, R., Chiodo, L. K., & Polk, M. J. (2004). Declining executive control in normal aging predicts change in functional status: the Freedom House Study. *Journal of the American Geriatrics Society, 52*(3), 346–352.

Rubin, O., & Meiran, N. (2005). On the origins of the task mixing cost in the cuing task-switching paradigm. *Journal of Experimental Psychology: Learning, Memory, and Cognition, 31*(6), 1477–1491.

Ruge, H., Brass, M., Koch, I., Rubin, O., Meiran, N., & von Cramon, D. Y. (2005). Advance preparation and stimulus-induced interference in cued task switching: Further insights from BOLD fMRI. *Neuropsychologia, 43*(3), 340–355.

Rush, B. K., Barch, D. M., & Braver, T. S. (2006). Accounting for cognitive aging: Context processing, inhibition or processing speed? *Aging, Neuropsychology and Cognition, 13*(3–4), 588–610.

Rypma, B., & D'Esposito, M. (2000). Isolating the neural mechanisms of age-related changes in human working memory. *Nature Neuroscience, 3*, 509–515.

Salthouse, T. A. (1990). Working memory as a processing resource in cognitive aging. *Developmental Review, 10*(1), 101–124.

Salthouse, T. A. (1992). Influence of processing speed on adult age differences in working memory. *Acta Psychologica, 79*(2), 155–170.

Salthouse, T. A. (1994). The aging of working memory. *Neuropsychology, 8*(4), 535–543.

Salthouse, T. A. (2000). Methodological assumptions in cognitive aging research. In F. I. M. Craik & T. A. Salthouse (Eds.), *Handbook of aging and cognition* (2nd ed., pp. 467–498). Hillsdale, NJ: Lawrence Erlbaum Associates, Inc.

Salthouse, T. A. (2001). A research strategy for investigating group differences in a cognitive construct: Application to ageing and executive processes. *European Journal of Cognitive Psychology, 13*(1/2), 29–46.

Salthouse, T. A. (2005a). Effects of aging on reasoning. In K. Holyoak & R. G. Morrison (Eds.), *The Cambridge handbook of thinking and reasoning* (pp. 589–605). New York: Cambridge University Press.

Salthouse, T. A. (2005b). Relations between cognitive abilities and measures of executive functioning. *Neuropsychology, 19*(4), 532–545.

Salthouse, T. A. (2006). Theoretical issues in the psychology of aging. In J. E. Birren & K. W. Schaie (Eds.), *Handbook of the psychology of aging* (6th ed.). New York: Academic Press.

Salthouse, T. A., Atkinson, T. M., & Berish, D. E. (2003). Executive functioning as a potential mediator of age-related cognitive decline in normal adults. *Journal of Experimental Psychology: General, 132*(4), 566–594.

Salthouse, T. A., Berish, D. E., & Siedlecki, K. L. (2004). Construct validity and age sensitivity of prospective memory. *Memory and Cognition, 32*(7), 1133–1148.

Salthouse, T. A., & Miles, J. D. (2002). Aging and time-sharing aspects of executive control. *Memory and Cognition, 30*(4), 572–582.

Salthouse, T. A., Mitchell, D. R., Skovronek, E., & Babcock, R. L. (1989). Effects of adult age and working memory on reasoning and spatial abilities. *Journal of Experimental Psychology: Learning, Memory, and Cognition, 15*(3), 507–516.

Servan-Schreiber, D., Cohen, J. D., & Steingard, S. (1996). Schizophrenic deficits in the processing of context: A test of a theoretical model. *Archives of General Psychiatry, 53*, 1105–1113.

Shilling, V. M., Chetwynd, A., & Rabbitt, P. M. (2002). Individual inconsistency across measures of inhibition: An investigation of the construct validity of inhibition in older adults. *Neuropsychologia, 40*(6), 605–619.

Shum, D., Valentine, M., & Cutmore, T. (1999). Performance of individuals with severe long-term traumatic brain injury on time-, event-, and activity-based prospective memory tasks. *Journal of Clinical Experimental Neuropsychology, 21*(1), 49–58.

Smith, E. E., & Jonides, J. (1999). Storage and executive processes in the frontal lobes. *Science, 283*, 1657–1661.

Smith, R. E. (2003). The cost of remembering to remember in event-based prospective memory: Investigating the capacity demands of delayed intention performance. *Journal of Experimental Psychology: Learning, Memory, and Cognition, 29*, 347–361.

Smith, R. E., & Bayen, U. J. (2004). A multinomial model of event-based prospective memory. *Journal of Experimental Psychology: Learning, Memory, and Cognition, 30*(4), 756–777.

Smith, R. E., & Bayen, U. J. (2006). The source of adult age differences in event-based prospective memory: A multinomial modeling approach. *Journal of Experimental Psychology: Learning, Memory, and Cognition, 32*(3), 623–635.

Spector, A., & Biederman, I. (1976). Mental set and shift revisited. *American Journal of Psychology, 89*, 669–679.

Spencer, W. D., & Raz, N. (1995). Differential effects of aging on memory for content and context: A meta-analysis. *Psychology of Aging, 10*(4), 527–539.

Spieler, D. H. (2001). Modeling age-related changes in information processing. *European Journal of Cognitive Psychology, 13*(1/2), 217–234.

Spieler, D. H., Balota, D. A., & Faust, M. E. (1996). Stroop performance in healthy younger and older adults and in individuals with dementia of the Alzheimer's type. *Journal of Experimental Psychology: Human Perception and Performance, 22*, 461–479.

Sternberg, S. (1966). High-speed scanning in human memory. *Science, 153*, 652–654.

Stine, E. A., & Wingfield, A. (1990). How much do working memory deficits contribute to age differences in discourse memory. *European Journal of Cognitive Psychology, 2*, 289–304.

Stroop, J. R. (1935). Studies of interference in serial verbal reactions. *Journal of Experimental Psychology, 18*, 643–662.

Stuss, D. T., Alexander, M. P., Floden, D., Binns, M. A., Levine, B., McIntosh, A. R., et al. (2002). Fractionation and localization of distinct frontal lobe processes: Evidence from focal lesions in humans. In D. T. Stuss & R. T. Knight (Eds.), *Principles of frontal lobe function* (pp. 392–407). New York: Oxford University Press.

Stuss, D. T., & Benson, D. F. (1986). *The frontal lobes.* New York: Raven Press.

Stuss, D. T., Bisschop, S. M., Alexander, M. P., Levine, B., Katz, D., & Izukawa, D. (2001). The Trail Making Test: A study in focal lesion patients. *Psychological Assessment, 13*(2), 230–239.

Stuss, D. T., Floden, D., Alexander, M. P., Levine, B., & Katz, D. (2001). Stroop performance in focal lesion patients: Dissociation of processes and frontal lobe lesion location. *Neuropsychologia, 39*(8), 771–786.

Stuss, D. T., Levine, B., Alexander, M. P., Hong, J., Palumbo, C., Hamer, L., et al. (2000). Wisconsin Card Sorting Test performance in patients with focal frontal and posterior brain damage: Effects of lesion location and test structure on separable cognitive processes. *Neuropsychologia, 38*(4), 388–402.

Stuss, D. T., Shallice, T., Alexander, M. P., & Picton, T. W. (1995). A multidisciplinary approach to anterior attentional functions. *Annals of the New York Academy of Sciences, 769,* 191–211.

Troyer, A. K., Graves, R. E., & Cullum, C. C. (1994). Executive functioning as a mediator of the relationship between age and episodic memory in healthy aging. *Aging, Neuropsychology and Cognition, 1,* 45–53.

Uttl, B., & Graf, P. (1997). Color-word Stroop test performance across the adult life span. *Journal of Clinical Experimental Neuropsychology, 19*(3), 405–420.

van Boxtel, M. P., ten Tusscher, M. P., Metsemakers, J. F., Willems, B., & Jolles, J. (2001). Visual determinants of reduced performance on the Stroop color-word test in normal aging individuals. *Journal of Clinical Experimental Neuropsychology, 23*(5), 620–627.

Verhaeghen, P., & Basak, C. (2005). Ageing and switching of the focus of attention in working memory: Results from a modified N-back task. *Quarterly Journal of Experimental Psychology: Section A, 58*(1), 134–154.

Verhaeghen, P., & Cerella, J. (2002). Aging, executive control, and attention: A review of meta-analyses. *Neuroscience and Biobehavioral Reviews, 26*(7), 849–857.

Verhaeghen, P., Cerella, J., Bopp, K. L., & Basak, C. (2005). Aging and varieties of cognitive control: A review of meta-analyses on resistance to interference, coordination, and task switching, and an experimental exploration of age-sensitivity in the newly identified process of focus switching. In R. W. Engle, G. Sedeek, U. v. Hecker, & D. M. McIntosh (Eds.), *Cognitive limitations in aging and psychopathology: Attention, working memory, and executive functions* (pp. 160–189). Cambridge: Cambridge University Press.

Verhaeghen, P., & De Meersman, L. (1998). Aging and the Stroop effect: A meta-analysis. *Psychology and Aging, 13*(1), 120–126.

Verhaeghen, P., Kliegl, R., & Mayr, U. (1997). Sequential and coordinative complexity in time-accuracy functions for mental arithmetic. *Psychology and Aging, 12*(4), 555–564.

Verhaeghen, P., Steitz, D. W., Sliwinski, M. J., & Cerella, J. (2003). Aging and dual-task performance: A meta-analysis. *Psychology and Aging, 18*(3), 443–460.

Viskontas, I. V., Morrison, R. G., Holyoak, K. J., Hummel, J. E., & Knowlton, B. J. (2004). Relational integration, inhibition, and analogical reasoning in older adults. *Psychology and Aging, 19*(4), 581–591.

Vogels, W. W., Dekker, M. R., Brouwer, W. H., & de Jong, R. (2002). Age-related changes in event-related prospective memory performance: A comparison of four prospective memory tasks. *Brain Cognition, 49*(3), 341–362.

Welford, A. T. (1952). The 'psychological refractory period' and the timing of high-speed performance—a review and a theory. *British Journal of Psychology, 43,* 2–19.

West, R. (1996). An application of prefrontal cortex function theory to cognitive aging. *Psychological Bulletin, 120*(2), 272–292.

West, R. (1999). Age differences in lapses of intention in the Stroop task. *Journal of Gerontology: Psychological Sciences, 54B*(1), P34–P43.

West, R. (2001). The transient nature of executive control processes in younger and older adults. *European Journal of Cognitive Psychology, 13*(1/2), 91–105.

West, R. (2004). The effects of aging on controlled attention and conflict processing in the Stroop task. *Journal of Cognitive Neuroscience, 16*(1), 103–113.

West, R., & Alain, C. (2000a). Age-related decline in inhibitory control contributes to the increased Stroop effect observed in older adults. *Psychophysiology, 37*, 179–189.

West, R., & Alain, C. (2000b). Effects of task context and fluctuations of attention on neural activity supporting performance of the Stroop task. *Brain Research, 873*, 102–111.

West, R., & Baylis, G. C. (1998). Effects of increased response dominance and contextual disintegration on the Stroop interference effect in older adults. *Psychology and Aging, 13*(2), 206–217.

West, R., & Bowry, R. (2005). Effects of aging and working memory demands on prospective memory. *Psychophysiology, 42*(6), 698–712.

West, R., Bowry, R., & Krompinger, J. (2006). The effects of working memory demands on the neural correlates of prospective memory. *Neuropsychologia, 44*(2), 197–207.

West, R., & Covell, E. (2001). Effects of aging on event-related neural activity related to prospective memory. *Neuroreport, 12*(13), 2855–2858.

West, R., & Craik, F. I. M. (1999). Age-related decline in prospective memory: The roles of cue accessibility and cue sensitivity. *Psychology and Aging, 14*(2), 264–272.

West, R., & Craik, F. I. M. (2001). Influences on the efficiency of prospective memory in younger and older adults. *Psychology and Aging, 16*(4), 682–696.

West, R., & Moore, K. (2005). Adjustments of cognitive control in younger and older adults. *Cortex, 41*(4), 570–581.

West, R., Murphy, K. J., Armilio, M. L., Craik, F. I. M., & Stuss, D. T. (2002). Lapses of intention and performance variability reveal age-related increases in fluctuations of executive control. *Brain Cognition, 49*(3), 402–419.

West, R., & Schwarb, H. (2006). The influence of aging and frontal function on the neural correlates of regulative and evaluative aspects of cognitive control. *Neuropsychology, 20*(4), 468–481.

Williams, B. R., Ponesse, J. S., Schachar, R. J., Logan, G. D., & Tannock, R. (1999). Development of inhibitory control across the life span. *Developmental Psychology, 35*(1), 205–213.

Wood, S., Busemeyer, J., Koling, A., Cox, C. R., & Davis, H. (2005). Older adults as adaptive decision makers: Evidence from the Iowa Gambling Task. *Psychology and Aging, 20*(2), 220–225.

Yeung, N., Cohen, J. D., & Botvinick, M. M. (2004). The neural basis of error detection: Conflict monitoring and the error-related negativity. *Psychological Review, 111*(4), 931–959.

Zacks, R. T., Hasher, L., & Li, K. Z. H. (2000). Human memory. In F. I. M. Craik & T. A. Salthouse (Eds.), *The handbook of aging and cognition* (2nd ed., pp. 293–357). Mahwah, NJ: Lawrence Erlbaum Associates, Inc.

Zelazo, P. D., Craik, F. I. M., & Booth, L. (2004). Executive function across the life span. *Acta Psychologica, 115*(2–3), 167–183.

8

Language and Aging

Deborah M. Burke
Pomona College

Meredith A. Shafto
University of Cambridge

Language in old age has been an active research area since early experimental investigations in cognitive aging (e.g., Craik & Masani, 1967; Riegel & Riegel, 1964). This is undoubtedly because of the profound importance of language throughout the lifespan not only in cognition, but in social interactions as well. Declines in language processing, such as increased difficulty in understanding spoken language or in producing a word while speaking, undermine older adults' ability and desire to communicate, and can erode evaluation of their language competence by themselves and by others (e.g., Hummert, Garstka, Ryan, & Bonnesen, 2004; Ryan, See, Meneer, & Trovato, 1994). Negative self-appraisal promotes withdrawal from social interaction, and negative appraisal by others promotes their use of oversimplified speech to older adults (Hummert et al., 2004; Kemper, Finter-Urczyk, Ferrell, Harden, & Billington, 1998). This downward cycle highlights the practical significance of identifying patterns of change in language during adulthood and old age, especially since there is good news about aging in this research. The aging pattern is characterized by stability and improvement during adulthood in some language functions, unlike other cognitive abilities such as episodic or working memory which are characterized by quite uniform age-related decrements.

Research on language processing has also played an important role in the development of theory in cognitive aging (e.g., Baltes, Staudinger, & Lindenberger, 1999; Burke, Mackay, & James, 2000; DeDe, Caplan, Kemtes, & Waters, 2004; Hasher, Lustig, & Zacks, 2007; Kemper, 2006;

Light, 1991; MacKay & Abrams, 1996; Madden, 2001; Murphy, Craik, Li, & Schneider, 2000; Stine-Morrow, Miller, & Hertzog, 2006; Tun, Wingfield, Stine, & Mecsas, 1992). We will briefly review six theories of cognitive aging that motivate much of the research reviewed in this chapter. These theories postulate age-related resource deficits, general slowing, inhibition deficits, transmission deficits, declining working memory, or sensory/perceptual deficits. Some of these theories are not independent inasmuch as resource deficits are sometimes specified as declines in processing speed, efficiency of inhibition, and working memory capacity. We distinguish these models, however, because they are conceptually distinct and vary in their relevance to different research paradigms.

Testing these aging theories is aided by the fact that language research in general is a theoretically well-developed area of cognitive science. There are a number of well-specified models of the organization of the language system and although there are areas of controversy (e.g., Caramazza, Costa, Miozzo, & Bi, 2001; Levelt, Roelofs, & Meyer, 1999), there is also agreement about aspects of the architecture and mechanisms. We outline basic principles of a modal model of comprehension and production that are relevant to aging research, and then turn to the six cognitive aging theories relevant to language comprehension and production in old age.

THE LANGUAGE SYSTEM

Figure 8.1 illustrates a tiny portion of the language system within a model with connectionist architecture and localist/symbolic representations. A vast network of pathways connects representational units organized into subsystems. The *semantic subsystem* represents proposition and word meanings and lexical information such as syntactic class. The *phonological/orthographic subsystem* represents word sounds and spellings (e.g., Burke, MacKay, Worthley, & Wade, 1991; Caramazza, 1997; Dell, 1986; Levelt et al., 1999; MacKay, 1987; Schwartz, Dell, Martin, Gahl, & Sobel, 2006). Although aging models have postulated distributed deficits in specific processes, for example, speed of propagation of excitation in the network (e.g., Salthouse, 1996), aging research has not used models with distributed representations wherein semantic, phonological, and orthographic information is represented by patterns of activation over sets of units (e.g., Rogers & McClelland, 2004). Because we emphasize here language models that have been used as a framework in cognitive aging research, our modal model has localist rather than distributed representation.

Retrieval of information encoded in a representation occurs when

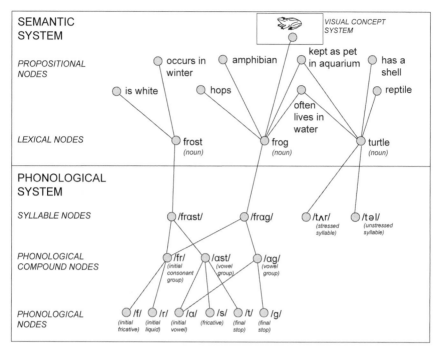

FIG. 8.1 Example of representation of some semantic, syntactic, and phonological information in an interactive activation model. Many nodes necessary for perceiving or producing these words have been omitted to simplify the figure.

excitation reaches a threshold, either absolute or relative to the level of excitation of other representations in the domain (Levelt, 2001). We use the term *priming* to refer to pre-threshold excitation that prepares a representational unit for activation, the process that triggers retrieval (MacKay, 1987). Relative thresholds explain, for example, neighborhood effects wherein words that have many phonologically related neighbors are more difficult to hear than words with few neighbors. This occurs because it takes more perceptual processing for the presented word to achieve threshold relative to its phonologically related neighbors, which have also accumulated priming (e.g., Luce & Pisoni, 1998). Interactive activation models of language feature parallel bottom-up and top-down connections between representations that transmit priming between semantic, lexical, and phonological/orthographic levels (see Figure 8.1) allowing feedback among representations at different levels (e.g., Cutting & Ferreira, 1999; Dell, Schwartz, Martin, Saffran, & Gagnon, 1997; MacKay, 1987; Rapp & Goldrick, 2000; Schwartz et al., 2006; but see Levelt et al., 1999). During lexical selection, priming spreads to connected units that share semantic or phonological characteristics with the target word (see Figure 8.1). Language comprehension and production depend on how fast and how much priming can be transmitted across the connections that link representations.

In comprehension of spoken language, the speech signal must be mapped onto abstract phonological representations such as phonemes and syllables. Priming is transmitted bottom-up from phonological representations to corresponding lexical and conceptual representations. This spread of excitation is interactive, cascading bottom-up from the phonological system to the semantic system and top-down from lexical and semantic representations to phonological representations. This interactive activation pattern provides the basis for top-down context effects on speech perception. For example, word recognition is more accurate when the target word is presented in a semantically relevant sentence that predicts the word than when it is in an unrelated sentence (e.g., Speranza, Daneman, & Schneider, 2000). Within these models, top-down excitation can compensate for reduced bottom-up excitation caused by degraded input as occurs with age-related loss of acuity (cf., Marslen-Wilson & Welsh, 1978).

Production of spoken language begins with the activation of a concept or message to be expressed. Excitation spreads top-down from conceptual representations to corresponding lexical and phonological representations. A word is produced when the lowest level representations, muscle movements, are activated (Dell, 1986; Levelt et al., 1999; MacKay, 1987). During production, top-down priming to the phonological level spreads back up to lexical representations for words phonologically related to the target word, and then back down to the target phonological representations, increasing their priming levels and moving them closer to threshold for retrieval. This interactive spread of priming explains, for example, why large phonological neighborhoods facilitate production: the larger the number of phonologically related neighbors of a word, the greater the cascade of priming to target phonological representations and the faster they will reach threshold (Vitevitch & Sommers, 2003).

Within current models, words and sentences are computed during comprehension and production, in contrast to having pre-existing unitary representations. The mechanism for encoding the correct serial order of sounds within a word and of words within a sentence is a highly significant problem (Lashley, 1951). Most interactive activation models postulate generative rules that define the sequencing possibilities of all representations at a given level. Rules are stated in terms of domains of representations, for example, syntactic rules govern lexical domains (noun, verb, etc.), and segmental rules govern phonological domains (initial consonant, vowel, end consonant, etc.). In production, generative rules determine which lexical domain may be activated at each point in construction of a sentence. The most primed word in a lexical domain is selected, and this explains why most word errors in production are from the same syntactic class as the intended word; only representations from a particular domain will be "eligible" for activation (Dell, 1986; MacKay, 1987). Thus transmission of priming and activation dynamics are critical for selection of the correct syntactic domain and the correct word within that domain. Indeed, errors in picture naming have been simulated by varying parameters of activation dynamics (Saffran, Dell, & Schwartz, 2000).

In comprehension, sentences must be syntactically parsed and a representation of the sentence meaning is created as well as a model of the discourse more globally. Selection of lexical meaning is influenced by both local and discourse level context. For example, the speed of word identification is affected by the compatibility of the word's meaning with the meaning of adjacent words as well as the meaning of the global discourse (see Ledoux, Camblin, Swaab, & Gordon, 2006 for a review). Comprehension models emphasize that the construction of sentence meaning occurs within a limited capacity system. In an influential model, Just and Carpenter (1992) argued that working memory stores perceptual input and the products of semantic and syntactic computations. Storage and computational processes require priming (spreading activation in their model) and the amount of priming available is limited, providing the basis for capacity limitations (for a different view see Caplan & Waters, 1999; Waters & Caplan, 2001, 2005; and cognitive aging models below). Thus, language deficits can be caused by limitations in working memory capacity. In contrast, capacity constraints are often absent from models of language production. This difference between comprehension and production models is reflected in explanations of age-related changes in language comprehension versus production. For example, capacity reductions figure prominently in accounts of age-related declines in language perception and comprehension, but not in production with the exception of production of complex syntax (e.g., Kemper & Kemptes, 1999).

COGNITIVE AGING MODELS OF LANGUAGE PROCESSING

We outline below the basic principles of several models of cognitive aging, emphasizing the characteristics of these models most relevant to research on language and aging. One important task for these models is to explain why some language functions decline with aging and others do not. For example, there is considerable evidence that semantic processing at a lexical and discourse level is maintained in old age whereas complex syntactic processing declines. Also, age-related decline is seen in retrieval of phonological and orthographic information about a word, but not in retrieval of lexical semantics (e.g., Burke & MacKay, 1997; Thornton & Light, 2006). As we will see, aging models tend to focus on decrements in language performance and there has been little attempt to evaluate the compatibility of models with both the positive and negative components of older adults' language functioning that we review below. Another challenge for cognitive aging models is to explain the impact of older adults' auditory and visual sensory deficits on higher level language functions. What is the mechanism whereby impairment at the sensory level affects processing at higher semantic or syntactic levels? Finally, cognitive aging models of language must be testable and this requires behavioral measures of critical mechanisms, for example, resources or inhibition. As we will see, there has been mixed success in locating these mechanisms within a language model and in identifying behavioral measures of each mechanism.

Resource theory is based on the idea that human capacity for processing information is limited (e.g., Miller, 1956) because a finite pool of attention or resources is shared by different mental processes that occur simultaneously or in close succession (Kahneman, 1973). Thus, under some conditions there may be insufficient resources to complete all the component processes necessary for accurate performance (e.g., Rabbitt, 1968). Resource theory explains age declines in performance by postulating that older adults have reduced resources compared to young adults and that certain operations are more resource demanding for older than young adults. Consequently, older adults reach the point where available resources are insufficient to complete a task before young adults do (Craik & Byrd, 1982; Hasher & Zacks, 1979; McCoy, Tun, Cox, Colangelo, Stewart, & Wingfield, 2005; Murphy et al., 2000).

What are resources? Definitions include processing speed, working memory, attention, and inhibition (Light, 1991; Salthouse & Craik, 2000; Wingfield & Stine-Morrow, 2000). There has been considerable criticism of the vacuity attached to definitions of resources and their underlying mechanisms (Light & Burke, 1988; MacKay, Hadley, & Abrams, 2007a; MacKay & James, 2001; McDowd & Shaw, 2000; Navon, 1984; Salthouse & Craik, 2000). Perhaps because of this criticism, recent studies of language and aging tend to focus on a specific resource, e.g., speed, inhibition, or working memory, and there has been some attempt to follow Salthouse and Craik's recommendation to conceptualize resources in terms of specific behavioral measures (for problems with these attempts see Burke & Osborne, 2007; MacKay et al., 2007a; Schneider, Daneman, & Murphy, 2005; Waters & Caplan, 2001).

The use of the broad term "resources" in Kahneman's (1973) sense of mental energy is used in language research to explain the relation between perception and memory. It is known that the difficulty of perceiving a word affects subsequent mental operations such as how well it is remembered (Aaronson, 1974; McCoy et al., 2005; Rabbitt, 1968). Within the resources framework, this is because difficult perceptual operations use more resources and this drains resources from subsequent cognitive operations, including language and memory processes. Age-related declines in sensory processing increase the difficulty of identifying words so that older adults, relative to young adults, have reduced resources remaining for subsequent cognitive operations involving those words (McCoy et al., 2005; Wingfield, Tun, & McCoy, 2005). Within the framework presented in Figure 8.1, resource limitations have been conceptualized as limitations in the amount of priming or activation that is shared among language processes and maintenance of items in memory (Haarmann, Just, & Carpenter, 1997; Just & Carpenter, 1992; Saffran et al., 2000). This level of specificity increases the predictive power of a resource model, but has not been developed in aging models which remain challenged by the need to specify resources in terms of a theoretical mechanism and a behavioral measure.

Theories focusing on a specific definition of resources, namely, speed, inhibition, or working memory, have attempted to identify underlying mechanisms and behavioral measures that isolate the resource. *General slowing theories* postulate that age-related declines in cognitive performance are caused by slowing of component processes (Birren, 1965; Cerella, 1985; Madden, 2001; Myerson, Hale, Wagstaff, Poon, & Smith, 1990; Salthouse, 1985, 1996, 2000) and are the most extensively researched of theories of cognitive aging. They are supported by findings showing that measures of perceptual-motor speed share much of the age-related variance in performance on a broad range of cognitive tasks, including some language tasks (e.g., Salthouse, 1985). There has been, however, disagreement about whether behavioral measures are successful in isolating speed from other processes, for example, memory processes (e.g., Parkin & Java, 2000).

There are different views on how general age-related slowing is. Some have argued that the amount of age-related slowing is the same for all cognitive operations (Cerella, 1985) and others have argued that slowing differs between verbal and spatial domains (Lima, Hale, & Myerson, 1991). Currently, it is acknowledged that the degree of age-related slowing varies considerably for different cognitive operations (Allen, Madden, & Slane, 1995; Fisher, Duffy, & Katsikopoulos, 2000). Slowing has been applied to older adults' language processing as an explanation, for example, of their greater difficulty in comprehending speeded speech

(Wingfield, 1996), their greater benefit from semantic context in word recognition (Madden, 1988), and their failure to use sentential context to disambiguate homophones (Dagerman, MacDonald, & Harm, 2006).

Salthouse (1996) postulated mechanisms through which general slowing causes errors. Some cognitive operations may be executed too slowly for their successful completion in the available time or their completion may spill over depleting the time available for successive operations. Both outcomes would cause an increase in speech comprehension errors. For example, speed of processing is critical with speech because the signal extends through time and no single moment is adequate for recognition. Rapid processing is essential for correct identification of fast changing components of the speech signal, such as voice onset time that distinguishes /pa/ from /ba/. If the processing is slowed, the stimulus may be gone before identification is possible. Within interactive activation models (see Figure 8.1) slowing would affect the dynamics of priming such as speed of transmission of priming. Slower transmission during a fixed interval would reduce the information that is prepared for activation and retrieval (Dell, 1986; Dell, Chang, & Griffin, 1999).

Slowing impairs functions requiring simultaneous availability of information because information from early processes may have decayed by the time information from later processes is produced. For example, sentence comprehension requires coactivation of successive words and their meaning in the sentence in order to build a representation of the sentence meaning. Comprehension will suffer if processing is so slow that the meaning of initial words has decayed before final words are represented (Saffran et al., 2000). Indeed, aging effects on language that have been attributed to older adults' smaller working memory capacity can be accounted for by slowing alone (MacDonald & Christiansen, 2002).

Inhibition deficit theory proposes that aging weakens inhibitory processes that regulate attention and the contents of working memory, thereby affecting a broad range of cognitive performance, including comprehension and production of language (Hasher et al., 2007; Hasher & Zacks, 1988). Inhibition deficit theory has been applied to older adults' language processing to explain, for example, why older adults' performance suffers more from distracting stimuli during reading (Connelly, Hasher, & Zacks, 1991) or listening (Hasher et al., 2007; Tun, O'Kane, & Wingfield, 2002), and why older adults' conversations are more likely to go off topic (e.g., Arbuckle, Nohara-LeClair, & Pushkar, 2000). Hasher and Zacks view inhibition as a controlled attentional process that occurs after automatic activation processes during the access function. Some language processing models postulate automatic inhibition of competitors during lexical selection (e.g., McClelland & Rumelhart, 1981), but such obligatory inhibition is not relevant to the Hasher and Zacks model (e.g., Zacks & Hasher,

1997). Nevertheless, inhibition deficits have been invoked to explain age differences in processes not under attentional control, such as competition between phonologically related neighbors and a target word during lexical selection in speech perception (e.g., Sommers & Danielson, 1999).

Working memory theories of cognitive aging build on models that postulate both storage and processing functions for working memory and subsume the principles of *resource theories* (e,g., Baddeley, 1986; Engle, Tuholski, Laughlin, & Conway, 1999; Just & Carpenter, 1992). It is proposed that older adults suffer reductions in working memory capacity and this constrains their ability to comprehend and produce complex semantic content and complex syntax (Kemper & Kemptes, 1999). For example, the computational demands of complex syntax such as left-branching sentences are hypothesized to require more working memory than simpler syntax such as right-branching sentences. A listener must retain a longer initial clause in the left-branching sentence "The gal who runs a nursery school for our church is awfully young" than in the right-branching sentence "She's awfully young to be running a nursery school for our church" (from Kemper, Thompson, & Marquis, 2001b). Older adults' preference for producing right-branching sentences has been attributed to their reduced working memory (Kemper & Kemtes, 1999).

Some researchers have argued that language and other cognitive functions share the same working memory capacity that is measured with traditional span tasks (e.g., Just & Carpenter, 1992). Caplan and Waters (1999; Waters & Caplan, 2001, 2005), however, have argued for a dedicated working memory that is specialized for online interpretive processing of sentences, in particular for resolving the syntactic structure and the meaning of the sentence, and is not related to traditional span measures. Traditional measures of working memory span are related to postinterpretive processes which are controlled and conscious, and are involved in, for example, offline tasks such as plausibility judgments and sentence recall. The Caplan and Waters approach emphasizes the distinction between online and offline language processes, with the latter but not the former affected by memory processes. This is an important distinction for aging research which aims to investigate language processes uncontaminated by age-related memory declines.

These working memory models of aging appear to differ conceptually from a general resources model in requiring a separate working memory component that is limited in terms of capacity rather than limited by the overall processing efficiency of the language system. MacDonald and Christiansen (2002) argue that this commits working memory theorists to explaining individual differences in language, including aging effects, in terms of changes in finite capacity (e.g., Just & Carpenter, 1992). An alternative approach is that the processing efficiency of the language system depends on properties such as the rate of transmission of excitation which in turn is influenced by experience or aging, with no working memory structure required. Less efficient processing would deplete finite resources sooner than efficient processing, but there is no difference among groups in finite capacity in this alternative to a working memory model (MacDonald & Christiansen, 2002; Saffran et al., 2000).

Transmission deficit theory is based on a model with connectionist architecture and localist/symbolic representations as in Figure 8.1 (MacKay, 1987). It postulates that connections among representational units in the network are strengthened by frequent and recent use (activation) and are weakened by aging. As connection strength weakens, it decreases the transmission of priming which may become so reduced that it is inadequate to activate connected representations. Aging weakens connection strength universally, causing general processing deficits, rather than deficits limited to a single process such as working memory or inhibition (Burke & MacKay, 1997; MacKay & Abrams, 1996; MacKay & Burke, 1990). Indeed, the theory does not include a resource mechanism and accounts for processing limitations through architecture and activation dynamics (cf. Dell et al., 1997; MacDonald & Christiansen, 2002). The transmission deficit theory is consistent with neurobiological characteristics of aging. For example, age-related atrophy of white matter has been linked to a reduction of the total length of the myelinated fibers of white matter, reducing neural connectivity (e.g., Marner, Nyengaard, Tang, & Pakkenberg, 2003; Tang, Nyengaard, Pakkenberg, & Gundersen, 1997; see Raz, 2000 for a review). At a functional level, consistent with weaker connections, somatosensory event-related potentials show that peripheral and central conduction time slows with aging in adulthood (Shaw, 1992; Tanosaki, Ozaki, Shimamura, Baba, & Matsunaga, 1999).

Although age-related transmission deficits are distributed across the representational system, the functional effects of transmission deficits depend on the architecture of the language system. For example, pathways diverge from the single lexical representation of a word (see Figure 8.1) to the phonological representations that are hierarchically organized in levels of syllables, phonological compounds, and down to the lowest level of phonological features (not shown in Figure 8.1). The single connections to phonological representations make them more vulnerable to transmission deficits during production, consistent with older adults' increased phonological retrieval failures in tip-of-the-tongue (TOT) experiences (e.g., Burke et al., 1991) and slips of the tongue (MacKay & James, 2004). In contrast to the phonological system, the semantic system is characterized by redundancy and converging of connections among representations that make them less vulnerable to transmission deficits, consistent with older adults' well-maintained semantic processing (e.g.,

Thornton & Light, 2006). For example, the representation of the semantic knowledge that *frogs spend time in water* would be an unlikely candidate for transmission deficit and retrieval failure after activation of the lexical representation for *frog*. It would receive excitation not just from the lexical representation but also from associated semantic information, for example, that frogs are amphibians, that they swim, etc.

The sensory/perceptual deficit account or *degraded signal* account is the least developed theory but it makes a straightforward prediction: age-related declines in sensory and perceptual processes yield incomplete or erroneous input to the computation of lower level phonological and orthographic codes; this impairs lexical selection and other subsequent linguistic processes so that older adults select incorrect words or none at all (e.g., Brown & Pichora-Fuller, 2000; Murphy, McDowd, & Wilcox, 1999; Pichora-Fuller & Singh, 2006; Schneider et al., 2005; Schneider, Daneman, Murphy, & Kwong See, 2000; Schneider & Pichora-Fuller, 2000). Under the degraded signal account, impairment in word recognition should be eliminated when accuracy of language perception is equated across age.

As we will see, there is controversy about the extent to which errors in higher level language processes should be attributed to a degraded signal alone, or if resources available for cognitive processes are also required to account for the results (Humes, 1996; Schneider & Pichora-Fuller, 2000; Scialfa, 2002; Tun et al., 2002). There is, however, agreement that age-related perceptual declines directly influence language processing, especially under difficult perceptual conditions (e.g., Madden & Whiting, 2004; Schneider & Pichora-Fuller, 2000; Wingfield et al., 2005).

Organization of this Review

Because of the interactive nature of language processes, it is difficult to isolate processing of phonological/orthographic, semantic, and syntactic information. These different types of knowledge, however, constitute different levels in linguistic theory, each with its own generative rules that guide production and understanding of familiar and novel constructions at each level. Within psycholinguistic models, the levels involve different architectures and mechanisms and thus may vary in their sensitivity to aging. We review relevant research for each of these three levels in separate sections. Within each section we organize our review by the units of analysis in the research, namely word, sentence, and discourse, where relevant, and by the language function, namely comprehension/perception or production. We tend to focus on research published since Wingfield and Stine-Morrow's (2000) excellent review of language and aging in the last *Handbook of Aging and Cognition*.

PERCEPTION OF PHONOLOGY AND ORTHOGRAPHY

Visual and auditory acuity show steady decline with aging during adult-hood with some studies showing an increased rate of decline after the age of 70 years (e.g., Baltes & Lindenberger, 1997; Committee on Hearing and Bioacoustics and Biomechanics [CHABA], 1988; Corso, 1971; Linden-berger & Baltes, 1994; Salthouse, Hancock, Meinz, & Hambrick, 1996). Baltes and Lindenberger (1997) pointed out that there had been little con-sideration of age differences in sensory functions in studies of aging effects on cognition. Indeed, Schneider and Pichora-Fuller (2000) reviewed 288 published articles measuring young and older adults' cog-nitive performance involving auditory or visual stimuli. Acuity was measured in only 18% of the studies using auditory stimuli and in only 21% of the studies using visual stimuli, and in only six studies was acuity covaried in the statistical analyses.

Thus, investigation of the sensory analysis of spoken or written lan-guage and investigation of higher level language processes have been carried out in remarkably separate domains of aging research. The rela-tive lack of contact between these two separate subfields, namely sensory aging and cognitive aging, is surprising in the investigation of language because models of language processing emphasize the interaction between sensory, lexical, and semantic processes (e.g., Dell, 1986; Marslen-Wilson & Welsh, 1978; McClelland & Rumelhart, 1981; Rapp & Goldrick, 2000). Moreover, it is well established that when perceptual processing becomes more difficult, higher level cognitive functions may suffer (Aar-onson, 1974; Rabbitt, 1968).

Recently, however, interest in the interaction between sensory and cognitive processes in language has grown (e.g., Murphy et al., 2000; Pichora-Fuller & Singh, 2006; Wingfield et al., 2005), stimulated in part by compelling evidence that decline in sensory processes strongly affects higher level cognitive processing of language in old age (see Schneider & Pichora-Fuller, 2000 for an excellent review). Several different investigative approaches link sensory declines to language performance.

Correlations between Visual/Auditory Acuity and Language Performance

Large-scale cross-sectional and longitudinal studies have demonstrated that considerable age-related variance in cognitive performance is shared with measures of auditory and visual acuity. Many of these studies included a few measures of language functions in their cognitive batter-ies, for example, vocabulary tests, category fluency, confrontation naming of pictures, and the National Adult Reading Test (NART) requiring pronunciation of irregularly spelled words (e.g., Anstey, Hofer, & Luszcz, 2003; Anstey, Luszcz, & Sanchez, 2001; Anstey & Smith, 1999; Baltes & Lindenberger, 1997; Christensen, Mackinnon, Korten, & Jorm, 2001; Ghisletta & Lindenberger, 2005; Lindenberger & Baltes, 1994). The tests primarily measure semantic and phonological retrieval at the word level, and are relatively undemanding in terms of sensory processes because they tend to be untimed and stimuli are available for repeated inspection (e.g., NART). Nonetheless, language tests and visual and auditory acuity share considerable age-related variance. For example, Baltes and Lindenberger (1997) reported that controlling for auditory and visual acuity produced a 20-fold decrease in the age-related variance in language measures, eliminating the significant effect of age.

Several accounts have been proposed to explain the relation between sensory acuity and cognitive performance, including language tests, in these large-scale studies (Baltes & Lindenberger, 1997; Lindenberger & Baltes, 1994; Salthouse et al., 1996). Although older adults' sensory declines may produce a degraded signal, this approach cannot explain why the link between language performance and sensory acuity occurs even when they involve different sensory modalities (Lindenberger & Baltes, 1994), or why language performance is correlated with physiological markers such as respiratory efficiency (Christensen et al., 2001). Moreover, degraded input would have little influence on tests such as fluency where the only sensory input is the instructions. In an experimental test of the degraded signal hypothesis, Lindenberger, Scherer, and Baltes (2001) reduced visual and auditory acuity of middle-aged adults to the level of adults aged 70 to 84 years but found no decline in their performance on the cognitive tests used in their earlier studies (e.g., Lindenberger & Baltes, 1994; but see Gilmore, Spinks, & Thomas, 2006 for a contrary result).

The dominant explanation of why sensory acuity shares age-related variance with cognitive performance in these large scale studies is that a *common cause* is responsible for age-related decline in sensory and cognitive functions, including language (but see Anstey et al., 2003). This account is supported by findings that sensory, language, and other cognitive measures load on a common cause factor in samples with a large or narrow age range (Christensen et al., 2001). Candidates for the common cause are the structural and physiological integrity of the brain (Baltes & Lindenberger, 1997; Li & Lindenberger, 2002) or the integrity of conscious cognitive processes (Salthouse, Hambrick, & McGuthry, 1998). However, age does not have a homogeneous effect on the neurophysiological integrity of different regions of the brain. Structural MRI analyses have demonstrated that the rate of gray matter atrophy with age varies for different brain regions (Good, Johnsrude, Ashburner, Henson, Friston, &

Frackowiak, 2001; Ohnishi, Matsuda, Tabira, Asada, & Uno, 2001; Resnick, Pham, Kraut, Zonderman, & Davatzikos, 2003; Sowell, Peterson, Thompson, Welcome, Henkenius, & Toga, 2003) and fMRI has demonstrated that age differences are found in neural activation of some brain regions and not others (see Raz, 2000 for an excellent review of differential vulnerability of neural regions). This differential age sensitivity of neural regions predicts that the amount of age-related variance accounted for by sensory acuity would depend on the neural substrate for the cognitive function, contrary to the common cause hypothesis. This is especially relevant to language functions where there is considerable regional specificity of semantic, phonological, and orthographic processes (e.g., Indefrey & Levelt, 2004).

The cross-sectional and longitudinal studies investigating the relation between sensory and cognitive performance used only a few language measures that depended heavily on vocabulary size. A far more extensive relationship between sensory functioning and language processes has been demonstrated in experimental studies that examine language performance after manipulating sensory processing either directly or statistically so that young and older adults' recognition accuracy is equivalent. These studies provide evidence that the efficiency of sensory processing directly affects the integrity of higher level language processes. This is a specific factor that may, in addition to a common cause, contribute to the relation between sensory and language functions. We consider first research on the effect of perceptual factors on older adults' auditory language processing.

Speech Recognition: Effect of Auditory Sensory and Perceptual Changes

Presbycusis is age-related hearing loss, influenced by both physiological and environmental factors, and is characterized by bilateral loss of higher frequencies, the frequencies important for speech (e.g., Cheesman, 1997; CHABA, 1988). In a sample of adults older than age 65, about one-third report significant hearing loss (Pichora-Fuller & Singh, 2006). The relation between acuity and speech recognition is well established. For example, in the Framingham Heart Study pure tone thresholds for 1662 participants aged 63–92 years predicted correct word recognition (Gates, Feeney, & Higdon, 2003; see also Humes, Watson, Christensen, Cokely, Halling, & Lee, 1994; van Rooij & Plomp, 1990). Consistent with this relation between acuity and speech intelligibility, older adults with hearing loss are poorer than normal hearing older adults at identifying speech stimuli ranging from syllables to sentences (Halling & Humes, 2000; Phillips, Gordon-Salant, Fitzgibbons, & Yeni-Kombshian, 2000).

There are, however, factors in addition to presbycusis that contribute to older adults' reduced ability to recognize speech (CHABA, 1988; Schneider, 1997; Schneider & Pichora-Fuller, 2000). Although much of the variance in speech intelligibility is accounted for by pure tone thresholds (Humes, 1996), age differences linger when young and older adults are matched on hearing loss, and for normal hearing adults when the speech is speeded or presented in noise (e.g., CHABA, 1988; Corso, 1971; Humes & Christopherson, 1991). These findings implicate age-related changes in auditory perceptual functions beyond acuity and higher level cognitive functions important for speech recognition. We turn to this issue next.

Auditory temporal processing is a critical perceptual function that declines with age and affects older adults' speech perception, especially for the fine structure of the speech signal (Fitzgibbons & Gordon-Salant, 1996; Humes & Christopherson, 1991; Schneider & Pichora-Fuller, 2001). Aging is associated with loss of auditory temporal synchrony in both the peripheral and central nervous system (e.g., Brown & Pichora-Fuller, 2000; Schneider, 1997). In an attempt to simulate age-related asynchrony in young adults, Brown and Pichora-Fuller (2000) presented sentences to young adults that had been "jittered" by changing slightly the timing of successive amplitudes in the speech signal. Young adults' performance in identifying and remembering the final word in the jittered sentences resembled older adults' performance with intact sentences, consistent with the hypothesis that older adults' speech processing is disrupted by internal jitter.

Detection of temporal gaps and the order of sounds are other aspects of auditory temporal processing that decline with aging (Fozard & Gordon-Salant, 2001; Schneider, Pichora-Fuller, Kowalchuk, & Lamb, 1994; Schneider, Speranza, & Pichora-Fuller, 1998; Trainor & Trehub, 1989). Older adults' gap detection threshold is about twice the size of young adults' (Schneider, Daneman, & Pichora-Fuller, 2002). Gap detection thresholds are negatively associated with recognition of syllables in noise (Phillips et al., 2000) and words in noise (Snell, Mapes, Hickman, & Frisina, 2002) but are uncorrelated with audiometric thresholds suggesting that temporal acuity is unrelated to hearing loss (Schneider et al., 1994). Perception of temporal acoustic cues is essential for distinguishing speech sounds that differ in voice onset time (VOT), as in /pa/ versus /ba/, because the initial phonemes differ primarily in the interval between the consonant stop release and the onset of voicing. Older adults performed more poorly than young adults in discriminating speech sounds that differ in VOT (Strouse, Ashmean, Ohde, & Grantham, 1998; Tremblay, Piskosz, & Souza, 2002), whereas age differences have not been found in discriminating vowels which are more steady state than consonants (Coughlin, Kewley-Port, & Humes, 1998). Despite the evidence for age-related declines in temporal processing of segmental and subsegmental speech cues, temporal processing at the supra-segmental level is well maintained in the use of prosody (Wingfield, Lindfield, & Goodglass, 2000).

Frequency discrimination also depends on temporal synchrony and is a critical component of speech perception; aging impairs frequency resolution ability (Schneider, 1997). Individual differences in the ability to resolve frequency may explain why some adults with hearing loss have good ability to recognize speech while others do not. Older adults with mild hearing loss and poor speech recognition were impaired in frequency resolution of complex stimuli compared to older adults also having mild hearing loss but with good speech recognition (Phillips et al., 2000).

These studies suggest a direct effect of age-related sensory and perceptual changes on language processing. The contribution of cognitive factors to speech recognition has been examined in experiments that degrade speech either with background distraction or by fast presentation rates. We turn to these studies next.

Speech Recognition: The Interaction of Perception and Cognition

Resources, Inhibition, and Word Recognition with Distraction

Older adults complain about the difficulty of perceiving speech under conditions where there is a noisy background or multiple people speaking at once. Laboratory research supports this complaint because older adults' speech recognition declines more than young adults' as the signal-to-noise ratio (SNR) decreases (CHABA, 1988; Snell et al., 2002; Tun, 1998), even when there are no detectable age differences in performance in quiet (e.g., Dubno, Dirks, & Morgan, 1984; Pichora-Fuller, Schneider, & Daneman, 1995; Tun & Wingfield, 1999). These studies find age deficits at a noise level typical of common everyday environments such as restaurants, subways, and parties, and thus we would expect older adults' speech recognition to be impaired in these environments.

Although it is generally acknowledged that older adults' sensory and perceptual deficits contribute to their vulnerability to noisy backgrounds (CHABA, 1988; Humes, 1996; Schneider & Pichora-Fuller, 2000; Tun & Wingfield, 1999; Wingfield et al., 2005), there is disagreement over the relative importance of sensory and cognitive factors. Some researchers argue that older adults' vulnerability to noise is primarily a consequence of auditory not cognitive deficits (Humes, 1996; Li, Daneman, Qi, & Schneider, 2004; Schneider et al., 2000, 2002). This position is consistent with the correlations found between the level of speech recognition in noise and perceptual functions, for example, gap detection (Snell et al., 2002). In contrast, other researchers have argued that cognitive deficits play a major role in noise effects (Hasher et al., 2007; Sommers & Danielson, 1999; Tun et al., 2002). Under the resources account, aging reduces resource capacity and increases resources required during word recognition because of sensory deficits, leaving older adults insufficient resources for comprehension and memory (Pichora-Fuller et al., 1995; Wingfield et al., 2005). Under the inhibition deficit account, perception of speech in noise is a selective attention task in which older adults' inhibition deficits impair their ability to selectively attend to the target speech and ignore the irrelevant background noise (Hasher et al., 2007; Tun et al., 2002; Tun & Wingfield, 1999). Under general slowing, older adults are impaired more in noise because fast processing is necessary to analyze bits of target speech that are available during pauses in the noise but that must be analyzed before being masked by subsequent input (Tun & Wingfield, 1999).

Some of the most powerful evidence supporting a primary role for age-related sensory deficits comes from experiments that eliminate older adults' sensory deficit by equating perceptibility of stimuli across age. If perceptual problems are responsible for older adults' impaired language processing in noise, then age differences observed when young and old are tested with no acuity adjustment should disappear when SNR is adjusted on the basis of each participant's threshold for word recognition in noise. On the other hand, if diminished inhibition or resources contribute to older adults' impaired language processing in noise, then this adjustment for acuity will not eliminate age differences in the negative effect of increased background noise levels. When Schneider et al. (2000) presented prose passages at an adjusted SNR, age differences in correct answers to detailed questions about the passage were eliminated at all SNRs except the lowest. Schneider et al. argued for the degraded signal account: age-related declines in perceptual processes produce errors in the perceptual representation of speech and these errors impair subsequent comprehension and memory, especially for details in the prose that may be easy to miss when audition is poor. Even when Schneider et al. added a secondary task, its effect on correct responses was the same for young and older adults.

Using the same SNR adjustment technique to compensate for age differences in hearing, Murphy, Daneman, and Schneider (2006) eliminated age differences in recall of dialogues presented in quiet and noise except when the two speakers were spatially separated. This suggests that older adults' difficulty in following conversations may be a consequence of perceptual deficits in word recognition and in using auditory cues to spatially differentiate the speakers. Murphy et al. (1999) equated speech intelligibility across age and in three experiments, each using a different distraction paradigm, found that when stimuli were equivalent in perceptibility across age, there was no age-related deficit in the effect of distracting information. These results are consistent with a degraded signal account, but not with either an inhibition deficit or a resource account which predict that older adults will show a greater effect of factors that tax inhibition or resources, namely noise, distraction, or a secondary task.

Tun et al. (2002) reached different conclusions about the role of inhibition deficits. They argued that if distracting irrelevant speech has a greater effect on older adults' speech processing because of their sensory declines, then the semantic content of the distracting background speech should be irrelevant to the age difference (Lustig & Hasher, 2001). They found that recall of sentences was impaired more for older than young adults when the distraction was meaningful text compared to random words or quiet. Recall in the distraction conditions was related to performance on the Trail Making Test which the authors interpreted as evidence that processing speech with distraction involves executive control processes (but see Salthouse et al., 2000 for alternative interpretations of the Trail Making Test). Li et al. (2004) reported comparable decline across age in sentence recall with syntactically correct but meaningless sentences as distraction compared to white noise. Moreover, spatial separation of target and distraction virtually eliminated the difference in interfering effect of speech and noise for both young and older adults, providing no evidence that older adults were less able to ignore distraction. Future research is needed to identify the critical characteristics of distracting speech that are required for age differences in the distraction effect. Moreover, online measures in addition to memory measures would indicate whether age differences in distraction effects occur during language processing, or after.

Finally, McCoy et al. (2005) manipulated the difficulty of word recognition not with noise, but by comparing normal and hearing impaired older adults and by manipulating the amount of predictive context. With words correctly identified, recall declined more for impaired than normal adults and more for the low versus high predictive contexts. Under the resources account, the greater perceptual difficulty imposed by hearing impairment and low context drains resources from memory processes. The results are not compatible with the degraded signal account alone because the words were perceived correctly.

In summary, the investigation of sensory and cognitive factors influencing age differences in language processing in noise has yielded results that are not consistent in their entirety with a single theoretical account. Much of the evidence suggests that equating word recognition across age removes age differences in the effects of noise, contrary to the inhibition deficit account. The strongest case, however, for the primary role of perceptual rather than inhibition deficits can be made when an interaction between age and noise level occurs without adjustment for acuity and then disappears with the acuity adjustment. This has not been demonstrated. The resources account of perceptual effects is supported by evidence that older adults' recall is impaired under conditions where they have correctly identified the signal, but word recognition is difficult because of hearing impairment or poor semantic context.

Phonological Neighborhood

Word recognition is also influenced by a "background" that is activated internally during word recognition, namely, words that share most phonemes with the target word, known as the phonological neighborhood. Words with dense neighborhoods have many phonological neighbors and are more difficult to perceive than words with sparse neighborhoods, an effect attributed to lexical competition for recognition among phonologically similar words in the lexicon (Luce & Pisoni, 1998). Sommers (1996; Sommers & Danielson, 1999) adjusted SNRs for young and older adults so that identification of sparse neighborhood (easy) words was the same across age. Using these adjusted SNRs, identification was poorer for dense neighborhood (hard) words, with greater decline in identification for older than young adults. Sommers attributed older adults' greater neighborhood density effect to inefficient inhibition of alternative words that competed during lexical selection. Consistent with this, young and older adults' ability to identify dense neighborhood words was negatively related to an interference score derived from tasks believed to measure inhibition such as Stroop (Sommers & Danielson, 1999). These findings suggest that inhibition occurring automatically during lexical selection (involved in the neighborhood effect) is related to inhibition that is under conscious control (involved in ignoring a Stroop baseword) and that both are negatively affected by aging (cf. Zacks & Hasher, 1997).

Studies testing young normal hearing adults and older adults with hearing loss, however, found comparable effects of high neighborhood density (plus low word frequency) on word recognition across age (Carter & Wilson, 2001; Takayanagi, Dirks, & Moshfegh, 2002). Clearly, the relation of aging and acuity to phonological neighborhood effects is an important area for future research. It is interesting to note in this context that strong *semantic* competitors that are primed internally during lexical selection because of shared semantic features, not sensory features, show equivalent effects on word production and recognition for young and older adults (Persson, Sylvester, Nelson, Welsh, Jonides, & Reuter-Lorenz, 2004; Prull, Godard-Gross, & Karas, 2004; Stine & Wingfield, 1994).

Effect of Speech Rates on Perception

When speech rates are accelerated, older adults decline more than young adults in speech perception (Gordon-Salant & Fitzgibbons, 1999), comprehension (Wingfield, Peelle, & Grossman, 2003), and recall (Stine, Wingfield, & Poon, 1986; Tun et al., 1992; Wingfield, Poon, Lombardi, & Lowe, 1985; Wingfield, Tun, Koh, & Rosen, 1999). Recall of accelerated speech improves with practice and the improvement is comparable for young and older adults, although older adults show less transfer of improvement to different accelerated speech rates (Peelle & Wingfield, 2005). Increasing meaningfulness and syntactic structure also improved speech processing at fast rates and the improvement is often greater for older adults (Gordon-Salant & Fitzgibbons, 2001; Wingfield et al., 1985). Indeed, age differences in comprehension of meaningful sentences often do not occur until speech rates become very fast, for example, at least 595 wpm for short sentences, a rate that would not be encountered in normal everyday conversation (Wingfield et al., 2003). As we saw in studies of background noise, older adults are adept at using linguistic context to aid processing. It is clear, however, that in general older adults perform better at slower speech rates and that they prefer them (Wingfield & Ducharme, 1999).

Both degraded signal accounts and cognitive accounts have been used to explain why fast speech rates affect older adults more than young adults and there is disagreement about which account is primary (e.g., Schneider et al., 2005; Wingfield et al., 2005). The usual method for speeding speech rates is to eliminate tiny segments of speech at regular intervals. The degraded signal account postulates that speeded speech primarily affects the difficulty of perceptual processing by making transient acoustic cues even briefer, compounding older adults' problems in processing temporal aspects of the speech signal that are critical for word recognition (Gordon-Salant & Fitzgibbons, 2001). Thus older adults may not correctly perceive compressed words. Adding a resource account, the increased difficulty of perception drains resources from higher level cognitive processes. On the other hand, faster speech rates reduce the time available for processing and this may directly disrupt older adults' syntactic, semantic, and memory processes, as well as perceptual processes, under general slowing.

Although hearing impairment increases speech compression effects for both young and older adults (Gordon-Salant & Fitzgibbons, 2001; Wingfield, McCoy, Peelle, Tun, & Cox, 2007), older adults perform more poorly than young adults with compression even when tone or speech thresholds are matched across age (Wingfield et al., 2003). These results do not eliminate the degraded signal account because older adults' deficit in processing transient cues may only be visible under speeded conditions; matching thresholds in unspeeded conditions would not control this deficit in temporal processing.

Wingfield and his colleagues reported that syntactically difficult sentences impaired comprehension compared to syntactically simpler sentences, and the impairment increased with compression and more so for older adults and hearing impaired adults (Wingfield et al., 2007; Wingfield et al., 2003). They argued that compression affects both the quality of the speech signal and higher level syntactic processes. Under the resource account, compression exacerbates older adults' sensory deficits and the greater difficulty of sensory analysis reduces time or resources available for subsequent syntactic processes. Under general slowing, compression may limit the time available for syntactic processing, independent of sensory analysis, which will impair older adults more because they are slower to complete syntactic analysis. The degraded signal account is inadequate because the quality of the stimulus should not be affected by syntactic complexity.

One approach to differentiating the degraded signal and slowing accounts is to increase speech rate by compressing different parts of the speech signal. Consonants are characterized by transient acoustic cues requiring rapid processing compared to vowels or pauses which are more steady state. Gordon-Salant and Fitzgibbons (2001) reported that selective compression of consonants produced greater age deficits in sentence recall than selective compression of vowels or pauses; performance with consonant compression was the best predictor of uniform compression performance. Schneider et al. (2005) reported comparable compression effects on word recognition across age when they compressed only steady state portions of the sentence (e.g., pauses, steady state portions of vowels), but greater compression effects for older adults when they compressed sentences in the usual way by deleting 10 ms segments at regular intervals. The former technique leaves intact cues for identifying phonemes, but eliminates time for higher level cognitive processes such as semantic and syntactic analysis. These results suggest that compression reduces older adults' performance not by reducing time for processing, but rather by reducing critical temporal features of speech. Wingfield et al. (1999) selectively *restored* deleted time to compressed speech by inserting silent intervals at random locations in a passage or at clause and sentence boundaries. Only the restored time at clause or sentence boundaries improved recall, and recall was lifted to the level for unaltered speech only for young adults, not older adults. The results are consistent with age-related decrements in processing at all levels but also with an age-specific perceptual decrement that cannot be corrected by adding time at linguistic boundaries.

In sum, the pattern of findings overall provides evidence that accelerated speech rates impair older adults' perceptual processing more than young adults', especially of transient acoustic cues. Acceleration of speech also impairs older adults' higher level processing, either directly by removing time needed for syntactic analysis (general slowing account) or indirectly by increasing the difficulty of perceptual analysis, thereby reducing available resources (resources account).

Visual Word Recognition: Effects of Sensory and Perceptual Processes

In addition to declines in visual acuity, older adults exhibit other visual processing deficits that are relevant to reading, for example, retinal blurring (Artal, Ferro, Miranda, & Navarro, 1993), reduced accuracy of voluntary saccadic eye movements (Scialfa, Hamaluk, Pratt, & Skaloud, 1999), and reduced retinal illumination and loss of contrast sensitivity (Haegerstrom-Portnoy, Schneck, & Brabyn, 1999). Aging reduces the amount of light transmitted to the retina so that under comparable viewing conditions retinal illumination is considerably lower for older than young adults, a factor likely to increase word recognition threshold (Scialfa, 2002; for excellent reviews of visual sensory and perceptual deficits in older adults, see Fozard & Gordon-Salant, 2001; Madden & Whiting, 2004; Schneider & Pichora-Fuller, 2000; Scialfa, 2002). Even corrected vision is negatively related to age (Salthouse et al., 1996).

Recent research suggests that such sensory and perceptual changes affect the ability to read text under certain conditions. Steenbekkers (1998) determined the font size required for adults aged 20 to 80+ years, wearing corrective lenses when appropriate, to read text that was presented with 4 levels of contrast and under 3 levels of room illumination. Font size varied from 3.2 to 12.6 points. There were age deficits under all conditions, with the greatest differences for lower illumination and lower contrast. Participants in their seventies required a font that was almost twice as large as that of 20–30-year-olds to read without excessive delays.

Studies of visual language processing often rely on participants' reports of corrected to normal vision to rule out effects of age-related sensory deficits. The results of MacKay, Taylor, and Marian (2007b) suggest that this procedure is inadequate. They administered a close vision acuity test to young and older participants who self-reported 20/20 corrected vision; 20% of the older adults and 79% of the young adults actually scored 20/20. Older adults who reported 20/20 vision were faster to read large words (30 point lower case and 24 point upper case) than small words (24 point lower case and 18 point upper case), whereas young adults showed no effect of word size and were faster overall. Akutsu, Legge, Ross, and Schuebel (1991) also reported that older adults with self-reported normal vision were slower than young adults to read text in the range used by MacKay et al. (2006b), and also to read very small and very large text. Clearly, studies of visual language processing should report levels of contrast and illumination, administer vision tests, and compensate for observed age differences in visual acuity.

There is also evidence that age-related sensory deficits are linked to age-related declines in activation of visual cortex during word recognition. Increasing word length slowed older adults' lexical decision latency more than young adults' and was associated with decreased visual cortex (BA 17) activation (Madden et al., 2002; Whiting, et al., 2003). Whiting et al. reported that the advantage in lexical decisions for high frequency words over low frequency words increased with activation of both anterior (BA 17 and 18) and posterior (BA 37) regions of the occipito-temporal pathway for older adults only. They suggest that the frequency effects indicate that older adults access lexical level features of words to aid in word recognition and compensate for age-related declines in sensory analysis of the visual stimulus (Madden, Whiting, & Huettel, 2005).

Evaluation of aging, visual acuity, and word recognition has been carried out within a larger framework to test whether aging affects perceptual, lexical, and semantic processes during word recognition to the same extent. General slowing models predict a general rather than a process-specific effect of aging on word recognition processes (e.g., Lima et al., 1991). A number of studies, however, have shown that variables differ in their effect on young and older adults depending on the processes involved. Degradation of visual words, for example, by presenting words in visual noise or with asterisks between letters, produces a greater effect on older than young adults, as was also true for auditory processing in noise (Allen, Madden, Weber, & Groth, 1993; Madden, 1992; Speranza et al., 2000). Madden (1992) reported this greater cost of degradation on lexical decision latency even when visual acuity was covaried. Statistical control of performance on a test of speed reduced age-related variance in lexical decision latency and in the degradation effect, although age effects remained for both measures. Madden found that the benefit for semantically related compared to unrelated words, and for words compared to nonwords, was equivalent across age, suggesting that these lexical and semantic components of word recognition are unaffected by general slowing (for similar conclusions see Allen, Lien, Murphy, Sanders, & McCann, 2002; Madden, Pierce, & Allen, 1993; see Semantics section below for further discussion).

Spieler and Balota (2000) reported that, relative to young adults, older adults' word reading latency showed a smaller effect of word length and neighborhood density, variables affecting perception, and a greater effect of word frequency, a lexical level variable. They argued that older adults rely less on perceptual analysis during recognition because of their sensory deficits and rely more on lexical level characteristics. However, other studies have not reported the same effects of these variables in word naming (Morrison, Hirsh, & Duggan, 2003) or lexical decision (Tainturier, Tremblay, & Lecours, 1989; Whiting et al., 2003). Although age of acquisition and frequency of occurrence are correlated, Morrison et al. (2003) argued that age of acquisition rather than frequency predicts word naming latency and that it has equivalent effects on young and older adults.

Visual Word Recognition: Cognitive Operations and Studies of Distraction

As was true for auditory language processing, background visual noise (known as distraction in reading research) has a greater effect on older than young adults' visual language processing. Targets are typically written in one font and the distracters in another so that to read correctly the participant must discriminate between italicized and normal font (Carlson, Hasher, Zacks, & Connelly, 1995; Connelly et al., 1991; Duchek, Balota, & Thessing, 1998; Dywan & Murphy, 1996; Earles et al., 1997; Li, Hasher, Jonas, May, & Rahhal, 1998). The dominant framework for explaining why visual noise slows reading time more for older than young adults has been the inhibition deficit account: older adults' inhibition deficits impair their ability to ignore the distracting material so that it enters working memory and undermines the reading of the target text (Hasher et al., 2007). Alternatively, under the degraded signal account, age-related declines in perceptual processing make differentiation of targets and distracters more difficult for older than young adults (Burke & Osborne, 2007). When targets were distinguished from distracters spatially so discrimination between italics and standard font was no longer required, no age differences in distracter interference were observed (Carlson et al., 1995). Distracters that are semantically related to the target text increase interference more for older than young adults, a finding consistent with inhibition deficits (Carlson et al. 1995; Connelly et al., 1991; Li et al., 1998). On the other hand, older adults compensate for sensory losses under conditions of difficult reading conditions by engaging in more top-down processing than young adults (e.g., Speranza et al., 2000) so this effect is also consistent with sensory deficits. Visual acuity for participants is not typically reported in reading with distraction studies so the impact of a degraded signal is an important question for future research.

Kemper and McDowd (2006) introduced a new approach for investigating age differences in the effect of distraction on reading, namely, measurement of online eye movements during reading. They hypothesized that inhibition deficits would produce greater eye fixation on distracters. Sentences with a distracter word were read more slowly and comprehended more poorly than sentences without a distracter, but these effects were the same across age. Participants looked back more at distracters related to the sentences than unrelated distracters and more at distracters distinguished by font than by color, but again the effect was age invariant. These results provide no support for age-related inhibition deficits.

In sum, older adults' visual word recognition is affected by their declining perceptual processing, but it remains for future research to determine whether perceptual declines also contribute to age differences in distraction.

Summary of Perception of Phonology and Orthography

There is consistent evidence that age-related declines in acuity and perceptual processes, especially temporal processes in audition, impair older adults' language performance. In studies of auditory processing, equating intelligibility of stimuli across age eliminates much of the age differences in identifying and remembering language when background noise is increased. The direct effect of a degraded signal in older adults is in addition to the common cause hypothesized as the basis for correlations between sensory acuity and a range of cognitive functions including language (e.g., Baltes & Lindenberger, 1997). There is also evidence for indirect effects of perceptual declines in older adults wherein their greater difficulty in perceptual processing affects subsequent processes by constraining available resources, according to a resource account. Overall, findings emphasize the necessity of equating across age the intelligibility of auditory or visual language before making inferences about age declines in nonperceptual processes important for language.

PRODUCTION OF PHONOLOGY AND ORTHOGRAPHY

Language production is an extraordinary skill that allows a speaker to retrieve words from a lexicon of 50–100,000 words and speak them at a quite normal rate of 2 to 4 words per second. Moreover, errors in word production occur rarely, once or twice in 1000 words (Levelt, 2001). Older adults know more words than young adults (Kemper & Sumner, 2001; see Vocabulary section below), but they are more likely than young adults to experience difficulty producing a specific word (see Burke et al., 2000; Kemper, 2006; Thornton & Light, 2006). What level of the language system is responsible for this age-related change in production? There has been consensus for a number of years that semantic representations and the processes that act on them are well maintained and some actually improve during adulthood until very old age (Botwinick, 1977; Burke & MacKay, 1997; Kemper, 1992; Light, 1991; Wingfield & Stine-Morrow, 2000). In contrast, retrieval of phonological and orthographic information appears to decline with aging (see Burke & Shafto, 2004; Mortensen, Meyer, & Humphreys, 2006 for reviews). A variety of evidence suggests that the locus of the deficit causing age-related increases in word finding failures is in the phonological and orthographic system. We now consider this evidence.

Phonological Production

Picture Naming

Dozens of studies over the last 30 years have examined aging effects on picture naming and there has been controversy about the conclusions (e.g., Connor, Spiro, Obler, & Albert, 2004; Feyereisen, 1997; Goulet, Ska, & Kahn, 1994; Schmitter-Edgecombe, Vesneski, & Jones, 2000). The evidence suggests that older adults make more errors in naming pictures of objects or actions than young adults, but this difference does not become significant until older adults are in their seventies (e.g., Barresi, Nicholas, Connor, Obler, & Albert, 2000; Connor et al., 2004; MacKay, Connor, Albert, & Obler, 2002; Morrison et al., 2003; Nicholas, Obler, Albert, & Goodglass, 1985; for a meta-analysis, see Feyereisen, 1997). Age deficits in picture naming, however, are not consistently found in individual studies (Goulet et al., 1994). One explanation of this inconsistency is that older adults' larger vocabulary (see Semantics section) allows them to identify pictures of rare objects better than young adults, e.g., *trellis, abacus* in the Boston Naming Test, compensating for errors caused by word retrieval deficits (Schmitter-Edgecombe et al., 2000). In the context of this account, it is interesting that vocabulary (Lindenberger & Baltes, 1997) as well as picture naming decline after age 70.

Although perceptual, semantic, lexical, and phonological deficits can cause naming errors, analyses of types of errors (Albert, Heller, & Milberg, 1988), patterns of errors over repeated presentations (Barresi et al., 2000), and the greater effectiveness of phonological cues over semantic cues (MacKay et al., 2002) suggest that older adults' naming errors reflect deficits in lexical or phonological access rather than semantic access (see Mortensen et al., 2006). It is difficult, however, to use picture naming to unambiguously locate the level of the deficit in the language system that causes a naming error (Hodgson & Ellis, 1998).

Older adults are also slower than young adults to name pictures and several studies have varied characteristics of the picture or its name in an attempt to identify the processes responsible for the age-related slowing. Morrison et al. (2003) reported that visual complexity of pictured actions affected latency to produce the appropriate verb for old but not young adults, suggesting age differences in perceptual recognition time. However, the age difference in latency was equivalent for word reading and picture naming when general slowing was taken into account, a finding inconsistent with a greater effect of visual complexity of pictures for older adults. Age of acquisition and name agreement also affected naming latency but with comparable effects for young and older adults (Mitchell, 1989; Morrison et al., 2003). In sum, although there is some evidence that older adults' picture naming errors reflect lexical or phonological retrieval problems, we lack comparable evidence for naming latency.

Tip-of-the-tongue Experiences

Perhaps the strongest evidence that older adults suffer deficits in phonological retrieval comes from studies of tip-of-the-tongue states (TOT) in which a person is temporarily unable to produce a well-known word. In the throes of a TOT, a person can produce semantic and grammatical information about the TOT target, but only partial information about the phonology of the word, such as number of syllables or first phoneme (e.g., Brown & McNeill, 1966; Burke et al., 1991; Miozzo & Caramazza, 1997). Older adults rate word finding failures as a cognitive problem that is most frequent, most affected by aging, and the most annoying (Lovelace & Twohig, 1990; Rabbitt, Maylor, McInnes, Bent, & Moore, 1995; Ryan et al., 1994; Schweich, Van der Linden, Brédart, Bruyer, Nelles, & Schils, 1992; Sunderland, Watts, Baddeley, & Harris, 1986).

Consistent with retrospective self-reports, in diary studies older adults record more spontaneous TOTs during their everyday life than young adults (Burke et al., 1991; Heine, Ober, & Shenaut, 1999). Older adults also report more TOTs than young adults when they are induced in the laboratory with pictures or definitions for relatively low frequency words (Gollan & Brown, 2006; Heine et al., 1999; Rastle & Burke, 1996; Shafto, Burke, Stamatakis, Tam, & Tyler, in press; see also Brown & Nix, 1996). TOTs for low frequency words in the laboratory, however, are relatively rare and the age difference in number of TOTs is not always obtained (Burke et al., 1991; Vitevitch & Sommers, 2003; White & Abrams, 2002). However, the majority of naturally occurring TOTs are for proper names for both young and older adults (Burke et al., 1991) and there are consistent age-related increases in TOTs for proper names in the laboratory (Burke, Locantore, Austin, & Chae, 2004; Cross & Burke, 2004; Maylor,

1990) with a greater age-related increase for proper names than for other types of words (Burke et al., 1991; Evrard, 2002; James, 2006; Rastle & Burke, 1996).

A leading account of TOTs is the transmission deficit theory that TOTs occur when connections between lexical and phonological representations in the language system are too weak to transmit adequate priming for phonological representations to reach threshold. Activation of a lexical representation produces a feeling of knowing the word and makes available syntactic information about the word, but awareness of the phonological code for the word requires activation of representations in the phonological system down to the lowest level. Infrequent or nonrecent use of a word and aging of the participant weaken connections to and within the phonological system (Burke et al., 1991; Burke & Shafto, 2004). Consistent with this account, Vitevitch and Sommers (2003) demonstrated that both young and older adults produced more TOTs for low than high frequency words. They also reported that in young adults words with few phonological neighbors were more susceptible to TOTs than words with dense neighborhoods. A paucity of phonologically related neighbors reduces the spread of priming to phonological representations for the target. In older adults, however, the density effect only occurred for low frequency neighborhoods, perhaps because transmission of priming in dense neighborhoods was already reduced by aging.

If aging reduces transmission of excitation to phonological representations, then older adults should recall less phonological information while in a TOT state, as observed (Brown & Nix, 1996; Burke et al., 1991; Heine et al., 1999). Moreover, TOTs should be decreased by production of words that share phonology but not meaning with the target word because activation of phonological representations, required for production, strengthens connections. This prediction was confirmed: when young and older adults pronounced words sharing a few phonemes with a target word, it decreased the probability of inducing a TOT for the target word, for example, saying *decreed* and *pellet* decreased the probability of a TOT for *velcro* (James & Burke, 2000). Prior production of a homophone (e.g., [cherry] *pit*) increased correct naming and reduced TOTs for the name of a famous person (e.g., *Brad Pitt*) for older but not young adults when there was no awareness of the homophone manipulation (Burke et al., 2004).

Pronunciation of phonologically related words not only reduces the likelihood of a TOT, but in the midst of a TOT state it actually increases resolution of a TOT for both young and older adults (James & Burke, 2000). Words sharing the initial syllable with the target are more effective than words sharing the middle or final syllable (White & Abrams, 2002). In the only phonological priming study to divide older adults into young-old and old-old groups, White and Abrams found that old-old adults, aged 73–80 years, showed no priming effect. In very old age connections to phonological representations may become so weak that multiple activations are required to overcome transmission deficits. This is consistent with reports that phonological cuing in picture naming is less effective for adults older than 70 years compared to younger adults (Au, Joung, Nicholas, Ober, Kass, & Albert, 1995).

There has been some controversy about whether older adults suffer a disproportionate impairment in producing known proper names compared to other types of words (James, 2006; Maylor, 1997; Rendell, Castel, & Craik, 2005). The transmission deficit model predicts that proper names are more susceptible to retrieval failures than common names because proper names carry reference but not meaning. Thus, proper name representations at the lexical level lack converging top-down semantic connections from representations of meaning and this makes them vulnerable to transmission deficits in the single connections from conceptual representations of their referents (see Burke et al., 1991, 2004). The strongest relevant evidence comes from studies that control familiarity of the names across age. Rendell et al. (2005) found older adults in their seventies named fewer famous people who were known than did younger adults, although there were no age differences in naming known objects. James (2006) asked young and older adults to name and give occupations for familiar famous people. Participants produced more TOTs for names than occupations, and the increase was greater for older than young adults. Thus, the evidence suggests that retrieval is more difficult for proper names than other types of words, especially for older adults.

An alternative explanation for TOTs is that they are caused by a more accessible but incorrect alternate word that comes spontaneously to mind and interferes with retrieval of the target word (e.g., Jones, 1989; Logan & Balota, 2003; Zacks & Hasher, 1997). Under the inhibition deficit model, older adults are impaired in the ability to inhibit the alternate irrelevant word and this increases interference and the likelihood of a TOT. Contrary to this prediction, older adults are less likely than young adults to experience an alternate word during a TOT (Burke et al., 1991; Heine et al., 1999; White & Abrams, 2002). Moreover, when young and older adults were cued to produce an alternate name (e.g., *Eliza Doolittle*) prior to producing the name of an actor/actress pictured depicting this character (e.g., *Audrey Hepburn*), the alternate name did not increase the probability of a TOT, even though older adults produced more TOTs than young adults (Cross & Burke, 2004).

In sum, there is considerable evidence for age-related increases in phonological retrieval failures in research on picture naming and TOTs. Phonological priming techniques have been used to show that strengthening phonological connections decreases the likelihood of a TOT and increases resolution of a TOT, without the participant's awareness of the phonological relation. There is some evidence that retrieval failures in adults in their seventies and older may involve connections so weak that they respond poorly to phonological cues or priming. The evidence is consistent with the transmission deficit model which postulates that aging weakens connections between semantic and phonological representations of verbal knowledge. This is counter to the view that existing knowledge representations, the basis for crystallized intelligence/ cognitive pragmatics, are insensitive to aging (e.g., Baltes et al., 1999; see Burke, 2006).

Competitor Priming in Phonological and Orthographic Production

If older adults are less efficient than young adults in inhibiting competitors during word production, then priming competitors should have a more deleterious effect on production for older than young adults. Wheeldon and Monsell (1994) defined competitors in picture naming as sharing both physical and conceptual similarity with a target word. When they elicited a competitor with a verbal cue, for example, *largest creature that swims in the sea*—response: *whale*, latency was slower to name a picture of a shark compared to when the verbal cue elicited an unrelated word. Results using a similar paradigm provide no evidence that the delay in picture naming caused by a primed competitor was greater for older than young adults (Burke, 1999; Tree & Hirsh, 2003). Examining the role of competitors in lexical retrieval more broadly, Logan and Balota (2003) reported that presentation of an orthographically related (but incorrect) competitor (e.g., *ANALOGY*) slowed the completion of a fragment (e.g., *A-L--GY*) with a previously studied correct word (e.g., *ALLERGY*) and increased errors. These effects were again comparable for young and older adults, but older adults made more intrusion errors by producing the competitor than young adults. Logan and Balota concluded that older adults have more difficulty differentiating the source of activation for competitors and targets.

Competitors do not have to be explicit but rather can be internally and implicitly generated. In a verb generation task, a *low competition* noun cue elicited a single dominant verb response (e.g., *broom → sweep*), and a *high competition* noun cue elicited no dominant verb response (e.g., *pill → swallow, take*, etc.). Under the inhibition deficit theory, age differences in retrieval time should be greater for high than low competition nouns because they require suppression of competing alternatives to select a response. Responses were slower for high than low competition nouns, but there was no age difference in the magnitude of this effect, contrary to the prediction (Persson et al., 2004; Prull et al., 2004). An alternative explanation of competitor effects is that they slow production because it takes longer for the lexical representation of target word to reach a critical threshold relative to the level of excitation of competitors (e.g., Burke, 1999; Wheeldon & Monsell, 1994). It is interesting that in auditory word perception the effect of internally generated competitors is greater for older than young adults (Sommers & Danielson, 1999; see above). Thus, there are age differences in effects of internal perceptual competitors but not of internal semantic competitors.

In sum, studies of the effect of implicit and explicit competitors on lexical production provide little evidence that older adults are less able to inhibit competitors for selection. We return to competitor effects in the Semantics section where we consider interference from semantically related words.

Slips of the Tongue and Dysfluencies

There are relatively few aging studies of a phenomenon that has been central to the study of language production: speech errors known as slips of the tongue. In a slip of the tongue, the speaker misproduces one or more sounds in an intended word, for example, saying "coffee cot" instead of *coffee pot*, or one or more words in a sequence, for example, saying "take the hands out of the guns of people" instead of "take the guns out of the hands of people." Slips have been critical in the development of language production models which must account for the systematic patterns in these errors, for example, sequential class regularity is when nouns replace other nouns and initial syllables replace other initial syllables.

Although slips are infrequent in spontaneous speech, techniques for inducing slips in the laboratory provide insight into the locus of age changes in language production. MacKay and James (2004) induced slips by asking young and older adults to change /p/ to /b/, or /b/ to /p/, when naming a visually presented word with a /p/ or /b/. Age differences in speech errors in their responses occurred for some error types but not others. Older adults were more likely than young adults to omit sounds (e.g., "beach" instead of breach) whereas young adults were relatively more likely to substitute a different sound ("puck" instead of pug). Studies using tongue twisters (e.g., "The Swiss wristwatch strap snapped") also reported more omissions for older than young adults (Taylor & Burke, 2000) or that older adults added pauses to produce responses (Vousden & Maylor, 2006). This pattern is predicted by the transmission deficit theory because omission errors are caused by insufficient transmission of priming to phonological representations so that they fail to reach threshold for production. Older adults' weaker connections increase the probability of such transmission deficits. Some transformations in the MacKay and James task required phonological accommodation for a suffix under English morphology, as when the stimulus "ribs" /ribz/ is correctly transformed to rips /rips/. Older adults made more errors when this accommodation was required than when it was not, e.g., "bugs" correctly transformed to "pugs." Phonological accommodations errors are predicted by the changes in activation dynamics caused by transmission deficits (see MacKay & James, 2004).

Dysfluencies are another type of speech error that interrupt the flow of speech and appear to indicate a word retrieval problem. In describing a picture or other stimulus, older adults produced more lexical fillers (e.g., *you know*), non-lexical fillers (e.g., *um*), word repetitions (e.g., *just on the left left side*), lengthy pauses, and empty words than young adults, although studies are not always consistent in the specific type of dysfluency showing an age difference (e.g., Bortfeld, Leon, Bloom, Schober, & Brennan, 2001; Heller & Dobbs, 1993; Kemper, Rash, Kynette, & Norman, 1990; Schmitter-Edgecombe et al., 2000). These dysfluencies have been interpreted as devices to secure time for word finding. Consistent with this, Bortfeld et al. reported that older adults produced more fillers than young adults within syntactic phrases where word finding failures might occur, but not between syntactic phrases where fillers can signal the intention to continue speaking.

In sum, speech error data provide evidence for an increase in lexical and phonological retrieval deficits in old age and are consistent with age-related transmission deficits affecting language production.

Orthographic Production

Older adults reported that they can no longer spell words they once knew how to spell, and despite their higher vocabulary and education in these studies, they were more likely than young adults to misspell words they read or heard (Abrams & Stanley, 2004; MacKay & Abrams, 1998). Older adults regularized irregularly spelled letter combinations more than young adults, e.g., *calendar* → *calender*, but only the old-old group (*M* age = 77 years) misspelled regularly spelled combinations, e.g., *calendar* → *kalendar* (MacKay & Abrams, 1998; MacKay, Abrams, & Pedroza, 1999). Margolin and Abrams (in press) reported that the age difference was found for poor spellers but not good spellers. The transmission deficit model predicted an age-related decline in orthographic production (i.e., spelling), parallel to the predicted decline in phonological production. Aging weakens connections, and orthographic representations like phonological representations are especially vulnerable to transmission deficits because of their architecture: orthography is accessed via single connections from lexical nodes (Burke & MacKay, 1997; MacKay et al., 1999).

Cortese, Balota, Sergent-Marshall, and Buckner (2003) reported that older adults made more errors than young adults in spelling spoken homophones with heterogeneous spellings, e.g., *vein, capitol*, and were more likely to produce a spelling that corresponded to the dominant meaning but was a nondominant spelling for that sound (e.g., *vein*). Young adults' production favored a spelling that corresponded to a non-dominant meaning but was a dominant spelling for that sound (e.g., *vane*). This suggests that semantics has a stronger effect than orthography on lexical selection for older but not young adults.

In sum, older adults are more vulnerable to lexical retrieval failures while speaking single words and during discourse. Lexical competitor effects in production seem to be comparable for young and older adults. Rather, findings are consistent with phonological retrieval failures caused by transmission deficits. Parallel age-related deficits on orthographic retrieval increase spelling errors in old age.

SEMANTICS

Reviews of language function have consistently concluded that conceptual representations underlying the meaning of language at the word, sentence, or discourse level are well preserved during adulthood (e.g., Botwinick, 1984; Burke et al., 2000; Kemper, 1992; Kliegl & Kemper, 1999; Thornton & Light, 2006; Wingfield & Stine-Morrow, 2000; Zacks & Hasher, 2006). Performance on tests of general knowledge improves during adulthood, suggesting that older adults have richer semantic representations than young adults (Ackerman & Rolfhus, 1999; Beier & Ackerman, 2001). In contrast to age-related declines in retrieval processes at the phonological/orthographic level, there is little evidence for age-related changes in semantic retrieval processes, except in their speed. Where there are age deficits, they tend to appear under specific circumstances, such as in very old age (e.g., Lindenberger & Baltes, 1997) or as measured by online electrophysiological techniques such as event-related potential (ERP; e.g., Cameli & Phillips, 2000). Moreover, some age-related changes may not reflect age-related deficits, but rather experience-based changes, for example, in communication goals (e.g., Radvansky, Zwaan, Curiel, & Copeland, 2001). This is especially relevant to semantic performance because experience with language continues to affect the representation and structure of the semantic network across the lifespan. Thus, it is a particular challenge for researchers in this area not only to identify age-related deficits which may affect semantic processing, but also to distinguish between the effects of age per se and the effects of a lifetime of language experience.

Lexical Semantics: Vocabulary

Cognitive aging studies often report vocabulary scores in descriptions of their participants' background characteristics and these scores are usually higher for older than young adults; this was confirmed in a meta-analysis of 210 studies published in *Psychology and Aging* between 1986 to 2001 (Verhaeghen, 2003). However, education is strongly related to vocabulary and older adults in the surveyed studies were more highly educated than young adults. When Verhaeghen took education into account, the superior performance of older adults was eliminated for multiple choice vocabulary tests, but not for those requiring production of a definition for a target word. In addition to standard vocabulary measures, the National Adult Reading Test (NART; Nelson, 1985), which requires pronunciation of irregularly spelled words (e.g., *leviathan*), yields superior performance for older than young adults, even after removing education effects (Uttl, 2002). In discourse, older adults demonstrate their larger vocabularies with a greater type-token ratio wherein they produce a greater number of different words relative to the total words produced compared to young adults (Kemper & Sumner, 2001).

There is some recent evidence that older adults' greater vocabulary and verbal experience may affect lexical processing by increasing the relative frequency of low frequency words. In a homophone priming paradigm, young adults had greater priming effects with high frequency than low frequency words, but older adults did not show this frequency effect. In addition, older adults produced the low frequency version of a homophone in an unprimed spelling task more often than young adults, consistent with an age-related increase in relative frequency of use for low frequency words (Gomez, 2002). Moreover, highly educated older participants (who would be likely to have larger vocabularies) show smaller differences in lexical decision response times to low and high frequency words than young adults (Caza & Moscovitch, 2005).

Although there is a great deal of support for age-related superiority in vocabulary, cohort effects complicate the interpretation of vocabulary differences in cross-sectional studies. Vocabulary scores have increased steadily through the twentieth century (e.g., Schaie, 2005), and in studies published between 1965 and 1995 the increase over time was greater for older than young adults (Uttl & Van Alstine, 2003). Some but not all of this age difference is because educational level at the time of testing rose for older but not young adults, who are typically college students, again highlighting the importance of controlling education in evaluating the effect of aging on vocabulary. Longitudinal studies, however, confirmed that independent of education and cohort, aging is associated with improved vocabulary during adulthood until very old age (e.g., Schaie, 1994, 2005).

Vocabulary does decline in very old age. Lindenberger and Baltes (1997) reported that vocabulary scores in the Berlin Aging Study declined from age 70 to 103 years in cross-sectional comparisons. However, 6-year longitudinal data showed that vocabulary scores were maintained and did not begin to decline until age 90 years (Singer, Verhaeghen, Ghisletta, Lindenberger, & Baltes, 2003). Alwin and McCammon (2001) found that after adjusting for cohort effects older adults' scores did not decline to the level of 20-year-olds until participants were in their eighties (see Schaie, 1994, 2005 for similar findings).

Why do vocabulary scores level off in late adulthood and start to decline sometime after the age of 70 years? Insight into this issue is provided by research on HM, the famous anterograde amnesic whose hippocampus was bilaterally removed in 1953. HM was tested at the age of 71 on a lexical decision task of circling words but not nonwords. HM's correct identification of high frequency words was similar to age and education matched controls, but controls outperformed him in identifying low frequency words by almost 5 standard deviations. Comparing HM's lexical decision performance at age 53 to his performance at age 71 showed that his accuracy in identifying words had declined over 6 standard deviations at age 71 relative to same-age controls. The decline was attributed to errors on low frequency words and constituted an exaggerated age-linked decline (James & MacKay, 2001).

Using the transmission deficit model, James and MacKay argue that frequent and recent use of high frequency words maintains the strong connections in their representations, aiding their retrieval. Connections for low frequency words, however, weaken from disuse and from aging which both cause transmission deficits that impair retrieval. In the case of extreme disuse, all connections to a lexical representation can weaken to the point of being nonfunctional for the transmission of priming so that the word is no longer in the lexicon. When this happens for controls with no hippocampal damage, new representations can be readily made when the word is encountered again. However, HM, because of his hippocampal damage, cannot readily form new connections. Thus, low frequency but not high frequency words disappear from his lexicon (James & MacKay, 2001; MacKay, 2006; MacKay & James, 2001). In normal old age, formation of new semantic representations declines (e.g., McIntyre & Craik, 1987; Schacter, Osowiecki, Kaszniak, Kihlstrom, & Valdiserri, 1994), although obviously on a much lower scale than for HM. Nonetheless, this impedes reconstruction of representations of low frequency words that have been lost from extreme transmission deficits. Within this framework, the changes in vocabulary in very old age reflect the weakening and eventual loss without reinstatement of low frequency words, an interesting prediction for future research.

Within this framework, proper names would be expected to be especially vulnerable to loss. In addition to their susceptibility to transmission deficits (see TOT section above), older adults learn the proper name of an unknown person more poorly than young adults when there are no age differences in learning the occupation (James, 2004). Moreover, other processes necessary for learning new vocabulary decline in very old age. Adults 75 years or older were less able than younger adults to derive the correct meaning of unknown words from context because of declines in inferential processes that are essential for abstraction (McGinnis & Zelinski, 2000, 2003).

In addition to changes in cognitive processes, Carstensen's socio-emotional selectivity theory postulates that there is a shift in old age to emotional goals that bring immediate satisfaction, and away from the goal of accumulating knowledge because the uncertainty of the future calls into question when this knowledge would be put to use (e.g., Carstensen, Isaacowitz, & Charles, 1999; Isaacowitz, Charles, & Carstensen, 2000).

In sum, education, cohort, and age range all contribute to age differences in vocabulary measures, but the evidence suggests that semantic and lexical knowledge accumulates during adulthood and remains stable until very old age. Further research is needed to understand why vocabulary does not continue to increase in very old age and begins to decline.

Semantic Organization

There is consensus that aging has little effect on the organization of semantic knowledge as revealed, for example, by word associations and the structure of taxonomic categories and scripts (Burke et al., 2000; Light, 1991; Thornton & Light, 2006; Wingfield & Stine-Morrow, 2000). Nonetheless, recent findings show that there is age variance in the strength of specific responses. Contrary to the inhibition deficit prediction that older adults would have more difficulty inhibiting esoteric responses in word production, Hirsh and Tree (2001) found that young adults produced more diverse word association responses than older adults and young and older adults agreed on the dominant response for only 36 out of 90 words. Previous studies have reported no age difference in variability (e.g., Burke & Peters, 1986). In a homophone association task, White and Abrams (2004a) found that young and older adults differed in their dominant response on one-third of items, and on their dominance ratings for homophones for one-half of items. These findings highlight the importance of using association norms based on both young and older adults in semantic research. Associative relationships are similar across age groups with higher levels of contextual support, as when participants generate (Lahar, Tun, & Wingfield, 2004) or rate the predictability of sentence-final words (Little, Prentice, & Wingfield, 2004).

Lexical Level Comprehension: Semantic Priming

Facilitory Effects of Semantic Relatedness

In addition to word associations, the integrity of semantic organization and processes is often evaluated with semantic priming tasks which show faster response times to a target when preceded by a semantically related prime word or picture compared to an unrelated prime word or picture. This facilitation is attributed to excitation that spreads via semantic connections between the representations of the prime and target, moving the representation for the target closer to threshold. Previous research has provided evidence for preserved priming effects in older adults (e.g., Burke, White, & Diaz, 1987; Howard, McAndrews, & Lasaga, 1981), and more recent findings support this conclusion (e.g., Balota, Watson, Duchek, & Ferraro, 1999; Faust, Balota, & Multhaup, 2004; Lazzara, Yonelinas, & Ober, 2002; Tree & Hirsh, 2003). Preserved semantic processing at the lexical level is also supported by studies of the effects of semantic relatedness on the N400 in ERP studies. The N400 is a negatively going potential which is larger in response to semantic anomaly. The N400 for pairs of semantically related words is reduced in magnitude compared to unrelated words and this reduction is the same in magnitude and timing for young and older adults (Federmeier, Van Petten, Schwartz, & Kutas, 2003).

As with the frequency effects discussed earlier, older adults' greater linguistic experience may explain some age-related changes to semantic processing, for example, the *greater* semantic priming effects for older than young adults in meta-analyses (Laver & Burke, 1993; Myerson, Ferraro, Hale, & Lima, 1992). One account of this age difference is that during adulthood the semantic network not only gains lexical representations, but additional connections are generated between existing lexical representations so they become more richly connected (Laver & Burke, 1993). Thus, a prime word would have more and stronger connections to a related target, increasing priming effects. An alternative explanation is that greater priming effects are simply a byproduct of age-related general slowing (Giffard, Desgranges, & Kerrouche, 2003; Myerson et al., 1992).

Recent studies have attempted to address the general slowing explanation by controlling age differences in response time. If priming effects are greater for older adults when baseline latency is the same across age, this cannot be explained by the general slowing argument that priming effects are proportional to latency. Laver (2000) used four response deadlines (from 100 to 600 ms) to control young and older adults' lexical decision latencies. He reported an age-related increase in the size of priming effects but no age difference in absolute latency. Giffard et al. (2003) controlled age-related slowing statistically rather than behaviorally by entering unrelated latency and age in a regression on absolute priming effect. Although older adults' absolute semantic priming effects were larger than young adults', unrelated latency but not age was a significant predictor of priming effects in the regression, consistent with the general slowing explanation of age differences. Another approach was taken in a recent word stem completion task (White & Abrams, 2004b), where the priming effect was the probability of stem completion with a target word (e.g., *sand*) following a semantically related word (*beach*) compared to an unrelated word (*batch*). Older adults had a larger priming effect, responding more often with the target word following a semantic prime. This was despite no age difference in the size of a mediated *phonological* priming effect, where the target word (*sand*) was produced more often following a word phonologically identical to the semantically related word (*beech*) compared to an unrelated word. It is not clear how this age increase in semantic priming could be explained by slowing. Thus, the evidence is inconclusive as to whether larger priming effects for older adults are caused by cognitive declines such as general slowing, or by an increase in the interconnected nature of the semantic network due to experience.

Interfering Effects of Semantic Relatedness

Older adults' reading or listening is disrupted more than younger adults' by visual or auditory distracting information when it is semantically related to the target language (Carlson et al., 1995; Connelly et al., 1991; Li et al., 1998; Tun et al., 2002). Under the inhibition deficit theory, this is because older adults are less efficient in inhibiting the distracting information which competes with the target for attention.

Recent studies provide mixed support for the inhibition deficit explanation. As we saw above in discussing phonological production, production of a semantic competitor before picture naming (e.g., production of *rope* before naming a picture of a *chain*) produces comparable slowing across age (Burke, 1999; Tree & Hirsh, 2003), except at a very short prime–target lag time where young but not older adults showed interference (Tree & Hirsh, 2003). When semantic competitors are implicit (i.e., internally generated without awareness) rather than explicit, production is also slower for both young and older adults with no age differences in the effect (see above: Competitor priming in phonological and orthographic production). In the picture-word interference paradigm, participants ignore a word presented with a picture they are to name. Slowing from unrelated word distracters (compared to a white noise condition) and facilitation from distracters phonologically related to the picture name (compared to unrelated distracters) was equivalent across age; only semantically related distracters showed greater slowing for older than young adults (Taylor & Burke, 2002). Under an inhibition deficit account, age-related inhibition deficits should apply to all irrelevant information regardless of its phonological or semantic relatedness to the target. Taylor and Burke argue that older adults' greater semantic interference reflects their more elaborate semantic network which increases the transmission of priming to related concepts, an explanation related to the "enriched semantics" account discussed earlier to explain age-related increases in semantic priming.

In sum, there is evidence for age-related increases in interference from semantically related distracters when they are presented, but not when they are implicit or produced by the participant. It is unclear how this overall pattern can be explained by age-related inhibition deficits. It has been suggested that age-related increases in perceptual interference, as in reading with distracters, are related to perceptual deficits (Burke & Osborne, 2007), but further investigation of the pattern of age differences with implicit and explicit distracters or competitors is needed.

Sentence Comprehension

Although the priming effect between semantically related words is a common measure of semantic network integrity, words are rarely comprehended in isolation, and efficient semantic processing at sentential and discourse levels is critical. Additionally, lexical level tasks may not provide a fair test of some models of cognitive aging which predict interactions of age and increasing processing complexity. For example, under the working memory model, older adults' capacity may be taxed during sentence comprehension by the requirement to integrate incoming information into a developing sentence level representation, but these coordinative efforts may not be required in single word processing. Moreover, under a general slowing account, impairment to semantic processes may only become apparent when multiple successive processes are required in time-sensitive online tasks, as with auditory sentence comprehension.

Conclusions about the integrity of semantic processes during comprehension differ for online and offline measures. Online measures minimize nonlinguistic memory requirements and meta-linguistic judgments about meaning; they occur during language processing and reflect semantic processes involved in computing a representation of a sentence. Offline measures of comprehension occur after computation of the representation and are vulnerable to age-related declines in episodic memory. Not surprisingly, retention of a sentence or text after it is read or heard declines with age (e.g., Johnson, 2003; Van der Linden et al., 1999), as does performance on comprehension measures that depend on memory for the text (Kemper & Sumner, 2001). Mackenzie (2000b), however, reported that accuracy in responding to questions about details, inferences, or metaphors in texts was comparable in middle-aged and young-old adults, but declined in adults 75 to 88 years of age. Although this may reflect a memory decline, aging effects on semantic processing of text may differ before and after the age of 75 years as is the case for aging effects in semantic processing at the lexical level (e.g., vocabulary).

Online measures usually show age equivalence in constructing semantic representations of sentences and using these representations top-down to prime relevant concepts (e.g., Light, Valencia-Laver, & Zavis, 1991; Roe et al., 2000; Stine & Wingfield, 1994; for review see Kemper, 1992; Light, 1991). Indeed, meaningful sentential contexts often facilitate word identification during language processing more for older than young adults, especially under difficult perceptual conditions (Manenti et al., 2004; Schneider et al., 2005; Sommers & Danielson, 1999; Speranza et al., 2000). When errors in an offline recognition task reflected the correct generation of inferences during sentence processing, older adults showed at least as much evidence of inference generation as young adults (Zipin, Tompkins, & Kasper, 2000).

Online studies that show priming of relevant meanings and suppression of irrelevant meanings are important because under the inhibition deficit model, older adults should be less able to inhibit contextually inappropriate meanings. Newsome and Glucksberg (2002) demonstrated that both young and older adults were faster to respond to a metaphor-relevant probe (e.g., *Sharks are tenacious*) after reading a metaphor prime (e.g., *The lawyer for the defense is a shark*) than after reading a literal prime (e.g., *The large hammerhead is a shark*). Responses to a metaphor-irrelevant probe (e.g., *Sharks are good swimmers*) were slower after metaphor primes than literal primes, suggesting suppression of attributes irrelevant to the metaphor, with no age effect. Similarly, when a homophone was presented in a sentence biasing one meaning, both young and older adults' word recognition was faster for a word related to the contextually appropriate meaning than the inappropriate meaning suggesting that only the appropriate meaning was available (Hopkins, Kellas, & Paul, 1995; Paul, 1996). Dagerman et al. (2006), however, reported that young but not older adults used context online to disambiguate noun–verb homophones. They presented an auditory fragment biasing the verb interpretation of the ambiguous word (e.g., *The union told the reporters that the corporation fires*) or the noun interpretation (e.g., *The union told the reporters that the warehouse fires*) followed immediately by a visual target word that was compatible with the verb interpretation (e.g., *us*). Young adults' naming latency for the target word was faster with the verb bias context than the noun bias context, whereas older adults showed no context effect. Both young and older adults showed context effects in an offline judgment about the compatibility of the fragment and the visual target. The authors argued that older adults' processing was too slow to use the context to resolve the ambiguity by the time the target was presented. This explanation was supported in a simulation of the age difference in use of sentential context that implemented a model which manipulated a speed parameter controlling activation of all nodes in the model.

Age differences in semantic processing are also suggested by recent research that makes inferences about semantic processing of sentences based on the N400 response in ERPs. N400s are negatively going potentials which are larger following a semantically anomalous word in a sentence than a semantically congruent word. Kutas and Federmeier (2001) argued that words which are congruent with the sentence are primed by the sentence context and this readies them for activation and lowers the N400. Because this priming is feature based, a sentence-incongruent word sharing semantic features with the congruent word will also receive some priming, reducing the N400 amplitudes compared to an incongruent and unrelated word. While young adults demonstrate this graded progression of N400 amplitudes, this pattern was reduced or absent in older adults. This age difference has been interpreted as older adults using the sentence context less effectively (Cameli & Phillips, 2000; Federmeier, McLennan, De Ochoa, & Kutas, 2002). In support of this conclusion, Federmeier et al. (2002) found that older adults with larger vocabularies and higher verbal fluency scores showed the young response pattern. However, in other studies, young and older adults showed comparable effects of sentence context on N400 to sentence congruent words (Federmeier et al., 2003; Phillips & Lesperance, 2003, Experiment 2), although the effect was delayed 200 ms in older adults compared to young adults in one study (Federmeier et al., 2003) but not the other. The delay is consistent with Dagerman et al.'s (2006) claim that older adults require more time for sentence context to affect word processing.

In sum, although lexical level semantic processing is at least as strong in older as young adults, there is some evidence that semantic processing of sentences may decline with aging, possibly because of age-related slowing. This is somewhat surprising given the consistent findings that sentential context aids older adults' perceptual processing of language. Further research is needed to determine if age-related changes in ERP during sentence processing are linked to behavioural deficits in older adults and to investigate what semantic properties of sentences constrain older adults' sentence processing and how these properties are related to slowing.

Discourse Comprehension

Discourse comprehension is particularly important for assessing the relative contributions of age-related processing deficits versus age-related increases in language experience. Discourse comprehension places demands on working memory because it requires integrating concepts and maintaining thematic information over multiple sentences. However, discourse comprehension also provides an opportunity for strong top-down influences, guiding comprehension with heuristics and real world knowledge which increases during adulthood. Part of discourse comprehension is the development of a situation model, namely, a multi-dimensional representation of the topic of the text, including information such as space, time, and causal relationships (Zwaan & Radvansky, 1998). A situation model goes beyond the literal content of the text by integrating the text with pre-existing knowledge (e.g., Stine-Morrow, Gagne, Morrow, & DeWall, 2004). Thus, situation model information is often contrasted with the *surface* information (i.e., the specific word content), and *textbase* information (i.e., the specific propositional content).

Older adults typically demonstrate preserved use of situation models. Although one study suggests older adults do not inhibit representations of irrelevant situation models as well as younger adults (Radvansky, Zacks, & Hasher, 2005), most studies demonstrate age constancy in constructing and using situation models during comprehension, for example, by updating them when there are changes to spatial or temporal information (Radvansky, Copeland, & Zwaan, 2003). Indeed, a number of studies indicate a *stronger* influence of situation models on older adults' comprehension than on younger adults'. Radvansky et al. (2001) gave participants history texts to read, and found that older adults had greater memory for situation model information than younger adults. This age-related superiority was eliminated when a narrative text was used, which encouraged all readers to form situation models, but a subsequent study (Radvansky et al., 2003) demonstrated age-related superiority for remembering situation model information even when participants read narratives.

In keeping with these findings, a number of established situation model effects are larger for older adults. Dijkstra, Yaxley, Madden, and Zwaan (2004) had participants read sentences which described objects (e.g., spaghetti), in a context (e.g., bowl/box) which implied specific form information (e.g., cooked/uncooked). Participants then saw a drawing of an object (e.g., cooked or uncooked spaghetti) and had to indicate whether it had been described in the sentence or not. If features of the drawing mismatched the implied features from the sentence, participants were slower to make this decision than when the features matched. Older adults showed a larger mismatch effect than young adults, suggesting that their situation models were stronger and had more of an impact when the model was violated. Another situation model effect demonstrated that reading times were faster and memory was better for text where items had a functional, interactive relationship compared to a nonfunctional relationship (e.g., Radvansky et al., 2003). This functionality effect was present in both age groups but was larger for older adults. Finally, the further a described object is from the protagonist, the longer it takes readers to process information about it. For participants with good comprehension, this "distance effect" was larger for older than younger adults (Stine-Morrow, Morrow, & Leno, 2002).

Stine-Morrow, Loveless, and Soederberg (1996) evaluated the allocation of resources to surface, textbase, and discourse processing by regressing word-by-word reading times onto factors associated with these different processing levels. For example, word length in syllables measured orthographic decoding, the number of propositions was a textbase variable, and the "serial position" indirectly indicated the strength of the global representation (which should increase as more of the passage is read). The critical assumption of this approach is that reading time allocation reflects relative allocation of cognitive processing. Using this approach, discourse factors influence older adults' processing more than young adults' because older adults' reading time depends more on these factors (e.g., Miller, Stine-Morrow, Kirkorian, & Conroy, 2004; Stine-Morrow, Miller, & Leno, 2001; Stine-Morrow et al., 2002). For example, Stine-Morrow et al. (2001) reported that better performing young adults allocated more time to textbase factors, while better performing older adults allocated more time to both textbase and discourse factors. For an excellent review of age-related changes to resource allocation during reading, see Stine-Morrow et al. (2006).

Applying a resource model to older adults' emphasis on discourse-level processing, raises the question of whether it is an attempt to optimize limited resources or a byproduct of insufficient processing resources (see Stine-Morrow et al., 2006 for discussion). Several results suggest that older adults attempt to optimize their performance. For example, Stine-Morrow et al. (1996) found that older adults who showed the same pattern of reading time allocation as young adults had *worse* subsequent recall, whereas older adults with better recall had allocated more time to "strong schema-based processing." A number of other studies have also found different allocation patterns for older adults in the context of equivalent memory (e.g., Miller et al., 2004; Smiler, Gagne, & Stine-Morrow, 2003; Stine-Morrow et al., 2001) or superior memory perform-ance compared to young (Miller et al., 2004). However, McGinnis and Zelinski (2003) demonstrated that when participants attempted to iden-tify the definition of an unfamiliar word which had appeared in a passage context, older adults over age 75 gave high ratings to precise definitions, but unlike young or young-old adults, also gave high ratings to definitions based on the general themes of the passage and irrelevant definitions. This implies, at least for very older adults, that the preference for discourse-level processing is not necessarily optimal. Additionally, during self-paced lis-tening, younger adults adjusted allocation of listening times to improve memory as task difficulty increased, but older adults were not as flexible in their resources allocation patterns, and demonstrated worse recall than younger adults (Titone, Prentice, & Wingfield, 2000).

Recent research has called into question the underlying assumption that there is a connection between older adults' resource allocation pat-terns and decreases in available resources, such as working memory. Stine-Morrow et al. (2001) found that age-related changes to allocation patterns were largely independent of working memory capacity (as assessed with reading and listening sentence span tasks), despite an age-related capacity decline. The role of working memory capacity was more directly addressed by Smiler et al. (2003) who had participants read pas-sages with or without a secondary memory task. Older adults had longer "wrap-up" times at the ends of sentences, thought to reflect time allocated to conceptual integration, and this age difference increased in the pres-ence of the secondary memory task. However, working memory capacity (i.e., sentence span) did not predict this pattern, despite the finding that working memory capacity was lower in the older group and did predict performance on the secondary memory task.

If age-related shifts towards discourse-level processing are not responses to decreasing processing resources, a ready alternative is that this shift is due to their greater pool of general knowledge, acquired across their lifespan. However, Radvansky et al. (2001) found no correl-ation between measures of prior knowledge and measures of situation model use, and many of the situation model effects depend on manipulat-ing and updating situation models based on new information given in the task (e.g., Dijkstra et al., 2004, Radvansky et al., 2003). In fact, under some circumstances, older adults use situation models differentially more than younger adults in the context of new information. For example, both young and older adults increase the time they allocate to the integration of concepts when they have pre-existing expertise on the topic at hand

(Miller, 2003), but only older adults are similarly affected by newly acquired knowledge (Miller et al., 2004). Additionally, Stine-Morrow et al. (2002) demonstrated that when new object information is introduced during text comprehension, only older adults integrate this information into the situation model, while younger adults rely on textbase processing to remember the new information. Finally, when reading a text multiple times, younger adults will tend to emphasize discourse-level processing only in the second reading after establishing a textbase representation in the first reading, whereas older adults focus on discourse-level processing beginning with the first reading (Stine-Morrow et al., 2004), a pattern which also leads to better comprehension performance in the older group.

Thus, older adults may have a bias towards top-down processing per se, but more research is clearly needed to determine why older adults prioritize situation model formation and other discourse-level processing during text comprehension. One possibility is that changes to older adults' performance may be due to their language "expertise." If the primary goal of comprehension is to form a situation model, older adults, who are more practiced at comprehension, may be better at identifying and focusing on the aspects of text that are relevant for forming situation models (Radvansky et al., 2001). In support of this view, Miller et al. (2004) reported that during passage reading older adults applied newly acquired domain knowledge more, which differentially slowed their reading, but they subsequently outperformed younger adults on a comprehension task that required forming inferences. Thus, as suggested by Radvansky et al. (2001), young and older adults may be equally influenced by textbase information during comprehension, but while younger adults retain it, older adults discard this information after using it to form a situation model, which may explain older adults' better inferential memory (Miller et al., 2004), but younger adults' better propositional memory.

In sum, text comprehension in old age appears to involve increased reliance on discourse structures such as situation models. However, recent studies suggest that this shift may be independent of declines in processing resources such as working memory, and may constitute an age-related shift in priorities during comprehension.

Elderspeak and Comprehension

Elderspeak is an adopted speech register used to address older adults that attempts to accommodate anticipated communication difficulties, similar to speech used to small children and foreigners. Elderspeak is characterized by exaggerated intonation, slower speech rates, more repetition and elaboration, and shorter sentences with simpler syntax. Is elderspeak a helpful accommodation to older adults' comprehension abilities? Kemper and Harden (1999) identified helpful and harmful aspects of elderspeak using a referential communication task in which participants were instructed on how to follow a route on a map. Semantic alterations in the speaker's language such as repetitions and elaborations improved performance and reduced older adults' reported communication difficulties. The same was true for some kinds of syntactic simplifications, such as reducing the use of embedded or subordinate clauses, but simply shortening sentences was not helpful. Moreover, changes to prosody such as exaggerated intonation and slowed speech rate increased older adults' reported communication difficulties and under some circumstances impaired performance.

The combination of helpful and harmful characteristics of elderspeak may explain some of the mixed reactions that elderspeak elicits. Older adults resent patronizing speech, and find it insulting and condescending (Ryan, Giles, Bartlucci, & Henwood, 1986). Despite older adults' negative reaction to being spoken to in a patronizing register, they may be blamed for its use, contributing to the view that they are less competent (La Tourette & Meeks, 2000). Moreover, older adults feel that they have more communicative difficulties themselves in response to patronizing speech (Kemper & Harden, 1999), suggesting that elderspeak can lead to a downward spiral that reinforces negative stereotypes (e.g., Nussbaum, Pitts, Huber, Raup Krieger, & Ohs, 2005). However, while patronizing speakers are typically preferred less than speakers who do not use patronizing speech (Brown & Draper, 2003), elderspeak can also be associated with affection and nurturance (Ryan et al., 1986). In fact, when observing a conversation, both young and older adults rate elderspeak higher than neutral speech on both negative and positive characteristics (Gould, Saum, & Belter, 2002). Interventions to reduce the use of elderspeak are motivated by findings that older adults prefer health-care workers who are not condescending (e.g., La Tourette & Meeks, 2000), and that patronizing speech to nursing home residents can encourage dependence and increase social isolation (Williams, Kemper, & Hummert, 2003; Nussbaum et al., 2005). Intervention effectively reduces some aspects of elderspeak but not others (Williams et al., 2003), and some improvements remain stable, but some deteriorate over time (Williams, 2006).

In sum, the way that older adults are spoken to dramatically affects how they feel about themselves and how they are perceived by others. It can also affect their performance on cognitive tasks, improving it under some conditions and impairing it under others. Components of elderspeak are either helpful or harmful, but as Kemper and Kemtes (2000) point out, it is unclear that speakers use helpful components to adjust their speech to the communicative needs of older adults.

Discourse Production

Much of the recent aging research on production of discourse investigates the semantic content, in particular, the number of ideas produced relative to a fixed number of words and the degree to which these ideas are relevant to the topic. The density of ideas declines with age in written autobiographical essays (Kemper, Greiner, Marquis, Prenovost, & Mitzner, 2001a), spoken responses to topics (Kemper & Sumner, 2001; Kemper et al., 2001a), and spoken descriptions of a picture (Mackenzie, 2000a). Juncos-Rabadan, Pereiro, and Rodriguez (2005) presented sequences of pictures and analyzed the semantic content of narratives about them by native speakers of Galician with no more than an eighth grade education. Although the overall content did not vary with age, the density of content declined with age. At present, there is no account of why idea density declines with age, but low idea density is associated with increased all-cause mortality and Alzheimer's disease (Snowdon, Greiner, Kemper, Nanayakkara, & Mortimer, 1999; Snowdon et al., 1996).

There is also evidence that under some conditions older adults produce more speech that is off topic. Arbuckle, Pushkar Gold, and colleagues examined the responses of 60 to 95-year-old adults in a life history interview and reported that off-topic verbosity (OTV) increased with aging (e.g., Arbuckle & Pushkar Gold, 1993; Gold, Andres, Arbuckle, & Schwartzman, 1988). High OTV was associated with reduced performance on tests involving the ability to ignore irrelevant information (e.g., Trailmaking test, Stroop test), and the authors attributed OTV to age-related deficits in the ability to inhibit irrelevant information (Arbuckle & Pushkar Gold, 1993; Pushkar Gold & Arbuckle, 1995).

James, Burke, Austin, and Hulme (1998) argued for an alternative pragmatic change account of discourse under which older adults produce more off-topic speech because of a shift in their conversational goals from the concise exchange of information, to an emphasis on personal narratives and identification of significant events in their lives. James et al. found that older adults produced more off-topic speech only during autobiographical storytelling, and although their stories were rated as less focused, they were also rated as more interesting and higher quality than young adults'.

The roles of age, inhibition, and pragmatic factors in OTV have become clearer through careful and systematic investigations of Arbuckle, Pushkar Gold, and colleagues. They selected adults who were in the top 15% of a panel of 455 older adults in terms of OTV, as well as samples with mid and low levels of OTV. To test the generality of OTV, as predicted by the inhibition deficit account, they used a referential communication task where participants gave descriptions to identify a nonsense figure to a listener. The high OTV group used more words, more hedges, and more redundant information than the low or medium OTV groups who did not differ. There was, however, no difference among groups in off-topic speech in the task and little difference in the effect on the performance of the listener (Arbuckle et al., 2000). In a "get acquainted" conversation with other participants, the high OTV participants spent more time talking and provided more information about themselves. In a condition where they received cues signalling listener boredom during the conversation, the high OTV participants still talked more than the other groups but all groups reduced the time they spent talking.

Arbuckle, Pushkar, and colleagues concluded that OTV characterizes only a minority of older adults and that "older people in general are not prone to verbose self-focused talk or to high levels of OTV" (p.373) (Pushkar et al., 2000). They argue that inhibitory deficits explain OTV, but also suggest that declining cognitive performance may trigger a pragmatic change by shifting conversational goals towards more personal narratives. As Kemper and Mitzner (2001) point out, the inhibitory deficits invoked in OTV differ from the pervasive age-related deficits postulated in the inhibition deficit model (Hasher & Zacks, 1988). The relation between OTV and inhibitory function is found only for older adults in the top 15% of OTV scores, and not for the remaining 85% of older adults. Moreover, even high OTV adults are able to curb off-topic speech in some situations, e.g., referential communication tasks and when conversational partners look bored.

Summary of Semantics

Evidence from studies of lexical semantics, including vocabulary knowledge and semantic priming, suggests that this aspect of the semantic system is well preserved in old age. Declines in vocabulary occur only in very old age and may reflect declines in learning rather than in semantic processing. The bulk of the evidence from studies of semantic processing of sentences and discourse suggests that older adults compute meaning online and use this meaning top-down in subsequent language processing. Some recent ERP findings indicate slower or incomplete computation of meaning of sentences, although supporting behavioral evidence is sparse (but see Dagerman et al., 2006). Older adults' greater language experience is relevant to several age-related changes including semantic priming and frequency effects at the lexical level and the use of situational models at the discourse level. Cognitive aging models of language have yet to address the question of why aging has a beneficial effect on lexical semantic processing but not on processing in other language subsystems. Older adults reduce the density of ideas in their discourse and produce more off-topic speech in autobiographical narratives. Further research is needed to determine if the change in idea density is related to a combination of changes in cognitive function and pragmatic principles as seems to be true for off-topic speech.

SYNTAX

The primary account of syntactic changes in adulthood is that they are driven by a shrinking working memory capacity which limits older adults' ability to process complex hierarchical structures such as those underlying some syntactic constructions. The assumption is that embedded clauses in general and certain types in particular, such as those in left-branching sentences, increase working memory load to a point that sometimes exceeds older adults' capacity, disrupting syntactic processes (Kemper & Kemtes, 1999). Caplan and Waters, however, have argued for a dedicated working memory that is specialized for automatic interpretive processing of sentences and is unrelated to standard working memory measures that show age-related declines. Under this model, the online computation of meaning and syntax during reading or listening is obligatory and shows little variation with age. In contrast, offline postinterpretive language processing such as plausibility or grammaticality judgments involve conscious, controlled processing that reflects age-related decrements in working memory capacity as measured by standard working memory tasks (Caplan & Waters, 1999; Waters & Caplan, 2001, 2005). Investigation of the relation of online and offline language performance to aging and to working memory measures has motivated much recent research on comprehension of syntax.

Comprehension of Syntax

Offline measures of comprehension that require participants to answer questions about a text after it is read have consistently found age-related declines in performance (e.g., Kemper & Sumner, 2001; Van der Linden et al., 1999), especially for text with greater syntactic complexity (Waters & Caplan, 2001, 2005; but see Feier & Gerstman, 1980). Online techniques measure word-by-word or phrase-by-phrase reading or listening time, for example, by using the auditory moving window paradigm in which participants control presentation of successive phrases of the sentence. More time was allocated when the text increased in syntactic complexity, but this slowing of presentation was comparable for young and older adults at the most demanding regions of the sentence (Stine-Morrow et al., 1996; Waters & Caplan, 2001, 2005). Moreover, Waters and Caplan reported that offline but not online measures were correlated with working memory span and that age effects in the offline measures were reduced when span effects were removed. DeDe et al. (2004) tested this pattern of age differences using a structural equation modeling approach. Although the final model showed that the effects of syntactic complexity on listening time were related to age, they were not related to working memory measures. In contrast, offline measures of comprehension were related to age and the age effects were mediated by working memory.

The effects of syntactic complexity can also be seen in sentences with temporary syntactic ambiguity as in garden path sentences: *The experienced soldiers warned about the dangers conducted the midnight raid*. Correct interpretation and avoidance of the garden path requires multiple interpretations of the ambiguous phrase, in particular, transformation of *warned* from main verb to the verb in a relative clause (Kemper, Crow, & Kemtes, 2004). If syntactic processing is related to working memory capacity, then older adults should be less able to hold multiple interpretations in working memory and more likely to show garden path effects. However, the effect of ambiguity on reading time did not differ by age although young adults were more accurate than older adults answering questions about ambiguous sentences, but not unambiguous sentences (Kemtes & Kemper, 1997). In a study tracking eye movements, there were no age differences in the pattern of first pass fixation times for successive words in garden path sentences. First pass fixations are believed to reflect immediate semantic and syntactic processing during reading, and thus these findings are consistent with the Waters and Caplan (2001) model. Regressions back to words already read are believed to represent postinterpretive processes and these were more numerous for older than young adults in garden path sentences, suggesting that older adults were less able to hold the words in memory (Kemper et al., 2004).

Overall, the evidence suggests few age differences in online measures of syntactic processing and age decrements in offline measures of syntactic processing. This pattern is consistent with the Caplan and Waters' (1999) model of a dedicated working memory for online language processing that is unrelated to working memory span. We turn now to production where virtually all measures have been online.

Production of Syntax

Kemper and her colleagues have produced considerable evidence from both longitudinal and cross-sectional research that the syntactic complexity of spoken and written language declines with age. Syntactic complexity, measured by counts of different types of embedded clauses and of clauses per utterance, declined in old age in samples of writing from diaries (Kemper, 1987) and essays (Kemper et al., 2001a) and spoken responses to questions (Kemper & Sumner, 2001; Kemper et al., 2001b). Syntactic complexity was not related to educational attainment or high school grades (Kemper et al., 2001a), but was related to working memory measures (Kemper, Kynette, Rash, Sprott, & O'Brien, 1989; Kemper & Sumner, 2001; Kemper et al., 2001b).

Experimental studies of language production provide more control over pragmatic aspects of language that may influence the structure and content of spontaneous language, and may also vary with age. Davidson, Zacks, and Ferreira (2003) used a constrained production task in which young and older adults constructed a sentence using a visually presented subject pronoun and verb followed by two or three other cue words. The verbs varied in the number of syntactic options they allowed. Having only one option for sentence construction slowed onset latency and increased dysfluencies, with no age difference in these effects. Thus, the ability to use grammatical options to increase efficiency in constructing a sentence is well maintained in old age.

Using a similar constrained production task and presenting two, three or four cue nouns, Kemper, Herman, and Lian (2003a) reported that latency to produce a sentence increased with the number of nouns presented and more so for older than young adults. Despite this apparent greater time planning the sentences when there were more cue words, older adults' grammatical complexity and idea density increased less than young adults' with four words, although there were no age differences with two or three cue words. Parallel findings were obtained when the complexity of a cue verb was varied by comparing complement-taking verbs, e.g., *wished, guessed*, which often yield multiclause sentences, with transitive verbs, e.g., *called, replaced* and intransitive verbs, *smiled, jumped*. Complement taking verbs increased latency more for older than young adults, and increased grammatical complexity and idea density, but again this increase was less for older than young adults. Kemper, Herman, and Lian argued that increasing the number of cue words or the complexity of a cue verb increases memory load. This constrains the complexity of older adults' sentences because their reduced working memory capacity is inadequate with this increased load to generate complex syntax. This conclusion is consistent with results from another constrained production task where sentences were generated from presented stems that cued right-branching or left-branching completions (Kemper, Herman, & Liu, 2004). Young adults' sentences, but not older adults' sentences, were longer, more grammatically complex and more dense in propositions for right-branching than left-branching stems. The authors argued that older adults' reduced working memory capacity creates a "ceiling" on sentence complexity so that it does not vary with verb type.

Consistent with this account, Altmann and Kemper (2006) found that while young adults' word order in sentences was influenced by cue word characteristics such as animacy, older adults tended to construct sentences based on the order in which cue words were presented, perhaps because this reduced memory load. It is somewhat surprising in the context of these results that Kemper, Herman, and Lian (2003b) found that language production of both young and older adults was affected by performance of a concurrent task, for example, walking or finger tapping. Young adults showed greater costs in reduction of grammatical complexity and length of utterance and older adults showed greater costs in slowing of speech rate. Although older adults' baseline language was less fluent and complex than young adults, it is unclear how the pattern of costs is consistent with the working memory account of age difference in grammatical complexity.

Miller and Johnson (2004) identified different types of working memory based on patient data, focusing on "lexical-semantic" short-term memory that is measured, for example, by the difference in memory span for words versus nonwords, and has been related to language production. Participants described the movement pattern of three pictures on a screen which varied so that the response required two nouns in the initial noun phrase "The ball and the tree move above the finger" or one noun in the initial noun phrase "The ball moves above the tree and the finger." Latency to begin the sentence was longer for the two noun initial phrases than the one noun and the size of the effect was the same across age. There were no age differences in measures of lexical-semantic short-term memory, but these measures predicted the complexity effect in onset latency whereas measures of phonological short-term memory did not. These results are compatible with the view that there may be different types of working memory that vary in their relevance to language tasks.

In sum, older adults produce sentences with lower syntactic complexity and propositional density than young adults in both spontaneous language and constrained language production tasks in the lab. This is readily explained under a working memory model in which older adults are less able to produce sentences with high complexity because of declines in working memory capacity. These conclusions are contrary to the conclusion reached in online comprehension studies that age has small effects on online syntactic processes and there is no relation between these processes and working memory. Clearly, future research needs to consider the reasons for this difference between online production and comprehension. It is unlikely that older adults construct simpler sentences as a pragmatic choice because they produce simpler sentences in constrained laboratory tasks and their reduced complexity compared to younger adults is accompanied by higher error rates (e.g., Kemper et al., 2004), suggesting that the simpler sentences were a response to processing difficulty. A recent attempt to identify different components of working memory that vary in how they are affected by age and in how they influence language production is a promising approach for understanding why some aspects of syntactic complexity are affected by age and others are not (Miller & Johnson, 2004).

CONCLUDING COMMENTS: IMPLICATIONS FOR COGNITIVE AGING RESEARCH

One of the most salient findings emerging from this review of language and aging is the profound effect that age differences in perceptual processing have on cognitive performance. Since Baltes and Lindenberger (1997) noted the paucity of research on the relation between sensory functioning and cognition in older adults, there has been a rapid increase in research activity in this area. On a theoretical level, the interaction between perception and cognition is consistent with interactive language models (see Figure 8.1) in which semantic activation depends on priming transmitted bottom-up from the phonological system; top-down priming from the semantic system is also transmitted to phonological representations during perception, aiding perceptual recognition. The permeability of sensory and cognitive systems in these models underscores the significance of age-related changes in sensory processes.

The methodological implications are very clear. The sensory acuity of young and older participants in language research must be measured and reported. Self-reports of acuity have been shown to be inaccurate and unreliable. The research record demonstrates that it is difficult to draw conclusions about age differences in higher level language processes on the basis of behavior that reflects age differences in sensory acuity (see Schneider & Pichora-Fuller, 2000). In recent research older adults' sensory decline has been compensated for by adjusting presentation of stimuli to equate baseline performance or by statistically removing age differences in acuity. These procedures would be useful in a broad range of language research.

Cognitive aging theories have had mixed success in explaining why variables affecting perceptual difficulty, such as background noise or accelerated speed, have a greater effect on older adults' cognitive performance. The degraded signal account explains some but not all of the findings. In particular, even when identification of incoming language is correct so the signal is not degraded, the difficulty of perceptual identification affects subsequent cognitive processes (McCoy et al., 2005). Such effects are often attributed to limits on resource capacity. The resource model, however, continues to be plagued by a lack of specification of the nature of resources and how they affect performance.

The inadequacy of the resource model as currently implemented is not a new criticism (e.g., Light & Burke, 1988; MacKay & James, 2001; McDowd & Shaw, 2000; Navon, 1984; Salthouse & Craik, 2000). One of the most serious problems is the absence of an independent measure of resources, creating a problem pointed out by Salthouse and Craik (2000): "when the same empirical results that are 'explained' by reduced resources, also serve as the primary evidence for inferring the existence of an age-related reduction of resources" (p. 690). Little progress has been made in identifying an independent measure of resources; indeed, there is additional evidence that is inconsistent with a single pool of processing resources which can be measured by a single general measure (e.g., Waters & Caplan, 2001).

The predictive inadequacy that results from the absence of a behavioral index or a theoretical mechanism for resources can be seen clearly in language research. Consider the effect on performance of difficult perceptual conditions such as background noise or accelerated presentation rate. Older adults' word recognition declines more than young adults', an age difference that has been attributed to difficult perceptual conditions requiring more resources than are available to older adults. When, however, the to-be-identified words are presented in a meaningful sentence context, identification improves compared to a low meaning or no context condition, often with a larger benefit for older than young adults (e.g., Schneider et al., 2005; Sommers & Danielson, 1999; Speranza et al., 2000). This result can be explained under a resource account only if it is assumed that computing a semantic and syntactic representation of the sentence and using this representation top-down during word recognition *reduces* the resources required for the task compared to a no sentence context condition. This assumption is undermined by the findings of Stine-Morrow and others that demonstrate that computation of a mental representation of a sentence requires resources (e.g., Smiler et al., 2003). This assumption is also undermined under resource models that postulate that capacity is the maximum amount of activation available for storage and processing, and this amount is smaller for older than young adults (Just & Carpenter, 1992). Under this account, the activation required for computation and representation of sentence meaning would place a greater burden on older than young adults.

The extent to which semantic processes are maintained in old age presents a provocative challenge to cognitive aging theories more generally. What is required is a principled basis for explaining the asymmetric effects of aging on language, for example, the well-maintained semantic retrieval of word meaning (e.g., Verhaeghen, 2003) and the impaired phonological retrieval of word sounds (James & Burke, 2000), or the preserved response to internal semantic competitors during lexical selection (Stine & Wingfield, 1994) but the impaired response to internal phonological competitors (Sommers & Danielson, 1999). Thus, the challenge is to account for the good news in language research as well as age-related deficits.

ACKNOWLEDGMENTS

The writing of this chapter was supported by grant AG 08835 from the National Institute on Aging. We thank Diana Rabut for her able assistance with references and Tim Salthouse, Gus Craik, and Don MacKay for their comments on earlier versions of this chapter.

REFERENCES

Aaronson, D. (1974). Stimulus factors and listening strategies in auditory memory: A theoretical analysis. *Cognitive Psychology, 6*, 108–132.

Abrams, L., & Stanley, J. H. (2004). The detection and retrieval of spelling in older adults. In S. P. Shohov (Ed.), *Advances in psychology research* (Vol. 33, pp. 87–109). Hauppauge, NY: Nova Science.

Ackerman, P. L., & Rolfhus, E. L. (1999). The locus of adult intelligence: Knowledge, abilities and nonability traits. *Psychology and Aging, 14*, 314–330.

Akutsu, H., Legge, G. E., Ross, J. A., & Schuebel, K. J. (1991). Psychophysics of reading: X. Effects of age-related changes in vision. *Journal of Gerontology: Psychological Sciences, 46*, 325–331.

Albert, M. S., Heller, H. S., & Milberg, W. (1988). Changes in naming ability with age. *Psychology and Aging, 3*, 173–178.

Allen, P. A., Lien, M.-C., Murphy, M. D., Sanders, R. E., & McCann, R. S. (2002). Age differences in overlapping-task performance: Evidence for efficient parallel processing in older adults. *Psychology and Aging, 17*, 505–519.

Allen, P. A., Madden, D. J., & Slane, S. (1995). Visual word encoding and the effect of adult age and word frequency. In P. A. Allen & T. R. Bashore (Eds.), *Age differences in word and language processing* (pp. 30–71). Amsterdam: North-Holland.

Allen, P. A., Madden, D. J., Weber, T. A., & Groth, K. E. (1993). Influence of age and processing stage on visual word recognition. *Psychology and Aging, 8*, 274–282.

Altmann, L. J. P., & Kemper, S. (2006). Effects of age, animacy and activation order on sentence production. *Language and Cognitive Processes, 21*, 322–354.

Alwin, D. F., & McCammon, R. J. (2001). Aging, cohorts, and verbal ability. *Journal of Gerontology: Social Sciences, 56B*, S151–S161.

Anstey, K. J., Hofer, S. M., & Luszcz, M. A. (2003). A latent growth curve analysis of late-life sensory and cognitive function over 8 years: Evidence of specific and common factors underlying change. *Psychology and Aging, 18*, 714–726.

Anstey, K. J., Luszcz, M. A., & Sanchez, L. (2001). A reevaluation of the common factor theory of shared variance among age, sensory function, and cognitive function in older adults. *Journal of Gerontology: Psychological Sciences, 56B*, 3–11.

Anstey, K. J., & Smith, G. A. (1999). Interrelationships among biological markers of aging, health, activity, acculturation and cognitive performance in late adulthood. *Psychology and Aging, 14*, 605–618.

Arbuckle, T. Y., Nohara-LeClair, M., & Pushkar, D. (2000). Effect of off-target verbosity on communication efficiency in a referential communication task. *Psychology and Aging, 15*, 65–77.

Arbuckle, T. Y., & Pushkar Gold, D. P. (1993). Aging, inhibition and verbosity. *Journal of Gerontology: Psychological Sciences, 48*, 225–232.

Artal, P., Ferro, M., Miranda, I., & Navarro, R. (1993). Effects of aging in retinal image quality. *Journal of the Optical Society of America* A, *10*, 1656–1662.

Au, R., Joung, P., Nicholas, M., Obler, L. K., Kass, R., & Albert, M. L. (1995). Naming ability across the adult life span. *Aging and Cognition, 2*, 300–311.

Baddeley, A. D. (1986). *Working memory*. New York: Oxford University Press.

Balota, D. A., Watson, J. M., Duchek, J. M., & Ferraro, F. R. (1999). Cross-modal semantic and homograph priming in healthy young, healthy old, and in Alzheimer's disease individuals. *Journal of the International Neuorpsychological Society, 5*, 626–640.

Baltes, P. B., & Lindenberger, U. (1997). Emergence of a powerful connection between sensory and cognitive functions across the adult life span: A new window to the study of cognitive aging? *Psychology and Aging, 12*, 12–21.

Baltes, P. B., Staudinger, U. M., & Lindenberger, U. (1999). Life span psychology: Theory and application to intellectual functioning. *Annual Review of Psychology, 50*, 471–507.

Barresi, B. A., Nicholas, M., Connor, L. T., Obler, L., & Albert, M. L. (2000). Semantic degradation and lexical access in age-related naming failures. *Aging, Neuropsychology, and Cognition, 7*, 169–178.

Beier, M. E., & Ackerman, P. L. (2001) Current-events knowledge in adults: An investigation of age, intelligence, and nonability determinants. *Psychology and Aging, 16*, 615–628.

Birren, J. E. (1965). Age changes in speed of behavior: Its central nature and physiological correlates. In A. T. Welford & J. E. Birren (Eds.), *Behavior, aging and the nervous system* (pp. 191–216). Springfield, IL: Thomas.

Bortfeld, H., Leon, S. D., Bloom, J. E., Schober, M. F., & Brennan, S. E. (2001). Disfluency rates in conversation: Effects of age, relationship, topic, role, and gender. *Language and Speech, 44*, 123–149.

Botwinick J. (1977). Intellectual abilities. In J. E. Birren & K. W. Schaie (Eds.), *Handbook of the psychology of aging* (pp. 580–605). New York: Van Nostrand Reinhold.

Botwinick, J. (1984). *Aging and behavior*. New York: Springer.

Brown, A., & Draper, P. (2003). Accommodative speech and terms of endearment: Elements of a language mode often experienced by older adults. *Journal of Advanced Nursing, 41*, 15–21.

Brown, R., & McNeill, D. (1966). The "tip of the tongue" phenomenon. *Journal of Verbal Learning Behavior, 5*, 325–337.

Brown, A. S., & Nix, L. A. (1996). Age-related changes in the tip-of-the-tongue experience. *American Journal of Psychology, 109*, 79–91.

Brown, S., & Pichora-Fuller, M. K. (2000). Temporal jitter mimicks the effects of aging on word identification and word recall in noise. *Canadian Acoustics, 28*, 126–128.

Burke, D. M. (1999). Language production and aging. In S. Kemper and R. Kliegl (Eds.), *Constraints on language: Aging, grammar and memory* (pp. 3–28). Boston: Kluwer.

Burke, D. M. (2006). Representation and aging. In E. Bialystok & F. I. M. Craik (Eds.) *Lifespan cognition: Mechanisms of change* (pp. 193–206). New York: Oxford University Press.

Burke, D. M., Locantore, J., Austin, A., & Chae, B. (2004). Cherry pit primes Brad Pitt: Homophone priming effects on young and older adults' production of proper names. *Psychological Science, 15*, 164–170.

Burke, D. M., & MacKay, D. G. (1997). Memory, language and ageing. *Philosophical Transactions of the Royal Society: Biological Sciences, 352,* 1845–1856.

Burke, D. M., MacKay, D. G., & James, L. E. (2000). Theoretical approaches to language and aging. In T. Perfect & E. Maylor (Eds.), *Models of cognitive aging* (pp. 204–237). Oxford: Oxford University Press.

Burke, D. M., MacKay, D. G., Worthley, J. S., & Wade, E. (1991). On the tip of the tongue: What causes word finding failures in younger and older adults. *Journal of Memory and Language, 30,* 542–579.

Burke, D. M., & Osborne, G. L. (2007). Aging and inhibition deficits: Where are the effects? In D. Gorfein & C. MacLeod (Eds.), *Inhibition in cognition* (pp. 163–183). Washington, DC: American Psychological Association Press.

Burke, D. M., & Peters, L. (1986). Word associations in old age: Evidence for consistency in semantic encoding during adulthood. *Psychology and Aging, 1,* 283–292.

Burke, D. M., & Shafto, M. A. (2004). Aging and language production. *Current Directions in Psychological Science, 13,* 21–24.

Burke, D. M., White, H., & Diaz, D. L. (1987). Semantic priming in young and older adults: Evidence for age constancy in automatic and attentional processes. *Journal of Experimental Psychology: Human Perception and Performance, 13,* 542–579.

Cameli, L., & Phillips, N. A. (2000). Age-related differences in semantic priming: Evidence from event-related brain potentials. *Brain and Cognition, 43,* 69–73.

Caplan, D., & Waters, G. S. (1999). Verbal working memory and sentence comprehension. *Behavioral and Brain Sciences, 22,* 77–126.

Caramazza, A. (1997). How many levels of processing are there in lexical access? *Cognitive Neuropsychology, 14,* 177–208.

Caramazza, A., Costa, A., Miozzo, M., & Bi, Y. (2001). The specific-word frequency effect: Implications for the representation of homophones. *Journal of Experimental Psychology: Learning, Memory, and Cognition, 27,* 1430–1450.

Carlson, M. C., Hasher, L., Zacks, R. T., & Connelly, S. L. (1995). Aging, distraction, and the benefits of predictable location. *Psychology and Aging, 10,* 427–436.

Carstensen, L. L., Isaacowitz, D. M., & Charles, S. T. (1999). Taking time seriously. *American Psychologist, 54,* 165–181.

Carter, A. S., & Wilson, R. H. (2001). Lexical effects on dichotic word recognition in young and elderly listeners. *Journal of the American Academy of Audiology, 12,* 86–100.

Caza, N., & Moscovitch, M. (2005). Effects of cumulative frequency, but not of frequency trajectory, in lexical decision times of older adults and patients with Alzheimer's disease. *Journal of Memory and Language, 53,* 456–471.

Cerella, J. (1985). Information processing rates in the elderly. *Psychological Bulletin, 98,* 67–83.

Cheesman, M. F. (1997). Speech perception by elderly listeners: Basic knowledge and implications for audiology. *Journal of Speech-Language Pathology and Audiology, 21,* 104–110.

Christensen, H., Mackinnon, A. J., Korten, A., & Jorm, A. F. (2001). The "common cause hypothesis" of cognitive aging: Evidence for not only a common factor but also specific associations of age with vision and grip strength in a cross-sectional analysis. *Psychology and Aging, 16,* 588–599.

Committee on Hearing and Bioacoustics and Biomechanics (CHABA, 1988). Speech understanding and aging. *Journal of the Acoustical Society of America, 83,* 859–895.

Connelly, S. L., Hasher, L., & Zacks, R. T. (1991). Age and reading: The impact of distraction. *Psychology and Aging, 6,* 533–541.

Connor, L. T., Spiro, A., Obler, L. K., & Albert, M. L. (2004). Change in object naming ability during adulthood. *Journal of Gerontology: Psychological Sciences, 59B,* P203–P209.

Corso, J. F. (1971). Sensory processes and age effects in normal adults. *Journal of Gerontology*, *26*, 90–105.

Cortese, M. J., Balota, D. A., Sergent-Marshall, S. D., & Buckner, R. L. (2003). Spelling via semantics and phonology: Exploring the effects of age. Alzheimer's disease and primary semantic impairment. *Neuropsychologia*, *41*, 952–967.

Coughlin, M., Kewley-Port, D., & Humes, L. E. (1998). The relation between identification and discrimination of vowels in young and elderly listeners. *Journal of the Acoustical Society of America*, *104*, 3597–3607.

Craik, F. I. M., & Byrd, M. (1982). Aging and cognitive deficits: The role of attentional resources. In F. I. M. Craik & S. E. Trehub (Eds.), *Aging and cognitive processes* (pp. 191–211). New York: Plenum Press.

Craik, F. I. M., & Masani, P. A. (1967). Age differences in the temporal integration of language. *British Journal of Psychology*, *58*, 291–299.

Cross, E. S., & Burke, D. M. (2004). Do alternative names block young and older adults retrieval of proper names? *Brain and Language*, *89*, 174–181.

Cutting, C. J., & Ferreira, V. S. (1999). Semantic and phonological information flow in the production lexicon. *Journal of Experimental Psychology: Learning, Memory, and Cognition*, *25*, 318–344.

Dagerman, K. S., MacDonald, M. C., & Harm, M. W. (2006). Aging and the use of context in ambiguity resolution: Complex changes from simple slowing. *Cognitive Science*, *30*, 311–345.

Davidson, D. J., Zacks, R. T., & Ferreira, F. (2003). Age preservation of the syntactic processor in production. *Journal of Psycholinguistic Research*, *32*, 541–566.

DeDe, G., Caplan, D., Kemptes, K., & Waters, G. (2004). The relationship between age, verbal working memory, and language comprehension. *Psychology and Aging*, *19*, 601–616.

Dell, G. S. (1986). A spreading-activation theory of retrieval in sentence production. *Psychological Review*, *93*, 283–321.

Dell, G. S., Chang, E., & Griffin, Z. M. (1999). Connectionist models of language production: Lexical access and grammatical encoding. *Cognitive Science*, *34*, 517–542.

Dell, G. S., Schwartz, M. F., Martin, N., Saffran, E. M., & Gagnon, D. A. (1997). Lexical access in aphasic and nonaphasic speakers. *Psychological Review*, *104*, 801–838.

Dijkstra, K., Yaxley, R. H., Madden, C. J., & Zwaan, R. A. (2004). The role of age and perceptual symbols in language comprehension. *Psychology and Aging*, *19*, 352–356.

Dubno, J. R., Dirks, D. D., & Morgan, D. E. (1984). Effects of age and mild hearing loss on speech recognition in noise. *Journal of the Acoustical Society of America*, *76*, 87–96.

Duchek, J. M., Balota, D. A., & Thessing, V. C. (1998). Inhibition of visual and conceptual information during reading in healthy aging and Alzheimer's disease. *Aging, Neuropsychology, and Cognition*, *5*, 169–181.

Dywan, J., & Murphy, W. E. (1996). Aging and inhibitory control in text comprehension. *Psychology and Aging*, *11*, 199–206.

Earles, J. L., Connor, L. T., Frieske, D., Park, D. C., Smith, A. D., & Zwahr, M. (1997). Age differences in inhibition: Possible causes and consequences. *Aging, Neuropsychology, and Cognition*, *4*, 45–57.

Engle, R. W., Tuholski, S. W., Laughlin, J. E., & Conway, A. R. A. (1999). Working memory, short-term memory, and general fluid intelligence: A latent-variable approach. *Journal of Experimental Psychology: General*, *128*, 309–331.

Evrard, M. (2002). Ageing and lexical access to common and proper names in picture naming. *Brain and Language*, *81*, 174–179.

Faust, M. E., Balota, D. A., & Multhaup, K. S. (2004). Phonological blocking during picture naming in dementia of the Alzheimer type. *Neuropsychology*, *18*, 526–536.

Federmeier, K. D., McLennan, D. B., De Ochoa, E., & Kutas, M. (2002). The impact of semantic memory organization and sentence context on spoken language processing by younger and older adults: An ERP study. *Psychophysiology, 39*, 133–146.

Federmeier, K. D., Van Petten, C., Schwartz, T. J., & Kutas, M. (2003). Sounds, words, sentences: Age-related changes across levels of language processing. *Psychology and Aging, 18*, 858–872.

Feier, C. D., & Gerstman, L. J. (1980) Sentence comprehension abilites throughout the life span. *Journal of Gerontology, 35*, 722–728.

Feyereisen, P. (1997). A meta-analytic procedure shows an age-related decline in picture-naming: Comments on Goulet, Ska, and Kahn. *Journal of Speech and Hearing Research, 40*, 1328–1333.

Fisher, D. L., Duffy, S. A., & Katsikopoulos, K. V. (2000). Cognitive slowing among older adults: What kind and how much? In T. Perfect & E. Maylor (Eds.), *Models of cognitive aging* (pp. 87–124). Oxford: Oxford University Press.

Fitzgibbons, P. J., & Gordon-Salant, S. (1996). Auditory temporal processing in elderly listeners. *Journal of the American Academy of Audiology, 7*, 183–189.

Fozard, J. L., & Gordon-Salant, S. (2001). Changes in vision and hearing with aging. In J. E. Birren and K. W. Schaie (Eds.), *Handbook of the psychology of aging* (pp. 214–266). New York: Academic Press.

Gates, G. A., Feeney, M. P., & Higdon, R. J. (2003). Word recognition and the articulation index in older listeners with probable age-related auditory neuropathy. *Journal of the American Academy of Audiology, 14*, 574–581.

Ghisletta, P., & Lindenberger, U. (2005). Exploring structural dynamics within and between sensory and intellectual functioning in old and very old age: Longitudinal evidence from the Berlin Aging Study. *Intelligence, 33*, 555–587.

Giffard, B., Desgranges, B., & Kerrouche, N. (2003). The hyperpriming phenomenon in normal aging: A consequence of cognitive slowing? *Neuropsychology, 17*, 594–601.

Gilmore, G. C., Spinks, R. A., & Thomas, C. W. (2006). Age effects in coding tasks: Componential analysis and test of the sensory deficit hypothesis. *Psychology and Aging, 21*, 7–18.

Gold, D., Andres, D., Arbuckle, T., & Schwartzman, A. (1988). Measurement and correlates of verbosity in elderly people. *Journal of Gerontology: Psychological Sciences, 43*, P27–33.

Gollan, T. H., & Brown, A. S. (2006) From tip-of-the-tongue (TOT) data to theoretical implications in two steps: When more TOTs means better retrieval. *Journal of Experimental Psychology: General, 135*, 462–483.

Gomez, R. (2002). Word frequency effects in priming performance in young and older adults. *Journal of Gerontology: Psychological Sciences, 57B*, P233–P240.

Good, C. D., Johnsrude, I. S., Ashburner, J., Henson, R. N. A., Friston, K. J., & Frackowiak, R. S. J. (2001). A voxel-based morphometric study of ageing in 465 normal adult human brains. *Neuroimage, 14*, 21–36.

Gordon-Salant, S., & Fitzgibbons, P. (1999). Profile of auditory temporal processing in older listeners. *Journal of Speech, Language, and Hearing Research, 42*, 300–311.

Gordon-Salant, S., & Fitzgibbons, P. J. (2001). Sources of age-related recognition difficulty for time-compressed speech. *Journal of Speech, Language, and Hearing Research, 44*, 709–719.

Gould, O. N., Saum, C., & Belter, J. (2002). Recall and subjective reactions to speaking styles: Does age matter? *Experimental Aging Research, 28*, 199–213.

Goulet, P., Ska, B., & Kahn, H. J. (1994). Is there a decline in picture naming with advancing age? *Journal of Speech and Hearing Research, 37*, 629–644.

Haarmann, H. J., Just, M. A., & Carpenter, P. A. (1997). Aphasic sentence comprehension as a resource deficit: A computational approach. *Brain and Language, 59*, 76–120.

Haegerstrom-Portnoy, G., Schneck, M. E., & Brabyn, J. A. (1999). Seeing into old age: Vision function beyond acuity. *Optometry and Vision Science, 76,* 141–158.

Halling, D. C., & Humes, L. E. (2000). Factors affecting the recognition of reverberant speech by elderly listeners. *Journal of Speech, Language, and Hearing Research, 43,* 414–439.

Hasher, L., Lustig, C., & Zacks, R. (2007). Inhibitory mechanisms and the control of attention. In A. Conway, C. Jarrold, M. Kane, A. Miyake, & J. Towse (Eds), *Variation in working memory* (pp. 227–249). New York: Oxford University Press.

Hasher, L., & Zacks, R. T. (1979). Automatic and effortful processes in memory. *Journal of Experimental Psychology: General, 108,* 356–388.

Hasher, L., & Zacks, R. T. (1988). Working memory, comprehension, and aging: A review and a new view. *Psychology of Learning and Motivation, 22,* 193–225.

Heine, M. K., Ober, B. A., & Shenaut, G. K. (1999). Naturally occurring and experimentally induced tip-of-the-tongue experiences in three adult age groups. *Psychology and Aging, 14,* 445–457.

Heller, R., B., & Dobbs, A. R. (1993). Age differences in word finding in discourse and non-discourse situations. *Psychology and Aging, 8,* 443–450.

Hirsh K. W., & Tree, J. J. (2001). Word association norms for two cohorts of British adults. *Journal of Neurolinguistics, 14,* 1–44.

Hodgson, C., & Ellis, A. W. (1998). Last in, first to go: Age of acquisition and naming in the elderly. *Brain and Language, 64,* 146–163.

Hopkins, K. A., Kellas, G., & Paul, S. (1995). Scope of word meaning activation during sentence processing by young and older adults. *Experimental Aging Research, 21,* 123–142.

Howard, D. V., McAndrews, M. P., & Lasaga, M. I. (1981). Semantic priming of lexical decisions in young and old adults. *Journal of Gerontology, 36,* 707–714.

Humes, L. E. (1996). Speech understanding in the elderly. *Journal of the American Academy of Audiology, 7,* 161–167.

Humes, L. E., & Christopherson, L. (1991). Speech identification difficulties of hearing-impaired elderly persons: The contributions of auditory processing deficits. *Journal of Speech and Hearing Research, 34,* 686–693.

Humes, L. E., Watson, B. U., Christensen, L. A., Cokely, C. G., Halling, D. C., & Lee, L. (1994). Factors associated with individual differences in clinical measures of speech recognition among the elderly. *Journal of Speech and Hearing Research, 37,* 465–474.

Hummert, M. L., Garstka, T. A., Ryan, E. B., & Bonnesen, J. L. (2004). The role of age stereotypes in interpersonal communication. In J. F. Nussbaum & J. Coupland (Eds.), *Handbook of communication and aging research* 2nd ed. (pp. 91–114). Hillsdale, NJ: Lawrence Erlbaum Associates, Inc.

Indefrey, P., & Levelt, W. J. M. (2004). The spatial and temporal signatures of word production components. *Cognition, 92,* 101–144.

Isaacowitz, D. M., Charles, S. T., & Carstensen, L. L. (2000). Emotion and cognition. In F. I. M., Craik & T. A. Salthouse (Eds.), *The handbook of aging and cognition* (pp. 593–631). Mahwah, NJ: Lawrence Erlbaum Associates, Inc.

James, L. E. (2004). Meeting Mr. Farmer versus meeting a farmer: Specific effects of aging on learning proper names. *Psychology and Aging, 19,* 515–522.

James, L. E. (2006). Specific effects of aging on proper name retrieval: Now you see them, now you don't. *Journal of Gerontology: Psychological Sciences, 61,* P180–P183.

James, L. E. &, Burke, D. M. (2000). Phonological priming effects on word retrieval and tip-of-the-tongue experiences in young and older adults. *Journal of Experimental Psychology: Learning, Memory and Cognition, 26,* 1378–1391.

James, L. E., Burke, D. M., Austin, A., & Hulme, E. (1998). Production and perception of "verbosity" in younger and older adults. *Psychology and Aging, 13,* 355–367.

James, L. E. & MacKay, D. G. (2001). H. M., word knowledge and aging: Support for a new theory of long-term retrograde amnesia. *Psychological Science, 12*, 485–492.

Johnson, R. E. (2003). Aging and the remembering of text. *Developmental Review, 23*, 261–346.

Jones, G. V. (1989). Back to Woodworth: Role of interlopers in the tip of the tongue phenomenon. *Memory and Cognition, 17*, 69–76.

Juncos-Rabadan, O, Pereiro, A. X., & Rodriguez, M. S. (2005). Narrative speech in aging: Quantity, information content, and cohesion. *Brain and Language, 95*, 423–434.

Just, M. A., & Carpenter, P. A. (1992). A capacity theory of comprehension: Individual differences in working memory. *Psychological Review, 98*, 122–149.

Kahneman, D. (1973). *Attention and effort.* Englewood Cliffs, NJ: Lawrence Erlbaum Associates, Inc.

Kemper, S. (1987). Life-span changes in syntactic complexity. *Journal of Gerontology, 42*, 323–328.

Kemper, S. (1992). Language and aging. In F. I. M. Craik & T. A. Salthouse (Eds.) *The handbook of aging and cognition* (pp. 213–270). Hillsdale, NJ: Lawrence Erlbaum Associates, Inc.

Kemper, S. (2006). Language in adulthood. In E. Bialystok & F. I. M. Craik (Eds.) *Lifespan cognition: Mechanisms of change* (pp. 223–238). New York: Oxford University Press.

Kemper, S., Crow, A., & Kemptes, K. (2004). Eye-fixation patterns of high- and low-span young and older adults: Down the garden path and back again. *Psychology and Aging, 19*, 157–170.

Kemper, S., Finter-Urczyk, A., Ferrell, P., Harden, T., & Billington, C. (1998). Using elder-speak with older adults. *Discourse Processes, 25*, 55–73.

Kemper, S., Greiner, L. H., Marquis, J. G., Prenovost, K., & Mitzner, T. L. (2001a). Language decline across the life span: Findings from the nun study. *Psychology and Aging, 16*, 227–239.

Kemper, S., & Harden, T. (1999). Experimentally disentangling what's beneficial about elder-speak from what's not. *Psychology and Aging, 14*, 656–670.

Kemper, S., Herman, R., & Lian, C. (2003a). Age differences in sentence production. *Journal of Gerontology: Psychological Sciences, 58B*, P260–P268.

Kemper, S., Herman, R. E., & Lian, C. H. T. (2003b). The costs of doing two things at once for young and older adults: Talking while walking, finger tapping, and ignoring speech or noise. *Psychology and Aging, 18*, 181–192.

Kemper, S., Herman, R. E., & Liu, C. J. (2004). Sentence production by young and older adults in controlled contexts. *Journal of Gerontology: Psychological Sciences, 59B*, P220–P224.

Kemper, S., & Kemtes, K. (1999). Limitations on syntactic processing. In S. Kemper & R. Kliegl (Eds.), *Constraints on language: Aging, grammar, and memory* (pp. 79–106). Boston: Kluwer.

Kemper, S., & Kemtes, K. (2000). Aging and message production and comprehension. In D. C. Park & N. Schwarz (Eds.), *Cognitive aging: A primer* (pp. 197–213). New York: Psychology Press.

Kemper, S., Kynette, D., Rash, S., Sprott, R., & O'Brien, K. (1989). Life-span changes to adults' language: Effects of memory and genre. *Applied Psycholinguistics, 10*, 49–66.

Kemper, S., & McDowd, J. (2006). Eye movements of young and older adults while reading with distraction. *Psychology and Aging, 21*, 32–39.

Kemper, S., & Mitzner, T. L. (2001). Language production and comprehension. In In J. E. Birren & K. W. Schaie (Eds.), *Handbook of the psychology of aging* (5th ed., pp. 378–398). San Diego, CA: Academic Press.

Kemper, S., Rash, S., Kynette, D., & Norman, S. (1990). Telling stories: The structure of adults' narratives. *European Journal of Cognitive Psychology, 2*, 205–228.

Kemper, S., & Sumner, A. (2001). The structure of verbal abilities in young and older adults. *Psychology and Aging, 16*, 312–322.

Kemper, S., Thompson, M., & Marquis, J. (2001b). Longitudinal change in language production: Effects of aging and dementia on grammatical complexity and propositional content. *Psychology and Aging, 16*, 227–239.

Kemptes, K. A., & Kemper, S. (1997). Younger and older adults' on-line processing of syntactically ambiguous sentences. *Psychology and Aging, 12*, 362–371.

Kliegl, R., & Kemper, S. (1999). Concluding observations. In S. Kemper and R. Kliegl (Eds.), *Constraints on language: Aging, grammar and memory* (pp. 299–307). Boston: Kluwer.

Kutas, M., & Federmeier, K. D. (2001). Electrophysiology reveals semantic memory use in language comprehension. *Trends in Cognitive Science, 4*, 463–470.

Lahar, C. J., Tun, P. A., & Wingfield, A. (2004). Sentence-final word completion norms for young, middle-aged, and older adults. *Journals of Gerontology: Psychological Sciences, 59*, P7–P10.

Lashley, K. S. (1951). The problem of serial order in behavior. In L. A. Jeffress (Ed.), *Cerebral mechanisms in behavior* (pp. 112–146). New York: Wiley.

La Tourette, T. R., & Meeks, S. (2000). Perceptions of patronizing speech by older women in nursing homes and in the community. Impact of cognitive ability and place of residence. *Journal of Language and Social Psychology, 19*, 463–473.

Laver, G. D. (2000). A speed-accuracy analysis of word recognition in young and older adults. *Psychology and Aging, 15*, 705–709.

Laver, G. D., & Burke, D. M. (1993). Why do semantic priming effects increase in old age? A meta-analysis. *Psychology and Aging, 8*, 34–43.

Lazzara, M. M., Yonelinas, A. P., & Ober, B. A. (2002). Implicit memory in aging: Normal transfer across semantic decisions and stimulus format. *Aging, Neuropsychology, and Cognition, 9*, 145–156.

Ledoux, K., Camblin, C. C., Swaab, T. Y., & Gordon, P. C. (2006). Reading words in discourse: The modulation of lexical priming effects by message-level context. *Behavioral and Cognitive Neuroscience Reviews, 5*, 107–127.

Levelt, W. J. M. (2001). Spoken word production: A theory of lexical access. *Proceedings of the National Academy of Sciences, USA, 98*, 13464–13471.

Levelt, W. J. M., Roelofs, A., & Meyer, A. S. (1999). A theory of lexical access in speech production. *Behavioral and Brain Sciences, 22*, 1–75.

Li, K. Z. H., Hasher, L., Jonas, D., May, C. P., & Rahhal, T. A. (1998). Distractibility, circadian arousal, and aging: A boundary condition? *Psychology and Aging, 13*, 574–583.

Li, K. Z., & Lindenberger, U. (2002). Relations between aging sensory/sensorimotor and cognitive function, *Neuroscience and Biobehavioral Reviews, 26*, 777–783.

Li, L., Daneman, M., Qi, J. G., & Schneider, B. A. (2004). Does the information content of an irrelevant source differentially affect spoken word recognition in younger and older adults? *Journal of Experimental Psychology: Human Perception and Performance, 30*, 1077–1091.

Light, L. L. (1991). Memory and aging: Four hypotheses in search of data. *Annual Review of Psychology, 42*, 333–376.

Light, L., & Burke, D. (1988). Patterns of language and memory in old age. In L. Light, & D. Burke (Eds.), *Language, memory and aging* (pp. 244–271). New York: Cambridge University Press.

Light, L. L., Valencia-Laver, D., & Zavis, D. (1991). Instantiation of general terms in young and older adults. *Psychology and Aging, 6*, 337–351.

Lima, S. D., Hale, S., & Myerson, J. (1991). How general is general slowing? Evidence from the lexical domain. *Psychology and Aging, 6*, 416–425.

Lindenberger, U., & Baltes, P. (1994). Sensory functioning and intelligence in old age: A strong connection. *Psychology and Aging, 9*, 339–355.

Lindenberger, U., & Baltes, P. B. (1997). Intellectual functioning in old and very old age: Cross-sectional results from the Berlin Aging Study. *Psychology and Aging, 12*, 410–432.

Lindenberger, U., Scherer, H., & Baltes, P. B. (2001). The strong connection between sensory and cognitive performance in old age: Not due to sensory acuity reductions operating during cognitive assessment. *Psychology and Aging, 16*, 196–205.

Little, D. M., Prentice, K. J., & Wingfield, A. (2004). Adult age differences in judgments of semantic fit. *Applied Psycholinguistics, 25*, 135–143.

Logan, J. M., & Balota, D. A. (2003). Conscious and unconscious lexical retrieval blocking in young and older adults. *Psychology and Aging, 18*, 537–550.

Lovelace, E. A., & Twohig, P. T. (1990). Healthy older adults' perceptions of their memory functioning and use of mnemonics. *Bulletin of the Psychonomic Society, 28*, 115–118.

Luce, P. A., & Pisoni, D. B. (1998). Recognizing spoken words: The neighborhood activation model. *Ear and Hearing, 19*, 1–36.

Lustig, C., & Hasher, L. (2001). Implicit memory is not immune to interference. *Psychological Bulletin, 127*, 618–628.

MacDonald, M. C., & Christiansen, M. H. (2002). Reassessing working memory: Comment on Just and Carpenter (1992) and Waters and Caplan (1996). *Psychological Review, 109*, 35–54.

MacKay, A. I., Connor, L. T., Albert, M. L., & Obler, L. K. (2002). Noun and verb retrieval in healthy aging. *Journal of the International Neuropsychological Society, 8*, 764–770.

MacKay, D. G. (1987). *The organization of perception and action: A theory for language and other cognitive skills*. New York: Springer-Verlag.

MacKay, D. G. (2006). Aging, memory and language in amnesic HM. *Hippocampus, 16*, 491–495.

MacKay, D. G., & Abrams, L. (1996). Language, memory, and aging: Distributed deficits and the structure of new-versus-old connections. In J. E. Birren & K. W. Schaie (Eds.), *Handbook of the psychology of aging* (4th ed., pp. 251–265). San Diego, CA: Academic Press.

MacKay, D. G., & Abrams, L. (1998). Age-linked declines in retrieving orthographic knowledge: Empirical, practical, and theoretical implications. *Psychology and Aging, 13*, 647–662.

MacKay, D. G., Abrams, L., & Pedroza, M. J. (1999). Aging on the input versus output side: Theoretical implications of age-linked asymmetries between detecting versus retrieving orthographic information. *Psychology and Aging, 14*, 3–17.

MacKay, D. G., & Burke, D. M. (1990). Cognition and aging: New learning and the use of old connections. In T. M. Hess (Ed.), *Aging and cognition: Knowledge organization and utilization* (pp. 213–263). Amsterdam: North-Holland.

MacKay, D. G., Hadley, C. B., & Abrams, L. (2007a). *Beyond soup stones: Testing the core assumptions of age-linked resource-capacity theories*. Manuscript submitted for publication.

MacKay, D. G., & James, L. E. (2001). The binding problem for syntax, semantics, and prosody: H. M. 's selective sentence-reading deficits under the theoretical-syndrome approach. *Language and Cognitive Processes, 16*, 419–460.

MacKay, D. G., & James, L. E. (2004). Sequencing, speech production, and selective effects of aging on phonological and morphological speech errors. *Psychology and Aging, 19*, 93–107.

MacKay, D. G., Taylor, J. K., & Marian, D. E. (2007b). *Unsuspected age-linked acuity deficits and research on reading: Practical and empirical implications*. Manuscript submitted for publication.

Mackenzie, C. (2000a). Adult spoken discourse: The influences of age and education. *International Journal of Language and Communication Disorders, 35*, 269–285.

Mackenzie, C. (2000b). The relevance of education and age in the assessment of discourse comprehension. *Clinical Linguistics and Phonetics, 14,* 151–161.

Madden, D. J. (1988). Adult age differences in the effects of sentence context and stimulus degradation during visual word recognition. *Psychology and Aging, 3,* 167–172.

Madden, D. J. (1992). Four to ten milliseconds per year: Age-related slowing of visual word identification. *Journal of Gerontology: Psychological Sciences, 47,* 59–68.

Madden, D. J. (2001). Speed and timing of behavioral processes. In J. E. Birren & K. W. Schaie (Eds.), *Handbook of the psychology of aging* (5th ed., pp. 288–312). San Diego, CA: Academic Press.

Madden, D. J., Langley, L. K., Denny, L. L., Turkington, T. G., Provenzale, J. M., & Hawk, T. C. (2002). Adult age differences in visual word identification: Functional neuroanatomy by positron emission tomography. *Brain and Cognition, 49,* 297–321.

Madden, D. J., Pierce. T. W., & Allen, P. A. (1993). Age-related slowing and the time course of semantic priming in visual word identification. *Psychology and Aging, 8,* 490–507.

Madden, D. J., & Whiting, W. L. (2004). Age-related changes in visual attention. In P. T. Costa & I. C. Siegler (Eds.) *Recent advances in psychology and aging* (pp. 41–88). Amsterdam: Elsevier.

Madden, D. J., Whiting, W. L., & Huettel, S. A. (2005). Age-related changes in neural activity during visual perception and attention. In R. Cabeza, L. Nyberg, & D. Park (Eds.), *Cognitive neuroscience and aging: Linking cognitive and cerebral aging* (pp. 157–185). New York: Oxford University Press.

Manenti, R., Repetto, C., Bentrovato, S., Marcone, A., Bates, E., & Cappa, S. F. (2004). The effects of ageing and Alzheimer's disease on semantic and gender priming. *Brain, 127,* 2299–2306.

Margolin, S. J. & Abrams, L. (in press). Individual differences in young and older adults' spelling: Do good spellers age better than poor spellers? *Aging, Neuropsychology, and Cognition.*

Marner, L., Nyengaard, J. R., Tang, Y., & Pakkenberg, B. (2003). Marked loss of myelinted nerve fibers in the human brain with age. *Journal of Comparative Neurology, 462,* 144–152.

Marslen-Wilson, W. D., & Welsh, A. (1978). Processing interactions and lexical access during word recognition in continuous speech. *Cognitive Psychology, 10,* 29–63.

Maylor, E. A. (1990). Recognizing and naming faces: Aging, memory retrieval and the tip of the tongue state. *Journal of Gerontology: Psychological Sciences, 45,* 215–225.

Maylor, E. A. (1997). Proper name retrieval in old age: Converging evidence against disproportionate impairment. *Aging, Neuropsychology, and Cognition, 4,* 211–226.

McClelland, J. K., & Rumelhart, D. E. (1981). An interactive activation model of context effects in letter perception: Pt. 1. An account of the basic findings. *Psychological Review, 88,* 375–407.

McCoy, S. L., Tun, P. A., Cox, L. C., Colangelo, M., Stewart, R. A., & Wingfield, A. (2005). Hearing loss and perceptual effort: Downstream effects on older adults' memory for speech. *Quarterly Journal of Experimental Psychology, 58A,* 22–33.

McDowd, J. M., & Shaw, R. J. (2000). Aging and attention: A functional perspective. In F. I. M. Craik & T. A. Salthouse (Eds.), *The handbook of aging and cognition* (pp. 221–292). Mahwah, NJ: Lawrence Erlbaum Associates, Inc.

McGinnis, D., & Zelinski, E. M. (2000). Understanding unfamiliar words: The influence of processing resources, vocabulary knowledge, and age. *Psychology and Aging, 15,* 335–350.

McGinnis, D., & Zelinski, E. M. (2003). Understanding unfamiliar words in young, young-old, and old-old adults: Inferential processing and the abstraction-deficit hypothesis. *Psychology and Aging, 18,* 497–509.

McIntyre, J. S., & Craik, F. I. M. (1987). Age differences in memory for item and source information. *Canadian Journal of Psychology, 41,* 175–192.

Miller, G. A. (1956). The magical number seven, plus or minus two: Some limits on our capacity for processing information. *Psychological Review, 63*, 81–97.

Miller, L. M. S. (2003). The effects of age and domain knowledge on text processing. *Journal of Gerontology: Psychological Sciences, 58B*, 217–P223.

Miller, L. M. S., Stine-Morrow, E. A. L., Kirkorian, H. L., & Conroy, M. L. (2004). Adult age differences in knowledge-driven reading. *Journal of Educational Psychology, 96*, 811–821.

Miller, M. D., & Johnson, J. S. (2004). Phonological and lexical-semantic short-term memory and their relationship to sentence production in older adults. *Aging, Neuropsychology, and Cognition, 11*, 395–415.

Miozzo, M., & Caramazza, A. (1997). Retrieval of lexical-syntactic features in tip-of-the-tongue states. *Journal of Experimental Psychology: Learning, Memory, and Cognition, 23*, 1410–1423.

Mitchell, D. B. (1989). How many memory systems? Evidence from aging. *Journal of Experimental Psychology: Learning, Memory, and Cognition, 15*, 31–49.

Morrison, C. M., Hirsh, K. W., & Duggan, G. B. (2003). Age of acquisition, ageing, and verb production: Normative and experimental data. *Quarterly Journal of Experimental Psychology: Human Experimental Psychology, 56*, 705–730.

Mortensen, L., Meyer, A. S., & Humphreys, G. W. (2006). Age-related slowing of object naming: A review. *Language and Cognitive Processes, 21*, 238–290.

Murphy, D. R., Craik, F. I. M., Li, K. Z. H., & Schneider, B. A. (2000). Comparing the effects of aging and background noise on short-term memory performance. *Psychology and Aging, 15*, 323–334.

Murphy, D. R., Daneman, M., & Schneider, B. A. (2006). Why do older adults have difficulty following conversations? *Psychology and Aging, 21*, 49–61.

Murphy, D. R., McDowd, J. M., & Wilcox, K. A. (1999). Inhibition and aging: Similarities between younger and older adults as revealed by the processing of unattended auditory information. *Psychology and Aging, 14*, 44–59.

Myerson, J., Ferraro, F. R., Hale, S., & Lima, S. D. (1992). The role of general slowing in semantic priming and word recognition. *Psychology and Aging, 7*, 257–270.

Myerson, J., Hale, S., Wagstaff, D., Poon, L. W., & Smith, G. A. (1990). The information-loss model: A mathematical theory of age-related cognitive slowing. *Psychological Review, 97*, 475–487.

Navon, D. (1984). Resources—a theoretical soupstone? *Psychological Review, 91*, 216–234.

Nelson, H. E. (1985). *National Adult Reading Test (NART): Test manual*. Windsor: National Foundation for Educational Research.

Newsome, M. R., & Glucksberg, S. (2002). Older adults filter irrelevant information during metaphor comprehension. *Experimental Aging Research, 28*, 253–267.

Nicholas, M., Obler, L. K., Albert, M. L., & Goodglass, H. (1985). Lexical retrieval in healthy aging. *Cortex, 21*, 595–606.

Nussbaum, J. F., Pitts, M. J., Huber, F. N., Raup Krieger, J. L., & Ohs, J. E. (2005). Ageism and ageist language across the life span: Intimate relationships and non-intimate interactions. *Journal of Social Issues, 61*, 287–305.

Ohnishi, T., Matsuda, H., Tabira, T., Asada, T., & Uno, M. (2001). Changes in brain morphology in Alzheimer disease and normal aging: Is Alzheimer disease an exaggerated aging process? *American Journal of Neuroradiology, 22*, 1680–1685.

Paul, S. T. (1996). Search for semantic inhibition failure during sentence comprehension by younger and older adults. *Psychology and Aging, 11*, 10–20.

Parkin, A. J., & Java, R. I. (2000). Determinants of age-related memory loss. In T. Perfect & E. Maylor (Eds.), *Models of cognitive aging* (pp. 188–203). Oxford: Oxford University Press.

Peelle, J. E., & Wingfield, A. (2005). Dissociations in perceptual learning revealed by adult age differences in adaptation to time-compressed speech. *Journal of Experimental Psychology: Human Perception and Performance, 31*, 1315–1330.

Persson, J., Sylvester, C.-Y. C., Nelson, J. K., Welsh, K. M., Jonides, J., & Reuter-Lorenz, P. A. (2004). Selection requirements during verb generation: Differential recruitment in older and young adults. *Neuroimage, 23*, 1382–1390.

Phillips, N. A., & Lesperance, D. (2003). Breaking the waves: Age differences in electrical brain activity when reading text with distractors. *Psychology and Aging, 18*, 126–139.

Phillips, S. L., Gordon-Salant, S., Fitzgibbons, P. J., & Yeni-Kombshian, G. (2000). *Journal of Speech, Language, and Hearing Research, 43*, 217–228.

Pichora-Fuller, M. K., Schneider, B. A., & Daneman, M. (1995). How young and old adults listen to and remember speech in noise. *Journal of the Acoustical Society of America, 97*, 593–608.

Pichora-Fuller, M. K., & Singh, G. (2006). Effects of age on auditory and cognitive processing: Implications for hearing aid fitting and audiologic rehabilitation. *Trends in Amplification, 10*, 29–59.

Prull, M. W., Godard-Gross, C., & Karas, E. M. (2004, April). *How verb generation repetition priming in adulthood is influenced by age and response competition.* Poster presented at the Cognitive Aging Conference, Atlanta, GA.

Pushkar, D., Basevitz, P., Arbuckle, T. Y., Nohara-LeClair, M., Lapidus, S., & Peled, M. (2000). Social behavior and off-target verbosity in elderly people. *Psychology and Aging, 15*, 361–374.

Pushkar Gold, D. P., & Arbuckle, T. Y. (1995). A longitudinal study of off-target verbosity. *Journal of Gerontology: Psychological Sciences, 50B*, P307–315.

Rabbitt, P. M. (1968). Channel-capacity, intelligibility and immediate memory. *Quarterly Journal of Experimental Psychology, 20*, 241–248.

Rabbitt, P., Maylor, E., McInnes, L., Bent, N., & Moore, B. (1995). What goods can self-assessment questionnaires deliver for cognitive gerontology? *Applied Cognitive Psychology, 9*, S127–S152.

Radvansky, G. A., Copeland, D. E., & Zwaan, R. A. (2003). Aging and functional spatial relations in comprehension and memory. *Psychology and Aging, 18*, 161–165.

Radvansky, G. A., Zacks, R. T., & Hasher, L. (2005). Age and inhibition: The retrieval of situation models. *Journals of Gerontology: Psychological Sciences, 60*, 276–278.

Radvansky, G. A., Zwaan, R. A., Curiel, J. M., & Copeland, D. E. (2001). Situation models and aging. *Psychology and Aging, 16*, 145–160.

Rapp, B., & Goldrick, M. (2000). Discreteness and interactivity in spoken word production. *Psychological Review, 107*, 460–499.

Rastle, K. G., & Burke, D. M. (1996). Priming the tip of the tongue: Effects of prior processing on word retrieval in young and older adults. *Journal of Memory and Language, 35*, 586–605.

Raz, N. (2000). Aging of the brain and its impact on cognitive performance: Integration of structural and functional findings. In F. I. M. Craik and T. A. Salthouse (Eds.), *Handbook of aging and cognition* (2nd ed., pp. 1–90). Mahwah, NJ: Lawrence Erlbaum Associates, Inc.

Rendell, P. G., Castel, A. D., & Craik, F. I. M. (2005). Memory for proper names in old age: A disproportionate impairment? *Quarterly Journal of Experimental Psychology, 58A*, 54–71.

Resnick, S. M., Pham, D. L., Kraut, M. A., Zonderman, A. B., & Davatzikos, C. (2003). Longitudinal magnetic resonance imaging studies of older adults: A shrinking brain. *Journal of Neuroscience, 23*, 3295–3301.

Riegel, K. F., & Riegel, R. M. (1964). Changes in associative behavior during later years of life: A cross-sectional analysis. *Vita Humana, 7*, 1–32.

Roe, K., Jahn-Samilo, J., Juarez, L., Mickel, N., Royer, I., & Bates, E. (2000). Contextual effects on word production: A lifespan study. *Memory and Cognition, 28*, 756–765.

Rogers. T. T., & McClelland, J. L. (2004). *Semantic cognition: A parallel distributed processing approach*. Cambridge, MA: MIT Press.

Ryan, E. B., Giles, H., Bartlucci, G., & Henwood, K. (1986). Psycholinguistic and social psychological components of communication by and with the elderly. *Language and Communication, 6*, 1–24.

Ryan, E. B., See, S. K., Meneer, W. B., & Trovato, D. (1994). Age-based perceptions of conversational skills among younger and older adults. In M. L. Hummert, J. M. Wiemann, & J. N. Nussbaum (Eds.), *Interpersonal communication in older adulthood* (pp. 15–39). Thousand Oaks, CA: Sage.

Saffran, E. M., Dell, G. S., & Schwartz, M. F. (2000) Computational modeling of language disorders. In M. S. Gazzaniga (Ed.), *The new cognitive neurosciences* (pp. 933–948). Cambridge, MA: MIT Press.

Salthouse, T. A. (1985). *A theory of cognitive aging*. Amsterdam: North-Holland.

Salthouse, T. A. (1996). The processing-speed theory of adult age differences in cognition. *Psychological Review, 103*, 403–428.

Salthouse, T. A. (2000). Steps towards the explanation of adult age differences in cognition. In T. Perfect & E. Maylor (Eds.), *Models of cognitive aging* (pp. 19–49). Oxford: Oxford University Press.

Salthouse. T. A. . & Craik. F. I. M. (2000). Closing comments. In F. I. M. Craik & T. A. Salthouse (Eds.), *The handbook of aging and cognition* (pp. 689–703). Mahwah, NJ: Lawrence Erlbaum Associates, Inc.

Salthouse, T. A., Hambrick, D. Z., & McGuthry, K. E. (1998). Shared age-related influences on cognitive and non-cognitive variables. *Psychology and Aging, 13*, 486–500.

Salthouse, T. A., Hancock, H. E., Meinz, E. J., & Hambrick, D. Z. (1996). Interrelations of age, visual acuity, and cognitive functioning. *Journal of Gerontology, 51B*, 317–330.

Salthouse, T. A., Toth, J., Daniels, K., Parks, C., Pak, R., Wolbrette, M., et al. (2000). Effects of aging on efficiency of task switching in a variant of the trail making test. *Neuropsychology, 2000*, 102–111.

Schacter, D. L., Osowiecki, D., Kaszniak, A. W., Kihlstrom, J. F., & Valdiserri, M. (1994). Source memory: Extending the boundaries of age-related deficits. *Psychology and Aging, 9*, 81–89.

Schaie, K. W. (1994). The course of adult intellectual development. *American Psychologist, 49*, 304–313.

Schaie, K. W. (2005). *Developmental influences on adult intelligence*. Oxford: Oxford University Press.

Schmitter-Edgecombe, M., Vesneski, M., & Jones, D. (2000). Aging and word finding: A comparison of discourse and nondiscourse tests. *Archives of Clinical Neuropsychology, 15*, 479–493.

Schneider, B. (1997). Psychoacoustics and aging: Implications for everyday listening. *Journal of Speech-Language Pathology and Audiology, 21*, 111–124.

Schneider, B. A., Daneman, M., & Murphy, D. R. (2005). Speech comprehension difficulties in older adults: Cognitive slowing or age-related changes in hearing? *Psychology and Aging, 20*, 261–271.

Schneider, B. A., Daneman, M., Murphy, D. R., & Kwong See, S. (2000) Listening to discourse in distracting settings: The effects of aging. *Psychology and Aging, 15*, 110–125.

Schneider, B. A., Daneman, M., & Pichora-Fuller, M. K. (2002). Listening in aging adults: From discourse comprehension to psychoacoustics. *Canadian Journal of Experimental Psychology, 56*, 139–152.

Schneider, B. A., & Pichora-Fuller, M. K. (2000). Implications of perceptual deterioration for cognitive aging research. In F. I. M. Craik & T. A. Salthouse (Eds.), *Handbook of aging and cognition* (pp. 155–220). Mahwah, NJ: Lawrence Erlbaum Associates, Inc.

Schneider, B. A., & Pichora-Fuller, M. K. (2001). Age-related changes in temporal processing: Implications for listening comprehension. *Seminars in Hearing, 22,* 227–239.

Schneider, B. A., Pichora-Fuller, M. K., Kowalchuk, D., & Lamb, M. (1994). Gap detection and the precedence effect in young and old adults. *Journal of the Acoustical Society of America, 95,* 980–991.

Schneider, B., Speranza, F., & Pichora-Fuller, M. K. (1998). Age-related changes in temporal resolution: Envelope and intensity effects. *Canadian Journal of Experimental Psychology, 52,* 184–191.

Schwartz, M. F., Dell, G. S., Martin, N., Gahl, S., & Sobel, P. (2006). A case-series test of the interactive two-step model of lexical access: Evidence from picture naming. *Journal of Memory and Language, 54,* 228–264.

Schweich, M., Van der Linden, M., Brédart, S., Bruyer, R., Nelles, B., & Schils, J. P. (1992). Daily-life difficulties in person recognition reported by young and elderly subjects. *Applied Cognitive Psychology, 6,* 161–172.

Scialfa, C. T. (2002). The role of sensory factors in cognitive aging research. *Canadian Journal of Experimental Psychology, 56,* 153–163.

Scialfa, C. T., Hamaluk, E., Pratt, J., & Skaloud, P. (1999). Age differences in saccadic averaging. *Psychology and Aging, 14,* 695–699.

Shafto, M. A., Burke, D. M., Stamatakis, E. A., Tam, P. P., & Tyler, L. K. (in press). Atrophy in insula predicts increased word-finding failures with ageing. *Journal of Cognitive Neuroscience.*

Shaw, N. A. (1992). Age-dependent changes in central somatosensory conduction time. *Clinical Electroencephalography, 23,* 105–110.

Singer, T., Verhaeghen, P., Ghisletta, P., Lindenberger, U., & Baltes, P. B. (2003). The fate of cognition in very old age: Six year longitudinal findings in the Berlin Aging Study (BASE). *Psychology and Aging, 18,* 318–331.

Smiler, A. P., Gagne, D. D., & Stine-Morrow, E. A. L. (2003). Aging, memory load, and resource allocation during reading. *Psychology and Aging, 18,* 203–209.

Snell, K. B., Mapes, F. M., Hickman, E. D., & Frisina, D. R. (2002). Word recognition in competing babble and the effects of age, temporal processing, and absolute sensitivity. *Journal of the Acoustical Society of America, 112,* 720–727.

Snowdon, D. A., Greiner, L., Kemper, S., Nanayakkara, N., & Mortimer, J. A. (1999). Linguistic ability in early life and longevity: Findings from the Nun study. In J. M. Robine, B. Forette, C. Franchesci, & M. Allard (Eds.), *The paradoxes of longevity* (pp. 103–113). Amsterdam: Springer.

Snowdon, D. A., Kemper, S., Mortimer, J. A., Greiner, L. H., Wekstein, D. R., & Markesbery, W. R. (1996). Cognitive ability in early life and cognitive function and Alzheimer's disease in late life: Findings from the Nun study. *Journal of the American Medical Association, 275,* 528–532.

Sommers, M. S. (1996). The structural organization of the mental lexicon and its contribution to age-related declines in spoken-word recognition. *Psychology and Aging, 11,* 333–341.

Sommers, M. S., & Danielson, S. M. (1999). Inhibitory processes and spoken word recognition in young and older adults: The interaction of lexical competition and semantic context. *Psychology and Aging, 14,* 458–472.

Sowell, E. R., Peterson, B. S., Thompson, P. M., Welcome, S. E., Henkenius, A. L., & Toga, A. W. (2003). Mapping cortical change across the human life span. *Nature Neuroscience, 6,* 309–315.

Speranza, F., Daneman, M., & Schneider, B. A. (2000). How aging affects the reading of words in noisy backgrounds. *Psychology and Aging, 15,* 253–258.

Spieler, D. H., & Balota, D. A. (2000). Factors influencing word naming in younger and older adults. *Psychology and Aging, 15,* 225–231.

Steenbekkers, L. P. A. (1998). Visual contrast sensitivity. In L. P. A. Steenbekkers & C. E. M. Beijsterveldt (Eds.), *Design-relevant characteristics of ageing users. Backgrounds and guidelines for product innovation* (pp. 131–136). Delft: Delft University Press.

Stine, E. A. L., & Wingfield, A. (1994). Older adults can inhibit high-probability competitors in speech recognition. *Aging and Cognition, 1*, 152–157.

Stine, E. L., Wingfield, A., & Poon, L. W. (1986). How much and how fast: Rapid processing of spoken language in later adulthood. *Psychology and Aging, 1*, 303–311.

Stine-Morrow, E. A. L., Gagne, D. D., Morrow, D. G., & DeWall, B. H. (2004). Age differences in rereading. *Memory and Cognition, 32*, 696–710.

Stine-Morrow, E. A. L., Loveless, M. K., & Soederberg, L. M. (1996). Resource allocation in on-line reading by younger and older adults. *Psychology and Aging, 11*, 475–486.

Stine-Morrow, E. A. L., Miller, L. M. S., Hertzog, C. (2006). Aging and self-regulated language processing. *Psychological Bulletin, 132*, 582–606.

Stine-Morrow, E. A. L., Miller, L. M. S., & Leno, R. (2001). Patterns of on-line resource allocation to narrative text by younger and older readers. *Aging, Neuropsychology, and Cognition, 8*, 36–53.

Stine-Morrow, E. A. L., Morrow, D. G., & Leno, R. (2002). Aging and the representation of spatial situations in narrative understanding. *Journals of Gerontology: Psychological Sciences, 57*, 91–97.

Strouse, A., Ashmean, D. H., Ohde, R. N., & Grantham, D. W. (1998). Temporal processing in the aging auditory system. *Journal of the Acoustical Society of America, 104*, 2385–2399.

Sunderland, A., Watts, K., Baddeley, A. D., & Harris, J. E. (1986). Subjective memory assessment and test performance in elderly adults. *Journal of Gerontology, 41*, 376–384.

Tainturier, M. J., Tremblay, M., & Lecours, A. R. (1989). Aging and the word frequency effect: A lexical decision investigation. *Neuropsychologia, 27*, 1197–1203.

Takayanagi, S., Dirks, D. D., & Moshfegh, A. (2002). Lexical and talker effects on word recognition among native and non-native listeners with normal and impaired hearing. *Journal of Speech, Language and Hearing Research, 45*, 585–597.

Tang, Y., Nyengaard, J. R., Pakkenberg, B., & Gundersen, H. J. (1997). Age-induced white matter changes in the human brain: a stereological investigation. *Neurobiology of Aging, 18*, 609–615.

Tanosaki, M., Ozaki, I., Shimamura, H., Baba, M., & Matsunaga, M. (1999). Effects of aging on central conduction in somatosensory evoked potentials: Evaluation of onset versus peak methods. *Clinical Neurophysiology, 110*, 2094–2103.

Taylor, J. K., & Burke, D. M. (2000, April). *Slips of the tongue: An examination of language production in old age.* Poster presented at the Cognitive Aging Conference, Atlanta.

Taylor, J. K., & Burke, D. M. (2002). Asymmetric aging effects on semantic and phonological processes: Naming in the picture-word interference task. *Psychology and Aging, 17*, 662–676.

Thornton, R., & Light, L. L. (2006). Language comprehension and production in normal aging. In J. E. Birren and K. W. Schaie (Eds.), *Handbook of the psychology of aging* (pp. 262–287). Burlington, MA: Elsevier.

Titone, D., Prentice, K. J., & Wingfield, A. (2000). Resource allocation during spoken discourse processing: Effects of age and passage difficulty as revealed by self-paced listening. *Memory and Cognition, 28*, 1029–1040.

Trainor, L. J., & Trehub, S. E. (1989). Aging and auditory temporal sequencing: Ordering the elements of repeating tone patterns. *Perception and Psychophysics, 45*, 417–426.

Tree, J. J., & Hirsh, K. W. (2003) Sometimes faster, sometimes, slower: Associative and competitor priming in picture naming with young and elderly participants, *Journal of Neurolinguistics, 16*, 489–514.

Tremblay, K. L., Piskosz, M., & Souza, P. (2002). Aging alters the neural representation of speech cues. *Neuroreport, 13*, 1865–1870.

Tun, P. A. (1998). Fast noisy speech: Age differences in processing rapid speech with background noise. *Psychology and Aging, 13*, 424–434.

Tun, P. A., O'Kane, G., & Wingfield, A. (2002). Distraction by competing speech in young and older adult listeners. *Psychology and Aging, 17*, 453–467.

Tun, P. A., & Wingfield, A. (1999). One voice too many: Adult age differences in language processing with different types of distracting sounds. *Journals of Gerontology: Psychological Sciences, 54B*, 317–327.

Tun, P. A., Wingfield, A., Stine, E. A. L., & Mecsas, C. (1992). Rapid speech processing and divided attention: Processing rate versus processing resources as an explanation of age effects. *Psychology and Aging, 7*, 546–550.

Uttl, B. (2002). North American Adult Reading Test: Age norms, reliability, and validity. *Journal of Clinical and Experimental Neuropsychology, 24*, 1123–1137.

Uttl, B., & Van Alstine, C. L. (2003). Rising verbal intelligence scores: Implications for research and clinical practice. *Psychology and Aging, 18*, 616–621.

Van der Linden, M., Hupet, M., Feyereisen, P., Schelstraete, M., Bestgen, Y., Bruyer, R., et al. (1999). Cognitive mediators of age-related differences in language comprehension and verbal memory performance. *Aging, Neuropsychology, and Cognition, 6*, 32–55.

van Rooij, J. C. G. M., & Plomp, R. (1990). Auditive and cognitive factors in speech perception by elderly listeners. II. Multivariate analyses. *Journal of the Acoustical Society of America, 88*, 2611–2624.

Verhaeghen, P. (2003). Aging and vocabulary score: A meta-analysis. *Psychology and Aging, 18*, 332–339.

Vitevitch, M. S., & Sommers, M. S. (2003). The facilitative influence of phonological similarity and neighborhood frequency in speech production in younger and older adults. *Memory and Cognition, 31*, 491–504.

Vousden, J. I., & Maylor, E. A. (2006). Speech errors across the lifespan. *Language and Cognitive Processes, 21*, 48–77.

Waters, G., & Caplan, D. (2001). Age, working memory and on-line syntactic processing in sentence comprehension. *Psychology and Aging, 16*, 128–144.

Waters, G. S., & Caplan, D. (2005). The relationship between age, processing speed, working memory capacity, and language comprehension. *Memory, 13*, 403–413.

Wheeldon, L. R., & Monsell S. (1994). Inhibition of spoken word production by priming a semantic competitor. *Journal of Memory and Language, 33*, 332–357.

White, K. K., & Abrams, L. (2002). Does priming specific syllables during tip-of-the-tongue states facilitate word retrieval in older adults? *Psychology and Aging, 17*, 226–235.

White, K. K., & Abrams L. (2004a). Free associations and dominance ratings of homophones for young and older adults. *Behavior Research Methods, Instruments, and Computers, 36*, 408–420.

White, K. K., & Abrams, L. (2004b). Phonologically mediated priming of preexisting and new associations in young and older adults. *Journal of Experimental Psychology: Learning, Memory, and Cognition, 30*, 645–655.

Whiting, W. L., Madden, D. J., Langley, L. K., Denny, L. L., Turkington, T. G., Provenzale, J. M., et al. (2003). Lexical and sublexical components of age-related changes in neural activation during word identification. *Journal of Cognitive Neuroscience, 15*, 475–487.

Williams, K. N. (2006). Improving outcomes of nursing home interactions. *Research in Nursing and Health, 29*, 121–133.

Williams, K., Kemper, S., & Hummert, M. L. (2003). Improving nursing home communication: An intervention to reduce elderspeak. *The Gerontologist, 43*, 242–247.

Wingfield, A. (1996). Cognitive factors in auditory performance: Context, speed of processing, and constraints of memory. *Journal of the American Academy of Audiology, 7,* 175–182.

Wingfield, A., & Ducharme, J. L. (1999). Effects of age and passage difficulty on listening-rate preferences for time-altered speech. *Journal of Gerontology: Psychological Sciences, 54,* 199–202.

Wingfield, A., Lindfield, K. C., & Goodglass, H. (2000). Effects of age and hearing sensitivity on the use of prosodic information in spoken word recognition. *Journal of Speech, Language, and Hearing Research, 43,* 915–925.

Wingfield, A., McCoy, S. L., Peelle, J. E., Tun, P. A., & Cox, L. C. (2007). Effects of adult age and hearing loss on comprehension of rapid speech varying in syntactic complexity. *Journal of the American Academy of Audiology, 17,* 487–497.

Wingfield, A., Peelle, J. E., & Grossman, M. (2003) Speech rate and syntactic complexity as multiplicative factors in speech comprehension by young and older adults. *Aging, Neuropsychology, and Cognition, 10,* 310–322.

Wingfield, A., Poon, L. W., Lombardi, L., & Lowe, D. (1985). Speed of processing in normal aging: effects of speech rate, linguistic structure, and processing time. *Journal of Gerontology, 40,* 579–585.

Wingfield, A., & Stine-Morrow, E. A. L. (2000). Language and speech. In F. I. M. Craik & T. A. Salthouse (Eds.), *The handbook of aging and cognition* (2nd ed., pp. 359–416). Mahwah, NJ: Lawrence Erlbaum Associates, Inc.

Wingfield, A., Tun, P. A., Koh, C. K., & Rosen, M. J. (1999). Regaining lost time: Adult aging and the effect of time restoration on recall of time-compressed speech. *Psychology and Aging, 14,* 380–389.

Wingfield, A., Tun, P. A., & McCoy, S. L. (2005). Hearing loss in older adulthood: What it is and how it interacts with cognitive performance. *Current Directions in Psychological Science, 14,* 144–148.

Zacks, R. T., & Hasher, L. (1997). Cognitive gerontology and attentional inhibition: A reply to Burke and McDowd. *Journal of Gerontology: Psychological Sciences, 52,* 274–283.

Zacks, R. T., & Hasher, L. (2006). Aging and long-term memory: Deficits are not inevitable. In E. Bialystok & F. I. M. Craik (Eds.), *Lifespan cognition: Mechanisms of change* (pp. 162–177). Oxford: Oxford University Press.

Zipin, L. M., Tompkins, C. A., & Kasper, S. C. (2000). Effects of foregrounding on predictive inference generation by normally ageing adults. *Aphasiology, 14,* 115–131.

Zwaan, R. A., & Radvansky, G. A. (1998). Situation models in language comprehension and memory. *Psychological Bulletin, 123,* 162–185.

9

Knowledge and Cognitive Aging

Phillip L. Ackerman
Georgia Institute of Technology

WHAT IS KNOWLEDGE?

After Ryle (1949/2000), experimental and cognitive psychologists traditionally parse the nature of knowledge into two forms—declarative knowledge (or knowing that) and procedural knowledge (knowing how). However, it has been argued (e.g., Polanyi, 1966/1983) that there is a third type of knowledge called "tacit" knowledge, that is not well incorporated by these former two types of knowledge. Broudy (1977) for example, has claimed that this form of knowledge, which he referred to as "knowing with," is an especially important aspect of an individual's knowledge base; it is of particular interest in terms of what the individual learns in school, and what the individual can bring to bear on novel problems. A more precise description of these types of knowledge should be the first order of business.

Knowing That

Factual knowledge about the world around us represents much of the essence of declarative knowledge. It encompasses many of the domains identified in Adler's (1974) wheel of knowledge (see Figure 9.1). This knowledge can be discrete (such as the name of the current president of Bolivia or the capital of South Dakota), or it can represent a set of principled or organized knowledge (such as the periodic table of the chemical elements, the positions played in a baseball or football game, the rankings

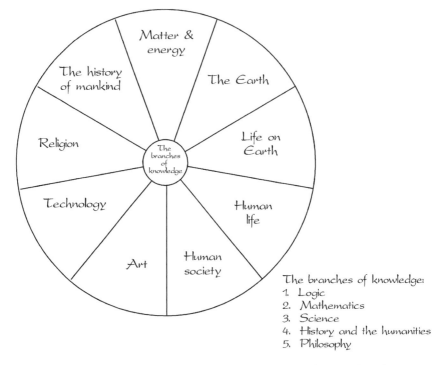

FIG. 9.1. Adler's (1974) wheel of knowledge. Copyright Encyclopædia Britannica, Inc.

of different hands in poker, and so on). Much of the information that we might need to recall on a day-to-day basis is declarative in nature (e.g., the names of our co-workers, the passwords needed to log on to our email or other computer accounts). On the one hand, as illustrated by Adler's wheel of knowledge, there is a great amount of declarative knowledge that is taught in school that is not ordinarily encountered in other situations. Knowledge of European history, medieval art, and the importance of fish exports to the economy of Iceland are exemplars of declarative knowledge that, while they may be of critical importance to an individual's occupation or avocational interests (e.g., hobbies), may not be needed shortly after the time the information is acquired. That is, once the school test is over, the knowledge may never be needed by the individual again in his or her lifetime. On the other hand, many declarative facts are critical to our survival (e.g., which mushrooms are poisonous) or to our relative well-being (e.g., a spouse's birthday or your anniversary date). For other declarative facts, however, it is often difficult to know, a priori, whether they are going to be needed in the future. The inability to determine the utility of declarative knowledge means that the learner sometimes may have to take the need to acquire facts at face value.

Knowing How

Procedural knowledge is typically associated with sequences of actions (e.g., playing a piece of music on a piano or operating an automobile). In some cases, knowledge of a sequence can be represented as declarative knowledge, such as when one follows a recipe for preparing a meal. When the sequence of actions must be completed in a short period of time and/or with high levels of precision, such as when a surgeon removes a patient's appendix, declarative knowledge alone is not ordinarily sufficient for accomplishing a task. That is, knowing the sequence needed to perform the task (e.g., reading the music on a page and knowing which piano keys correspond to the notes on the page, or knowing that the golf ball must be hit with just enough force to reach the hole but not overshoot it) is not the same thing as being able to perform the sequence in a competent manner. It is with such examples that the different nature of procedural knowledge becomes clear. Procedural knowledge is acquired through consistent and extensive practice. The knowledge may be represented in a declarative fashion when learning starts, such as when the driving instructor provides a schema for the novice driver to follow (e.g., insert the key, make sure the car is in "park" or "neutral," start the car, check the mirrors, look left, right and forward before releasing the parking brake, and so on). Even these instructions, though, presume a high level of knowledge on the part of the learner, in that the instructor presumes that the learner knows how to open the car door, how to orient the limbs to sit in the car seat, and so on. These kinds of procedural knowledge are not usually mediated by explicit cognitive articulation—as the learner has effectively "automatized" the process of these intermediate, but critical steps in the process of getting into the car prior to the task of driving.

Knowing With

By the time individuals reach adulthood, they have acquired large amounts of knowledge that are not readily decomposed into declarative or procedural categories. Much of this knowledge is "tacit" in that it is not usually spontaneously articulated nor is it often easily accessible to verbal reports. Broudy (1977) noted that the educated individual "thinks, perceives, and judges with everything that he has studied in school, even though he cannot recall these learnings on demand" (Broudy, 1977, p. 12; see also Bransford & Schwartz, 2000 for a discussion of knowing with and transfer).

Polanyi's "tacit knowing" and Broudy's conceptualization of "knowing with" share similarities with Gestalt principles of perceptual organization and problem solving (e.g., see Köhler, 1947). This type of knowledge has overlap with subsequent proposals of a third kind of knowledge, such as the Wagner and Sternberg (1985) concept of "tacit knowledge" and the Baltes, Smith, and Staudinger (1992) concept of "wisdom." However, in both of these examples, the domains of knowledge are considerably more narrowly defined than that proposed by Polanyi and Broudy. Specifically, Sternberg's operationalization of tacit knowledge is occupationally or academically specific, and it relates to particular strategies for success. The Baltes construct of wisdom has been *operationalized* in contexts that are limited to novel problem solving, or what traditional learning theories would call "distant transfer." The patterns of growth, maintenance, and decline in the context of adult aging may differ for these three kinds of knowledge, so it will be useful to consider each kind of knowledge separately in the discussion to follow.

INTELLIGENCE, KNOWLEDGE, AND AGE

Over the first half of the twentieth century in particular, theory and empirical research on knowledge and aging have been very much integrated into the domain of intelligence theory and assessment. It is thus appropriate to provide a basic overview of the relations among intelligence and knowledge in the context of aging. This review, however, is necessarily brief. More extensive historical discussions of these issues can be found in other sources (e.g., Botwinick, 1967; Schaie, 1996a; Wechsler, 1944).

Early Intelligence Theory

Two theoretical approaches to human intelligence arrived at almost diametrically opposed considerations of knowledge as a fundamental component of the construct. The first approach is identified with Spearman (1904), and the second approach is identified with Binet and Simon (1905/1973). These approaches are reviewed in turn below.

Spearman

Spearman's (1904, 1927; Spearman & Jones, 1950) theory of intelligence evolved over the course of the first half of the twentieth century. In his initial empirical and theoretical exposition of the construct of general intelligence (g), Spearman noted that the measure most highly associated with the construct of general intelligence was knowledge of "Classics" (e.g., Latin and Greek)—in fact, this measure had a 0.99 correlation with the general factor of intelligence (where 1.00 would represent a perfect linear correspondence between individual differences in Classics grades and the hypothetical construct of general intelligence [g]—see Spearman, 1904, p. 276). Spearman later identified another measure that is closely associated with knowledge, namely verbal fluency, as highly associated with g ($r = .97$; see Krueger & Spearman, 1907). The measure designed to assess this kind of knowledge and context inference was designed by Ebbinghaus (1896–1897), and is called the Completion Test. The test presents the examinee with a passage of text, where letters, syllables, and whole words have been replaced with blanks. The examinee must infer what to place in the blanks in order to have a coherent and complete text passage. As such, it clearly depends on two important components of knowledge: knowledge of the structure of grammar, and the range of vocabulary knowledge.

By the 1930s, Spearman had largely discarded any notion that knowledge was an important component of general intelligence, despite the lack of evidence to contradict his earlier empirical findings of the high associations of Classics knowledge or Completion Test performance with g (e.g., see Spearman, 1930, p. 562). Instead, Spearman came to endorse a measure of nonverbal abstract reasoning (call the Progressive Matrices Test) as the sine qua non of intelligence (e.g., see Spearman, 1938). The reasons behind this choice are somewhat obscure, but in terms of our current concerns, Spearman's stated reason for removing knowledge as a central aspect of intelligence was that level of knowledge was obviously related to prior experience and education; but in contrast abstract reasoning measures appeared (at least on the surface) to represent something about intelligence that was unaffected by such background issues. Spearman also disliked the notion that g could grow or develop during childhood and adolescence (Spearman, 1930, 567–568), in that he was mainly interested in a quality of an individual that was genetically fixed and unchanging. Considerations of knowledge and aging thus fall mainly outside of the domain of Spearman's g.

Binet and Simon

In contrast to Spearman's approach to intelligence, the work by Binet and Simon (1905/1973) both endorsed the notion of knowledge as an important component of intelligence, and explicitly provided for developmental changes in the level and breadth of intelligence. Binet and Simon developed a battery of tests to assess the intelligence of children and adolescents as a means toward predicting academic success or failure.

Although their aim was not to directly assess the "sum of acquired knowledge" (Binet & Simon, 1905/1973, p. 40), which they identified as the pedagogical method of intelligence assessment, several component measures of their scales included declarative knowledge (e.g., a variant of the Ebbinghaus Completion Test, the Verbal Definition of Known Objects Scale) and procedural knowledge (e.g., picking up and manipulating objects, drawing objects, paper cutting). It might also be argued that performance on many of the intelligence scales required varying degrees of "knowing that," such as in answering the Comprehension Scale questions, for example "When one has missed the train what must one do?" or "When one breaks something belonging to another what must one do?" (p. 224), or questions related to Interpreting Pictures.

The aspect of Binet and Simon's approach that is critical for the assessment of knowledge and aging is that they explicitly considered that intelligence levels *change* as a function of age of the individual. In fact, their approach was a normative approach, in that each individual's intelligence level was interpretable only in the context of that individual's age peers. An individual who correctly answered an equivalent number of questions as the average child of the same age was considered to have a normal level of intelligence (identified as an equal mental age and chronological age), and those individuals who answered fewer questions correctly had a lower mental age than their chronological age, while other individuals who answered more questions correctly had a higher mental age compared to their chronological age. One major criterion for the inclusion of items on the Binet-Simon scales was "age differentiation"—which means that the probability of a correct answer to the question must increase with an increase in the age of the children being tested. This means that, ceteris paribus (i.e., all other things being equal), older children are expected to have a greater body of stored knowledge, when compared to younger children.

Adult Intelligence Assessment

The notion of cumulative increases in knowledge was critical for the Binet-Simon approach to the construct of intelligence, but the Binet-Simon scales and various revisions developed by others were initially only used for assessment of children and adolescents. The application of this approach to the study of adults and aging in the 1910s created serious interpretational problems. By the mid-1910s, new intelligence tests were introduced that were predicated on many of the Binet-Simon scales, but were modified to make them more interesting and relevant to adults (e.g., the Otis test, see Otis, 1919). The most widely used intelligence assessment measure for adults was the Army Alpha test, which was developed in World War I, and administered to 1,700,000 men conscripted into the US Army (e.g., see Yoakum & Yerkes, 1920). There was only a brief discussion of age-related differences among those tested (Yerkes, 1921), mainly because there were relatively few older draftees compared to young draftees (only 1.7% of the principal sample of 15,385 officers was older than 50 years of age), and because it was assumed that the older group was not representative of the population at large (in that these individuals were more likely to be trained professionals, such as medical doctors, dentists, and engineers; Yerkes, 1921, pp. 813–818). However, substantial controversy was elicited when the entire sample was identified as having an average mental age of 13, based on a comparison of scores between the Army Alpha test and the Binet-Simon test (e.g., see Lippmann, 1922; Terman, 1922). There were several problems with such a representation (e.g., see Brigham, 1923). The two main difficulties with this simplistic presentation of an average mental age statistic are that there were no reference norms for the Binet-Simon scales for adults of various ages and that the whole construct of "mental age" is only meaningful if age differentiation were to be found across the entire age span of children *and* adults. Clearly, one inference from this statistic is that there may be a limit of increasing performance that is reached at some point in adulthood, after which performance levels off or declines with increasing age. Whether this pattern pertains to all aspects of intelligence or to knowledge in particular, was an open question in the 1920s.

Later Empirical Studies with the Army Alpha

The first in-depth study of the relationship between adult age and intelligence test performance from a community-dwelling sample was collected by Jones and initially reported by Hsiao (1927) in a masters thesis. This research represented an impressive effort to assess the intelligence levels of 1191 community-dwelling persons with a wide range of ages (from 10 to 60). The Army Alpha test was administered to this sample, and scores reported for a set of reasonably homogeneous age groups. The overall Alpha test scores showed a rapid rise with age until about age 20, and then a less steep but consistently declining mean score with increased adult ages. However, two tests from the Alpha in particular did not show the general trend of decline with increasing adult ages—Test 4 (a test of vocabulary called Synonym/Antonym) and Test 8 (the test of General Information). The results from these two tests provided the most substantive evidence that knowledge is well preserved in middle age, even when one factors in the likelihood that cohort differences (where older participants likely had less formal education than younger participants) masked an underlying positive association between adult age and level of knowledge. The data set was subsequently described by others (e.g., Conrad, 1930; Jones & Conrad, 1933). Hsiao (1927, and later Conrad, 1930) highlighted that at least within the range of ages he examined (up to age 54), performance on the general information scale from the Army Alpha test increased or remained stable with increasing age. Both Hsiao and later Conrad also noted the difference between Spearman's approach (that excluded knowledge from the construct of general intelligence) and other approaches where knowledge was considered an essential if not the *"main"* component of intelligence (p. 593, italics in original). Conrad (1930) identified several key issues and questions that transcend attempts to assess and understand the relationship between knowledge and adult aging, as follows. First, Conrad noted that an "ideal general information test would represent the acquisition and retention by an individual of information which is equally interesting and available to all individuals" (p. 593). Conrad identified this as a test of "practical general information." Second, Conrad asked the following questions: "Does intelligence decline sharply in advanced old age? Does the intelligence of the individual of 120 IQ decline less rapidly than that of the person of 100 IQ? Does the intelligence of those engaged in heavy manual labor decline more rapidly than the intelligence of clerks?" (pp. 596–597). Although these questions were posed quite some time ago, the answers are still somewhat elusive, depending on the kind of knowledge under consideration.

Jones and Conrad (1933)

The more in-depth write-up of the data set collected by Jones was reported by Jones and Conrad in 1933. Based on the same data, Jones and Conrad concluded:

> From the point of view of measuring basic or native intelligence, the information tests of the Alpha (Test 4 and 8) present an unfair advantage to those in the upper age brackets. Exclusion of Subtests 4 and 8 from the Alpha gives a picture of comparatively more rapid growth among the adolescents and more rapid decline among the adults.

That is, the data reported by Hsiao (1927), Conrad (1930), and Jones and Conrad (1933) show well-preserved performance of adults up to age 60 in terms of vocabulary knowledge and knowledge of general information. But because these two scales differ from the pattern of decline after age 18–20 found for tests of analogies, arithmetic, and other such abilities, Jones and Conrad essentially de-emphasized the integrality of knowledge for the construct of intelligence—ultimately presenting an approach that was similar to Spearman's conceptualization.

Hebb (1939, 1942)

Based on a series of examinations of intellectual functioning of individuals after removal of brain tumors or other operations that removed brain tissue, the noted neuropsychologist D. O. Hebb came to the conclusion that intellectual abilities were differentially affected by such operations, and that the effects also depended on the age of the individual when the operations were performed. Hebb identified two broad types of intellectual abilities, called "A" and "B." Intelligence A represented "direct intellectual power" (Hebb, 1942, p. 289) and this kind of intelligence is involved in novel learning, abstract reasoning, and similar kinds of tasks. Intelligence B represented "the establishment of routine modes of response to common problems" (p. 289), and this kind of intelligence is involved in vocabulary and general information kinds of tasks. Hebb noted, based on the work by Jones and Conrad, that in normal aging Intelligence A tends to decline with increasing adult age, but that Intelligence B tends to be well preserved with advanced age. Hebb fundamentally disagreed with Jones and Conrad about the useful interpretation of these results. Specifically, he said: "In condemning these tests of 'acquired information,' Jones and Conrad neglect the fact that they may be the best indices, even in senescence, of an important part of intellectual function" (p. 289). Moreover, Hebb noted that the loss of neural tissue through surgical removal, ceteris paribus, for adults was more likely to result in poorer performance on measures of Intelligence A, but not for relatively well-preserved knowledge—namely, Intelligence B.

Cattell (1943)

R. B. Cattell, working mostly from a review of research on normal adults and the relationship between adult age and performance on intelligence tests, but also from the work by Hebb, proposed a division of intellectual abilities similar in many ways to Hebb's Intelligence A and Intelligence B. Cattell called these two intelligences "fluid" and "crystallized," respectively. Cattell noted that the main differences between his representation and Hebb's theory were that "fluid ability" was proposed to be equivalent to Spearman's construct of g, and that the intelligence of children is largely synonymous with fluid ability. Cattell also specifically argued that crystallized ability consists of knowledge developed "through the operation of fluid ability, but not [sic] longer requiring insightful perception for their successful operation" (Cattell, 1943, p. 178). Over the next several decades, further expansions and refinements were made by Cattell and his colleagues, which will be discussed in more detail later in this chapter.

Summary

The empirical research by Conrad, Jones, and others in the 1930s (e.g., Miles & Miles, 1932; Christian & Paterson, 1936), and the theoretical contributions made by Hebb and Cattell in the early 1940s point to a few basic findings and propositions with regard to knowledge and aging, as follows:

(1) Measures of intellectual ability that pertain to declarative knowledge (e.g., vocabulary and general information) appear to be generally well preserved in the context of normal aging through middle age to later adulthood. (In contrast, measures of intellectual ability that require more novel processing [e.g., abstract reasoning] are much more likely to show declines with increasing adult age.)
(2) When brain injuries or diseases occur in adulthood, previously acquired declarative knowledge appears to be most resilient, in that it is least likely to be impaired, in comparison to other kinds of intellectual abilities.
(3) Knowledge, as an expression of crystallized intelligence, is posited to develop out of the operation of fluid intelligence, especially during childhood and adolescence.
(4) A corollary to Cattell's (1943) initial explication of the theory of fluid and crystallized intelligence (later made explicit, see Cattell, 1957) is that as early adulthood is reached, fluid intelligence starts a pattern of decline, which in turn is expected to make it more difficult for middle-aged and older adults to acquire new knowledge, in comparison to children and young adults.

In addition to these findings, it is important to note that despite the substantial interest in the role of aging on knowledge-related abilities from the 1930s onward, by 1950 there was still almost no empirical data on fundamental issues associated with this topic, namely:

(1) The relationship between adult age and acquisition of new declarative knowledge or procedural knowledge.
(2) The extent of stability or change in retained declarative knowledge over the course of adult aging.
(3) The extent of stability or change in previously acquired procedural knowledge over the course of adult aging.
(4) The relationship between aging and domain-specific knowledge (i.e., knowledge other than verbal [vocabulary] or general information knowledge).

From mid-century onwards, however, there has been an explosion of empirical research on cognitive and motor aspects of aging. Research on each of the above issues is reviewed in turn below.

AGE AND ACQUISITION OF NEW KNOWLEDGE

Perhaps the most widely researched aspect of the topic of knowledge and adult aging has been in the area of acquisition of new knowledge. Early psychological research on these issues was relatively sparse. The studies of adult aging and learning in the literature up to the 1930s can be characterized mainly as: (a) small-scale studies (fewer than 20 participants); (b) narrow age ranges (e.g., up to age 50); (c) unrepresentative samples across age groups; (d) measures of individual differences in learning that were inconsistent or subject to statistical artifacts (e.g., see Ackerman, 1987, for a review of this issue). Nonetheless, the general consensus from such studies was that adults between the ages of 40 and 50 tended to perform less well, on average, compared to young adults, on knowledge acquisition tasks as varied as associative memory (e.g., Hollingworth, 1927; Ruch, 1934) and acquisition of Esperanto (an artificial language; Thorndike, Bregman, Tilton, & Woodyard, 1928). For an extensive review of research during this period, see Ruch (1933).

In more recent decades, almost every variety of laboratory task used by experimental psychologists has been given to groups of young adults (typically college students) and older adults (typically over the age of 60 or 70), and contrasts between them have been made. Such tasks include simple associative learning procedures (e.g., rehearsing arbitrary paired associates for later recall) and random motor sequences. An extensive review by Light (1991) illustrates that in nearly every standard laboratory learning paradigm, memory retained of older adults (over 60) after learning exposure is, on average, poorer than that of younger adults. Although less frequently studied, acquired memory for tasks that have real-world analogues (e.g., remembering "information from simulated medicine labels"—see Morrell, Park, and Poon, 1989) also indicate that older adults, on average, perform less well at retention testing compared to young adults.

Micro

In a comprehensive meta-analysis of age differences in memory performance Verhaeghen, Marcoen, and Goossens (1993) provided a specific breakdown of average effect sizes across several standard tasks of learning and retention, including short-term memory (digit span), paired-associate recall, incidental learning, and prose recall. Across all of these different task types, and their various different instantiations, the obtained results reflect a single general conclusion—that is, knowledge retained in strictly controlled laboratory learning conditions is less accurate for older adults than for young adults. Actual effect sizes were in the medium-to-large range (e.g., $d = 0.5$ to 1.3). A more recent meta-analysis by Johnson (2003) that focused only on recall of text information showed a largely similar pattern of age-related deficits to those in other specific learning/memory domains ($d = .69$). The analysis provided by Johnson did point to several factors that attenuated the differences between younger and older adults. Some of the most salient factors included educational achievement (with more highly educated older adults showing comparatively less impaired performance), size of vocabulary, intelligence, text characteristics (e.g., older adults were comparatively less poor performers when the text to be remembered included connected prose, in contrast to unrelated sentences). In some ways, these results provide an answer to Conrad's question about the relationship between intelligence level and rate of decline with age—that is, those individuals with lower levels of intelligence do appear to retain less than those individuals with higher levels of intelligence.

Because the comparatively poorer performance of older adults compared to younger adults on tasks that require short-term acquisition and retention of new knowledge is so ubiquitous for these various laboratory tasks, it is difficult to localize the source of the relative deficits. Several theories have been proposed to account for such differences; two current theories are cognitive slowing (e.g., Salthouse, 1996), and decline in working memory capacity (for a review, see Phillips & Hamilton, 2001). These theoretical approaches do not make differential predictions for outcomes of the experiments described above, meaning that studies of this type are not diagnostic for the validity of the theories. Nonetheless, the extant data and theories support the notion that with increasing adult age there are likely to be mean deficits in acquisition and retention of new declarative knowledge, and that the deficits are exacerbated for lower ability learners and for more arbitrary learning material.

There have been far fewer investigations of short acquisition and retention of *meaningful* procedural knowledge in the context of aging than there are for declarative knowledge. In addition, as with other nonage-related studies of procedural knowledge, the tasks under consideration cannot be uniquely identified with procedural knowledge, but rather represent some combination of declarative, procedural, and knowing-with components. Perhaps the most widely studied class of tasks that involve acquisition of procedural knowledge are those that study aspects of computerized text processing (or word processing) and military tasks (such as procedures in using and maintaining guns or piloting skills). In these studies (e.g., see Charness, Kelley, Bosman, & Mottram, 2001 for a review and empirical data), there are two general findings: (1) for novice learners (i.e., those with minimal exposure to either typewriting or computer use), older adults are at a significant and substantial disadvantage in terms of speed of learning, degree of retention, and speed/accuracy of performance after training; (2) for expert learners (e.g., those who already have high levels of typewriting skills), the differences between older and younger adults are attenuated on the training and retention measures.

There is an apparent dissociation between the performance of older adults on word processing tasks and the more traditional typing tasks. When older adults are expert typists, there appear to be minimal differences in overall transcription typing performance when compared to younger expert typists (e.g., see Salthouse, 1984). However, when older and younger expert typists are compared on word processing tasks (where the tasks included more editing components than straightforward typing), there are significant differences in overall performance between the age groups, with younger adults performing better than older adults, on average (though there is a question about whether the individuals at the same occupational level, but with different ages, are equally representative of the population). One explanation for this difference is that transcription typing is much more of a "pure" procedural knowledge task, and word processing has more strategic and declarative knowledge components—where older adults are most likely to show diminished performance, compared to young adults (e.g., see Bosman, 1993).

In areas of knowledge and skill acquisition research outside of the laboratory, comparative data regarding older and younger adults are more difficult to obtain, and even when available, are less clear because of various uncontrolled factors. In areas of classroom instruction and organizational training, there are problems of nonrandom sampling (through self-selection or prior institutional/organizational selection), motivation or attitude toward the material to be learned, differential degrees of relevant prior knowledge and experience, and so on.

Macro

Perhaps the first large-scale systematic examination of the educational achievement of adults with a wide range of age was conducted by Sorenson (1933, 1938). Sorenson described the pattern of abilities and other characteristics (such as motives) among several thousand university extension course students, and he generally concluded that older adults are indeed capable learners in educational settings across a variety of different domains. However, Sorenson noted that there were two critical determinants of a successful learning experience for adult learners in the educational context—abilities and motivation (the latter mainly attributed to the meaningfulness of the content of the learning experience). Similar points were made by Lorge (1937), based on a secondary analysis of data collected by Thorndike on learning "Esperanto (an artificial language) . . . in learning stenography, and in learning facts of biography" (p. 28). In a subsequent review of the literature on lifespan development and education, Schaie and Willis (1978) also commented on the possibility that there are substantial age differences in learning, dependent on the "meaningfulness of content." It should be noted that the evidence cited by Schaie and Willis was somewhat mixed on this topic, and that the meaningfulness of content was limited to relatively narrow laboratory tasks, rather than knowledge domains relevant to real-world concerns. A few more recent attempts have been made that attempt to address the special issues associated with adult learners in educational settings (e.g., see Longworth & Davies, 1996; Smith & Pourchot, 1998), but the relative paucity of systematic study of adult learners in the literature is notable from the perspective of higher education, especially given that there is a substantial representation of adult learners in the college classroom. According to recent statistics (Chronicle of Higher Education, 2005–2006), 23.8% of all college and graduate school students in the USA were aged 30 or older (roughly 4 million students) as of Fall, 2003—a percentage that is expected to increase over the next few decades (e.g., see Dychtwald & Flower, 1989).

Research from the organizational training domain is somewhat more extensive than in the educational domain, but perhaps the main difference in samples is that, whereas one can assume that many or most adult students in educational programs are participating because of a high level of interest in the topic domain, such an assumption is not often warranted in the case of industrial training. That is, variability in terms of endorsement or resistance to new technology or new procedures in the workplace is anecdotally ubiquitous (e.g., when text processing was introduced to managers in close temporal proximity to the elimination of typing pools from the organization). Such resistance to new technology is also generally supported empirically as well (e.g., see Morris, Venkatesh, & Ackerman, 2005). Many organizations often provide numerous opportunities for *voluntary* acquisition of new knowledge and skills to employees, but there is substantial variation within age groups and also substantial differences between younger and older workers in terms of interest and enrollment patterns. Older adults tend to express less interest in such opportunities, and enroll less frequently than younger adults. The explanations for such differences involve multiple influences, such as differences between age groups in terms of self-efficacy for success, perceived difficulty, evaluation apprehension, and even managerial decisions based on negative stereotypes of the ability of older workers to acquire new knowledge (e.g., see Rosen & Jerdee, 1976).

With the above caveats in mind, a meta-analysis of training studies for older and younger adults by Kubeck, Delp, Haslett, and McDaniel (1996) indicated that there is a consistent pattern of lower levels of knowledge and skill mastered among older adults when compared with younger adults in the context of training ("the mean correlation between age and training mastery was $r = -.26$" [p. 95]). Although this correlation may look relatively small, it is important to note that the implication of this correlation is that advancing age is associated with increasingly poor performance on training mastery tasks, so that when young and older adults are compared in terms of mean performance, the effect size of the difference between the two groups is $d = .88$, which is a large effect (Cohen, 1988). In addition, the Kubeck et al. meta-analysis indicated that it takes longer for older adults to complete the same training than younger adults ($r = .42$).

RETAINED KNOWLEDGE AND AGING

The evaluation of the effects of aging on retained knowledge is much more difficult, if not occasionally impossible, in comparison to the study of the association between age and new learning. The reasons for this difficulty are relatively straightforward. First, there is typically a lack of experimental control over the initial learning of a particular body of declarative knowledge or set of procedural skills. Whether or not an individual learns how to play the piano at age 4, learns how to ride a bicycle at age 6, or learns Spanish at age 12 is not traditionally something that can be decided by random assignment to an experimental or control condition. Furthermore, much of the kinds of knowledge that adults have previously acquired is a function of some unknown combination of formal (e.g., school) instruction and informal influences (e.g., self-study, use over the course of development). Without random assignment to conditions of learning and conditions of practice after learning, it is impossible to directly ascertain the causal influences of various age-related factors on knowledge retention at adulthood.

The investigator who wants to evaluate the relationship between aging and retained knowledge is left with examining the products of "nature's experiments" (Cronbach, 1957), that is, by examining correlations between variables that he or she has no control over. In addition, unless objective records of prior learning are available (such as enrollment data and course curricula specifications, or prior tests of achievement), it is difficult to determine what the individual's level of initial knowledge acquisition was. Retrospective reports by adults for knowledge obtained in childhood or adolescence are likely to be subject to many different influences that serve to distort or obscure the key information, even when the individual could be expected to be able to remember when and where specific knowledge was acquired. For example, for semantic memory (e.g., vocabulary), individuals rarely have any accurate memory trace for when and where the knowledge was obtained (e.g., see Tulving, 1989). Other kinds of knowledge may have boundary conditions, such as knowledge of current events or recent advances in science, medicine, and technology, simply because the "knowledge" did not exist prior to a specific date or range of dates. Thus, while a currently living adult might have acquired knowledge of Isaac Newton's principles of gravity at any age, no person could have acquired knowledge about Sputnik or that Neil Armstrong walked on the moon until those events had actually happened.

One potential solution to this difficulty would be to provide arbitrary facts or train a novel sequence of movements to individuals and then test them for retention after some long period of time. If the facts or sequences have no connection to anything in the real world, one can presume that only internal processes (such as an individual's reflection on the prior learning) will influence the later tests of retention. Such an approach might be preferred to the examination of knowledge and skills that are relevant to real-world activities, but it is important to note that this strategy does not remove the potential influences of "knowing with" and the inherent aspects of general transfer. As noted by Ferguson (1956), only the newborn infant can be considered to be engaged in new learning; everyone else's performance on a learning task is determined to a greater or lesser degree by transfer of prior knowledge and skills. Therefore, even in the learning of arbitrary facts in a laboratory task, prior knowledge (of language comprehension, strategy development and application, etc.) is likely to play a transfer role in both initial learning and later knowledge retention performance.

To further complicate matters, it is impossible to simultaneously equalize initial learning levels and amount of practice across learners of different ability levels, because different learners will require different amounts of practice to reach the same asymptotic levels of performance (if indeed all learners do eventually achieve such performance—see Ruch, 1936). Experimenters are faced with either having to allow for different initial levels of learning (which most certainly will affect level of later recall) or different amounts of practice (and excluding learners who do not reach an acceptable level of performance), which similarly may result in different recall levels. Neither approach is particularly attractive, in that results of later knowledge assessments cannot yield unambiguous results. A pessimistic view is that any of these studies will be overly ambiguous in terms of informing one about the effects of aging on knowledge. But, the view taken here is that as long as we are cognizant of these potential threats to validity or generalizability, it may be possible to seek convergence of findings from these different approaches.

STABILITY AND CHANGE IN RETAINED DECLARATIVE KNOWLEDGE DURING AGING

General Semantic Knowledge Assessed with Intelligence Tests

Owens (1953)

The first longitudinal study of adult intelligence over an extended period of time was conducted by Owens (1953). A group of men who had completed the Army Alpha test in 1919 as an entrance examination at Iowa State College (now Iowa State University) when they were on average 19 years old were re-examined on the same test in 1950, 31 years after the initial test. Sixty-five percent of the total population of former students were tested in 1950, which means that one cannot provide a certainty to the generalization of the results. That is, as with any longitudinal study with some attrition over time, the generalizability of the results is partly predicated on whether the causes for attrition are not in some way correlated with the variables being measured. With that qualification in mind, the results of this study are striking, especially in the context of conclusions from cross-sectional studies about knowledge and aging. That is, after 31 years, the average overall intelligence score of these individuals actually increased. Of particular relevance to the current concerns, the largest increase in subtest performance was on Test 8 (Information), with the overall gain in performance estimated to be nearly a one standard deviation in mean improvement. Test 4 (Synonym/Antonym) showed a significant, but smaller increase of about one half of a standard deviation in mean improvement. One variable that correlated significantly with the relative gains in performance on these tests was the number of hobbies and recreational activities reported by the participants. Those participants with a greater number of hobbies showed substantially greater gain in performance on the Information and Synonym/Antonym tests.

Schaie—Seattle Longitudinal Study

Schaie started his investigation with a cross-sectional study of intellectual abilities in 1956, and expanded the study to include longitudinal retesting of the original sample, along with new cohort groups in the decades that followed (for comprehensive reviews, see Schaie, 1996a, 1996b, 2005). This research program provides perhaps the most comprehensive joint examination of cohort differences and age-related changes over several waves of retesting (7-year intervals) in intellectual abilities during adulthood. In terms of knowledge and aging issues, like most studies of intellectual abilities, most of the information available is through intelligence scales of verbal ability (e.g., synonym/antonym and vocabulary). Schaie has noted that there are substantial age cohort differences in average performance on such tests, which undoubtedly indicates that previous cross-sectional studies provide a somewhat skewed notion of adult declines in general vocabulary knowledge with increased age (or, in contrast, may underestimate any improvements in such knowledge with increasing age). In 1996 Schaie reported that the longitudinal data indicate that scores on the synonym/antonym test increase with age, reaching a maximum performance around age 60, followed by an accelerating decline through the seventies and eighties. After adjusting for cohort differences, the peak performance for this kind of general verbal knowledge is still around age 60, but the decline with increasing age is somewhat attenuated (e.g., the average adult at age 73 would be expected to perform as well as the average adult at age 25, ceteris paribus). Changes in the battery of tests and additional data have led Schaie (2005) to conclude that significant declines in the verbal memory abilities may not occur until somewhat later (i.e., age 74).

Other Sources of Data on Retained Knowledge

In an extensive series of studies starting in the 1970s, Bahrick and his colleagues have provided important evidence on the preservation of declarative knowledge over long periods of time. In an early study of name and face recognition for high-school classmates, Bahrick, Bahrick, and Wittlinger (1974) noted that even at 35 years after graduation, participants were able to correctly recognize 90% of their high-school classmates, and that women tend to perform better on such tests than men.

In a study of retention of Spanish language learned during high school and college, Bahrick (1984) tested a sample of 773 participants from 1 to 50 years after they completed Spanish language instruction. The results indicated that although a substantial amount of declarative knowledge is lost in the first 6 years after instruction is completed, there is little further decline in knowledge until about 25 years after the instruction is completed. Bahrick refers to knowledge maintained over these long periods of time as existing in a sort of "permastore." The degree of knowledge retained appears to be a function of the length of initial instruction (more is better) and the achievement level at initial instruction (students with "A" grades recall much more than students with a "C" grade). In fact, students with poor grades appear to retain relatively little of their initial knowledge after extended periods of time, perhaps indicating the long-term perils of incomplete initial learning.

In a study of mathematical knowledge, Bahrick and Hall (1991) administered algebra or geometry tests to 1726 participants from 19 to 84 years of age. Individuals who originally completed only the initial algebra and geometry courses evidenced a rapid decline in retained knowledge, but those individuals who had several additional math courses (e.g., calculus) beyond the initial instruction retained good performance even with retention intervals as long as 50 years.

In a recent study of 829 adults between the ages of 35 and 80 (at initial testing), Rönnlund, Nyberg, and Bäckman (2005) administered a set of brief episodic memory tests (involving the retention of new declarative knowledge) and semantic memory tests (general knowledge, vocabulary, and fluency). After a 5-year delay, the tests were readministered to the same sample, along with a control group (to provide an assessment of practice effects). The general findings from these results were that cross-sectional comparisons tended to show a decline in both general knowledge and episodic memory performance, starting around age 50 and age 40, respectively. However, the estimated changes in performance for the longitudinal comparisons, after factoring in practice effects, suggest that: (a) general declarative knowledge (semantic memory) increases until about age 60, and then slowly declines; (b) episodic memory tends to be stable up to about age 50–60 and then shows a somewhat steeper decline than general knowledge with increasing age.

STABILITY AND CHANGE IN RETAINED PROCEDURAL KNOWLEDGE DURING AGING

Adults typically have a large repertoire of procedural skills, ranging from those that are performed almost every day (e.g., putting on one's socks and shoes) to those that may have been learned early in life, but may not be performed over long periods of time (e.g., riding a bicycle). Perhaps partly because casual introspection indicates that many of these skills are either retained over long periods of time, or are very quickly reacquired (e.g., getting on the bicycle after a 20-year period of time), there are far fewer investigations of retained procedural knowledge and aging than there are of investigations of declarative knowledge. As with other kinds of knowledge, however, it is difficult for an investigator to ascertain how well the initial procedural skills were performed during original learning, except in a small number of situations. For example when there is some kind of permanent record of prior execution of procedural skills, it is possible to make a relatively objective comparison of skill retention. One might compare the technical execution of a famous musician by comparing his or her performance of a piece of music recorded at an early period of the career, and then again later in life. Of course, such a comparison would be confounded by whatever new learning has taken place over the course of the individual's career, such as differences in artistic interpretation, or the acquisition of new skills. Few records exist that would allow a comparison between an individual's musical performance at age 20 and again at age 60, without any intervening practice.

Other procedural skills are highly integrated with physical abilities. Thus, examining the batting performance of a professional baseball player 10 years after retiring would undoubtedly indicate substantial loss of skill, but such a loss would not be clearly interpretable as an indication of poor retention of procedural knowledge, even though that may be a partial determinant of lower performance levels. The loss of perceptual speed abilities with increasing adult age (e.g., see Salthouse, 1996) would exclude an unambiguous interpretation of speeded procedural knowledge retention over the course of adult aging. These considerations ultimately lead to a focus of procedural knowledge retention in the context of well-practiced and familiar tasks, such as procedural tasks of everyday activities (e.g., cooking, dressing, and so on), or tasks that are occupationally (e.g., surgery, watch repair) or avocationally specific (e.g., typewriting or playing bridge) to particular individuals.

There is an additional issue that makes retention of declarative and procedural knowledge difficult to compare. That is, when one attempts to assess declarative knowledge retention, either recall or recognition approaches may be used. Many if not most studies of retained declarative knowledge use one of these forms (e.g., multiple choice questions on a vocabulary test). For procedural knowledge, reproduction (recall) is almost universally used as an assessment technique (e.g., see discussion by Annett, 1979). With the exception of discrete motor tasks, it is also critical to evaluate the entire sequence of retained procedural knowledge. Partly for this reason, an additional tool for assessing retained procedural knowledge is to assess both initial performance after a period of nonuse, but also the number of retraining trials needed to achieve performance levels equivalent to the final training level. The "savings" in retraining (that is, the comparison between the number of trials to criterion in training and the number of trials to criterion in retraining) are often used as an index of the efficacy of retained procedural knowledge.

Early Studies

Perhaps the first study of long-term retention of procedural knowledge was reported by Swift (1905, 1910). Swift trained himself in the task of "tossing two balls with one hand, one ball being caught and thrown while the other was in the air" (Swift, 1910, p. 17). Initial training included 42 daily sessions of practice. Five monthly tests were made after initial training, and an additional test was made 1.5 years after the last monthly test. A final retention and retraining sequence was completed 6 years after the initial training. At the start of the retention and retraining, performance was nearly equivalent to the first trial of initial training. However, relearning of the sequence was quite rapid. By the seventh retraining session, he performed at a level equivalent to 37 days of initial practice. At the tenth retraining session, he performed as well as he had at the final initial training session (session 42). Similar results were obtained with typewriting skills, although the retention interval was only 1 year (Swift, 1906), and by Book (1908) who noted that performance on the retention test after 1 year of nonuse was equivalent to performance at the end of initial practice.

In another case study of typewriting retention, Hill acquired typewriting skills over the course of 5 months of daily practice (Hill, Rejall, & Thorndike, 1913). He later assessed his retained procedural knowledge after a 25-year period of nonuse (Hill, 1934), and then again 50 years after the initial training (Hill, 1957), when the author/subject was 80 years old. In the first 25-year retention test, he performed at a level equivalent to that which had been achieved after 27 days of initial practice. In the 50-year retention test, it took him only 8 days of retraining to reach the same level of performance.

In these and other studies of much shorter duration, it appears that procedural knowledge is not fully retained during the course of aging (i.e., in the sense that performance levels at initial retention trials are not identical to the last initial practice trial performance), but that clearly *something* is retained to a remarkable degree.

More Recent Reviews and Studies

Adams (1964) in a seminal review of the literature on motor skills lamented the fact that there were few studies that concerned the retention of motor skills (procedural knowledge) over long periods of time. At the time, the existing literature on motor skills retention was almost exclusively in the domain of military studies of skills involved in tasks like tracking or assembling machine guns. Furthermore, retention intervals were relatively brief (on the order of days), and there were no studies that examined retention beyond 1 year of nonuse of the skill. With these qualifications in mind, Adams reported that the majority of investigations indicated two general findings. First, motor skill retention tended to be quite good, on average—especially when the skills were continuous, rather than discrete. Second, level of performance at retention was highly correlated with level of skill at the conclusion of initial training.

A more recent review of the literature on long-term retention of procedural skills (Farr, 1987) noted that most of the studies conducted in the two decades after the Adams review were also performed in a military context, and the periods of nonuse of the skills were still quite modest in length. As such, the more recent studies provide few clues for evaluating the forgetting curves of procedural skills over a time period that would be relevant to adult aging concerns. Both Adams (1987) and Farr (1987) indicated that one might get the "impression that long-term motor retention is a domain empty of productive ideas in which only a little research is done" (Adams, 1987, pp. 64–65). The consensus opinion from the literature is that "forgetting increases as a positive function of the retention interval, overlearning is beneficial for retention, relearning after a retention interval is more rapid than the original learning, discrete procedural responses are forgotten more readily than continuous motor skills" (p. 65). The final point is a significant aspect of procedural knowledge that deserves special attention for the study of aging and knowledge retention concerns. That is, while discrete procedural knowledge (e.g., pressing an arbitrary sequence of buttons) appears to decay substantially even over brief retention intervals (at a rate similar to the decay of lists of meaningless verbal/ declarative material; e.g., see Neumann & Ammons, 1957), continuous procedural knowledge appears to be comparatively more robust after a period of nonuse.

In the context of real-world procedural knowledge, continuous procedural knowledge is a more central concern than arbitrary discrete procedural knowledge. The issue is that continuous procedural knowledge is typically made up of a sequence of actions, and that retention of the sequence may be sensitive to the fact that after the first action in the sequence, subsequent actions are linked (that is, the sequence is "chained" such that the successful performance of one action will increase the likelihood of successful performance of subsequent actions). The prototypical example for this kind of procedural knowledge is a piece of music. As the individual performs the piece, each note or sequence of notes is linked in memory. In addition to specific procedural memory, there is also the more general issue of constraints in the actions to be performed. That is, in most real-world tasks, the sequences of actions involved in the procedural skill are not equally likely, but are more or less constrained by the nature of the task. This particular aspect of procedural knowledge is especially salient. For example, one cannot drive off in a car without starting the engine; one cannot (or should not) suture the patient until the repair of the arteries is completed; and the cook who turns off the stove before cooking the items in the pot is likely to end up with a less than satisfying outcome. Scripts or schemas are certainly part of the knowledge structure underlying such skills, but these sequences may be represented as entirely procedural, entirely declarative, or some combination of the two.

An excellent example of continuous procedural knowledge learning and retention with a sample that had a wide range of ages (18 to 95) at initial acquisition was reported by Smith, Walton, Loveland, Umberger, Kryscio, and Gash (2005). In this study, subjects were trained to retrieve steel nuts from four different objects, by reaching through a plexiglass portal. Initial training involved five trials with each of the four stimuli, repeated with each hand. After a 2-year retention interval, the motor tasks were repeated. Although older subjects performed the task much more slowly at initial training than the younger adult subjects, at retention they performed the task just as well (in fact slightly faster) as they did at the last training trial 2 years before. These results are all the more remarkable in that fine motor coordination and dexterity tend to show deterioration in adults over the age of 65 (e.g., see Carmeli, Patish, & Coleman, 2003).

KNOWING WITH/TACIT KNOWLEDGE

As discussed earlier, there is quite an extensive body of research on declarative knowledge and aging, but far less research on procedural knowledge and aging. For the third kind of knowledge, there is almost no direct research on the topic. In contrast, there is a handful of studies that purport to assess some aspects of tacit knowledge or implicit knowledge in adults, and a few that consider the relationship between these aspects of knowledge and aging. A brief review of these research programs is provided here, to illustrate both the difficulties of attempting to assess tacit knowledge, and to consider what is yet not known about the topic.

The first instantiation of a test of practical intelligence (i.e., items that tap tasks that are "indigenous" to adults) was created by Demming and Pressey (1957). In their study, items that related to everyday activities (e.g., using a telephone directory, getting professional assistance, etc.) were administered to a sample of individuals from 15 years of age to older adults in "golden age" clubs. Although the samples were by no means randomly selected across the age groups, the general pattern of results indicated that the older groups showed substantially higher average scores on these test items, in comparison to young adult groups. The general essence of this work is that when questions related to tacit know-ledge about the everyday world are administered to adults of varying ages, older adults (at least up to age 40 or 50) perform better, on average, than young adults. More recent investigations of tacit knowledge involve research programs by Sternberg and his colleagues, and by Baltes and his colleagues. Each is reviewed below.

In Sternberg's triarchic theory of intelligence (e.g., Sternberg, 1985), one domain is called "practical intelligence" and it has become loosely linked to a set of tacit knowledge tests (e.g., see Wagner, 1987; Wagner & Sternberg, 1985). These tests are generally domain specific (e.g., managers, professors), and involve scenarios for qualitative problem solving in situations that arise in those domains. Although these tests have shown some limited promise for predicting criterion-related performance (e.g., see Sternberg, Wagner, Williams, & Horvath, 1995 for a review), the construct validity of these tests for assessing something unrelated to domain-specific declarative knowledge has yet to be demonstrated (also see Jensen, 1993, Schmidt & Hunter, 1993 for critical comments). One study has examined age-related differences on the Tacit Knowledge for Managers (Colonia-Willner, 1998). In a study of bank managers, Colonia-Willner found negative correlations between age and performance on traditional reasoning tests, but smaller or negligible correlations between age and performance on the test of management tacit knowledge, suggesting that this aspect of domain-specific tacit knowledge may have an age-related pattern of growth and decline that differs from the more traditional g_f-related abilities. These results are consistent with other measures of domain knowledge and aging (see below), but there is no evidence reported to date that establishes whether there are substantive differences between tacit knowledge and the other two kinds of knowledge.

In the work by Baltes and his colleagues on the construct of "wisdom" (e.g., see Baltes & Staudinger, 2000, for a review), criterion tasks are open-ended, in contrast to the multiple-choice questions used in the tacit knowledge measures of Wagner and Sternberg. Typically, an individual is given a scenario and a question about life planning (e.g., see Baltes & Staudinger, 1993; Smith & Baltes, 1990; Staudinger, Smith, & Baltes, 1992). The assigned task is to prepare an action plan recommendation for the individual described in the scenario. In a series of studies, these researchers have found that some aspects of wisdom are well preserved in adults up to relatively advanced age (e.g., to age 75—see Baltes & Staudinger, 2000). However, the construct of wisdom as represented in this framework is such that it is fundamentally dependent on an extensive foundation of declarative and procedural knowledge related to life issues. That is, wisdom is construed to be something that can only exist if the individual already has a body of relevant knowledge from the other two domains. In this context, one would expect that especially middle-aged adults would have an advantage over younger adults on such tasks, something that is not generally found in these studies. One reason for this apparent discrepancy is that the problems posed as wisdom questions involve a nontrivial amount of new information processing, rather than the recall of previous solutions to problems encountered in the past (such as comprehension of the problem, delineating the range of possible solutions, exploring the consequences of various options—generally in domains where the individual cannot be expected to have had any domain-specific experience). As such, there may be a tradeoff between age-related decrements in abstract reasoning abilities and age-related increments in foundation declarative and procedural knowledge.

Ultimately, it may be that a new operationalization of tacit knowledge is needed. The problem is to spell out what tacit knowledge is, and to better distinguish tacit knowledge from declarative and procedural knowledge. Although it seems straightforward to state that tacit knowledge represents the general or domain-specific tools that can be used for problem solving, outside of explicit declarative and procedural knowledge, it is not clear how one can separate, for example, knowledge of language (declarative knowledge) from the internal construction of a problem representation and the planning of a solution. In addition, it will also be necessary to establish a new assessment paradigm needed to assess tacit knowledge or knowing with than is represented by current and previous efforts. The ideal assessment of tacit knowledge must somehow establish both convergent and discriminant validity (with other tacit knowledge measures, with other measures of declarative and procedural knowledge, and with traditional intellectual abilities) to provide for a clear evaluation of age-related differences. In the larger context of knowledge and aging research, however, these are still early days, and it might be expected that further research along the lines discussed above will be illuminating in the determination of how tacit knowledge/knowing with changes over the course of adult development and aging.

INDIVIDUAL DIFFERENCES

To this point, the main focus of this chapter has been on general or average changes with age in adult knowledge acquisition and knowledge retention. It is important to note that large individual differences are found in these domains. Even when there are large differences between mean knowledge retention of 20 year olds and 70 year olds, the distributions of the two groups almost always show some overlap. That is, some 20 year olds perform worse than the average 70 year old, and some 70 year olds perform better than the average 20 year old. There are several key constructs that account for some of the within and between age group differences, and these will be explored below, in the context of theory and empirical evidence.

Determinants of Individual Differences in Knowledge—Theory

In terms of development of knowledge structures in adulthood, one important theoretical perspective was proposed by Cattell (1971) and has been referred to as the "Investment Theory." The origins of the theory appear to lie with earlier psychologists and their attempts to merge Spearman's ideas of g with conative (or motivational) constructs (e.g., Alexander, 1935; Webb, 1915). McDougall (1933), for example, made a case for the importance of the linkage between cognitive (ability) and conative determinants of knowledge acquired by the individual, based on both human and animal studies. Similarly, Hayes (1962) noted that, even with identical ability levels, individuals who devote more time to intellectual activities will be more likely to acquire larger vocabularies and "a larger store of linguistically transmitted information" than those individuals who are less oriented toward reading and more oriented towards other activities (Hayes, 1962, p. 302). Where McDougall argued for a relatively equal balance of cognitive and conative processes in intellectual attainment, Hayes argued that motivational and experiential differences between individuals are perhaps even more important than the individual's initial intellectual endowment. Ultimately, each of these researchers was proposing that an individual's orientation to, and investment of, effort towards or away from knowledge acquisition are of critical importance in determining level of knowledge attained.

Cattell's (1971) Investment Theory builds on these earlier perspectives and provides a general outline of the kinds of constructs that determine whether fluid intellectual abilities are devoted to or away from acquisition of crystallized intellectual knowledge. The theory (shown in Figure 9.2) illustrates that the prior investment of fluid intelligence (g_f), determined by variables of Time, Interests, and Memory, will in turn determine individual differences in crystallized intelligence (g_c). Current levels of g_c, along with current interests and memory, will in turn determine individual differences in scholastic achievement measures, which represent assessments of declarative and procedural knowledge. Cattell also proposed that various personality constructs will have positive influences on such knowledge-related variables as school achievement (e.g., Need Achievement, Constructiveness, and Protectiveness), while others will be negatively correlated with such knowledge variables (e.g., Pugnacity, Narcissism; see p. 389), and that individual differences in motivation will also account for a significant amount of school achievement variance. However, the data presented by Cattell (1971) were portrayed as mainly

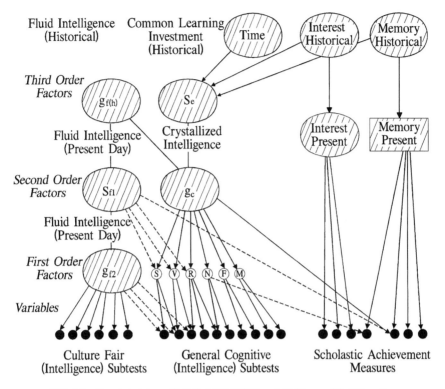

FIG. 9.2. Reprinted from Cattell (1971/1987), p. 146, Figure 6.3. "Hypothesized causal action in the investment theory." Reprinted by permission. Copyright 1971 Houghton Mifflin.

suggestive rather than well established, given the paucity of empirical studies on which these points were made.

Ackerman's (1996) theory of the individual differences determinants of adult intellectual development takes these earlier approaches as the starting point for an investment framework to individual differences in knowledge across the adult lifespan. It especially draws on Cattell's proposal that g_c grows out of the investment of g_f, and that nonability constructs provide the direction and level of cognitive investment in acquiring and maintaining knowledge. The theory also considers an important aspect of Cattell's theory of g_c, in that after adolescence crystallized knowledge becomes increasingly differentiated, such that traditional measures of child or young adult g_c (e.g., vocabulary and general information) become increasingly distinct from the large array of different knowledge structures that are acquired through academic, occupational, or avocational investment. (As Cattell (1957) noted, assessments of adult g_c must either focus mainly on "historical g_c"—which is knowledge that was acquired at a relatively early phase of development, when one can reasonably assume that most individuals are well exposed to a body of general knowledge and vocabulary), or one can focus on "present g_c"—which for adults would mean as many different knowledge tests as there are different domains of knowledge (e.g., physics, art, law, psychology, music, math, etc.)

Figure 9.3 illustrates the hypothesized pattern of growth and decline of g_f, g_c, and two sources of domain knowledge—occupational and avocational (e.g., hobbies) across the adult lifespan. The patterns of growth and decline for g_f and g_c are based on Horn's (1965) instantiation of the Cattell theory. The key aspect of this pattern is that although g_c increases with age during much of adulthood, the gains in g_c do not fully balance the losses in g_f with increasing age. Including occupational and avocational knowledge in an overall representation of adult intelligence—that is, giving the adults credit for *what they know* outside of broad vocabulary and general cultural knowledge–might suggest that middle-aged adults are in fact more intelligent than younger adults.

Ackerman's theory diverges from these earlier approaches in that it

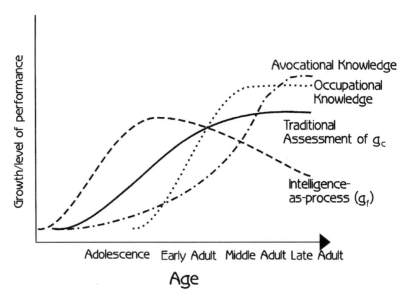

FIG. 9.3. Hypothetical growth/level of performance curves across the adult life span, for intelligence-as-process, traditional measures of g_c (crystallized intelligence), occupational knowledge, and avocational knowledge. (Intelligence-as-process [g_f] and g_c modeled after Horn [1965], Figure 1, p. 185.)

provides for a relatively small set of facilitative and impeding influences, and it attempts to map these influences to differentiated knowledge structures. Ackerman's approach also differs from the traditional approach to assessment of g_c in that it attempts to address "present g_c" in addition to the traditional forms of "historical g_c." Thus, the approach is especially suitable for the examination of adult intellectual development, in contrast to other research that focuses only on what the individual has retained from early experiences or general exposure to the dominant culture. This theory, illustrated in Figure 9.4, is called PPIK for intelligence-as-Process, Personality, Interests, leading to intelligence-as-Knowledge. Intelligence-as-process is similar to Cattell's g_f, except it represents an attempt to more fully separate the basic processes of intellect (e.g., short-term and working memory, speed of encoding, processing information, and executing responses) from content (e.g., general problem-solving strategies, aspects of "knowing with," etc.). The key constructs of personality and interests that relate to orientation towards or away from acquiring and maintaining

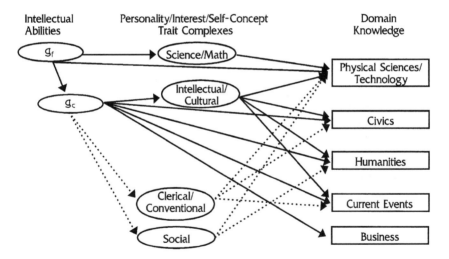

FIG. 9.4. Illustration of constructs and influences in the PPIK theory (Ackerman, 1996). g_f (fluid intelligence) represents "intelligence-as-process;" g_c = crystallized intelligence; Trait complexes (including: personality, interests, self-concept, ability) from Ackerman and Heggestad (1997). Positive and negative influences derived from the theory and supported by prior empirical data (Ackerman, 2000; Ackerman & Rolfhus, 1999; Beier & Ackerman, 2001; Rolfhus & Ackerman, 1999). Note: "Negative influences" mean that lower levels of one construct (e.g., g_c) lead to higher levels of the other construct (e.g., Clerical/Conventional trait complex). From Ackerman, Beier, and Bowen (2002). Copyright American Psychological Association. Reprinted by permission.

knowledge are based on a large scale meta-analysis and review of personality–interest–ability relations (Ackerman & Heggestad, 1997). This
review indicated that there is sufficient commonality among affective and
conative traits to allow for a small set of "trait complexes" that, in turn,
appear to jointly determine direction and level of effort towards intellectual activities. Ackerman and Heggestad (1997) proposed the existence
of four trait complexes, called Social, Clerical/Conventional, Intellectual/
Cultural, and Math/Science. These trait complexes and their constituent
traits are shown in Figure 9.5.

Empirical Studies of Age and Individual Difference Determinants of Domain Knowledge

In a series of studies, Ackerman and his colleagues have investigated both
the nature of age-related differences in levels of domain knowledge and
the tenets of the PPIK framework in delineating the ability and nonability

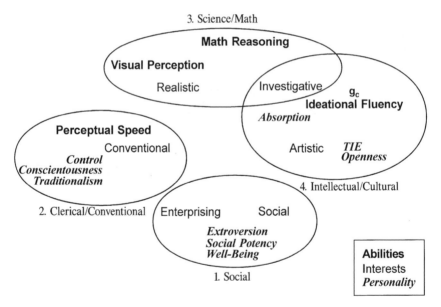

FIG. 9.5. Trait complexes, including abilities, interests, and personality
traits, showing positive commonalities. Shown are: (1) Social, (2) Clerical/
Conventional, (3) Science/Math, (4) Intellectual/Cultural trait complexes.
Ability traits = bold; Interests = Roman font; Personality traits = Italic font.
(Figure 7 on p. 239 from Ackerman and Heggestad, 1997, "Intelligence,
personality, and interests: Evidence for overlapping traits." *Psychological
Bulletin, 121,* 219–245). Copyright American Psychological Association.
Reprinted by permission.

determinants of domain knowledge. First, a series of domain knowledge tests were created that covered a range from very low levels of knowledge to knowledge equivalent to the content of a first-year college sequence (Rolfhus & Ackerman, 1999). The tests were administered to young (age 18–27) and middle-aged (30–59) adult university students. Ackerman and Rolfhus (1999) found that the average performance of the middle-aged adults on 19 of 20 knowledge domains exceeded that of the younger adults. Figure 9.6 shows the mean differences between the two groups in term of Cohen's d effect sizes. The overall advantage to middle-aged adults was highest in humanities knowledge domains (e.g., Literature, Art, Music) and Civics (e.g., US Government, US History). Smaller, but still medium-to-large effect size differences were found favoring middle-aged adults for several social and physical sciences domains (e.g.,

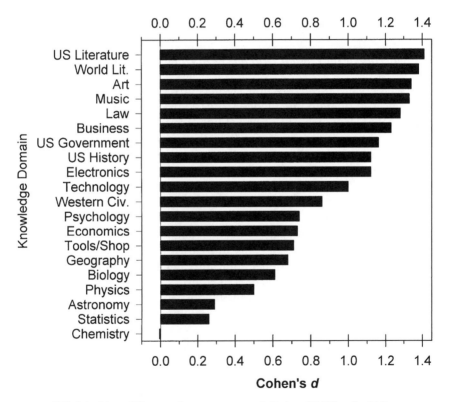

FIG. 9.6. Mean differences between young adults (age 18–27) and middle-aged adults (age 30–59) on domain knowledge scores, expressed in terms of Cohen's d. (A d score of 1.0 indicates that the middle-aged group mean performance exceeded that of the young adult group by 1 standard deviation unit.) Based on data reported in Ackerman and Rolfhus (1999).

Psychology, Biology, Geography). The only knowledge domain that showed negligible differences between the younger and older groups was Chemistry. A follow-up study of similar domain knowledge tests was conducted with a group of adults who had all attained at least a BA/BS level of educational achievement (Ackerman, 2000). The study was conducted partly to eliminate educational achievement differences as a possible explanation for the differences between the younger and middle-aged groups on the various domain knowledge tests. In this study of 228 adults between the ages of 21 and 62, the pattern of positive correlations of age with level of domain knowledge was largely replicated. Older adults tended to perform better on most of the knowledge tests, except for those in the domain of physical sciences (e.g., Chemistry, Physics). It is important to note that the advantage of older adults on domain knowledge tests was found, *even though age correlations with g_f were negative ($r = -0.39$) and correlations with g_c were positive ($r = .14$), but not large enough to offset the negative correlations with g_f.*

Prediction of Individual Differences in Domain Knowledge

g_f scores were positively and significantly correlated with individual differences in domain knowledge scores across the twenty or so domains investigated. However, the correlations between g_c and domain knowledge scores were mostly larger than they were for g_f—again with the exception of the physical sciences domain, where older adults were at an overall disadvantage compared with younger adults (Ackerman, 2000; Ackerman & Rolfhus, 1999). Assessment of nonability traits in these studies also provided for an examination of the trait complex determinants of individual differences in domain knowledge. First, it should be noted that for the three trait complexes under investigation—Science/Math, Intellectual/Cultural, and Social—only individual differences in the Science/Math trait complex correlated significantly negatively with age ($r = -.17$). Figure 9.7 shows the patterns of trait complex correlations with composites of domain knowledge tests in the areas of Physical Science, Civics, Humanities, and Business. As the figure illustrates, both the Science/Math and Intellectual/Cultural trait complexes are facilitative or supportive of domain knowledge. The Science/Math trait complex was most highly positively associated with knowledge in the physical sciences, and the Intellectual/Cultural trait complex was most highly associated with Humanities domain knowledge. In contrast, individuals who scored high on the Social trait complex performed less well on all of the knowledge domains assessed, suggesting that the trait complex represents an impeding factor for acquisition and retention of knowledge, especially for academically related domains. The PPIK approach to adult intellectual

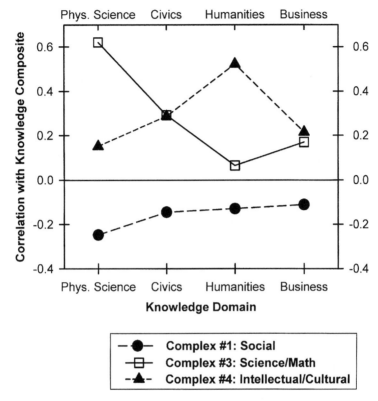

FIG. 9.7. Correlations between trait complex scores and domain knowledge composites of Physical Sciences (e.g., Physics, Chemistry, Astronomy), Civics (US Government, US History, Economics), Humanities (US Literature, Art, Music), and Business (Business/Management, Law). From data reported in Ackerman (2000).

development, which includes process (g_f), traditional (historical) g_c, personality, and interest trait complexes, provided an effective prediction of individual differences in domain knowledge. Amount of total variance accounted for by these variables ranged from 31% in Business domain knowledge to 63% in Humanities domain knowledge. Moreover, after accounting for individual differences in these key predictor variables, age of respondent accounted for almost no additional variance (0–3%) in domain knowledge scores, which suggests that age in and of itself is not a particularly important determinant of individual differences in domain knowledge, once the other key variables are taken into account (at least within a range of ages from 18 to 62).

The key findings from these studies were as follows: (1) middle-aged adults have higher levels of domain knowledge across a variety of domains, compared to younger adults; (2) even though older adults had lower g_f scores on average compared to younger adults, g_f did not appear to be nearly as important a determinant of domain knowledge, compared to g_c, except in the physical sciences; (3) nonability traits and trait complexes made up of correlated constructs provided evidence for facilitative and impeding influences on the level of performance on domain knowledge tests. These trait complexes provide at least an historical indication of both direction of effort and intensity of effort in acquiring domain knowledge. It is important to note that one finding from these research studies that was not expected was a significant and substantial pattern of gender differences in domain knowledge test scores. That is, even though men and women tend to score similarly on the measures of g_f and g_c, there were large average differences in domain knowledge test performance, favoring men across nearly all of the domains investigated (e.g., see Ackerman, Beier, & Bowen, 2002). These gender differences in domain knowledge are largely concordant with larger samples of young adults (e.g., see Ackerman, 2002; Ackerman, Bowen, Beier, & Kanfer, 2001; College Board, 2000; Willingham & Cole, 1997).

Nonacademic Knowledge

The studies described above, with a few exceptions, could be considered to represent mostly declarative knowledge in academic domains, rather than the kinds of knowledge that one could be expected to acquire more or less outside schoolroom settings. To determine whether the PPIK approach can account for individual and age-related differences in domain knowledge beyond academic topics, two additional studies were conducted. The first study (Beier & Ackerman, 2001) considered the domain of current events knowledge, and it included tests that spanned the decades from the 1930s to the 1990s, and subareas of art/humanities, politics/economics, popular culture, and nature/science/technology. In this study of 153 adults between the ages of 20 and 69, age was again negatively correlated with g_f ($r = -.21$), marginally correlated with g_c ($r = .13$), but positively and significantly correlated with current events knowledge ($r = .36$). Older adults had higher levels of knowledge across all four current events domains, with the largest positive correlations for Politics/Economics ($r = .42$) and the smallest correlations for Art/Humanities ($r = .24$). Only very recent current events (those that took place in the 1990s) showed no significant advantage for older adults compared to younger adults.

Scores on g_c were substantially more highly correlated with overall current events knowledge ($r = .81$) than were scores on g_f ($r = .45$). In addition, key variables of personality and self-concept derived from the PPIK framework also showed significant correlations with levels of current events domain knowledge. The pattern of positive and negative correlations of these trait measures was largely consistent with those of previous studies. An interesting aspect of current events knowledge was that there was no overall significant relationship between gender and domain knowledge scores (though men performed somewhat better than women on the Politics/Economics and Science current events knowledge).

A similar pattern of results was obtained in a study of health-related domain knowledge (Beier & Ackerman, 2003). In this study, a battery of 10 domain knowledge tests that covered a range of health-related issues (e.g., common illnesses, childhood illnesses, mental health, nutrition, reproduction, etc.) was administered to 176 adults between the ages of 19 and 70. As with current events knowledge, older adults on average performed better than younger adults on nearly all of the health-related knowledge tests ($r = .28$). Also, g_c measures better predicted individual differences in health-related domain knowledge ($r = .84$) compared to g_f prediction of knowledge ($r = .49$). PPIK-based measures of personality, interest, and self-concept traits also accounted for a significant amount of variance in health-related knowledge. Together, these measures accounted for 82% of the individual differences variance in domain knowledge scores. Gender differences were also found on these measures, but in this case women performed, on average, better than men on nearly all of the health domain knowledge tests ($r = .28$). Nearly all of the variance attributable to age and gender, however, was explained by individual differences in the key cognitive ability and nonability predictors of domain knowledge.

Summary

Together this set of cross-sectional studies provides evidence for several observations about knowledge and aging. First, despite marked declines in g_f with increasing age, and only small increases in g_c with age, older adults tend to have higher levels of domain knowledge than younger adults. Second, even though g_f is predictive of domain knowledge, individual differences in g_c (e.g., vocabulary, general information, fluency) are much more influential in determining which adults will have higher levels of domain knowledge. Third, a small set of trait complexes (e.g., science/math, intellectual/cultural) appear to play a supportive role in orientation and level of effort allocated to acquisition of domain knowledge across a wide range of adult ages. Finally, examination of gender differences suggests that men are more likely to have higher levels of academically related domain knowledge, women are more likely to have higher levels of health-related domain knowledge, and there are few differences between genders when it comes to current events domain knowledge. These differences are clearly mediated by gender differences in the pattern of personality, self-concept, and interests.

INDIVIDUAL DIFFERENCE DETERMINANTS OF THE ACQUISITION OF NEW KNOWLEDGE

Recent examination of the PPIK framework in the context of acquiring real-world relevant knowledge (as opposed to disconnected sentences or memorizing letters and numbers) suggests that there is an important interplay between existing knowledge structures, abilities, and age. In a study of 199 adults between 19 and 68, Beier and Ackerman (2005) administered ability and existing domain knowledge tests prior to exposure to a constrained classroom instruction and self-study (of articles that ranged from nontechnical to technical levels) on topics of health (cardiovascular disease, CVD) and technology (xerography and duplicating). g_f and g_c provided substantial predictive validity for existing knowledge structures in the two topic domains (g_c was significantly more highly correlated with CVD knowledge, g_f and g_c were equivalent predictors for technology knowledge). Both classes of abilities increased in their prediction of domain knowledge after the constrained classroom instruction, and domain knowledge after a 3-day period of self-study. However, older adults were at more of a disadvantage when compared to young adults on the measure that assessed the information provided in the classroom, while there was no significant association between age and performance on the self-study materials. The implication of this study is that when faced with a knowledge acquisition task that taxes the information processing system (i.e., when the learner has no control over the rate of information provided), older adults have more difficulties, even when they have equal or higher levels of prior domain knowledge. In contrast, when the learner is allowed to process new information at his or her own pace, the disadvantage to older adults may be diminished or eliminated, even though there were no significant differences between quality or quantity of notes taken by the older and younger learners on the self-study materials. The relationship between age and domain knowledge after independent study is positive and significant, even when individual differences in g_c are statistically controlled ($r = .28$).

In a study of 141 adults aged from 18 to 69, Ackerman and Beier (2006) administered ability, nonability trait, and existing domain knowledge tests prior to a 1-week self-study of personal financial issues knowledge (e.g., financial planning, stocks, bonds, retirement plans, educational savings plans, etc.). Learners were provided with an audio CD with narration for a binder of associated PowerPoint handouts, and a set of 20 printed articles on various aspects of financial planning, insurance, retirement, credit, and so on. They were also provided a 1-week period to study the CD/PowerPoint materials, articles, and any other information on the topic they might wish to study. At the conclusion of the study period, the learners returned to the laboratory for extensive domain knowledge testing (using both multiple choice and open-ended scenario tests). As with previous investigations based on the PPIK framework, prediction of individual differences in domain knowledge (both prior to and after the opportunity for self-study) were well predicted by individual differences on g_f and g_c, with g_c having a significantly higher correlation ($r = .56$) than did g_f ($r = .40$). Together, these ability measures accounted for 32% of the total variance in the existing knowledge prior to self-study. Adding in variance associated with the facilitative and impeding trait complexes raised the amount of pretest variance accounted for to 43%.

After the 1-week self-study opportunity (i.e., the posttest), there was a significant increase in the amount of variance accounted for by g_f and g_c, with a larger gain in influence by g_f. Together the abilities accounted for 48% of the variance in posttest performance. Adding in trait complex influences raised the amount of posttest variance accounted for to 53%. Age was a significant positive predictor of pretest knowledge of financial issues ($r = .23$), but was a nonsignificant predictor of posttest knowledge of financial issues ($r = .16$), and gender was not a significant predictor of either pretest or posttest knowledge of financial issues.

These two studies represent a relatively early phase of research exploring the ability, nonability, and prior knowledge correlates of age differences in acquiring new real-world relevant knowledge. However, they point to some tentative conclusions, as follows. First, in terms of real-world knowledge, older adults may perform at least as well as younger adults, if not better overall. Second, prior knowledge gives a clear advantage to knowledge available after a period of either classroom or self-study. Third, g_f and g_c also play an important role in both prior knowledge and exposure to new knowledge. The evidence collected to date suggests that both g_f and g_c increase in their prediction of knowledge after new learning opportunities. Nonability trait complexes do appear to partially determine the direction and amount of cognitive effort and the level of acquired knowledge. Although the validation of the PPIK perspective is incomplete (areas of occupational knowledge, for example, have yet to be addressed), there is a substantial amount of convergent evidence that supports the general approach to understanding and accounting for age-related differences in domain knowledge.

CONCLUSIONS

Nearly a hundred years of investigation into the nature of knowledge and the relationship between knowledge and cognitive aging has provided important findings regarding what knowledge is likely to be retained during adult development, what knowledge is likely to be lost, and how difficult it is to acquire new knowledge at various adult ages. In general, the overall sense of the literature is that as far as declarative knowledge is concerned, the better the knowledge traces initially established during childhood, adolescence, or early adulthood, the more likely the knowledge will be retained well into middle age and perhaps beyond that. Individuals who only learn declarative knowledge well enough to "get by" a course final exam will undoubtedly be at a disadvantage when asked to recall material long after the original learning, compared to the more diligent learners who devote sufficient time and effort to acquire a deep and thorough knowledge in the original learning. Nonetheless, even though much declarative knowledge can be retained years or decades after original learning, there is most certainly a cost to nonuse of the knowledge. Lack of use of such knowledge acquired in early adulthood can lead to substantial decline in later retention (e.g., see the study by Schmidt et al., 2000 on retention of "street names from one's childhood neighborhood"). Thus, the cup of retained declarative knowledge could be considered half-full or half-empty, depending on one's level of optimism/pessimism.

In contrast, general information (such as vocabulary in one's main language and knowledge about the world) that is used and/or updated frequently throughout much of the adult lifespan shows much better resiliency through middle age and beyond, compared to declarative knowledge that once learned is rarely used (e.g., foreign language vocabulary or algebra knowledge). Research on these areas of declarative knowledge indicates that middle-aged adults tend to perform better than young adults, even taking declines in g_f with increasing adult age into account. On the one hand, most of these studies have been cross-sectional in design, so it is important to qualify this point in that one doesn't know how much day-to-day knowledge is lost along the road of adult development. On the other hand, the few studies that have been performed with longitudinal designs (e.g., Owens, 1953) do indicate that the identical tests of general knowledge and vocabulary show good retention across the decades.

Investigations of aging and procedural knowledge show generally similar results to those of aging and declarative knowledge. These studies indicate that meaningful motor skills (as opposed to less meaningful discrete motor sequences) are well retained over long periods of time. Even when they are not retained perfectly (as indeed is the case), relearning of procedural skills is much faster than initial learning. In addition to the few empirical studies, there are also substantial anecdotal reports of the notion that once one learns how to ride a bicycle, operate a typewriter, or acquire some other procedural skill, one doesn't readily forget the skill, even if one is a bit wobbly in the first few minutes of riding the bicycle or rusty on the typewriter after a decade or two of nonexposure to the task.

Research on the acquisition of *new* declarative and procedural knowledge as adult age progresses provides a less bright and rosy picture. Generally speaking, middle-aged and older adults have progressively greater difficulty acquiring new declarative knowledge and skills, compared to adolescents and younger adults. After training, older adults still typically perform such tasks at a lower level than younger adults. The salient qualification to this general finding is that both prior knowledge and individual differences in abilities and other trait determinants of prior knowledge also appear to play a role in determining who profits from exposure to new knowledge. Middle-aged adults who have higher levels of prior knowledge or high levels of facilitative personality and interest trait complexes tend to perform better than others of the same age group, and may perform better than the average young adult. The picture that has emerged from this body of research is that a history of positive cognitive investment to acquire knowledge is beneficial to the acquisition of knowledge in middle age and beyond, at least in a wide variety of domains, but a history of avoidance of such things will, ceteris paribus, result in poorer acquisition of new knowledge. The exception to middle-aged advantage is that expert levels of knowledge about domains that are highly dependent on g_f, such as math and some domains of the physical sciences, appear to mostly favor the young adult.

The literature on tacit knowledge or "knowing with" is too sparse to yield any overall sense of how this kind of knowledge is acquired, maintained, or lost over the course of adult development. What can be suggested at this point is that it appears that there may be a dissociation between the generalized knowledge of problem-solving strategies and task-specific tacit knowledge, which is used to solve relatively familiar real-world occupational or avocational problems. The former domain of tacit knowledge may be tied more closely to g_f-related abilities (such as reasoning and working memory), and as such seems to put the middle-aged or older adult at a disadvantage, compared to younger adults. The latter domain of tacit knowledge appears to be much more robust well into middle age and beyond, as it is tied more closely to g_c-related domain knowledge. The best evidence for the preservation of this kind of knowledge is probably illustrated by case studies of domain-specific problem solving of older experts.

In the final analysis, however, the preponderance of evidence on knowledge and cognitive aging indicates that once individuals reach age 70 and beyond, the more general effects of aging on cognitive processes are associated with a concomitant decline in retention of declarative knowledge. Similarly, the general effects of aging on physical capabilities (such as motor control, dexterity, and precision) will yield concomitant declines on the expression of procedural skills. Nonetheless, there are large individual differences within age groups that may mitigate these effects for some individuals.

CHALLENGES AND FUTURE DIRECTIONS

The brief survey of the literature on knowledge and aging presented here shows that even after several decades of empirical research and theory there is much that is not known about the topic. Most clearly, there is a lack of longitudinal data on the effects of aging on procedural knowledge and there is a lack of both cross-sectional and longitudinal data on the effects of aging and tacit knowledge. Even the domain of declarative knowledge, while there is much more longitudinal data, is not particularly robust, in terms of examining knowledge beyond the kinds of questions that relate to either general information, vocabulary, or information acquired in school. The few studies that address real-world knowledge (such as street names or recognition of classmates from school) suggest many positive aspects of knowledge retention, but there is much to learn about how declarative knowledge (especially that which is used on a relatively frequent basis) is retained into middle age and beyond. The research described in this chapter illustrates some of the difficulties in assessing such knowledge (given the problems associated with assessing both the time and extent of initial knowledge acquisition and the objective assessment of exposure and use of such knowledge in the intervening years), but there is substantial value to the examination of these topics. In addition, the field is ripe for theories and models for the maintenance and retention of declarative, procedural, and tacit knowledge across the adult lifespan. One can only hope that the next decade or two may yield some significant contributions in these areas.

REFERENCES

Ackerman, P. L. (1987). Individual differences in skill learning: An integration of psychometric and information processing perspectives. *Psychological Bulletin, 102*, 3–27.
Ackerman, P. L. (1996). A theory of adult intellectual development: Process, personality, interests, and knowledge. *Intelligence, 22*, 229–259.

Ackerman, P. L. (2000). Domain-specific knowledge as the "dark matter" of adult intelligence: gf/gc, personality and interest correlates. *Journal of Gerontology: Psychological Sciences, 55B*(2), P69–P84.

Ackerman, P. L. (2002). Gender differences in intelligence and knowledge: How should we look at achievement score differences? *Issues in Education: Contributions from Educational Psychology, 8*(1), 21–29.

Ackerman, P. L., & Beier, M. E. (2006). Determinants of domain knowledge and self-regulated learning in an adult sample. *Journal of Educational Psychology, 98*, 366–381.

Ackerman, P. L., Beier, M. B., & Bowen, K. R. (2002). What we really know about our abilities and our knowledge. *Personality and Individual Differences, 34*, 587–605.

Ackerman, P. L., Bowen, K. R., Beier, M. B., & Kanfer, R. (2001). Determinants of individual differences and gender differences in knowledge. *Journal of Educational Psychology, 93*, 797–825.

Ackerman, P. L., & Heggestad, E. D. (1997). Intelligence, personality, and interests: Evidence for overlapping traits. *Psychological Bulletin, 121*, 219–245.

Ackerman, P. L., & Rolfhus, E. L. (1999). The locus of adult intelligence: Knowledge, abilities, and non-ability traits. *Psychology and Aging, 14*, 314–330.

Adams, J. A. (1964). Motor skills. *Annual Review of Psychology, 15*, 181–202.

Adams, J. A. (1987). Historical review and appraisal of research on the learning, retention, and transfer of human motor skills. *Psychological Bulletin, 101*, 41–74.

Adler, M. (1974). The circle of learning. *Encyclopædia Britannica—Propædia* (pp. 5–7). Chicago, IL: Encyclopædia Britannica.

Alexander, W. P. (1935). Intelligence, concrete and abstract: A study in differential traits. *British Journal of Psychology Monograph, 6*, 19.

Annett, J. (1979). Memory for skill. In M. M. Gruneberg & P. E. Morris (Eds.), *Applied problems in memory* (pp. 215–247). New York: Academic Press.

Bahrick, H. P. (1984). Fifty years of second language attrition: Implications for programmatic research. *Modern Language Journal, 68*(2), 105–118.

Bahrick, H. P., Bahrick, P. O., & Wittlinger, R. P. (1974). Long-term memory: Those unforgettable high-school days. *Psychology Today, 8*(7), 50–56.

Bahrick, H. P., & Hall, L. K. (1991). Lifetime maintenance of high school mathematics content. *Journal of Experimental Psychology: General, 120*(1), 20–33.

Baltes, P. B., Smith, J., & Staudinger, U. M. (1992). Wisdom and successful aging. *Nebraska Symposium on Motivation, 39*, 123–167.

Baltes, P. B., & Staudinger, U. M. (1993). The search for a psychology of wisdom. *Current Directions in Psychological Science, 2*(3), 75–80.

Baltes, P. B., & Staudinger, U. M. (2000). Wisdom: A metaheuristic (pragmatic) to orchestrate mind and virtue toward excellence. *American Psychologist, 55*, 122–136.

Beier, M. E., & Ackerman, P. L. (2001). Current events knowledge in adults: An investigation of age, intelligence and non-ability determinants. *Psychology and Aging, 16*, 615–628.

Beier, M. E., & Ackerman, P. L. (2003). Determinants of health knowledge: An investigation of age, gender, abilities, personality, and interests. *Journal of Personality and Social Psychology, 84*(2), 439–448.

Beier, M. E., & Ackerman, P. L. (2005). Age, ability and the role of prior knowledge on the acquisition of new domain knowledge. *Psychology and Aging, 20*, 341–355.

Binet, A., & Simon, T. (1905/1973). *The development of intelligence in children* (E. Kite, Trans.). New York: Arno Press.

Book, W. F. (1908). *The psychology of skill: With special reference to its acquisition in typewriting.* Missoula: University of Montana.

Bosman, E. A. (1993). Age-related differences in the motoric aspects of transcription typing skill. *Psychology and Aging, 8*, 87–102.

Botwinick, J. (1967). *Cognitive processes in maturity and old age*. New York: Springer.

Bransford, J. D., & Schwartz, D. L. (2000). Rethinking transfer: A simple proposal with multiple implications. *Review of Research in Education, 24*, 61–100.

Brigham, C. C. (1923). *A study of American intelligence*. Princeton: Princeton University Press.

Broudy, H. S. (1977). In R. C. Anderson, R. J. Spiro, & W. E. Montague (Eds.), *Schooling and the acquisition of knowledge* (pp. 1–17). Hillsdale, NJ: Lawrence Erlbaum Associates, Inc.

Carmeli, E., Patish, H., & Coleman, R. (2003). The aging hand. *Journal of Gerontology: Medical Sciences, 58*(A), 146–152.

Cattell, R. B. (1943). The measurement of adult intelligence. *Psychological Bulletin, 40*, 153–193.

Cattell, R. B. (1957). *Personality and motivation structure and measurement*. Yonkers-on-Hudson: World Book Company.

Cattell, R. B. (1971). *Abilities: Their structure, growth, and action*. New York: Houghton Mifflin.

Charness, N., Kelley, C. L., Bosman, E. A., & Mottram, M. (2001). Word-processing training and retraining: Effects of adult age, experience, and interface. *Psychology and Aging, 16*(1), 110–127.

Christian, A. M., & Paterson, D. G. (1936). Growth of vocabulary in later maturity. *Journal of Psychology: Interdisciplinary and Applied, 1*, 167–169.

Chronicle of Higher Education Almanac, 2005–2006. Washington, DC: Author.

Cohen, J. (1988). *Statistical power analysis for the behavioral sciences*. Hillsdale, NJ: Lawrence Erlbaum Associates, Inc.

College Board (2000). *ACE [American Council on Education] recommendations*. World Wide Web (www.collegeboard.org).

Colonia-Willner, R. (1998). Practical intelligence at work: Relationship between aging and cognitive efficiency among managers in a bank environment. *Psychology and Aging, 13*, 45–57.

Conrad, H. S. (1930). General-information, intelligence, and the decline of intelligence. *Journal of Applied Psychology, 14*, 592–599.

Cronbach, L. J. (1957). The two disciplines of scientific psychology. *American Psychologist, 12*, 671–684.

Demming, J. A., & Pressey, S. L. (1957). Tests "indigenous" to the adult and older years. *Journal of Counseling Psychology, 4*(2), 144–148.

Dychtwald, K., & Flower, J. (1989). *Age wave: The challenges and opportunities of an aging America*. New York: St. Martin's Press.

Ebbinghaus, H. (1896–97). Über eine neue Methode zur Prüfung geistiger Fähigkeiten und ihre Anwendung bei Schulkindern [On a new method for testing mental abilities and its use with school children]. *Zeitschrift für Psychologie und Psyiologie der Sinnesorgane, 13*, 401–459.

Farr, M. J. (1987). *The long-term retention of knowledge and skills: A cognitive and instructional perspective*. New York: Springer-Verlag.

Ferguson, G. A. (1956). On transfer and the abilities of man. *Canadian Journal of Psychology, 10*, 121–131.

Hayes, K. J. (1962). Genes, drives, and intellect. *Psychological Reports, 10*, 299–342.

Hebb, D. O. (1939). Intelligence in man after large removals of cerebral tissue: Report of four left frontal lobe cases. *Journal of General Psychology, 21*, 73–87.

Hebb, D. O. (1942). The effect of early and late brain injury upon test scores, and the nature of normal adult intelligence. *Proceedings of the American Philosophical Society, 85*(3), 275–292.

Hill, L. B. (1934). A quarter century of delayed recall. *Journal of Genetic Psychology, 44*, 231–238.

Hill, L. B. (1957). A second quarter century of delayed recall, or relearning at eighty. *Journal of Educational Psychology, 48*, 65–69.

Hill, L. B., Rejall, A. E., & Thorndike, E. L. (1913). Practice in the case of typewriting. *Pedagogical Seminary, 20,* 516–529.

Hollingworth, H. L. (1927). *Mental growth and decline: A survey of developmental psychology.* New York: Appleton.

Horn, J. L. (1965). *Fluid and crystallized intelligence: A factor analytic study of the structure among primary mental abilities.* Ann Arbor, MI: University Microfilms International.

Hsiao, H.-h. (1927). *The performance of the Army Alpha as a function of age.* Unpublished master's thesis. New York: Columbia University.

Jensen, A. R. (1993). Test validity: *g* versus "tacit knowledge". *Current Directions in Psychological Science, 1,* 9–10.

Johnson, R. E. (2003). Aging and the remembering of text. *Developmental Review, 23*(3), 261–346.

Jones, H. E., & Conrad, H. S. (1933). The growth and decline of intelligence: A study of a homogeneous group between the ages of ten and sixty. *Genetic Psychology Monographs: Child Behavior, Animal Behavior, and Comparative Psychology, 13,* 223–275.

Köhler, W. (1947). *Gestalt psychology.* New York: Liveright Publishing.

Krueger, F., & Spearman, C. (1907). Die Korrelation zwischen verschiedenen geistigen Leistungsfähigkeiten. *Zeitschrift für Psychologie (Leipzig), 44,* 50–114.

Kubeck, J. E., Delp, N. D., Haslett, T. K., & McDaniel, M. A. (1996). Does job-related training performance decline with age? *Psychology and Aging, 11*(1), 92–107.

Light, L. L. (1991). Memory and aging: Four hypotheses in search of data. *Annual Review of Psychology, 42,* 333–376.

Lippmann, W. (1922). The mental age of Americans. *New Republic, 32,* 213–215.

Longworth, N., & Davies, W. K. (1996). *Lifelong learning.* London: Kogan Page.

Lorge, I. (1937). Never too late to learn: Some findings concerning interests and attitudes in adult education. *Journal of the American Association of University Women, 31,* 27–32.

McDougall, W. (1933). *The energies of man: A study of the fundamentals of dynamic psychology.* New York: Charles Scribner's Sons.

Miles, C. C., & Miles, W. R. (1932). The correlation of intelligence scores and chronological age from early to late maturity. *American Journal of Psychology, 44,* 44–78.

Morrell, R. W., Park, D. C., & Poon, L. W. (1989). Quality of instructions on prescription drug labels: Effects on memory and comprehension in young and old adults. *Gerontologist, 29,* 345–354.

Morris, M. G., Venkatesh, V., & Ackerman, P. L. (2005). Gender and age differences in employee decisions about new technology: An extension to the theory of planned behavior. *IEEE Transactions on Engineering Management, 52*(1), 69–84.

Neumann, E., & Ammons, R. B. (1957). Acquisition and long-term retention of a simple serial perceptual-motor skill. *Journal of Experimental Psychology, 53,* 159–161.

Otis, A. S. (1919). *Otis Group Intelligence Scale.* Yonkers-on-Hudson: World Book Co.

Owens, W. A., Jr. (1953). Age and mental abilities: A longitudinal study. *Genetic Psychology Monograph, 48,* 3–54.

Phillips, L. H., & Hamilton, C. (2001). The working memory model in adult aging research (pp. 101–125). In J. Andrade (Ed.), *Working memory in perspective.* New York: Psychology Press.

Polanyi, M. (1966/1983). *The tacit dimension.* Gloucester, MA: Peter Smith.

Rolfhus, E. L., & Ackerman, P. L. (1999). Assessing individual differences in knowledge: Knowledge structures and traits. *Journal of Educational Psychology, 91,* 511–526.

Rönnlund, M., Nyberg, L., & Bäckman, L. (2005). Stability, growth, and decline in adult life span development of declarative memory: Cross-sectional and longitudinal data from a population-based study. *Psychology and Aging, 20,* 3–18.

Rosen, B., & Jerdee, T. H. (1976). The nature of job-related age stereotypes. *Journal of Applied Psychology, 61,* 180–183.

Ruch, F. L. (1933). Adult learning. *Psychological Bulletin, 30,* 387–414.

Ruch, F. L. (1934). The differential decline of learning ability in the aged as a possible explanation of their conservatism. *Journal of Social Psychology, 5,* 329–336.

Ruch, F. L. (1936). The method of common points of mastery as a technique in human learning experimentation. *Psychological Review, 43,* 229–234.

Ryle, G. (1949/2000). *The concept of mind.* Chicago: University of Chicago Press.

Salthouse, T. A. (1984). Effects of age and skill in typing. *Journal of Experimental Psychology: General, 113,* 345–371.

Salthouse, T. A. (1996). The processing-speed theory of adult age differences in cognition. *Psychological Review, 103,* 403–428.

Schaie, K. W. (1996a). Intellectual functioning in adulthood. In J. E. Birren & K. W. Schaie (Eds.), *Handbook of the psychology of aging* (4th ed., pp. 266–286). New York: Academic Press.

Schaie, K. W. (1996b). *Intellectual development in adulthood: The Seattle Longitudinal Study.* New York: Cambridge University Press.

Schaie, K. W. (2005). *Developmental influences on adult intelligence: The Seattle Longitudinal Study.* New York: Oxford University Press.

Schaie, K. W., & Willis, S. L. (1978). Life span development: Implications for education. *Review of Research in Education, 6,* 120–156.

Schmidt, F. L., & Hunter, J. E. (1993). Tacit knowledge, practical intelligence, general mental ability, and job knowledge. *Current Directions in Psychological Science, 1,* 8–9.

Schmidt, H. G., Peeck, V. H., Paas, F., van Breukelen, J. P., et al. (2000). Remembering the street names on one's childhood neighborhood: A study of very long-term retention. *Memory, 8,* 37–49.

Smith, J., & Baltes, P. B. (1990). Wisdom-related knowledge: Age/cohort differences in response to life-planning problems. *Developmental Psychology, 26,* 494–505.

Smith, M. C., & Pourchot, T. (Eds.). (1998). *Adult learning and development: Perspectives from educational psychology.* Mahwah, NJ: Lawrence Erlbaum Associates, Inc.

Smith, C. D., Walton, A., Loveland, A. D., Umberger, G. H., Kryscio, R. J., & Gash, D. M. (2005). Memories that last in old age: Motor skill learning and memory preservation. *Neurobiology of Aging, 26*(6), 883–890.

Sorenson, H. (1933). *Adult abilities in extension classes: A psychological study.* Minneapolis: University of Minnesota Press.

Sorenson, H. (1938). *Adult abilities: A study of university extension students.* Minneapolis: University of Minnesota Press.

Spearman, C. (1904). "General intelligence," objectively determined and measured. *American Journal of Psychology, 15,* 201–293.

Spearman, C. (1927). *The abilities of man: Their nature and measurement.* New York: Macmillan.

Spearman, C. (1930). Disturbers of tetrad differences: Scales. *Journal of Educational Psychology, 21,* 559–573.

Spearman, C. E. (1938). Measurement of intelligence. *Scientia Milano, 64,* 75–82.

Spearman, C., & Jones, L. W. (1950), *Human ability: A continuation of "the abilities of man".* London: Macmillan.

Staudinger, U. M., Smith, J., & Baltes, P. B. (1992). Wisdom-related knowledge in a life review task: Age differences and the role of professional specialization. *Psychology and Aging, 7,* 271–281.

Sternberg, R. J. (1985). *Beyond IQ: A triarchic theory of human intelligence.* Cambridge: Cambridge University Press.

Sternberg, R. J., Wagner, R. K., Williams, W. M., & Horvath, J. A. (1995). Testing common sense. *American Psychologist, 50,* 912–927.

Swift, E. J. (1905). Memory of a complex skillful act. *American Journal of Psychology, 16,* 131–133.

Swift, E. J. (1906). Memory of skillful movements. *Psychological Bulletin, 3,* 185–187.

Swift, E. J. (1910). Relearning a skillful act: An experimental study in neuro-muscular memory. *Psychological Bulletin, 7,* 17–19.

Terman, L. (1922). The great conspiracy or the impulse imperious of intelligence testers, psychoanalyzed and exposed by Mr. Lippmann. *The New Republic, 12,* 116–120.

Thorndike, E. L., Bregman, E. O., Tilton, J. W., & Woodyard, E. (1928). *Adult learning.* New York: Macmillan.

Tulving, E. (1989). Memory: Performance, knowledge, and experience. *European Journal of Cognitive Psychology, 1,* 3–26.

Verhaeghen, P., Marcoen, A., & Goossens, L. (1993). Facts and fiction about memory aging: A quantitative integration of research findings. *Journal of Gerontology, 48*(4), 157–171.

Wagner, R. K. (1987). Tacit knowledge in everyday intelligent behavior. *Journal of Personality and Social Psychology, 52,* 1236–1247.

Wagner, R. K., & Sternberg, R. J. (1985). Practical intelligence in real-world pursuits: The role of tacit knowledge. *Journal of Personality and Social Psychology, 49,* 436–458.

Webb, E. (1915). Character and intelligence. *British Journal of Psychology Monograph Supplement, III.*

Wechsler, D. (1944). *The measurement of adult intelligence.* Baltimore: Williams & Wilkins.

Willingham, W. W., & Cole, N. S. (1997). *Gender and fair assessment.* Mahwah, NJ: Lawrence Erlbaum Associates, Inc.

Yerkes, R. M. (1921). *Memoirs of the National Academy of Science* (Vol. XV). Washington, DC: Government Printing Office.

Yoakum, C. S., & Yerkes, R. M. (1920). *Mental tests in the American Army.* London: Sidgwick & Jackson.

Intraindividual Variability, Cognition, and Aging

David F. Hultsch
Esther Strauss
Michael A. Hunter
University of Victoria

Stuart W. S. MacDonald
Karolinska Institute

Researchers examining cognitive functioning in adulthood have typically focused their attention on average age-related effects. Methodologically, this emphasis has translated into comparisons of mean level performance across different age groups using cross-sectional designs or examination of average changes in performance over time using longitudinal designs. Research on average age-related differences and changes in cognition has been useful, but it reflects certain assumptions about the nature of human development. Specifically, this emphasis is rooted in the assumption that either the behaviors of interest are stable over time or that the trajectory of change that does occur is similar for all persons. This assumption with respect to level of performance represents one instantiation of a more general stability perspective that has dominated developmental research (Gergen, 1977; Nesselroade & Featherman, 1997). By contrast, variability in performance, particularly variability within persons, has received less attention. However, as noted by Nesselroade and Boker (1994), the concepts of stability and variability are logically dependent on one another — defining one demands consideration of the other.

There are multiple classifications of types of variability and stability (e.g., Alwin, 1994; Buss, 1974; Cattell, 1957; Nesselroade & Featherman, 1997), and sometimes the same label has been applied to different types (e.g., Christensen, Mackinnon, Korten, Jorm, Henderson, & Jacomb, 1999; Shammi, Bosman, & Stuss, 1998). However, basic types of variability may be considered with reference to a generalized data box defined by persons, measures, and occasions (Cattell, 1966; Nesselroade & Ford, 1985;

Nesselroade & Ram, 2004). This data box can be used to define the minimum conditions for observing variability in relation to the three dimensions. First, one can consider differences between persons measured on a single task on a single occasion (sometimes referred to as individual differences). Second, one can examine variability associated with measuring a single person once on multiple tasks (sometimes referred to as intraindividual differences). The third type of variability is defined by the minimum condition of measuring a single person on a single task on multiple occasions (sometimes labeled intraindividual variability). These latter two types of variability refer to variability within persons. Although these configurations represent the minimum conditions necessary to observe variability, in practice it is common to select subsets of observations across more than one dimension which results in the opportunity to observe more than one type of variability. For example, selection of a subset of observations including persons, tasks, and occasions can yield information on all three types of variability (e.g., Hultsch, MacDonald, & Dixon, 2002).

Developmentalists, of course, are particularly interested in change over time. Therefore, our focus in this chapter will be on variability within persons across occasions, or intraindividual variability. There are different ways to conceptualize intraindividual variability, and therefore it is useful to narrow our focus a bit more. Two key features that have been used to differentiate changes within persons over time include the permanence of the change and the timescale over which the change occurs (Cattell, 1957; Fisk & Rice, 1955; Li, Huxhold, & Schmiedek, 2004a; Nesselroade, 1991; Wohlwill, 1973). For example, Nesselroade (1991) distinguished between intraindividual change and intraindividual variability. Intraindividual change refers to changes that are more or less enduring and occur relatively slowly (usually across months, years, or decades). Examples would include progressive changes associated with development and aging and long-term learning and skill acquisition. Intraindividual variability refers to relatively reversible fluctuations in functioning over shorter periods of time (usually across seconds, minutes, days, or weeks). Examples would include variability in physical performance, fluctuations in cognitive processing speed or accuracy, and shifts in emotional state.

Both of these types of within-person change are central to our understanding of development and aging in general, and the description and explanation of cognitive changes in later life in particular (Dixon & Hertzog, 1996). Indeed, it has been suggested that there are dynamic relationships between intraindividual change and intraindividual variability (Nesselroade, 1991; Lindenberger & von Oertzen, 2006). One implication of this perspective is that the parameters of short-term intraindividual variability distributions can change over time and these changes may influence long-term intraindividual change outcomes. Thus, intraindividual variability may be both an outcome and an antecedent of developmental change.

Although we have just argued that it is important to consider both intraindividual change and intraindividual variability in order to understand cognitive changes in adulthood and aging, our focus in this chapter is specifically on intraindividual variability or short-term fluctuations in individuals' behavior (particularly cognitive performance) and its relationship to various outcomes. This type of within-person variability has also been denoted by several other terms, including wobble (Nesselroade & Featherman, 1997), lability (Butler, Hokanson, & Flynn, 1994), fluctuation (West, 2001), noise (Hendrickson, 1982), processing robustness (Li et al., 2004a), and inconsistency (Hultsch, MacDonald, Hunter, Levy-Bencheton, & Strauss, 2000). In this chapter, we will use the terms intraindividual variability and inconsistency.

There are three major parts to the chapter. First, we begin with an expanded examination of different conceptualizations of intraindividual variability and the potential relevance of the phenomenon for understanding aging and cognition. In the second part, we review several strands of existing research, including work describing between-person differences in intraindividual variability as a function of age and neurological status, and the association of intraindividual variability with cognitive functioning, functional competence, and mortality. In the final part, we examine a number of unresolved issues in this area of research including appropriate statistical indicators of intraindividual variability, whether intraindividual variability provides unique information above and beyond what is carried by measures of central tendency, and potential mechanisms that might cause changes in intraindividual variability over the life course.

CONCEPTUALIZATIONS OF INTRAINDIVIDUAL VARIABILITY

Dimensions of Intraindividual Variability

We have offered a basic definition of intraindividual variability as relatively reversible fluctuations in behavior over relatively short time intervals such as seconds, minutes, days, or weeks. This is a very broad definition, and it is likely that there are multiple types of intraindividual variability that may be distinguished on a variety of dimensions.

Timescale

Intraindividual variability can be observed across a variety of time frames as long as the changes are relatively reversible. Some studies have examined fluctuations in performance over very short intervals; for example, inconsistency in response latency on reaction time (RT) tasks (e.g., Anstey, 1999; Hultsch et al., 2002; Nesselroade & Salthouse, 2004). Other studies have measured intraindividual variability across longer periods such as days or weeks (e.g., Li, Aggen, Nesselroade, & Baltes, 2001a; Salthouse, Nesselroade, & Berish, 2006). A small number of investigations have examined variation across multiple time frames (e.g., Hultsch et al., 2000; Rabbitt, Osman, Moore, & Stollery 2001; Ram, Rabbitt, Stollery, & Nesselroade, 2005b). This begs the question of whether variability measured across these different time frames represents the same underlying phenomenon (e.g., Martin & Hofer, 2004). This issue may be informed by examining the results of studies that have assessed variability across different time frames on the same task in the same sample. For example, several studies have measured both trial-to-trial and week-to-week variability in performance on a variety of RT tasks (e.g., Hultsch et al., 2000; Rabbitt et al., 2001). Rabbitt et al. (2001) attempted to directly assess whether variability across the two intervals provided the same information. Although measures of within- and between-session variability were positively and significantly correlated, additional simulation analyses suggested that individual differences in within-session variability did not account for all the variance in between-session variability. Related to this, Hultsch and his colleagues (Fuentes, Hunter, Strauss, & Hultsch, 2001; Hultsch et al., 2000) have observed that group differences in inconsistency of RT performance as a function of age and neurological status were substantially larger when measured from trial to trial than when measured from week to week. In most cases, the magnitude of intraindividual variability observed across trials was approximately twice as large as that observed across weeks. These findings along with the results of Rabbitt et al.'s (2001) analyses suggest that moment-to-moment and week-to-week fluctuations in response time may be telling us somewhat different things.[1]

---

[1] Related to this, Ram et al. (2005b) recently suggested labeling variability across trials within a session as inconsistency and variability across sessions (e.g., days, weeks) as intraindividual variability. Note that the basic definition and mechanics of calculation of variability across different time frames is identical. However, given the possibility that measures of variability across different time frames may provide different information, the suggestion by Ram and his colleagues has merit.

Source of Influence

The above point leads to the consideration of potential sources of intraindividual variability. For example, variability in cognition might be influenced at the neurobiological level by a number of mechanisms such as the speed of neural transmission or the functioning of neurotransmitter systems. Alternatively, variability in performance might be affected at the behavioral level by fluctuations in affective or somatic states (e.g., depressive affect, perceived stress level, and fatigue). Although the neurobiological and behavioral levels are intertwined, some functions are influenced more by endogenous mechanisms, whereas others are driven more by changes in the external environment. The impact of these different sources of influence is probably better captured within some time frames than others. For example, it seems plausible that neurological functioning might show very rapid changes from one moment to the next as a function of various putative mechanisms such as fluctuations in connectivity of network pathways or the efficacy of neurotransmitter systems. In contrast, it seems unlikely that other sources of intraindividual variability such as affective states, fatigue, stress, and pain will show significant fluctuations over such short intervals. Rather, we would expect to see variability in these domains over longer intervals such as hours, days, or weeks. As a result, measurement of variability over very short intervals (e.g., trial-to-trial inconsistency in RT) may be a more useful approach to capture neurobiological sources of variability, whereas assessment of intraindividual variability over longer intervals may be necessary to examine the impact of more exogenous sources of influence.

Scope

In their taxonomy of intraindividual dynamics Li et al. (2004a) presented a four-fold classification based on timescale and scope. Similar to Nesselroade and others, they distinguished between developing or ontogenetic change and functioning or microgenetic change; the former terms refer to progressive and relatively permanent changes (intraindividual change), whereas the latter refer to short-term changes that are relatively reversible (intraindividual variability). The other dimension they identified refers to the scope of the change. One can contrast variations in a single function (i.e., univariate changes) with transformations of the functional organization of behavior (i.e., multivariate changes). Li and her colleagues suggested that, at the microgenetic timescale, variations in a single function are reflected by processing lability, neural or behavioral plasticity, and resilience to environmental perturbations. In contrast, transformations in organization refer to shifts in resource allocation, coordination and compensation, and variations in mental set and functional organization. Thus, trial-to-trial fluctuations in RT on a visual search task would illustrate change in a single function, whereas shifts in resource allocation between a visual search task and a memory task in a dual task paradigm would be an example of multivariate variability. To date, most of the work on intraindividual variability has been univariate in nature. Lindenberger and von Oertzen (2006) argue that a major challenge for cognitive aging researchers is to examine how fluctuations in a single function result in transformations in global organization and vice versa.

Adaptive/Maladaptive Variability

Several writers have pointed out that intraindividual variability may be adaptive or maladaptive in the sense that it is associated with positive versus negative outcomes (Allaire & Marsiske, 2005; Siegler, 1994). For example, Siegler (1994) noted that cognitive change in children may facilitate learning. Such variability may reflect changes in strategic processing that are part of the learning process. Indeed, he suggests that variability is most pronounced in infancy and early childhood when learning rather than efficiency of performance is most important. Li and her colleagues (2004a) proposed that there are several types of intraindividual variability associated with different stages of acquisition of an ability from initial learning through acquired function as illustrated in Figure 10.1. This model implies that variability associated with the acquisition of a skill (plasticity) is quite different than the variability observed about average performance once asymptote of the skill has been reached. As expertise increases, variability of performance decreases. Other aspects such as the ability to recover from a significant perturbation of a typical range of functioning may constitute other specific types of intraindividual variability.

Thus, there may be different types of intraindividual variability associated with different phases of task acquisition (or opportunity for acquisition), and they are likely to tell us different things. For example, Allaire and Marsiske (2005) recently examined variability in accuracy of performance across multiple occasions for a sample of older adults (60–87 years) on three cognitive tasks that permitted implementation of new performance strategies with practice. Consistent with Li's model, they found that intraindividual variability on any given task was associated positively with level of performance on the task and the amount of a person's practice-related gain across sessions. In contrast, when a task provides little opportunity for strategic processing, or where performance has reached asymptote (or practice effects have been statistically

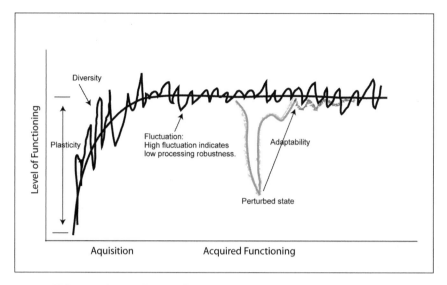

FIG. 10.1. Some subtypes of short-term intraindividual variation in functioning. Adapted from Li, S.-C., Huxhold, O., and Schmiedek, F. (2004).
Aging and attenuated processing robustness: Evidence from cognitive and
sensorimotor functioning. *Gerontology, 50,* 28–34. Reproduced by permission of S. Karger AG, Basel.

controlled), intraindividual variability is more likely to be associated with
maladaptive outcomes. For example, multiple studies have shown that
inconsistency in latency of response on relatively simple RT tasks is
associated with lower performance on other cognitive tasks, neurological
damage and illness, and mortality (e.g., Hultsch & MacDonald, 2004;
Rabbitt, 2000).

Cyclicality

Fisk and Rice (1955) distinguished between changes that are ordered in
some fashion such as oscillations or cycles and changes that do not show
any systematic pattern of fluctuation. There are a number of examples of
intraindividual variability that are characterized by some form of periodicity, for example, circadian rhythms related to alertness (e.g., Webb, 1982)
and monthly hormonal cycles in women (e.g., Hamson, 1990). Such
within-person fluctuations may have important implications for cognitive
functioning. For example, there is increasing evidence that people tested
at peak circadian periods perform better compared with people who
are tested at off-peak times of the day (Intons-Peterson, Rocchi, West,
McLellan, & Hackney, 1998; May & Hasher, 1998). Preferred times of day

vary with age, with most older adults preferring mornings and most younger adults preferring later times of the day (May, Hasher, & Stoltzfus, 1993). Moreover, age differences in performance on some tasks, particularly those requiring careful, deliberate, or strategic processing, are smaller when individuals are tested at their preferred times and larger when they are tested at their nonpreferred times (Intons-Peterson et al. 1998; West, Murphy, Armilio, Craik, & Stuss, 2002). Interestingly, a recent study by May, Hasher, and Foong (2005) suggests that both younger and older adults showed better performance on an implicit memory task when tested at off-peak compared with peak times of the day—a reversal of the pattern of results found with explicit tasks. Thus, both type and time of testing can have an impact on assessment of behavior. Beyond theoretical implications related to variability of behavior, these results suggest that normative clinical data may need to be re-evaluated with time of testing controlled.

Magnitude and Reliability of Intraindividual Variability

Although some types of intraindividual variability appear to be ordered in some way as in the circadian patterns discussed above, other within-person changes appear to be more "random" in the sense that cyclical or other patterns cannot be detected. The observation that within-person changes over short periods may appear random raises an important issue. Is intraindividual variability in cognitive performance a legitimate phenomenon for study? Traditional views of psychological measurement associated with a stability perspective assume that an observed score is composed of a true score and error. Test–retest correlations are one key indicator of the reliability of measurement operations and any intraindividual variability over short intervals is typically treated as error. However, as Nesselroade and Featherman (1997) note, low test–retest correlations may reflect poor reliability of the measures, substantial intraindividual variability of the attribute, or both.

Is there evidence for the existence of significant amounts of intraindividual variability in cognitive functions that are often considered to be trait-like endowments of the person? One approach to this question is to evaluate the magnitude of intraindividual variability on a given task relative to the amount of between-person variability observed on the same task. Using this approach, several studies have found that the magnitude of intraindividual variability is about half that of interindividual variability (Li et al., 2001a; Nesselroade & Salthouse, 2004; Salthouse et al., 2006). For example, Nesselroade and Salthouse (2004) asked adults ranging in age from 20 to 91 years to perform three speeded perceptual-motor tasks on three separate occasions over a period of about two weeks.

For each task, they computed three measures of variability: (a) between-person variability computed as the standard deviation of mean scores of the sample; (b) within-person variability computed as the average of a person's trial-to-trial standard deviations for the three sessions; (c) within-person variability computed as the standard deviation of a person's three mean scores for the three sessions. Examination of the ratio of both types of within-person variability to between-person variability revealed values ranging from .31 to .85 with the majority ranging from .40 to .55. Similar results have been reported by Salthouse et al. (2006) for accuracy of performance on multiple cognitive tasks from four cognitive domains (perceptual speed, fluid abilities, episodic memory, vocabulary) administered to a sample of adults across a wide range of ages (18–97 years) on three separate occasions over a two-week period. Both of these studies sampled a wide age range, but similar results have been reported within a much narrower older adult age range. Li et al. (2001a) examined intraindividual variability for a set of memory and sensorimotor variables across 13 biweekly sessions in a sample of older adults aged 64 to 86 years. Consistent with the previously reported studies, the magnitude of intraindividual fluctuation in both the memory and sensorimotor domains was half or more of the magnitudes of interindividual differences in the sample. These results suggest that there is substantial intraindividual variability in what are typically considered to be relatively stable cognitive abilities. Moreover, it is interesting that the magnitude of this intraindividual variability appears to be relatively similar across different cognitive tasks and age ranges.

There still remains the question of whether within-person variability reflects lawful but fluctuating sources of influence, or whether it is better characterized as error. There are several lines of evidence that suggest that much of the intraindividual variability observed in cognitive performance is a signal in its own right rather than error. One line of evidence comes from studies that have treated multiple observations as a time series. For example, spectral analysis transforms the time domain into a frequency domain and examines the data for periodicity. If the series is random, the power spectrum should have no slope; that is, all frequencies should be equally evident indicating "white noise." In contrast, if the series is periodic, the resulting power spectrum should reveal a peak at the "driving frequency." This would indicate the presence of systematic variation, sometimes labeled colored or pink noise. Recent analyses of time series data generated by multiple tasks including time estimation (Gilden, Thornton, & Mallon, 1995) and choice RT tasks (Clayton & Bruhns Frey, 1997) have shown that trial-to-trial fluctuations are inconsistent with the view that variability is due to a large number of independent random variables (i.e., white noise). Rather, spectrum analysis indicates two components: a white noise component and a colored noise component indicating the presence of lawful variation in the data.

Additional evidence for the argument that intraindividual variability can be measured reliably comes from studies examining intercorrelations of measures of variability obtained on separate occasions and/or derived from different tasks. A number of studies have shown that the magnitude of within-person variability appears to be somewhat characteristic of the individual. Two results in line with this view have been observed in several studies (e.g., Fuentes et al., 2001; Hultsch et al., 2002; Rabbitt et al., 2001). First, measures of inconsistency computed for a given task across different time intervals (e.g., trials versus weeks, or earlier versus later sessions) are positively correlated (Allaire & Marsiske, 2005; Hultsch et al., 2000; Rabbitt et al., 2001). Second, individuals who are more inconsistent on one task are also more inconsistent on other tasks, at least in the case of RT tasks (Fuentes et al., 2001; Hultsch et al., 2000; 2002). Table 10.1 shows an example of intercorrelations among measures of inconsistency in performance for four different tasks performed by a sample of older adults (Hultsch et al., 2000). All but two of these correlations are significant and all are positive. Allaire and Marsiske (2005) note that variability in different cognitive domains may not be positively correlated if the tasks differ in difficulty or strategic requirements as reflected in their acquisition curves. Even in this case, however, they observed substantial trait-like consistency across time within tasks. Similar results showing relative

TABLE 10.1

Intercorrelations among Measures of Inconsistency in Performance for Four Different Tasks by Sample of Older Adults

Variable	(1)	(2)	(3)	(4)	(5)	(6)	(7)	(8)
ISD Across Trials								
(1) SRT	—							
(2) CRT	.76**	—						
(3) Word	.69**	.73**	—					
(4) Story	.69**	.79**	.90**	—				
ISD Across Occasions								
(5) SRT	.58**	.60**	.52**	.49**	—			
(6) CRT	.42**	.75**	.51**	.53**	.33*	—		
(7) Word	.54**	.60**	.71**	.63**	.18	.54**	—	
(8) Story	.46**	.64**	.62**	.68**	.15	.62**	.84**	—

* $p < .05$. ** $p < .01$. *Note.* The top panel of the table shows intercorrelations of trial-to-trial inconsistency among the four tasks averaged across four testing occasions. The last three columns of the bottom panel show intercorrelations of week-to-week inconsistency, and the first four columns of the bottom panel show the correlations of trial-to-trial and week-to-week inconsistency.

stability of individual differences in intraindividual variability over time have been observed in studies examining different domains of functioning such as physical functioning and cognition (Strauss, MacDonald, Hunter, Moll, & Hultsch, 2002) and self-rated health and activities (Ghisletta, Nesselroade, Featherman, & Rowe, 2002).

Consistent with the relationships summarized above, studies that have computed reliability for odd and even trials (e.g., Jensen, 1992; Sliwinski, Smyth, Hofer, & Stawski, 2006) indicate that measures of intraindividual variability show good reliability. For example, Sliwinski et al. (2006) computed reliabilities for several RT tasks based on each individual's odd and even trials partialed for practice and time of day effects. Reliability levels were acceptable, ranging from .65 to .78 across different task and age groups.

Finally, perhaps the most compelling evidence for the reliability of measures of intraindividual variability is their systematic association with personal characteristics such as age and with performance outcomes such as changes in cognitive functioning and proximity to death.

Potential Relevance of Intraindividual Variability for Aging and Cognition

If one accepts the argument that both level and variability of performance are important indicators of human behavior, it follows that it may be useful to examine variability in order to further our understanding of many phenomena. However, intraindividual variability may be of particular relevance to researchers interested in cognitive aging for several reasons. We will explore this issue further in the remainder of the chapter, but here wish to mention two generic issues that point to the potential relevance of intraindividual variability for understanding cognitive changes in aging.

First, one possibility is that intraindividual variability represents an important indicator of cognitive aging. Specifically, several theorists have proposed that performance inconsistency at the behavioral level may be an indicator of central nervous system (CNS) functioning. For example, it has been suggested that inconsistency in RT could be caused by random errors or neural "noise" in the transmission of signals in the CNS (Hendrickson, 1982). This view maps on to earlier hypotheses in the gerontological literature that proposed aging-related cognitive declines are a function of increased information loss due to neural noise (Crossman & Szafran, 1956; Welford, 1965; Myerson, Hale, Wagstaff, Poon, & Smith, 1990) or random breaks in neural networks (Cerella, 1990). More recently, Li and her colleagues have suggested that the signal-to-noise ratio of neural information processing may be regulated by the functioning of catecholaminergic neurotransmitters such as epinephrine, norepin-ephrine, and dopamine (Li & Lindenberger, 1999; Li, Lindenberger, & Sikström, 2001b). Consistent with these arguments linking variability and CNS dysfunction at the neurobiological level, behavioral studies have shown that inconsistent performance is associated with multiple mani-festations of neurological disturbance including Parkinson's disease (e.g., Burton, Strauss, Hultsch, Moll, & Hunter, 2006a), traumatic brain injury (e.g., Stuss, Pogue, Buckle, & Bondar, 1994), and dementia (e.g., Gordon & Carson, 1990). Such findings have led some writers to suggest that intraindividual variability represents an indicator of processing efficiency that may provide unique information about cognitive functioning above and beyond that provided by indicators of average performance (Hultsch, Hunter, MacDonald, & Strauss, 2005; Hultsch & MacDonald, 2004; Rabbitt, 2000).

In contrast, others have suggested the possibility that intraindividual variability may be an agent of developmental change (Lindenberger, & von Oertzen, 2006). More specifically, this view suggests that variability in neural activation or neural noise may be a source of influence driv-ing a wide variety of aging-related cognitive changes. For example, Li and her colleagues have used neurocomputational simulations to simu-late the effects of aging-related changes in neuromodulation on cogni-tive functioning (Li & Lindenberger, 1999; Li, Lindenberger, & Frensch, 2000; Li et al., 2001b). Specifically, variations in the gain parameter of connectionist models were used to simulate the effects of age differ-ences in neuromodulation on neural network processing and outcomes. Decrements in the gain parameter led to increased intra-network vari-ability and decrements in the distinctiveness of network activation pat-terns. Comparison of "young" and "old" networks revealed several interesting parallels to well-known behavioral findings. Specifically, old networks were characterized by a lower level of mean performance, larger interindividual differences, and higher intercorrelations between tasks than young networks. No other assumptions other than increased variability at the intra-network level were required to produce these results.

Of course, the distinction between indicator and outcome versus agent or cause of change is, to some degree, arbitrary. Indeed, it is possible for intraindividual variability to be both an outcome and an agent of developmental change. Leaving this argument aside for the moment, we believe it is possible to conclude that it is an important phenomenon to consider for both theory and clinical practice related to cognition and aging. We turn now to existing evidence to support this assertion.

EXISTING RESEARCH

Age Differences and Changes in Intraindividual Variability

If intraindividual variability in RT is an indicator of either neural or information processing efficiency, we would obviously expect to observe greater inconsistency for older adults compared with younger adults. Indeed, this seems to be the case across a range of timescales and tasks.

Age Differences across the Lifespan

To place the examination of age differences in its largest developmental context, we first consider the results of several recent studies that have examined inconsistency across the lifespan (Li et al., 2004b; Williams, Hultsch, Strauss, Hunter & Tannock, 2005; Williams, Strauss, Hultsch, & Hunter, in press). These studies suggest that intraindividual variability in performance is high in both childhood and old age. For example, Williams et al. (2005) measured inconsistency in choice RT performance in a sample of individuals ranging in age from 6 to 81 years. As shown in Figure 10.2, rapid decreases in inconsistency of performance were observed from age 6 through young adulthood followed by increases in inconsistency throughout adulthood to approximately 80 years of age. Although both children and older adults evinced greater intraindividual variability, there is evidence that this quantitative similarity does not reflect similar processes. Williams et al. (2005) demonstrated that the age-related differences in inconsistency in adulthood were observed primarily in the slow portion of the RT distribution, and partialing inconsistency from the fast portion of the distribution did not reduce the age-related variation in inconsistency in the slow portion of the distribution. Such findings have been interpreted as reflecting the operation of some specific variability-producing process such as attentional blocks that result in a relatively high number of very slow responses rather than a general slowing process (Bunce, Warr, & Cochrane, 1993). The outcome is different for the childhood years. Here Williams et al. (2005) found evidence for age differences in both the fast and slow ends of the distribution, and partialing inconsistency from the fast end of the distribution resulted in a partial attenuation of age-related differences in the slow end. This suggests both general and specific variability-producing processes may be operating in childhood.

Adult Age Differences

Studies examining variability within the adult age range are consistent with these lifespan studies, and also suggest the presence of significant

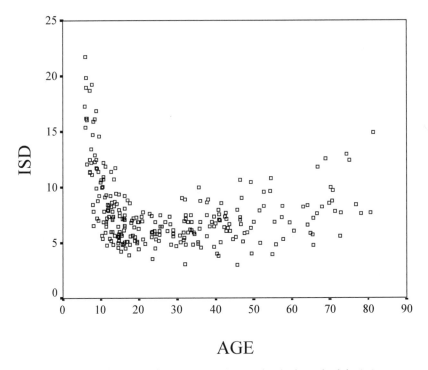

AGE

FIG. 10.2. Scatter plot of inconsistency (intraindividual standard deviation of residualized CRT) across the life span. From Williams, B. R., Hultsch, D. F., Strauss, E., Hunter, M. A., and Tannock, R. (2005). Inconsistency in reaction time across the lifespan. *Neuropsychology, 19*, 88–96. Copyright © 2005 by the American Psychological Association. Reprinted with permission.

age differences in inconsistency within the adult age range. A relatively sizable number of studies have observed that older adults exhibit greater inconsistency in performance latency across trials on various RT tasks than younger adults (e.g., Anstey, 1999; Fozard, Vercruyssen, Reynolds, Hancock, & Quilter, 1994; Hultsch et al., 2002; Nesselroade & Salthouse, 2004; West et al., 2002). Age differences may also be observed within the older adult age range, with inconsistency being particularly pronounced after approximately age 75 (Hultsch et al., 2002).

The cross-sectional results reported by Hultsch et al. (2002) illustrate this pattern of age effects. They examined age differences in RT inconsistency for younger adults (19–36 years, $n = 99$) and three groups of older adults (young-old, 54–64 years, $n = 178$; mid-old, 65–74 years, $n = 361$; and old-old, 75–94 years, $n = 224$). Participants completed two nonverbal RT tasks (simple RT and choice RT) and two more verbal RT tasks (lexical decision and semantic decision), and within-person standard deviations were computed across trials for each task. As shown in Figure 10.3, greater inconsistency was observed for older compared with younger adults on all tasks, particularly for individuals over age 75. Participants in this group showed greater inconsistency than all other age groups on all tasks. Effect sizes associated with the age group differences ranged from medium to large in most cases.

Age differences in trial-to-trial inconsistency in performance on speeded tasks appear to be larger on more complex tasks, particularly those requiring executive processes such as inhibition, set switching, or working memory. For example, West et al. (2002) examined age differences in trial-to-trial inconsistency in performance on RT tasks that placed varying demand on executive control processes (e.g., a basic choice RT task versus a 1-back choice RT). Performance variability was similar for younger and older adults under task conditions requiring minimal

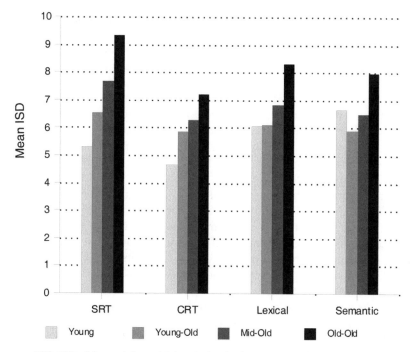

FIG. 10.3. Mean trial-to-trial intraindividual standard deviation (ISD) T-scores for four RT tasks by age group. SRT = simple reaction time; CRT = choice reaction time. Young = 19–36 years, Young-Old = 54–64 years, Mid-Old = 65–74 years, Old-Old = 75–94 years. From Figure 3, Hultsch, D. F., MacDonald, S. W. S., and Dixon, R. A. (2002). Variability in reaction time performance of younger and older adults. *Journal of Gerontology: Psychological Sciences, 57B*, P101–P115. Copyright © The Gerontological Society of America. Reproduced by permission of the publisher.

executive control, but greater for older than younger adults under task conditions that required active recruitment of executive control processes. In a recent study using similar tasks, Dixon, Garrett, Lentz, MacDonald, Strauss, and Hultsch (2007) reported significant age differences in inconsistency on all tasks (simple, 4-choice, and 1-back 4-choice RT tasks), but the largest differences were observed on the more complex 1-back task. Similarly, Bunce, MacDonald, and Hultsch (2004) found that inconsistency was greater for older adults for decision RTs (as opposed to motor RTs) when task demands relating to the number of choices and fatigue from time-on-task were high. In a different vein, Figure 10.3 shows that age differences were somewhat smaller for the two verbally based RT tasks than for the two nonverbally based tasks. Hultsch et al. (2002) speculated that the relatively preserved verbal ability of older adults may have provided them with access to compensatory mechanisms that reduced their relative inconsistency to some degree.

In addition to studies examining inconsistency in response speed from one trial to the next within a single session, a smaller number of studies have looked at intraindividual variability in performance across different sessions separated by days or weeks. Evidence for age differences is less systematic here. In general, studies that have examined inconsistency in response time computed across sessions show similar, although attenuated, results to studies that compute variability from trial to trial within sessions. For example, Nesselroade and Salthouse (2004) examined intraindividual variability on a number of perceptual-motor tasks in a sample ranging in age from 20 to 91 years of age. Measures of intraindividual variability were computed based on the individual's standard deviation across within-session trial scores averaged across the three sessions (within-person, within-session variability) and the standard deviation of the individual's three mean session scores (within-person, between-session). Nesselroade and Salthouse found that age was positively correlated with both measures of within-person variability, but the correlations were consistently higher for the measures of within-session variability than for the measures of between-session variability. Other studies examining age and patient-group differences have also reported greater differences in within-session compared with between-session variability (Fuentes et al., 2001; Hultsch et al., 2000).

In contrast, studies examining variability in accuracy of performance across sessions have found less evidence for age differences. For example, Salthouse et al. (2006) recently investigated intraindividual variability in performance in a sample of adults aged 18 to 97 years who completed different versions of 13 cognitive tests on three separate occasions. Although there was evidence for substantial within-person variability in cognitive performance across sessions (relative to between-person variability), there was little evidence that within-person variability was associated with age. Similarly, Li et al. (2001a) found only partial evidence for age differences in intraindividual variability in accuracy of perform- ance across sessions. In this study, measures of within-person variability were obtained for multiple sensorimotor and memory measures across 13 biweekly sessions in a sample of adults aged 64 to 86 years. The investiga- tors found that intraindividual variability in performance was positively correlated with age for most of the sensorimotor measures, but only for one of the memory measures.

There are probably several reasons why age differences are more likely to be found for measures of response speed compared with response accuracy. First, latency measures may simply provide a more sensitive scale compared to indicators of accuracy. Most cognitive tasks directed principally at assessing accuracy of response contain a limited number of items. As a result, variability in accuracy across sessions may consist of fluctuations on only one or two items. Such a scale may not be sensitive enough to measure intraindividual variability reliably. In contrast, latency measures have substantial range, and often rather small changes in response speed may be detected reliably. Second, accuracy measures are often derived from relatively complex power tasks which may be quite sensitive to strategy use. In contrast, latency measures are often obtained from relatively simpler speeded tasks where accuracy is relatively high. We noted earlier that intraindividual variability may be affected by stra- tegic processing, and in some cases may be related to better rather than poorer performance (Allaire & Marsiske, 2005). Finally, and perhaps most important, is the issue of the time frame over which intraindividual vari- ability is assessed. If moment-to-moment fluctuations represent the best time frame to assess efficacy of neurological functioning, then measures of intraindividual variability over such very short intervals may be the "purest" indicator of age-related processing efficiency.

Having said this, another issue that must be considered in evaluating the age or other between-group differences in intraindividual variability is the impact of group differences in overall speed of performance and systematic changes in speed related to practice and other time-related processes (this issue applies to measures of accuracy as well, but it is particularly relevant in the case of tasks assessing response speed). The simplest and most frequently used index of intraindividual variability is the intraindividual standard deviation (ISD) computed across time (trials or occasions). However, computation of ISDs using raw-score responses (e.g., reaction time latencies) is potentially problematic. Group differences in average level of performance as well as systematic changes over time (e.g., across trials or occasions) associated with practice or different materials therefore represent potential confounds for the analysis of intraindividual variability. For example, older adults may exhibit increased ISDs computed on raw RT scores simply as a function of their slower average response latencies (i.e., higher mean RTs are typically associated with higher standard deviations). Similarly, practice often markedly reduces response times and may do so at a differential rate for different age groups.

The importance of this issue is illustrated by a recent pair of papers. Deary and Der (2005) reported significant gender differences in inconsistency with women showing more variability in choice RT than men. Deary and Der controlled for mean RT, but were not able to assess systematic trial effects because of the way the data were recorded. Reimers and Maylor (2006) recently tested the hypothesis that the gender effect was due to differences between men and women in their rate of performance improvement across trials. Using data from a large online choice RT study, Reimers and Maylor replicated the finding that women are more variable than men. However, women were also slower than men on the initial trials, but became faster than men with practice. When the initial trials were excluded, the gender effect disappeared. To the extent that intraindividual variability is defined as fluctuations in performance independent of systematic (nonreversible) effects such as learning (Hultsch & MacDonald, 2004; Nesselroade & Featherman, 1997), these findings suggest that it is critical to address such potential confounds. There are multiple ways to address these potential problems (Hultsch & MacDonald, 2004), and we will return to this issue in a later section. However, for now we simply note the issue and the fact that some studies have not addressed it at all, whereas others have employed various strategies to remove group and systematic time-related effects from the data prior to or following computation of indices of intraindividual variability.

Longitudinal Changes

Cross-sectional age differences are, of course, subject to a host of caveats (Baltes, Reese, & Nesselroade, 1977), and the demonstration of simple age differences is not very meaningful theoretically (Perfect & Maylor, 2000). Longitudinal data provide somewhat stronger evidence for age-related increases in intraindividual variability. The few studies that are available suggest that there are average longitudinal increases in intraindividual variability, particularly in the older age ranges (Deary & Der, 2005; Fozard et al., 1994; MacDonald, Hultsch, & Dixon, 2003). For example, MacDonald et al. (2003) examined longitudinal changes in inconsistency on four RT tasks administered three times over 6 years to a sample of 446 adults from the Victoria Longitudinal Study. Participants were divided into three age groups based on age at initial testing, and inconsistency scores were computed based on residual trial-to-trial latency scores partialed for age group differences in average speed as well as practice and other systematic time-related effects. Figure 10.4 shows there were significant increases in average within-person inconsistency over the longitudinal interval as implied by cross-sectional comparisons of younger and older adults. However, longitudinal increases across the 6 years were evident only in the oldest participants (75–94 years) compared with young-old (55–64 years) and mid-old adults (65–74 years) who showed little evidence for average change. Interestingly, Deary and Der (2005) recently reported longitudinal increases in intraindividual variability in simple and choice RT for both middle-aged and older adults. Their population-based sample was probably less select than the Victoria sample which

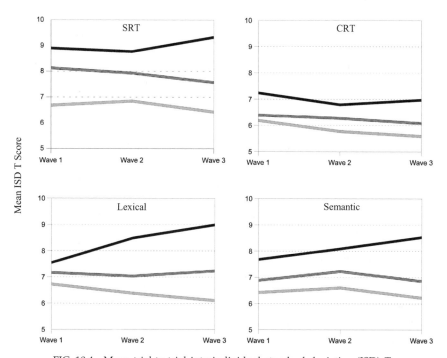

FIG. 10.4. Mean trial-to-trial intraindividual standard deviation (ISD) T-scores for four RT tasks by age group and longitudinal wave of testing. Young-Old = 55–64 years indicated by light lines, Mid-Old = 65–74 years indicated by medium lines, Old-Old = 75–94 years indicated by dark lines at Wave 1. From Figure 3, MacDonald, S. W. S., Hultsch, D. F., and Dixon, R. A. (2003). Performance variability is related to change in cognition: Evidence from the Victoria Longitudinal Study. *Psychology and Aging, 18,* 510–523. Copyright © 2003 by the American Psychological Association. Reprinted with permission.

may account for the observation of significant changes at younger ages.

Overall, the age-related results are consistent with the proposition that measures of intraindividual variability may be a useful indicator of cognitive aging. However, examination of other group and individual difference patterns of performance inconsistency can help shed more light on the issue.

Neurological Status

Historically, a number of authors have emphasized the association of inconsistency and neurological disturbance. Harlow (1868) provides an excellent description of this phenomenon (1868) in his famous study of Phineas Gage whose accident caused significant medial frontal pathology. Prior to the accident, Gage was "persistent in executing all his plans of action." Subsequently, however, he was "capricious and vacillating." The importance of the phenomenon was also noted by Henry Head (1926) who proposed that "an inconsistent response is one of the most striking results produced by a lesion of the cerebral cortex." In addition to these clinical observations, there were hints in the research literature suggesting the importance of this phenomenon. Benton and Blackburn (1957) reported that a group of brain-damaged individuals, most with vascular disease or neoplasms, showed a significant increase in intraindividual variability in simple but not choice RT in comparison to patient controls. Bruhn and Parsons (1977) also found greater within-person variability across RT trials in people with epilepsy and individuals suffering from unspecified types of brain damage in comparison to controls.

It has only been in recent years, however, that researchers have begun to explore systematically the proposal that intraindividual variability represents a behavioral marker of underlying central nervous system dysfunction. Much of this research has focused on head injury, and aging-related conditions such as dementia and mild cognitive impairment (MCI). Table 10.2 provides a summary of the results of recent studies. As detailed below, this literature reveals greater intraindividual variability in patients diagnosed with a variety of neurological, but not nonneurological, conditions. Further, the research suggests an association between intraindividual variability and severity of neurological dysfunction, with more severe disturbance demonstrating greater inconsistency. Intraindividual variability appears to be a relatively general phenomenon because it is observed with central nervous system compromise arising from various etiologies although it may be more pronounced in certain disorders. Finally, there is evidence, for many of these conditions, that increased variability reflects reduced attentional/executive efficiency.

TABLE 10.2
Summary of Results of Recent Studies

Condition	Authors	Contrast Groups	Tasks/Procedure	Findings
Traumatic Brain Injury	Burton, Hultsch, Strauss, and Hunter (2002)	Mild TBI Mod/severe TBI Healthy adults Note: All patients in chronic stages of recovery.	Physical performance. Affect/stress. Assessed on 10 occasions.	Increased variability in physical functioning in TBI compared to healthy controls.
	Bleiberg, Garmoe, Halpern, Reeves, and Nadler (1997)	Mild/moderate TBI Healthy controls	RT tasks varying from SRT to complex reasoning tasks.	Increased variability in TBI in their within- and across-day performances.
	Collins and Long (1996)	TBI patients Healthy controls	SRT and CRT tasks.	Increased variability in TBI. Variability better than speed in discriminating non-impaired TBI patients and controls.
	Hetherington, Stuss, and Finlayson (1996)	Mod/severe TBI patients 5 and 10 years post-TBI Healthy controls	RT tasks varying from simple RT to complex choice RT. Tasks repeated one week later.	Increased variability in TBI; increased variability on the more complex tasks; the shorter the time since injury, the greater the variability.
	Perbal, Couillet, Azouvi, and Pouthas (2003)	Severe TBI patients Healthy controls	Time estimation.	Increased variability in TBI in duration of reproduction and production tasks; working memory and speed scores correlated with variability.
	Segalowitz, Dywan, and Unsal (1997)	Mod/severe TBI patients Healthy controls	Oddball CRT and ERP components (P300 and CNV).	Increased variability in TBI; increases in RT variability related to P300 amplitude and to the pre-response component of CNV.

(Continued)

TABLE 10.2
(Continued)

Condition	Authors	Contrast Groups	Tasks/ Procedure	Findings
	Stuss, Stethem, Hugenholtz, Picton, Pivik, and Richard (1989)	TBI patients of varying severity Mildly concussed patients Normal controls	RT tasks varying from simple RT to complex choice RT. Tasks given 1–5 times, depending on the sample.	Increased variability within and across occasions in TBI patients compared to healthy controls; the shorter the time since TBI, the greater the variability.
	Stuss, Pogue, Buckle, and Bondar (1994)	TBI of varying severity Healthy controls	RT tasks varying from simple RT to complex choice RT. Tasks repeated one week later.	Increased variability in the TBI group; no relation between variability and indices of TBI severity, age, or education.
Dementia	Burton, Strauss, Hunter, and Hultsch (2006)	Patients with PD Patients with mild AD Healthy controls	SRT, CRT, word recognition, story recognition. Tasks repeated on four separate occasions spaced about a week apart.	AD cases more variable than PD cases and both more variable than healthy controls; lower MMSE and FSIQ scores associated with increased variability.
	Hultsch, MacDonald, and Dixon (2000)	Mild dementia Individuals with arthritis Healthy controls	SRT, CRT, word recognition, story recognition. Tasks repeated on four separate occasions spaced about a week apart.	Increased variability in mild dementia cases.
	Knotek, Bayles, and Kaszniak (1990)	Mild and moderate AD patients Healthy controls	PPVT (picture naming) was repeated following a 7-day interval.	Moderate AD patients gave more inconsistent responses than normals; a similar trend evident in mild AD cases.
	Murtha, Cismaru, Waechter, and Chertkow (2002)	Patient with AD Patients with frontal lobe dementia Healthy controls	Stroop test, SRT, CRT; tasks given weekly for 5 weeks.	Greater variability with increasing dementia severity, with more effortful tasks, and in those with frontal lobe dementia.

	Study	Sample	Measures/Tasks	Findings
	Strauss, MacDonald, Hunter, Moll, and Hultsch (2002)	Mild dementia Individuals with arthritis Healthy controls	Measures of physical status (balance/gait, fine motor dexterity, blood pressure, respiratory function) and affect/beliefs. Tasks repeated on four separate occasions spaced about a week apart.	Increased variability in physical performance in mild dementia cases.
	Walker et al. (2000)	Patients with AD Patients with DLB Patients with vascular dementia Healthy elderly controls	Choice RT. Digit vigilance RT.	Greater variability in patients with DLB
Other				
	Stuss, Murphy, Binns, and Alexander (2003)	Patients with frontal and nonfrontal lesions, Normal controls	RT tasks varying in complexity.	Greater variability in patients with frontal lesions except those with exclusively inferior medial damage.
Mild Cognitive Impairment	Christensen, Dear, Anstey, Parslow, Sachdev, and Jorm (2005)	Community-dwelling individuals aged 60–64	SRT, CRT.	Greater variability in those with MCI, but variability did not contribute uniquely to identifying MCI beyond mean RT.
	Dixon, Garrett, Lentz, MacDonald, Strauss, and Hultsch (2007)	Two samples of community-dwelling adults aged 64–90+	Study 1: SRT, CRT, lexical and semantic decision RT; Study 2: SRT, CRT, one-back.	Within-person variability better than mean level in distinguishing cognitive status groups, particularly in those aged 74+ and when complex RT tasks used.
	Strauss, Bielak, Bunce, Hunter, and Hultsch (in press)	Community-dwelling adults aged 64–92	RT tasks varying in complexity.	Those with multiple areas of impairment more variable, particularly on more cognitively demanding tasks.

Head Injury

A number of reports have suggested that intraindividual variability is increased in persons with traumatic brain injuries (TBI) at least for some tasks and at some points in the recovery process. For example, Stuss and his colleagues (Hetherington, Stuss, & Finlayson, 1996; Stuss, Stethem, Hugenholtz, Picton, Pivik, & Richard, 1989; Stuss et al., 1994) compared patients with TBI and healthy controls on a variety of RT tasks. They found greater inconsistency in the performance of brain-injured individuals compared with controls on the more complex RT tasks, both within a test session and across assessments. In addition, individuals with a shorter time since injury showed greater inconsistency on the RT tasks than those with a longer time since injury. That is, intraindividual variability may be sensitive to recovery of function, with individuals demonstrating more inconsistency when disorders are more severe in the early postinjury period.

Measures of inconsistency on RT tasks appear to bring additional information to the assessment process; that is, they are sensitive to residual processing deficits often overlooked by traditional neuropsychological tests. For example, Collins and Long (1996) reported increased inconsistency across trials in simple and choice RT tasks in people who had suffered a TBI, even though they were not impaired in their standard neuropsychological test performance as assessed by the Impairment Index of the Halstead-Reitan Neuropsychological Test Battery. Intraindividual variability proved better than overall speed in distinguishing these mildly impaired patients from controls. Similar findings have also been reported by Bleiberg, Garmoe, Halpern, Reeves, and Nadler (1997).

The increased inconsistency of RT in TBI patients does not appear to be due to increased variability in the time taken to evaluate information; rather, it appears to reflect some defect in more effortful, attention-demanding processes. Segalowitz, Dywan, and Unsal (1997) found that latency and variability in behavioral RT were correlated with the latency and variability of electrophysiological measures of attention and information processing (the P300 ERP). Among normal controls, RT was related to allocation of attention as indexed by the P300 amplitude; higher amplitude was associated with shorter behavioral response times. For the TBI patients, variability of behavioral response time (but not response speed) was associated with electrophysiological indicators of allocation of attention (P300 amplitude) and control (CNV E-wave); higher P300 amplitude and CNV E-wave were associated with less variability (Segalowitz et al., 1997). These findings are consistent with the notion that intraindividual variability is sensitive to central nervous system disturbance, particularly in conditions requiring executive processes (Bunce et al., 2004; Strauss, Bielak, Bunce, Hunter, & Hultsch, in press; West et al., 2002). Related to this, there are some suggestions in the head injury literature relating inconsistency to frontal disturbances. Stuss (1991) has observed that TBI patients, although suffering from diffuse damage, may predominantly have frontotemporal pathology. This hypothesis requires verification.

TBI patients also show more intraindividual variability than controls when making judgments of temporal duration (Perbal, Couillet, Azouvi, & Pouthas, 2003). The increased variability appears highly correlated with performance on measures of attention, working memory, and processing speed, suggesting that in patients with TBI deficits do not relate specifically to timing but rather are due to problems in these other areas (Perbal et al., 2003).

Increased intraindividual variability in persons with TBI also extends to other domains. For example, Burton, Hultsch, Strauss, and Hunter (2002) examined physical functioning and self-perceived affect/stress in three groups of adults: adults with mild head injuries, adults with moderate/severe head injuries, and healthy adults. Individuals with head injuries (of a chronic nature) showed greater intraindividual variability on certain physical tasks (finger dexterity, grip strength but not gait, blood pressure, peak expiratory flow) than healthy controls. Burton and her colleagues suggested that intraindividual variability represented an attribute of the person as individuals who were more variable on one task tended to be more variable on other tasks in the same domain of functioning as well as in other domains (e.g., in physical status and in emotional status). Further, consistent with the notion that intraindividual variability is a marker of neurobiological compromise, those individuals with poorer levels of physical functioning were more variable than those with higher levels of physical functioning.

Dementia

Increased intraindividual variability also appears to be characteristic of persons diagnosed with dementia. In fact, fluctuations in cognition occur in about 20% of Alzheimer disease (AD) cases, 35–50% of people with vascular dementia, and in 80–90% of those with dementia with diffuse Lewy bodies (Walker et al., 2000). One patient with diffuse Lewy body disease described by Byrne, Lennox, Lowe, and Godwin-Austen (1989) had day-to-day changes of more than 50% on the Mini Mental State Examination (MMSE); another individual experienced episodes of confusion that were so catastrophic that she varied from being mute, confused, and unable to stand without assistance to being capable of carrying on a conversation (cited in Walker et al., 2000). These clinical observations are supported by a number of empirical studies.

Knotek, Bayles, and Kaszniak (1990) examined mildly and moderately impaired patients with probable AD and healthy individuals on a picture-naming task, the Peabody Picture Vocabulary Test. Each individual was tested twice with a 7-day intertest interval. AD patients responded less consistently to the items than did the normal participants. Moreover, the moderately impaired AD patients had a higher rate of response inconsistency than the mildly impaired individuals. The authors suggested that impaired attention and an inability to access semantic memory contents may underlie the response inconsistency observed in the patients with AD.

Hultsch et al. (2000) contrasted mildly demented patients, most with a diagnosis of probable AD, with healthy individuals and with neurologically intact individuals who were suffering from significant somatic disturbance (arthritis) on a number of reaction time and episodic memory tasks. As illustrated in Figure 10.5, individuals with dementia showed increased intraindividual variability in latency both within and across four weekly test sessions relative to the adults who were neurologically intact, regardless of their health status. Further, intraindividual variability was related to level of performance on other cognitive tasks and proved uniquely predictive of neurological status independent of level of performance. The implication is that short-term intraindividual variability in cognitive performance is a stable trait of individuals, evident both within and across test sessions, and reflects primarily a central nervous system phenomenon rather than general health-related conditions.

Strauss et al. (2002) extended the study of intraindividual variability into the domains of physical status and self-perceived affect/beliefs. They examined the same individuals (that is, adults with mild dementia, arthritic adults, healthy controls) as in Hultsch et al. (2000), but focused on physical and emotional functioning. Greater intraindividual variability in physical performance was observed in those with mild dementia. By contrast, fluctuations in affect appeared to reflect other more transient sources, such as pain. In general, increased intraindividual variability in noncognitive domains was associated with poorer cognitive function. That is, those who fluctuated more physically performed worse on measures of memory, whereas those who were more stable physically had better memory. There were also cross-domain links between intraindividual variability in physical functioning and fluctuations in cognitive performance, but typically only for those with dementia. The observation that these cross-domain linkages are present in patients with dementia and less evident in neurologically normal groups suggests that there may be specific pathophysiological mechanisms underlying these associations.

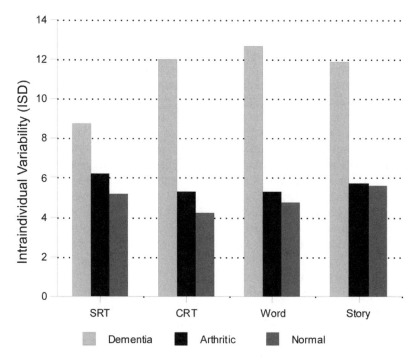

FIG. 10.5. Mean trial-to-trial intraindividual standard deviation (ISD) T-scores by group and task. SRT = simple reaction time; CRT = 2-choice reaction time. From Hultsch, D. F., MacDonald, S. W. S., Hunter, M. A., Levy-Bencheton, J., and Strauss, E. (2000). Intraindividual variability in cognitive performance in older adults: Comparison of adults with mild dementia, adults with arthritis, and healthy adults. *Neuropsychology, 14,* 588–598. Copyright © 2000 by the American Psychological Association. Reprinted with permission.

One way to explore the issue of underlying mechanisms is to determine whether the fluctuations in performance are more characteristic of some neurological disorders than others. Burton et al. (2006a) found AD patients showed more inconsistency in latency of performance on simple, choice, and episodic memory tasks than patients with Parkinson's disease (PD). However, differences in overall severity of cognitive impairment (AD patients more severely impaired) and drug regimen (PD patients were medicated) complicated interpretation of the results. Murtha, Cismaru, Waechter, and Chertkow (2002) evaluated two groups of dementia patients (those with probable AD versus those with frontal lobe dementia), matched in terms of dementia severity, and normal elderly controls. Participants were tested once a week for five consecutive weeks on a Stroop test and three reaction-time tasks varying in complexity (simple, cued choice, choice). Inconsistency in performance over the five test sessions was greater with increasing dementia severity and in task situations which demanded more effortful processing. Further, inconsistency was more marked in the frontal lobe dementia group than the AD group, suggesting an association with frontal rather than temporal lobe pathologies.

Consistent with this, Walker et al. (2000) reported greater fluctuations in cognition (evaluated by clinical ratings of alertness, concentration, confusion) and in attention (measured via vigilance and choice RT tasks) in patients with diffuse Lewy body dementia than in those with vascular dementia or AD. A similar fluctuating profile was observed in the mean electrocortical (EEG) rhythms. Of note, diffuse Lewy body dementia is characterized by visual-perceptual and attentional-executive impairments and the most frequent locations of Lewy bodies are in the frontal, cingulate, and inferior temporal cortex (Collerton, Burn, McKeith, & O'Brien, 2003). Individuals with AD have the least involvement of the frontal lobes and the least intraindividual variability. In line with this proposal are recent findings by Stuss, Murphy, Binns, and Alexander (2003). They studied patients with focal frontal or nonfrontal lesions— all with an acute acquired etiology (infarction, hemorrhage, trauma, or resection of a benign tumor). Patients with frontal lobe lesions, except those with inferior medial damage, showed increased intraindividual variability on reaction time tasks. This suggests that increased intraindividual variability may not be a general effect of brain damage, but rather may depend on the involvement of specific frontal circuits.

However, such findings do not rule out the possibility of increased variability that is specific to impairments in other brain regions. Patients with right brain damage and spatial neglect show increased variability on line bisection tasks (Anderson et al., 2000) and patients with left brain damage and aphasia show increased variability on lexical decision task (Milberg et al., 2003). Thus, there are likely multiple routes to increased variability, with disturbances of the frontal lobes playing a prominent role (see also Stuss et al., 2003).

Mild Cognitive Impairment

The term mild cognitive impairment is typically used to refer to a transitional state between normal cognitive function and clinically probable AD or other type of dementia (Tuokko & McDowell, 2006; Winblad et al., 2004). Traditionally, studies on the prediction of individuals at risk for dementia have focused on mean level of performance. However, the finding of greater intraindividual variability in patients with a variety of neurological conditions (see above) suggests the possibility that inconsistency in performance may be an early indicator of decline that may be detectable prior to clinically significant change in level of performance.

To date, three studies have evaluated whether inconsistency in response speed is a useful indicator of mild cognitive impairment (see Table 10.2). Unfortunately, the studies have yielded somewhat contradictory results. Christensen, Dear, Anstey, Parslow, Sachdev, and Jorm (2005) evaluated community-dwelling individuals aged 60–64 years on both simple and choice reaction time (RT) tasks and found that variability was greater in individuals who showed some form of mild cognitive disorder—a finding consistent with the notion that variability is an indicator of central nervous system compromise. When subtypes of cognitive disorder were considered, variability was greater for those meeting criteria for Age-Associated Cognitive Decline (Levy, 1994; 1 SD below age group on any of a number of tasks) and Mild Cognitive Impairment (Petersen, Smith, Waring, Ivnik, Tangalos, & Kokmen, 1999; objective and subjective memory impairment adjusted for age and education), but not for those classified with Age-Associated Memory Impairment (Crook, Bartus, Ferris, Whitehouse, Cohen, & Gershon, 1986; 1 SD below mean of young adults on memory tests). However, variability did not add to the precision of diagnostic classification (screened positive versus negative for cognitive disorder) beyond that contributed by mean RT performance.

On the other hand, Dixon et al. (2007) examined two separate samples of community-dwelling older adults spanning a wider age range (64–90+ years) on a more extensive battery of tasks (e.g., simple and choice RT tasks, lexical and semantic decision making, one-back RT). They found that inconsistency increased with advancing age as well as with the extent of cognitive impairment. Further, among old-old participants (aged 74–92 years), a stepwise increase in inconsistency was seen on the more cognitively demanding RT tasks (e.g., choice RT, one-back) with increasing extent of cognitive impairment; that is, those older adults with multiple domains of impairment were more variable than those who showed a single area of impairment. Among the mid-old adults (64–73 years), those with multiple domains of impairment were more inconsistent than those classed as intact or showing impairment in a single domain, with the latter two groups not differing from one another. In contrast to Christensen et al. (2005), inconsistency reliably predicted cognitive group differences (intact, single domain, multiple domain) over and above mean level, particularly when the more complex RT tasks (e.g., one-back) were used to assess variability.

These findings are reinforced by a recent study by Strauss et al. (in press). They examined one of the samples described in Dixon et al. (2007) on a range of reaction-time tasks spanning a continuum from simple to complex (Motor [tapping], Basic [2- and 4-choice RT], Complex [4-choice 1-back RT, task switching], Interference [spatial Stroop]). Inconsistency was greater in those with multiple domains of cognitive impairment in comparison to those who showed an isolated area of impairment (e.g., memory only). Further, the effect was stronger when more cognitively demanding tasks were used (Complex, Interference). Finally, group differentiation was better achieved when variability as opposed to mean level of performance was considered.

The discrepancy in findings is likely due to a number of factors. First, Christensen et al.'s (2005) sample represents a restricted, younger age range (60–64), whereas both Dixon et al. (2006) and Strauss et al. (in press) included older participants (64 to 92 years)—a group in which variability appears to be accentuated. Second, different measures of intraindividual variability were used with Dixon et al. and Strauss et al. employing a wider range of RT measures, varying in terms of complexity. Third, the studies used different approaches to analyzing the data as well as different methods of classifying mild cognitive impairment. For analyses bearing on the utility of variability versus level of performance, Christensen et al. (2005) used a fairly broad definition of mild cognitive impairment, classifying individuals as impaired who screened positive on *any one* of a number of different cognitive indicators (MMSE [Folstein, Folstein, & McHugh, 1975], speed, memory). By contrast, Dixon et al. (2006) and Strauss et al. (in press) grouped participants according to the presence *and extent* of impairment (single versus multiple domains) with increased variability more evident in those with more extensive impairment.

The mechanisms underlying increased intraindividual variability are not certain. However, commonalities with findings from patients with other neurological conditions (e.g., TBI, dementia) are intriguing. In the Strauss et al. study (in press), group differences were more marked in cognitively demanding situations, that is, when individuals had to manipulate information held briefly in mind, switch cognitive set, or inhibit an automatic response. Thus, at the psychological level, increased inconsistency evident in those with mild cognitive impairment may reflect inefficiencies in executive control mechanisms.

Examination of the risk factors for increased within-person variability may also provide some clues regarding causes. Christensen et al. (2005) found that lower education, a risk factor for faster cognitive deterioration in old adults (Anstey & Christensen, 2000), was associated with increased variability. Strauss et al. (in press), however, found only relatively small correlations between education and within-person variability (r values ranging from −.13 to −.18). The link between lower education and increased within-person variability is of interest since it may suggest that lower variability can index increased cognitive reserve (Christensen et al., 2005).

Brain–Behavior Relationships

If intraindividual variability is a behavioral manifestation of neuro-biological functioning, there should be associations between variability in performance and brain-based measures. Established links between intraindividual variability and brain correlates are sparse, with the preponderance of evidence being descriptive and indirect. In a recent review of available evidence, MacDonald, Nyberg, and Bäckman (2006) argue that increases in intraindividual variability likely reflect multiple neural determinants. Plausible structural brain correlates of intraindividual variability include white matter demyelination (Britton, Meyer, & Benecke, 1991) as well as lesions to frontal gray matter (Stuss et al., 2003). For example, increased intraindividual variability could reflect differences in cortical pathway lengths along which evoked potentials travel for executing a correct response, implicating the importance of white matter integrity (Reed, 1998). Moreover, decreasing variability in cognitive performance through childhood and adolescence followed by increases in later years may implicate the importance of gray matter. Specifically, the constraints of maturation and senescence represent logical correlates of intraindividual variability. Decreasing intraindividual variability from childhood through adolescence (Williams et al., 2005) coincides with reductions in gray matter density due to synaptic pruning (e.g., Gogtay et al., 2004), a process which increases neural efficiency and may decrease neural noise in cognitive functioning. Thus, larger performance fluctuations for younger children could reflect immature neural systems (Kray, Eber & Lindenberger, 2004). In contrast, reductions of gray matter in the elderly (e.g., due to neurodegenerative disease processes) are linked to functional impairments (Raz, Gunning-Dixon, Head, Rodrigue, Williamson, & Acker, 2004). Thus, the developmental evolution and involution of the brain corresponds, at least grossly, to increasing then decreasing intellectual functioning (Li et al., 2004b) as well as decreasing then increasing intraindividual variability (Williams et al., 2005) across young, middle-aged, and elderly participants.

Functional brain imaging correlates of intraindividual variability have also been identified. A review of neuroscientific perspectives on aging implicates intraindividual variability as a marker of age-related cognitive impairment (Hedden & Gabrieli, 2004), with less efficient blood oxygen level dependent (BOLD) activations observed for older adults who nonselectively recruit task-irrelevant brain regions (Logan, Sanders, Snyder, Morris, & Buckner, 2002). Variability in both behavioral performance and

BOLD activations is also an intrinsic property of schizophrenia (Manoach, 2003). Schizophrenics exhibit excessive activation of dorsolateral prefrontal cortex during working memory tasks, a pattern that connotes inefficient neural processing that may reflect abnormal prefrontal cortex neurons (Callicott et al., 2000). Although promising, these patterns of variability reflect between-person differences in BOLD activations for mean level performance—not across-trial variability. However, recent findings from an fMRI investigation are among the first to directly link intraindividual variability in behavior to the magnitude and anatomical brain location of BOLD activations (MacDonald, Nyberg, Sandblom, Fischer, & Bäckman, 2007). Nineteen older adults (70–79 years) were presented with 80 words at encoding, with brain scans and response latencies obtained during subsequent word recognition. Intraindividual standard deviations (ISDs) were computed across successful latency trials per individual. Consistent with previous findings, high ISDs were associated with poorer recognition sensitivity and slower response latencies. Of particular significance, low variability for successful word retrieval was also linked to bilateral BOLD activations in the supramarginal gyrus of the parietal lobe, a structure implicated in sustained attention, deep semantic encoding, and retrieval success (e.g., Cabeza & Nyberg, 2000). Thus, increased brain activation in this region may reflect an advantage of low-variability individuals for these three factors, with such patterns supporting the hypothesis that behavioral intraindividual variability represents a proxy for neural integrity.

Select investigations have also examined cognitive performance in relation to event-related oscillations (on a trial-by-trial basis) in the EEG band. One recent EEG study examined whether increased variability of prefrontal physiological responses was associated with frontal lobe deficits in schizophrenia (Winterer et al., 2004). Increased frontal broadband noise during information processing was negatively correlated with working memory performance. Moreover, cortical noise in frontal lobe activity was characteristically trait-like for those with schizophrenia, but to a lesser extent for their siblings without schizophrenia, and even less so for normal controls. Such increases in prefrontal cortical noise may be a function of asynchronous field potential oscillations for cortical pyramidal neurons (Winterer et al., 2004). Similarly, psychometric intelligence has been found to share an inverse relationship with event-related potential variability in the parieto-temporal lobes (Barrett & Eysenck, 1994).

Predicting Cognitive Performance

Significant increases in performance variability are seen with increasing age and appear to be moderated by neurological dysfunction and decline.

Not surprisingly, then, greater intraindividual variability is associated with lower levels of general intelligence (Jensen, 1982, 1992; Li et al., 2004b; Rabbitt et al., 2001) and poorer level of performance on multiple cognitive tasks (e.g., Anstey, 1999; Hultsch et al., 2002; Li et al., 2001a; Nesselroade & Salthouse, 2004; West et al., 2002). For example, in their population-based study of individuals aged 6 to 89 years, Li et al. (2004b) found that a composite measure of inconsistency based on 10 RT tasks predicted fluid intelligence over and above average speed of performance in old age but not childhood. This finding again points to the potential usefulness of measures of inconsistency as an indicator of cognitive functioning in later life (see also Williams et al., 2005, in press). Similarly, Rabbitt et al. (2001) found that greater inconsistency in RT performance computed over both shorter (trial-to-trial) and longer term (week-to-week) intervals was associated with poorer performance on the Culture Fair Intelligence Test. Importantly, the participants in this sample were selected so that age was not related to intelligence level, thus providing an examination of the relationship between inconsistency and intelligence independent of age. Recently, Ram et al. (2005b) reanalyzed the data previously reported by Rabbitt et al. (2001) using a variety of multivariate techniques. Using growth curve analysis, they showed that inconsistency declines with practice, and the final level of inconsistency can be interpreted as the limit of the individual's capacity. Individuals with higher scores on fluid intelligence reached lower asymptotic levels of inconsistency compared with individuals with lower scores. Moreover, even after controlling for the systematic effects of practice, variability in inconsistency from week to week was more pronounced for individuals with lower fluid intelligence scores compared to individuals with higher scores.

Consistent with the above link between intraindividual variability and general ability, other studies have shown greater inconsistency is associated with poorer performance on more specific cognitive abilities as well. For example, Hultsch et al. (2002) reported that poorer cognitive performance on measures of perceptual speed, working memory, episodic memory, and crystallized abilities was associated with greater trial-to-trial inconsistency for four different RT measures. Table 10.3 reports the correlations for the youngest (17–36 years) and oldest (75–94 years) age groups in this study, showing that significant relationships were more widespread for the older compared with the younger group.

The association of concurrent measures of inconsistency in RT and level of performance on a range of other cognitive measures is consistent with the view that performance variability might be an important indicator of cognitive aging. However, it is not very compelling evidence. A key issue is not simply whether inconsistency predicts concurrent level of cognitive

TABLE 10.3
Correlations for Youngest and Oldest Age Groups in Study by Hultsch *et al.* (2002)

Cognitive Measure	RT-ISD (trials)			
	SRT	CRT	Lexical	Semantic
Young				
Perceptual speed	−.15	−.20*	−.41**	−.33**
Working memory	−.02	−.09	−.16	−.11
Episodic memory	−14	−.15	−.31**	−.48**
Crystallized ability	−.11	−.04	−.13	−.14
Old-Old				
Perceptual speed	−.35**	−.34**	−.42**	−.27**
Working memory	−.23**	−.15*	−.31**	−.28**
Episodic memory	−.21**	−.21**	−.29**	−.24**
Crystallized ability	−.24**	−.13	−.28**	−.28**

* $p < .05$ ** $p < .01$.

performance, but whether it also predicts changes in level of cognitive performance. MacDonald et al. (2003) provided a more stringent longitudinal test of the relationship between inconsistency and level of cognitive performance. This study examined whether age differences and change in inconsistency were related to changes in multiple cognitive abilities. Data were available from 446 participants from two samples of the Victoria Longitudinal Study tested on three occasions over 6 years. Participants were divided into three age groups based on age at initial testing (55–64 years, $n = 135$; 65–74 years, $n = 225$; 75–89 years, $n = 86$). Trial-to-trial inconsistency scores for a single occasion were computed from four RT tasks: two nonverbal RT tasks (simple RT and choice RT) and two verbal RT tasks (lexical decision and semantic decision). Cognitive performance was assessed using a continuum of measures spanning processes to products of cognition, including indicators of perceptual speed (identical pictures), working memory (computation span), fluid reasoning (letter series), episodic memory (word recall and story recall), and crystallized verbal ability (vocabulary).

Two related analyses shed light on the linkage between inconsistency and cognitive change. First, there were associations between inconsistency at the first wave of measurement and subsequent cognitive change over the 6 years. Significant declines in cognitive performance were observed for all six measures. However, a repeated measures analysis of covariance revealed that longitudinal declines were no longer significant after controlling for Time 1 level of inconsistency. Up to 96% of the variance associated with wave and 42% of the variance associated with the age by wave interaction were attenuated. As expected, the inconsistency covariate significantly predicted cognitive change for all six measures. Second, in a more stringent test of the link between inconsistency and cognitive change, MacDonald et al. (2003) used hierarchical linear modeling to examine covariation between inconsistency and cognitive performance. As expected, they found that individuals had lower cognitive performance for waves on which they were more inconsistent relative to those on which they were less inconsistent. Over three waves of testing, increasing inconsistency was associated with declining cognitive performance for five of the six measures (all but vocabulary, the measure of crystallized ability). Notably, these observed covariations were independent of the average linear trend across waves. For example, for the measure of perceptual speed (identical pictures test) the average individual identified 28.08 correct match-to-targets for Wave 1 at the sample mean on inconsistency and subsequently declined 0.57 matches for each increment in inconsistency. This covariation between changes in inconsistency and changes in cognition implies that the association of inconsistency and performance is not an artifact of initial level, and further supports the view that performance variability represents a useful marker of cognitive aging.

Predicting Everyday Functioning

An increasing body of research has been devoted to examining the performance of older adults in everyday situations (e.g., Allaire & Marsiske, 1999; Cornelius & Caspi, 1987; Willis & Marsiske, 1991). In large part, this reflects the growing number of older adults who require nursing home placement, community-based services, and/or family support, and the financial and psychosocial implications of such arrangements for the individual and their families and friends. Two major categories of functional abilities are typically distinguished: (a) activities of daily living, commonly known as ADLs, that focus primarily on overlearned self-care activities such as feeding, bathing, toileting, and basic mobility (Katz, Ford, Moskowitz, Jackson, & Jaffe, 1963; Odenheimer & Minaker, 1994); and (b) instrumental activities of daily living, IADLs, that involve fairly complex cognitive abilities and include activities such as managing medication, managing finances, using transportation, using the telephone, housekeeping, meal preparation, and nutrition (Fillenbaum, 1985; Lawton and Brody, 1969). It is the IADLs that are of primary interest in studies of aging because loss of competence in complex tasks of daily living is a defining diagnostic feature of AD and related dementing disorders (APA, 2000). Recently, there have also been reports of subtle changes, according to self or other ratings or observed on performance-based measures, in complex everyday life activities of individuals classi-fied with Mild Cognitive Impairment (e.g., Artero, Touchon, & Ritchie, 2001; Tabert et al., 2002). Given the links between inconsistency and level of cognitive performance, as well as the associations between basic cogni-tive abilities and functional abilities (e.g., Allaire & Marsiske, 1999; Bur-ton, Strauss, Hultsch, & Hunter, 2006a; Cornelius & Caspi, 1987), one might expect inconsistency in performance to be predictive of everyday functioning.

Burton, Strauss, Hunter, and Hultsch (in press) examined a sample of community-dwelling older adults, ranging in age from 62 to 92. Based on a series of benchmark cognitive tasks, participants were categorized into three groups, ranging from cognitively intact to mildly impaired but not yet demented. In addition to a series of reaction-time tasks, participants also completed a measure of everyday competence, the Everyday Prob-lems Test (EPT; Willis & Marsiske, 1999), a paper and pencil task that requires participants to solve problems associated with daily living. For example, with respect to meal preparation, participants are provided with a nutritional information chart for cereal and are asked to determine how many calories are in a serving of cereal if whole milk is used instead of skim milk. For a question on transportation, participants are provided with a chart of taxi rates and are asked to determine how much they would have to pay if they traveled 1 mile in a suburban area. Both mean latencies and inconsistency scores were significantly associated with EPT performance, such that slower and more inconsistent reaction times were associated with poorer everyday problem solving abilities. Even after accounting for age, education, and mean level performance, inconsistency in reaction time continued to account for a significant proportion of the variance (about 5–10%) in EPT scores. Mean latencies failed to account for a significant proportion of the variance above and beyond inconsistency.

These findings suggest that inconsistency has functional relevance even in those with very mild levels of cognitive impairment. However, its clin-ical importance requires additional study. First, it would be important to evaluate the link between inconsistency and functional status, using other measures of everyday performance, such as self and other ratings. Second, the observed link between inconsistency in reaction time and everyday performance in this cross-sectional sample raises the question of whether inconsistency predicts declines in everyday functioning. Finally, it is also important to note that functional status is influenced by cognitive abilities such as memory, executive function, visual-spatial ability, and language (e.g., Allaire & Marsiske, 1999; Burton et al., 2006a). An import-ant area for further investigation is to determine whether inconsistency makes a unique contribution in predicting functional status over and above these cognitive abilities. That is, after accounting for other cognitive abilities that have been found to be important determinants of everyday performance, such as memory, executive function, visuospatial ability, and language, does inconsistency provide additional predictive utility?

Predicting Mortality

Given links between intraindividual variability and neurological impairment, it stands to reason that inconsistency may also foreshadow impending death. Considerable evidence documents the association between accelerated cognitive decline and proximity to death in older adults (Bosworth & Schaie, 1999; Johansson & Zarit, 1997; Kleemeier, 1962). Such precipitous changes in cognitive performance may reflect general CNS disturbances and/or declining biological vitality (Berg, 1996) as well as specific causes of death such as cardiovascular disease (Hassing et al., 2002). Thus, it is plausible to expect that inconsistency in performance might be associated with proximity to death, and possibly with specific causes of death. MacDonald (2003) recently examined this question using data from the Victoria Longitudinal Study spanning five waves of measurement. The sample consisted of 707 older adults (aged 59 to 95 years at final testing). Whereas 442 survivors completed all waves and relevant measures, 265 decedents participated on at least one occasion and subsequently died. Decedents' date and cause of death information were obtained from Vital Statistics records of the province of British Columbia, Canada. Participants were grouped by age (59–79 years and 80–95 years) and presence or absence of cardiovascular and cerebrovascular conditions (CVD; current diagnosis for survivors and cause of death for decedents). Measures of trial-to-trial response time inconsistency were available for two speeded verbal decision tasks (lexical decision and semantic decision).

Consistent with expectations, greater inconsistency at the last wave of testing was observed for older adults, individuals with CVD, and decedents. Significant interactions among these factors were observed for both inconsistency measures. Figure 10.6 shows select patterns for the lexical decision task. For the younger group, inconsistency across trials was comparable across mortality status and disease classification. Decedents with CVD were more variable than both survivor groups, but no other comparisons were significant. In contrast, for the older group, all pairwise comparisons were significant with the exception of the two survivor groups. These results suggest that, in addition to general neurological disturbances, specific disease processes such as CVD magnify differences in inconsistency in late life.

As was the case for the earlier section summarizing inconsistency as a predictor of cognitive performance, the cross-sectional results linking

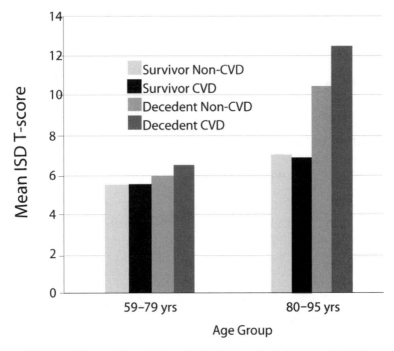

FIG. 10.6. Mean trial-to-trial intraindividual standard deviation (ISD) T-scores for lexical decision RT by age group, disease classification, and mortality status. CVD = cardiovascular and cerebrovascular disease.

inconsistency to mortality are intriguing, but limited. More compelling evidence comes from longitudinal analyses which also indicated differential increases in performance inconsistency over time as a function of age, disease condition, and mortality status. As shown in Figure 10.7, increases in inconsistency over 6 years were observed for older individuals, and these increases were particularly notable for individuals who died of CVD-related causes. Moreover, multilevel analyses of change were employed to examine the time-varying covariation between longitudinal changes in performance inconsistency with increasing proximity to death. Inconsistency increased per additional year closer to death, with significantly higher rates of change for older adults and for decedents. In summary, these longitudinal patterns point to a systematic relationship between inconsistency in RT and proximity to death, perhaps reflecting an early behavioral marker of neurological dysfunction.

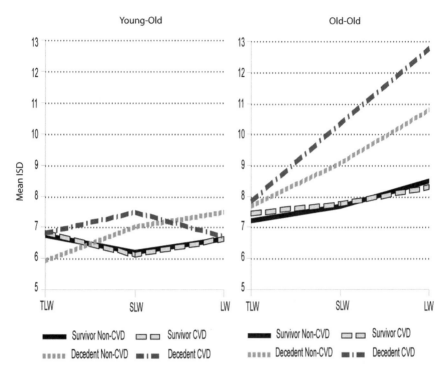

FIG. 10.7. Six-year change in mean trial-to-trial intraindividual standard deviation (ISD) T-scores for lexical decision RT by age group, disease classification, and mortality status. CVD = cardiovascular and cerebrovascular disease. TLW = third last wave, SLW = second-last wave, LW = last wave.

UNRESOLVED ISSUES

The research reviewed above suggests that indicators of intraindividual variability are predictive of multiple outcomes. In particular, measures of moment-to-moment inconsistency in response time appear to be associated with lower performance on multiple cognitive tasks, poorer functional capacity in a variety of instrumental activities of daily living, and proximity to death. However, there are many issues that require clarification before the contribution of intraindividual variability to understanding cognitive aging can be fully assessed. We now turn to some of these issues.

Statistical Indicators of Intraindividual Variability

We mentioned previously that there are two major types of intraindividual variation: systematic within-person changes, often called intraindividual change; and within-person fluctuations over relatively short periods of time, which we refer to as intraindividual variability or inconsistency. Methods that focus on systematic change are typically interested in describing and modeling the *form* of intraindividual variability (e.g., Moskowitz & Hershberger, 2002), whereas analyses that focus on short-term fluctuations in behavior are typically interested in the *amount* of intraindividual variability. Our focus is on methods for measuring and modeling the amount of intraindividual variability, although we will briefly return to discuss the dynamic structure of intraindividual variability at the end of this section.

Indices of Amount of Intraindividual Variability

The most frequently used measure of amount of intraindividual variability is the intraindividual standard deviation computed across time (trials or occasions) using raw-score responses (the raw-score ISD). Although this method is direct computationally, it is indirect conceptually and can be difficult to interpret. Consider the structural model associated with the data from a study of group differences in individual performance across time:

$$Y_{ijk} = \mu + g_i + t_j + (gt)_{ij} + p_{k(i)} + e_{ikj}$$

where Y_{ijk} is the performance score for person k, in group i taken on the jth occasion; μ is the grand mean; g_i is the effect of group i; t_j is the effect of time j; $(gt)_{ij}$ is the interaction effect of group i and time j; $p_{k(i)}$ is the individual difference component for subject k within group i; and e_{ijk} is the residual for subject k in group i at time j. From this decomposition it can be seen that each score potentially contains systematic and unsystematic within-subject components, as well as systematic between-group and residual within-group components, and that combining these scores into a raw-score ISD will produce a measure of an individual's total intraindividual variability containing a mixture of all of these sources of variation. Accordingly, if one were to compare raw-score ISDs between groups (e.g., age groups), they could differ due to group differences in systematic within-subject variability (practice effects, fatigue, etc.), group differences in unsystematic within-subject variability (e.g., inconsistency), or systematic overall between-group differences (group differences in overall mean performance).

That group comparison of raw-score ISDs is likely affected by group differences in mean performance has been well recognized among researchers who study variability (Hale, Myerson, Smith, & Poon, 1988; Shammi et al., 1998). Two relatively common procedures used to address this issue are Analysis of Covariance (ANCOVA), and use of the Intra-individual Coefficient of Variation (ICV). We consider each of these procedures below.

ANCOVA is run in an attempt to control statistically for mean perform-ance differences by using an index of intraindividual variability $ISD_{residual}$ rather than raw-score ISD, where $ISD_{residual}$ is equal to the raw-score ISD minus that part of it that is predictable from mean performance. ANCOVA is run in hopes of asking whether groups differ in inconsistency were they not different in mean performance. The use of ANCOVA to equate nonequivalent groups that differ on the covariate has many critics whose opinions range from recommending caution (e.g., Campbell & Stanley, 1963; Howell, 1992) to recommending that it be avoided altogether (e.g., Elashoff, 1969; Huitema, 1980; Maxwell and Delaney, 1990; and Pedhazur, 1997). The severest critics argue that the results of ANCOVA are valid only if the grouping variable (e.g., age) and the cov-ariate (e.g., mean performance) are independent. Otherwise, not only is the covariate partialed from the dependent variable, it is also partialed from the group variable to produce $Group_{residual}$, which at best no longer has the same meaning as Group (although it is interpreted as such by most users), and at worst is not interpretable (e.g., what would have to be done in order to make older and younger adults equal on the covariate, and is it possible? If it is possible, would our results represent the same population of old and young adults that we started with and want to generalize to?). Even those who merely recommend caution agree that at a minimum data on the covariate should be gathered before treatments are administered or groups are formed. Failure to do this means that the covariate and dependent variable are equally affected by group such that ANCOVA removes some portion of the effect of interest (i.e., group) from the dependent variable when the covariate adjustment is calculated. In the case of inconsistency data, both mean performance and inconsistency are measured after groups are formed and indeed both are based on the same scores. Thus, using ANCOVA on such data does not "control for" mean performance, but instead removes from the group sum of squares part of the effect of interest.

We side with those experts who recommend caution in the use of ANCOVA and suggest that if it is used to analyze group differences in inconsistency while partialing mean performance, the logic of interpret-ation should be one of direct and indirect effects, not one of statistical control. For example, a pattern of results that shows group differences in both mean performance and inconsistency, a relationship between mean performance and inconsistency, and attenuated group differences in inconsistency when both group and mean performance are used as pre-dictors is consistent with a model in which group effects on inconsistency are mediated by mean performance. Of course one should have a reasonable theory or argument for such a model. It is also possible that differences in inconsistency produce differences in mean performance, in which case inconsistency would be considered the mediator. A third option, and one that we prefer (see Cohen, Cohen, West, & Aiken, 2003, pp. 452–454), is that both mean performance and inconsistency, although collinear, might provide independent information for differentiating groups. Testing this notion requires assigning Group as the dependent variable and then evaluating the direct effects of mean performance and inconsistency.

Unfortunately, there is another potentially more serious problem with using ANCOVA to analyze group differences in raw-score ISDs even if partialing mean performance could be unambiguously interpreted as a statistical control technique. The problem is that it still does nothing to control for the mixture of systematic and unsystematic *within-subject variation* inherent in the raw-score ISD (see the structural model above). Even after partialing individual means, between-group comparisons in raw-score ISDs could still reflect group differences in practice effects, fatigue, etc., group differences in inconsistency, or both. This is particularly problematic because it is possible that the systematic portion (e.g., practice-effects, learning) might have a very different, perhaps opposite, relationship to grouping variables such as age, neurological status, etc., compared to the unsystematic portion (see Allaire & Marsiske, 2005). This is also a problem for the coefficient of variation as it is typically calculated, a topic to which we turn next.

The intraindividual coefficient of variation (ICV) attempts to control for mean performance by dividing individual raw-score ISDs by individual performance means. The idea is that if the standard deviation increases proportional to mean performance, and if there are group differences in mean performance, the ICV will not show a group effect. One problem with the ICV is that it is a cross-product term and thus contains an ambiguous combination of the main effect of the raw-score ISD, the main effect of (the inverse of) mean performance, and the interaction between the two. Thus even if the data suggest that group differences in (or the effects of) the raw-score ISD are dampened in proportion to the mean, an unambiguous test would have to include along with the ICV the main effects of mean performance and raw-score ISD in the model. Otherwise, the model is misspecified and the results could reflect any of these three effects. These issues aside, we believe the most serious problem with using the ICV as an index of inconsistency is that, like ANCOVA adjustment, it still does not distinguish between systematic and unsystematic within-subject sources of variability.

Given the ambiguity of using ANCOVA and the ICV to control for mean performance, and in particular given the fact that neither of these procedures disentangles systematic from unsystematic within-subject sources of variation (and between-subject interactions with them), researchers are turning to an alternative index of intraindividual variability. This index is based on decomposing the structural model shown above into its constituent parts (systematic and unsystematic within-subject variability, and systematic and unsystematic between-subject variability) using either mixed-model ANOVA or a random regression model, and then computing intraindividual variability as the standard deviation of each subject's unsystematic portion (i.e., each subject's e_{ikj}). We call the index the residual ISD (as opposed to ISD$_{residual}$ from ANCOVA), and it has two advantages over the ANCOVA and ICV indices. First, although by definition groups cannot show mean differences on these residuals (nor can there be any systematic trends or group differences in those trends), they can differ in the extent to which their residuals deviate relative to their de-trended and equated group means and therefore in their average residual ISD. If groups do differ in average residual ISD, it cannot be due to group differences in practice, fatigue, etc., nor to between-group variation in mean performance, which is important for those researchers who define inconsistency as intraindividual variability that is independent of systematic between- and within-subject effects.

The second advantage is more philosophical than computational. It seems to us preferable to decompose (partial) the data first and then base an index of intraindividual variability directly on the unsystematic portion, rather than to compute a measure of total intraindividual variability first and then try to derive a measure of unsystematic intraindividual variability via partialing (or dividing) after the fact. As an analogy to these different strategies, consider investigating age differences in verbal and performance IQ. One would most likely first "decompose" the overall IQ test into scales/items measuring PIQ and scales/items measuring VIQ and then compute separate scores for VIQ and PIQ directly from their constituent scales/items. One would not likely consider analyzing FSIQ with VIQ partialed and calling that an analysis of PIQ, or FSIQ with PIQ partialed and calling that VIQ. The former procedure is akin to residual ISD, and the latter to ISD$_{residual}$.

The Dynamic Structure of Intraindividual Variability

Recently, measures of the amount of intraindividual variability have been supplemented by assessments of its dynamic structure via measures of cyclicity, autocorrelation, approximate entropy, and pink noise (Clayton & Bruhns Frey, 1997; Ram, Chow, Bowles, Wang, Grimm, Fujita, &

Nesselroade, 2005a; Slifkin & Newell 1998; Van Orden, Holden, & Turvey, 2003). Most of these techniques come from the tradition of time series analysis and as such are applied to data from which external sources of variability such as group effects and systematic time effects have been removed (i.e., the same data that form the basis of residual ISD; data that historically have been considered error or background noise). Two recent examples of this tradition show its promise for the study of intraindividual variability, cognition, and aging. Van Orden et al. (2003) investigated the dynamic structure of simple reaction times and speeded word naming times. They applied spectral analysis to each subject's de-trended time series to transform the time domain into a frequency domain, then plotted frequency against power (amplitude squared) in Base-10 logarithmic units, and finally calculated the slope of the frequency/power relationship. They found that the slopes were all negative in a range consistent with pink noise. The significance of these analyses lies in the fact that pink noise is indicative of systems that self-organize their behavior. Given that this analysis produces a separate slope for each individual subject, one can imagine applying it to the reaction time data of different age groups either cross-sectionally or longitudinally to evaluate age-related differences or changes in self-organization, and whether self-organization is correlated with other cognitive domains.

Ram et al. (2005a) also applied spectral analysis to de-trended time series data, and then evaluated interindividual differences in cyclicity by fitting a multilevel sinusoidal model of change. Their model provides parameter estimates of periodicity (amplitude and cycle length) for each subject, again allowing for mean comparisons among groups as well as providing variables for individual difference analyses. An additional feature of their method is that it incorporates an Item Response model for use with data that are not on interval or ratio scales (they illustrated their procedure with ratings of emotional states). Clearly a full characterization of intraindividual variability will require assessing both the amount and dynamic structure of performance variability. Thus, these newer methods represent an exciting addition to the field.

Structure of Intraindividual Variability

We noted previously that simple correlational analyses have suggested there is relative stability of individual differences in intraindividual variability over time within tasks, as well as positive associations among measures of intraindividual variability across different tasks or domains of functioning. These univariate relationships imply the possibility that there is an underlying structure of intraindividual variability. To date, only a few studies have attempted to address this issue using multivariate approaches.

Some analyses have examined whether inconsistency in response speed can be differentiated from average speed. In an early effort of this type, Jensen (1992) used principal component factor analysis to determine if the median (md) and standard deviation (SD) of RT reflect the same or different sources of variance. This analysis used data from multiple studies of children and university students who had performed two different RT tasks. The results for both tasks showed a large general factor shared in common by md and SD and a second bipolar factor that corresponded to the md and SD sources of variance. Jensen concluded that measures of RT central tendency and variability reflect distinct sources of variance, in addition to the large proportion that they have in common.

More recently, Ram et al. (2005b) used contemporary analytic techniques to address the same question. In this analysis, Ram and his colleagues examined 12 indicators of inconsistency and 12 measures of memory speed derived from letter search tasks varying in difficulty administered across 36 weekly sessions to a sample of adults aged 52 to 79 years. Chain p-technique factor analysis was used to develop and test a measurement model. The analysis indicated that the 24 measures were represented parsimoniously by two underlying latent factors: one accounting for the common variation between the 12 inconsistency measures, and one accounting for the common variation between the 12 memory speed factors. Additional analyses indicated that attempting to model the data as a single factor reduced the fit of the model. That is, memory speed and inconsistency represented different and separable constructs.

These studies suggest that inconsistency can be differentiated from speed of processing. As well, it might be possible to identify several dimensions of inconsistency based on processing demands that impinge on task difficulty. However, substantially more research is required before drawing any firm conclusions about the underlying structure of inconsistency in response time or intraindividual variability associated with other metrics.

Mean versus Variability

The fact that average speed and inconsistency appear to be separable constructs immediately raises the question of their relative contribution as predictors of outcomes of interest (Bereiter, 1963). When intraindividual variability in an attribute is small, interindividual differences in that attribute supply the bulk of useful information and measures of central tendency will suffice. However, when intraindividual variability is large, interindividual differences will not capture most of the relevant variance, and measures of variability will provide additional predictive power. We have seen that the magnitude of intraindividual variability associated with many cognitive abilities is relatively large. Similarly, our review of existing studies has shown that measures of intraindividual variability, particularly inconsistency in response speed, are predictive of cognitive performance, functional capacity in everyday activities, and mortality. However, to what extent do measures of intraindividual variability provide us with information over and above the predictive power associated with measures of central tendency? Although measures of central tendency and intraindividual variability are typically correlated (often highly), thereby indicating substantial shared variance, a number of analyses indicate that each of these indicators may provide unique and valuable information.

In one approach to this question, some studies have used variance component analysis to examine the unique and shared contributions of intraindividual variability estimates and mean estimates as predictors of performance. For example, Hultsch et al. (2002) used partial set correlation (Cohen, 1982) to examine the unique and shared influences of unpurified intraindividual mean (IM) and purified intraindividual standard deviation (ISD) estimates for two groups of RT tasks (nonverbal and verbal) as predictors of cognition, including measures of perceptual speed, working memory, episodic memory, and crystallized ability. Three set correlations were computed: regression of cognitive measures onto IM without partialing any variables, regression of cognitive measures onto ISD partialing out IM performance, and regression of cognitive measures onto IM performance partialing out ISD. Not surprisingly, mean and variability estimates shared a considerable amount of overlapping variance as indexed by R^2. However, mean and variability estimates also made unique predictive contributions. For both categories of RT measures, mean level performance significantly predicted cognitive performance independent of variability. Of particular interest, inconsistency estimates (unique ISD) for nonverbal estimates (based on simple RT and choice RT tasks) significantly predicted variance in cognitive performance over and above mean level influences for all four cognitive domains. Specifically, ISDs for nonverbal RT uniquely accounted for 16% (perceptual speed), 11% (working memory), 12% (episodic memory), and 20% (crystallized ability) of total R^2. Other studies have also reported that estimates of intraindividual variability predict outcome measures over and above measures of average level of performance. For example, Li et al. (2001a) found that fluctuations in physical performance (walking steps) made more of a unique contribution to accounting for individual differences in text and spatial memory than the level score (number of walking steps). The results of this analysis are summarized in Figure 10.8.

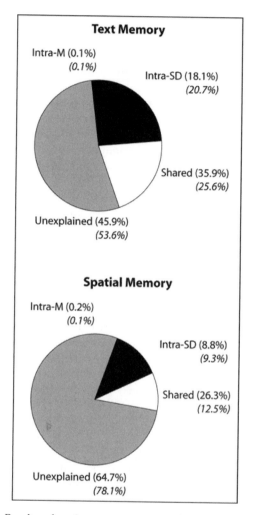

FIG. 10.8. Results of variance component analyses involving walking steps. The pie charts depict the amounts of unique and shared variances of level and fluctuation scores of walking steps in predicting individual differences with respect to text or spatial memory. Italicized values are the age-partialed results. From Li, S.-C., Aggen, S. H., Nesselroade, J. R., and Baltes, P. B. (2001). Short-term fluctuations in elderly people's sensorimotor functioning in predict text and spatial memory performance: The MacArthur successful aging studies. *Gerontology, 47*, 100–116. Reproduced by permission of S. Karger AG, Basel.

Given that inconsistency is associated with specific neurological disturbances, another approach to this issue is to ask whether measures of inconsistency predict group membership independent of measures of average level of performance. For example, Hultsch et al. (2000) used discriminant function analysis to estimate the extent to which dementia and nondementia groups could be differentiated by measures of inconsistency and level of performance. Separate analyses were run for four tasks using multiple indicators of inconsistency (across trials, across occasions) and level of performance (average accuracy, average latency). For all tasks, the combined performance and variability information differentiated the dementia from the nondementia groups, correctly classifying from 87% to 100% of participants depending on the task. Across-trial latency ISD was the most consistent independent predictor overall, making a significant independent contribution to classification on all four tasks. In contrast, average speed did not make a unique contribution, although it approached significance for the choice RT task. Measures of average accuracy also uniquely contributed to group classification for the word and story recall tasks.

In a similar approach, MacDonald, Hultsch, and Dixon (2007) used Cox regression models to evaluate whether inconsistency provides unique predictive information about impending death beyond that contributed by mean level performance. Table 10.4 presents the results from a survival analysis predicting mortality status as a function of covariates entered in five hierarchical blocks. Demographic variables (age, education, self-reported health) and indicators of cardiovascular disease (presence of CVD, number of CVD medications) were entered in Blocks 1 and 2, respectively. Mean level cognitive performance was entered in Block 3, with separate models computed for indicators of working memory (computation span, listening span, sentence construction), episodic memory (word recall, story recall), semantic memory (fact recall), and verbal ability (vocabulary). Next, each of two indicators of average RT (lexical decision speed, semantic decision speed) were entered separately in Block 4, followed by individual entry of the corresponding RT inconsistency indicators (e.g., lexical level followed by lexical ISD) for Block 5. Not surprisingly, the results demonstrated that age, number of CVD medications, and performance inconsistency all shared significant associations with mortality status. Examination of the Block 3 results shows that no measures of mean level cognitive performance significantly predicted increased risk of mortality; the odds ratios were all approximately 1, indicating that mortality risk was unrelated to mean performance. Examination of the results from Blocks 4 and 5 indicated that both level and variability indicators were predictive of mortality independent of demographic indicators, CVD measures, and mean level cognitive

TABLE 10.4

Results for Survival Analysis Predicting Mortality Status as Function of Covariates Entered in Five Hierarchical Blocks

Covariates	β	Odds Ratio	95% CI	p
Block 1				
Age	0.026	1.026	1.008–1.045	0.005
Education	0.024	1.024	0.989–1.061	0.173
Relative health	0.013	1.013	0.864–1.188	0.870
Block 2				
CVD conditions	−0.033	0.967	0.808–1.158	0.717
CVD medications	0.229	1.257	1.065–1.483	0.007
Block 3				
Computation span[a]	−0.004	0.996	0.981–1.011	0.582
Block 4: RT Level Semantic	−0.020	0.981	0.967–0.994	0.006
Block 4: RT Level Lexical	−0.018	0.982	0.971–0.994	0.002
Block 5: RT ISD Semantic	0.119	1.127	1.044–1.216	0.002
Block 5: RT ISD Lexical	0.088	1.092	1.035–1.153	0.001
Listening span[a]	−0.007	0.993	0.978–1.009	0.412
Block 4: RT Level Semantic	−0.019	0.982	0.968–0.995	0.009
Block 4: RT Level Lexical	−0.017	0.983	0.971–0.994	0.004
Block 5: RT ISD Semantic	0.118	1.126	1.043–1.214	0.002
Block 5: RT ISD Lexical	0.088	1.092	1.035–1.152	0.001
Sentence construction	−0.003	0.997	0.985–1.008	0.592
Block 4: RT Level Semantic	−0.011	0.989	0.977–1.001	0.079
Block 4: RT Level Lexica	−0.013	0.987	0.977–0.998	0.024
Block 5: RT ISD Semantic	0.068	1.070	1.001–1.145	0.048
Block 5: RT ISD Lexical	0.034	1.034	0.987–1.034	0.156
Story recall	−0.001	0.999	0.985–1.014	0.919
Block 4: RT Level Semantic	−0.013	0.987	0.974–1.000	0.052
Block 4: RT Level Lexical	−0.013	0.987	0.976–0.998	0.018
Block 5: RT ISD Semantic	0.070	1.072	1.002–1.147	0.042
Block 5: RT ISD Lexical	0.035	1.035	0.988–1.035	0.145
Word recall	−0.002	0.998	0.986–1.011	0.813
Block 4: RT Level Semantic	−0.012	0.988	0.976–1.001	0.065
Block 4: RT Level Lexical	−0.013	0.987	0.976–0.998	0.021
Block 5: RT ISD Semantic	0.069	1.071	1.001–1.146	0.046
Block 5: RT ISD Lexical	0.034	1.034	0.987–1.083	0.158
Fact recall	−0.003	0.997	0.983–1.010	0.626
Block 4: RT Level Semantic	−0.012	0.988	0.974–1.001	0.072
Block 4: RT Level Lexical	−0.013	0.987	0.976–0.998	0.024
Block 5: RT ISD Semantic	0.069	1.071	1.001–1.146	0.046
Block 5: RT ISD Lexical	0.034	1.035	0.988–1.084	0.149
Vocabulary	0.008	1.008	0.996–1.020	0.185
Block 4: RT Level Semantic	−0.019	0.982	0.969–0.994	0.005
Block 4: RT Level Lexical	−0.016	0.984	0.973–0.994	0.003
Block 5: RT ISD Semantic	0.066	1.068	1.000–1.141	0.050
Block 5: RT ISD Lexical	0.047	1.048	0.999–1.099	0.055

Note. Statistical models were computed separately for each cognitive and RT measure. Results represent parameters for a given regression block controlling for the influence of all predictors on previous blocks. Mortality status was coded as either 0 (survivor) or 1 (decedent). CI = confidence interval; CVD = cardiovascular disease; RT = response time. Subjects rated their health relative to same-aged peers on a 5-point scale ranging from (0) very good to (4) very poor. CVD conditions represent self-reported presence of four cardiovascular diseases (heart disease, stroke, arteriosclerosis, and high blood pressure) for any wave of testing. CVD medications reflect self-reported use of medications prescribed to treat cardiovascular symptoms and disease (heart, chest, high blood pressure, and anticoagulants). ISD = intraindividual standard deviation. [a] N = 707 for all measures except computation span and listening span (n = 635).

performance. Importantly, the contrasting patterns of significance between Blocks 4 and 5 indicated that response speed level was not uniquely significant for any models that included response speed inconsistency, whereas inconsistency predicted mortality independent of level. Moreover, the association between intraindividual variability and mortality was present as many as 15 years prior to the death event.

The results summarized above indicate that, in many cases, indicators of inconsistency predict performance or group membership above and beyond indicators of mean level performance. Not all studies have found this result (e.g., Christensen et al., 2005; Salthouse, 1993, 1998). For example, Christensen et al. (2005) reported that although RT variability was greater for individuals classified as having mild cognitive impairment (MCI), it did not contribute uniquely to group membership over and above mean RT. However, the age range of this study was relatively restricted (60–64 years). Given that we have repeatedly seen that inconsistency effects appear to be particularly robust after approximately age 75, it may be the case that effects were attenuated in this relatively young sample. In fact, when a wider age range (64 to 92 years) and a broader array of RT tasks were examined recently by Strauss et al. (in press), the results showed group differentiation (normals versus MCI) was better achieved with measures of inconsistency compared with measures of mean speed. Differing methods for controlling group differences in mean speed and practice or other systematic time-related effects may also contribute to the discrepancies in results related to this issue.

Intraindividual Change in Intraindividual Variability

We suggested earlier that different types of intraindividual variability may be associated with different points in the acquisition curve (see Figure 10.1). In general, it is suggested that as individuals become more skilled at a task, intraindividual variability will decline (or alternatively, performance will become more consistent). Indeed, several studies have shown that average levels of inconsistency decrease across multiple testing sessions (Fuentes et al., 2001; Hultsch et al., 2000; Ram et al., 2005b; West et al., 2002). In perhaps the most comprehensive examination of this issue to date, Ram et al. (2005b) analyzed data from 91 adult participants (aged 52 to 79 years) who completed multiple memory speed (letter recognition) tasks on 36 separate occasions. Multivariate techniques were used to compute a "true score" measure of inconsistency based on trial-to-trial variability within sessions. Within-person change in this variability was then examined across occasions. Figure 10.9 shows that, on average, inconsistency decreases with exposure to the task, but there are substantial individual differences in intraindividual change across the 36 ses-

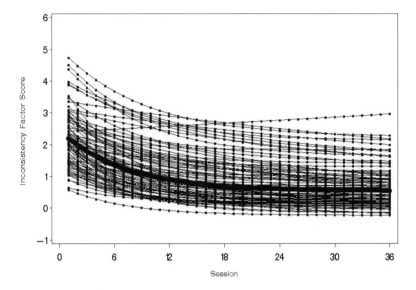

FIG. 10.9. Predicted exponential growth curves representing intraindividual change in inconsistency. Each individual is represented by a single line connecting their week-to-week scores illustrating "practice effects." The prototypical trajectory is indicated as the thick bold line. From Ram, N., Rabbitt, P., Stollery, B., and Nesselroade, J. R. (2005b). Cognitive performance inconsistency: Intraindividual change and variability. *Psychology and Aging*, *20*, 623–633. Copyright © 2005 by the American Psychological Association. Reprinted with permission.

sions. Importantly, individuals with higher fluid intelligence scores were more likely to attain greater consistency of performance over time than individuals with lower scores. However, intelligence scores were not systematically related to the total amount of increase in consistency or the rate at which it occurred.

Ram et al. (2005b) also examined the data to determine if there were any systematic state-like patterns in the intraindividual variability of inconsistency across time. To separate intraindividual change from intraindividual variability, the systematic effects associated with practice or learning shown in Figure 10.9 were removed. These residual scores were subjected to individual time series to determine if there were systematic patterns present, or whether they were better characterized as "white noise." Ram and his colleagues concluded that there was little evidence for state-like changes in inconsistency scores that have been partialed for practice effects. However, this "noise" appears to contain meaningful information. The gross amount of each individual's residual noise was quantified by computing the individual standard deviation across weeks.

There were substantial and relatively normally distributed interindividual differences in this measure of "noise." Moreover, noise was significantly and negatively correlated with performance on fluid intelligence. These results are consistent with the argument of Hultsch and his colleagues that measures of intraindividual variability derived from trial-to-trial inconsistency in latency of performance that have been partialed for group speed and systematic practice effects may be one of the most powerful and useful measures of intraindividual variability (Hultsch et al., 2005).

Mechanisms of Intraindividual Variability

We have shown that intraindividual variability in cognitive performance can be measured reliably, is substantial in magnitude, exhibits intraindividual change over time, and is predictive of a number of important outcomes in a variety of domains. However, a major unresolved question is: what are the mechanisms that are responsible for intraindividual variability, and particularly for age-related differences or changes in intraindividual variability? This question may be approached at several levels of analysis, including the neurological, cognitive, and affective.

For example, at the neurobiological level, theorists have proposed inconsistency in performance could be caused by random errors or neural "noise" in the transmission of signals in the CNS (Hendrickson, 1982; Welford, 1980), a decrease in the frequency of neuronal oscillation reflecting the excitatory potential of neurons (Jensen, 1992), or dysfunctions in the functioning of neurotransmitters such as epinephrine, norepinephrine, and dopamine (Li & Lindenberger, 1999; Li et al., 2001b). Many of the groups that show increased intraindividual variability (e.g., dementia patients, schizophrenics, attention deficit and hyperactivity disorder children, older adults), for example, also exhibit changes in dopaminergic neurotransmission. The dopamine system is clearly implicated in cognitive aging with marked and consistent declines in dopamine binding in the brain (Bäckman & Farde, 2004) and corresponding declines in cognitive abilities (e.g., executive functions) in brain regions (e.g., prefrontal cortex) subserved by dopaminergic pathways that serve to activate and maintain neural representations independent of environmental cues (Miller & Cohen, 2001). More generally, alterations in dopamine neuromodulation result in increased neural noise (Bäckman & Farde, 2004; Cohen & Servan-Schreiber, 1992), less distinct cortical representations, and subsequent decreases in cognitive performance and increases in behavioral intraindividual variability (Li et al., 2001b). In support of a neural noise interpretation, variation in catechol O-methyltransferase activity for the Val or Met genotypes is linked to performance stability for a rapid perceptual comparison task (Stefanis, van Os, Avramopoulos, Smyrnis, Evdokimidis, & Stefanis, 2005). Participants (young men, mean age = 21 years) responded whenever two identical 4-digit numbers appeared in a row for 300 trials over a 5-minute session. Intraindividual variability of response latencies to target was computed, with Met carriers exhibiting reduced intraindividual variability in response latencies. Among possible interpretations, Met carriers exhibit more dopamine signaling in the prefrontal cortex relative to Val carriers who exhibit much higher enzymatic activity resulting in faster degradation of dopamine in the synaptic cleft. Thus, the observed performance advantage for Met carriers implicates the potential importance of genotype and dopamine neuromodulation for conferring greater stability in cognitive performance, perhaps related to more stabilized neural representations in the prefrontal cortex (Stefanis et al., 2005).

Cognitive mechanisms that have been suggested include lapses of attention (e.g., Bunce et al., 1993), failures of executive control (e.g., West et al., 2002), or more conservative settings of response criteria (Ratcliff, Thapar, & McKoon, 2001). For example, whereas healthy elderly tend to exhibit significant correlations between intraindividual variability and cognitive performance regardless of task load, associations for younger adults are more likely to be observed only on more difficult tasks (e.g., frontally based executive processes; Bunce et al., 2004; Hultsch et al., 2002). Such results support the interpretation that limited attentional resources are available for older relative to younger adults (Murphy, Craik, Li, & Schneider, 2000), with intraindividual variability for the elderly perhaps a behavioral manifestation of more frequent attentional lapses (Bunce et al., 1993) or fluctuations in executive control (West et al., 2002). Such observed patterns are consistent with the frontal-lobe deficit hypothesis of aging (Dempster, 1992; West, 1996) postulating that age-related cognitive deficits are a function of age-related changes in the frontal lobes (Raz et al., 2004). Consistent with this interpretation, ordered variations in the magnitude of intraindividual variability as a function of head injury location parallel differences observed for the dementias: those with focal injuries to the frontal lobes, or frontal-temporal dementia, exhibit more intraindividual variability in cognitive performance relative to conditions with less involvement of the frontal lobes including nonfrontal lesions or Alzheimer's dementia (Stuss et al., 2003). Converging evidence from multiple sources supports the central importance of the frontal lobes and associated cognitive processes in mediating intraindividual variability (Murtha et al., 2002; Stuss et al., 2003; Winterer et al., 2004). In contrast, Robertson, Myerson, and Hale (2006) recently failed to find significant age differences in intraindividual variability on several working memory tasks despite replicating the typical finding that older participants showed more inconsistency on a RT task. They conclude that their results fail to support arguments that the frontal lobes may be critical for consistency of performance. As we noted earlier, however, others have observed discrepancies in results between more latency-based measures and accuracy-based measures; the latter may be less reliable indicators and may be more affected by strategic processing. Moreover, as suggested by Stuss et al. (2003), all aspects of frontal functioning may not be equally important.

Finally, some writers have suggested that changes in the external environment that contribute to fluctuations in affective (e.g., depression, stress) or somatic states (e.g., pain, sleep deprivation) might drive intraindividual variability in cognition or other performance domains. There is relatively little evidence linking intraindividual variability in cognition to fluctuations in affect (e.g., Strauss et al., 2002). In one of the best demonstrations of this link, however, Sliwinski et al. (2006) recently examined within-person relationships of variability in daily stress and daily variability in cognitive performance. A sample of younger ($M = 20.21$ years) and older adults ($M = 80.23$ years) completed a self-report measure of their experience of daily hassles and two RT tasks varying in attentional demand on six different occasions. The results showed that variability in daily stressors covaried with variability in cognitive performance. That is, within individuals, RTs were slower on high stress days compared with low stress days. This relationship appeared to be magnified for older adults relative to younger adults as it was observed on both of the more demanding tasks in the case of the old, but only on one task in the case of the young. Additional analyses suggested that high stress days were associated with a larger number of slow trials, but there was little relationship between stress and fast responses. Sliwinski et al. (2006) suggested that stress might result in lapses of attention that produce a larger number of very slow trials. This latter finding suggests that the various explanations for intraindividual variability may well be related. Multiple directions of influence might be involved. For example, stress might induce attentional lapses thus increasing inconsistency in performance. Similarly, increased neural noise might contribute to degradation of executive control resulting in increased intraindividual variability.

SUMMARY AND CONCLUSION

Our review of the work on intraindividual variability, cognition, and aging leads us to offer several preliminary conclusions:

(1) There are multiple types of intraindividual variability and they will

tell us different things. Researchers should be sensitive to the dimensions of intraindividual variability (e.g., timescale, scope) that they are examining.

(2) There is a substantial amount of intraindividual variability in cognitive abilities that are typically considered to be trait-like characteristics of persons. Much of the observed intraindividual variability in cognitive performance appears to reflect lawful sources of influence rather than error of measurement.

(3) There are substantial age differences in intraindividual variability, particularly when assessed as trial-to-trial inconsistency in response latency. Inconsistency is very high in childhood, declines through adolescence to young adulthood, and increases again into old age. In adulthood, inconsistency seems particularly prevalent in the older age ranges above 75 years. Age differences appear to be exacerbated on more complex tasks that place demands on executive functions and may be ameliorated by tasks that allow older adults to employ preserved crystallized knowledge or expertise. There is some evidence for longitudinal increases in inconsistency, but additional data are needed.

(4) Intraindividual variability appears to be primarily a central nervous system phenomenon. Specifically, greater intraindividual variability is observed in persons diagnosed with a wide variety of neurological conditions including traumatic brain injury, Parkinson's disease, epilepsy, dementia, and mild cognitive impairment. Importantly, it is not observed in nonneurological conditions such as arthritis. Further, there appears to be a possible dose–response relationship between neurological disturbance and intraindividual variability; the more severe (or extensive) the disturbance, the greater the intraindividual variability. There is also some evidence that inconsistency is particularly pronounced in those conditions that impact executive/attentional functions governed by particular frontal systems. However, the fact that impairments in other functions (e.g., language) also result in increased intraindividual variability suggests that intraindividual variability likely reflects multiple neural determinants.

(5) Intraindividual variability is predictive of multiple outcomes. In particular, inconsistency in response time is associated with lower intellectual ability (particularly fluid ability), poorer performance on more complex cognitive tasks such as episodic memory and reasoning, decreased functional capacity on a variety of instrumental activities of daily living, and proximity to death. However, intraindividual variability is not always maladaptive. Intraindividual variability may be associated with better performance in the early

stages of acquisition, particularly for complex tasks that have substantial opportunity for strategic processing.

(6) There are a number of conceptual and statistical issues that need to be considered in computing indices of intraindividual variability. Differences between persons in level of performance and systematic changes in performance across occasions (trials, testing sessions) related to practice or materials can be potential confounds for the measurement of intraindividual variability. If one is interested in "unsystematic" fluctuations over time, it is preferable to decompose (partial) the data first and then base an index of intraindividual variability on the unsystematic portion of the variance, rather than to compute a measure of total intraindividual variability and then try to divide the unsystematic portion from the systematic portion.

(7) Measures of central tendency and measures of intraindividual variability reflect distinct sources of variance. Consistent with this, there is evidence that measures of intraindividual variability provide predictive power above and beyond measures of central tendency for many outcomes of interest. However, beyond demonstrating that the mean and variability can be separated, little work on the structure of intraindividual variability has been done.

(8) Multiple suggestions have been offered to explain the descriptive differences and changes in intraindividual variability observed with age and other grouping variables. At the neurobiological level, theorists have suggested that inconsistency in performance could be caused by multiple mechanisms, including white matter demyelination, gray matter lesions, and dysfunctions in neurotransmitter systems. Cognitive mechanisms that have been suggested focus on problems in executive control such as lapses of attention. Finally, intraindividual variability may be driven, in part, by changes in affective or somatic states such as depression, stress, pain, and fatigue.

(9) To date, the bulk of the work examining intraindividual variability has focused on differences in the amount of intraindividual variability and its relationship to various outcomes. Although this research is informative, more work examining intraindividual variability at the within-person level is needed. For example, to what extent are there within-person changes in intraindividual variability? Is there covariation in intraindividual variability from different domains over time?

(10) Overall, there is accumulating evidence that intraindividual variability may be a good indicator of cognitive aging. In addition, it is possible that it represents an antecedent of developmental change

as well. However, there is little evidence to address this latter hypothesis at the present time.

This summary of research findings suggests that measures of intraindividual variability may be plausible behavioral indicators of aging-induced deterioration of neurobiological mechanisms which compromise the integrity of the brain across a wide range of areas and functional circuitry. For example, it has been suggested that older brains may need to recruit additional resources to manage executive functions of otherwise relatively simple tasks (Cabeza, 2002; Dixon & Bäckman, 1999). Thus, even localized neural deficits may be expressed as a generalized impairment (Raz, 2000). Such changes have been hypothesized as the common cause for aging-associated losses in cognitive capacity and plasticity (Baltes & Lindenberger, 1997; Lindenberger & Baltes, 1994).

At a methodological level, these findings argue that it is important to attend to both level and variability of performance. Each of these indices provides useful information that the other does not. Because a stability orientation tends to guide research, the current task is to supplement the dominant view by increasing attention to cycles, oscillations, and fluctuations in behavior, and to explore how these can contribute to the development of theories of cognitive aging. At the same time, it is important not to ascribe more significance to the concept of intraindividual variability than is warranted. For example, we do not wish to suggest that behavioral inconsistency represents some type of psychological "primitive" that will account for all or most of the age-related variance in cognitive performance. Rather, we suggest that this phenomenon is an integral part of cognitive functioning that needs to be considered both in theory development and in clinical assessment.

In closing, we offer a final caveat. Research on intraindividual variability, cognition, and aging is growing rapidly. However, relative to the corpus of work based on mean level performance, the amount of information is miniscule. We believe that it is important not to reach premature conclusions about the theoretical or practical significance of intraindividual variability for the study of aging. We believe there is enough evidence to assert that it is useful to consider variability as an important phenomenon. However, substantial work will be needed to determine the ultimate contribution of this phenomenon (or phenomena) to our understanding of the aging process.

REFERENCES

Allaire, J. C., & Marsiske, M. (1999). Everyday cognition: Age and intellectual ability correlates. *Psychology and Aging, 14,* 627–644.

Allaire, J. C., & Marsiske, M. (2005). Intraindividual variability may not always indicate vulnerability in elders' cognitive performance. *Psychology and Aging, 20,* 390–401.

Alwin, D. F. (1994). Aging, personality, and social change: The stability of individual differences over the adult life span. In D. L. Featherman, R. M. Lerner, & M. Perlmutter (Eds.), *Life-span development and behavior* (Vol. 12, pp. 135–185). Hillsdale, NJ: Lawrence Erlbaum Associates, Inc.

American Psychological Association (2000). *Diagnostic and statistical manual of mental disorders* (4th. ed.). Washington, DC: American Psychological Association.

Anderson, B., Mennemeier, M., & Chatterjee, A. (2000). Variability not ability: Another basis for performance decrements in neglect. *Neuropsychologia, 38,* 785–796.

Anstey, K. J. (1999). Sensorimotor and forced expiratory volume as correlates of speed, accuracy, and variability in reaction time performance in late adulthood. *Aging, Neuropsychology, and Cognition, 6,* 84–95.

Anstey, K. J., & Christensen, H. (2000). Education, activity, health, blood pressure and apolipoprotein E as predictors of cognitive change in old age: A review. *Gerontology, 46,* 163–177.

Artero, S., Touchon, J., & Ritchie, K. (2001). Disability and mild cognitive impairment: A longitudinal population-based study. *International Journal of Geriatric Psychiatry, 16,* 1092–1097.

Bäckman L., & Farde L. (2004). The role of dopamine functions in cognitive aging. In R. Cabeza, L. Nyberg, & D. C. Park (Eds.), *Cognitive neuroscience of aging: Linking cognitive and cerebral aging* (pp. 58–84). New York: Oxford University Press.

Baltes, P. B., & Lindenberger, U. (1997). Emergence of a powerful connection between sensory and cognitive functions across the adult lifespan: A new window to the study of cognitive aging? *Psychology and Aging, 12,* 12–21.

Baltes, P. B., Reese, H. W., & Nesselroade, J. R. (1977). *Life-span developmental psychology: Introduction to research methods.* Monterey, CA: Brooks/Cole.

Barrett P. T., & Eysenck H. J. (1994). The relationship between evoked potential component amplitude, latency, contour length, variability, zero-crossings, and psychometric intelligence. *Personality and Individual Differences, 16,* 3–32.

Benton, A. L., & Blackburn, H. L. (1957). Practice effects in reaction-time tasks in brain-injured patients. *Journal of Abnormal and Social Psychology, 54,* 109–113.

Bereiter, C. (1963). Some persisting dilemmas in the measurement of change. In C. W. Harris (Ed.), *Problems in measuring change* (pp. 3–20). Madison, WI: University of Wisconsin Press.

Berg, S. (1996). Aging, behavior, and terminal decline. In J. E. Birren & K. W. Schaie (Eds.), *Handbook of the psychology of aging* (4th ed., pp. 323–337). New York: Springer.

Bleiberg, J., Garmoe, W. S., Halpern, E. L., Reeves, D. L., & Nadler, J. D. (1997). Consistency of within-day and across-day performance after mild brain injury. *Neuropsychiatry, Neuropsychology, and Behavioral Neurology, 10,* 247–253.

Bosworth, H. B., & Schaie, K. W. (1999). Survival effects in cognitive function, cognitive style, and sociodemographic variables in the Seattle Longitudinal Study. *Experimental Aging Research, 25,* 121–140.

Britton, T. C. Meyer, B. U., & Benecke, R. (1991) Variability of cortically evoked motor responses in multiple sclerosis. *Electroencephalography and Clinical Neurophysiology, 81,* 186–194.

Bruhn, P., & Parsons, O. A. (1977). Reaction time variability in epileptic and brain damaged patients. *Cortex, 13,* 373–384.

Bunce, D. MacDonald, S. W. S., & Hultsch, D. F. (2004). Inconsistency in serial choice responding decision and motor reaction times dissociate in younger and older adults. *Brain and Cognition, 56*, 320–327.

Bunce, D. J., Warr, P. B., & Cochrane, T. (1993). Blocks in choice responding as a function of age and physical fitness. *Psychology and Aging, 8*, 26–33.

Burton, C. L., Hultsch, D. F., Strauss, E., & Hunter, M. A. (2002). Intraindividual variability in physical and emotional functioning: Comparison of adults with traumatic brain injuries and healthy adults. *The Clinical Neuropsychologist, 16*, 264–279.

Burton, C. L., Strauss, E., Hultsch, D. F., & Hunter, M. A. (2006a). Cognitive functioning and everyday problem solving in older adults. *The Clinical Neuropsychologist, 20*, 432–52.

Burton, C. L., Strauss, E., Hultsch, D. F., Moll, A., & Hunter, M. A. (2006b). Intraindividual variability as a marker of neurological dysfunction: A comparison of Alzheimer's disease and Parkinson's disease. *Journal of Clinical and Experimental Neuropsychology, 28*, 67–83.

Burton, C. L., Strauss, E., Hunter, M. A., & Hultsch, D. F. (in press). The relationship between everyday problem solving and inconsistency in reaction time in older adults. *Aging, Neuropsychology, and Cognition.*

Buss, A. R. (1974). A general developmental model for interindividual differences, intraindividual differences, and intraindividual changes. *Developmental Psychology, 10*, 70–78.

Butler, A. C., Hokanson, J. E., & Flynn, H. A. (1994). A comparison of self-esteem lability and low trait self-esteem as vulnerability factors for depression. *Journal of Personality and Social Psychology, 66*, 166–177.

Byrne, E. J., Lennox, G., Lowe, J., & Godwin-Austen, R. B. (1989). Diffuse Lewy body disease: Clinical features in 15 cases. *Journal of Neurology, Neurosurgery and Psychiatry, 52*, 709–717.

Cabeza, R. (2002). Hemispheric asymmetry reduction in old adults: The HAROLD model. *Psychology and Aging, 17*, 85–100.

Cabeza R., & Nyberg L. (2000). Imaging cognition II: An empirical review of 275 PET and fMRI studies. *Journal of Cognitive Neuroscience, 12*, 1–47.

Callicott J. H., Bertolino A., Mattay V. S., Langheim F. J. P., Duyn J., Coppola R., et al. (2000). Physiological dysfunction of the dorsolateral prefrontal cortex in schizophrenia revisited. *Cerebral Cortex, 10*, 1078–1092.

Campbell, D. T., & Stanley, J. C. (1963). *Experimental and quasi-experimental designs for research.* Boston: Houghton Mifflin.

Cattell, R. B. (1957). *Personality and motivation: Structure and measurement.* New York: World Book.

Cattell, R. B. (1966). The data box: Its ordering of total resources in terms of possible relational systems. In R. B. Cattell (Ed.), *Handbook of multivariate experimental psychology* (pp. 67–128). Chicago: Rand McNally.

Cerella, J. (1990). Aging and information-processing rate. In J. E. Birren & K. W. Schaie (Eds.), *Handbook of the psychology of aging* (3rd ed., pp. 201–221). San Diego: Academic Press.

Christensen, H., Dear, K. B. G., Anstey, K. J., Parslow, R. A., Sachdev, P., & Jorm, A. F. (2005). Within-occasion intra-individual variability and pre-clinical diagnostic status: Is intra-individual variability an indicator of mild cognitive impairment? *Neuropsychology, 19*, 309–317.

Christensen, H., Mackinnon, A. J., Korten, A. E., Jorm, A. F., Henderson, A. S., & Jacomb, P. (1999). Dispersion in cognitive ability as a function of age: A longitudinal study of an elderly community sample. *Aging, Neuropsychology, and Cognition, 6*, 214–228.

Clayton, K., & Bruhns Frey, B. (1997). Studies of mental "noise". *Nonlinear Dynamics, Psychology, and Life Sciences, 1*, 173–180.

Cohen, J. (1982). Set correlation as a general multivariate data-analytic method. *Multivariate Behavioral Research, 17*, 301–341.

Cohen, J., Cohen, P., West, S. G., & Aiken, L. S. (2003). *Applied multiple regression/correlation analysis for the behavioral sciences* (3rd ed.). Hillsdale, NJ: Lawrence Erlbaum Associates, Inc.

Cohen J. D., & Servan-Schreiber D. (1992). Context, cortex, and dopamine: A connectionist approach to behavior and biology in schizophrenia. *Psychological Review, 99*, 45–77.

Collerton, D., Burn, D., McKeith, I., & O'Brien, J. (2003). Systematic review and meta-analysis show that dementia with Lewy bodies in a visual-perceptual and attentional-executive dementia. *Dementia and Geriatric Cognitive Disorders, 16*, 229–237.

Collins, L. F., & Long, C. J. (1996). Visual reaction time and its relationship to neuropsychological test performance. *Archives of Clinical Neuropsychology, 11*, 613–623.

Cornelius, S.W., & Caspi, A. (1987). Everyday problem solving in adulthood and old age. *Psychology and Aging, 2*, 144–153.

Crook, T., Bartus, R. T., Ferris, S. H., Whitehouse, P., Cohen, G. D., & Gershon, S. (1986). Age associated memory impairment: Proposed diagnostic criteria and measures of clinical change: report of a National Institute of Mental Health Work Group. *Developmental Neuropsychology, 2*, 261–276.

Crossman, E. R. F. W., & Szafran, J. (1956). Changes with age in the speed of information intake and discrimination. *Experientia Supplementum, 4*, 128–135.

Deary, I. J., & Der, G. (2005). Reaction time, age, and cognitive ability: Longitudinal findings from age 16 to 63 years in representative population samples. *Aging, Neuropsychology, and Cognition, 12*, 187–215.

de Carli, C. (2003). Mild cognitive impairment: Prevalence, prognosis, aetiology, and treatment. *Lancet Neurology, 2*, 15–21.

Dempster, F. N. (1992). The rise and fall of the inhibitory mechanism: Toward a unified theory of cognitive development and aging. *Developmental Review, 12*, 45–75.

Dixon, R. A., & Bäckman, L. (1999). Principles of compensation in cognitive neurorehabilitation. In D. T. Stuss, G. Winocur, & I. H. Robertson (Eds.), *Cognitive neurorehabilitation* (pp. 59–72). Cambridge: Cambridge University Press.

Dixon, R. A., Garrett, D. D., Lentz, T. L., MacDonald, S. W. S., Strauss, E., & Hultsch, D. F. (2007). Neurocognitive resources in cognitive impairment: Exploring markers of speed and inconsistency. *Neuropsychology, 21*, 381–399.

Dixon, R. A., & Hertzog, C. (1996). Theoretical issues in cognition and aging. In F. Blanchard-Fields & T. M. Hess (Eds.), *Perspectives on cognitive change in adulthood and aging* (pp. 25–65). New York: McGraw-Hill.

Elashoff, J. D. (1969). Analysis of covariance: A delicate instrument. *American Educational Research Journal, 6*, 383–401.

Fillenbaum, G. G. (1985). Screening the elderly: A brief instrumental activities of daily living measure. *Journal of the American Geriatrics Society, 33*, 698–706.

Fisk, D. W., & Rice, L. (1955). Intra-individual response variability. *Psychological Bulletin, 52*, 217–250.

Folstein, M., Folstein, S., & McHugh, P. R. (1975). Mini-mental state: A practical method for grading the cognitive state of patients for the clinician. *Journal of Psychiatric Research, 12* 189–198.

Fozard, J. L., Vercruyssen, M., Reynolds, S. L., Hancock, P. A., & Quilter, R. E. (1994). Age differences and changes in reaction time: The Baltimore Longitudinal Study of Aging. *Journal of Gerontology: Psychological Sciences, 49*, P179–P189.

Fuentes, K., Hunter, M. A., Strauss, E., & Hultsch, D. F. (2001). Intraindividual variability in cognitive performance in persons with chronic fatigue syndrome. *The Clinical Neuropsychologist, 15*, 210–227.

Gergen, K. J. (1977). Stability, change, and chance in understanding human development. In N. Datan & H. W. Reese (Eds.), *Life-span developmental psychology: Dialectical perspectives on experimental research* (pp. 135–158). New York: Academic Press.

Ghisletta, P., Nesselroade, J. R., Featherman, D. L., & Rowe, J. W. (2002). The structure, validity, and predictive power of weekly intraindividual variability in health and activity measures. *Swiss Journal of Psychology, 61,* 73–83.

Gilden, D. L., Thornton, T., & Mallon, M. W. (1995). 1/f noise in human cognition. *Science, 267,* 1837–1839.

Gogtay, N., Giedd, J. N., Lusk, L., Hayashi, K. M., Greenstein, D., Vaituzis, A. C., et al. (2004). Dynamic mapping of human cortical development during childhood through early adulthood. *Proceedings of the National Academy of Sciences USA, 101,* 8174–8179.

Gordon, B., & Carson, K. (1990). The basis for choice reaction time slowing in Alzheimer's disease. *Brain and Cognition, 13,* 148–166.

Hale, S., Myerson, J., Smith, G. A., & Poon, L. W. (1988). Age, variability, and speed: Between-subjects diversity. *Psychology and Aging, 3,* 407–410.

Hamson, E. (1990). Variations in sex related cognitive abilities across the menstrual cycle. *Brain and Cognition, 14,* 26–43.

Harlow, J. M. (1868). Recovery after severe injury to the head. *Publications of the Massachusetts Medical Society, 2,* 327–346.

Hassing, L. B., Johannson, B., Berg, S., Nilsson, S. E., Pedersen, N. L., Hofer, S. M., et al. (2002). Terminal decline and markers of cerebro- and cardiovascular disease: Findings from a longitudinal study of the oldest old. *Journal of Gerontology: Psychological Sciences, 57,* 268–276.

Head, H. (1926). *Aphasia and kindred disorders of speech.* Cambridge: Cambridge University Press.

Hedden, T., & Gabrieli, J. D. E. (2004). Insights into the ageing mind: A view from cognitive neuroscience. *Nature Reviews Neuroscience, 5,* 87–97.

Hendrickson, A. E. (1982). The biological basis of intelligence Part I: Theory. In H. J. Eysenck (Ed.), *A model for intelligence* (pp. 151–196). Berlin: Springer-Verlag.

Hetherington, C. R., Stuss, D. T., & Finlayson, M. A. J. (1996). Reaction time and variability 5 and 10 years after traumatic brain injury. *Brain Injury, 10,* 473–486.

Howell, D. C. (1992). *Statistical methods for psychology* (3rd ed.). Belmont, CA: Duxbury.

Huitema, B. E. (1980). *The analysis of covariance and alternatives.* New York: Wiley.

Hultsch, D. F., Hunter, M. A., MacDonald, S. W. S., & Strauss, E. (2005). Inconsistency in response time as an indicator of cognitive aging. In J. Duncan, L. Phillips, & P. McLeod (Eds.), *Measuring the mind* (pp. 33–58). New York: Oxford University Press.

Hultsch, D. F., & MacDonald, S. W. S. (2004). Intraindividual variability in performance as a theoretical window onto cognitive aging. In R. A. Dixon, L. Bäckman, and L.-G. Nilsson (Eds.), *New frontiers in cognitive aging* (pp. 65–88). New York: Oxford University Press.

Hultsch, D. F., MacDonald, S. W. S., & Dixon, R. A. (2002). Variability in reaction time performance of younger and older adults. *Journal of Gerontology: Psychological Sciences, 57B,* P101–P115.

Hultsch, D. F., MacDonald, S.W.S., Hunter, M. A., Levy-Bencheton, J., & Strauss, E. (2000). Intraindividual variability in cognitive performance in older adults: Comparison of adults with mild dementia, adults with arthritis, and healthy adults. *Neuropsychology, 14,* 588–598.

Intons-Peterson, M. J., Rocchi, P., West, T., McLellan, K., & Hackney, A. (1998). Aging, optimal testing times, and negative priming. *Journal of Experimental Psychology: Learning, Memory, and Cognition, 24,* 362–376.

Jensen, A. R. (1982). Reaction time and psychometric g. In H. J. Eysenck (Ed.), *A model for intelligence* (pp. 93–132). Berlin: Springer-Verlag.

Jensen, A. R. (1992). The importance of intraindividual variation in reaction time. *Personality and Individual Differences, 13,* 869–881.

Johansson, B., & Zarit, S. H. (1997). Early cognitive markers of the incidence of dementia and mortality: A longitudinal population-based study of the oldest old. *International Journal of Geriatric Psychiatry, 12,* 53–59.

Katz, S., Ford, A., Moskowitz, R., Jackson, B., & Jaffe, M. (1963). Studies of illness in the aged: The Index of ADL, a standardized measure of biological and psychological function. *Journal of the American Medical Association, 185,* 94–99.

Kleemeier, R. W. (1962). Intellectual changes in the senium. *Proceedings of the American Statistical Association, 1,* 290–295.

Knotek, P. C., Bayles, K. A., & Kaszniak, A. W. (1990). Response consistency on a semantic memory task in persons with dementia of the Alzheimer type. *Brain and Language, 38,* 465–475.

Kray, J., Eber J., & Lindenberger, U. (2004) Age differences in executive functioning across the lifespan: The role of verbalization in task preparation. *Acta Psychologica, 115,* 143–165.

Lawton, M. P., & Brody, J. (1969). Assessment of older people: Self-maintaining and instrumental activities of daily living. *Gerontologist, 9,* 179–185.

Levy, R. (1994). Aging-associated cognitive decline. Working Party of the International Psychogeriatric Association in collaboration with the World Health Organisation. *International Psychogeriatrics, 6,* 63–68.

Li, S.-C., Aggen, S. H., Nesselroade, J. R., & Baltes, P. B. (2001a). Short-term fluctuations in elderly people's sensorimotor functioning in predict text and spatial memory performance: The MacArthur successful aging studies. *Gerontology, 47,* 100–116.

Li, S.-C., Huxhold, O., & Schmiedek, F. (2004a). Aging and attenuated processing robustness. Evidence from cognitive and sensorimotor functioning. *Gerontology, 50,* 28–34.

Li, S.-C., & Lindenberger, U. (1999). Cross-level unification: A computational exploration of the link between deterioration of neurotransmitter systems and dedifferentiation of cognitive abilities in old age. In L.-G. Nilsson & H. Markowitsch (Eds.), *Cognitive neuroscience and memory* (pp. 103–146). Toronto: Hogrefe & Huber.

Li, S.-C., Lindenberger, U., & Frensch, P. A. (2000). Unifying cognitive aging: From neuromodulation to representation to cognition. *Neurocomputing, 32–33,* 879–890.

Li, S.-C., Lindenberger, U., Hommel, B., Aschersleben, G., Prinz, W., & Baltes, P. B. (2004b). Transformations in the couplings among intellectual abilities and constituent cognitive processes across the life span. *Psychological Science, 15,* 155–163.

Li, S.-C., Lindenberger, U., & Sikström, S. (2001b). Aging and cognition: From neuromodulation to representation. *Trends in Cognitive Science, 5,* 479–486.

Lindenberger, U., & Baltes, P. B. (1994). Sensory functioning and intelligence in old age: A strong connection. *Psychology and Aging, 9,* 339–355.

Lindenberger, U., & von Oertzen, T. (2006). Variability in cognitive aging: From taxonomy to theory. In F. I. M. Craik & E. Bialystok (Eds.), *Lifespan cognition: Mechanisms of change* (pp. 297–314) Oxford: Oxford University Press.

Logan, J. M., Sanders, A. L., Snyder, A. Z., Morris, J. C., & Buckner, R. L. (2002). Underrecruitment and non-selective recruitment: Dissociable neural mechanisms associated with aging. *Neuron, 33,* 827–840.

MacDonald, S. W. S. (2003). *Longitudinal profiles of terminal decline: Associations between cognitive decline, age, time to death, and cause of death.* Unpublished dissertation, Department of Psychology, University of Victoria, Victoria, BC, Canada.

MacDonald, S. W. S., Hultsch, D. F., & Dixon, R. A. (2003). Performance variability is related to change in cognition: Evidence from the Victoria Longitudinal Study. *Psychology and Aging, 18,* 510–523.

MacDonald, S. W. S., Hultsch, D. F., & Dixon, R. A. (2007). *Intraindividual variability in neurocognitive performance predicts impending death.* Manuscript under review.

MacDonald, S. W. S., Nyberg, L., & Bäckman, L. (2006). Intraindividual variability in behavior: Links to brain structure, neurotransmission, and neuronal activity. *Trends in Neurosciences, 29,* 474–480.

MacDonald, S.W.S., Nyberg, L., Sandblom, J., Fischer, H., & Bäckman, L. (2007). Increased response-time variability is associated with reduced inferior parietal activation in successful recognition. Manuscript under review.

Manoach, D. S. (2003). Prefrontal cortex dysfunction during working memory performance in schizophrenia: Reconciling discrepant findings. *Schizophrenia Research, 60,* 285–298.

Martin, M., & Hofer, S. M. (2004). Intraindividual variability, change, and aging: Conceptual and analytical issues. *Gerontology, 50,* 7–11.

Maxwell, S. E., & Delaney, H. D. (1990). *Designing experiments and analyzing data: A model comparison perspective.* Belmont, CA: Wadsworth.

May, C. P., & Hasher, L. (1998). Synchrony effects in inhibitory control over thought and action. *Journal of Experimental Psychology: Human Perception and Performance, 24,* 363–379.

May, C. P., Hasher, L., & Foong, N. (2005). Implicit memory, age, and time of day. Paradoxical priming effects. *Psychological Science, 16,* 96–100.

May, C. P., Hasher, L., & Stoltzfus, E. R. (1993). Optimal time of day and the magnitude of age differences in memory. *Psychological Science, 4,* 326–330.

Milberg, W., Blumstein, S., Sullivan Giovanello, K., & Misiurski, C. (2003). Summation priming in aphasia: Evidence for alterations in semantic integration and activation. *Brain and Cognition, 51,* 31–47.

Miller, E. K., & Cohen, J. D. (2001). An integrative theory of prefrontal cortex function. *Annual Review of Neuroscience, 24,* 167–202.

Moskowitz D. S., & Hershberger S. L. (Eds.). (2002) *Modeling intraindividual variability with repeated measures data: Methods and applications.* Mahwah, NJ: Lawrence Erlbaum Associates, Inc.

Murphy, D. R., Craik, F. I. M., Li, K. Z. H., & Schneider, B. (2000). Comparing the effects of aging and background noise on short-term memory performance. *Psychology and Aging, 15,* 323–334.

Murtha, S., Cismaru, R., Waechter, R., & Chertkow, H. (2002). Increased variability accompanies frontal lobe damage in dementia. *Journal of the International Neuropsychological Society, 8,* 360–372.

Myerson, J., Hale, S., Wagstaff, D., Poon, L. W., & Smith, G. A. (1990). The information-loss model: A mathematical theory of age-related cognitive slowing. *Psychological Review, 97,* 475–487.

Nesselroade, J. R. (1991). The warp and woof of the developmental fabric. In R. Downs, L. Liben, & D. S. Palermo (Eds.), *Visions of aesthetics, the environment, and development: The legacy of Joachim F. Wohlwill* (pp. 213–240). Hillsdale, NJ: Lawrence Erlbaum Associates, Inc.

Nesselroade, J. R., & Boker, S. M. (1994). Assessing constancy and change. In T. F. Heatherton & J. L. Weinberger (Eds.), *Can personality change?* (pp. 121–147). Washington, DC: American Psychological Association.

Nesselroade, J. R., & Featherman, D. L. (1997). Establishing a reference frame against which to chart age-related changes. In M. A. Hardy (Ed.), *Studying aging and social change: Conceptual and methodological issues* (pp. 191–205). Newbury Park, CA: Sage.

Nesselroade, J. R., & Ford, D. H. (1985). P-technique comes of age: Multivariate, replicated, single-subject designs for research on older adults. *Research on Aging, 7,* 46–80.

Nesselroade, J. R., & Ram, N. (2004). Studying intraindividual variability: What have we learned that will help us understand lives in context? *Research in Human Development, 1,* 9–29.

Nesselroade, J. R., & Salthouse, T. A. (2004). Methodological and theoretical implications of intraindividual variability in perceptual-motor performance. *Journal of Gerontology: Psychological Sciences, 59B*, P49–P55.

Odenheimer, G. L., & Minaker, K. L. (1994). Functional assessment in geriatric neurology. In M.L. Albert & J.E. Knofel (Eds.), *Clinical neurology of aging* (2nd edition, pp. 181–189). New York: Oxford University Press.

Pedhazur, E. J. (1997). *Multiple regression in behavioral research* (3rd ed.). Orlando, FL: Harcourt Brace.

Perbal, S., Couillet, J., Azouvi, P., & Pouthas, V. (2003). Relationships between time estimation, memory, attention, and processing speed in patients with severe traumatic brain injury. *Neuropsychologia, 41*, 1599–1610.

Perfect, T. J., & Maylor, E. A. (2000). Rejecting the dull hypothesis: The relation between method and theory in cognitive aging research. In T. J. Perfect & E. A. Maylor (Eds.), *Models of cognitive aging* (pp. 1–18). New York: Oxford University Press.

Petersen, R. C., Smith, G. E., Waring, S. C., Ivnik, R. J., Tangalos, E. G., & Kokmen, E. (1999). Mild cognitive impairment: Clinical characterization and outcome. *Archives of Neurology, 56*, 303–308.

Rabbitt, P. M. A. (2000). Measurement indices, functional characteristics, and psychometric constructs in cognitive aging. In T. J. Perfect & E. A. Maylor (Eds.), *Models of cognitive aging* (pp. 160–187). New York: Oxford University Press.

Rabbitt, P., Osman, P., Moore, B., & Stollery, B. (2001). There are stable individual differences in performance variability, both from moment to moment and from day to day. *Quarterly Journal of Experimental Psychology A, 54*, 981–1003.

Ram, N., Chow, S., Bowles, R. P., Wang, L., Grimm, F. F., & Fujita, F. et al. (2005a). Examining the interindividual differences in cyclicity of pleasant and unpleasant affect using spectral analysis and item response modeling. *Psychometrika, 70*, 773–790.

Ram, N., Rabbitt, P., Stollery, B., & Nesselroade, J. R. (2005b). Cognitive performance inconsistency: Intraindividual change and variability. *Psychology and Aging, 20*, 623–633.

Ratcliff, R., Thapar, A., & McKoon, G. (2001). The effects of aging on reaction time in a signal detection task. *Psychology and Aging, 16*, 323–341.

Raz, N. (2000). Aging of the brain and its impact on cognitive performance: Integration of structural and functional findings. In F. I. M. Craik & T. A. Salthouse (Eds.), *The handbook of aging and cognition* (2nd ed., pp. 1–90). Mahwah, NJ: Lawrence Erlbaum Associates, Inc.

Raz, N., Gunning-Dixon, F., Head, D., Rodrigue, K. M., Williamson, A., & Acker, J. D. (2004). Aging, sexual dimorphism, and hemispheric asymmetry of the cerebral cortex: Replicability of regional differences in volume. *Neurobiology of Aging, 25*, 377–396.

Reed, T.E. (1998) Causes of intraindividual variability in reaction times: A neurophysiologically oriented review and a new suggestion. *Personality and Individual Differences, 25*, 991–998.

Reimers, S., & Maylor, E. A. (2006). Gender effects on reaction time variability and trial-to-trial performance. Reply to Deary and Der (2005). *Aging, Neuropsychology, and Cognition, 13*, 479–489.

Robertson, S., Myerson, J., & Hale, S. (2006). Are there age differences in intraindividual variability in working memory performance? *Journal of Gerontology: Psychological Sciences, 61B*, P18–P24.

Salthouse, T. A. (1993). Attentional blocks are not responsible for age-related slowing. *Journal of Gerontology: Psychological Sciences, 48*, P263–P270.

Salthouse, T. A. (1998). Relation of successive percentiles of reaction time distributions to cognitive variables and to age. *Intelligence, 26*, 153–166.

Salthouse, T. A., Nesselroade, J. R., & Berish, D. E. (2006). Short-term variability in cognitive performance and the collaboration of longitudinal change. *Journal of Gerontology: Psychological Sciences, 61B*, P144–P151.

Segalowitz, S. J., Dywan, J., & Unsal, A. (1997). Attentional factors in response time variability after traumatic brain injury: An ERP study. *Journal of the International Neuropsychological Society, 3*, 95–107.

Siegler, R. S. (1994). Cognitive variability: A key to understanding cognitive development. *Current Directions in Psychological Science, American Psychological Association*, 1–5.

Shammi, P., Bosman, E., & Stuss, D. T. (1998). Aging and variability in performance. *Aging, Neuropsychology, and Cognition, 5*, 1–13.

Slifkin, A. B., & Newell, K. M. (1998). Is variability in human performance a reflection of system noise? *Current Directions in Psychological Science, 6*, 170–177.

Sliwinski, M. J., Smyth, J., Hofer, S. M., & Stawski, R. S. (2006). Intraindividual coupling of daily stress and cognition. *Psychology and Aging, 21*, 545–557.

Stefanis, N. C., van Os, J., Avramopoulos, D., Smyrnis, N., Evdokimidis, I., & Stefanis, C. N. (2005). Effect of COMT Val 158 Met polymorphism on the continuous performance test, identical pairs version: Tuning rather than improving performance. *American Journal of Psychiatry, 162*, 1752–1754.

Strauss, E., Bielak, A., Bunce, D., Hunter, M. A., & Hultsch, D. F. (in press). Is within-person variability a better indicator of mild cognitive impairment than processing speed? *Aging, Neuropsychology, and Cognition*.

Strauss, E., MacDonald, S. W. S., Hunter, M. A., Moll, A., & Hultsch, D. F. (2002). Intraindividual variability in cognitive performance in three groups of adults: Cross-domain links to physical status and self-perceived affect and beliefs. *Journal of the International Neuropsychology Society, 8*, 893–906.

Stuss, D. T. (1991). Disturbance of self-awareness after frontal system damage. In G. P. Prigatano & D. L. Schacter (Eds.), *Awareness of deficit after brain injury: Clinical and theoretical issues* (pp. 63–83). New York: Oxford University Press.

Stuss, D. T., Murphy, K. J., Binns, M. A., & Alexander, M. P. (2003). Staying on the job: The frontal lobes control individual performance variability. *Brain, 126*, 2363–2380.

Stuss, D. T., Pogue, J., Buckle, L., & Bondar, J. (1994). Characterization of stability of performance in patients with traumatic brain injury: Variability and consistency on reaction time tests. *Neuropsychology, 8*, 316–324.

Stuss, D. T., Stethem, L. l., Hugenholtz, H., Picton, T., Pivik, J., & Richard, M. T. (1989). Reaction time after head injury: Fatigue, divided and focused attention, and consistency of performance. *Journal of Neurology, Neurosurgery, and Psychiatry, 52*, 742–748.

Tabert, M. H., Albert, S. M., Borukhova-Milov, L., Camacho, Y., Pelton, G., Liu, X., et al. (2002). Functional deficits in patients with mild cognitive impairment: Prediction of AD. *Neurology, 58*, 758–764.

Tuokko, H., & McDowell, I. (2006). An overview of mild cognitive impairment. In H. Tuokko & D. F. Hultsch (Eds.), *Mild cognitive impairment: International perspectives* (pp. 3–28). New York: Taylor & Francis.

Van Orden, G. C., Holden, J. G., & Turvey, M. T. (2003). Self-organization of cognitive performance. *Journal of Experimental Psychology: General, 132*, 331–350.

Walker, M. P., Ayre, G. A., Cummings, J. L., Wesnes, K., McKeith, I. G., O'Brien, J. T., et al. (2000). Quantifying fluctuation in dementia with Lewy bodies, Alzheimer's disease, and vascular dementia. *Neurology, 54*, 1616–1624.

Webb, W. B. (1982). Sleep in older persons: Sleep structure of 50- to 60-year-old men and women. *Journal of Gerontology, 37*, 581–586.

Welford, A. T. (1965). Performance, biological mechanisms and age: A theoretical sketch. In A. T. Welford & J. E. Birren (Eds.), *Behavior, aging, and the nervous system* (pp. 3–20). Springfield, IL: Thomas.

Welford, A. T. (1980). Relationships between reaction time and fatigue, stress, age and sex. In A. T. Welford (Ed.), *Reaction time* (pp. 321–354). New York: Academic Press.

West, R. (1996). An application of prefrontal cortex function theory to cognitive aging. *Psychological Bulletin, 120,* 272–292.

West, R. (2001). The transient nature of executive control processes in younger and older adults. *European Journal of Cognitive Psychology, 13,* 91–105.

West, R., Murphy, K. J., Armilio, M. L., Craik, F. I. M., & Stuss, D. T. (2002). Lapses of intention and performance variability reveal age-related increases in fluctuations of executive control. *Brain and Cognition, 49,* 402–419.

Williams, B. R., Hultsch, D. F., Strauss, E., Hunter, M. A., & Tannock, R. (2005). Inconsistency in reaction time across the lifespan. *Neuropsychology, 19,* 88–96.

Williams, B. R., Strauss, E., Hultsch, D. F., & Hunter, M. A. (in press). Reaction time inconsistency in a spatial Stroop task: Age-related differences through childhood and adulthood. *Aging, Neuropsychology, and Cognition.*

Willis, S. L., & Marsiske, M. (1991). Life span perspective on practical intelligence. In K. D, Cicerone (Ed.), *The neuropsychology of everyday life: Issues in development and rehabilitation* (pp. 183–197). Boston: Kluwer Academic.

Willis, S. L., & Marsiske, M. (1999). *Manual for the everyday problems test.* University Park, PA: Pennsylvania State University.

Winblad, B., Palmer, K., Kivipelto, M., Jelic, V., Fratiglioni, L., Wahlund, L.-O., et al. (2004). Mild cognitive impairment—beyond controversies, towards consensus: a report of the International Working Group on Mild Cognitive Impairment. *Journal of Internal Medicine, 256,* 240–246.

Winterer G., Coppola R., Goldberg T. E., Egan M. F., Jones D. W., Sanchez C. E., et al. (2004). Prefrontal broadband noise, working memory, and genetic risk for schizophrenia. *American Journal of Psychiatry, 161,* 490–500.

Wohlwill, J. F. (1973). *The study of behavioral development.* New York: Academic Press.

11

Lifespan Cognitive Development

The Roles of Representation and Control

Fergus I. M. Craik
Rotman Research Institute

Ellen Bialystok
York University

It is a curious fact that studies of cognitive aging and studies of cognitive development make little contact with each other. The findings, methods, and concepts from each area have typically emerged and existed in isolation, despite the obvious point that children develop into young adults and finally into older adults. Given this continuity, it seems necessary to assume some corresponding continuities in the mechanisms and processes that underlie cognitive performance, yet the great majority of investigations have either stopped at adolescence (in the case of cognitive development) or started at young adulthood (in the case of cognitive aging). The cultural isolation between the two subareas of lifespan cognitive development is even more difficult to understand when the few studies that do cover all ages report substantial similarities between the cognitive mechanisms in children and adults. As one recent example, Salthouse and Davis (2006) analyzed the structural organization of cognition in 3400 individuals ranging in age from 5 to 93 years and reported a qualitatively similar organizational structure of cognitive variables between children (5–17 years), students (18–22 years), and adults (23–93 years). The investigators concluded that "at least with respect to these aspects of cognition, age differences across the lifespan appear to be more quantitative than qualitative" (p. 52).

One reason for the division between researchers in child development and aging may be the different evolutionary histories of the two areas. Work on cognitive development evolved from observational studies of children's intellectual growth on the one hand and from studies of educational abilities and attainments on the other. In contrast, the two main sources of current work on cognitive aging are psychometric studies of abilities, and the findings, methods, and theories of experimental cognitive psychology. Despite these differences in history and emphasis, the potential benefits of an integrated approach to the study of lifespan cognition are enormous. As we point out elsewhere (Craik & Bialystok, 2006), these benefits go beyond the obvious advantages of sharing a common knowledge base and common methodologies and include such possibilities as improved understanding of the linkages between cognitive processes and brain functions. For example, both fields are concerned with understanding variability in performance and how such variability may serve as a mechanism of change. A coordinated investigation which aims to capture developmental changes in cognitive processing at different stages of the lifespan will potentially reveal a deeper view of the nature and function of change itself.

Exceptions to the general state of two separate cultures certainly exist. Paul Baltes and his colleagues have taken a lifespan approach to developmental psychology for many years (e.g., Baltes, 1987; Baltes, Reese, & Lipsitt, 1980), and Baltes and O.G. Brim edited a 10-volume series on Life-Span Development and Behavior between 1979 and 1990. Students and colleagues of Baltes at the Max Planck Institute in Berlin have also carried on this tradition with influential publications by Ulman Lindenberger (2001), Shu-Chen Li (2004), and others. Timothy Salthouse has stressed the fundamental role played by speed of processing in cognitive performance and how that speed first quickens throughout childhood and then slows in old age (Salthouse, 1991, 1998). Theories of child development have occasionally been applied to the aging process; for example, some attempts were made to extend Piaget's stage theory to adult development and aging (Hooper, Fitzgerald, & Papalia, 1971). Theorists have reached out in the other direction too; in an influential chapter, Klaus Riegel (1977) described the "dialectics of development"—the growth-related interactions between individuals and their inner biology on the one hand and their outer sociological conditions on the other. This dialectical approach is rooted in the study of adult development but is clearly applicable as well to childhood and adolescence (Riegel, 1977, p. 86). The emphasis on interactions among biology, individuality, and the social context has also been stressed by Baltes and his colleagues in a recent book entitled *Lifespan development and the brain: The perspective of biocultural co-constructivism* (Baltes, Reuter-Lorenz, & Rösler, 2006). Finally, we have edited a book in which pairs of authors address topics in cognitive psychology—attention, memory, thinking, language, etc.—with one member of each pair from the perspective of child development and the other from the perspective of cognitive aging (Bialystok & Craik, 2006). The aim was to initiate a set of fruitful dialogs between members of the two cultures. In summary, while the "two separate cultures" situation still clearly exists, there are now hopeful signs that the barriers between them are beginning to break down. We hope that the present chapter will contribute to the process.

MECHANISMS OF CHANGE: CONTEXT, REPRESENTATION, AND CONTROL

Recently we proposed that continuities between child development, adult development, and aging could be organized under the general headings of changes in representation and control (Craik & Bialystok, 2006). The argument was that both cognitive representations and cognitive control change during development and aging, but each is predominant at a different life stage. Early child development is dominated by the acquisition of knowledge of various types—sensory-motor, procedural, declarative, and episodic—and thus by the growth and organization of representations. In contrast, the decline of cognitive functioning in the elderly is more dominated by changes in control functions operating on the knowledge base.

The context in which behavior occurs is crucially important at both ends of the life course. The external environment is obviously the source of new information at all stages of life, and in that sense the context establishes, shapes, and confirms the knowledge incorporated in the representational systems. This function of context is particularly important during childhood, but the external context also has an important role in older age. Young children (like simple animals perhaps) are heavily affected by the current environment to influence feelings, thoughts, and behavior, but as they mature and accumulate internal representations, such thoughts and behaviors are progressively more dominated by these internal schemas. In this way, the maturing child is able to act independently of the pressures of "here and now," famously noted by Piaget (1959) and more in response to longer term plans and goals. In older adulthood, the support of the environment is again needed to compensate for the increasing difficulty in accessing representational knowledge. Thus, environmental support again becomes progressively more necessary at older ages, both to complement self-initiated behaviors that are difficult to manage, and to guide thoughts and actions appropriately (Craik, 1983).

The general theme of this chapter, then, is that lifespan cognitive development can be understood largely in terms of the growth and decline of representational structures and control systems, the interactions between them, and their joint interactions with the environmental context. It is clear that "context" in this sense must include social and cultural aspects

(Baltes et al., 2006; Vygotsky, 1978) although a thorough analysis of their profound effects on cognition is beyond the scope of the present chapter. The framework provided by this interactional scheme further suggests a number of general questions, some of which we pose in this introductory section and return to later in light of the empirical evidence described in subsequent sections.

We have already alluded to the first question, namely, whether the balance between representation and control remains constant or changes through different periods of life. A tentative answer is that representations play a dominant role when they are first established in early childhood and then become more "crystallized" (Cattell, 1971; Horn, 1982). These representational systems are well developed in adults, and the use of this represented knowledge is guided by effective control systems. In old age, representations are again dominant but for a different reason; on the assumption that representational systems include schematic habit patterns as well as structures representing abstract knowledge, the declining power of control systems leaves behavior influenced predominantly by previously established habits, which may no longer guide behavior adaptively. Does this mean that control is dominant in middle life and representations are dominant in both early and later life? Presumably the two sets of factors *interact* at all stages, although the balance may tilt from one to the other.

A second question is the extent to which aging can be regarded as "development in reverse." Superficially this seems to be an attractive idea, given that cognitive abilities obviously increase throughout childhood and generally wane from middle age on, although with markedly different trajectories depending on the relative involvement of such factors as fluid versus crystallized abilities, automatic versus controlled processes, and the like (Craik & Bialystok, 2006; Park, Lautenschlager, Hedden, Davidson, Smith, & Smith, 2002; Salthouse, 1991). We considered this possibility in an earlier paper (Craik & Bialystok, 2006) but rejected it on the grounds that even though overall performance first rises and then falls, the *components* of cognitive performance vary at different stages in life. That is, intellectual abilities in young children are relatively poor largely because they have not yet built up adequate knowledge structures, whereas cognitive inefficiencies in older adults stem principally from failures of control. This analysis suggests that equivalent overall performance between 12-year-olds and 80-year-olds is the result of substantially different component processes.

A third question concerns changes in the neural underpinnings of cognitive performance across the lifespan. Although research in the area of cognitive neuroscience is still at an early stage, there may be some hints about this question to be gleaned from a consideration of brain changes related to development and aging. For example, planning and control are functions generally considered to depend on frontal lobe processes. Therefore, before surveying lifespan changes in cognitive areas, we briefly consider some relevant findings and concepts from cognitive neuroscience.

Our suggestion is that lifespan changes in cognitive performance can be understood in terms of the growth and decline of mental representations, executive control, and the interactions between them and the current context. The nature of these interactions depends on the stage of life; in particular, on the potential for change afforded by neural structures and brain organization at that stage. Specifically, the execution of a successful cognitive action at a given moment depends on the interactions among knowledge representations, control processes, and context, resulting in a fluent act that is not readily decomposed into its components. It exists as a gestalt at a higher level, much as a winning shot in tennis depends on past knowledge of how to prepare for a particular stroke, current knowledge of the opponent's likely moves, the speed of the ball, the surface, and the racquet, all interacting to give rise to the final fluent action. It is in this sense that it is somewhat artificial to decompose mental processes into their constituent representational, control, and contextual components. Nonetheless, for ease of analysis and clarity of exposition we propose to do just that. We will examine evidence from language, memory, and executive processing to illustrate the roles of representation and control in development and aging and consider the implications of each domain for determining the mechanisms of change across the lifespan.

NEURAL PLASTICITY AND COGNITIVE CHANGE

One factor that is clearly *asymmetrical* across the lifespan is brain structure and function. There are approximately 10 billion neurons in the human brain, and these are all present at birth. This number remains relatively constant, at least until young adulthood, but the number of synapses changes dramatically—from roughly 2500 per cortical neuron at birth to 15,000 at age 2–3 years (Goswami, 2002). This explosive growth of connectivity is seen as an increase in synaptic density in the cerebral cortex (gray matter). It produces an overabundance of connections that are then pruned by experience—essentially a strengthening of connections that are used, and an elimination of connections that are not used. The balance between progressive synapse formation and increasing dendritic arborization on the one hand, and synaptic pruning on the other hand, results in an inverted U-shaped rise and fall of gray matter that peaks at different ages for different brain regions (Casey, Tottenham, Liston, & Durston,

2005; Gogtay et al., 2004). These peaks occur at approximately 11½ years for the frontal lobes, 11 years for the parietal lobes, and 16½ years for the temporal lobes (Giedd et al., 1999). In contrast to the growth and decline of gray matter during childhood, white matter (representing increasing myelinization and neuronal conductivity) increases linearly with age throughout childhood and young adulthood (Giedd et al., 1999) although again following a different timetable for different brain regions (Konner, 1991; Taylor, 2006). In older age there is a decline in white matter, attributable to the gradual process of demyelinization (Raz, 2000). The combined effects of synaptic growth, synaptic pruning, and increasing myelinization result in high levels of plasticity and learning ability in infants and young children; these abilities level off in middle life and then decline at older ages.

From early adulthood and progressively for the remainder of the lifespan, there is a decrease in plasticity but not an absence of brain modifiability. Further dendritic loss, and loss of cells themselves, is no longer adaptive as it is in childhood but limits rapid acquisition of new learning (Buckner, Head, & Lustig, 2006). A useful metaphor in this regard is that synaptic pruning in childhood may be regarded as a form of sculpture in which the extraneous raw material is removed in order to create the desired structure. Further removal of material from this structure in older age, however, is more analogous to erosion, depleting and distorting the original form. Synaptic loss and the consequent shrinkage of cortical gray matter in older age can be accelerated by hypertension and stress (Raz & Rodrigue, 2006). Other systems also decline in the course of aging, a prominent example being the dopamine system, which has been linked recently to cognitive performance (Bäckman, Nyberg, Lindenberger, Li, & Farde, 2006; Li, Lindenberger, Hommel, Aschersleben, Prinz, & Baltes, 2004).

In spite of this trend, a growing number of reports have found evidence for the beneficial effects of environmental and behavioral factors in reducing the rate of cognitive decline. Engagement in both intellectual and physical activities appears to be the key component, with higher levels of cognitive functioning associated with higher occupational status, continuing involvement in education, stimulating leisure activities, and physical fitness (see Kramer, Bherer, Colcombe, Dong, & Greenough, 2004 and Valenzuela & Sachdev, 2006 for reviews). Cognitive reserve (Stern, 2002) is the notion that stimulating mental activities can delay the onset of dementia, although whether such activities slow the rate of cognitive decline or simply raise the level of performance for the same rate of decline is still a matter of debate. One large-scale meta-analysis by Valenzuela and Sachdev (2006) found evidence for the former position whereas a second large-scale review by Salthouse (2006) showed strong evidence for the latter conclusion. Further analyses are clearly needed, but one possibility is that the pattern of outcomes may differ between normal aging and aging complicated by the presence of dementia (T.A. Salthouse, personal communication).

One notion related to plasticity is compensation, the idea that both neural and behavioral systems change their functional organization in order to cope better with age-related declines. At the level of brain organization, there is growing agreement about the changes that take place, but also some interesting debates on how best to characterize these changes. The evidence suggests that some functions represented unilaterally in the brains of young adults are bilaterally represented in the brains of older adults. Grady, McIntosh, Horwitz, and Maisog (1995) and Cabeza (2002) have shown that retrieval from episodic memory is typically associated with activity in the right dorsal prefrontal cortex in young adults (the HERA model suggested by Tulving et al., 1994), but episodic retrieval in older adults is associated with *bilateral* activity in the frontal lobes. This shift from unilateral to bilateral representations has been termed the HAROLD model (Hemispheric Asymmetry Reduction in Older Adults) by Cabeza (2002; Dennis & Cabeza, chapter 1). Although the shift to bilaterality is well recognized, whether or not the shift is compensatory is still an open question. The main alternative is that representations dedifferentiate in the older brain, and cognitive systems change from precisely focused representations in younger adults to fuzzier, less well focused representations in older adults. One argument in favor of dedifferentiation is that representations progressively *differentiate* in the developing child. This process of differentiation happens both in terms of cognitive structures (e.g., "doggy" used to name all animals, to "doggy" for dogs alone, to "terrier," "poodle," etc. for specific breeds of dog) and also in terms of brain representations where there is a developmental shift from diffuse to focal, lateralized representations (Casey et al., 2005).

One obvious way to decide whether the age-related trend towards bilateral representation is compensatory or not is to examine individual differences in some relevant cognitive ability and see whether higher levels of ability are associated with greater degrees of bilaterality. The evidence obtained by following this approach is not clear, however. Another possible form of brain-related compensation in older adults is the increasing reliance on frontal lobe strategies to bolster the waning efficiency of memory and other cognitive functions. Dennis and Cabeza (chapter 1) call this trend the "posterior to anterior shift with aging" or PASA. A puzzle, though, is why older people would use their frontal lobes *more* when there is good evidence that frontal-lobe functions (executive functions at the cognitive level) show rather steep declines with age (Raz, 2000; Rubin, 1999; Stuss et al., 2002). The evidence for and against the HAROLD and PASA models is discussed in chapter 1 by Dennis and Cabeza.

LANGUAGE

Theories of Language Acquisition

The acquisition of language is one of the more dramatic developments in childhood. In a breathtakingly short time, infants progress from babbling (about 6 months old), to single words (about 1 year old), with word combinations before 2 years old, and complex syntax and rich vocabulary by the time they start school. Their use of language by about the age of 5 years observes rules of grammar and indicates mastery of several thousand words spoken with native-like pronunciation, following the constraints of pragmatic usage. With aging, the speech of older adults is marked by difficulties in word retrieval and a noticeably simplified grammar, both for production and comprehension. Thus, the changes that characterize linguistic performance at both ends of the lifespan are vast. They are also roughly similar: children learn words and older adults forget them; children increase grammatical complexity and older adults reduce it. Is there a mechanism that unites the lifetime changes in linguistic ability? To what extent does the notion of symmetrical development and decline discussed earlier apply to language abilities across the lifespan? As Kemper (2006) points out, parallel change in linguistic ability may be caused by different mechanisms, so superficial evidence of similarity is insufficient evidence for the continuity of development and decline in the same processes.

Theories of language acquisition can be positioned along a dimension that varies in the extent to which this process is driven primarily by innate biases in the system to learn language or by experiences that lead the child to language through meaningful interactions. Theories that rely more strongly on biological biases to ensure learning are domain specific in that these biases apply only to language; the linguistic representations that emerge from this development will inevitably be unique to language and possibly idiosyncratic in form and structure. The syntax of natural languages is an example of a representational system that is considered to be a unique construction constrained by linguistic universals, as in the account proposed by Pinker (1994). Theories that rely more strongly on experience and interaction appeal to all-purpose cognitive and social processes to guide language acquisition. The linguistic representations that develop in response to these experiences will be continuous with other representational forms and largely integrated with them, as in the account proposed by Tomasello (2003). On these views, there is little in the representation of language that is distinct from other representational systems, even though much of it is unique. Along this dimension that describes the process of language acquisition in vastly different ways, the salient problem to be solved is how the child establishes the underlying knowledge system that defines the forms and structures of language.

The decline of linguistic ability with aging is similarly different under these two perspectives, appealing either to the decline of language-specific mechanisms that require more salient input and longer processing times, or to the decline of general cognitive mechanisms that define the overall changing cognitive profile that occurs with age. For example, a language-specific explanation of decline, such as that by Caplan and Waters (1999), points to the decline in components of working memory that are involved only in language processing, whereas the explanation offered by Wingfield (1996) based on the effect of cognitive slowing leads to a more domain-general account of decline that connects changes in language ability with other cognitive systems. Again, however, the central problem addressed by these different explanatory mechanisms is an account of how access to linguistic knowledge and the productive use of linguistic knowledge changes with aging. Unlike the problem in explaining children's acquisition of representational structures that form the core of linguistic knowledge, the problem in aging is to understand changes in the control systems that interact with that knowledge.

The difference in emphasis on the identification of the linguistic problem converges on a differential focus at each end of the lifespan in considering representational structure (children) or control processes (older adults) as the primary locus of change. When development and aging are examined independently, the isolation of only one of these components can be interpreted as providing a sufficient account of changes in language behavior, and complementary changes in the less salient component are often neglected. However, a complete account of language change across the lifespan will need to integrate the role of both representation and control at all points in the lifespan. Moreover, the bias for attention on one or the other of these components has also led to a bias for accepting theories that are more biological and domain specific (children) or more experiential and domain general (older adults) as the more useful perspective. Again, however, a complete account will ultimately require a synthesis that addresses the contribution of both biology and experience. With a more fully elaborated account, the mechanisms of change responsible for linguistic ability throughout the lifespan will be clearer. These ideas will be illustrated by considering explanations for changes in vocabulary and syntax in development and aging.

Vocabulary Learning and Semantic Knowledge

Vocabulary acquisition proceeds at a stunning rate through childhood. Bates, Dale, and Thal (1995) report that by 16 months of age children could reliably understand a mean of 191 words and produce a mean of 64 words; by 30 months, the mean number of words in productive vocabulary was 534. This period of rapid vocabulary growth during the second year of life has been called the "vocabulary burst" (Bloom, 1973; Dromi, 1987; Nelson, 1973), and researchers have calculated different rates for this achievement, ranging from about 5 words (Anglin, 1993) to 10 words per day (Clark, 1993) during the school years. Other researchers describe word acquisition in terms of an accelerated rate of learning with no identifiable burst (Bloom, 2002; Elman, Bates, Johnson, Karmiloff-Smith, Parisi, & Plunkett, 1996), but the outcome is the same for the present purposes.

Biologically based accounts of this development rely on mechanisms that guide children to understand how labels heard in the speech around them are the names for specific objects, a process called fast mapping (Carey, 1978; Markson & Bloom 1997). The mechanisms enabling this one-trial learning of new words are posited as biological constraints and include taxonomic constraints, mutual exclusivity, and whole object constraint (Clark, 1993; Markman, 1989). However, the same outcome can be achieved without biases that are dedicated to the language system. For example, Smith, Jones, and Landau (1996) propose that simple attention processes automatically focus on the correct level of description for a new word and guarantee the correct representation, a point that Bloom (2000) takes as evidence for the importance of domain-general cognitive constraints in language acquisition. Similarly, Golinkoff and Hirsh-Pasek (2006) attribute word learning to a fortunate confluence of children's attentional biases and developing cognitive systems in interaction with adults who guide the process of word learning.

In these accounts of vocabulary development, the focus is on explaining the rapid and efficient acquisition of a complex system of symbols to denote the full range of meanings that humans intend to express. The problem, therefore, is about building representations, but the solution invokes various degrees and types of control to establish that representational system. The solutions differ in whether the mechanisms are specific to language or general cognitive processes, but they share the feature of addressing the single most crucial issue in vocabulary development: how do children figure out how words refer and solve the mapping problem between words and their meanings? In none of these proposals are the cognitive and executive monitoring systems (e.g., working memory) involved in vocabulary acquisition either complex or central to the story.

Evidence on the fate of vocabulary knowledge in old age is more mixed. There is consensus that vocabulary continues to increase throughout middle age and holds up well, but eventually begins to decline in older age (Hultsch, Hertzog, Dixon, & Small, 1998; Schaie, 1996). However, these deficits in vocabulary knowledge are not reported until individuals are 70 (Au, Joung, Nicholas, Kass, Obler, & Albert, 1995), 80 (Alwin & McCammon, 2001), or even 90 years old (Singer, Verhaeghen, Ghisletta, Lindenberger, & Baltes, 2003), an achievement that attests to the durability of the representations. Therefore, the eventual decline of vocabulary in older age cannot be attributed to the same factors responsible for the increase of vocabulary in childhood when children are establishing representational structures connecting symbols to concepts.

The main diagnostic experience of vocabulary failures in older age is the problem of word retrieval (Burke, MacKay, Worthley, & Wade, 1991; Cohen & Faulkner, 1986; Mortensen, Meyer, & Humphreys, 2006). Inherent in this description is an assumption about its locus: word retrieval implies that the knowledge is present but inaccessible, and the responsibility for accessibility is control. Not surprisingly, therefore, most explanations of the word retrieval problem appeal to failures in aspects of control, including reductions in processing speed, working memory, and inhibitory control (Burke & Shafto, chapter 8; Wingfield & Stine-Morrow, 2000).

In contrast to these control-based views, Burke and her colleagues propose an explanation for vocabulary failure in older age that is based on the representational system and called the "transmission deficit hypothesis" (Burke & Laver, 1990; Burke et al., 1991). The essence of the model is that the connections between concepts and lexical details, especially phonological and orthographic information, are strengthened by use but weakened by aging. These weak connections are characteristics of the representation but are experienced as general processing deficits. Put another way, aging causes deterioration in the connectivity of the representational structure, making word retrieval problematic. Aspects of the system that are based on single connections, such as the links between a word and its phonology, are vulnerable to decay and result in word retrieval failures; but aspects of the system that are connected through built-in redundancy, such as lexical–semantic links, are more robust, preserving semantic processing for older adults. Thus, age-related changes in representational structures account for changes in lexical processing in older age. This view is contrary to those claiming that knowledge representations are insensitive to aging (e.g., Baltes, Staudinger, & Lindenberger, 1999). An intermediate position might be that they are *relatively* insensitive to the effects of aging.

To summarize, both representation and control are involved in the acquisition of vocabulary for children and the failure to access vocabulary in older age. What is different is the balance between them and the mechanism required by each. For children, the primary challenge for representation is to solve the mapping problem between concepts and symbols so that a representational structure can be created and developed. For adults, the primary challenge for representation is to maintain the connections between ideas and the specific lexical details as those links weaken in older age. The control restrictions on vocabulary acquisition and decline are defined by the processing resources required for access to specific items. These resources may be insufficient for young children, so limiting the extent of new vocabulary acquisition, and diminished for older adults, so reducing access to vocabulary that has been previously represented but is now weakly activated or confusable with competing terms. Thus both representation and control define the richness and accessibility of vocabulary knowledge throughout the lifespan.

Syntax and Grammatical Processing

The second major index of language ability in both children's development and older age is mastery of the complex syntax that defines natural language. At about 2 years old, children begin to produce two-word utterances, and syntactic complexity emerges as the utterance length, generally measured as Mean Length of Utterance (MLU), increases (Brown, 1973). The usual explanations for this increase in grammatical competence appeal to children's improvements in processing capacity and cognitive resources, either in terms of domain-general mechanisms for processing complex information or language-specific information for discovering the rules of language. The majority of the explanations fall into the latter category (e.g., Meisel, 1995). These accounts of syntactic development begin with the assumption that the brain is strongly biased for language learning through its innate structure (Pinker, 1994) and rely on the growing processing capacity of children to uncover those rules and allow children to produce increasingly complex linguistic utterances that conform to those rules (de Villiers & de Villiers, 1992).

An empirical demonstration of this approach has been supplied by Valian and her colleagues, who have shown that the restrictions on the grammaticality and completeness of children's utterances are determined more by processing limitations than by knowledge failures. For example, children find it easier to imitate complex sentences that have predictable objects that serve to reduce the processing load (Valian, Prasada, & Scarpa, 2006) and are more likely to drop subjects from their utterances as a function of sentence length, indicating performance deficits, and not grammatical complexity, indicating competence deficits (Valian,

Hoeffner, & Aubry, 1996). Children are capable of reproducing complex syntax if the sentence falls within their resource capacity.

This processing-based view of syntactic development fits well with evidence from children's developing cognitive resources and the appearance of increasingly complex grammatical forms in their speech. However, it is possible to consider the acquisition of grammar in terms of the representation system and not the control system. Bates and colleagues (Bates & Goodman, 1999; Elman et al., 1996) have noted that children begin to combine words and demonstrate grammatical constraints at the point at which their vocabulary exceeds a base level of 50 words, and the development of both vocabulary and syntax from that point is entirely intertwined; they argue in fact that they are aspects of the same development. For example, in a longitudinal study of children between 10 and 28 months old, the correlations between measures of grammar and measures of vocabulary were just as high as measures within one of those domains, and generally greater than +.75. The explanation is that grammar emerges as a natural organizational property of representations of words and the need to use those words in a linear speech channel for communication. Thus, increasing grammatical complexity is a reflection of the growth of representations of the lexicon.

Changes in grammatical competence become apparent again in older age, although basic syntactic processes appear to be unaffected by aging (Kemper, Herman, & Nartowitz, 2003). Part of this may reflect the ability of adults to recruit representations of context and meaning as a support for more detailed linguistic structures. In several studies, the facilitating effect of context on the ability to interpret complex language has been shown to be greater for older adults than younger ones (Schneider, Daneman, & Murphy, 2005), suggesting the reliance on larger representational structures for language processing in older adults.

In contrast to intact comprehension, there is a characteristic simplification of speech production in older age (Cooper, 1990; Kemper, Kynette, Rash, Sprott, & O'Brien, 1989; Shewan & Henderson, 1988). Kemper, Thompson, and Marquis (2001) quantified this age-related simplification by computing values for Developmental Level (D-Level) and Propositional Density (P-Density) indexing syntactic and propositional complexity, respectively, and showed declines for both in older age. Kemper (2006) attributes this decline to working memory limitations (Kemper et al., 1989), reductions in processing speed (Wingfield, 1996), and reduced inhibitory control (Hasher & Zacks, 1988). A large-scale study by Van der Linden et al. (1999) confirmed a model in which age-related differences in language comprehension and verbal memory were mediated through changes in working memory, indirectly incorporating reduced processing speed and decreased resistance to interference. Similarly, Burke and

Shafto (chapter 8) offer six explanations for age-related change in syntactic complexity—resource deficits, general slowing, inhibition deficits, transmission deficits, declining working memory, and sensory/perceptual deficits—all of which are based on reductions in control processes that occur with aging.

As in the explanation for development, the issue of whether the relevant processes are specific to language or part of general cognitive systems applies as well to aging. In contrast to the views described above in which general resource reduction is responsible, some theorists identify processing declines in systems that are specific to language processing. Caplan and Waters (1999), for example, consider that linguistic processing is carried out by dedicated systems involved only in the processing of language, and the reduction in syntactic complexity in older age is attributable to the changes in the working memory components of these language-specific processors. Again, the scope of the processes as being general cognitive or language-specific functions is different from the thematic argument that it is reduction in such control systems that is responsible for declining complexity in syntactic structure for older adults.

It is apparent in this brief review that no account of language acquisition and decline is possible without considering the contributions of both representation and control. In this sense, the development and decline of language processing abilities are indeed symmetrical, rising and falling for reasons rooted in the same ultimate mechanisms. However, it is equally apparent that the changes in linguistic abilities that characterize each end of the lifespan are dramatically different from each other. Our view is that these differences reflect two aspects of the functioning of representation and control systems. The first is that the bias for each of these systems is different at the two ends of the lifespan, with greater emphasis on representation in childhood and on control in older adulthood. The second is that the precise responsibility of each of these systems is different, with representation changing from establishing concepts to maintaining them, and control changing from directing attention to language-relevant events in the environment to monitoring attention and working memory for online processing.

These differences in the responsibilities for representation and control come from different linguistic challenges in childhood and in older age. Language acquisition is defined by the development of the linguistic system and the accumulation of language-specific knowledge about the forms and functions of language. Language decline is defined by a decrease in the cognitive systems that support language, not necessarily in the language systems themselves. For these reasons, children's challenges are not with control but with representation, the most important being the need to establish conceptual structures that can relate abstract symbolic forms and structures to meanings. The depth of this problem has led many researchers to invoke a large degree of biological preparedness as a means of overcoming the formidable problem of creating such representational structures from nothing. In contrast, the challenges of older adulthood come from the diminishing resources that are available to carry out the comprehension and production of a system as complex as language.

Language Ability across the Lifespan

The case of language makes clear the joint involvement of representation and control across the lifespan. As the balance between them shifts and demands of mastering a linguistic system grow, different aspects of these processes are highlighted. Even taking the same evidence, for example, reduced vocabulary in childhood and older age, the explanation for children's deficit is predominantly lack of knowledge or representation of words, but for adult deficits it is lack of access to words. Development and decline are different to be sure, but their progress and dynamic rest on the same small set of processes that define all human cognition.

MEMORY

Procedural Learning and Implicit Memory

Much of the research on learning and memory in infants over the past 30–40 years has been devoted to showing that they possess more powerful learning abilities than Piaget (1959) had acknowledged in his claim that infants lack the means to represent information from the outside world until they are 18–24 months old. Nonetheless, Piaget's view that infants necessarily live in the "here and now"—a conscious present with little access to the past or future—may still be largely correct, given that infants' abilities may be characterized as adaptive *learning* rather than *memory* in the usual sense. Although perceived events and infants' consequent reactions to them certainly change subsequent behavior, infants do not necessarily *recollect* those events in the sense of consciously re-experiencing them.

A significant problem facing researchers of memory and learning in preverbal infants and very young children is how to assess those abilities. Rovee-Collier and colleagues devised an ingenious solution (reviewed by Rovee-Collier & Hayne, 2000). They had infants aged 2–6 months lie in their cribs with one foot tied by a ribbon to an attractive mobile suspended above the crib. Initially, spontaneous footkicks moved the mobile, thereby reinforcing further kicking movements. Learning was revealed 24 hours later when the infant kicked in the presence of the original mobile, even though it no longer moved. This learning was specific to the original mobile, as kicking did not occur in response to a different mobile. A study by Timmons (1994) demonstrated how this "hyperspecificity" of learning is modified later by conditioning 6-month-old infants to move a mobile by kicking and to activate a music box by performing an arm movement. These learned responses were apparently forgotten after 3 weeks, but when the child was reminded of the learning by again allowing the music box to be activated by an arm movement, footkicks to the mobile were also emitted. In other words, the representations of the actions to activate the mobile and the music box were somehow associated, presumably through the common training context, allowing a form of generalization to take place. Rovee-Collier and Hayne (2000) give further examples of how with age infants' responses can increasingly generalize to novel task cues. The supportive effects of context are therefore quite specific at first but can be overridden by training in multiple contexts. By 8 months old, infants learn to generalize, decreasing the dependency on exact context reinstatement to support retrieval of the learned response.

Another method used to study infants' learning is novelty preference, sometimes in a paired comparison setting. The infant is familiarized with one stimulus and then exposed to the choice of that stimulus or a novel stimulus; the infant demonstrates learning by attending more to the novel stimulus. This phenomenon reflects a mechanism for learning new patterns and objects—the starting point for a system of representations. When the same pattern is exposed on repeated occasions, it becomes habituated, no longer attracting attention but presumably gaining in familiarity. As children mature, they can deal with more complex patterns and retain them for longer periods. At the age of 5 months, children will select a novel black and white pattern after 2 days but will select a novel facial photograph after 2 weeks (Fagan, 1973). It seems likely that the advantage to faces reflects some relatively innate ability that has obvious biological value.

These examples of early learning, while impressive, are unlikely to involve memory in the sense of recollecting anything about the original event but are more akin to demonstrations of procedural memory or priming in adults (Mandler, 1998). As Tulving (1983) has also pointed out, some forms of memory and learning appear to be more fundamental and primitive, occurring in lower animals and also occurring early in ontogeny. Does this mean that they are also the last to survive in the aging brain?

In general, the answer is yes; most studies show that older adults are essentially unimpaired on implicit or procedural tasks of memory and learning. In the serial reaction time task, for example, participants must press the key corresponding to one of several lights in a display. Over a long continuous series of stimuli and responses, some conditions contain a repeated sequence of 8–12 stimuli whereas other series are random. Learning is exhibited by faster responding to the repeated series, and older participants show as much learning as young adults in this task although they are less able to explicitly report knowledge of the repetitions (Howard & Howard, 1989). A similar age-related dissociation between implicit and explicit memory occurs in the word-stem completion paradigm. In this task, participants first study a long list of words, often under conditions of incidental learning in which they simply make decisions about each studied word. In the test phase the first three letters of studied and unstudied words (e.g., PAR_, LEA_) are presented, either with the instruction to use the word stem as a cue to recall studied words (explicit memory) or with the instruction to complete the stem with "the first word that comes to mind." In this second condition, implicit learning is shown to the extent that stems of studied words are completed correctly more often than stems of comparable unstudied control words. The typical result is that older adults show a deficit relative to young participants in the explicit condition but none in the implicit condition (Light & Singh, 1987; La Voie & Light, 1994).

Although age constancy in priming and related tasks is generally a good thing, the likelihood that older adults have intact implicit but impaired explicit memory means that the older person's experience of past events tends to be dominated by feelings of familiarity rather than by recollection of specific detail. For this reason, feelings of familiarity may be misconstrued as genuine memories or known facts. Dywan and Jacoby (1990) presented a list of fictitious names to older and younger adults and later gave them a test in which names of famous people were mixed with the previously presented fictitious names. Older adults were more likely to misattribute the familiarity of fictitious names to fame in the real world. Similarly, Jennings and Jacoby (1997) found that older adults were more likely to confuse repetitions of words on a test list with words previously presented in a study list. Thus, the early development and late retention of implicit modes of learning and memory are clearly advantageous in general, yet have their costs in terms of vulnerability to error.

The finding that young children and older adults perform well on tasks of procedural or implicit memory and learning does *not* mean that their learning is as good as that of young adults. Encoding processes are likely to be less deep and elaborate in children and the elderly, sufficient to support a feeling of familiarity and to bias certain responses, but insufficient to support conscious recollection that the word or other event has been perceived recently. This explanation accounts for lifespan differences in terms of the quality of the representation underlying the memory or learning. An alternative account is that children and older adults utilize their developed representations (of perceptual motor sequences or words at a later stage in children) but do not possess the control processes that would enable retrieval of the stored event plus its context in a way that yields the experience of recollection.

Semantic Memory

Tulving (1983) has suggested that memory systems have evolved in the order procedural, semantic, and finally episodic. The growth of semantic memory, or general knowledge of the world, is obviously one of the major achievements of development. Semantic memory is a complex system of representations that are (like episodic memory) declarative in the sense that the stored pieces of information may be contemplated consciously and expressed to others. Our contention is that semantic memory is one major area of *asymmetry* between young children and older adults. That is, knowledge of facts, number, and language all increase markedly during child development but remain relatively stable in older adults (Light, 1992; Nilsson, 2003). What *does* change in the course of aging is the ability to access information quickly—or even at all. A difficulty in retrieving names is reported universally by adults over 60 years of age, as discussed above in the section on Language.

Children and older adults undoubtedly differ in their ability to add new information to their knowledge store. Younger children rapidly acquire both vocabulary and grammar, as described above, but even the acquisition of interesting new facts is less efficient in older than in younger adults (McIntyre & Craik, 1987). As Keil (2006) pointed out, there are adaptive reasons why certain core functions should be preserved in early childhood, whereas there are no such evolutionary pressures on retention of these abilities in old age. Second language learning is an example of an ability in which young children outperform adults of all ages; this ability appears to decline steadily throughout life (Hakuta, Bialystok, & Wiley, 2003). Thus both the acquisition of new information and the ability to access that information rapidly and effectively appear to favor children over older adults.

One factor that may tilt the balance in favor of older adults is the benefit associated with expertise; it is well established that new learning is facilitated when it is congruent with existing schematic knowledge (Bransford, Franks, Morris, & Stein, 1979). It seems reasonable to suppose that older adults possess more schematic knowledge and will therefore outperform children if the new material is relevant to their current knowledge base. However, if a child is an expert in some domain of knowledge, that child will show a correspondingly good ability to learn and remember new material in that domain. For example, Chi (1978) showed that chess-playing 10-year-olds were better at remembering chess positions than non-chess-playing adults, although the adults were better at remembering digit strings. Bäckman, Small, Wahlin, and Larsson (2000) point out an interesting parallel between fluid and crystallized intelligence on the one hand and the learning of completely new versus schema-relevant information on the other hand. Just as fluid intelligence declines with age, so does the ability to learn new information; in contrast, crystallized intelligence holds up well with age, as does the ability to learn using pre-existing knowledge structures (Bäckman et al., 2000, p. 503).

One final point of comparison with regard to semantic memory is the access to different levels of specificity of stored information. Brainerd and Reyna (1990) have proposed "fuzzy trace theory" in which acquired information is represented both in a literal verbatim form and in terms of gist or conceptual meaning. The verbatim form is dominant in early childhood but gradually gives way to the encoding and retrieval of gist. The consequence is that young children tend to recall events in terms of their surface form but older children interpret incoming information to a greater degree and therefore show a greater tendency to recall the meaning of events. Efficient memory performance in older children and young adults reflects both types of representation—gist and inference as well as perceptual and contextual detail. As adults age, specific detail becomes less accessible and recall of both factual and episodic material reflects abstracted generalities (Craik, 2002; Dixon, Hultsch, Simon, & von Eye, 1984). This developmental sequence moving from verbatim to gist, to conceptual plus specific, to abstract/general, reflects the interplay of representation and control processes at different ages. Young children represent incoming events largely in terms of surface form; as conceptual representations develop, events are interpreted in those terms, and control processes allow access to both general and specific levels of detail. In older adults, representational systems remain intact but control processes are less effective, affording easy access to generalities but not to specifics.

Episodic and Strategic Memory

The developmental course for the recollection of autobiographical events is clear, but explanations for that pattern vary substantially. By the end of the first year of life infants can reproduce a sequence of actions. Bauer (2002) points out that such deferred imitations reflect declarative memory in that a complex sequence can be recalled and expressed. Recall becomes increasingly reliable during the second year, and by the age of 3–4 years the child's personal memories are primarily expressed in verbal terms (Bauer, 2002). However, for these forms of declarative memory to indicate control of episodic memory as formulated by Tulving (1983), they would need to include "mental time travel" (Tulving, 1993), that is, the ability to relive the experience through recollection of details of the original event. This seems unlikely for such declarative recall as deferred imitation or remembering where a toy is hidden. Thus, Tulving (1983) suggests that episodic memory does not develop until the age of 4 years (see also Perner & Ruffman, 1995).

Episodic memory ability continues to increase until the teenage years and then levels off by the age of 25–30 years (Ornstein, Haden, & Elischberger, 2006; Schneider, 2002) when it begins a steady decline through adulthood (Nilsson, 2003; Park et al., 2002). Again, however, this surface symmetry likely conceals important differences between children of 10–12 years and older adults of 70–80 years. First, good episodic memory performance reflects good encoding in terms of the person's organized schematic knowledge base, especially expert knowledge in such specialized domains as chess, physics, music, or sport (Chi, 1978; Schneider & Bjork-lund, 1998). This is the basis for the levels-of-processing effect discussed by Craik and Lockhart (1972) and Craik and Tulving (1975). As described above, schematic knowledge develops over childhood but remains relatively intact in the course of aging, so the decline of episodic memory in older adults must have another major cause. Two other linked factors are the use of strategies and the efficiency of executive control processes. Viewing material passively results in poor memory performance, so between the ages of 5 and 10 years, children learn to use such strategies as rehearsal and organization (see Harnishfeger & Bjorklund, 1990 for review). Children younger than this neither use strategies nor profit from them when they are taught, a situation labeled *mediation deficiency*. Older children can and do use strategies but often do not produce them spontaneously, a situation labeled *production deficiency* (Schneider & Pressley, 1997). The probable reason for this latter deficiency is that strategy use is effortful and costly in terms of attentional resources (Guttentag, 1984), and exactly this pattern of production deficiency has also been reported for older adults (e.g., Naveh-Benjamin, Craik, Guez, & Kreuger, 2005).

Knowledge of strategies and their use is part of metamemory, a type of knowledge that increases in the course of child development. Metamemory knowledge is effective; Schneider and Pressley (1989) found a correlation of +0.41 between levels of metamemory and levels of memory performance in a large sample of children and young adults. With aging, metamemory knowledge remains largely intact, but knowledge of such memory strategies does not guarantee they will be used (Hertzog &

Hultsch, 2000). Older adults exhibit production deficiencies much as children do, and probably for the same reason, namely, strategies are laborious, time consuming, and effortful to use. In one classic study, Kliegl, Smith, and Baltes (1990) taught older adults to use the method of loci (Berlin landmarks), increasing their recall substantially over the course of extensive training. The problem, however, is that this strategic skill did not generalize to other memory situations in real life. In summary, strategy use develops in children aged 10 and above, and falls off in older adults because of the associated processing resource costs. Case (1985) commented that in younger children the use of strategies leaves little capacity for processing the material. The trick is to integrate new material into existing schematic knowledge, and to practice this skill until it becomes at least somewhat automatic and effortless.

Memory performance typically benefits from the reinstatement of the original learning context at the time of retrieval, a benefit labeled "environmental support" in the aging literature (Craik, 1983, 1986). Craik has shown that memory tasks such as free recall and time-based prospective memory lack such support and therefore require self-initiated activities by the rememberer and that such mental activities are especially difficult for older adults. The consequence is that age-related memory decrements are typically greatest in tasks that require the greatest amount of self-initiation and least in tasks such as recognition memory where the environment helps to cue the appropriate retrieval processes (Craik & McDowd, 1987). Interestingly, although older adults benefit substantially from reinstatement of the original encoding context at the time of recollection, they are considerably worse than young adults when asked to *recall* the original context (Schloerscheidt, Craik, & Kreuger, 2007; Spencer & Raz, 1994; but see also Siedlecki, Salthouse, & Berish, 2005 for evidence suggesting equivalent age-related declines in memory for context and content).

Children's memory retrieval is also helped by reminders of aspects of the original situation. In a useful discussion of these effects, Ornstein et al. (2006) describe how a mother's questions and prompts act as a scaffolding to support her child's narrative recall. Apart from the obvious effect of providing retrieval cues, this type of mother–child interaction can help the child's *understanding* of the situation, thereby providing a framework that acts to facilitate retrieval. Ornstein and colleagues go on to suggest that schooling in older children provides similar benefits to aid strategy development. That is, just as the young child's memory development is facilitated by "parent talk," so older children's further development is facilitated by "teacher talk," which provides semantic structure via hints, suggestions, and formal requirements.

Addressing another important aspect of memory retrieval, Jacoby and his colleagues (e.g., Jennings & Jacoby, 1993, 1997) have pointed out that recognition memory comprises two components—familiarity and conscious recollection—that can be dissociated in various ways, as described below in the section on Cognitive Control. Although the feeling of familiarity of a studied item, person, or event is not very affected by aging, the ability to recollect the original encoding context decreases substantially with aging (Jennings & Jacoby, 1993, 1997). The age-related decrease in recollection has obvious similarities to the age-related difficulty in retrieving context (referred to as "source amnesia" in more severe cases). This difficulty of recollection may reflect an age-related inefficiency in "binding" or associating two events at the time of learning (Chalfonte & Johnson, 1996; Naveh-Benjamin, 2000). We return to a discussion of familiarity and recollection in the section on Cognitive Control.

Summary of Lifespan Changes in Memory

The three aspects of memory we have discussed—procedural, semantic, and episodic—each show a different trajectory across the lifespan. In general, procedural and implicit learning remain relatively constant across the lifespan, semantic memory increases rapidly in childhood and then remains relatively intact, and episodic memory displays the symmetrical inverted U-shaped pattern of rising in childhood and declining in aging. These patterns can be explained by considering the reliance of each of these types of memory on representational and control processes: semantic memory is largely based on knowledge representations that increase in development and then remain intact whereas episodic memory is largely based on control and is most reliable for young adults for whom control processes are at their peak efficiency, as we discuss in the next section. However, interactions between representation and control affect all three types of memory, changing their pattern of development and decline. For example, both younger children and older adults profit from environmental or schematic support to bolster memory performance. Although context reinstatement is especially helpful to children and the elderly, both groups also show some impairment in binding or associative memory (Chalfonte & Johnson, 1996; Cowan, Naveh-Benjamin, Kilb, & Saults, 2006; Naveh-Benjamin, 2000). Finally, more detailed descriptions that isolate the relevant aspects of representation and control are required to understand memory performance across the lifespan, as Jacoby has demonstrated through his process-dissociation technique that distinguishes between familiarity and recollection. The success with which individuals can demonstrate control and flexibility of memory depends on the availability of representation and control processes at that developmental stage of life.

COGNITIVE CONTROL

An understanding of the development, maintenance, and deterioration of the processes involved in the regulation of mental functions is central to the study of cognitive changes over the lifespan. Despite this pivotal role of the executive functions, the nature of cognitive control is still poorly understood. Is there a single domain-general controller, or does each content area have its own mechanisms of selection, inhibition, goal setting, and conflict resolution? Are the representational and control systems independent or interdependent? What is the role of the external environment in guiding behavior, and does that role change as a function of development and aging? Similar questions can be raised about the role of schematized past learning in controlling choices and actions. In this section we survey some current findings and concepts, and relate them to our overall theme of understanding lifespan cognitive changes in terms of interactions between representations and control processes. The topic of age-related differences in cognitive control is also addressed by Braver and West (chapter 7).

One Controller or Many?

The question of whether there is one general controller or a family of task-specific controllers is a matter of current debate. On the one hand, Luria (1973) proposed that the prefrontal cortex (PFC) performed a set of general regulatory functions (manifested as inhibition, activation, planning, conflict resolution, etc.) that acted on posterior areas of the brain devoted to representations and associations. On the other hand, more recent work in neuropsychology and neuroanatomy has made it progressively clearer that the frontal lobes do not act in a holistic manner but are composed of regions having specific functions (Petrides & Pandya, 1999; Stuss et al., 2002). The finding that various tasks claiming to measure executive functions typically correlate poorly with each other also seems at odds with the idea of one controller (see Daniels, Toth & Jacoby, 2006 for a review). The interesting notion that executive control is not a thing in itself but rather an emergent property from the interactions among representational systems (Barnard, 1985) also suggests that such interactions would result in characteristics specific to the particular systems involved. However, two recent proponents of the unity view concede that only certain areas of the PFC are concerned with executive control (specifically, dorsal and ventral lateral regions), but claim that these areas have a *general* regulatory function. Thompson-Schill, Bedny, and Goldberg (2005) make a case for the left ventrolateral PFC acting to regulate various functions in working memory and language, and Duncan and colleagues

(Duncan et al., 2000; Duncan & Miller, 2002) have presented compelling data showing that a variety of executive function tasks activate similar areas of the lateral PFC and dorsal anterior cingulate. Duncan and Miller (2002, p. 281) make the further suggestion that "to some extent at least, the same frontal neurons may be configured to aid in solution of many different cognitive challenges." That is, the same PFC areas may be involved in the control of different tasks, but using different network configurations. Thompson-Schill and colleagues (2005) take the view that specificity of function is achieved as a result of connectivity between the same frontal regions and different domain-specific posterior regions.

Bases of Cognitive Control

It is important to understand the relationship between the PFC and other brain areas when examining lifespan changes in executive functions because it is universally agreed that the frontal lobes are the primary locus of control. It is also well established that the frontal lobes are the last areas of the brain to develop fully (Casey et al., 2005; Diamond, 2002) and among the first to decline (Raz, 2000; Raz et al., 2005). These latter conclusions suggest a degree of symmetry between development and aging, but whereas cortical development involves much sculpting of networks through *selective* loss of dendritic connectivity, the losses accompanying aging are less selective and therefore less adaptive.

At the cognitive/behavioral level, the functions of executive control processes are largely agreed upon. Their essential task is to overcome the "default mode" of automatic habitual perceptual-motor tendencies (Mesulam, 2002) in situations where an alternative response would be beneficial. The possession of efficient control processes thus enables the person (or other animal) to break free from rigid, stereotyped behaviors, and exhibit flexibility, adaptability, choice, and planning. Studies of control processes have focused on a variety of supposed components of executive functions: for example, inhibition, conflict resolution, decision making, selection, concentration, and resistance to interference. It is often essential to hold information in mind temporarily, to manipulate or transform that information mentally, and to integrate pieces of information from a variety of sources. These functions are performed by working memory, which thus combines the short-term storage of incoming or recently retrieved information with controlled operations performed on or with that information (see Diamond, 2006, for a useful discussion of the relations between working memory and executive functions).

Cognitive theorists agree on these components of executive functioning but stress different aspects when defining the fundamental roots of mental control. Current candidates include processing speed (Salthouse,

1996), attentional resources (Craik & Byrd, 1982), inhibition (Hasher & Zacks, 1988; Hasher, Zacks, & May, 1999), the ability to reflect consciously on integrated higher order rules (Zelazo, 2004), and recollection (Daniels et al., 2006; Jacoby, 1991; Jennings & Jacoby, 1997). All of these constructs are well described and analyzed, and lifespan changes in all of them are well documented, but it is reasonable to conclude that no one aspect is the crucial root cause of cognitive success and failure, and that all of them play some part in the overall regulation of behavior and thought.

Cognitive Control and the External Environment

The behavior of lower animals is largely controlled by the external environment, in that appropriate responses to salient stimuli are genetically wired into the organism. One major accomplishment of evolution is to relocate control within the animal, thereby giving behavior more independence and flexibility. Nonetheless, the external environment continues to play some part in control at the human level, and its importance is greater at the two ends of the lifespan than in later childhood and adulthood (Piaget, 1959). An obvious difference between young children and old adults is that the latter have acquired rich stores of schematic knowledge, with the result that environmental influences are filtered through these systems of habitual responses. As an example, an older person's actions and reactions become attuned and finally become over-dependent on domestic surroundings, so when the person moves into sheltered housing there is often a period of disorientation and confusion before new habit systems are learned. Craik (1983, 1986) has discussed the related notion of environmental support as the mechanism by which the older person relies on local contexts to guide behavior because of the declining efficiency of executive functions (self-initiated activities). The behavior of some severely impaired frontal patients is occasionally *over*-determined by the current context in interaction with learned schemas, so that patients will automatically eat when food is presented or attempt to sew if sewing materials are presented. These are the "utilization behaviors" described by Lhermitte (1986). Infants lack such schematic knowledge, so environmental control may be seen in more direct reflex behaviors such as sucking and rooting reflexes. In summary, the external environment acts on the young child and older adult to support appropriate behaviors. The older child is progressively freed from this influence as the frontal lobes develop, but the reliance on environmental support re-emerges in the older adult, although with the difference that the influence is now mediated and modified by schematic habits.

One corollary of lifespan changes in environmental dependence is the changing vulnerability to interference of distraction from external stimuli.

As a speculation, if young children and older adults are more dependent on the external environment to support appropriate behaviors, they may also be prone to the misleading effects of external stimuli when such stimuli are *not* in accord with optimal thoughts or actions. This idea was suggested by Dempster (1992) who argued that the ability to resist interference is a major function of the frontal lobes and therefore waxes and wanes over the lifespan. In what might be considered an extension of Dempster's view, Enns and Trick (2006) propose that the key feature of attention is *selection*, and that selective attention may be classified in terms of two dimensions: automatic-controlled and exogenous-endogenous. Enns and Trick use the terms exogenous and endogenous to refer to the contrast between external stimuli whose selection is not learned, and selection in terms of learned expectations and goals. Their framework generates a 2 × 2 classification in which automatic-exogenous selection is labeled Reflex, automatic-endogenous selection is labeled Habit, controlled-exogenous selection is termed Exploration, and controlled-endogenous selection is termed Deliberation (Figure 11.1). Like Dempster (1992), Enns and Trick attribute lifespan changes in their automatic-controlled dimension to the growth and decline of frontal lobe processes. Their exogenous-endogenous dimension, however, depends on degree of relevant learning. The Enns and Trick framework thus suggests that automatic-exogenous behaviors (Reflex) will show the least amounts of lifespan developmental change and controlled-endogenous behaviors (Deliberation) will show the greatest degree of change, but also the greatest degree of variability (Enns & Trick, 2006, p. 46).

In line with the general position advocated in this chapter, the Enns and Trick framework stresses the interactions between raw control as mediated by the frontal lobes, and representations in the sense of learned schemas. Indeed, learned representations can act as mechanisms of control, for example, in situations where the person is set to expect a specific stimulus configuration on the basis of past experience. Typically, however, accumulated past experiences push the person to respond in the habitual manner associated with current circumstances. In many cases this default mode may be the best option, but a major function of executive processes is to monitor the situation and either proceed with the habitual response or substitute a more appropriate one. In fact, most methods that have been used to assess the development, integrity, and deterioration of executive control processes have measured the effectiveness of control in overcoming the prepotent influences of both environmental and schematic pressures. The Stroop task fits this description, as does the ability to overcome the tendency to move the eyes towards a visual object appearing suddenly in peripheral vision and instead move the eyes *away* from the object in the antisaccade task. The

Reflex	Habit
• Innately specified	• Learned when goal repeated in specific environment
• Triggered by stimuli given priority by the nervous system	• Triggered by stimuli associated with specific goals in past
• Unconscious, automatic, fast, obligatory, effortless	• Unconscious, automatic, fast, obligatory, effortless
• Avoided only with deliberation	• Avoided only with deliberation
• Emerges on a developmental timetable	• Can emerge at any time
• Stable once acquired	• Can fade or be replaced at any time – strength varies with practice
Exploration	Deliberation
• Innately specified generic goal for novel situations	• Goal is internally generated and specific to the individual and context
• Default mode for controlled processing	• Occurs when individuals are carrying out specific goals in a specific context
• Conscious, controlled, slow, optional, effortful	• Conscious, controlled, slow, optional, effortful
• Occurs when the only goal is exploration	• Specific goals changed at will, but switches in goals take time
• Generic goal easily replaced by specific goal (switch to deliberation)	• Needed to overcome unwanted automatic processes
	• Interferes with other deliberately selected goals

FIG. 11.1. Aspects of four modes of selective attention. The vertical axis is controlled-automatic; the horizontal axis is exogenous-endogenous. (Reprinted from Enns & Trick, 2006 with the permission of Oxford University Press, Inc.)

automatic-exogenous (Reflex) tendency to look towards a visual target is so strong that the ability to perform antisaccadic eye movements does not develop until the child is 6 or 7 years old (Diamond, 2006).

Process Dissociation Procedures

The process dissociation (PD) procedure developed by Jacoby and his colleagues (Daniels et al., 2006; Jacoby, 1991; Jennings & Jacoby, 1997) provides a means of separating the controlled and automatic aspects of responses. The method yields estimates of Recollection (R) reflecting cognitive control, and a second measure that has been variously termed "automatic," "unconscious," "familiarity," and "accessibility bias," reflecting the pull exerted by recent learning or deeply ingrained habits. Jennings and Jacoby (1997) showed that R estimates decline from young to old adulthood in a memory paradigm, whereas automatic estimates do not change with age. In a similar demonstration, Zelazo, Craik, and Booth (2004) found that R estimates in a word-stem completion task rose from a group of children aged 8–10 years to young adults (22.3 years on average) and then fell to a group of older adults (71.1 years on average), but that estimates of automatic influences in the task showed no lifespan differences.

Jacoby has also applied his PD analysis to young children. In the classic Piagetian "A-not-B task," infants up to 12 months old will continue to search for a desired object in the place that it has been successfully found on previous trials in spite of watching as it was rehidden in a different location. This behavior has been attributed to an inability on the part of younger infants to maintain the correct information in working memory long enough to carry out the appropriate action (Diamond, 2006), but Jacoby argues that location information from previous trials is well learned and so creates an accessibility bias which influences the direction of the current choice (Daniels et al., 2006). In this way, the initial trials create a temporary habit which must be overruled by an efficiently functioning control mechanism (R) to avoid the error.

Jacoby, Debner, and Hay (2001) have used this method to evaluate age-related differences in recollection and accessibility bias at the other end of the age scale. They asked older and younger adults to learn related word pairs with two possible second words, e.g., knee-BONE or knee-BEND. In a series of training trials, one response (e.g., BONE) was presented 75% of the time and the other (BEND) was presented 25% of the time. After biasing this learned habit, participants were given short lists of the word pairs to be studied for a following cued-recall test. In this retrieval test, first words were presented with a word fragment cue for the second word (e.g., knee -B_N_) that could cue either response. The pairs presented in the to-be-remembered list were either congruent or incongruent with the previously biased (75%) response. Jacoby and colleagues argue that successful recall of congruent responses could be due to either recollection or habit, but correct recall of incongruent responses demonstrates that recollection overruled the accessibility bias created by the training phase. After applying the PD formulas (see Daniels et al., 2006; Jacoby, 1991), the authors found that aging decreased conscious control (lower R values) but left accessibility bias unchanged. In contrast, training in the 75% condition increased accessibility bias relative to a 50% control condition, but left R unchanged. Jacoby and his colleagues conclude that this result points to an age-related deficit in recollection, rather than to an age-related failure of inhibition being the reason for older adults' increased vulnerability to interference. That is, older adults do not differ from younger adults in their reliance on accessibility bias when recollection fails. The difference in performance between the age groups is attributable to more failures of recollection in the older adults caused by less efficient control.

The PD perspective illustrates how behavior can be governed both by control (R) and by learned representations (accessibility bias) acting either in concert or in opposition. The illustrations provided by Jacoby and colleagues have focused on situations in which accessibility bias is manipulated by varying *new* habit learning, and in these cases age-related differences are slight (cf., similarly slight age differences in priming and other cases of automatic learning such as the generation effect, Mitchell, Hunt, & Schmitt, 1986; Rabinowitz, 1989; and the self-performed task paradigm, Rönnlund, Nyberg, Bäckman, & Nilsson, 2003). It might be expected, however, that in situations where accessibility bias is provided by long-standing real-life habits, older adults would show larger effects of accessibility bias than younger adults. As the effectiveness of control processes declines with age in adulthood, behavior is progressively more influenced by accumulated habits rather than by the contingencies of the current situation.

Working Memory

The construct of working memory (WM) has played an increasingly important role in theories of cognitive performance since it was proposed by Baddeley and Hitch some 30 years ago (Baddeley & Hitch, 1974). These authors have focused largely on the short-term storage aspects of WM, but others have explored the role of WM in governing ongoing behavior. Over the lifespan, the data are clear on the general point that WM abilities increase throughout development (Diamond, 2006; Hitch, 2006) and decrease with age in adulthood (Gick, Craik, & Morris, 1988). Performance on WM tasks may begin to decline as early as the thirties, although initial declines may be slight (Park & Payer, 2006). As with other complex cognitive constructs, the exact nature of WM appears to depend on the task being performed. For example, span tasks for relatively meaningless material (e.g., digit or letter span) largely reflect control processes of the central executive and speed of processing (Case, Kurland, & Goldberg, 1982; Hitch, Towse, & Hutton, 2001), although speed of processing is unlikely to be the whole story (Diamond, 2006). However, when the WM task involves meaning, as with sentence span or reading span (where participants judge the truth or falsity of short statements and then attempt to remember the final words in each statement), long-term memory representational systems are clearly involved. In these latter cases, developmental changes depend on the development and organization of the relevant representational system. Commenting on individual differences in WM, Hitch (2006) suggests that "domain-specific variance might be explained by assuming that complex span tasks involve a general resource interacting with domain-specific knowledge representations" (Hitch, 2006, p. 120). A similar point was made by Ericsson and Kintsch (1995) to account for why WM capacity in adults is larger for domains in which the participants have expertise. These ideas, and the data behind them, make it quite unlikely that WM is a single thing, or even one fixed system. It seems more likely that the term applies to a family of related functions whose exact characteristics will depend on the representational systems involved.

Diamond (2006) and Kane and Engle (2003) have stressed the control functions of WM. One such function is goal maintenance, the ability to keep key aspects of the task in mind across a time delay or during performance of the task itself. This ability is tied to the maturity and integrity of frontal lobe functioning (Duncan, Emslie, Williams, Johnson, & Freer, 1996) and therefore improves during childhood (Diamond, 2006) and declines in later adulthood (Phillips, MacLeod, & Kliegel, 2005). Self-initiated activities were described by Craik (1983, 1986) as a group of processes brought online in memory retrieval situations when the information provided by the task and context is insufficient to support recollection. In these cases, such as free recall, the participant must actively generate information related to the context of learning or to the items themselves. Described in this way, self-initiated activities involve "going beyond the information given" in Bruner's (1973) useful phrase, and are clearly similar to the control processes of conscious recollection (R) described by Jacoby and others. Craik's point was that such self-initiated activities appear to decline with age in adulthood. Recent work by Engle and Kane (2004) has also stressed the executive role of WM and the important part played by the ability to generate relevant information from long-term memory.

Two further sets of studies relevant to cognitive control, WM, and aging will be described briefly. First, Braver and his colleagues have developed an ingenious paradigm to study control successes and failures in a WM context (Braver, Cohen, & Barch, 2002; Braver et al., 2001; Braver & West, chapter 7). Participants view a long sequence of letters presented as a series of successive cue–probe pairs and the task is simply to respond rapidly to each letter X, but only if the X probe is preceded by the cue letter A. Such AX events occur on 70% of trials; the remaining 30% are composed of BX, AY, and BY pairs, none of which should receive a response. Braver argues that failure to maintain the context cue B in working memory will result in a false alarm to the succeeding X in BX trials producing a "context-failure error"; in contrast, false alarms to Y in AY trials represent "context-induced errors." If older adults are less able to maintain context information in WM to control ongoing behavior, then they should make more BX errors but *fewer* AY errors than young adults, and this was the pattern observed (Braver et al., 2001, 2002). As described by Braver and West (chapter 7) these age-related results have been tied both to frontal lobe functions and the efficiency of dopamine regulation in older adults.

The second set of studies concerns the idea that WM in older adults is compromised by a failure to delete irrelevant information from this mental workspace (Hasher & Zacks, 1988; Hasher et al., 1999; Zacks & Hasher, 1994). These authors follow Cowan (1988) in suggesting that conscious awareness is restricted to some highly activated subset of representations (the focus of attention) and that it is this active fragment that controls thought and action. In order to maximize efficiency, and therefore control, Hasher and colleagues suggest that inhibition serves three functions in WM: access, deletion, and restraint. First, inhibition controls *access* to WM by monitoring and screening out irrelevant sources of activation from the environment and from intruding mental processes; failure to do so will result in interference and "loss of concentration." Second, inhibition acts to *delete* or suppress information in WM that is no longer relevant to the current goal; if the goal shifts (commencing a new task, for example), this function is crucial to maintain mental flexibility. Third, inhibition has a *restraining* function by dampening down habitual or prepotent stimulus–response tendencies, again in the service of keeping thought and action focused on the task at hand. Hasher and colleagues illustrate these notions in cognitive aging research by showing that older adults have less effective inhibitory functions, with a consequent reduction in the efficiency of WM as a control mechanism.

Task Switching and Mental Flexibility

Mental flexibility, defined as the ability to switch attention among two or more sources of information or to switch between alternative stimulus–response mappings with changes in task demands, is also central to cognitive control. This ability has been explored in studies of task switching in which participants respond to stimuli on the basis of two different rules, for example, respond to a display of colored shapes either on the basis of color or shape. Zelazo and colleagues (2004) carried out such an experiment on three groups: children aged 8–9 years, young adults aged 19–26 years, and older adults aged 65–74 years. Each trial presented a visual stimulus that was one of four shapes in one of four colors, and participants classified the stimulus by color if it was presented with the letter X and by shape if it was presented with the letter Y. Eighty percent of the trials required color responses to bias that classification. The primary dependent measure was the proportion of perseverative errors—a response that would have been correct according to the other rule. This proportion declined from 10% in children to 4% in young adults, and then rose again to 10% in older adults. Flexible control was therefore symmetrically poor in children and older adults, relative to younger adults.

Cepeda, Kramer, and Gonzalez de Sather (2001) reported a task-switching study in which displays of three digits (e.g., 111 or 333) were preceded by the question "How many?" or "What number?" Cognitive control varies with the display, since 333 yields the same response regardless of the question, whereas the display 111 requires different responses to the different questions. The authors measured speed of response in participants ranging in age from 7 to 82 years and found a U-shaped function, with higher switch costs for children and older adults. Switch costs were defined as the time to switch between tasks relative to a repeated-task baseline. All participants benefited from practice, with children and older adults showing the greatest benefits. Task set inertia was assessed by varying the time between one response and the cue for the next display; older adults benefited more than younger adults as this interval was lengthened, showing that older adults take longer to disengage from the current task set. Interestingly, children benefited less than older adults as the response–cue interval was lengthened, but both groups benefited from longer preparation times—the interval between the cue and the relevant display. The study thus demonstrated both symmetries (equivalent decrements in active preparation times in children and older adults relative to young adults) and asymmetries (children were less able than older adults to disengage from a previous task set) across the lifespan.

Several studies have now shown that specific switch costs show comparatively slight lifespan changes whereas general switch costs decline from children to young adults and then rise in older adults. Specific switch cost is the difference in response speed between successive trials requiring a switch to the other rule, and successive trials requiring the same rule; general switch cost or mixing cost is the difference in response speed between trials in a mixed block containing two rules and single blocks containing only one rule. Thus, perhaps unexpectedly, children and older adults can easily switch between rules on successive trials but their responses are slowed in mixed blocks, even on nonswitch trials, where the *possibility* of a switch is present. This pattern was shown in a large-scale internet study of over 5000 participants ranging in age from 10 to 66 years (Reimers & Maylor, 2005). Their results showed that general switch costs declined from children aged 10–11 years to adolescents aged 16–17 years. Thereafter, costs increased monotonically to a group aged 61–66 years, that is, performance peaked at age 17. However, specific switch costs showed no age-related trend across the age range 10–60 years, although the 61–66 year group showed slight amounts of slowing. The changes in general switch costs may be attributed to the developmental rise and fall of working memory abilities; the necessity to bear two rules in mind slows performance in children and in older adults.

Another method used to assess inhibitory control is the stop-signal procedure (Williams, Ponesse, Schachar, Logan, & Tannock, 1999). In this task, participants perform a long series of visual 2-choice reaction-time (RT) trials, but if a tone sounds they must inhibit their response on that trial. Williams and colleagues measured both the RTs to perform go-trials successfully and the shortest time between the visual go-stimulus and the auditory stop-signal for which participants could inhibit their responses on 50% of occasions. Both go-stimulus and stop-signal RTs showed lifespan developmental trends (measured on participants ranging in age from 6 to 81 years), but the trends were very different. Whereas go-signal RTs declined from 675 ms in early childhood to an average of 362 ms in young adulthood and then rose to 538 ms in participants aged 60–81 years, stop-signal RTs declined from 274 ms in early childhood to approximately 200 ms in late adolescence, but then rose only 30 ms to 230 ms in the elderly group. In this case, inhibition is equivalent to a simple (1-choice) RT, however, as opposed to the 2-choice go-signal, so the conclusion that response execution shows a more symmetrical lifespan trend than does inhibitory control should be tempered by that difference in the degree of choice involved.

Summary of Lifespan Changes in Cognitive Control

Across the various tasks described above, cognitive control over behavior improves from infancy to young adulthood and then declines throughout the adult years. This inverted U-shaped function parallels the growth and decline of efficient frontal lobe functioning. It is generally agreed that specific areas of the PFC interact with parietal and other brain areas to mediate control processes, but the exact manner in which these neural networks function to regulate behavior is still quite poorly understood. Different theorists have emphasized different aspects of controlled behavior and their developmental changes; for example, Salthouse (1996) has focused on speed and slowing, Hasher and Zacks (1988) emphasize inhibition, Craik and Byrd (1982) stress processing resources, and Jacoby and colleagues (Daniels et al., 2006) have emphasized conscious control. These interpretations are not necessarily mutually exclusive, and Dennis and Cabeza (chapter 1) explore the relations between them and how they relate to current ideas about brain structure and function. Thus, it seems likely that *all* of these factors play some role in the mechanisms of cognitive control across the lifespan, rather than one being correct and the others wrong.

REPRESENTATION AND CONTROL ACROSS THE LIFESPAN

In the cognitive domains we have discussed, change across the lifespan takes different forms, sometimes appearing to follow a symmetrical pattern of rising and falling ability, sometimes best characterized as childhood development of a skill that is well maintained through older age, and sometimes requiring a more complex description based on interactions between systems of knowledge and control. Our contention is that what unites these trajectories through the diverse domains is their reliance on the same basic cognitive mechanisms that themselves have a predictable evolution through the lifespan and a unique relationship to neural organization and development.

Processes involved in establishing representational structure and organization develop rapidly through childhood, consolidating knowledge structures and schemas that become available to guide further acquisition of knowledge and to participate in the control of behavior. This latter function becomes especially important with aging when the processes that comprise cognitive control begin to wane. In addition, these representational processes appear to be largely specific to different domains of thought, allowing for the development of expertise in certain areas in which attention, memory, and learning are enhanced by virtue of more elaborate schemas for that domain. More highly developed representational structures are also associated with more focal activation in the cortex, as neural connectivity becomes more specialized. This *increasing* localization of skill in the developing brain may be related to the finding that aging is associated with greater bilateral activity, in other words, *decreasing* localization, although the reasons for these changes at the two ends of the lifespan are likely quite different.

Processes involved in cognitive control are associated with the prefrontal cortex, an area of the brain that develops late and declines early, limiting the availability of these processes at the endpoints of life. In addition, control processes demand high levels of resources for attention and capacity, limiting the extent to which they can operate on a specific task at any time in the lifespan. Thus, the development and decline of cognitive control is constrained both neurologically and cognitively, shaping the type of mental activity that can be engaged at each stage of life.

Cognitive control includes a variety of skills and abilities, such as processing speed, inhibition, and working memory, and the relationship among them is a matter of debate, as we described in the previous section. Whatever that relationship is ultimately determined to be, however, all of the proposed components follow this common path of rising in childhood and waning in older age, and all are associated to some degree with the maturation and decline of the prefrontal cortex. Therefore, it is reasonable to assume that even under a model attributing the greatest independence to each component, there is some common core underlying their function. It is likely, in fact, that no one of these control components overrides the others for its centrality to cognitive processing. In his classic *Textbook of Psychology* (1972), Hebb pointed to the dual roles of sensory stimulation in guiding behavior, one being a nonspecific arousal function and the other being a behavioral steering or cue function. Similarly, it may be that cognitive functions require both sufficient processing resources and adequate cognitive control to be effective. Processing speed may be a *consequence* of these resource and control factors rather than being causative. In turn, all these factors reflect the integrity of brain mechanisms and functions and how they change across the lifespan.

In all the domains of cognitive function that we discussed, changes in ability throughout the lifespan depended not only on changes in representations and control but also on their interaction. Representations and control are inherently interdependent, and their degree of interdependence depends on the stage of life and on the task in question. Some tasks (an *n*-back RT task, for example) require little schematic support from past learning but a lot of raw cognitive control. Fluid intelligence tasks (e.g., Cattell & Cattell, 1960) are another example. Other tasks require a great deal of past learning, and such schematic knowledge (e.g., arithmetic, music, driving, chess) provides control by way of set and expectancy, as well as through the exploitation of well-learned routines. These last examples typify expertise and are adaptive, but schematized knowledge and behavioral routines can also become stereotyped, rigid, and inflexible—the downside of crystallized intelligence. We purchase automaticity and ease of processing at the cost of flexibility.

The interaction between representations and control is also evident in the manner in which lifespan development in each of the areas we discussed needs to be considered in a more fine-grained manner. For example, vocabulary development and decline is largely a reflection of representational change but syntactic development and decline is more dependent on cognitive control; semantic memory is primarily based on representational structure but episodic memory requires more control;

and working memory assumes established representational schemas but task switching involves high levels of cognitive control. There is no single formula that associates each of these two central processes with a higher cognitive function.

Another manifestation of the interdependence of representations and control is in their further interaction with the external environment in guiding behavior. Our suggestion is that this also follows a lifespan trajectory, being particularly necessary to support behavior in both childhood and old age. The cognitive system, in other words, is not confined to the internal mechanisms that direct behavior but reaches outward to incorporate the external environment into the normal cognitive routines associated with such activities as speaking, remembering, and planning, particularly when internal resources are inadequate or in decline. In all three domains we examined, there is a greater reliance on environmental support in older age to maintain performance.

The cognitive changes that occur across the lifespan are vast, and we do not suggest that a simple framework based on only two underlying processing mechanisms can account for those changes in all their complexity. However, we do believe that these two mechanisms allow us to understand both what is similar and what is different about the significant changes that occur over the lifespan. The observation that development and decline appear to share certain features needs to be explained in a way that allows the mechanisms underlying those shared descriptions to be quite different from each other—adults do not lose the ability to process complex syntactic structures for the same reason that children acquire that ability—but the explanations nonetheless need to be compatible. It would be extraordinary to think that the *types* of mechanisms responsible for cognitive development and decline were completely different in the young child and the older adult. Our purpose is to discover the continuity of these processes by attempting to examine the details of children's development and older adults' decline in specific areas of cognitive performance. We hope that this approach will reveal a clearer understanding of how thinking evolves and how the brain supports those developments.

REFERENCES

Alwin, D. F., & McCammon, R. J. (2001). Aging, cohorts, and verbal ability. *Journal of Social Sciences, 56B*, S151–S161.

Anglin, J. M. (1993). Vocabulary development: A morphological analysis. *Monographs for the Society for Research in Child Development, 58* (10, Serial No. 238).

Au, R., Joung, P., Nicholas, M., Kass, R., Obler, L. K., & Albert, M. L. (1995). Naming ability across the lifespan. *Aging and Cognition, 2*, 300–311.

Bäckman, L., Nyberg, L., Lindenberger, U., Li, S., & Farde, L. (2006). The correlative triad among aging, dopamine, and cognition: Current status and future prospects. *Neuroscience & Biobehavioral Reviews, 30*, 791–807.

Bäckman, L., Small, B. J., Wahlin, Å., & Larsson, M. (2000). Cognitive functioning in very old age. In F. I. M. Craik & T. A. Salthouse (Eds.), *The handbook of aging and cognition* (2nd ed., pp. 499–558). Mahwah, NJ: Lawrence Erlbaum Associates, Inc.

Baddeley, A. D., & Hitch, G. (1974). Working memory. In G. H. Bower (Ed.), *The psychology of learning and motivation: Advances in research and theory* (Vol. 8, pp. 47–89). New York: Academic Press.

Baltes, P. B. (1987). Theoretical propositions of life-span developmental psychology: On the dynamics between growth and decline. *Developmental Psychology, 23*, 611–626.

Baltes, P. B., Reese, H. W., & Lipsitt, L. P. (1980). Life-span developmental psychology. *Annual Review of Psychology, 31*, 65–110.

Baltes, P. B., Reuter-Lorenz, P. A., & Rösler, F. (Eds.). (2006). *Lifespan development and the brain: The perspective of biocultural co-constructivism*. New York: Cambridge University Press.

Baltes, P. B., Staudinger, U. M., & Lindenberger, U. (1999). Lifespan psychology: Theory and application to intellectual functioning. *Annual Review of Psychology, 50*, 471–507.

Barnard, P. J. (1985). Interacting cognitive subsystems: A psycholinguistic approach to short term memory. In A. Ellis (Ed.), *Progress in the psychology of language* (Vol. 2, pp. 197–258). Hove, UK: Lawrence Erlbaum Associates Ltd.

Bates, E., Dale, P. S., & Thal, D. J. (1995). Individual differences and their implications for theories of language development. In P. Fletcher & B. MacWhinney (Eds.), *Handbook of child language* (pp. 96–151). Oxford: Blackwell.

Bates, E., & Goodman, J. C. (1999). On the emergence of grammar from the lexicon. In B. MacWhinney (Ed.), *The emergence of language* (pp. 29–70). Mahwah, NJ: Lawrence Erlbaum Associates, Inc.

Bauer, P. J. (2002). Early memory development. In U. Goswami (Ed.), *Blackwell handbook of childhood cognitive development*. (pp. 127–146). Malden, MA: Blackwell.

Bialystok, E., & Craik, F. I. M. (Eds.). (2006). *Lifespan cognition: Mechanisms of change*. New York: Oxford University Press.

Bloom, L. (1973). *One word at a time*. The Hague: Mouton

Bloom, P. (2000). *How children learn the meaning of words*. Cambridge, MA: MIT Press.

Bloom, P. (2002). Mindreading, communication, and the learning of names for things. *Mind and Language, 17*, 37–54.

Brainerd, C. J., & Reyna, V. F. (1990). Gist is the grist: Fuzzy-trace theory and the new intuitionism. *Developmental Review, 10*, 3–47.

Bransford, J. D., Franks, J. J., Morris, C. D., & Stein, B. S. (1979). Some general constraints on learning and memory research. In L. S. Cermak & F. I. M. Craik (Eds.), *Levels of processing in human memory* (pp. 331–354). Hillsdale, NJ: Lawrence Erlbaum Associates, Inc.

Braver, T. S., Barch, D. M., Keys, B. A., Carter, C. S., Cohen, J. D., Kaye, J. A., et al. (2001). Context processing in older adults: Evidence for a theory relating cognitive control to neurobiology in healthy aging. *Journal of Experimental Psychology: General, 130*, 746–763.

Braver, T. S., Cohen, J. D., & Barch, D. M. (2002). The role of prefrontal cortex in normal and disordered cognitive control: A cognitive neuroscience perspective. In D. T. Stuss & R. T. Knight (Eds.), *Principles of frontal lobe function* (pp. 428–447). New York: Oxford University Press.

Brown, R. (1973). *A first language: The early stages*. Cambridge, MA: Harvard University Press.

Bruner, J. S. (1973). *Beyond the information given: Studies in the psychology of knowing*. New York: Norton.

Buckner, R. L., Head, D., & Lustig, C. (2006). Brain changes in aging: A lifespan perspective.

In E. Bialystok & F. I. M. Craik (Eds.), *Lifespan cognition: Mechanisms of change* (pp. 27–42). New York: Oxford University Press.

Burke, D. M., & Laver, G. D. (1990). Aging and word retrieval: Selective age deficits in language. In E. A. Lovelace (Ed.), *Aging and cognition: Mental processes, self-awareness, and interventions* (pp. 281–300). New York: Elsevier-North Holland.

Burke, D. M., MacKay, D. G., Worthley, J. S., & Wade, E. (1991). On the tip of the tongue: What causes word finding failures in young and older adults? *Journal of Memory and Language, 30,* 542–579.

Cabeza, R. (2002). Hemispheric asymmetry reduction in older adults: The HAROLD model. *Psychology and Aging, 17,* 85–100.

Caplan, D., & Waters, G. (1999). Verbal working memory and sentence comprehension. *Behavioral and Brain Sciences, 22,* 114–126.

Carey, S. (1978). The child as word learner. In M. Halle, J. Bresnan, & G. A. Miller (Eds.), *Linguistic theory and psychological reality* (pp. 264–293). Cambridge, MA: MIT Press.

Case, R. (1985). *Intellectual development: Birth to adulthood.* New York: Academic Press.

Case, R., Kurland, D. M., & Goldberg, J. (1982). Operational efficiency and the growth of short-term memory span. *Journal of Experimental Child Psychology, 33,* 386–404.

Casey, B. J., Tottenham, N., Liston, C., & Durston, S. (2005). Imaging the developing brain: What have we learned about cognitive development? *Trends in Cognitive Sciences, 9,* 104–110.

Cattell, R. B. (1971). *Abilities: Their structure, growth, and action.* Oxford: Houghton Mifflin.

Cattell, R. B., & Cattell, A. K. S. (1960). *The individual or group Culture Fair test.* Champaign, IL: Institute for Personality and Ability Testing.

Cepeda, N. J., Kramer, A. F., & Gonzalez de Sather, J. C. M. (2001). Changes in executive control across the life span: Examination of task-switching performance. *Developmental Psychology, 37,* 715–730.

Chalfonte, B. L., & Johnson, M. K. (1996). Feature memory and binding in young and older adults. *Memory & Cognition, 24,* 403–416.

Chi, M. T. H. (1978). Knowledge structure and memory development. In R. S. Siegler (Ed.), *Children's thinking: What develops?* (pp. 73–96). Hillsdale, NJ: Lawrence Erlbaum Associates, Inc.

Clark, E. V. (1993). *The lexicon in acquisition.* Cambridge: Cambridge University Press.

Cohen, G., & Faulkner, D. (1986). Memory for proper names: Age differences in retrieval. *British Journal of Developmental Psychology, 4,* 187–197.

Cooper, P. V. (1990). Discourse production and normal aging: Performance on oral picture tasks. *Journal of Gerontology: Psychological Sciences, 45,* P210–P214.

Cowan, N. (1988). Evolving conceptions of memory storage, selective attention, and their mutual constraints within the human information-processing system. *Psychological Bulletin, 104,* 163–191.

Cowan, N., Naveh-Benjamin, M., Kilb, A., & Saults, J. S. (2006). Life-span development of visual working memory: When is feature binding difficult? *Developmental Psychology, 42,* 1089–1102.

Craik, F. I. M. (1983). On the transfer of information from temporary to permanent memory. *Philosophical Transactions of the Royal Society of London, Series B, 302,* 341–359.

Craik, F. I. M. (1986). Selective changes in encoding as a function of reduced processing capacity. In F. Klix, S. Hoffmann, & E. Van der Meer (Eds.), *Cognitive research in psychology* (pp. 152–161). Berlin: Deutscher Verlag der Wissenshaften.

Craik, F. I. M. (2002). Human memory and aging. In L. Bäckman & C. von Hofsten (Eds.), *Psychology at the turn of the millennium, vol. 1: Cognitive, biological, and health perspectives* (pp. 261–280). Hove, UK: Psychology Press.

Craik, F. I. M., & Bialystok, E. (2006). Cognition through the lifespan: Mechanisms of change. *Trends in Cognitive Sciences, 10*, 131–138.

Craik, F. I. M., & Byrd, M. (1982). Aging and cognitive deficits: The role of attentional resources. In F. I. M. Craik & S. E. Trehub (Eds.), *Aging and cognitive processes* (pp. 191–211). New York: Plenum Press.

Craik, F. I. M., & Lockhart, R. S. (1972). Levels of processing: A framework for memory research. *Journal of Verbal Learning and Verbal Behavior, 11*, 671–684.

Craik, F. I. M., & McDowd, J. M. (1987). Age differences in recall and recognition. *Journal of Experimental Psychology: Learning, Memory, and Cognition, 13*, 474–479.

Craik, F. I. M., & Tulving, E. (1975). Depth of processing and the retention of words in episodic memory. *Journal of Experimental Psychology: General, 104*, 268–294.

Daniels, K., Toth, J., & Jacoby, L. (2006). The aging of executive functions. In E. Bialystok & F. I. M. Craik (Eds.), *Lifespan cognition: Mechanisms of change* (pp. 96–111). New York: Oxford University Press.

Dempster, F. N. (1992). The rise and fall of the inhibitory mechanism: Toward a unified theory of cognitive development and aging. *Developmental Review, 12*, 45–75.

de Villiers, P. A., & de Villiers, J. G. (1992). Language development. In M.H. Bornstein & M. E. Lamb (Eds.), *Developmental psychology: An advanced textbook* (pp. 337–418). Hillsdale, NJ: Lawrence Erlbaum Associates, Inc.

Diamond, A. (2002). Normal development of prefrontal cortex from birth to young adulthood: Cognitive functions, anatomy, and biochemistry. In D. T. Stuss & R. T. Knight (Eds.), *Principles of frontal lobe function* (pp. 466–503). New York: Oxford University Press.

Diamond, A. (2006). The early development of executive functions. In E. Bialystok & F. I. M. Craik (Eds.), *Lifespan cognition: Mechanisms of change* (pp. 70–95). New York: Oxford University Press.

Dixon, R. A., Hultsch, D. F., Simon, E. W., & von Eye, A. (1984). Verbal ability and text structure effects on adult age differences in text recall. *Journal of Verbal Learning & Verbal Behavior, 23*, 569–578.

Dromi, E. (1987). *Early lexical development*. Cambridge: Cambridge University Press

Duncan, J., Emslie, H. Y., Williams, P., Johnson, R., & Freer, C. (1996). Intelligence and the frontal lobe: The organization of goal-directed behavior. *Cognitive Psychology, 30*, 257–303.

Duncan, J., & Miller, E. K. (2002). Cognitive focus through adaptive neural coding in the primate prefrontal cortex. In D. T. Stuss & R. T. Knight (Eds.), *Principles of frontal lobe function* (pp. 278–291). New York: Oxford University Press.

Duncan, J., Seitz, R. J., Kolodny, J., Bor, D., Herzog, H., Ahmed, A., et al. (2000). A neural basis for general intelligence. *Science, 289*, 457–460.

Dywan, J., & Jacoby, L. (1990). Effects of aging on source monitoring: Differences in susceptibility to false fame. *Psychology and Aging, 5*, 379–387.

Elman, J. L., Bates, E. A., Johnson, M. H., Karmiloff-Smith, A., Parisi, D., & Plunkett, K. (1996). *Rethinking innateness: A connectionist perspective on development*. Cambridge, MA: MIT Press.

Engle, R. W., & Kane, M. J. (2004). Executive attention, working memory capacity, and a two-factor theory of cognitive control. *The psychology of learning and motivation* (Vol. 44, pp. 145–199). Oxford: Academic Press.

Enns, J. T., & Trick, L. M. (2006). Four modes of selection. In E. Bialystok & F. I. M. Craik (Eds.), *Lifespan cognition: Mechanisms of change* (pp. 43–56). New York: Oxford University Press.

Ericsson, K. A., & Kintsch, W. (1995). Long-term working memory. *Psychological Review, 102*, 211–245.

Fagan, J. F. (1973). Infants' delayed recognition memory and forgetting. *Journal of Experimental Child Psychology, 16*, 424–450.

Gick, M. L., Craik, F. I. M., & Morris, R. G. (1988). Task complexity and age differences in working memory. *Memory & Cognition, 16*, 353–361.

Giedd, J. N., Blumenthal, J., Jeffries, N. O., Castellanos, F. X., Liu, H., Zijdenbos, A., et al. (1999). Brain development during childhood and adolescence: A longitudinal MRI study. *Nature Neuroscience, 2*, 861–863.

Gogtay, N., Giedd, J. N., Lusk, L., Hayashi, K. M., Greenstein, D., Vaituzis, A. C., et al. (2004). Dynamic mapping of human cortical development during childhood through early adulthood. *Proceedings of the National Academy of Sciences of the United States of America, 101*, 8174–8179.

Golinkoff, R. M., & Hirsh-Pasek, K. (2006). The emergentist coalition model of word learning in children has implications for language in aging. In E. Bialystok & F. I. M. Craik (Eds.), *Lifespan cognition: Mechanisms of change* (pp. 207–222). New York: Oxford University Press.

Goswami, U. (Ed.). (2002). *Blackwell handbook of childhood cognitive development*. Malden, MA: Blackwell Publishing.

Grady, C. L., McIntosh, A. R., Horwitz, B., & Maisog, J. M. (1995). Age-related reductions in human recognition memory due to impaired encoding. *Science, 269*, 218–221.

Guttentag, R. E. (1984). The mental effort requirement of cumulative rehearsal: A developmental study. *Journal of Experimental Child Psychology, 37*, 92–106.

Hakuta, K., Bialystok, E., & Wiley, E. (2003). Critical evidence: A test of the critical-period hypothesis for second-language acquisition. *Psychological Science, 14*, 31–38.

Harnishfeger, K. K., & Bjorklund, D. F. (1990). Children's strategies: A brief history. In D. F. Bjorklund (Ed.), *Children's strategies: Contemporary views of cognitive development* (pp. 1–22). Hillsdale, NJ: Lawrence Erlbaum Associates, Inc.

Hasher, L., & Zacks, R. T. (1988). Working memory, comprehension, and aging: A review and a new view. In G. H. Bower (Ed.), *The psychology of learning and motivation* (Vol. 22, pp. 193–226). New York: Academic Press.

Hasher, L., Zacks, R. T., & May, C. P. (1999). Inhibitory control, circadian arousal, and age. In D. Gopher & A. Koriat (Eds.), *Attention and performance XVII: Cognitive regulation of performance: Interaction of theory and application* (pp. 653–675). Cambridge, MA: MIT Press.

Hebb, D. O. (1972). *Textbook of psychology* (3rd ed.). Philadelphia: Saunders.

Hertzog, C., & Hultsch, D. F. (2000). Metacognition in adulthood and old age. In F. I. M. Craik & T. A. Salthouse (Eds.), *The handbook of aging and cognition* (2nd ed., pp. 417–466). Mahwah, NJ: Lawrence Erlbaum Associates, Inc.

Hitch, G. J. (2006). Working memory in children: A cognitive approach. In E. Bialystok & F. I. M. Craik (Eds.), *Lifespan cognition: Mechanisms of change* (pp. 112–127). New York: Oxford University Press.

Hitch, G. J., Towse, J. N., & Hutton, U. (2001). What limits children's working memory span? theoretical accounts and applications for scholastic development. *Journal of Experimental Psychology: General, 130*, 184–198.

Hooper, F. H., Fitzgerald, J., & Papalia, D. (1971). Piagetian theory and the aging process: Extensions and speculations. *Aging & Human Development, 2*, 3–20.

Horn, J. L. (1982). The theory of fluid and crystallized intelligence in relation to concepts of cognitive psychology and aging in adulthood. In F. I. M. Craik & S. Trehub (Eds.), *Aging and cognitive processes* (pp. 237–278). New York: Plenum Press.

Howard, D. V., & Howard, J. H. (1989). Age differences in learning serial patterns: Direct versus indirect measures. *Psychology and Aging, 4*, 357–364.

Hultsch, D. F., Hertzog, C., Dixon, R. A., & Small, B. J. (1998). *Memory change in the aged*. New York: Cambridge University Press.

Jacoby, L. L. (1991). A process dissociation framework: Separating automatic from intentional uses of memory. *Journal of Memory and Language, 30*, 513–541.

Jacoby, L. L., Debner, J. A., & Hay, J. F. (2001). Proactive interference, accessibility bias, and process dissociations: Valid subject reports of memory. *Journal of Experimental Psychology: Learning, Memory, and Cognition, 27*, 686–700.

Jennings, J. M., & Jacoby, L. L. (1993). Automatic versus intentional uses of memory: Aging, attention, and control. *Psychology and Aging, 8*, 283–293.

Jennings, J. M., & Jacoby, L. L. (1997). An opposition procedure for detecting age-related deficits in recollection: Telling effects of repetition. *Psychology and Aging, 12*, 352–361.

Kane, M. J., & Engle, R. W. (2003). Working-memory capacity and the control of attention: The contributions of goal neglect, response competition, and task set to Stroop interference. *Journal of Experimental Psychology: General, 132*, 47–70.

Keil, F. (2006). Patterns of knowledge growth and decline. In E. Bialystok & F. I. M. Craik (Eds.), *Lifespan cognition: Mechanisms of change* (pp. 264–273). New York: Oxford University Press.

Kemper, S. (2006). Language in adulthood. In E. Bialystok & F. I. M. Craik (Eds.), *Lifespan cognition: Mechanisms of change* (pp. 223–238). New York: Oxford University Press.

Kemper, S., Herman, R. E., & Nartowitz, J. (2003). The costs of doing two things at once for young and older adults: Talking while walking, finger tapping, and ignoring speech or noise. *Psychology and Aging, 18*, 181–192.

Kemper, S., Kynette, D., Rash, S., Sprott, R., & O'Brien, K. (1989). Life-span changes to adults' language: Effects of memory and genre. *Applied Psycholinguistics, 10*, 49–66.

Kemper, S., Thompson, M., & Marquis, J. (2001). Longitudinal change in language production: Effects of aging and dementia on grammatical complexity and propositional density. *Psychology and Aging, 16*, 600–614.

Kliegl, R., Smith, J., & Baltes, P. B. (1990). On the locus and process of magnification of age differences during mnemonic training. *Developmental Psychology, 26*, 894–904.

Konner, M. (1991). Universals of behavioral development in relation to brain myelination. In K. R. Gibson & A. C. Petersen (Ed.), *Brain maturation and cognitive development* (pp. 181–223). New York: Aldine de Gruyer.

Kramer, A. F., Bherer, L., Colcombe, S. J., Dong, W., & Greenough, W. T. (2004). Environmental influences on cognitive and brain plasticity during aging. *Journals of Gerontology: Series A: Biological Sciences and Medical Sciences, 59*, 940–957.

La Voie, D., & Light, L. L. (1994). Adult age differences in repetition priming: A meta-analysis. *Psychology and Aging, 9*, 539–553.

Lhermitte, F. (1986). Human autonomy and the frontal lobes. Part II: patient behavior in complex and social situations—the "environmental dependency" syndrome. *Annals of Neurology, 19*, 335–343.

Li, S., Lindenberger, U., Hommel, B., Aschersleben, G., Prinz, W., & Baltes, P. B. (2004). Transformations in the couplings among intellectual abilities and constituent cognitive processes across the life span. *Psychological Science, 15*, 155–163.

Light, L. L. (1992). The organization of memory in old age. In F. I. M. Craik & T. A. Salthouse (Eds.), *The handbook of aging and cognition* (pp. 111–165). Hillsdale, NJ: Lawrence Erlbaum Associates, Inc.

Light, L. L., & Singh, A. (1987). Implicit and explicit memory in young and older adults. *Journal of Experimental Psychology: Learning, Memory, and Cognition, 13*, 531–541.

Lindenberger, U. (2001). Lifespan theories of cognitive development. In N. J. Smelser & P. B. Baltes (Eds.), *International encyclopedia of the social and behavioral sciences* (1st ed., pp. 8848–8854). Amsterdam: Elsevier.

Luria, A. R. (1973). *The working brain: An introduction to neuropsychology.* New York: Basic Books.

Mandler, J. M. (1998). Representation. In W. Damon (Ed.), *Handbook of child psychology: Volume 2: Cognition, perception, and language* (pp. 255–308). Hoboken, NJ: Wiley.

Markman, E. M. (1989). *Categorization and naming in children: problems of induction.* Cambridge, MA: MIT Press.

Markson, L., & Bloom, P. (1997). Evidence against a dedicated system for word learning in children. *Nature, 385,* 813–815.

McIntyre, J. S., & Craik, F. I. M. (1987). Age differences in memory for item and source information. *Canadian Journal of Psychology, 41,* 175–192.

Meisel, J. M. (1995). Parameters in acquisition. In P. Fletcher & B. MacWhinney (Eds.), *The handbook of child language* (pp. 10–35). Oxford: Blackwell.

Mesulam, M. (2002). The human frontal lobes: Transcending the default mode through contingent encoding. In D. T. Stuss & R. T. Knight (Eds.), *Principles of frontal lobe function* (pp. 8–30). New York: Oxford University Press.

Mitchell, D. B., Hunt, R. R., & Schmitt, F. A. (1986). The generation effect and reality monitoring: Evidence from dementia and normal aging. *Journal of Gerontology, 41,* 79–84.

Mortensen, L., Meyer, A. S., & Humphreys, G. W. (2006). Age-related slowing of object naming: A review. *Language and Cognitive Processes, 21,* 238–290.

Naveh-Benjamin, M. (2000). Adult age differences in memory performance: Tests of an associative deficit hypothesis. *Journal of Experimental Psychology: Learning, Memory, and Cognition, 26,* 1170–1187.

Naveh-Benjamin, M., Craik, F. I. M., Guez, J., & Kreuger, S. (2005). Divided attention in younger and older adults: Effects of strategy and relatedness on memory performance and secondary task costs. *Journal of Experimental Psychology: Learning, Memory, and Cognition, 31,* 520–537.

Nelson, K. (1973). Structure and strategy in learning to talk. *Monographs of the Society for Research in Child Development, 38* (1 and 2), Serial No. 149.

Nilsson, L. (2003). Memory function in normal aging. *Acta Neurologica Scandinavica, 107,* 7–13.

Ornstein, P. A., Haden, C. A., & Elischberger, H. B. (2006). Children's memory development: Remembering the past and preparing for the future. In E. Bialystok & F. I. M. Craik (Eds.), *Lifespan cognition: Mechanisms of change* (pp. 143–161). New York: Oxford University Press.

Park, D. C., Lautenschlager, G., Hedden, T., Davidson, N. S., Smith, A. D., & Smith, P. K. (2002). Models of visuospatial and verbal memory across the adult life span. *Psychology and Aging, 17,* 299–320.

Park, D. C., & Payer, D. (2006). Working memory across the adult lifespan. In E. Bialystok & F. I. M. Craik (Eds.), *Lifespan cognition: Mechanisms of change.* (pp. 128–142). New York: Oxford University Press.

Perner, J., & Ruffman, T. (1995). Episodic memory and autonoetic consciousness: Developmental evidence and a theory of childhood amnesia. *Journal of Experimental Child Psychology. Special Issue: Early memory, 59,* 516–548.

Petrides, M., & Pandya, D. N. (1999). Dorsolateral prefrontal cortex: Comparative cytoarchitectonic analysis in the human and the macaque brain and corticocortical connection patterns. *European Journal of Neuroscience, 11,* 1011–1036.

Phillips, L. H., MacLeod, M., & Kliegel, M. (2005). Adult aging and cognitive planning. In G. Ward & R. Morris (Eds.), *The cognitive psychology of planning* (pp. 111–134). Hove, UK: Psychology Press.

Piaget, J. (1959). *The language and thought of the child* (3rd ed.). London: Routledge & Kegan Paul.

Pinker, S. (1994). *The language instinct.* New York: William Morrow.

Rabinowitz, J. C. (1989). Judgments of origin and generation effects: Comparisons between young and elderly adults. *Psychology and Aging, 4*, 259–268.

Raz, N. (2000). Aging of the brain and its impact on cognitive performance: Integration of structural and functional findings. In F. I. M. Craik & T. A. Salthouse (Eds.), *The handbook of aging and cognition* (2nd ed., pp. 1–90). Mahwah, NJ: Lawrence Erlbaum Associates, Inc.

Raz, N., Lindenberger, U., Rodrigue, K. M., Kennedy, K. M., Head, D., Williamson, A., et al. (2005). Regional brain changes in aging healthy adults: General trends, individual differences and modifiers. *Cerebral Cortex, 15*, 1679–1689.

Raz, N., & Rodrigue, K. M. (2006). Differential aging of the brain: Patterns, cognitive correlates and modifiers. *Neuroscience & Biobehavioral Reviews, 30*, 730–748.

Reimers, S., & Maylor, E. A. (2005). Task switching across the life span: Effects of age on general and specific switch costs. *Developmental Psychology, 41*, 661–671.

Riegel, K. F. (1977). History of psychological gerontology. In J. E. Birren & K. W. Schaie (Eds.), *Handbook of the psychology of aging* (1st ed., pp. 70–102). New York: Van Nostrand Reinhold.

Rönnlund, M., Nyberg, L., Bäckman, L., & Nilsson, L. (2003). Recall of subject-performed tasks, verbal tasks, and cognitive activities across the adult life span: Parallel age-related deficits. *Aging, Neuropsychology, and Cognition, 10*, 182–201.

Rovee-Collier, C., & Hayne, H. (2000). Memory in infancy and early childhood. In E. Tulving & F. I. M. Craik (Eds.), *The Oxford handbook of memory* (pp. 267–282). New York: Oxford University Press.

Rubin, D. C. (1999). Frontal-striatal circuits in cognitive aging: Evidence for caudate involvement. *Aging, Neuropsychology, and Cognition, 6*, 241–259.

Salthouse, T. A. (1991). *Theoretical perspectives on cognitive aging.* Hillsdale, NJ: Lawrence Erlbaum Associates, Inc.

Salthouse, T. A. (1996). The processing-speed theory of adult age differences in cognition. *Psychological Review, 103*, 403–428.

Salthouse, T. A. (1998). Independence of age-related influences on cognitive abilities across the life span. *Developmental Psychology, 34*, 851–864.

Salthouse, T. A. (2006). Mental exercise and mental aging. evaluating the validity of the "use it or lose it" hypothesis. *Perspectives on Psychological Science, 1*, 68–87.

Salthouse, T. A., & Davis, H. P. (2006). Organization of cognitive abilities and neuropsychological variables across the lifespan. *Developmental Review, 26*, 31–54.

Schaie, K.W. (1996). Intellectual development in adulthood: The Seattle longitudinal study. New York: Cambridge University Press.

Schloerscheidt, A. M., Craik, F. I. M., & Kreuger, S. (2007). The influence of aging and context change on the recognition of pictures and words. (submitted for publication).

Schneider, W. (2002). Memory development in childhood. In U. Goswami (Ed.), *Blackwell handbook of childhood cognitive development* (pp. 236–256). Malden, MA: Blackwell.

Schneider, W., & Bjorklund, D. F. (1998). Memory. In W. Damon (Ed.), *Handbook of child psychology: Volume 2: Cognition, perception, and language* (pp. 467–521). Hoboken, NJ: Wiley.

Schneider, B. A., Daneman, M., & Murphy, D. R. (2005). Speech comprehension difficulties in older adults: Cognitive slowing or age-related changes in hearing? *Psychology and Aging, 20*, 261–271.

Schneider, W., & Pressley, M. (1989). *Memory development between 2 and 20* (1st ed.). New York: Springer-Verlag.

Schneider, W., & Pressley, M. (1997). *Memory development between two and twenty* (2nd ed.). Mahwah, NJ: Lawrence Erlbaum Associates, Inc.

Shewan, C. M., & Henderson, V. L. (1988). Analysis of spontaneous language in the older normal population. *Journal of Communication Disorders, 21*, 139–154.

Siedlecki, K. L., Salthouse, T. A., & Berish, D. E. (2005). Is there anything special about the aging of source memory? *Psychology and Aging, 20,* 19–32.

Singer, T., Verhaeghen, P., Ghisletta, P., Lindenberger, U., & Baltes, P. B. (2003). The fate of cognition in very old age: Six-year longitudinal findings in the Berlin aging study. *Psychology and Aging, 18,* 318–331.

Smith, L. B., Jones, S. S., & Landau, B. (1996). Naming in young children: A dumb attentional mechanism? *Cognition, 60,* 143–171.

Spencer, W. D., & Raz, N. (1994). Memory for facts, source, and context: Can frontal lobe dysfunction explain age-related differences? *Psychology and Aging, 9,* 149–159.

Stern, Y. (2002). What is cognitive reserve? Theory and research application of the reserve concept. *Journal of the International Neuropsychological Society, 8,* 448–460.

Stuss, D. T., Alexander, M. P., Floden, D., Binns, M. A., Levine, B., McIntosh, A. R., et al. (2002). Fractionation and localization of distinct frontal lobe processes: Evidence from focal lesions in humans. In D. T. Stuss & R. T. Knight (Eds.), *Principles of frontal lobe function* (pp. 392–407). New York: Oxford University Press.

Taylor, M. (2006). Neural bases of cognitive development. In E. Bialystok & F. I. M. Craik (Eds.), *Lifespan cognition: Mechanisms of change* (pp. 27–42). New York: Oxford University Press.

Thompson-Schill, S. L., Bedny, M., & Goldberg, R. F. (2005). The frontal lobes and the regulation of mental activity. *Current Opinion in Neurobiology, 15,* 219–224.

Timmons, C. R. (1994). Associative links between discrete memories in early infancy. *Infant Behavior & Development, 17,* 431–445.

Tomasello, M. (2003). *Constructing a language: A useage-based theory of language acquisition.* Cambridge, MA: Harvard University Press.

Tulving, E. (1983). *Elements of episodic memory.* New York: Oxford University Press.

Tulving, E. (1993). What is episodic memory? *Current Directions in Psychological Science, 2,* 67–70.

Tulving, E., Kapur, S., Craik, F. I. M., Moscovitch, M., & Houle, S. (1994). Hemispheric encoding/retrieval asymmetry in episodic memory: Positron emission tomography findings. *Proceedings of the National Academy of Sciences, 91,* 2016–2020.

Valenzuela, M. J., & Sachdev, P. (2006). Brain reserve and dementia: A systematic review. *Psychological Medicine, 36,* 441–454.

Valian, V., Hoeffner, J., & Aubry, S. (1996). Young children's imitation of sentence subjects: Evidence of processing limitations. *Developmental Psychology, 32,* 153–164

Valian, V., Prasada, S., & Scarpa, J. (2006). Direct object predictability: Effects on young children's imitation of sentences. *Journal of Child Language, 33,* 247–269.

Van der Linden, M., Hupet, M., Feyereisen, P., Schelstraete, M.-A., Bestgen, Y., Bruyer, R., et al. (1999). Congitive mediators of age-related differences in language comprehension and verbal memory performance. *Aging, Neuropsychology, and Cognition, 6,* 32–55.

Vygotsky, L. S. (1978). *Mind in society: The development of higher psychological processes.* Cambridge, MA: Harvard University Press.

Williams, B. R., Ponesse, J. S., Schachar, R. J., Logan, G. D., & Tannock, R. (1999). Development of inhibitory control across the life span. *Developmental Psychology, 35,* 205–213.

Wingfield, A. (1996). Cognitive factors in auditory performance: Context, speed of processing, and constraints of memory. *Journal of the American Academy of Audiology, 7,* 175–182.

Wingfield, A., & Stine-Morrow, E. A. L. (2000). Language and speech. In F. I. M. Craik & T. A. Salthouse (Eds.), *The handbook of aging and cognition* (2nd ed., pp. 359–416). Mahwah, NJ: Lawrence Erlbaum Associates, Inc.

Zacks, R. T., & Hasher, L. (1994). Directed ignoring: Inhibitory regulation of working memory. In D. Dagenbach & T. H. Carr (Eds.), *Inhibitory processes in attention, memory, and language* (pp. 241–264). New York: Academic Press.

Zelazo, P. D. (2004). The development of conscious control in childhood. *Trends in Cognitive Sciences, 8*, 12–17.

Zelazo, P. D., Craik, F. I. M., & Booth, L. (2004). Executive function across the life span. *Acta Psychologica, 115*, 167–183.

Author Index

Subject Index